P9-DES-959

REWIND

JEREMY MYERSON & GRAHAM VICKERS
WITH ESSAYS BY JEREMY BULLMORE, ALAN FLETCHER, MICHAEL JOHNSON, RICHARD SEYMOUR, JOHN WEBSTER & PETER YORK

REWIND FORTY YEARS

OF DESIGN & ADVERTISING

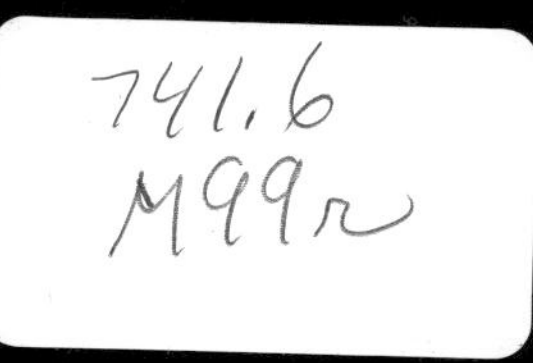

Phaidon Press Limited
Regent's Wharf
All Saints Street
London N1 9PA

Phaidon Press Inc.
180 Varick Street
New York, NY 10014

www.phaidon.com

First published 2002

ISBN 0 7148 4271 0

A CIP catalogue record for this book
is available from the British Library.

Designed by johnson banks
Printed in Italy

Foreword 07
Introduction 08
1960s 16
1970s 84
1980s 180
1990s 296
2000s 424
Cover story 468
Fact file 476
Index 504

D&AD (British Design & Art Direction) is a professional association and charity representing the UK's thriving design and advertising communities. Established in 1962, D&AD's purpose is to set creative standards, educate and inspire the next creative generation, and promote the importance of good design and advertising to the business arena. The D&AD Awards, familiarly known as the Yellow Pencils, are the largest and most internationally respected awards in the industry. They receive over 20,000 entries from around the world each year. These are judged by 250 senior practitioners in the business. At the same time D&AD places a high priority on education, investing over £1.5 million each year on a range of innovative programmes that seek to identify talented graduates, support colleges and develop and train young creatives.

www.dandad.org

D&AD would like to thank the patrons of its 40th anniversary year:

Design Council
EHS Brann
The Mill
Newspaper Publishers Association
O_2
Outdoor Advertising Association
Premier Paper Group
Ventura
Virgin Radio

How to use this book
All of the work shown has a key code relating to the D&AD Award it received from the jury of that year:

Gold Silver Silver Nomination Featured in D&AD Annual

There is also a reference number (e.g. 1963.01) for each selection, be that an individual piece or campaign, which refers to the fact file at the rear of the book in which all available creative credits for the work have been listed. The first four digits of the reference number relate to the year in which the work was entered into the D&AD Awards, the last two digits refer to the project number within that year. As a rule the work would have run or been launched in the previous year.

Unless indicated, reference numbers and captions relate to the images on a given page following a 'clockwise from top' convention.

Foreword
Michael Johnson

This project began in the late eighties when I sat at the back of a ballroom on Park Lane, peering though dense cigarette smoke, trying to watch some event called the D&AD Awards. As far as I could tell, people would occasionally walk up onto the stage and come away clutching small pieces of yellow wood, usually (but not always) accompanied by loud applause.

I didn't entirely understand it, but they looked important. I knew I wanted to try and win one. In order to do so I needed to see what had won before.

Luck was on my side. I tracked down and purchased a full set of D&AD Annuals and set about studying every single page of every single year since it started in 1963.

At first they were hoarded, everyone could keep their hands off and hunt down their own set. But it slowly began to dawn on me that it was selfish to keep them to myself and sad that so few others could learn from them.

It also became apparent that D&AD was more than just a pat-on-the-back award scheme. The chance to be recognized by your peers is one thing, but to become part of history? Now, that's serious.

I began to think that finding a way to rewind back through design and advertising history would provide the chance for us all to stop, take stock and evaluate where we are. And it became progressively clear throughout the nineties that design and advertising were no longer misunderstood professions.

The dreaded 'so what do you do?' question at dinner parties became easier and easier to answer. Television channels devoted whole evenings to the public's favourite 30-second stings. National newspapers began to introduce regular design columns and a plethora of characters arrived on TV to help us redesign our front room, our garden, even ourselves.

Slowly but surely, great design and advertising has become an integral part of our visual and verbal culture. It has shown that it can solve significant cultural problems, open our eyes to evils we never understood, even enhance our quality of life. (It can also oil the cogs of capitalism, sell more breakfast cereal and persuade you to buy too many pairs of trainers, but that tells us as much about human fallibility as it does the power of advertising.)

However, when I set off a chain of events that eventually led to this book and an exhibition at the Victoria and Albert Museum, all I then wanted to do was to provide a record of the 'story so far'.

It started with a letter to the individuals then running D&AD suggesting a *30th* birthday project. The reply was blunt and read something like 'Yes, we know, we're dealing with it, goodbye.'

Well, it wasn't dealt with – my pet project remained unrequited until, a decade later, older, wiser and, crucially, a little better connected I managed to resurrect it.

This time around I knew that this should be more than just a gentle jog down memory lane. Everyone involved was beginning to see that *Rewind* could be a landmark project for both D&AD and the whole profession.

In the nineties, one of the ad industry's most gifted directors, Tony Kaye, had stated publicly that he thought TV ads should be seen as art in their own right, coveted, collected and shown by museums. Now his wish has come true.

The most challenging part of the project was selecting the items for inclusion, knowing that we couldn't reproduce all the work. We spent many gruelling days re-living all the winners, and nearly winners.

Over the following pages the authors of *Rewind* explain their selection criteria in detail, but suffice to say that we knew we had space for 15 to 25 projects per year. Consequently we tried to include the pieces of work with 'real' historical significance over the ones that had won 'easy' prizes (if there can be such a thing).

If you've won many times, the chances are they won't all be here (but hey, you're famous enough not to worry, aren't you?). If we've missed a piece of work you think is timeless, well, sorry. History is the harshest of judges, and unless it proved an interesting cultural or sociological point, something that won and now seems 'time-locked' may not have made it.

We've debated how the D&AD archive has necessarily driven the content, and there are occasional holes in the collection, it's true.

But however flawed it may be, the archive is the closest we have to an accurate benchmark of creative excellence in communication of the last four decades, initially British based, now completely international.

If you want to study how the best companies and organizations have communicated at the highest level through their designs, products, advertising, packs, environments, websites – you name it – here it is, all in one book.

As for D&AD, the last ten years have seen it turn a corner from a small team of back-patters to the glue that holds the world's communication businesses together.

As the industry has grown from its original roots to one dominated by worldwide conglomerates, D&AD now finds itself in the position of pre-eminent global standard-setter.

Wherever you go in the world, from Melbourne to Mexico City, someone will ask you 'so how can I win a yellow pencil?'. (The answer, as ever, is to do the most amazing, fantastically unique and appropriate work, send it to London by January, then sit back and hope like hell).

But success in terms of size and fame hasn't led to a nice fat bank balance. D&AD's charitable remit compels it to pour millions back into education, encouraging and nurturing the creative brains of the future. Communications students the world over enter the Student Awards and you are as likely to see a winner from Florida as you are from Farnham.

One of my challenges, as the organization's incoming president, is how D&AD should start to look forwards again. The edges between design, advertising and the media continue to blur as these previously separate disciplines cross over. I don't profess to know where it will lead, but I know D&AD should be involved in the process.

But back in the present, I hope you enjoy rewinding through the past 40 years of design and advertising. By studying what has gone before, I guarantee you'll have better ideas in the future.

INTROD

UCTI D&AD N

When the interests of the British design and advertising communities coincided in London in the early sixties, one result of this dynamic interaction was a new organization – Designers & Art Directors Association (D&AD) – founded in 1962 and dedicated to celebrating creative communication, rewarding its practitioners and raising standards throughout the two industries. Four decades later, the media landscape has changed beyond all recognition but D&AD is still fulfilling that same fundamental role, and, in shrewdly recognizing that for things to remain the same they have to change, it has become a body with an international remit and a reputation that extends far beyond the original confines of a few streets in London's Soho. Its awards for international creative excellence – famously known as the 'Yellow Pencils' – still look much the same as when Lou Klein devised them in 1966, but they are now coveted throughout the world.

From the start, D&AD published annuals in support of its awards and so it is the proprietor of a unique archive that brings together large amounts of outstanding design and advertising work uniquely representative of industry trends and contemporary concerns over the years. Numerous examples drawn from this archive form the main visual core of this book, although here there is a cautionary note to strike. All of the images used are from a selection of work that either won D&AD Gold and Silver Awards or was featured for its special merit in one of the D&AD Annuals spanning a 40-year period. This, combined with the benefit of hindsight, means that there are a few omissions (and perhaps one or two inclusions) that some may find surprising.

This hardly requires any excuse, since there is probably no field of activity where contemporaneous judgment always chimes exactly with the findings of considered historical retrospection. What is perhaps remarkable though, is that a succession of D&AD juries (drawn exclusively from the leading creative practitioners of the era) was, through the years, so consistently accurate in identifying those design projects and advertising campaigns that hindsight would endorse as having been outstanding, groundbreaking or influential.

As a result, this book provides a remarkably rich and felicitous visual commentary of 40 years of design and advertising, supported by a main text that seeks to put the works in context, to provide some background that adds understanding or simply to explain how some of the work came about. Context, of course, is the key to appreciating how any aspect of popular culture turned out the way it did. Nothing happens in a vacuum and design and advertising have always developed in very direct response to the social, political and economic tenor of the times. In this case, the times in question are less than half a century long and have been utterly unlike any other period in history. The world has undergone many seismic changes that have proliferated at a staggering rate. In particular, there has been the revolution of the internet, a quantum leap in communications of at least equal historical importance as the invention of the printing press. When communications change, everything changes and there are those who say that they knew that world order could never be the same again when it emerged that Mikhail Gorbachev had worked out the details of *perestroika* using an Apple Macintosh. Vietnam, space exploration, an emergent European Union, AIDS, high-tech warfare, globalization, terrorism... the single lesson emerging from it all is that the global village is now finally with us, with all that implies; an end to geographical and cultural insularity.

Accordingly, in the world of communications explored in this book there is a progressive shift of emphasis from the mainly British perspective of the first half of the book to a much more international feel in the second half. There are certain pleasing symmetries, too. In the early sixties, the most creative minds agreed that British advertising had everything to learn from the Americans in general and Doyle Dane Bernbach in particular... whereas Madison Avenue could hardly hope to profit from studying the mainly dull and formulaic advertising techniques then being applied in Britain. A decade later, London would be the world centre for great advertising. Today, the pendulum has swung again and, as the more recent D&AD Awards have reflected, it is once again American agencies like Cliff Freeman & Partners, TBWA\Chiat\Day and Wieden + Kennedy which are in the driving seat.

Where the word 'advertising' has always had a fairly consistent meaning, design is a more problematic word that at different points in time has frequently meant very different things to different people. Up until the fifties, most British discussions about design had been academic and historical in nature, focusing mainly upon industrial design considered in the context of mass production and the rise of the consumer society. The mid-nineteenth century Arts and Craft movement, with its hierarchy of guilds, its moralistic advocacy of fitness to purpose and its essentially socialist agenda, exemplified how 'design' could be a vehicle for a worldview, just as the Modern Movement, uniting art and technology, embodied a very different vision of how society might consider its built environment, its artefacts and therefore itself.

By the early twentieth century, the Modern Movement had more or less appropriated 'design', effectively dismissing the future relevance of the decorative arts practitioners. In 1936 Nikolaus Pevsner reinforced this view in his influential *Pioneers of the Modern Movement*, a book which widely disseminated and promoted the famous dictum 'form follows function'. It remained for other commentators to develop Pevsner's somewhat rigid Germanic and architectonic interpretation of design, and then go on to explore the possibilities of a more fluid interaction between industry, technology and society's needs.

By the mid-forties, the British government, mindful of the proven value of propaganda posters during the war, began seeking to co-opt the power of effective design for the task of post-war reconstruction and trade. The assumption was that 'good design' would boost sales of British goods in post-war international markets. To help publicize this message, design exhibitions began in 1956 at the London headquarters of the newly opened Design Council. This initiative set the scene for design's assimilation into mainstream British culture where, by the eighties (the 'designer decade'), it would become associated with not always desirable notions of style and fashion that led to the final indignity of turning the word 'designer' from a noun into a shoddy commercial adjective: designer glasses, designer water, designer anything.

But while some strands of design activity were destined to coalesce into a lifestyle mush, the broader output of the design community happily proved more distinctive, more pluralistic, more muscular and more durable so that today, despite cyclical peaks and troughs, the British design industry, in all its varied disciplines, is a vital and internationally influential force. Indeed, a persistent cry in recent years has been one of regret that British design talent is so highly sought abroad that the home market is deprived of the outstanding designers it has trained. Meanwhile, advertising has always seemed to enjoy (if that is the word) an almost mythical reputation as being simultaneously the province of the snake-oil salesman and the sophisticated social analyst. Ever since people first made things or tendered services they realized that you had to inform prospective customers of what was on offer, and you used the best technology available to you at the time. The growth of large industrial concerns in Britain in the nineteenth century resulted in mass production which in turn required mass consumption if the full benefits of the economies of scale were to be enjoyed. The shift of emphasis from individual salesman to mass advertising was an inevitable one and something that was helped by the growth of literacy resulting from The Education Act of 1870. This (plus an earlier abolition of tax on newspapers) was largely responsible for an explosion in the sales of printed periodicals, giving advertisers access to a brand new mass market.

The rise of branding was another significant factor in the history of advertising. Until the end of the nineteenth century, most loose dry goods and provisions were weighed and packaged by the retailer. However, as regulatory trading bodies came into being at the start of the twentieth century, manufacturers and importers began to pre-package and brand their goods, applying standardized pricing and so achieving more predictable profits. In the early twentieth century, distinctive brand packaging was already starting to engage the consumer in a way that was quite different from the era when the only customer allegiance was to the independent retailer and the products themselves were largely of anonymous provenance.

In 1920 a public exhibition celebrating international advertising was held at London's White City. People were admitted at a cost of one shilling and threepence (about seven pence) a head and the Underground Railway poster promoting the exhibition featured a perspective drawing including a dozen or so famous advertising characters of the day standing on a station platform. This strongly suggests that the general public was already very familiar with, and well-disposed towards, the new culture of advertising. (It also reminds us of the remarkable longevity of characters such as The Bisto Kids, Nipper the HMV dog and The Michelin Man, all of whom were depicted in that 1920 poster.)

In Britain, World War II and the period of austerity, that followed it were, of course, inimical to any encouragement of mass consumption – or indeed any consumption at all that was not essential to keeping body and soul together – and the advertising industry that slowly re-established itself in the later fifties was inherently cautious, dull and formulaic. This was in direct contrast to the American experience where the consumer society was booming, so it is hardly surprising that Britain's early post-war creative influences all came from the other side of the Atlantic.

What is clear is that towards the end of the fifties, despite all the austerity, Britain began to experience the first pangs of dissatisfaction with the status quo. Prosperity was slowly returning, youth was empowered as never before and the stage was set for a revolt into style and a process of transformation that would make the last four decades of the twentieth century a vibrant period of rapid and extraordinary change, in which different design disciplines enjoyed varying fortunes and advertising gradually became accepted almost as an honorary entertainment medium in its own right.

Of course, design and advertising were only two of the indicators of times that were definitely changing, but they were important ones, each being inextricably woven into the nation's economic fabric as well as reflecting the spirit of the age. Accordingly, the sixties produced design and advertising that was eager to push the boundaries, blur lines of demarcation and generally shake up the establishment. By the seventies, the party was over, although the previous decade's legacy of iconoclasm and experiment could now be fully exploited and the door was pushed open for some remarkable talents to build international reputations. Nowhere was this more evident than in advertising, where, for a time, London led the world and the agency of Collett Dickenson Pearce led London.

Design would take centre stage in the eighties, dripping with entrepreneurialism and decorative revival. As the late Tibor Kalman reminded us, designers and art directors, who had banished history in the sixties and saw what the world looked like without it in the seventies, welcomed it back with a vengeance in all its illustrative glory. Communication would become increasingly complex and contradictory in the eighties, against the backdrop of the policies of the *eminence grise* of the decade, Margaret Thatcher, who led a powerful and socially divisive Conservative government. The nineties saw the pendulum swing again, with the advent of globalization, the rise of brand management and the many seismic realignments resulting from the widespread impact of digital technology. TV commercials adopted big cinematographic values that would cross all borders without the need for dialogue. Elsewhere, communication cleverly turned real, edgy and ugly – anti-design and anti-advertising that would prepare the ground for the post-millennial shocks of the Seattle anti-capitalism riots and Naomi Klein's *No Logo*.

These, at least, are the shorthand summaries of those years, although as always, the reality was less clear-cut, more finely nuanced and rarely conformed to the neat demarcations of the decades. This book attempts to explore some of those nuances, looking at the highlights, texture, and trends of 40 extraordinary years of design and advertising and identifying the key creative personalities involved. As the awards handed out by D&AD reveal, those lazy generalizations of pop, punk and post-modernism don't adequately sum up the sixties, seventies and eighties, just as digital technology didn't dominate the look of the nineties even though it challenged the very core of practice.

D&AD started out in what is now seen in retrospect as a golden age of British print – of glorious press ads, book covers, posters and magazines. In the seventies, the art of the TV commercial was brilliantly honed and, in the subsequent decades, the blossoming of the design disciplines came to embrace first environmental design (as the late eighties high street boomed) and later product design and interactive media. All the time, D&AD was widening its brief in order to remain relevant to an increasingly international design and advertising community. In 2002 the organization welcomed its first non-English language advertising entries as the logical next step in its continuing international growth.

The evolution of the D&AD Awards and what categories were included, however, masks a broader point about the centrality of creative communication. For those generations which grew up in the post-war years, the work shown in this book may reawaken memories and confirm (if confirmation were needed) that design and advertising are not abstract, specialized activities pursued by a minority, but part of the fabric of all our lives. To a younger generation of designers and advertising practitioners, one can only hope it affords some broader insights into how their industries got where they are today and by what combination of circumstances and vision the very best work of any period may come about.

196

60s

The design and advertising explosion of sixties Britain gave us a uniquely powerful visual commentary on a radical decade. More than any other period in recent history, the sixties can be instantly evoked by its contemporary images of communication; by this iconic poster or that classic album sleeve. Later, the decades would overlap and blur as real time does, but the communication culture of the sixties, based on challenge and dissent, was by nature spontaneous and iconoclastic and its look was distinctive in every way. This, at least, is the popular perception of the communication culture aspect of 'swinging sixties London', a catch-all phrase broadly suggesting ascendant youth culture and a new generation of home-grown popular heroes like The Beatles, Twiggy, The Rolling Stones and Mary Quant. This received wisdom about the sixties catches the spirit but misses much of the point. It casually perpetuates the myth of a spontaneous revolution apparently generated by little more than turning over the December page of the 1959 calendar.

In fact, what we now often think of as quintessential sixties culture only came into its own in the second half of the decade, the first half being a rather more gradual segue from what had gone before. For every paradigmatic sixties image like the poster for Andy Warhol's 1967 film *Chelsea Girls* there were many more that represented far more gradual incursions into traditional taste and style.

1969.01
Designers: **Derek Burton, Harry Willock, Small Faces**
Client: **Immediate Records**
In a typical piece of sixties design grave-robbing, this album for the Small Faces used the nostalgic image of a circular tobacco tin for its packaging.

1969.02
Design group: **Ink Studios**
Client: **Arts Laboratory**
Alan Aldridge's memorable UK poster for Andy Warhol's 1967 twin-projector experimental film, *Chelsea Girls,* has worn rather better than the movie itself.

1969.03
Design group: **Bentley/Farrell/Burnett**
Client: **Bosie's**
More nostalgia from the decade that took delight in adapting yesterday's soulful faces and sinuous typefaces to contemporary needs, this time in the identity programme for a fashion store.

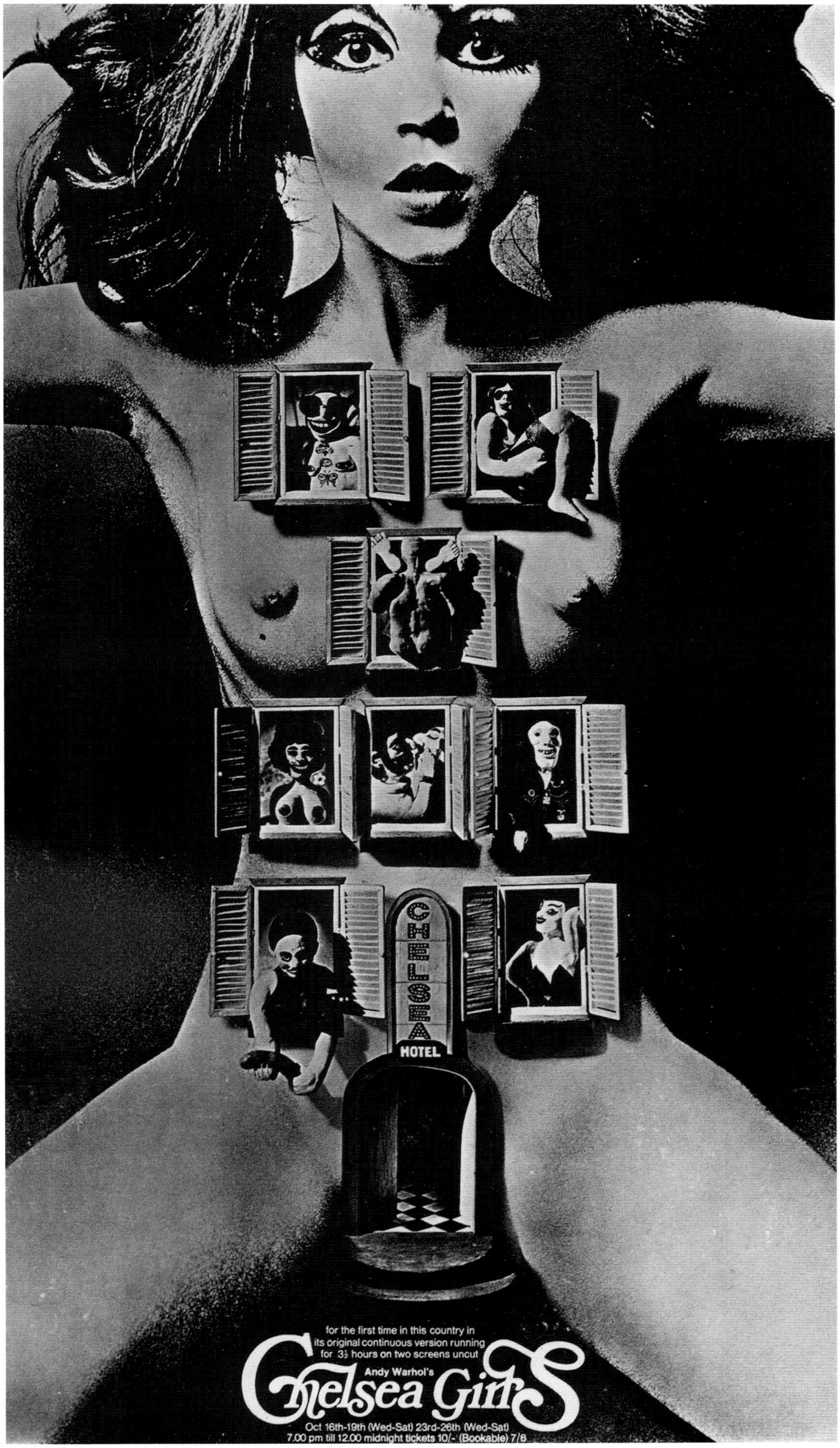

CHELSEA
HOTEL
for the first time in this country in
its original continuous version running
for 3½ hours on two screens uncut
Andy Warhol's
Chelsea Girls
Oct 16th-19th (Wed-Sat) 23rd-26th (Wed-Sat)
7.00 pm till 12.00 midnight tickets 10/- (Bookable) 7/6

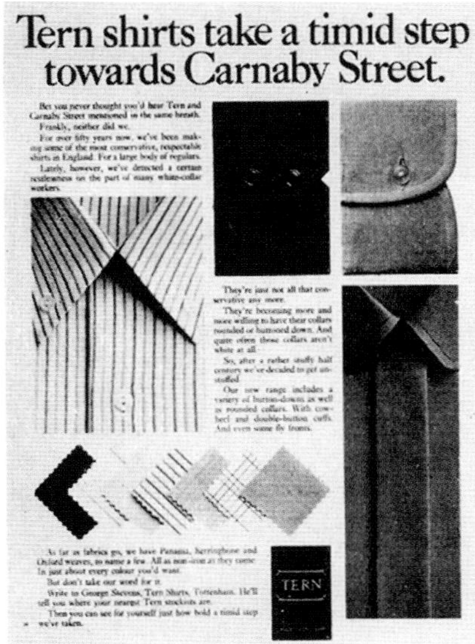

Tern shirts take a timid step towards Carnaby Street.
TERN

1969.04
Agency: **Doyle Dane Bernbach**
Client: **London Weekend Television**
DDB used a contemporary celebrity, ex-agent Tito Burns, to symbolize go-getting corporate qualities in this newspaper ad.

this page

1964.01
Agency: **Benton Bowles**
Client: **IBM Computers**
A new expression of the old sci-fi idea of computers taking over from people was here shown as a plausible scenario enabled by IBM.

1967.01
Agency: **Doyle Dane Bernbach**
Client: **Tern Consulate**
Early Neil Godfrey art direction for DDB's Silver-winning bid to position Tern Consulate shirts as being cautiously *à la mode.*

The key to the sixties lay in the fifties, a period usually characterized as 'grey' and one in which war-damaged Britain was defined by qualities like prudence, stability and austerity. The adult generation which set about rebuilding its life and that of the nation had neither the money nor the appetite for daring lifestyle adventures. To have emerged from the war with a life, let alone a lifestyle, was something to be grateful for. And yet, paradoxically, it was the subdued fifties that saw the first popular stirrings of 'design' being more widely recognized and celebrated.

In the early fifties, the British government had embraced the opportunity to use design in a celebratory way for the central event of The Festival of Britain (1951) on London's South Bank. Yet, the festival still seemed to retain a certain air of starchy official sanction, an invitation to celebrate, but only in the national good. No one could know it, but these were the last knockings of an old cultural order that would be revolutionized in the next decade, when earnings would rise, governments would become mistrusted and rebellion would come into vogue. Popular taste would at last begin to call the shots.

Bubbling under all this authorized activity were much looser design and advertising influences, many of them originating in the US where the economy, relatively unscathed by World War II, meant that the fifties was a decade of consumer boom. And design flourished in that boom; Charles and Ray Eames helped to introduce design thinking to manufacturing processes, Paul Rand began his influential corporate identity programme for IBM and Madison Avenue advertising man William Bernbach set the standards with his superb fifties press ads for Volkswagen. Bernbach (who would present the D&AD awards in 1968) pioneered an original approach – cool, droll, self-deprecating and entirely at odds with the hyperbole of most US car advertising of the time – that not only endured in print but also set the tone for four decades of successful Volkswagen TV commercials. In British terms, Bernbach in particular, and American advertising in general, were way ahead of the game.

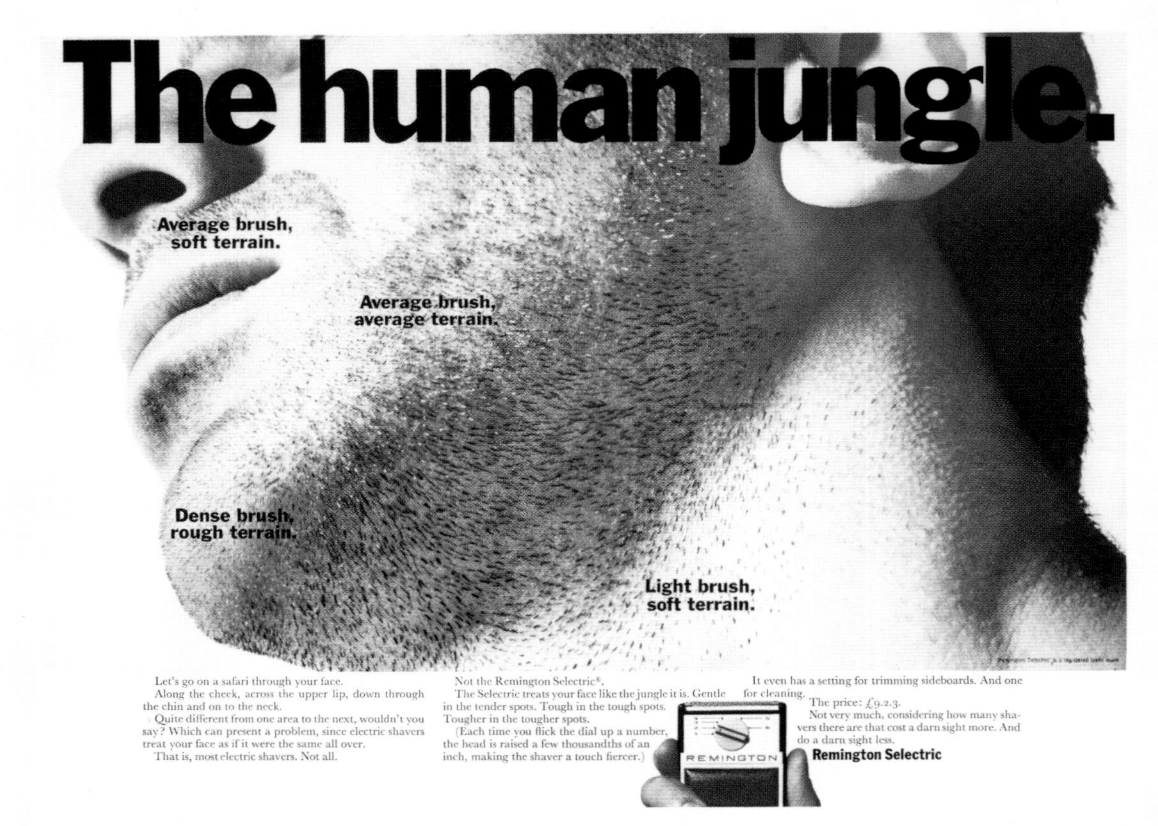

The human jungle.
Average brush, soft terrain.
Average brush, average terrain.
Dense brush, rough terrain.
Light brush, soft terrain.
Let's go on a safari through your face.
Along the cheek, across the upper lip, down through the chin and on to the neck.
Quite different from one area to the next, wouldn't you say? Which can present a problem, since electric shavers treat your face as if it were the same all over.
That is, most electric shavers. Not all.
Not the Remington Selectric®.
The Selectric treats your face like the jungle it is. Gentle in the tender spots. Tough in the tough spots. Tougher in the tougher spots.
(Each time you flick the dial up a number, the head is raised a few thousandths of an inch, making the shaver a touch fiercer.)
It even has a setting for trimming sideboards. And one for cleaning.
The price: £9.2.3.
Not very much, considering how many shavers there are that cost a darn sight more. And do a darn sight less.
REMINGTON
Remington Selectric

Our cordless shaver costs 14 gns.
We'd have liked to shave our price, but your face comes first.

If your kid buys you a Remington 25 for Christmas, he's getting altogether too much pocket money.

A few coins clutched in a grubby palm don't go far towards any electric shaver.
But the Remington 25 requires a special affluence, which is seldom achieved during childhood.
It costs ten quid. (About thirty shillings more than the other best-seller.)
Why should anybody, however well-heeled, fork out so much?
Glad you asked.
The Remington 25 has the largest shaving head you can get. And it stands to common sense that the larger the area a shaver shaves, the faster it will do the job.
Into the head we tuck 348 cutting edges. Far more than in any other shaver.
They're driven by the most powerful motor there is. A cool 8,000 times a minute.
The Remington 25 is the only shaver with adjustable Roller-Combs.
When they're up, our shaver is gentle. For the tender spots. When they're down, it ploughs smartly through the thickets.
Now the only way you're going to own a shaver this grand is by getting a near and dear one to part with ten pounds
If that's too much to hope for, we have a more modest proposal:
The Remington Rollershave, which costs £5.19.6.
It has a smaller head and a less powerful motor. So it takes a bit longer to shift the stubble.
But it's a lot quicker to save up for.
And time is running out.

1967.02
Agency: **Doyle Dane Bernbach**
Client: **Remington Electric Shavers**
A timeless ad pitched at the kind of tough-bearded customer who needs the analogy of agricultural equipment to persuade him.

1966.01
Agency: **Doyle Dane Bernbach**
Client: **Remington Electric Shavers**
A no-expense-spared pitch identifies the Remington cordless shaver as a superior product, priced in pre-decimal guineas.

1965.01
Agency: **Doyle Dane Bernbach**
Client: **Remington Electric Shavers**
DDB deploys an early version of the approach later used to sell 'reassuringly expensive' Stella Artois lager [as featured on page 365].

opposite

1968.01
Agency: **Doyle Dane Bernbach**
Client: **Uniroyal**
Donald Silverstein's photograph for this 'public interest' poster from Uniroyal anticipated the charity look that would later become a prevalent style.

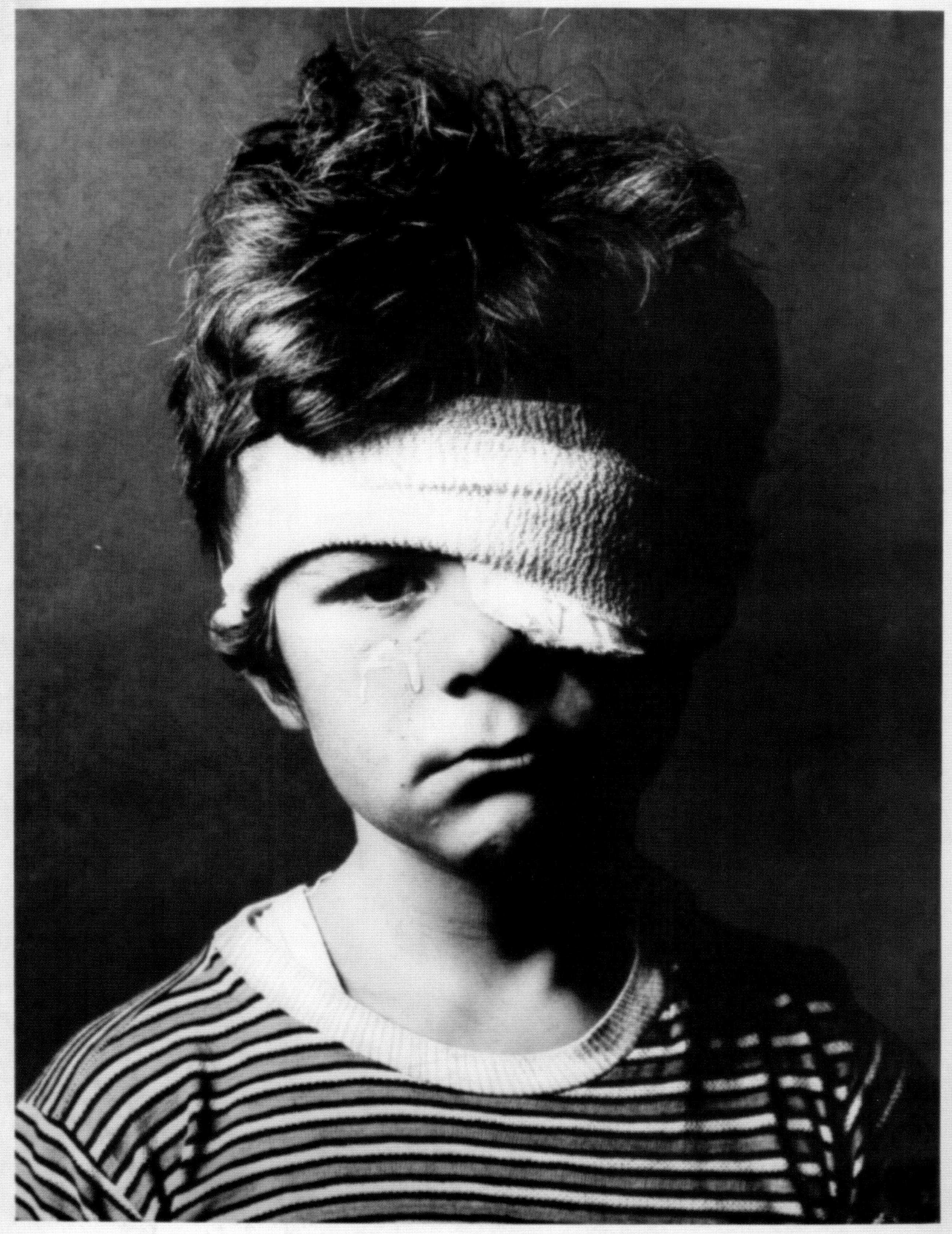

Make sure the wrong guy doesn't get burnt tonight.

By the time firework day was over last year, 1,289 children had been taken to hospital. Hundreds of those children had their eyes burned. Tonight, please make sure your kids take care. If they don't, they may never see November the fifth again.

This advertisement is issued in the public interest by Uniroyal Ltd.

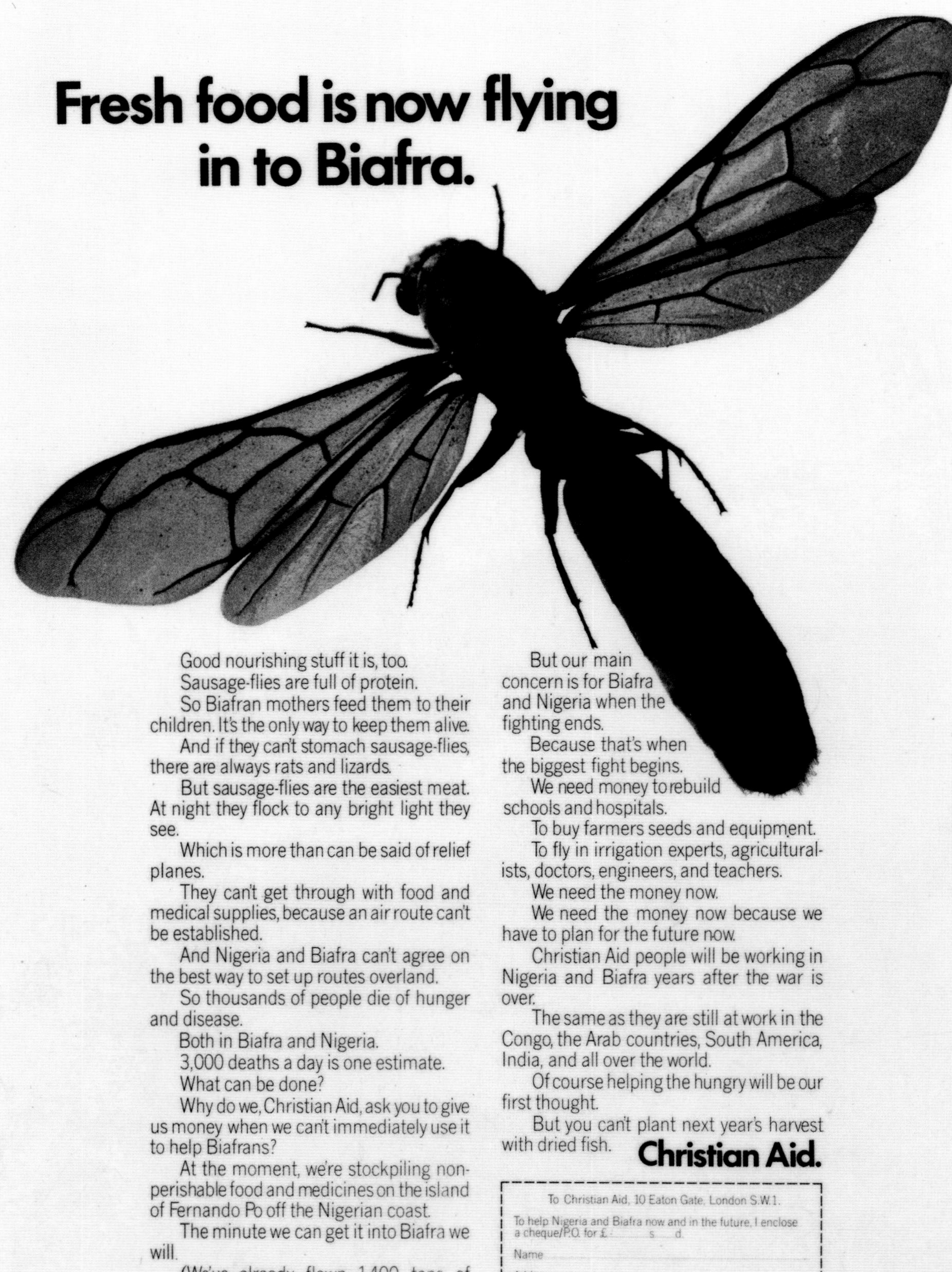
Fresh food is now flying in to Biafra.
Good nourishing stuff it is, too.
Sausage-flies are full of protein.
So Biafran mothers feed them to their children. It's the only way to keep them alive.
And if they can't stomach sausage-flies, there are always rats and lizards.
But sausage-flies are the easiest meat. At night they flock to any bright light they see.
Which is more than can be said of relief planes.
They can't get through with food and medical supplies, because an air route can't be established.
And Nigeria and Biafra can't agree on the best way to set up routes overland.
So thousands of people die of hunger and disease.
Both in Biafra and Nigeria.
3,000 deaths a day is one estimate.
What can be done?
Why do we, Christian Aid, ask you to give us money when we can't immediately use it to help Biafrans?
At the moment, we're stockpiling non-perishable food and medicines on the island of Fernando Po off the Nigerian coast.
The minute we can get it into Biafra we will.
(We've already flown 1,400 tons of stockfish into starvation areas now held by Federal troops.)
But our main concern is for Biafra and Nigeria when the fighting ends.
Because that's when the biggest fight begins.
We need money to rebuild schools and hospitals.
To buy farmers seeds and equipment.
To fly in irrigation experts, agriculturalists, doctors, engineers, and teachers.
We need the money now.
We need the money now because we have to plan for the future now.
Christian Aid people will be working in Nigeria and Biafra years after the war is over.
The same as they are still at work in the Congo, the Arab countries, South America, India, and all over the world.
Of course helping the hungry will be our first thought.
But you can't plant next year's harvest with dried fish.
Christian Aid.
To Christian Aid, 10 Eaton Gate, London S.W.1.
To help Nigeria and Biafra now and in the future, I enclose a cheque/P.O. for £ s d.
Name
Address

1969.05
Agency: **Doyle Dane Bernbach**
Client: **Christian Aid**
Martyn Walsh's image and Malcolm Gluck's copy made early use of shock tactics to jolt the public into giving money to a Third World aid programme.

this page

1966.02
Agency: **Doyle Dane Bernbach**
Client: **Remington Electric Shavers**

1967.03
Agency: **Doyle Dane Bernbach**
Client: **Remington Electric Shavers**

Two early examples of men's grooming commercials, both written by John Withers. The focus of these ads was the technical specifications of the shaver, and the effect of a clean shave on the opposite sex. Some things never change.

1968.02
Agency: **Doyle Dane Bernbach**
Client: **Tern Consulate**
Aided by David Montgomery's wide-angle shot, DDB continued to encourage cautious sartorial rebellion in the office.

Advertisement
ORPINGTON
THE TIMES
Tern invite the white collar worker to stick his neck out.
When it comes to office clobber, the British don't exactly go to town.
They've been wearing the same old white shirt for years. And we think it's time for a change.
To this end, we introduce our new coloured range.
Particularly suitable for dazzling the typing pool is the red cutaway. (As worn by the gent on the far left.)
We also make this shirt in pink, lilac, gold, and blue.
Another daring soul is the chap in the pin-stripe suit. His blue shirt has a button-down collar and angled cuffs.
Altogether, we have a hundred shades, checks and stripes in our range. (In non-iron cotton and nylon.)
With eight collar styles and seven cuff designs.
Of course, we realise that some of you are never going to wear the idea of wearing a coloured shirt to the office.
So our new range also includes white shirts with button-down collars and white on white stripes.
If we can't talk you into a coloured shirt, maybe we can get you into a more colourful white one.

The fifties had sown the seeds for a sixties cultural revolution in the UK, and when it came that revolution would embrace far more than design and advertising. Art, fashion, music, movies, graphic design, theatre, television, furniture, shopping, publishing, architecture and cars all at first reflected and then defined the *zeitgeist*. The movement was powered by youth, full employment and a sense of sudden release from the drabness and rationing of the post-war years. And its energy was so potent as to cut across hidebound techniques and production practices, freeing up commerce and the media to reflect and celebrate contemporary tastes and concerns. That liberating spirit was clearly evident in the intention, if not exactly in the phraseology, of the original D&AD mission: 'To encourage the understanding and commission of good design in publicity, graphic communications and advertising material of every nature. To demonstrate and to gain recognition for the part that imaginative design and art direction play in the context of modern society. To define and improve the current standards of all forms of graphic design in practice in Great Britain.'

The language may sound like that of a trade delegation, but the driving spirit was both radical and prescient; it was time to celebrate and promote the style, pizzazz and effectiveness of commercial communications, and acknowledge its true creative spirits.

The newly assembled D&AD juries, composed entirely of the leading designers and advertising art directors of the period, immediately began to seek out what they considered to be the groundbreaking work, although award selections were naturally restricted to what had been entered (and, in retrospect, it's clear that sometimes the most significant designs and campaigns were not entered into the awards at all).

These images show some of the members of the first D&AD judging sessions in 1963.

this page, left to right
Robert Brownjohn – *art director & designer*
John Pearce – *agency director, Collett Dickenson Pearce*
Barry Trengrove – *art director, Harper's Bazaar*
Tom Wolsey – *art director, Town*

opposite, left to right
Germano Facetti – *art director, Penguin Books*
Bob Pethick – *copywriter, Bensons*
Derek Birdsall – *designer*
Malcolm Hart – *art director, Bensons*

In this respect, it is worth recalling that from all of the examples of images used in The Beatles' album covers, which as a body of work perhaps summed up the cultural revolution of the sixties most vividly, D&AD's sole selection was arguably one of the least compelling: *Beatles For Sale*, photographed by Robert Freeman. The gatefold album was released at the end of 1964, and despite earlier press reports that it would feature The Beatles standing beneath the Arc de Triomphe at night holding lighted matches beneath their faces, the actual cover image was a considerably more routine piece of colour portraiture.

Looking back, it seems a more likely candidate for an award should have been Freeman's 1963 minimalist black and white cover for *With The Beatles*. Improvised in the dining room of a Bournemouth hotel, it was this grainy image that first defined the meeting of pop music and sophisticated packaging, a sixties process that would peak four years later with *Sergeant Pepper's Lonely Hearts Club Band*.

However, hindsight offers a perspective not always evident at the time and it was in a pioneering and occasionally improvisational spirit that the Designers

☐ 1965.02
Designer: **Robert Freeman**
Client: **EMI Records**
The Beatles' albums usually managed to evoke a sense of style not normally associated with pop albums prior to the sixties.

D&AD logo
The orientation of the D&AD logo has altered somewhat since it was first employed in the poster and exhibition catalogue for the 1963 Awards. To gain the desired perspective, Colin Forbes cut out the letters and placed them on a cube. Unfortunately, the photographs all fell out of focus so they were sent to Wolfgang Spoerl who re-drew the letters.

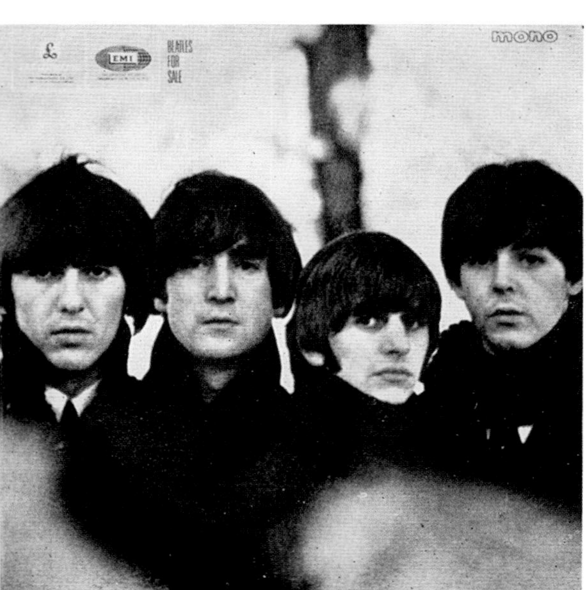

Poster
The 1963 'call for entries' poster for D&AD's first awards was designed by Fletcher/Forbes/Gill and listed both the awards categories and the jurors.

Exhibition catalogue
D&AD's first awards scheme yielded one Gold Award, for a TV ad for Shell by Geoffrey Jones, and 15 Silver Awards which were displayed, along with other entries, at the London Hilton Hotel. An exhibition catalogue, again designed by Fletcher/Forbes/Gill, included the credits for the work on display. The first D&AD Annual, complete with illustrations, wouldn't be produced until the following year.

and Art Directors Association of London (as it was then called) had been formed under the chairmanship of John Commander, an art director at the printing firm of Balding & Mansell. The founding members had looked to the US for some sort of lead, and graphic designer Alan Fletcher simply adapted an entry form from the New York Art Directors' Club. Colin Forbes designed the D&AD logo, using the decidedly pre-digital 3-D modelling technique of sticking the four characters onto the visible sides of a wooden cube and photographing the result.

Now equipped with a mission, an entry form and a logo, D&AD was in a position to codify the common concerns and aspirations of London's advertising and graphic design community. It began with an exhibition in the summer of 1963 that featured 403 items of print and 38 films selected from some 3,500 entries. The exhibition was opened by Lord Snowdon, focusing on what it labelled 'graphic design' and 'advertising art'. There was no book, just an exhibition booklet, yet two public exhibitions alone attracted a total of 25,000 visitors. As it turned out, John Commander's leadership would only extend until October of the following year, when he announced his resignation.

Design & Art Direction '63 The first annual exhibition of the Designers & Art Directors Association of London

A union, Jack!

Young Commonwealth Artists 1962. 4th Annual Exhibition. RBA Galleries, 6½ Suffolk Street, (off Haymarket), London SW1. Mondays to Saturdays 10 to 5.30, Sundays 2 to 6. From Monday, April 2 until Tuesday, April 24.

Barrie Bates

1963.01
Designer: **Barrie Bates**
Client: **Young Commonwealth Artists**
Once the British flag was a sacred thing. This poster design is one of the earliest attempts to put it into the service of commerce.

this page

1964.02
Production company: **Nicholas Cartoons**
Client: **Shell International**
An early attempt to introduce animated humour to selling an inherently unglamorous product.

1964.03
Production company: **Nordisk reklamefilm**
Client: **Shell International**
A D&AD European winner, this TV ad uses live action to make engine oil the focus of a little entertainment.

1963.02
Agency: **Colman Prentis & Varley**
Client: **Yardley**
The idea was Robert Brownjohn's (although he was uncredited) and the visual pun perfectly caught the feisty self-image that young women aspired to in the sixties.

Edward Booth-Clibborn, an art director at advertising agency J Walter Thompson (JWT), was elected chairman and went on to run D&AD in an idiosyncratic fashion for a quarter of a century.

That first year's Gold Award went to a Shell promotional film by Geoffrey Jones. One of 15 Silver Awards went to Barrie Bates for his poster design, promoting an exhibition of Young Commonwealth Artists. His modified Union Jack, its lineaments only partially coloured in with crayon, captured the emerging spirit of the sixties counter-culture; before long, the previously sacrosanct British flag would be hijacked and subverted by virtually every faction of that culture; eventually it would adorn underpants. Also honoured with a D&AD Silver in 1963 was Colman Prentis & Varley's ad for Yardley's lipsticks, a classic example of a visual pun – lipsticks masquerading as bullets in a gunbelt – giving rise to copy that doggedly sustains the conceit, 'Go great guns with Yardley ... be fore-armed ... sure-fire lipsticks.' In both cases the wit may look heavy-handed now, but it is nevertheless wit, something that was to characterize and shape some of the best sixties graphics.

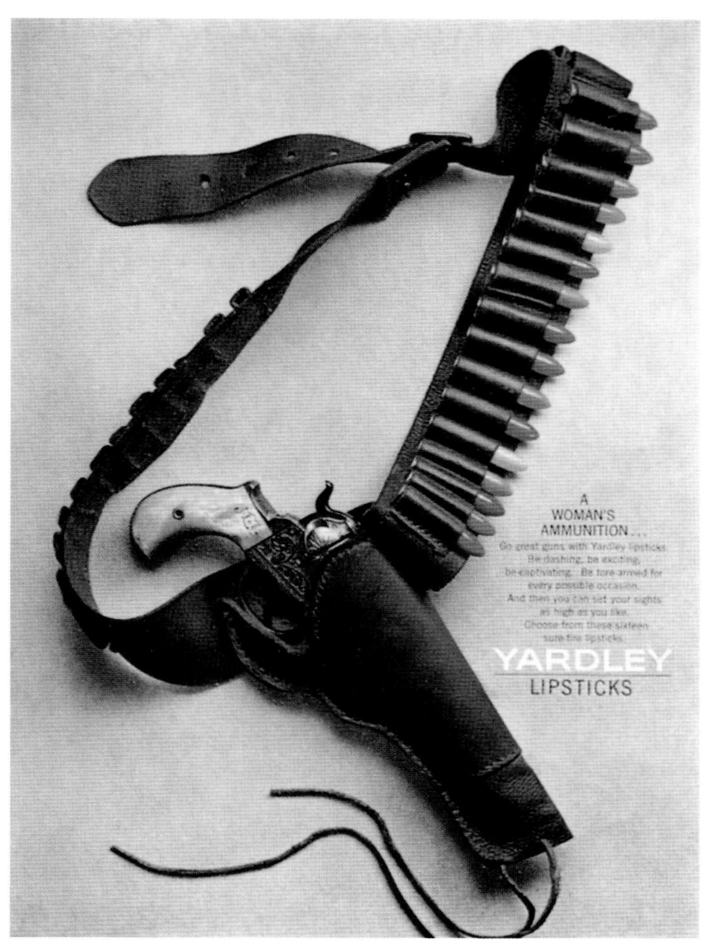

Right from the beginning of the decade, it was graphic design that showed the way forward. Here was a medium where inventive design did not have to cost any more than dull design and where the status quo was anyway crying out to be challenged. Hitherto, most graphic designers had been either freelance commercial artists or backroom boys toiling over type in the basements of large advertising agencies. Design consultancies did not really exist in the sense that we know them today. It was in the sixties that a new generation of designers began to emerge from the advertising agencies and to establish a fresh approach that would eventually significantly reshape the communication industries.

One of these new-style design consultancies was the exemplary Minale Tattersfield, founded in 1964. Marcello Minale and Brian Tattersfield had met at advertising agency Young & Rubicam (Y&R), where the visually-led Minale worked as a specialist designer while Tattersfield devised ads that were frequently language-based. Gradually their complementary talents would broaden to embrace and absorb one another. By 1964 they were ambitious and impatient enough to create their own company, one where they could, for the first time, meet with and explain their communication ideas directly to clients, something they had never been able to do under the prevailing protocol at Y&R. They declared themselves in business (working from an A4-depth windowsill in a tiny office in London's Edgware Road), ran a challenging advertisement in the trade publication *Ad Weekly* ('Who the devil are Minale Tattersfield?') and enshrined their approach in a famous graphic scribble indicating that they valued the hastily jotted but inspired idea more than the good manners of slick but soulless finished artwork.

Minale Tattersfield could not have come about as it did without the change of climate signalled by the burgeoning D&AD. It is therefore hardly surprising that the consultancy would go on to become a regular award winner. Its first was for Ocean Oil, in which a droplet descends from the initial 'O' to turn it into a kind of liquefied exclamation mark.

1967.04
Design group:
Minale Tattersfield Provinciali
Client: **The Ocean Oil Company**
This paradigmatic Marcello Minale graphic solution emblemizes the client company by effortlessly evoking its product.

1968.03
Design group:
Minale Tattersfield Provinciali
Client: **Osram-GEC**
An imaginative promotional calendar for Osram-GEC, a lightbulb manufacturer, that diverts the form of the product to a new and surprising end.

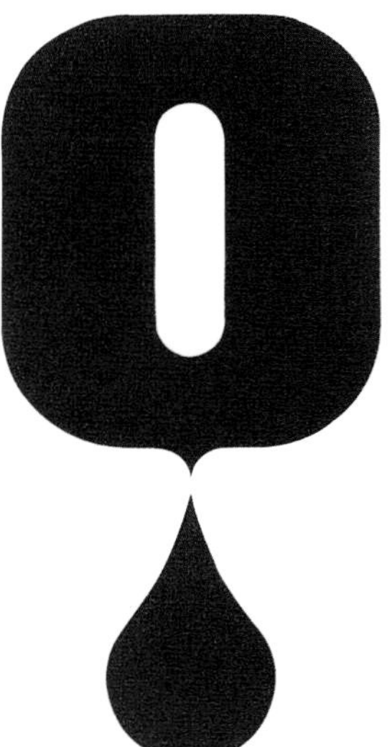

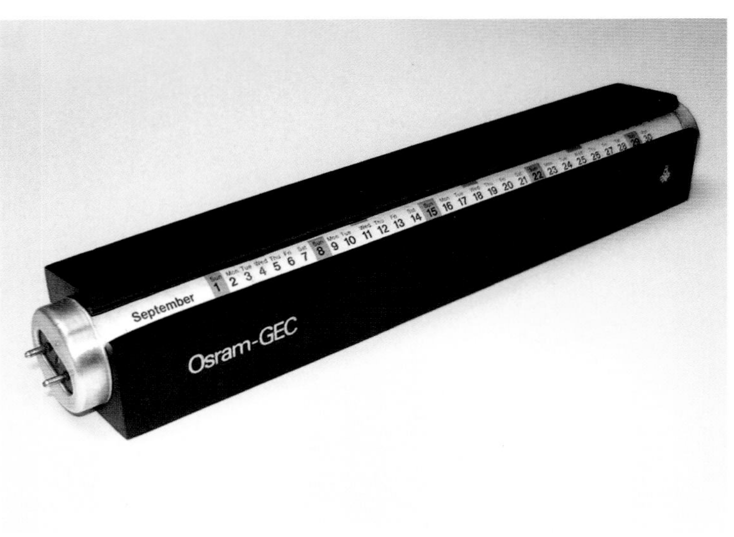

1964.04
Design group: **Fletcher/Forbes/Gill**
Client: **Penguin Books**
This cover for one of Penguin's non-fiction Pelican imprint titles elegantly married two images and their associated ideas.

1965.03
Designer: **Bob Gill**
Client: **The Kynoch Press**
Two drawings from 'Bob Gill's New York', a direct mail promotion from The Kynoch Press.

1964.05
Design group: **Fletcher/Forbes/Gill**
Client: **International Scientific Systems**
In the sixties, the square punched hole was one of the few recognizable symbols of automated data recognition, here incorporated into the logo design for ISS.

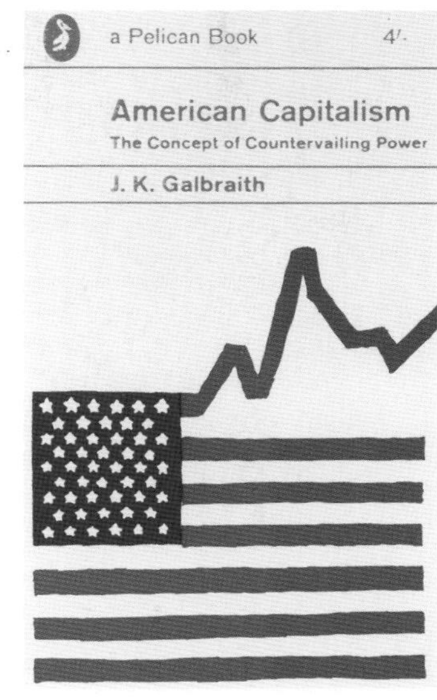

Two years earlier, another highly influential team had been formed. After stints in the US and Italy, Alan Fletcher returned to London in 1959 to work as a part-time design consultant to *Time* and *Life* magazines in Europe and to teach one day a week at Central School of Arts and Crafts. The young head of the graphic design department there was Colin Forbes, who four years later would design D&AD's logo. In 1962 Fletcher and Forbes teamed up with the American designer Bob Gill to form Fletcher/Forbes/Gill, an alliance that in some ways defined the pattern for the modern graphic design consultancy. Fletcher/Forbes/Gill took graphic design out of the province of the advertising agency, making it humorous, irreverent and effective in the process. Typically, its 1964 book cover for J K Galbraith's *American Capitalism: The Concept of Countervailing Power* made a performance graph out of the topmost stripe of the US flag, suggesting a level of wit perhaps absent from the book itself. When architect Theo Crosby joined the group to help realize a piece of environmental design in which buildings were to be constructed in the shape of letters, the practice seemed to be moving towards a multi-disciplinary approach that soon alienated Bob Gill. Crosby would later design offices for Collett Dickenson Pearce (CDP), Geers Gross, Boase Massimi Pollitt (BMP) and French Gold Abbott, but when he told Gill that his designs for a town centre would be built in eight years time, Gill allegedly replied, 'That's a long time to wait for a proof.' Gill left in 1965, but Fletcher/Forbes/Gill had already proved itself an influential force in the creation of a new pecking order within London's creative communication services. It had also generated the seed of what would prove to be an exceptionally successful and durable consultancy – Pentagram, to be launched a decade later.

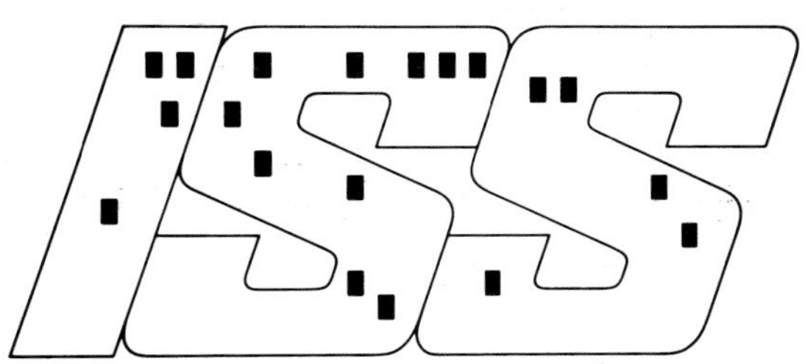

A third influential force in the sixties design revolution was Michael Wolff, who had worked at Crawfords advertising agency and the BBC before embarking on a series of doomed design businesses. However, in 1964 he and designer Jimmy Main set up Wolff Main, which contained the kernel of commercial success if not exactly success itself. The consultancy was saved by the arrival of Wally Olins, a shrewd operator who was able to bring a stabilizing business sense to Wolff's visionary brand of creativity. In the mid-sixties the mix was exactly right and resulted in some notable Wolff Olins design successes – including an award-winning 1966 corporate identity for Hadfields Paint & Chemicals that typified Wolff's highly personal approach. 'We got away from abstract logos, and used an image of a fox in several different ways, always with wit and humour.' At Wolff Olins a new design approach was beginning to emerge in which sixties humanistic concerns looked as if they might, after all, be able to co-exist with effective commercial strategies.

1969.06
Design group: **Wolff Olins**
Client: **Bowyers**
Michael Wolff's passion for using animals in corporate identities was for once defeated by the client, who, in this instance, had already used them in the product.

opposite

1968.04
Design group: **Wolff Olins**
Client: **Hadfields**
One of Wolff Olins' early examples of using an animal to make the product range memorable. The paint was water-based and the fox was the variable emblem within a fully integrated identity.

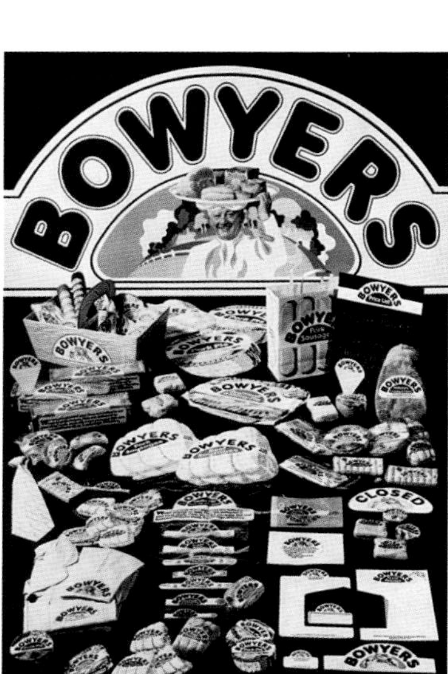

A paint so amazing yet so tried and tested, that **Hadfields** make this challenge to the public

*If you didn't read the test results on the previous page: Double back and have a look at them before you go any further

Lou Klein, one more of those American practitioners who had decamped to London, was another sixties creative design force whose influence recurred throughout the decade, and who enjoyed unique links with D&AD. Working for a number of major advertising agencies he won two Silver Awards in 1966 at Charles Hobson & Grey (for clients Spicers and Reed Paper) and a further two Silvers the following year. In partnership with Michael Peters (Klein Peters) he worked on a number of projects for Collett Dickenson Pearce & Partners, an advertising agency destined for world fame and whose star was already rising. These projects included a piece for Sexton's Charley boots which was a 1968 D&AD Silver Award winner. Michael Peters went on to form his own influential design consultancy while Klein continued to operate independently both as an art director and a designer with his own consultancy, Klein Design. However, perhaps Klein's most enduring legacy was the creation of the D&AD yellow pencil which has famously come to symbolize the organization and its awards. He is also the only person to have contributed to the design of two covers of D&AD annuals in 1966 and 1969.

1966.03
Art director: **Lou Klein**
Client: **Reed Paper & Board Sales**
In 1964 Lou Klein began work at Charles Hobson & Grey which counted among its clients the Reed Paper group as shown below in this promotional mailer.

1966.04
Art director: **Lou Klein**
Client: **Spicers**
In a bid to persuade printers to try new paper stock, Lou Klein was given the task of creating colourful poster proposals. The man in this promotion for Spicers paper was found in a tattoo parlour in London's Soho. The photograph was taken by Bob Brooks.

Venus was born
Printed on Reedart 20×30 50lbs 117gsm

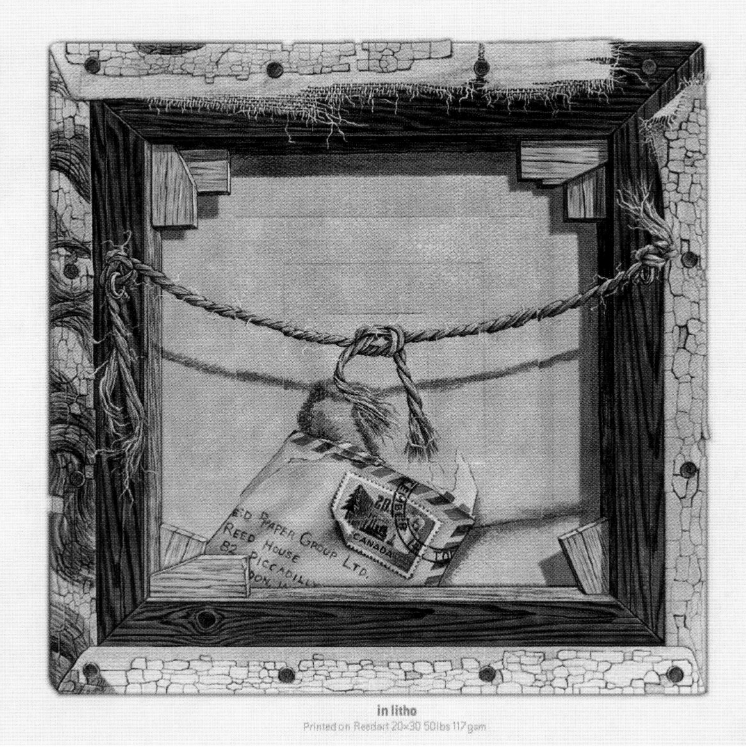

in litho
Printed on Reedart 20×30 50lbs 117gsm

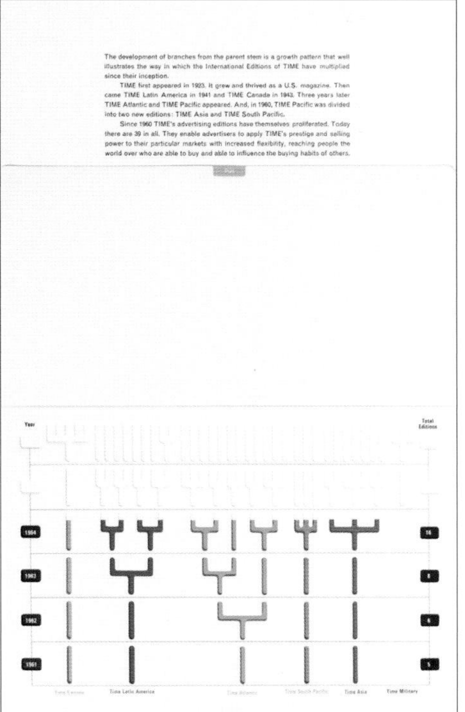
The development of branches from the parent stem is a growth pattern that well illustrates the way in which the International Editions of TIME have multiplied since their inception.

TIME first appeared in 1923. It grew and thrived as a U.S. magazine. Then came TIME Latin America in 1941 and TIME Canada in 1943. Three years later TIME Atlantic and TIME Pacific appeared. And, in 1960, TIME Pacific was divided into two new editions: TIME Asia and TIME South Pacific.

Since 1960 TIME's advertising editions have themselves proliferated. Today there are 39 in all. They enable advertisers to apply TIME's prestige and selling power to their particular markets with increased flexibility, reaching people the world over who are able to buy and able to influence the buying habits of others.

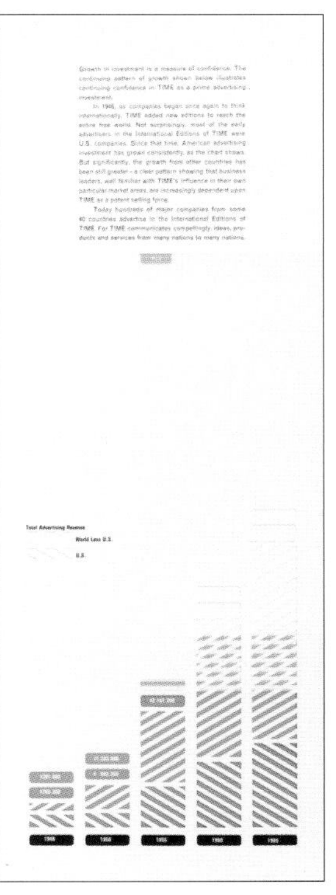

1967.05
Art director: **Lou Klein**
Client: **Reed Paper Group**
Another promotional paper sample for the Reed Paper Group, again done while Klein was at advertising agency Charles Hobson & Grey.

1967.06
Art director: **Lou Klein**
Client: **Time International**
These two pieces of direct mail showed the sales performance of *Time International* in coloured graphs that were only visible by pulling out an inserted sheet of card.

The D&AD Award
Though the yellow pencil is now synonymous with the D&AD Awards, there was a precursor designed by Minale Tattersfield – an ebony pencil box with sliding lid which held a regular-sized grey pencil with silver lettering. Unfortunately, D&AD could no longer afford the ebony, and the box fell apart quite quickly. The problem was discussed at a board meeting in 1966 at JWT's offices where Klein began scribbling. Upon showing these initial sketches to the group they immediately gave him the go-ahead to develop what has become one of the creative industry's most sought-after prizes.

As design continued to inject new creative life into the best print advertising, magazines were also embarking upon a form and content revolution. The 1963 Awards had already recognized two notable magazine revamps which were to prove catalytic; the titles were *Queen* and *Town* and they had been early reinventions of hitherto unadventurous metropolitan magazines. *Queen* and *Town*, at one point both art directed by Tom Wolsey, were rejuvenated by two publishing houses, respectively Stevens Press and Cornmarket. When Mark Boxer was art director of *Queen* he claimed that in Stevens Press's Jocelyn Stevens he had found 'an art director's essential requirement – a boss who was young, enthusiastic [and with] a real feeling for exciting layouts.' *Town* magazine, born out of the unpromising tailoring trade magazine *Man About Town*, combined a new edge and sharp wit with visual flair provided by Tom Wolsey.

1964.06
Art director: **Max Maxwell**
Publication: **Queen**
Queen was highly influential in British publishing and was originally art directed by Max Maxwell, who won Silver for this feature on horses.

1965.04
Art director: **Barry Trengrove**
Publication: **Harper's Bazaar**
Even the graffiti is chic in this surprisingly timeless mid-sixties fashion feature.

this page

1964.07
Art director: **Tom Wolsey**
Publication: **Town**
A typical *Town* feature in which a human face is put upon a foreign political piece and the result elegantly organized by Tom Wolsey.

SEA OF TROUBLES 2: PAUL JOHNSON ON INDONESIA'S BROWN IMPERIALISM

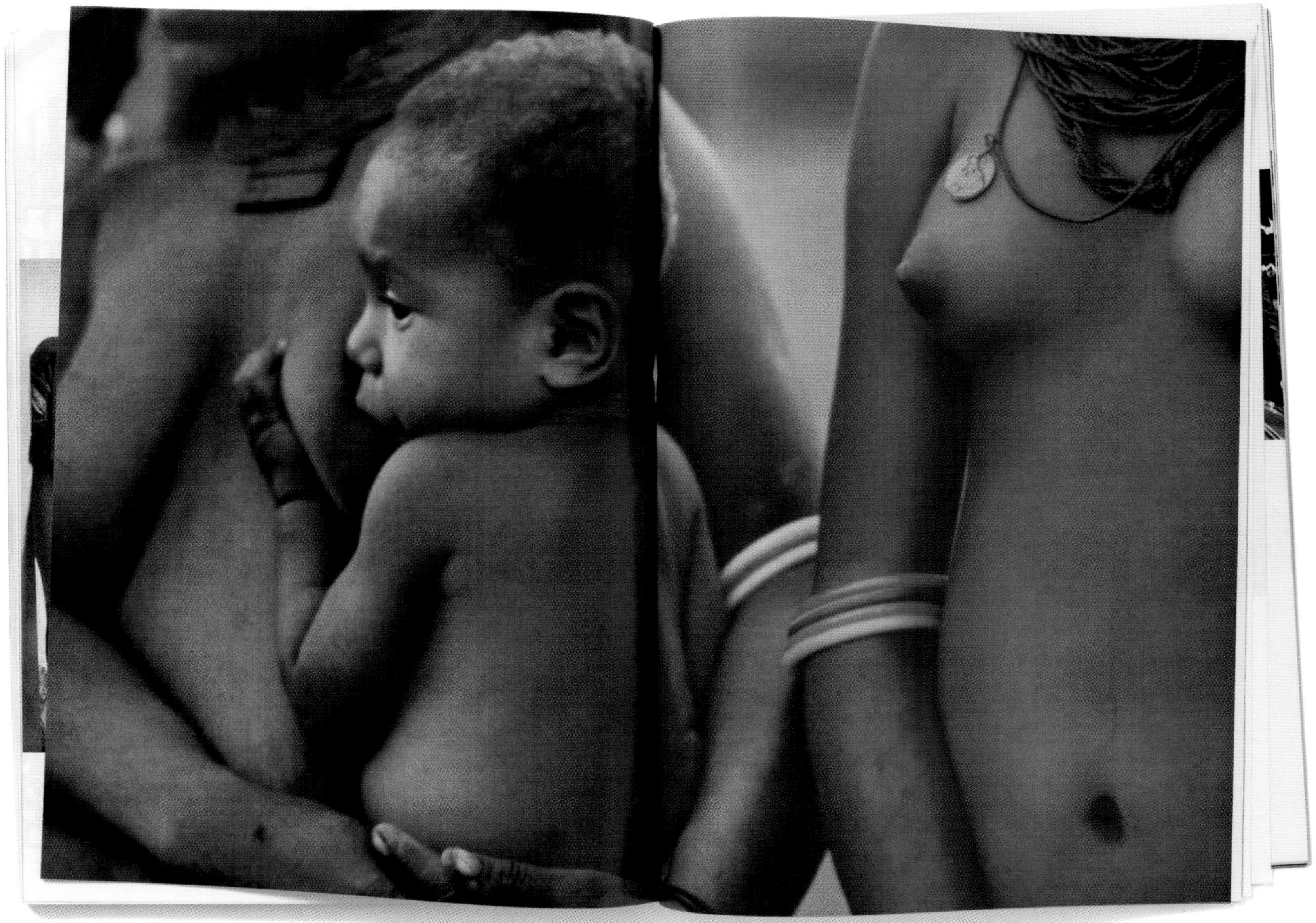

German-born Wolsey was an influential figure who had studied at Leeds College of Art and worked at Crawfords advertising agency before joining Michael Heseltine and Clive Labovitch's Cornmarket publishing house. His design approach was avowedly 'to stop people in their tracks' and 'make them think twice about some aspect of society.' It was a dramatic and revolutionary approach that contrasted with the prim manners of most British magazine design of the time, an approach whose contemporary impact is hard to appreciate today, when its lessons have been so thoroughly absorbed into the mainstream.

Wolsey's achievement and the success of the magazines he worked on stimulated the emerging Sunday supplements market and opened the door for titles like *Nova*, magazines that managed to focus on subject matter that really engaged their readers' imaginations instead of merely addressing them. The Sunday supplements, in particular, were influential in that, while they eventually came to provide a reason for buying a particular newspaper, initially they reached people who normally might not buy magazines at all.

When *The Sunday Times magazine* first adopted colour, this in itself became a key selling point. Tom Wolsey's assistant at *Queen* had been David King who, along with Michael Rand, would be responsible for the aggressive, polemical style of *The Sunday Times magazine*. King was an alumnus of the London School of Printing where Richard Hollis and Derek Birdsall had been among the tutors of the refocused and rechristened graphic and typographical design course (which was previously known as commercial art). Suddenly, middle-class lifestyle preoccupations were being interspersed with edgy photojournalism that explored uncomfortable political and social issues. There was something in the air and it had to do with social change combined with technical advance; suddenly, colour printing was cheap and its wide use gave new impact to black and white images if monochrome was deemed to suit the subject matter better. Challenging editorial subjects frequently became visually led... or at least shared the honours between text and image. Art directors were now becoming part of the editorial engine, not just graphic decorators.

1964.08
Agency: **Thomson Organisation**
Client: **The Sunday Times**
As these two posters advertised, *The Sunday Times magazine* was the first in the UK to be printed in colour.

opposite

1969.07
Art director: **Michael Rand**
Publication:
The Sunday Times magazine
'America Hurrah!' was one of a five-part series on the US. The special issues included a Walker Evans retrospective and an issue on Vietnam [see page 50]. It was also the first time that the magazine used photographer Diane Arbus.

1966.05
Art director: **Michael Rand**
Publication:
The Sunday Times magazine
Alan Aldridge was a junior in the promotions department of *The Sunday Times* when he showed his portfolio to Michael Rand. Less than six months later, he created this cover, using water-based paints on a silver Mini belonging to Rand's assistant, David Nathanson, who promptly hosed the car down after the shoot.

1965.05
Art director: **Michael Rand**
Publication:
The Sunday Times magazine

1969.08
Art director: **Jeanette Collins**
Publication:
The Times Women's Page

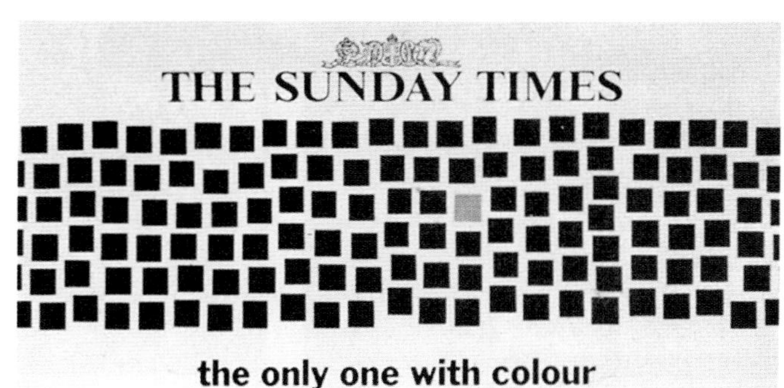

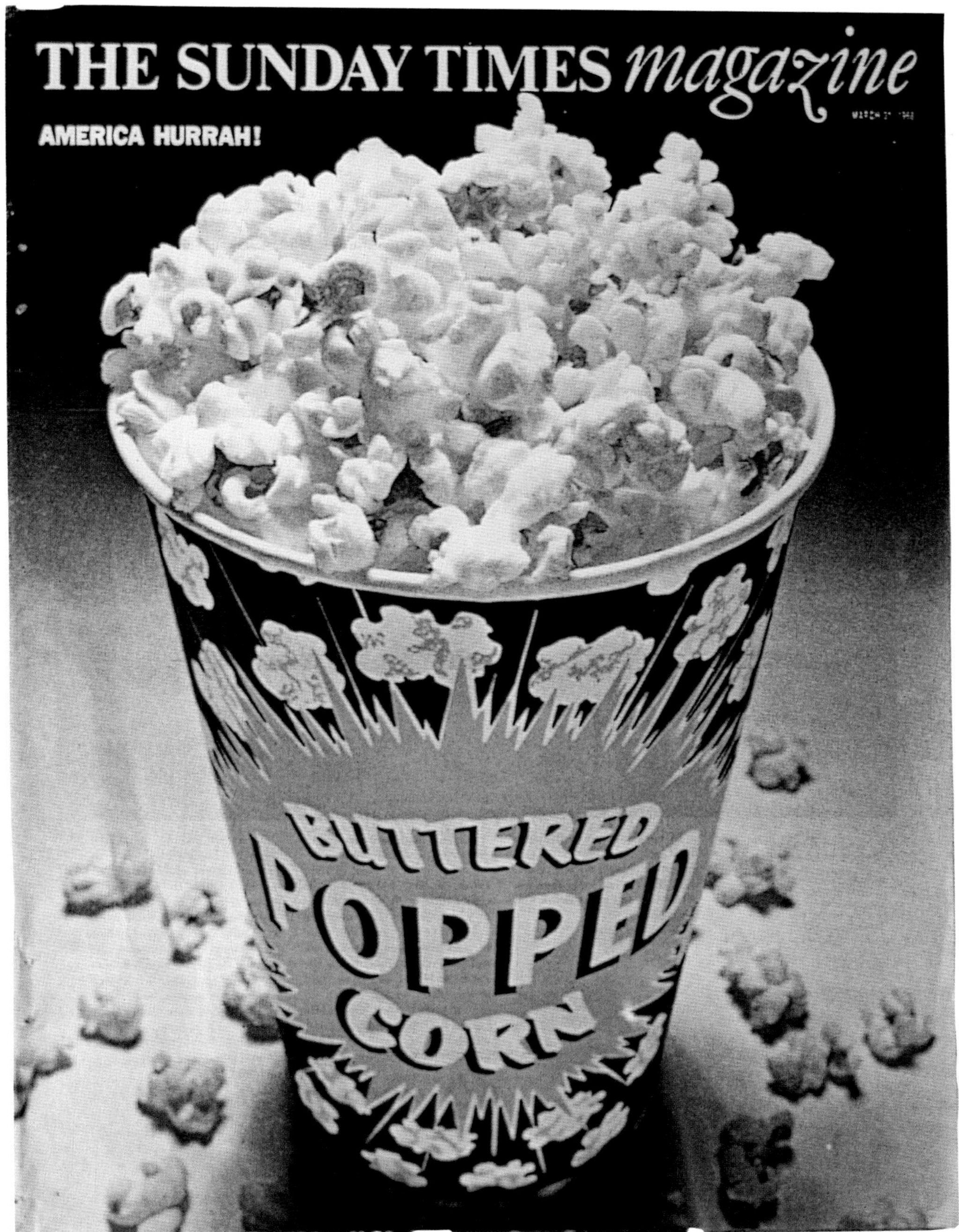

overleaf

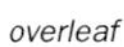 1968.05
Art director: **Michael Rand**
Publication:
The Sunday Times magazine
A classic feature that anticipated how celebrities of the day would look in their forties, courtesy of Michael Leonard's prescient illustrations.

THE SUNDAY TIMES *magazine*
NOVEMBER 12, 1967

The Middle Age of Jackie Kennedy - and YOU

Who's afraid of Middle Age? And if you are, why should you be? Of course it's inevitable but, as we hope to show in this and the following issue, it need not be intolerable. It seems odd that the years from 40 to 60 – perhaps the most responsible of our lives – have up till now been so neglected by sociologists, medical researchers and administrators. They are always debating the frustrations and problems of youth and old age – there have even been government committees to study them. But nobody has felt the need for a committee to investigate middle age. It might not be a bad idea, because this is a period of life which can be rich in the quality of its ideas, its judgment and its freedom. One eminent psychiatrist described it as "the crisis point of growth or regression. If middle-aged people give up their omnipotence wishes and gain a sense of perspective about their own place and power to influence the course of events they can enter into the enjoyment of life at 50".* Many of the people in this series are experiencing this enjoyment – women freed from the restrictions of child-bearing and rearing; men taking stock of their unfulfilled ambitions and deciding to make a dramatic and rewarding change of career. Below, Dr Alex Comfort suggests that the forties are now taking the form of a second adolescence. To answer the fascinating question of what those in their twenties and thirties today will look like in middle age, artist Michael Leonard makes predictions for 18 famous people, beginning with Jackie Kennedy. How many others do you recognise? The answers are on page 57. And for further insight into middle age, read on

Life can begin at 40

By Alex Comfort, Director, Medical Research Council Group on Ageing

Middle age is physically the late period of adult vigour, and longer survival has fundamentally altered our attitude towards it. Our fathers tended to regard it as the levelling-off time, and 40 or 45 in our residual mythology is the point at which disengagement from competitive enterprise – financial, sexual, everything except political – should begin. For the present generation, which has a good chance of reaching 80 if it avoids war, accident and lung cancer, 40 is halftime. In consequence the forties are coming more and more to take on the guise of a second adolescence.

At puberty we normally determine our goals in life and test our powers of attaining them. We have fantasies, fulfilled and unfulfilled, derived from our childhood and our environment. Life tests the desirability and practicability of these fantasies – we may or may not get insight into them, we may or may not attain them. Middle age brings a fresh access of energy to those fantasies that we have not realised or abandoned. It is the time when we realise things have not gone according to plan, and the realisation has the added force that comes from knowing that we have not too much time left. At the same time, unlike our predecessors, we know that it is still not too late.

Reactions to the 'second puberty' are diverse. Sexual reassessment, ranging from the appearance of repressed elements like homosexuality to the pursuit of reassurance with new partners, is common. Social opportunity for change is high – the middle-aged have the means and experience to do things they feared or could not afford to do in youth.

The woman, approaching the end of her fertility, though not of her sexuality, has raised her children and may find herself distanced from what she regarded in the past as a life work. As at puberty, some react to these forces by insightful change, others by thrashing about, and yet others by mental or physical illness. Although late middle age does bring physical changes, these are probably less important to those undergoing them than the psychological changes – at least in our culture – and they disturb us because they point to us that we are no longer young. How much of the psychosomatic stress which some women experience at the menopause is hormonal and how much a matter of attitude, is doubtful. Some regard it as the end of womanhood, others as a happy release of sexuality from childbearing. The facetious remark that women have a menopause, but men do not have a womenopause, is both true and wide of the mark. Both may pass through a period of anxiety about their continued identity and competitiveness as desirable people – castration fear in its Freudian sense, arising from the primacy of sexual ideas in our sense of selfhood. A radical reshaping of life in pursuit of unattained satisfactions is harder in our society for women than for men, and particularly hard when these satisfactions are sexually expressed: a man of any age can hope for a new partner, while a woman cannot.

Lowered mortality at all ages has made lifelong monogamy a 60- or 70-year stint. Often an outburst of non-sexual experiment in middle life bears the marks of being a displacement activity, or an assertion of separate identity against the image of 'togetherness', very like the adolescent's salutary break with parents. Continued sexual performance, contrary to folklore, depends very little on age or physical considerations and almost wholly on attitude. Impotence and frigidity are hardly ever direct consequences of age in people not obviously sick. They are more likely to be the outcome of anxieties, reservations or renunciations at the unconscious level.

Late middle age still belongs to the period of adult vigour, and can be one of its most rewarding passages, when selfhood is really attained. Fitting it together with 'second adolescence' and subsequent old age requires some inevitable degree of withdrawal if only from athletic pursuits and competition with the young, and it is something our culture gives us no real help in managing. We no longer dress our young grandmothers in mobcaps, but we still retire healthy people compulsorily. Those with resources of interest can survive, but for many it is a trap-door through which they fall, to become non-persons, devoid of social content and wished away by those who formerly valued them. In planning our society we need insights into these undiscussed attitudinal changes quite as much as we need medical and social services (without the insights we shall misplan the services).

We need to lose the mythology of ageing as inevitable decline without substituting an unreal cheerfulness which dresses grandmothers in mini-skirts and refuses – as in one American settlement for the retired – to permit hospitals or cemeteries to be constructed. We need to make a human and productive role in society for our old people without overtaxing or exploiting them. And we need, I feel, to avoid edifying philosophical statements about the compensations of old age. It has compensations, but, as every old man knows, it is a deteriorative process, the loss

"of every beautiful thing
that made a catch in the breath . . ."

to be faced with dignity, like death itself, but not to be accepted or romanticised.

The measure of ageing is the increased liability to die with increasing age, and the evidence of it is the fact of having a fixed and roughly foreseeable maximum lifespan – there is a date by which, however lucky I am, I shall almost certainly be dead. This deteriorative ageing is one of the oldest human enemies. It is of growing importance today because, unlike our forefathers who often died accidentally in youth, we are increasingly likely to live to exhibit it, along with its ➞

* Dr Henry Dicks *The Seven Ages of Man*. New Society Publications

In ten years we should know what makes us age

familiar symptoms of weakness of muscle, weakening of mind, wrinkling of skin, and hankering infirmity.

The conquest of ageing is a mythical human ambition. The early magicians attempted it; the middle reaches of developing rational science put it out of mind as an impracticable fantasy. Over the last ten or 20 years it has increasingly returned to the human agenda as a subject for serious operational research. Work on the fundamental nature of age processes, with a view to controlling them, now rates a very large scientific and monetary investment in several countries. America is spending heavily on it. The Soviet Union is beginning to do the same. I believe, as a professionally interested party, that Britain should invest in it more heavily. The point is, however, that with the progress of biology in general, and concentration on the study of age processes in particular, we shall almost certainly know within ten years what these processes are – and, depending upon what they are, we may well be able to interfere with them. There is no certainty of success, but the likelihood of some success – another five or ten years of adult vigour – is reasonably high.

Basic research on ageing is concerned with the clock mechanisms which causes us to lose vigour with age. If there is one such leading mechanism, and it proves accessible to interference, ageing could be slowed. Damage to the molecular blueprints which control the function of cells – particularly cells like those of the brain, which, like our adult teeth, we cannot replace – is a possible 'clock' of this kind. Such a clock could be slowed down. If there is more than one clock, then the nature and symptoms of ageing might be changed by serial interference with some or all of them. It is already known that the lifespan of rats and mice can be nearly doubled by simple dietary manipulations – not that these could be applied directly to ourselves, but they indicate that we are not attempting to modify a fundamental absolute. The speed of this advance will depend almost entirely on the priority we give it, and the public awareness of its feasibility.

If we could prolong adult vigour, we should still, eventually, age. A man of 75 then might have the vigour and mortality of a man of 70 today, but at 80 he would have the vigour and mortality of a man of 75. While ➞

At present we neglect and dislike old people

gerontology aims at basic interference with age processes, geriatrics aims to palliate the weaknesses and miseries of age as we now see them. All old men tend to infirmity, but not all are decrepit, demented and in pain. Medical measures can lighten the burden of infirmity, and there is even evidence that the degree of failure in mental powers can be reduced by making use of them fully in earlier life. Above all, the social role we assign to the old can make the difference between second childhood and active old age. At present we neglect and dislike old people, we exclude them socially and fiscally from rewarding activity, and we store them in chronic wards where they will not hamper the life of their children. In this we are less humane than the Eskimo, who allowed the incurably sick to die with dignity by exposing them on an icefloe – and far less humane than the peasant communities which allow them dignity and employment in the houses of their family. Dislike of the idea of ageing ourselves, the hostility of the generations, and the unconscious anxieties of doctors who see the incurable and the ageing as a reproach to their humane wish to heal, have all contributed to prevent us from treating our elders decently. We have a good geriatric hospital service, and excesses like those reported in *Sans Everything* are rare, though not rare enough. In addition to investment in fundamental research and in the medicine of old age, we need a new attitude, as a culture, towards the worth of old people. Self interest, if we care to think for a moment, demands that we take this matter seriously.

For many years yet, and perhaps perpetually, old age will be a part of life to be endured. Science offers the chance of postponing and palliating it, if not of controlling it completely, and these possibilities, when they become actual, should be accepted as wholly good, without any anxieties about it being arrogant to wish for longer vigorous life. Problems there will indeed be, if we are able to control ageing, but in a few generations the fears and the philosophising which have been our cultural posture so far will probably look as obsolete as the anxieties of Biblical fundamentalists over Simpson's introduction of chloroform.

The gain we envisage will be in the productive years. We spend a third of our present lifespan attaining full performance, whether as a doctor ➞

SEPTEMBER 1967 THREE SHILLINGS
NOVA
I was
not amused
by last
issue.
too far
CAMBRIDGE CLASS OF '67:
THE BOY MOST LIKELY TO SUCCEED.
Guess who's back in town – page 88

☐ 1968.06
Art director: **Bill Fallover**
Publication: **Nova**
Barry Fantoni's cover artwork illustrated an article, written by Kingsley Martin, on Prince Charles' fresher year at Trinity College, Cambridge in 1967.

this page

● 1967.07
Art director: **Harri Peccinotti**
Publication: **Nova**
This cover from August 1966 is one of a number of issues for which *Nova* won a Gold Award for Design of a Complete Unit.

☐ 1966.06
Art director: **Harri Peccinotti**
Publication: **Nova**
Nova seen here following the model of George Lois, who did a number of provocative cover designs for the US magazine *Esquire* in the sixties, including some that raised the issue of racism to its white middle-class audience.

Nova, founded in 1965, also marked a radical change, this time in women's magazines. Edited by Denis Hackett and art directed by Harri Peccinotti, *Nova* featured an intelligent and bracing mix of sex, art, fashion, politics, health and travel, all boldly designed by Peccinotti and richly printed on high-quality coated paper. The contrast with the insipid and condescending women's magazines that went before was complete. When, in 1967, *Nova* asked 'where are all the three-piece suites?' it was commenting on a shift in furniture-buying habits, but exactly the same kind of generational shift was already happening throughout the magazine world and *Nova* was part of the revolution. The visual furniture of the previous generation was being jettisoned in favour of a snappier, sexier brand. It was a shift that combined radical imagery with radical politics; the generation of practitioners who shaped the graphic look of the sixties were, by nature, sympathizers with the Left.

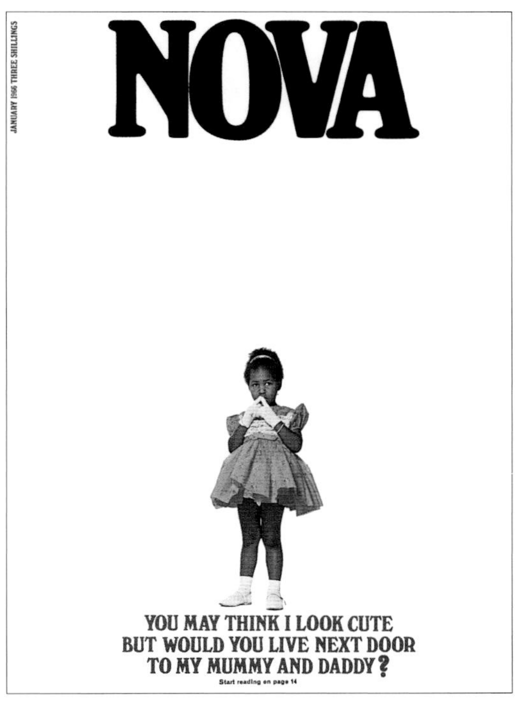

Shopping for winter holiday clothes in a grey-sky Britain which will survive the brilliance of a foreign sun can be disconcerting. Hot intense colours and vivid design can seem disturbingly bright, even garish, in our cold winter light. Picture them instead flattering a tan, glowing under a sizzling sun beating down on boat-deck or beach—pastels in these conditions would only keep you firmly in the fashion shade. So go for colours clear and strong.
Apply the same principle in choosing clothes for colder climates. Aim for intensity there, too. The success of Op Art design in clothes has proved convincingly the basic excellence of black and white—see for yourself how striking they can be against a snowy landscape. If your skiing is below standard, make sure your appearance is Gold Medal level. Since there's not much variation in basic ski outfits, excel individually with good definite colour and interesting texture. Sunglasses are an indispensable addition to your wardrobe for either sort of holiday. Superlative design in the past few seasons has made them as much a fashion item as a shield from the sun.
On pages 78-88 we give you a travel guide for the season 1966; on the opposite and following pages you can start choosing your winter holiday wardrobe now

1967.07
Art director: **Harri Peccinotti**
Publication: **Nova**
Spreads from *Nova's* deserved Gold Award, this time a Molly Parkin article on how to shop for winter or summer holidays – H&C, hot and cold.

opposite

1967.08
Art director: **Harri Peccinotti**
Publication: **Nova**
Jean-Loup Sieff was the photographer for this Molly Parkin article. Nearly 30 years later he would photograph Elle Macpherson naked, except for jewellery.

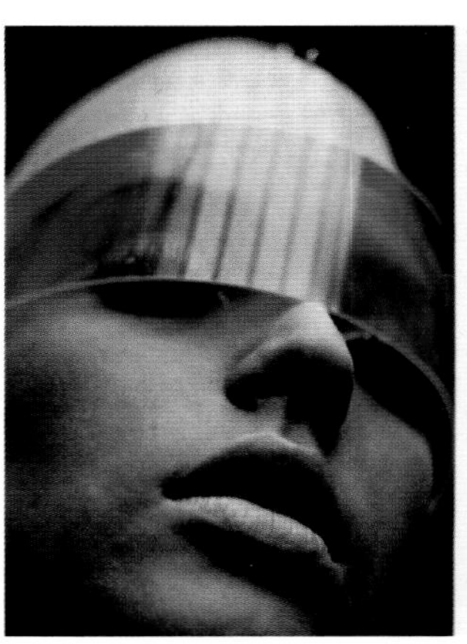

HOW PARIS SEES YOU THIS SPRING

Paco Rabanne gold bathing dress and ear-rings opposite. Pagan jewellery by Christine Burri

1968.07
Art director: **Bill Fallover**
Publication: **Nova**
After a career as an art director in the early sixties, Hans Feurer became a regular photographer for *Nova, Elle, Vogue* and *The Sunday Times.*

1967.07
Art director: **Harri Peccinotti**
Publication: **Nova**
Another example from *Nova*'s Gold Award-winning year, this feature was photographed by Harri Peccinotti.

opposite

1967.09
Art director: **Harri Peccinotti**
Publication: **Nova**
Roger Law's three-dimensional 'illustration' was soon to become a familiar sight in print and later, in partnership with Peter Fluck, on TV in *Spitting Image.*

TRAVEL FUR

Nova Fashion by Caroline Baker. Photographs: Hans Feurer. Hair by Christophe of Elrhodes at the Ann Bruton Salon. Lips and nails by Revlon

There is something about possessing a luxurious fur, whether in the mind or in the cupboard, that is slightly unnatural when you think of our natural spontaneous love for furry animals, and yet every woman wants a fur, and the more expensive and exotic the animal the better. Not only because a fur is warm and friendly to wear, but for psychological reasons. It is an obvious outward sign of success, either your own, your husband's or your lover's, and though people may laugh at keeping up with the Jones's, most of the time they are wondering how to overtake them. Envy is difficult to shake off. You can't help envying a film star dripping in furs and diamonds, or a model dragging a mink behind her, and until Pandora puts the lid and its evil contents back in the box, or worse still Beauty Without Cruelty win their battle, we shall all go on dreaming and desiring. If you haven't the ready money HP does make it easier but paying on the never never only complicates life more. You are continually under the threat of having your fur snatched away if you forget to pay an instalment or two. So to help your dreams on the next pages are a collection of sumptious, expensive and highly desirable furs: mink, highest in the name dropping game and very hardwearing; a leopard a lynx and a beaver in traditional shapes; a fox, sly as ever appears in four different colours, red fox jacket, ideal for wearing with short short skirts, a blonde fox and suede in horizontal stripes, a silver fox stole and for first impressions, impact and slimmer people, a big fluffy white fox; and a few others, all will make you green with envy, and wonder whether you are paid enough/married to the right man/living with the wrong man. Stockists for all furs shown are on page 125.☆

79

PREPARE TO FACE YOUR FIGURE

Make no mistake, the beach is one fashion area in which your best accessory is a good figure. Each year thousands of women undress for sea, sand and sun and without careful planning it can for many prove a harrowing experience. The success of summer holiday dressing depends more than any other on common sense and a sound knowledge of your own body. Remember that the comforting concealments of corsetry and shoes will not be at your disposal; that the initial walk from crowded beach to water's edge can seem the longest in the world to those not too confident of their back view. Plan ahead. However much of a rush it is to get away, do spend adequate time looking from every angle in front of a mirror at home, alone. Today's bikinis with briefest of pants and tops equivalent to no-bra bras are only for those with the firmest of flesh. If stretch marks and caesarians have cancelled out bikinis for you, be content to consider them as mere battle scars and the children themselves as more than adequate compensation for this one small area of lost vanity. Pay attention to the body length of one-piece swimsuits; it can be both an aggravation and an embarrassment to be split in two by one that is too short. Also make sure that the bust outline remains constant when straps are dropped for sunbathing. A towelling tunic is more use with sleeves than without as a protection from both sun and wind. These are very simple to make and most large stores now stock extremely well-designed towelling by the yard. Bags must be tough with wide comfortable handles, adequate room, and not ruined by a dip in the sea. See to it that your sunglasses are not so heavy that they leave a red weal on the bridge of your nose. Your sandal heels should be as near the height of your normal shoes as possible – it can be quite painful for leg muscles to adapt to too drastic a change. Accommodate the swelling of your feet by wearing backless sandals with solid wedge heels for comfort – they come in all heights. Children's cotton sunhats make excellent shields for adult hair and can be easily dyed to match your other beachwear. Finally, the matching is important: do try to get some consistency in colour or pattern in towel, bag and swimsuit rather than a haphazard mixture, which cancels out the impact of each article. Model: Ceylonese actress Champa Liyanage. Stockists: page 88

Right: Tricel cami-knickers with separate wrap-around skirt by Quorum, 9 gns. Matching cotton printed sunhat by Marimekko, from a selection at Vasa, £3 15s

What may be 'a good confession' to the penitent can be a tormenting perplexity to the priest, haunted as he always is by the fear of giving wrong advice. Is this a heavier burden than any sin? Norman Price reconstructs eight confessions of sins trivial, sins mortal, sins original and sins not-so-original. Step into the confessional box, sit where the priest sits, put your ear to the grille. This is what it might be like to be the voice of God's forgiveness on earth

'BLESS ME, FATHER, FOR I HAVE SINNED'

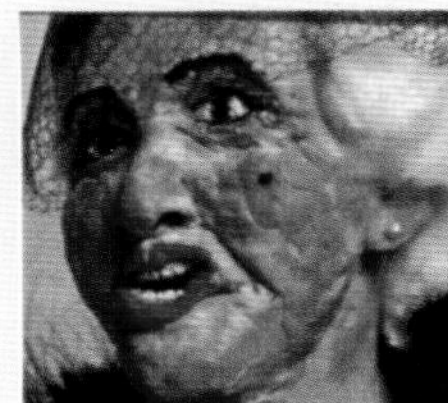

A confessional box has three doorways – two for penitents and one for the priest. Imagine yourself seated where the priest sits, in the middle box, with a curtained grille at each side. Above you is a small shaded light so you can peruse your breviary in spare moments. A shuffle, and a deep sigh. Shut your book now and pull back the little curtain.

'Bless me, father, for I have sinned. I stole a handbag from a shop.' Through the grille it is more of a groan than a voice.

'What made you do it?'

'I don't know.'

It seems to be the voice of an older woman. You decide to take a chance on this. 'Are you going through the change of life?'

'Yes, father.'

So she must be old enough to be my mother.

'Well, my daughter, this may be a case of diminished responsibility – do you understand me?'

'I – I think so, father.'

'You have not stolen before?'

'Oh, never – not in my whole life!'

'Then you must send the value of the handbag anonymously to the shop, and –'

She breaks in, her agitation beyond control. 'But I can't, father – the price-ticket said £45 – it was a crocodile handbag – and my husband is an old-age pensioner – we're on National Assistance.'

'Then send the handbag back.'

'But – when I got home I threw it on the fire – a thief, at my age! Please help me, father.'

Yet I cannot forgive her until she has made restitution. This is the rule of the confessional. I have given years of my life to learning these rules in all their complexity. Once each month the priests of my district gather for supper and bombard each other with such problems as this, real or imagined, sharpening our knowledge against the wits and experience of others around the big table. I have heard the answer repeatedly – 'In dubio standem est pro lege' – 'In all cases of doubt the law must stand.'

I tell her 'just a moment.' And that is all I have – just a moment – for unlike a judge I cannot stalk off in a rustle of robes to some private chamber to consider the problem, else the queues outside the confession box would be unending.

I know that since the value of the stolen property is worth more than a week's income to this penitent, the rules declare her theft to be 'a grave matter.' In 1946 the sum of £3 was accepted as 'a grave matter.' By 1948 it had spiralled with the cost of living to £5. Now, it is about £10. The novice thief, entering the confession box with a heavy conscience, must find it disconcerting to be subjected to a barrage of questions such as: 'How much do you earn?' – 'Do you value the loot at more than £10?'

Oh, why hadn't she stolen a pair of stockings or a tin of cat food?

Must I tell her that she has branded herself 'thief' and cannot hope for forgiveness in Christ's name until she has repaid what she stole? I am tempted. I try to remember the exact words of the Book of Precepts – did it say a week's income to the thief, or a week's income to the victim? Is a tramp who swipes a bike more guilty in God's eyes than a millionaire who steals ten thousand pounds?

This is sly, tricky, dishonest arguing, and nobody knows it better than I do. But it will have to suffice. I mumble an absolution and hear her sigh of relief and she departs and I stay there in my sultry little cubicle with her guilt now yoke-heavy upon my shoulders. She has sinned. I have sinned. Two wrongs do not make a right.

The priest, hidden like the manipulator of a Punch and Judy cabinet, may seem to be a disembodied Voice of Wisdom that infallibly absolves, forgives, inflicts penances and guidance – the Front Office representative of God. But he is discomfortingly aware that he is human. He has just finished his meal and can be in the throes of indigestion. If he is a heavy smoker, he is suffering. Approaching the confession box he sees the waiting queues and privately does a bit of mental arithmetic – how long will it take to get through them all – shall I miss Morecambe and Wise or get my sermon written tonight? If several priests are 'hearing' in one church, he compares the queue outside his 'box' with the others, to see how he fares in the parish Pop List . . . So there we sit in our dark little box (and you might be moved to know how many priests dispense with a cushion so that by enduring a mild discomfort they might draw nearer to the anguish of the penitent beyond the grille).

There is a crackle of knees like splintered firewood, and another woman's voice: 'Bless me, father, for I have sinned –'

Long pause. I prompt her gently. 'What did you do?'

'I haven't done it yet, father. I'm thinking about it.'

'But if it's a sin, daughter, you mustn't do it.'

'It's the doctor, he says I must.'

It has to be coaxed from her. She is thirty-three years old, was married at seventeen and has nine living children, several still-born and three dead. She has been in an almost continual condition of pregnancy for over fifteen years. By her wheezing breath I gather that she must be gross and thick, her abdominal muscles limp from over-stretching of them.

'My husband, he's fed up. The kids get on his nerves. It's a two-up, two-down house, he gets drunk. He comes home and bashes me – or the other, you know, father. I'd sooner, I mean it's better he bashes me – a black eye, well, it's gone in a week, I mean, but the other . . .'

Then, nothing to do with her confession, but perhaps because a human ear is listening in silence which is the nearest she can get to sympathy, she tells me urgently: 'I used to be good-looking once – you should see me now, father – I look fifty an' he knocked my teeth out. You should see my hands! Well the doctor says he won't answer if I have another, my veins are slack, you see?'

I don't see. Not about her veins being slack. But the rest I can see all too vividly. A woman more clever, more subtle, less blatantly honest, would have had the sterilising operation done under the National Health, a fortnight's precious rest in bed, and then come to tell her father-confessor. What's done can't be undone, in such a case. I get them often enough from the more affluent homes up the hill where trees shade the roads and the cars have garages. With such women (and I can smell the whiff of their scent through the grille – frail, exotic perfumes that haunt my memory, wraithlike, after they have gone) the slick patter comes and goes as brusque and unfeeling as a ping-pong ball –

'Father, I have been sterilised.'

'You know that was wrong?'

'Yes, father, and I am penitent.'

'Then I forgive you in Christ's name

CONTINUED OVERLEAF

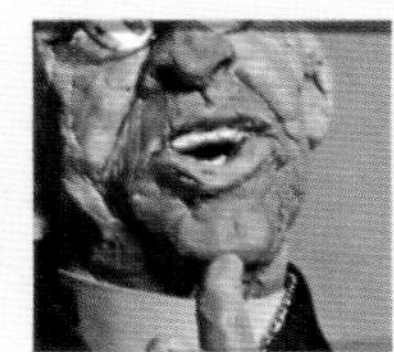

– now go and say three Hail Marys.'

But here crouches Mrs Whatever-her-name-is, not guilefully telling me that she has done it, but telling me that she is going to do it and needing her absolution beforehand! A better Christian – a better Catholic? Why, yes, I suppose she must be. But she leaves me no choice than to tell her that such operations are contrary to the law of God, a mortal sin both to her and to the doctor who performs it.

Did she dare to hope that the answer might be different in her case? I can only suppose that she did. But it can't be different. It never is. She expostulates – 'but I must do it, father, don't you see? My old man, he won't take much more – me falling for a kid every time he breathes on me – he'll be off, father, he'll be gone, next thing I know he'll have shoved off. I'll be left with the kids and no money.'

I, being merely human and fallible, can see that this could be an act of love – giving her husband and herself a slim, gambling chance of happiness. The surgeon's knife would never restore her thickened body to lissome beauty, nor restore her teeth and her vivacity. But at least she'd be able to surrender to her man tranquilly and unafraid. Do that much for him, and his desperate need. But I am forbidden to tell her this, for it is wrong.

'You must not have this operation. It is the temptation of the devil. God in his love will take care of you and your family. To doubt this is to doubt the teaching of the Church and to doubt the love of God.'

'But I'm a good Catholic – we never use what-you-call-thems – we all go to church regular –'

'Then be assured that God's grace and strength will be given to you, my daughter, and in His name I absolve you from the sin of having thought of this evil deed.'

She rises from her knees heavily and limps away. What have I done? Have I snatched her last hope from her, condemned her to misery in the name of God? Or will there be a miracle in that crowded house? My hands are sweating and the box is stuffily hot, the seat unbearably hard, my robes suffocating.

Most Catholics pass fairly humdrum, decent lives. But now and then the smoothworn prattle of ritual and absolution is dramatically interrupted. You realise that a tormented soul is out there – a moan, a plea: 'Oh, in God's mercy, father, help me!'

Sometimes it can be wry humour, as once I recall when the grille was almost melted by a blast of booze from slurred breath: 'Blesh me, fa-azer, I have shinned . . .' and a mumbled story so incoherent that after a few moments I interrupt:

'Perhaps – it might be better – if you came back – I mean, when the effects of alcohol have passed off – I can't very well hear your confession in this drunken condition.' A pause. Then – 'Shertainly, father, I'll come back when you're sober.' Well, that was very decent of him!

I open the curtain for a young male voice, husky with self-reproach.

'Father, I been nicking these women's underwear and such from off of clothes-lines.'

My brain flicks through the card-index of priesthood-trained responses. What to say? To the victim of this pitiable urge, it is stark tragedy. He will end up in the magistrates' court and the local newspaper probably.

I ask him: 'Is this an obsession?'

'Is it a what, father?'

'I mean, why do you do this?'

'I dun't rightly know, father.'

'Does it give you a sexual satisfaction?' I ask then.

'I dun't know about satisfaction, father – it does give me – well, yes, I suppose so.'

'Do you plan these thefts?'

'No, they just seem to happen.'

'Well, my son, this is wrong, yet an act done under impulse is less than a human sin' (and to myself I think, what good is it to this boy to know that?). 'Is it when you think about sex that these thefts happen?'

'No, it's like whenever I've had a row with me dad.'

Here, despite the careful training in modern psychotherapy that I have undergone as a priest, the long-established rules of the confessional immediately hamstring me. For in all sex matters the priest is obliged to ask too few, rather than too many, questions.

I can understand why this should be. A priest must be saved from any temptation to wallow in a blow by blow description by the penitent of his or her sexual trespasses. The priest must also discourage a sort of 'indecent exposure via word of mouth.' And with the experience of many centuries behind it, the Directive of the Sacred Office, 1943, is adamant that the priest must err on the side of reticence.

So – clank! – I must shut the door of hope upon this hapless young victim of obsession, and return to the safety of glib, customary patter. I tell him: 'What you did was sinful. Such sinful acts can only be overcome by trust in God. You must pray to God whenever the temptation comes to you.' I know that a psychiatrist would warn me that the more this boy thinks about stealing undies, the more likely he is to do it again. And to pray about it is to think about it. I am simply adding guilt to his obsession. Perhaps I should say to him: 'Forget the whole thing, sonny. What have the neighbourhood ladies' knickers got to do with you? Go join a youth club, get a girl friend – get several if you can. But don't come here putting on a display of sin when you are just a young clot who's got his targets mixed up.' And if I told him that, I might find myself before my Bishop. And upon my personal record file in the Holy Office at Rome would forever afterwards be a black mark: 'Wrong advice in the confession box.'

This haunts every priest. At any hint that the person beyond the grille could be mentally deranged or hysterical, the priest's main concern is to play it cool – to avoid at all costs his Bishop getting a letter of complaint. The Bishop might be a very understanding man. But his duty is to send all such complaints – right or wrong, fallacious or justifiable – to the Holy Office. And not all a priest's tears can wash out one word of them.

The voice of the true alcoholic through the grille is unmistakable and heartrending. This one was an educated voice. I could smell the fevered, sour-apple rottenness of his breath.

'. . . I get no joy from it, father – can't face a day without the stuff – it has cost me my wife's love – the respect of my children – I've just lost the last half-way decent job I'm ever likely to hold – I hate the taste and stench of drink – please help me, father!'

The rules say that drinking is a mortal sin, and before I can grant absolution in God's name, this penitent must first promise he will never drink to excess again. But where is the alcoholic who does not make this vow in the middle of every haunted night, when he

CONTINUED ON PAGE 78

The photojournalism that was now beginning to make graphic scenes of poverty and warfare regular Sunday morning reading matter for the educated middle-classes was, by nature, both political and accusatory. Its influence was enormous and its most famous practitioner was Don McCullin.

McCullin photographed almost every major conflict in the world, from inter-communal violence in Cyprus, Vietnam and Cambodia to the Biafran catastrophe, Northern Ireland and El Salvador. His haunting pictures were unrelentingly stark and seemed to demand responses of outrage and sympathy. Once, they might have appeared only in expensive photography books or in exhibitions visited by a handful of people. Now, they were in common currency. Inevitably they began to inform a whole movement that equated harsh, grainy, contrasty monochrome photography with a culture of silent witness that invited guilt and compassion. When, in 1968, the advertising agency KMP Partnership hired photographers to provide black and white images of socially deprived people for its client The Salvation Army, it was impossible for the public not to invest those images with some of the bleakness and despair shot by the heroic photojournalists who had travelled further than Britain's deprived inner cities to capture them.

1969.09
Art director: **Michael Rand**
Publication:
The Sunday Times magazine
Ironic echoes of Iwo Jima underscored this scene from a conflict that was to be celebrated with few heroic tableaux but many frozen images of horror.

1969.10
Agency: **Geer, Du Bois**
Client: **Mental Health Trust**
The shock-tactics of this 1969 image still have relevance three decades later.

opposite

1968.08
Agency: **The KMP Partnership**
Client: **Salvation Army**
Part of a Silver Award-winning series, this KMP ad blended the stark photography of Ray Rathborne with deliberate use of *faux* amateur printing techniques, simultaneously evoking associations with childhood and low budgets.

THE SUNDAY TIMES
VIETNAM: OLD GLORY, YOUNG BLOOD

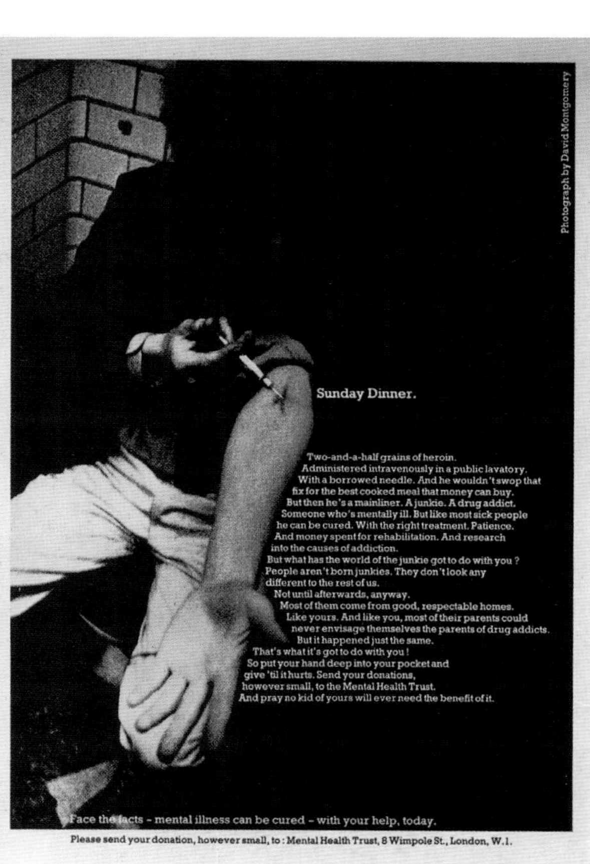

Photograph by David Montgomery
Sunday Dinner.
Two-and-a-half grains of heroin.
Administered intravenously in a public lavatory.
With a borrowed needle. And he wouldn't swop that
fix for the best cooked meal that money can buy.
But then he's a mainliner. A junkie. A drug addict.
Someone who's mentally ill. But like most sick people
he can be cured. With the right treatment. Patience.
And money spent for rehabilitation. And research
into the causes of addiction.
But what has the world of the junkie got to do with you ?
People aren't born junkies. They don't look any
different to the rest of us.
Not until afterwards, anyway.
Most of them come from good, respectable homes.
Like yours. And like you, most of their parents could
never envisage themselves the parents of drug addicts.
But it happened just the same.
That's what it's got to do with you !
So put your hand deep into your pocket and
give 'til it hurts. Send your donations,
however small, to the Mental Health Trust.
And pray no kid of yours will ever need the benefit of it.
Face the facts – mental illness can be cured – with your help, today.
Please send your donation, however small, to : Mental Health Trust, 8 Wimpole St., London, W.1.

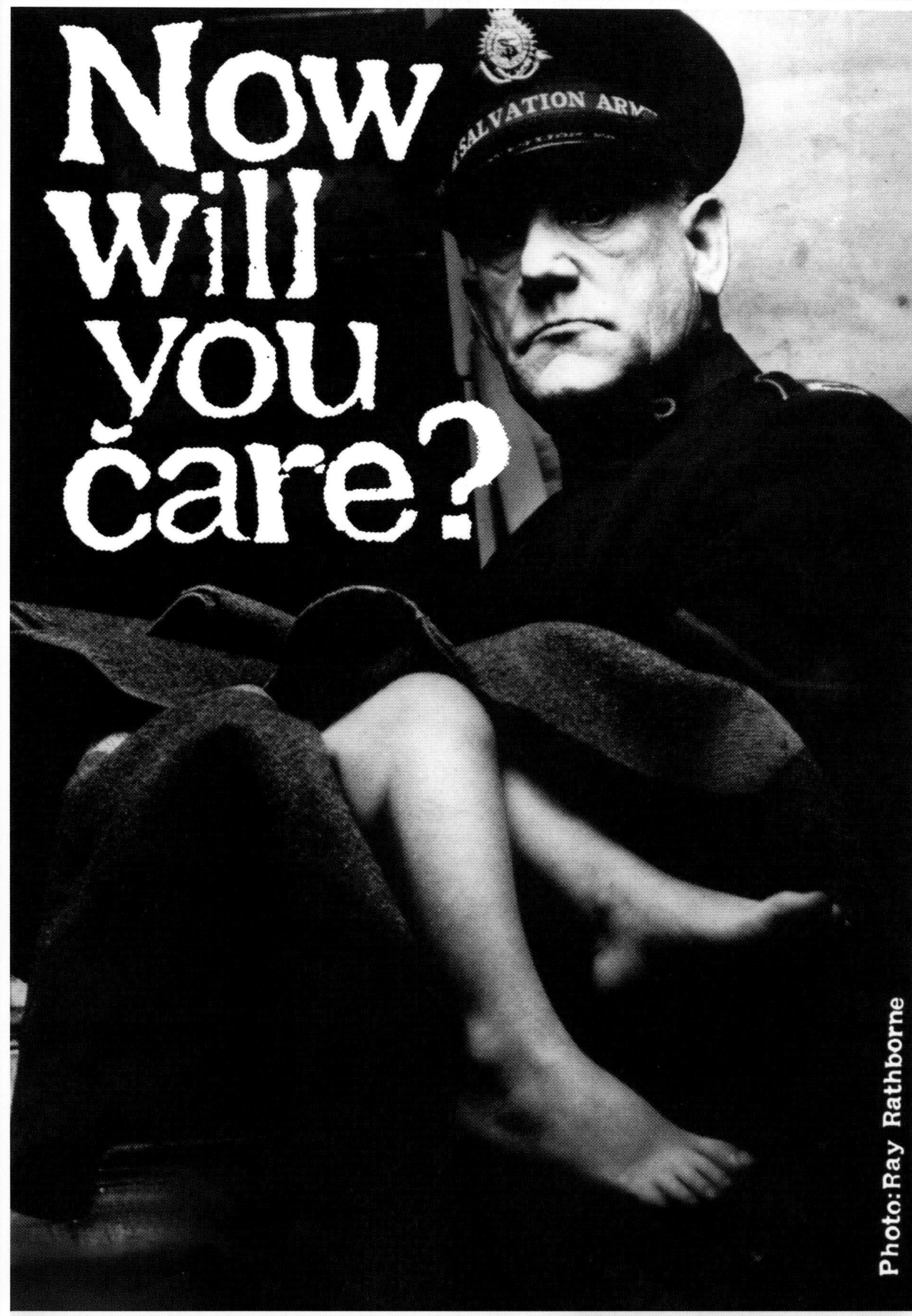

For God's saKe caRe give us a pound. Buy a Salvation Bond at your Bank
or direct from Dept. 24, Salvation Army, 101 Queen Victoria Street, LONDON, E.C.4

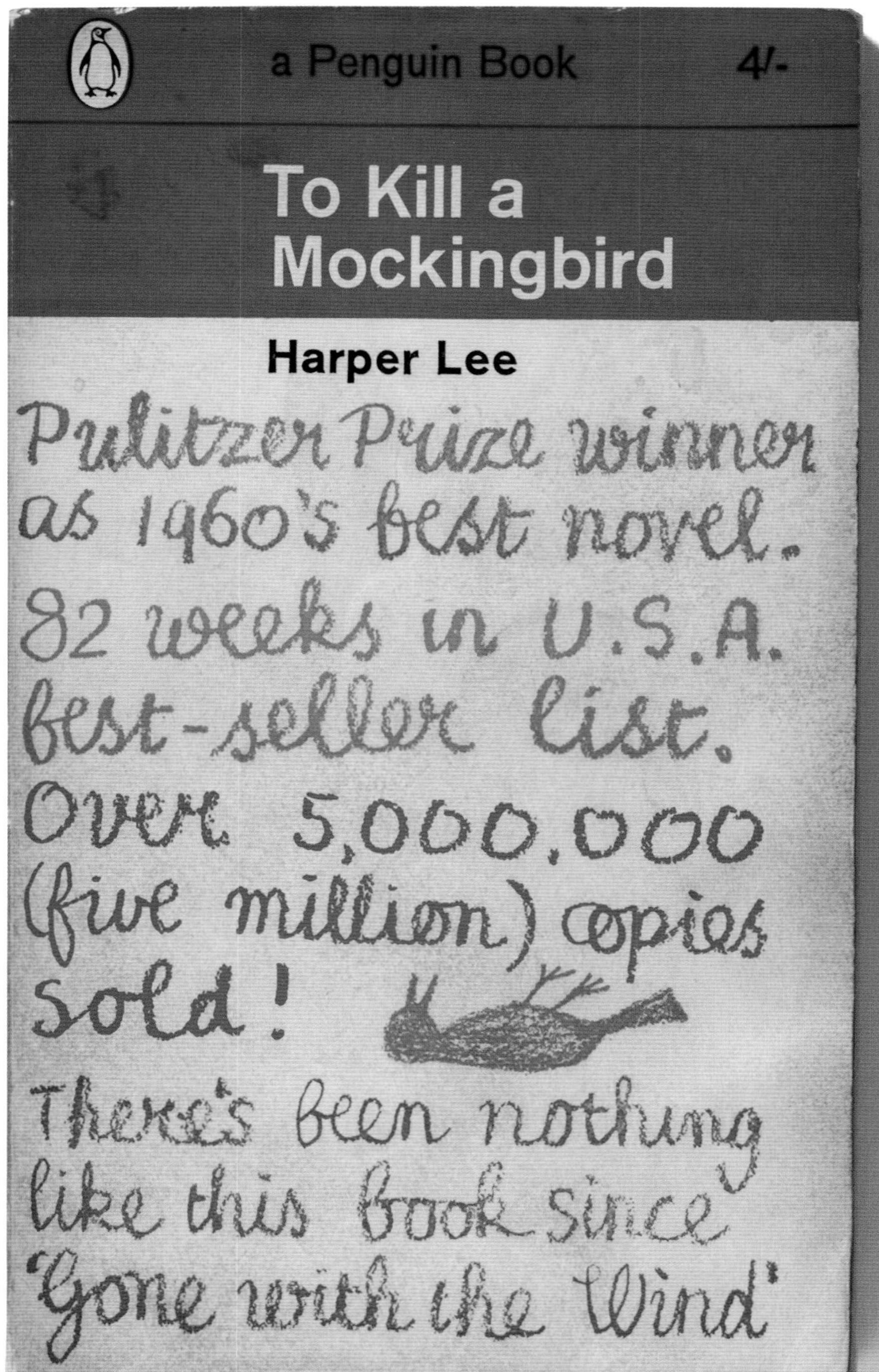
a Penguin Book
4/-
To Kill a Mockingbird
Harper Lee
Pulitzer Prize winner as 1960's best novel.
82 weeks in U.S.A. best-seller list.
Over 5,000,000 (five million) copies sold!
There's been nothing like this book since 'Gone with the Wind'

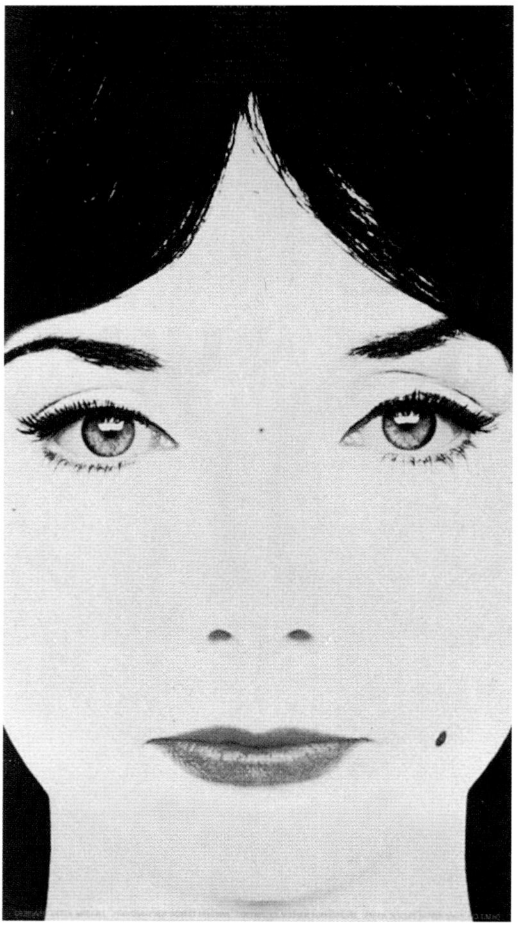

1964.09
Art director: **Derek Birdsall**
Client: **Penguin Books**
Another pastiche of unsophisticated typography here signalled the book's theme of childhood.

1964.10
Agency: **Waddicors & Clark Wilkinson**
Client: **Spicers**
Robert Freeman, famed for his work with The Beatles, was the photographer on this Silver Award-winning promotion for paper stock, designed by Derek Birdsall.

this page

1964.11
Art director: **Germano Facetti**
Client: **Penguin Books**
Facetti's stark, contrasty book cover images often looked like part of a sixties movie title sequence where graphic illustrations suddenly morph into live action.

The graphic revolution spread to book publishing too. The paperback book, first popularized by Allen Lane's 1935 Penguin imprint, was always intended to be easily and widely available. As such, it was inherently radical in that it put once prohibitively expensive books into the hands of many more people. By the early sixties the paperback also had been adapted to project the sort of imagery that placed it alongside fashionable magazines and movies. A number of 1964 D&AD book-jacket winners virtually came to define the new era of the paperback novel or textbook. Derek Birdsall's Penguin cover for *To Kill A Mockingbird* used childlike handwriting and a rudimentary drawing to convey the child's perspective of the novel. Meanwhile, Germano Facetti's many covers for crime thrillers usually owed more to Saul Bass' starkly effective movie title sequences than to traditional book illustration.

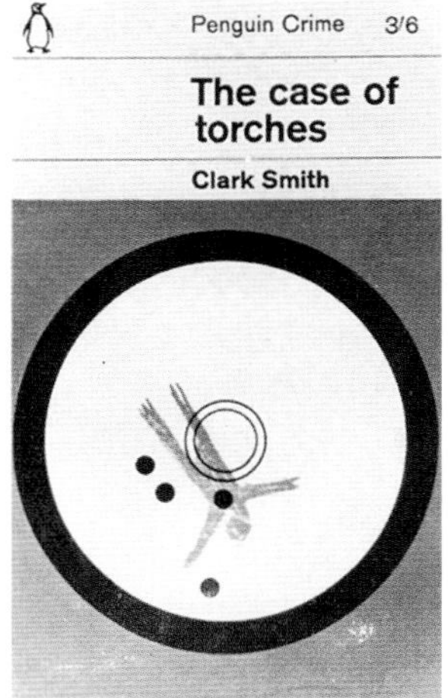

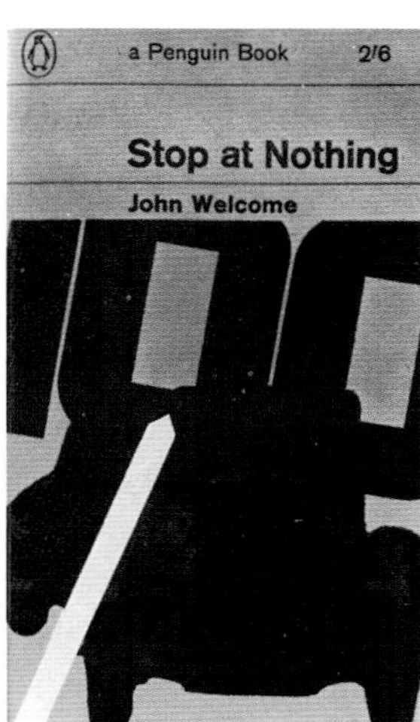

The new graphic sensibilities were also penetrating public communications. The Design Research Unit (DRU), founded in 1945 by Misha Black and Milner Gray, had grown out of the UK's first multi-disciplinary design consultancy (The Industrial Design Partnership) and had its roots in the governmental design thinking of the forties. However, its corporate redesign for British Rail (begun in 1965) proved to be fully in tune with the lively spirit of the decade. In the sixties there was optimism surrounding a national railway system that aspired to being streamlined and integrated. If subsequent events have made that optimism seem more than a little misplaced, DRU's award-winning identity, at least, was a success, neatly emblemized with a logo comprising a stylized piece of track and some dynamic arrowheads, and deploying a consistent, legible typeface.

That face echoed another one that may fairly claim to be among the most influential ever created. Jock Kinneir and Margaret Calvert devised a signage system and typeface for a British road system that in the mid-sixties was already beginning to be augmented with a network of high-speed motorways. An exemplary exercise in conveying vital information in the most efficient and unambiguous way possible, Kinneir Associates' 1964 solution has subsequently been adopted and adapted internationally.

1966.07
Design group: **Design Research Unit**
Client: **British Railways Board**
A move at the end of the fifties to unify many strands of Britain's railway network and related services resulted in a harmonious identity – if not exactly a coherent rail system.

1965.06
Design group: **Design Research Unit**
Client: **British Railways Board**
The famous British Rail symbol has proved itself a durable one and a graphic point of reference for rail companies worldwide. The man who drew it, Gerry Barney, left DRU for Wolff Olins, where he also drew the Audi logo.

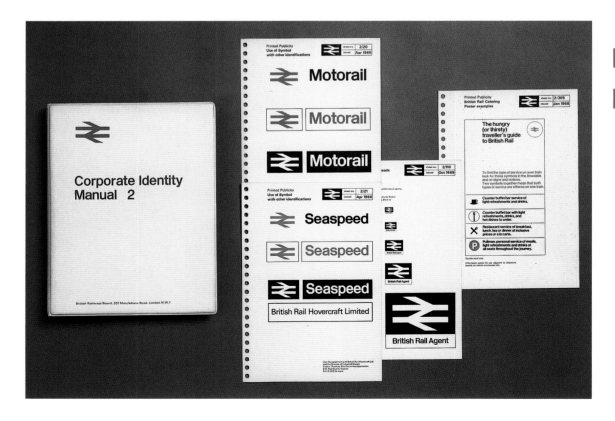

1964.12

Design group: **Kinneir Associates**
Client: **Ministry of Transport**
When legibility can be a matter of life and death, 'good design' takes on a whole new meaning. In Jock Kinneir and Margaret Calvert's classic road signage typeface, ambiguity was avoided by circular, rather than square, dots above the *i* and the *j* and the addition of an otherwise inconsistent tail on the lower case *l*.

ABCDEFGHI
JKLMNOPQ
RSTUVWXYZ

abcdefghijk
lmnopqrstuv
wxyz'.-,()

With even the traditionally slow-moving public sector embracing the spirit of change, it was only to be expected that the retail sector would also respond in the area of consumer durables. Revitalized paperback books and magazines were about to be joined by furniture and other home merchandise. If, in retrospect, this seems a natural progression, it should be remembered that reactionary forces were very strong in relation to the British home. It was an unquestioned tradition that ageing family furniture was handed down and that young married couples would be grateful to receive the dark, heavy tables, chairs and dressers that had originally suited their grandparents or even earlier generations. In truth, until the sixties there had been little choice anyway, since money was scarce and new furniture (which anyway usually mimicked the old styles) was expensive to buy.

By 1964 a 33-year-old entrepreneur was about to change all that. Terence Conran had already been a restaurateur and a designer with experience in textiles and architecture, and he was now an entrepreneur with his own furniture-making business. His bright, modern furniture caught the spirit of the times – but not the imagination of the traditionally-minded buyers in the department stores. They refused to consider stocking his furniture, so in response Conran decided to open his own store – Habitat – on London's Fulham Road. Conran is perhaps the pivotal figure in sixties design and commerce, mainly because of his Habitat achievement. He claimed that the ideal situation was one in which 'manufacturer, designer, retailer and consumer are involved in a balanced and integrated relationship.' If the notion was idealistic, the achievement was real. To have challenged and outdone the traditional retailers was as important as breaking the design mould. To have demonstrated that design sensibility could co-exist with successful entrepreneurial skills was to offer a role model to many who followed. That Habitat's sole recognition by D&AD came in 1965 and took the form of stationery designed by the Conran Design Group suggests that in the mid-sixties the emphasis was still very much upon graphics, and that Conran's full legacy was yet to be fully appreciated.

1969.11
Design group: **John McConnell**
Client: **Biba**
This early version of Biba's logotype, shown here on stationery and packaging, was later revised but it introduced the store's defining image of revamped Art Deco, a style that had always lent itself both to luxury (ivory and enamel) and a low-cost approximation of luxury (bakelite and coloured glass).

this page

1965.07
Design group: **Conran Design Group**
Client: **Habitat**
This depiction of Habitat wares tapped into an illustrative style of the times, usually used to suggest straightforward information as opposed to misleading hype. The distorted type on the bag – another favourite sixties device – added the illusion of depth and volume.

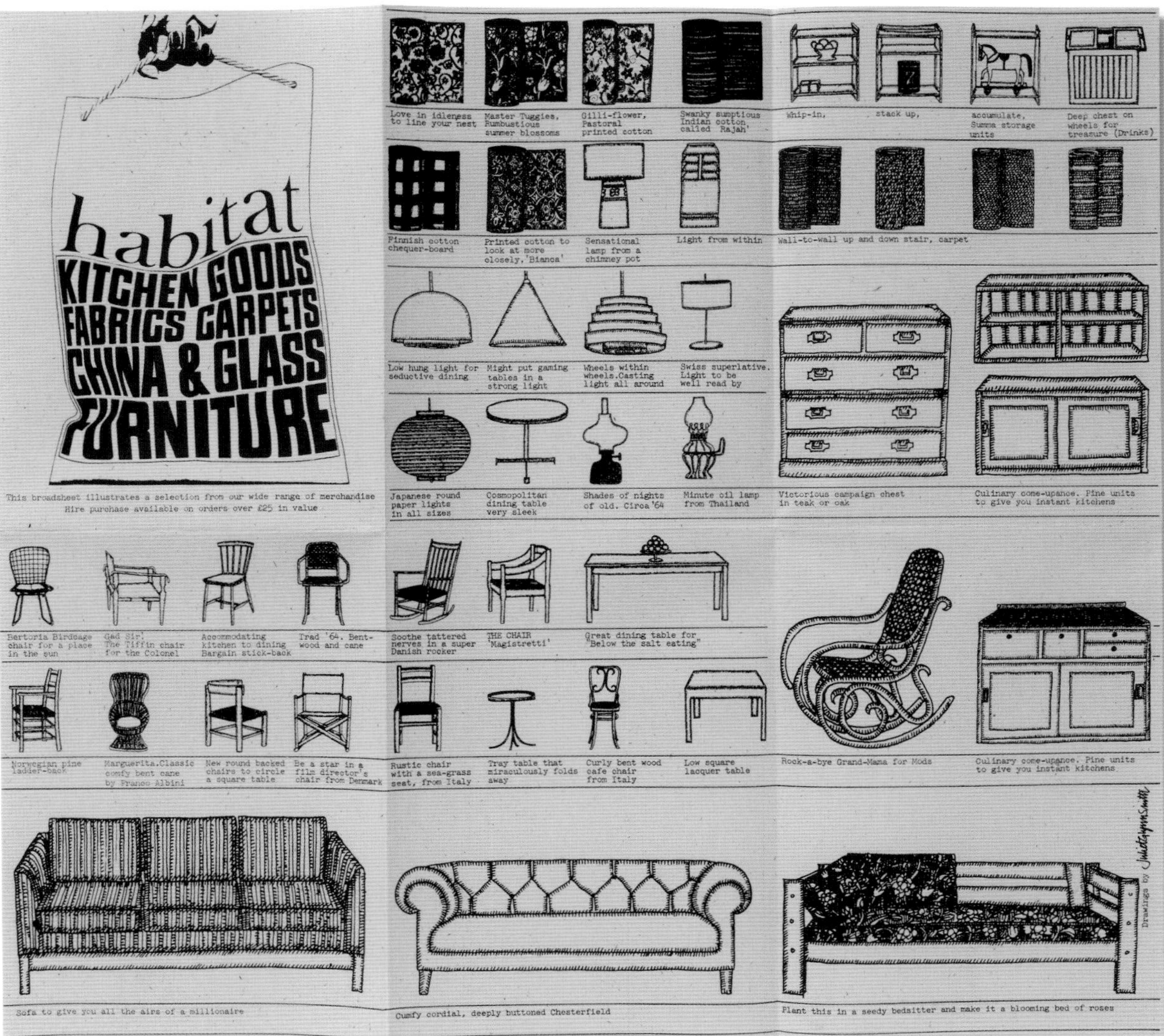

Zandra Rhodes Des RCA
32 St Stephens Gardens
London W2
BAYswater 1703

1965.08
Designer: **Richard Doust**
Client: **Zandra Rhodes**
Dating from the days before Rhodes established her own solo collections (and when London telephone numbers still had district prefixes) this stationery by Richard Doust gave a distinctive taste of an influential textile and fashion designer.

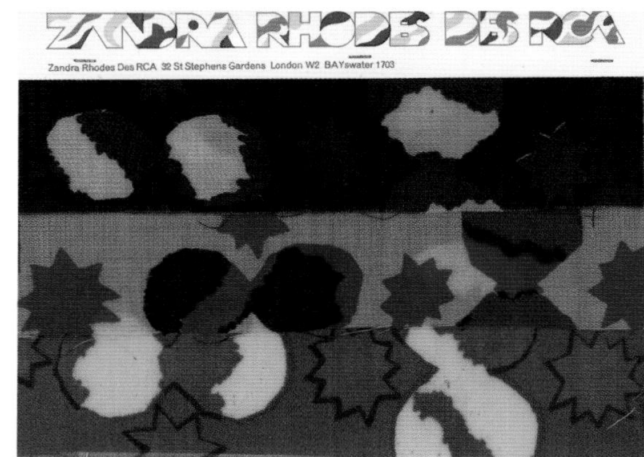

Print designed by Zandra Rhodes Des RCA
32 St Stephens Gardens London W2
BAYswater 1703

length ____________ design ____________

width ____________ colour ____________

Zandra Rhodes Des RCA 32 St Stephens Gardens London W2

☐ 1967.10
Design group: **Fargo Design Associates**
Client: **Mary Quant Cosmetics**
Mary Quant was an icon of her times, an entrepreneur with an intuitive sense of flair, rather than a designer or even a great champion of design. The stylized flower was her imprint and her legacy for one generation of young women was a heady sense of freedom achieved through radical personal style.

A long-time friend of Conran was fashion designer Mary Quant, whose King's Road shop, Bazaar, Conran had designed as early as 1955. Quant did for fashion what Conran did for furnishings, introducing a new order characterized by wit and accessibility. The now familiar scenario of a drab status quo overturned by an iconoclastic newcomer here resulted in the revolutionary concept of the mini-skirt and a whole culture of sexually driven self-reinvention for women. Once more, events have subsequently conspired to make the Quant-inspired sixties fashion revolution seem more innocuous than it appeared at the time. For example, Quant famously identified the aspirational shift of 20-year-old women to no longer appear older and more sophisticated than they were but younger and more available, as follows: 'Suddenly every girl with a hope of getting away with it is aiming to look not only under voting age but under the age of consent.'

D&AD's only Quant design-related selection was for Fargo Design Associates' packaging for a Quant cosmetics range in 1967, perhaps reflecting the fact that Quant's design contribution was perceived as controlling the overall ambience of her shops rather than creating exceptional products. She was certainly a pioneer of the now familiar concept that shopping should be an entertainment, not a chore.

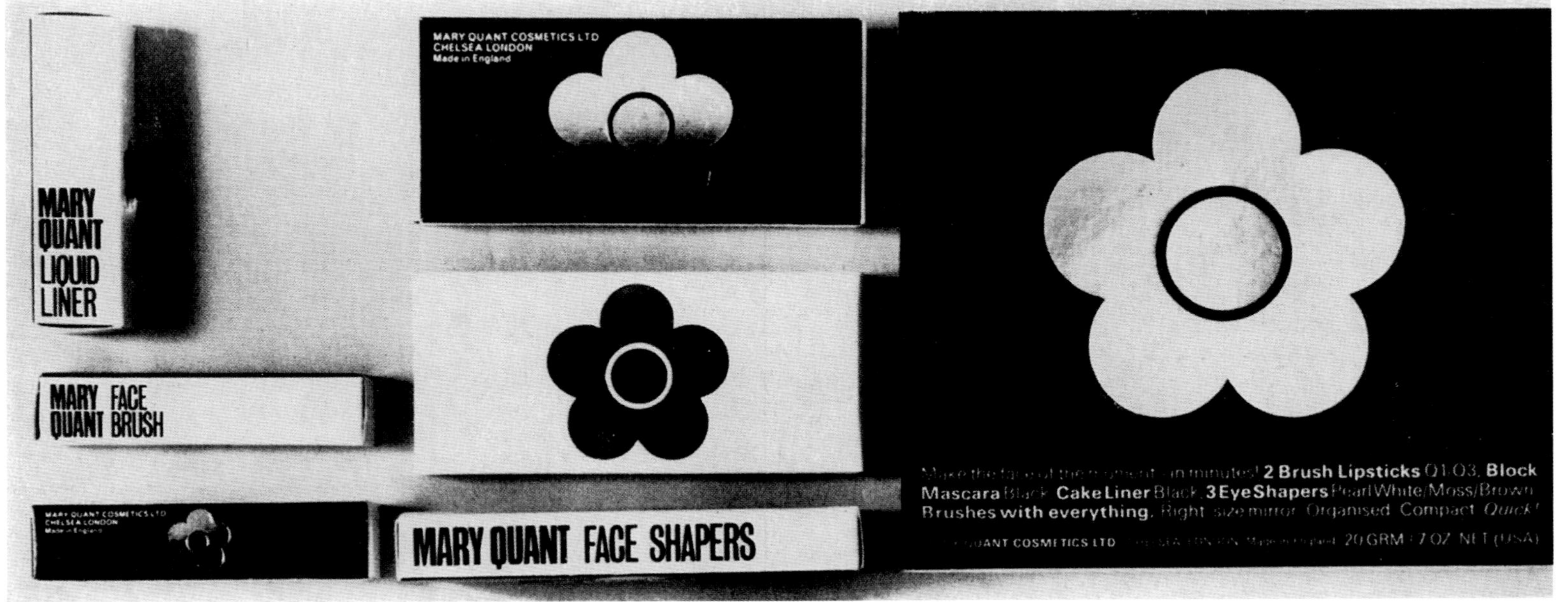

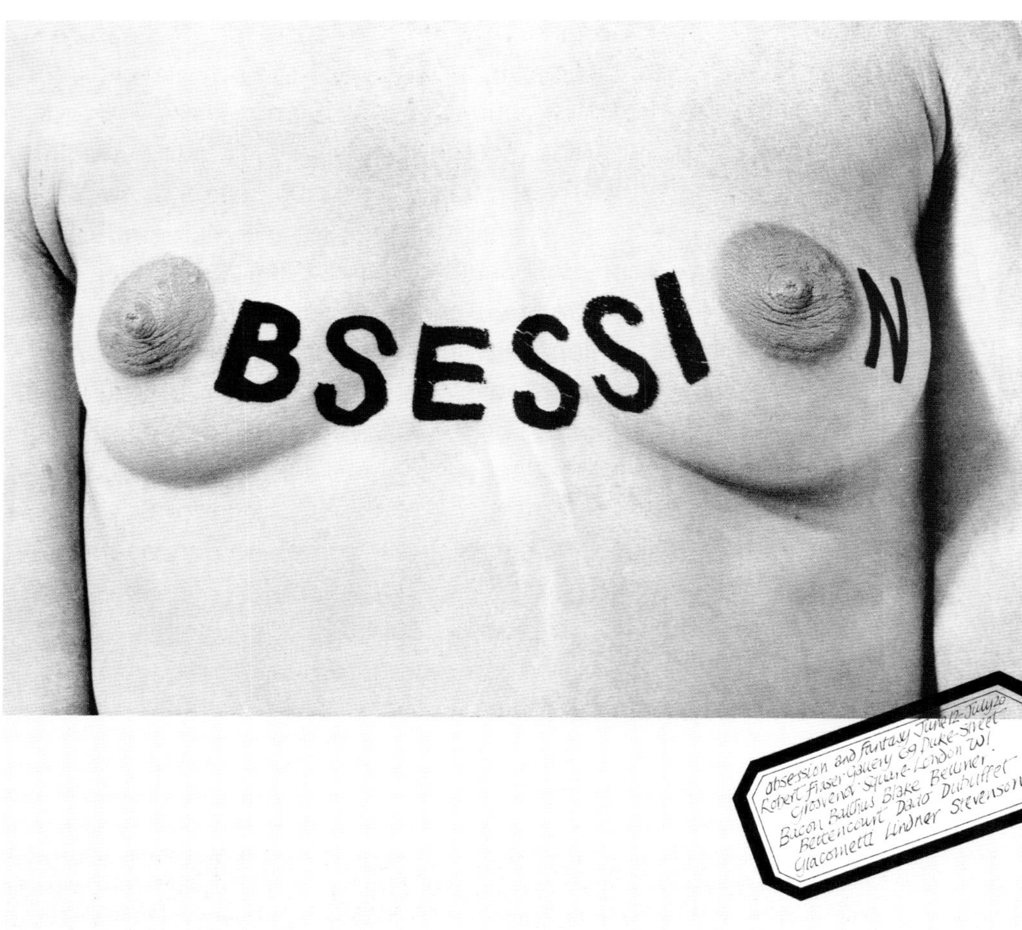

1964.13
Designer: **Robert Brownjohn**
Client: **Robert Fraser Gallery**
Attention-grabbing shock tactics early in the decade from Robert Brownjohn in this poster for an art exhibition.

1964.14
Agency: **McCann-Erickson**
Client: **Taylor-Woods: Lifelons**
More remarkable in 1964 than it may look now, this exercise in minimal copy and spare imagery in an ad for tights marked a radical departure in the promotion of this type of product.

1964.15
Agency: **Cammell-Hudson Associates**
Client: **Apple & Pear Publicity Council**
A Robert Brownjohn bid to make the humble apple into a movie star by means of an intricate and organic alphabet.

1967.11
Agency: **McLaren Dunkley Friedlander**
Client: **Fisons Foods**
A rare example of two expatriate American art directors – Bob Gill and Robert Brownjohn – combining their talents in the service of Pickerings pie products.

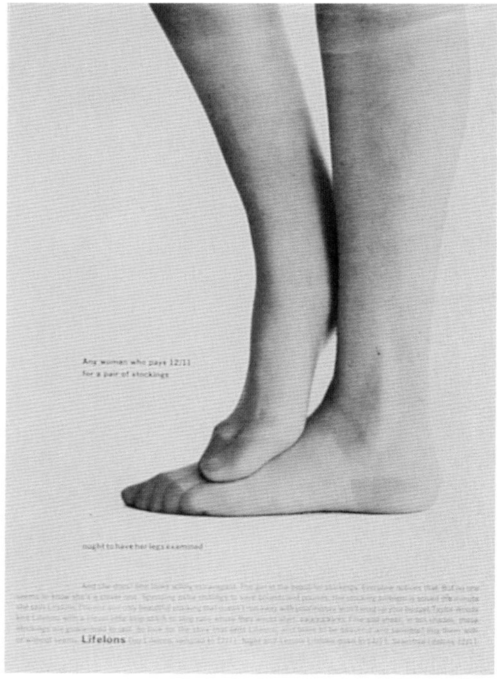

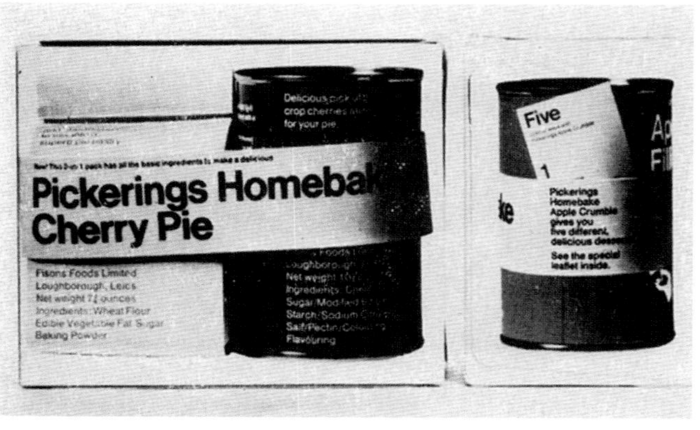

● 1965.09
Designer: **Robert Brownjohn**
Client: **Eon Productions**
Brownjohn's title sequence for *Goldfinger* provided one of the Bond franchise's more memorable moments. Despite using a stand-in for Golden Girl Shirley Eaton and having to compete with another Shirley's daunting vocals, the images remain powerful today.

Alan Fletcher recalls how Robert Brownjohn presented the idea to Cubby Broccoli, producer of the Bond films: 'The presentation was held in a small viewing theatre in Wardour Street. Brownjohn arrived with a handful of 35mm slides of the title and credits. He put them in the carousel, took off his shirt and stood in front of the screen, slowly gyrating to the music. Luckily Broccoli was able to make the required leap of imagination.'

More traditional entertainment, in the form of feature films, was just beginning to reflect the new concerns of popular communication. The British movies of Richard Lester, Ken Russell and Michelangelo Antonioni would all tap into the pacy, snappy, stylized sixties imagery that was increasingly being seen in the print medium. Yet even conventional action films, like the earliest in the emerging James Bond franchise, could stake their claim to fashionability in the credit sequences. Graphic designer Robert Brownjohn had switched his allegiance from New York to London in 1960 on the grounds that 'this is the place where the ideas are'. Brownjohn's 1965 D&AD Award-winning title sequence for Guy Hamilton's *Goldfinger* actually contained only one idea – paint everything gold – but was immediately identifiable as a superior title sequence if only because it looked as if it cost more than the entire budget of most British films of the time.

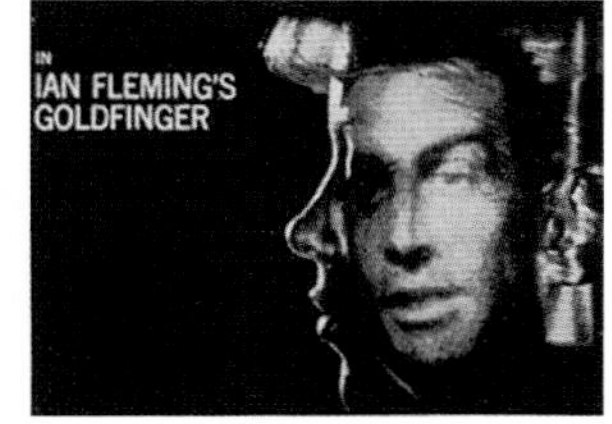

The Moving Image category of the D&AD Awards had encompassed TV programme titles, feature film titles and cinema and TV commercials. It initially tended to celebrate the graphic design aspect of the work, partly because that is what it set out to do, and partly because the language of the commercial was not yet fully developed. In fact, in the early days of ITV – Britain's only commercial TV station at the time – the commercial was the popular butt of exclusively derisive jokes. That changed in the course of the sixties and by the seventies TV commercials had even become a recognized and respected route into movies. Today, the list of commercials directors who subsequently moved into feature films is well known and includes Adrian Lyne, Alan Parker, Ridley Scott and Hugh Hudson. All of them began in some department of advertising, and Scott even started making modest commercials as early as 1968. Hudson, too, enjoyed some success in the sixties with his co-owned Cammell-Hudson company mainly making short films, and although the company went bankrupt in 1969 Hudson went on to work for Scott's RSA production company (formed in 1968) where his commercials career – and that of Scott – took off. Alan Parker's start in advertising was as a copywriter with the obscure Maxwell Clark agency and he only got his chance to move into commercials in the early seventies after a spell at advertising agency CDP had allowed him to direct test commercials in the basement.

Pre-dating all of them and their achievements was Philadelphia-born Richard Lester, director of a 1964 D&AD Award-winning commercial for Acrilan blankets.

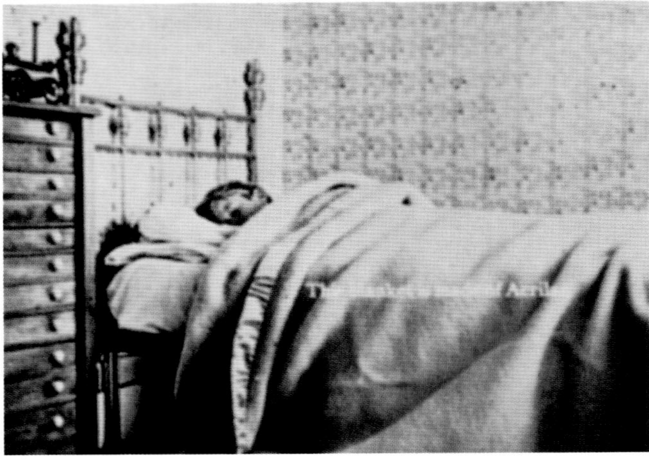

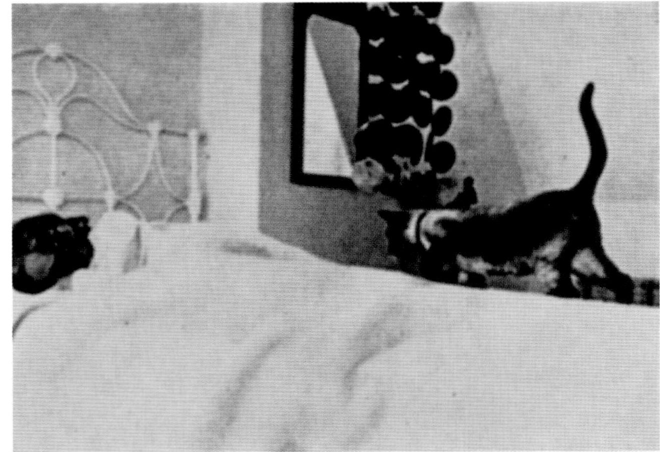

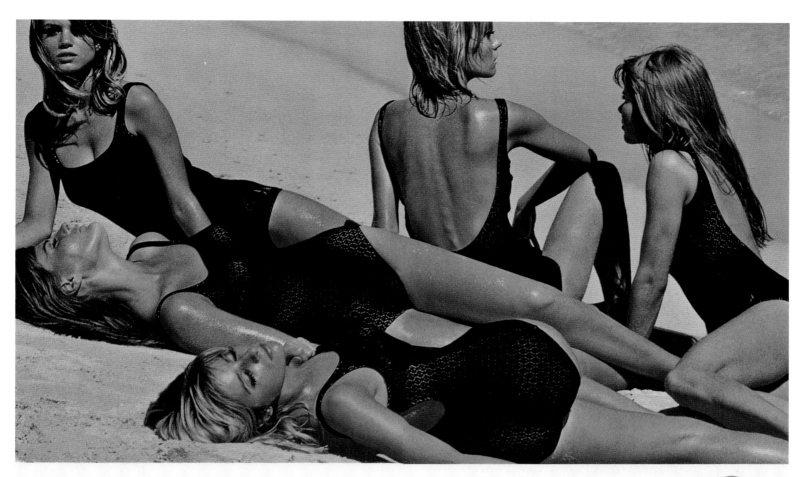

Netted: five black-and-tans.

When Jantzen and Blue C Nylon go fishing together: fishing with brilliant black lace: chances are they'll catch something *five times more gorgeous than usual.* They're out to get girls. No secret. Not just any girl, but the sunniest, slinkiest girls in the whole wide sea. You?

jantzen Mystique swimsuit in brilliant Blue C Nylon. Sizes 34"-38". Best catch this season 95/-.

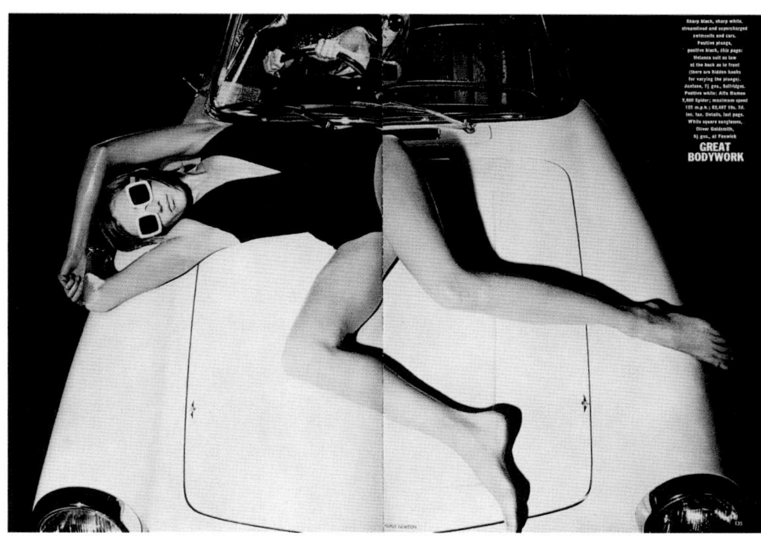

1968.09
Agency: **Collett Dickenson Pearce**
Client: **Monsanto**
This cinema commercial matched Charles Saatchi's mock-heroic voice-over ('Rodney anxiously raised a powerful arm in warm salute') to a prosaic wait at the bus stop. The product was an Acrilan coat.

1965.10
Agency: **Collett Dickenson Pearce**
Client: **Chemstrand**
Future film director Richard Lester directed this discreetly sensual CDP commercial for Acrilan blankets.

this page

1967.12
Agency: **Collett Dickenson Pearce**
Client: **Chemstrand**
Rather less discreetly sensual were Chemstrand's bathing suits as photographed by the young Helmut Newton.

1966.08
Art director: **Terence Whelan**
Client: **Vogue**
Helmut Newton brings his unique gift to the pages of *Vogue.*

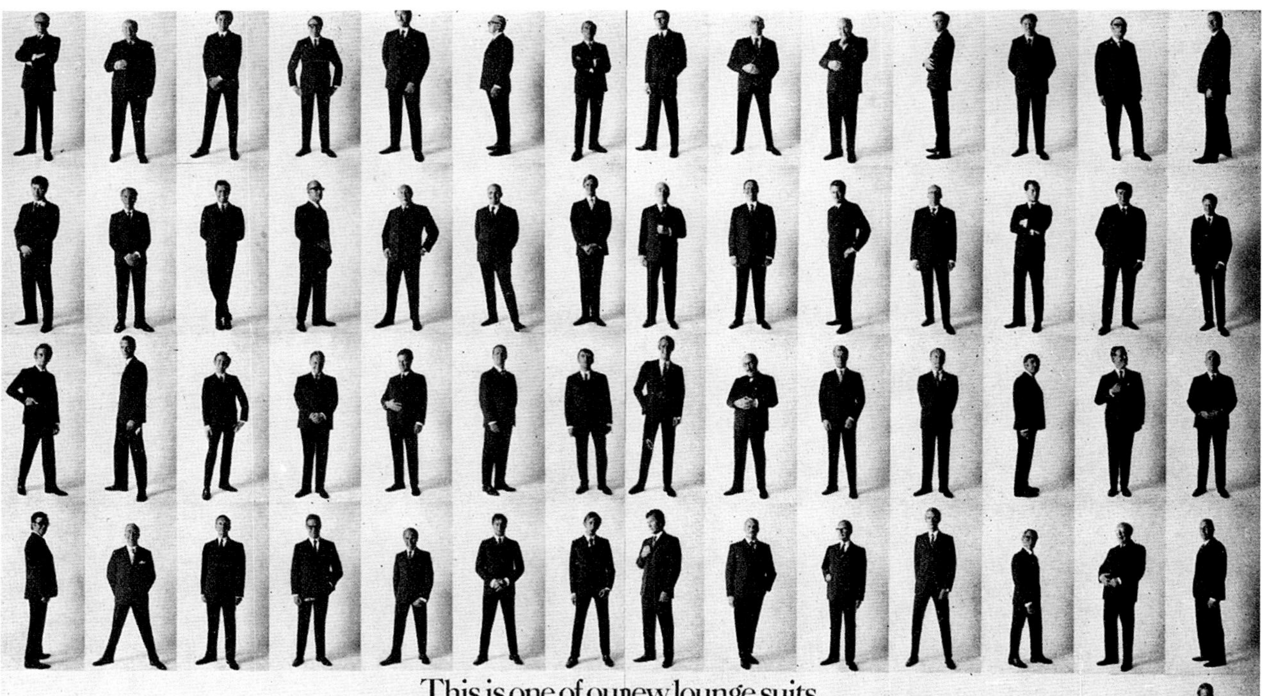

1968.10
Agency: **Collett Dickenson Pearce**
Client: **John Harvey & Sons**
This award winner for photography reflected CDP's perfectionism. The agency would always take as long as was needed, sometimes involving many reshoots, to ensure the best results.

1969.12
Agency: **Collett Dickenson Pearce**
Client: **Dunn & Co**
CDP took the ineffably dull outfitter Dunn & Co and made a reassuring virtue out of its innate conservatism.

opposite

1968.11
Design group: **Klein Peters**
Client: **Sexton Shoe Company**
Sexton shoes rarely excited the young. However, with the aid of trendy sub-branding expressed by Klein Peters' packaging, this was its bid to rival more fashionable footwear retailers.

1967.13
Agency: **Collett Dickenson Pearce**
Client: **Chemstrand**
Point-of-sale for bedding by Michael Peters, who was a recurring presence at CDP during the Klein Peters days.

1965.11
Agency: **Papert Koenig Lois**
Client: **J Player & Sons**
Papert Koenig Lois was co-founded by famous American art director George Lois. This cigarette campaign was singular in that it made a point of not showing the product packaging.

Charley
Boots by
Sexton

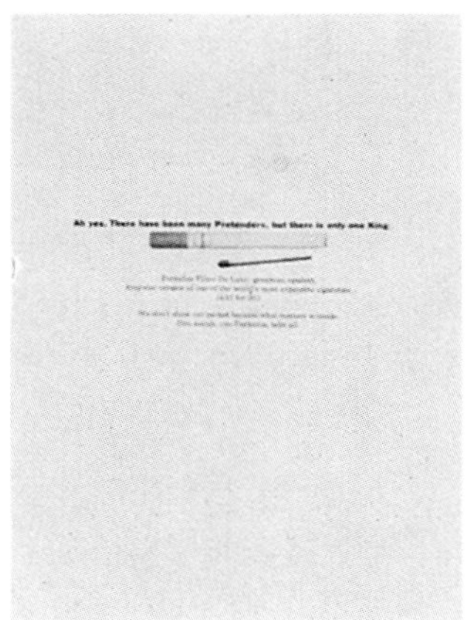
Ah yes. There have been many Pretenders, but there is only one King.

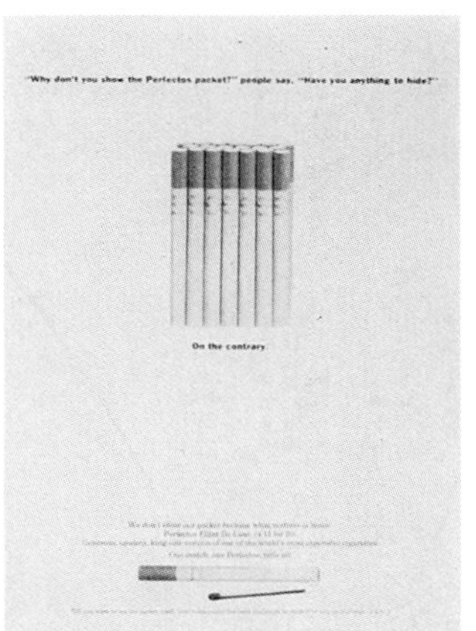
"Why don't you show the Perfectos packet?" people say. "Have you anything to hide?"
On the contrary

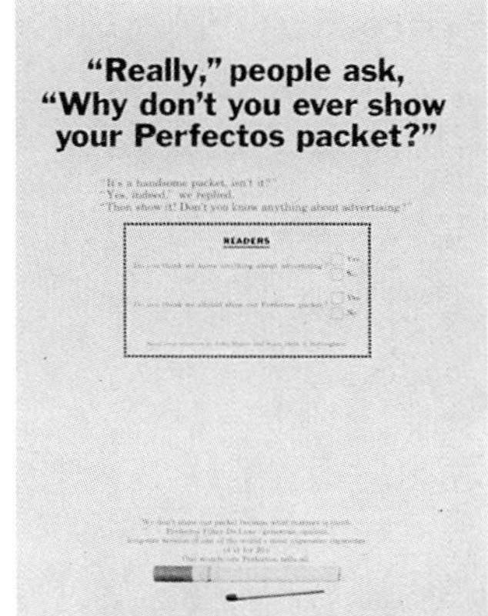
"Really," people ask,
"Why don't you ever show
your Perfectos packet?"
READERS

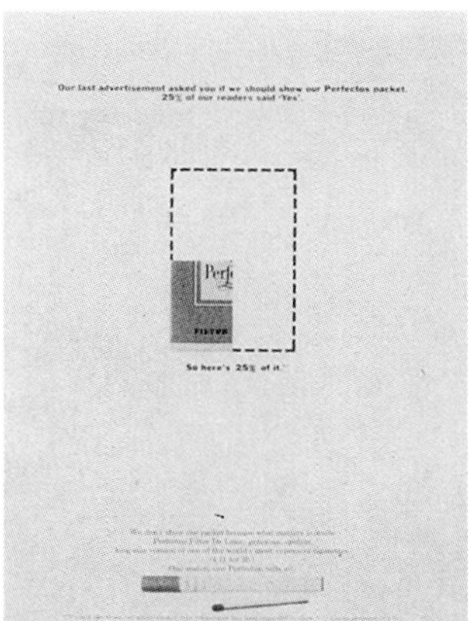
Our last advertisement asked you if we should show our Perfectos packet.
25% of our readers said 'Yes'.
So here's 25% of it.

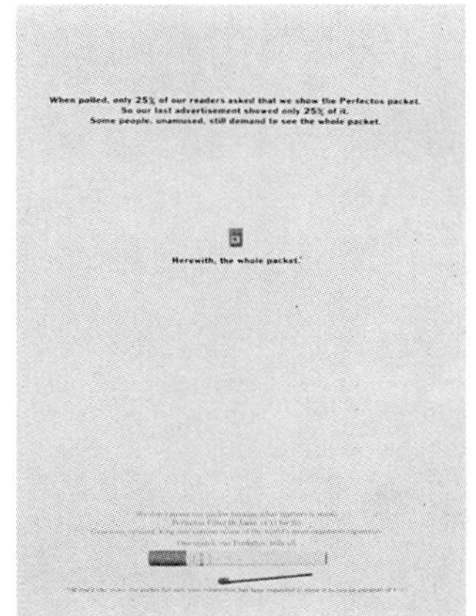
When polled, only 25% of our readers asked that we show the Perfectos packet.
So our last advertisement showed only 25% of it.
Some people, unamused, still demand to see the whole packet.
Herewith, the whole packet.

In the same year, Lester would direct *Hard Day's Night* to huge acclaim, following it with *Help!* and *The Knack*, films that together formed a paradigmatic 'swinging sixties' trilogy that owed as much to the spirit of the witty graphic design of the time as to any prevailing trend in commercials. Full of quick cuts, stylized images and jokey juxtapositions, Lester's mid-sixties British films were a hybrid of TV shorts, commercials and pop promos – witty, exuberant and very much of their time.

Bernard Lodge won a Silver Award for his strongly typographic BBC *Teletale* titles in 1964, reinforcing the 'printed graphics' look of many moving image titles and idents. Of course, it is worth remembering that in Britain the introduction of colour and 625-line TV transmission was gradual. Coarse resolution was a continuing factor in the presentation of type on the domestic TV screen and it was left to cinema ads to exploit the superior resolution of film.

However, by 1968 Lodge – and television – had progressed to some highly atmospheric credits for the popular science-fiction series *Dr Who*. Much enhanced by a woozy electronic score from The BBC Radiophonic Workshop, Lodge's animated Rorschach blots set the futuristic tone for the fantasy series with dynamic manipulated imagery that left static graphics way behind. With electronic engineer Ben Palmer, Lodge again won a Silver and in the process gave a long-running TV series its most unforgettable identity.

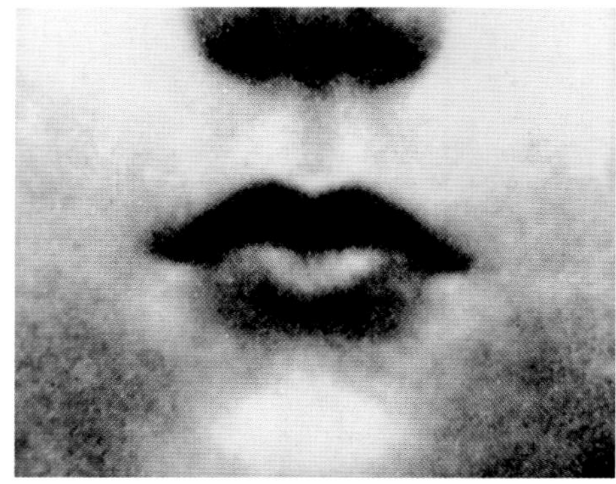

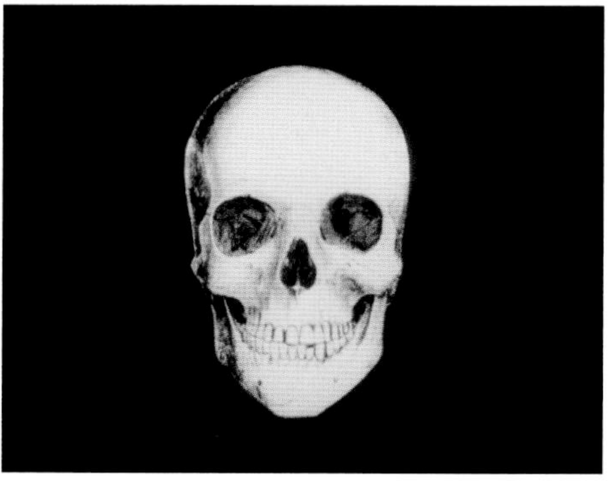

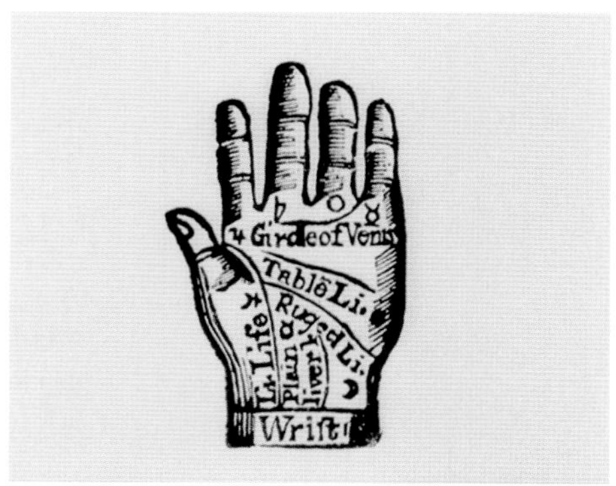

1963.03
Designer: **Geoff Brayley**
Client: **BBC**
Unlike today, in the early sixties the TV channel ident had a relatively simple job to perform: there were just two television providers and three channels.

1964.16
Designer: **Bernard Lodge**
Client: **BBC**
Bernard Lodge's clean and clear progression of symbolic images for *Teletale* owed more to print graphics than the language of moving images.

this page

1968.12
Designer: **Bernard Lodge**
Client: **BBC**
Lodge devised the second version of the *Dr Who* credits for Patrick Troughton's incarnation of the character. This sequence first ran in March 1967.

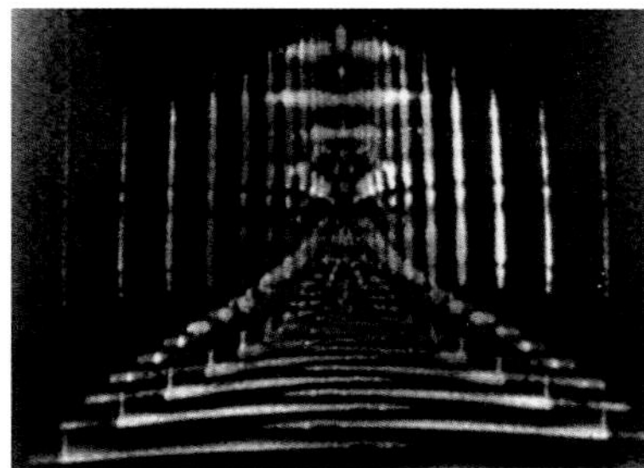

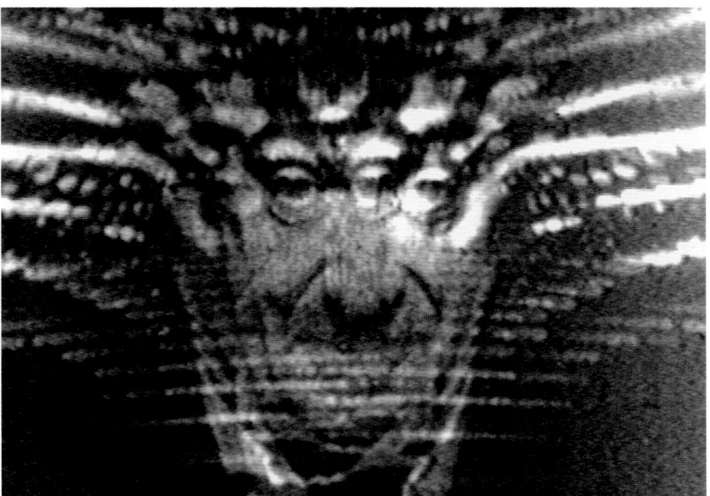

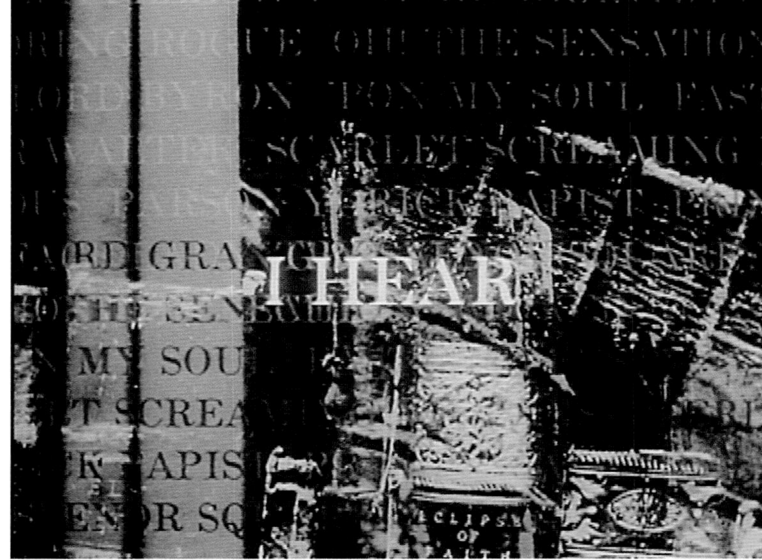
I HEAR

THAT SOME SAID

FAMOUS

TUT TUT TUT

FAMOUS
GOSSIPS

1966.09
Designer: **Alan Jeapes**
Client: **BBC**
Alan Jeapes' style was to use type and images in a way that combined the clear communication of information with an elegant visual quality. *Famous Gossips* was a television special that aired in 1965.

this page

1963.04
Art director: **Arnold Schwartzman**
Client: **Associated-Rediffusion**
Associated-Rediffusion was an independent TV company whose drama programmes often had a snappier look than the equivalent BBC product.

1963.05
Art director: **Arnold Schwartzman**
Client: **Associated-Rediffusion**
The broken *pince-nez* derived not from Eisenstein's *Battleship Potemkin* but from a literal detail in the Arthur Koestler book on which the drama was based.

Martin Lambie-Nairn, who would in later years give TV some of its most memorable idents and graphics, recalls the transitional period of TV graphics.

'The BBC graphic design department in the mid-sixties was a world leader in the craft of television design and employed the very best people in the industry,' he recalls. 'There was, however, a great deal of friction between the two distinct camps. The old guard from the Ealing Studios era of caption writing, maps and hand lettering bitterly resented the new generation of graphic designers; they called us Letraset designers.' Lambie-Nairn was seconded to Alan Jeapes who, along with Lodge, was to be a profound influence upon him. 'Jeapes, whose own work reflected the influence of the great Saul Bass, taught me that craft and technique were useless unless they could convey ideas,' Lambie-Nairn says.

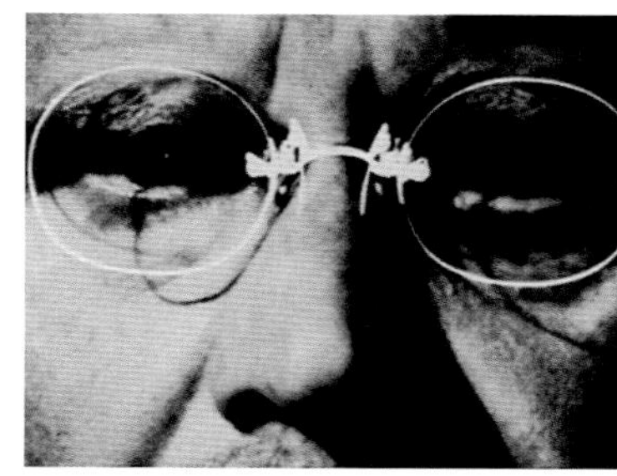

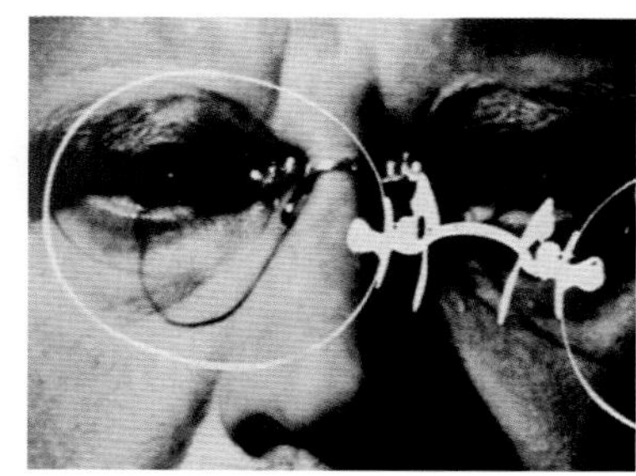

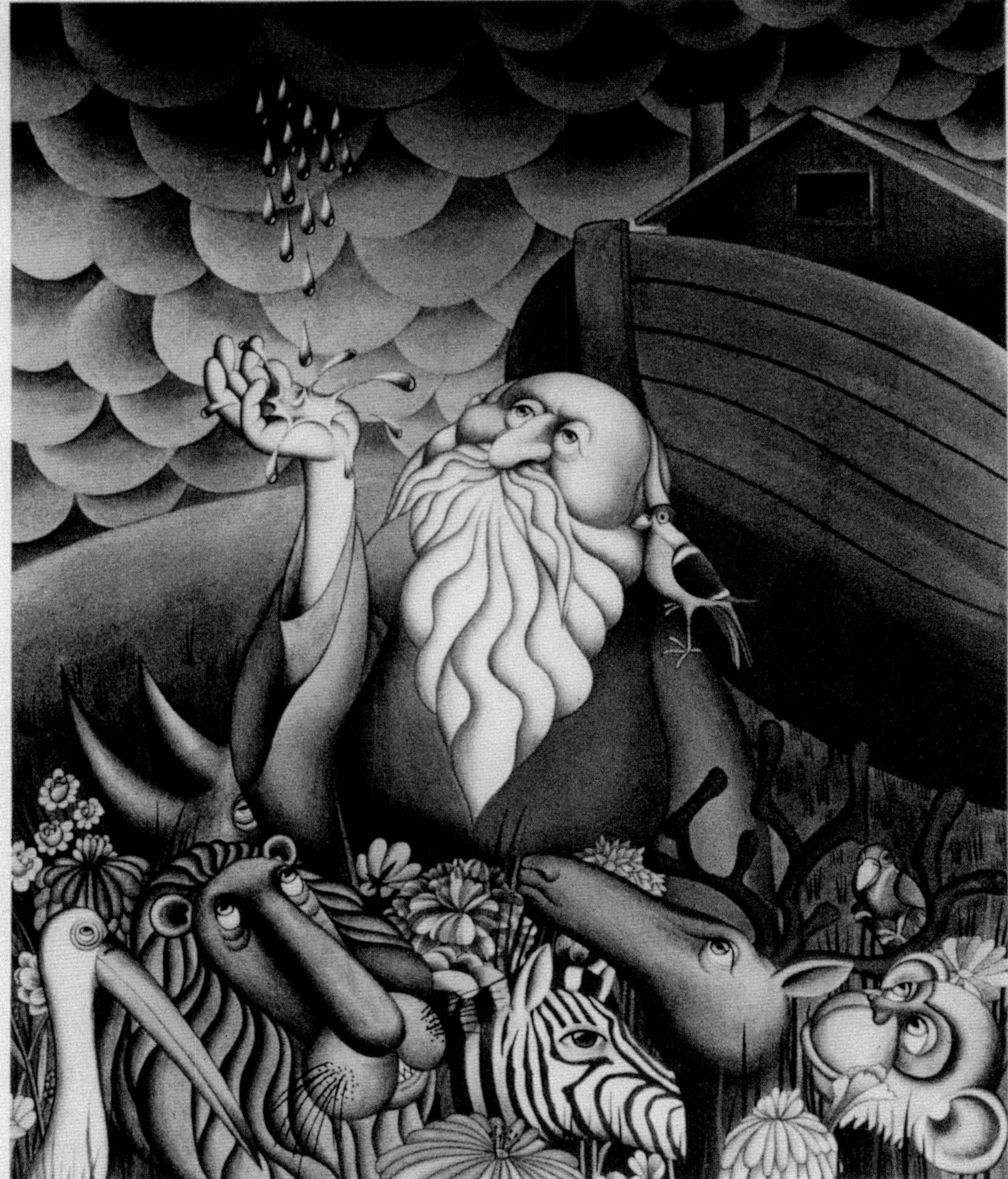

Yes, it has been known to rain in Israel.

Once upon a time we had quite a lot of it. Forty days and forty nights by all accounts.

Since then, the weather seems to have cleared up quite a bit. The old millibars, isobars and anti-cyclones etc. are all in our favour.

Most of the country can rely on 9 months uninterrupted sunshine a year. And Eilat, a lush resort on the Red Sea, only gets 5 days rain out of 365.

If you want to bake gently till a golden brown you'll find plenty of beaches to do it on.

We have four seas (Med., Dead, Red and Galilee), scores of sandy beaches and modern resorts like Nathanya, Ashkelon and Herzlia.

When you get browned-off sunbathing there are plenty of other things to see and do.

There are three thousand years of history to browse through. Biblical place names to bring to life. Colourful street markets and fashionable shops. Classical concerts in Roman amphitheatres. Wining, dining and dancing in bars, bistros and discotheques.

And all this is only 4½ hours away from London by EL AL's non-stop Boeings. Any day of the week.

Talk to your local travel agent. He says the nicest things.

Like, 'Yes, sir. Of course you can afford it. Even after devaluation. There are special low cost holidays which include 14 days in a hotel as well as return air fare. Sign here.

Sign there. And go.

And don't worry about the rain. If it ever happens again everyone will be in the same boat, anyway.

EL AL

EL AL. The Airline of the People of Israel.

If you fly EL AL it serves you right.

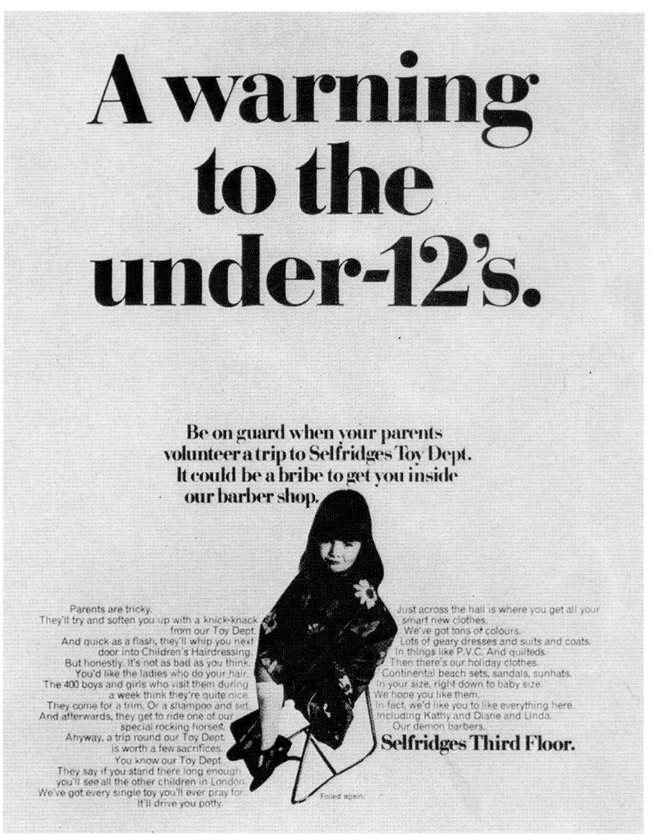

Ideas were also increasingly at the heart of British advertising, and press ads flourished as social awareness and sometimes difficult subject matter were treated with imagination and intelligence. In 1967 the young ad man John Hegarty was working for John Collings & Partners which had the unenviable task of luring sun-and-fun seeking tourists back to Israel after the Six-Day War. A press ad that blended Israel's biblical credentials with a statistically low chance of rain may not have been the obvious route, but Hegarty argued forcefully for the client to accept that it was the most effective one. 'The history of the region was by far its strongest card,' he says. 'You don't have to be a brain surgeon to work that out, you just have to be bloody-minded to get the client to buy it.'

Hegarty went on to join the Cramer Saatchi consultancy in 1967, later co-founding TBWA and then Bartle Bogle Hegarty (BBH). In addition to numerous awards, he would also receive the D&AD President's Award, the association's equivalent of a lifetime achievement award, in 1994. Cramer Saatchi could claim a star-studded sixties beginning and Alan Fletcher recalls the period when a visit to its one-room office would reveal 'Charlie Saatchi in one corner writing copy, Alan Parker in another doing the same. Ross Cramer was in the third and overseeing them was David Puttnam in-between agenting for photographers.' Cramer Saatchi would become Saatchi & Saatchi in 1970 and exert an unparalleled influence on the advertising of that decade.

1968.13
Agency: **John Collings & Partners**
Client: **El Al Israel Airlines**
This early piece of work from a future giant of British advertising, John Hegarty, helped to establish him as the dogged champion of a good idea.

1967.14
Agency: **John Collings & Partners**
Client: **El Al Israel Airlines**
An early example of the attention-grabbing possibilities of a copy line based on the *double entendre.*

this page

1967.15
Agency: **Collett Dickenson Pearce**
Client: **Selfridges**
In addition to using sting-in-the-tail headlines, CDP seemed to be reinforcing the varied nature of the famous department store by using inconsistent type styling in these ads.

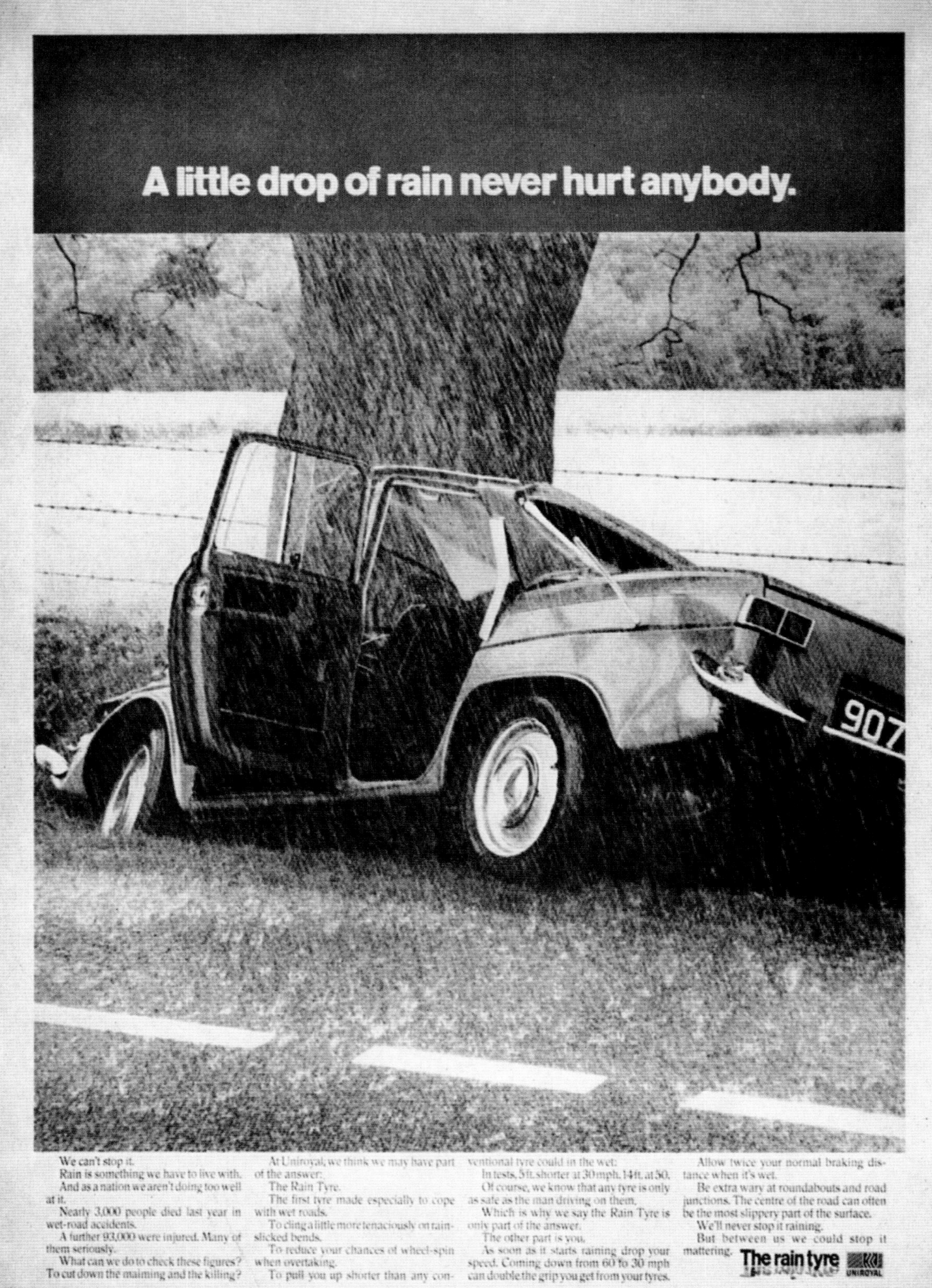

A little drop of rain never hurt anybody.
907
We can't stop it.
Rain is something we have to live with.
And as a nation we aren't doing too well at it.
Nearly 3,000 people died last year in wet-road accidents.
A further 93,000 were injured. Many of them seriously.
What can we do to check these figures? To cut down the maiming and the killing?
At Uniroyal, we think we may have part of the answer:
The Rain Tyre.
The first tyre made especially to cope with wet roads.
To cling a little more tenaciously on rain-slicked bends.
To reduce your chances of wheel-spin when overtaking.
To pull you up shorter than any conventional tyre could in the wet:
In tests, 5ft. shorter at 30mph. 14ft. at 50.
Of course, we know that any tyre is only as safe as the man driving on them.
Which is why we say the Rain Tyre is only part of the answer.
The other part is you.
As soon as it starts raining drop your speed. Coming down from 60 to 30 mph can double the grip you get from your tyres.
Allow twice your normal braking distance when it's wet.
Be extra wary at roundabouts and road junctions. The centre of the road can often be the most slippery part of the surface.
We'll never stop it raining.
But between us we could stop it mattering.
The rain tyre
UNIROYAL

1968.14
Agency: **Doyle Dane Bernbach**
Client: **Uniroyal**
David Abbott, who wrote this ad for Uniroyal rain tyres, started his agency career in the early sixties as a copywriter at Mather & Crowther. Later recruited by DDB, London, he was soon shipped off to the fountainhead, DDB's New York office, returning to the London office to become Creative Director and then Managing Director. Abbott was to become one of the great names in advertising, launching French Gold Abbott in 1971 and, seven years later, Abbott Mead Vickers. He became famous for a clutch of memorable copy lines, including this one and 'It's lonely at the top, but at least there's something to read' for *The Economist* in 1990.

opposite

1968.15
Agency: **Doyle Dane Bernbach**
Client: **Uniroyal**
The ongoing campaign for Uniroyal's rain tyres was created by art director Doug Maxwell and copywriter Dawson Yeoman. This campaign was given a Silver Award for the advertising campaign of the year by the D&AD Press jury.

In 1968, copywriter David Abbott gave an early indication of his talent for using language laced with irony and ambiguity in the Silver Award-winning newspaper ad for Uniroyal's rain tyre (the line 'A little drop of rain never hurt anybody' appears above the image of a wrecked car). John Webster came up with an even more minimalist take on the dangers of seasonal drink driving ('Have a New Year') and the magazine *New Society* also won in 1968, its bold covers further highlighting the way in which political and social awareness had come to the forefront of sixties sensibilities.

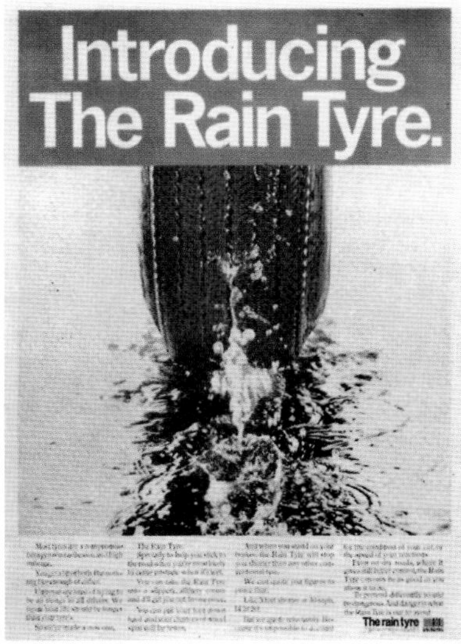

BL 446
It's taken long enough. Ever since cars started, in fact.
But at last a tyre maker's woken up to the fact that wet roads are dodgier than dry ones.
They deserve special attention.
So Uniroyal have made a tyre that's in it. element in the wet.
The Rain Tyre.
We've made it to cling onto treacherous bends for dear life. (Your life, perhaps.)
We've made it to give you grip to spare when you need acceleration in a hurry.
And we've made it to stop in a hurry, too.
When we tested it, the Rain Tyre stopped faster than any other conventional tyre.
5 feet faster at 30 mph. 14 ft. at 50.
But this doesn't give you the go-ahead to cut things 5 feet finer. (Even on dry roads, where our safety margins are higher still).
Because tests can never take every emergency into account.
What the Rain Tyre does, is help you reduce the number of emergencies you get into.
And a tyre like that's worth waiting for.
Even 70 years
UNIROYAL
The rain tyre
70 years late: The Rain Tyre.

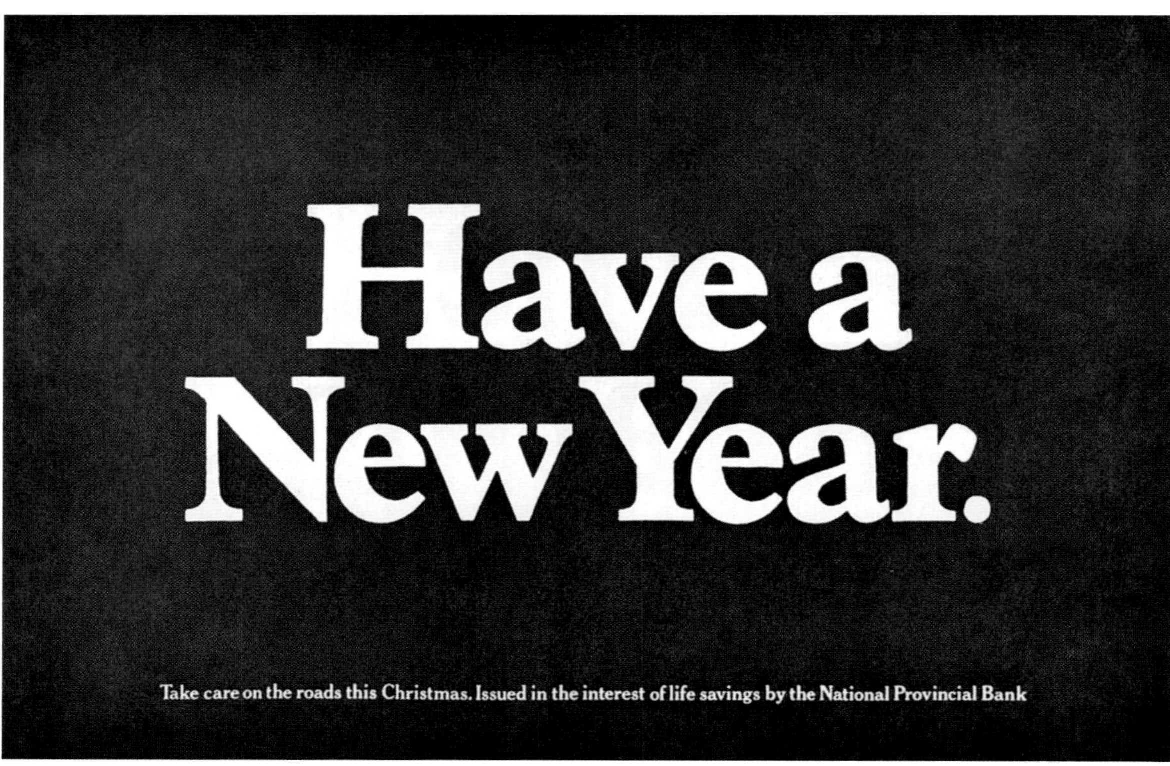

Have a
New Year.
Take care on the roads this Christmas. Issued in the interest of life savings by the National Provincial Bank

You can start a savings account
at the National Provincial Bank
for a few shillings

1968.16
Agency: **Pritchard Wood**
Client: **National Provincial Bank**
John Webster devised 'Have a New Year', an early example of his unfailing talent to distil a message into an effective line or image.

1965.12
Design group:
Churchill/Holmes/Kitley
Client: **Shell BP News**
Another simple idea well executed: the distorting effect of a recently emptied glass expresses the danger.

1968.17
Designer: **Romek Barber**
Client: **New Society**
Prime Minister Harold Wilson, the ultimate political pragmatist, depicted as an uncharacteristically forceful political figure with the aid of a superimposed fist on the cover of *New Society* from June 1967.

1969.13
Agency: **Pritchard Wood**
Client: **National Provincial Bank**
A frame from a TV ad shot by John Webster in which the little girl was judged most photogenic when animated by an urgent need to visit the bathroom.

opposite

1969.14
Agency: **Vernon Stratton**
Client: **Debenham & Freebody**
Tony Evans took the original shot for this press ad. It was painstakingly montaged in a photolab and in the late sixties it dazzled in a way that must be unimaginable by a generation brought up on digital image manipulation.

Are you a she, or a sheep?

Some London shopping streets make you feel like an extra in a cast-of-thousand's spectacular. Some London shopping streets make you feel as though the whole world is treading on your toes, grabbing your bargain, hailing your cab and screaming down your car.

That's some London Streets. Migraine Alleys. Not Wigmore Street.

Wigmore Street is four minutes walk from Oxford Circus.

Wigmore Street is where you'll find Debenham and Freebody. A quiet shop. Calm. What shopping was like before the flocks hit town. Or before shops ever opened on Saturday mornings, a time when we stay shut.

There are lots of beautiful clothes to try on in our spacious store. The cream of European couturiers including Givenchy, Ricci, Paton and Valentino.

But we also have 6 guinea dresses and 13 guinea coats. And desirable furs hats, lingerie, separates, baby and children's clothes. Shoes, stockings, knitwear, handbags and gifts. Cosmetics, china and glass, a limitless linen department, and a very chic hairdresser.

And, if all that gives you an appetite, we've a delicious restaurant called "The Golden Pheasant".

Next time you're in town, start your shopping trip in Wigmore Street. At Debenham and Freebody.

And don't be surprised if you find everything you need in our shop.

Including your patience, your equilibrium and your self-respect.

Debenham & Freebody.
Wigmore Street, W.1. 01-580 4444
A step up from Oxford Street.

A DICTIONARY OF THE REVOLUTION

What is loosely termed the Russian Revolution was not a single event, not even a single period in time, but a protracted, painful disintegration of a backward, autocratic government unable to function in the 20th century. The roots can be found in late 19th-century protests against the appalling conditions of Russia's peasants and industrial workers – recently liberated from serfdom but in many cases actually worse off. The Revolution had its dress rehearsal in 1905 when a surge of protest achieved a Constitution and superficial reforms. These, however led not to political and social evolution but to another period of reaction. In February 1917 the sclerotic Tsarist autocracy collapsed under the pressure of the first world war. This led to a futile attempt at a constitutional government under impossible conditions. The final revolution was that of the Bolsheviks nine months later – exactly 50 years ago. A savage civil war followed, and it was 1922 before Soviet rule prevailed everywhere in Russia. Here is an illustrated guide to some of the events of those cataclysmic years

Agitation is "the exercise of political influence on the masses by means of talks, reports, speeches, through newspapers, books, brochures, leaflets, radio, the cinema . . ." (*Political Dictionary*, Moscow, 1958). Posters below call for the defeat of exploiting classes, the defeat of the Whites, full participation at elections and (below left) attention to a State Publisher's books

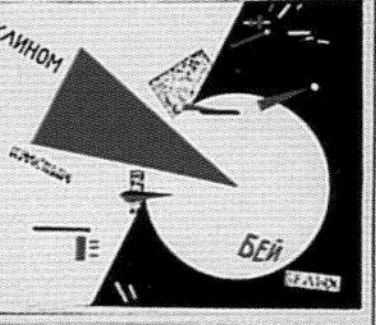

If Hegarty, Abbott and Webster exploited language as a medium for communicating ideas, David King (employed by the hugely influential art director Tom Wolsey, and designer of *The Sunday Times magazine* in its heyday) claimed to see typography 'simply as a vehicle for visual communication' and began a love affair with Soviet Constructivism that he would only fully develop in the seventies.

Alongside the strands of social awareness and thoughtful communication, the late sixties also saw a number of playful ads, companion pieces to the wit shown by many graphic designers at the start of the decade.

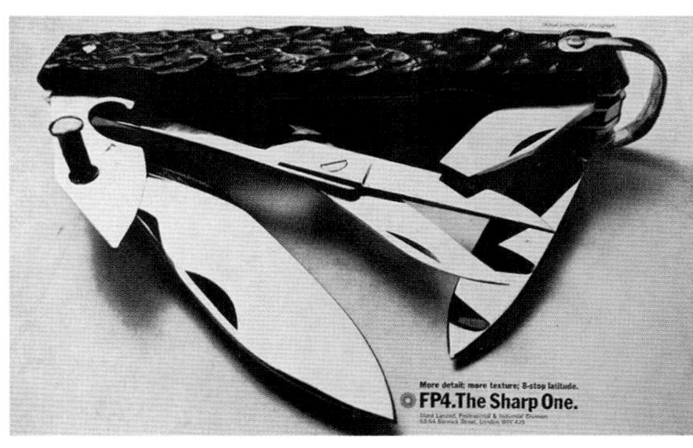

1968.18
Art director: **Michael Rand**
Publication:
The Sunday Times magazine
A watershed edition of the famous magazine gave David King (designer and cover artist of this October 1967 issue – 50 years on from the Russian Revolution) a chance to indulge in the pseudo-constructivism that would obsess him well into the seventies.

this page

1969.15
Agency:
Davidson Pearce Berry & Tuck
Client: **Ilford**
Ilford's FP4 promised high levels of sharpness in a medium-speed black and white film. An impossible virtue to demonstrate in reproduction, sharpness is here suggested metaphorically.

1967.16
Agency:
Davidson Pearce Berry & Tuck
Client: **Wates**
This audacious bid to align building company Wates with a 'new Jerusalem' scheduled for completion by the year 2000 may not have been entirely borne out by history, but it deserved full marks for *chutzpah* on the part of DPBT.

Many ads were becoming channels of communication that used catchphrases, puns and snappy confections of words and images. Witty and dynamic, the best also slipped into the popular consciousness like the hook of a catchy pop tune. Novelist and erstwhile copywriter Fay Weldon is popularly credited with dreaming up the slogan 'Go to work on an egg' for Ogilvy & Mather, and that award winner, like Mo Drake's 'Beanz Meanz Heinz' copy line for Y&R, proved that familiar foodstuffs and products could be promoted not by making exaggerated claims for them, but by associating them with snappy slogans.

Schweppes' 'Schhh...you know who' and Cadbury's 'Everyone's a fruit & nut case' joined the canon, reinforcing in a more populist way Alan Fletcher's view that graphics are obliged to provide not just solutions but solutions that contain wit and an element of surprise.

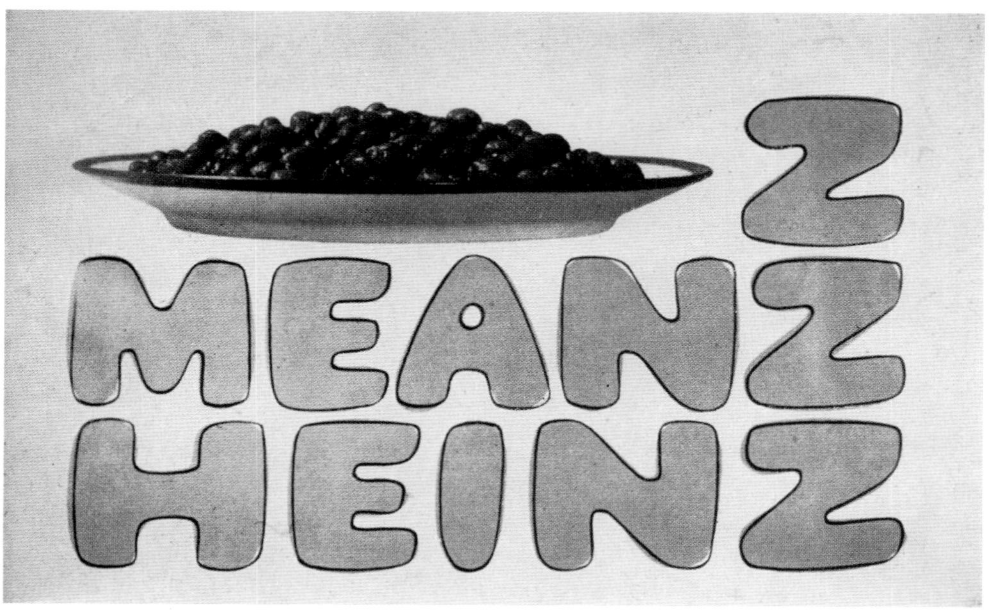

1967.17
Agency: **Young & Rubicam**
Client: **HJ Heinz**
A catchphrase that seeped into the mind of a generation: Mo Drake's susurrating slogan for the baked bean was allegedly composed during a drinking session at a pub. There seems no reason to doubt this.

opposite

1965.13
Agency: **Young & Rubicam**
Client: **Cadbury Brothers**
Starting in the mid-sixties the classic slogan 'Everyone's a fruit & nut case' did Cadbury's proud. Had it come two decades later it would probably have been withdrawn in response to complaints by mental health groups. This campaign was used on London Underground trains.

1968.19
Agency: **Young & Rubicam**
Client: **Cadbury Brothers**
One step further for the Fruit & Nut case campaign sees a London Underground ad thinly masquerading as an optical illusion. Whether or not bleary morning rail commuters were up for this prank is not recorded.

1967.18
Agency: **Young & Rubicam**
Client: **Cadbury Brothers**
Evidence that a memorable slogan is adaptable to as much variation as the campaign will stand, even stretching to mathematics.

1967.19
Agency: **Young & Rubicam**
Client: **Cadbury Brothers**
This slightly more oblique ad parodies airline advertising, always a signal of self-assured advertising.

1966.10
Agency: **Young & Rubicam**
Client: **Cadbury Brothers**
Another example of a London Underground poster relating the basic joke to the nature of the immediate environment.

"Hello, fruit"

"You fond of chocolate?"
"If it's Cadbury's"

"Good. I'll see you in the bar"

Cadbury's
Fruit & Nut
1/-
MILK CHOCOLATE
Everybody's a Cadbury's fruit & nut case

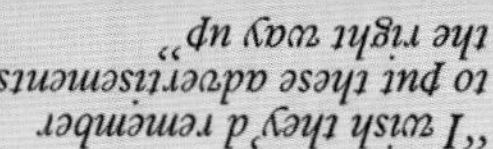

"I wish they'd remember to put these advertisements the right way up"

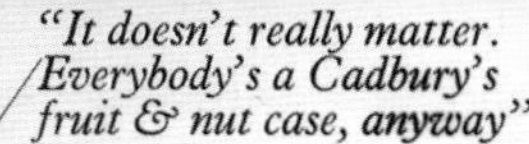

"It doesn't really matter. Everybody's a Cadbury's fruit & nut case, anyway"

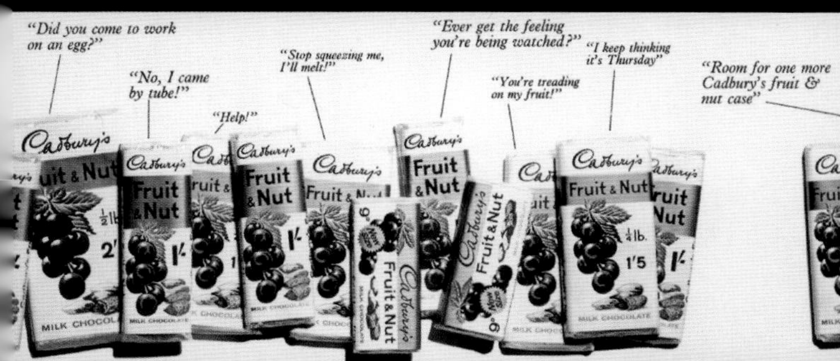

"Did you come to work on an egg?"
"No, I came by tube!"
"Help!"
"Stop squeezing me, I'll melt!"
"Ever get the feeling you're being watched?"
"You're treading on my fruit!"
"I keep thinking it's Thursday"
"Room for one more Cadbury's fruit & nut case"

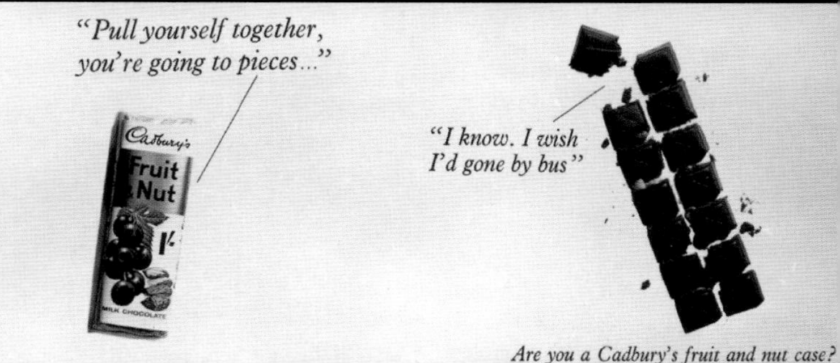

"Pull yourself together, you're going to pieces..."
"I know. I wish I'd gone by bus"
Are you a Cadbury's fruit and nut case?

Let's get out of here this bar is full of nuts!
Everybody's a Cadbury's fruit & nut case.

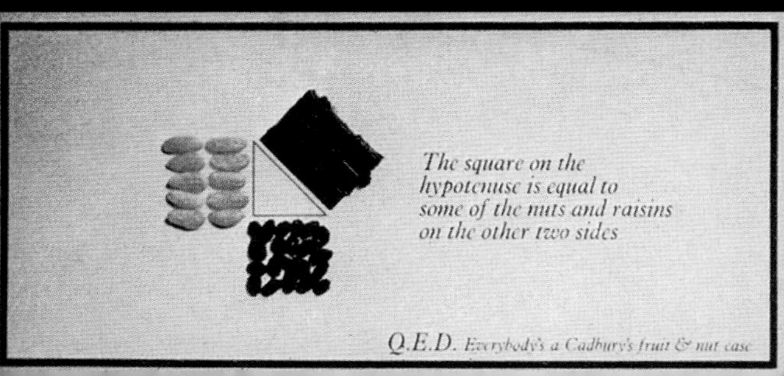

The square on the hypotenuse is equal to some of the nuts and raisins on the other two sides
Q.E.D. Everybody's a Cadbury's fruit & nut case

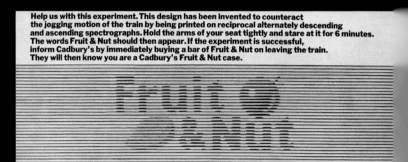

Help us with this experiment. This design has been invented to counteract the jogging motion of the train by being printed on reciprocal alternately descending and ascending spectrographs. Hold the arms of your seat tightly and stare at it for 6 minutes. The words Fruit & Nut should then appear. If the experiment is successful, inform Cadbury's by immediately buying a bar of Fruit & Nut on leaving the train. They will then know you are a Cadbury's Fruit & Nut case.

Fruit & Nut

Bob Isherwood extended the Cadbury catchphrase to include teasing adverts that played little visual practical jokes on the reader. Geers Gross helmed a long-running campaign that made uncharismatic Homepride flour the charming focus of a little bowler-hatted character who became a miniature star in his own right. TV sitcom characters like Alf Garnett could now cross over into commercials (in this case for Findus peas) with some confidence that the context would be a humorous extension of their popular personae. So now we had self-referential jokes, a sure sign of self-confidence in any medium, so that by the end of the decade advertising was developing a language and a set of references of its own in which the myriad visual and social influences of the turbulent sixties were being reflected and refracted.

Advertising was also transforming itself into a serious business, far removed from what it had been in 1960 when the first stirrings of D&AD were being felt.

1969.16
Agency: **Geers Gross**
Client: **Spillers**
The appeal of the Homepride flour man Fred and his friends was to prove enduring. Here the drawings for this TV ad are by Tony Cattaneo, father of *The Full Monty* film director, Peter Cattaneo.

1969.17
Agency: **J Walter Thompson**
Client: **Findus Eskimo Food**
Now that Samuel L Jackson and Ed Harris appear in TV ads, it is hard to recall a time when celebrities simply did not do that sort of thing.

1969.18
Agency: **J Walter Thompson**
Client: **Beecham Products**
Campari is presented as a kind of striptease in this TV ad, the name of the product being gradually revealed only after macro shots of clinking ice and swirling liquid.

1969.19
Art director: **Roland Schenk**
Client: **Campaign**
From Switzerland via France and Germany, Roland Schenk came to London and Michael Heseltine's Haymarket Publishing Group, where he designed the British advertising industry's groundbreaking trade magazine *Campaign*.

In 1968 the Haymarket Publishing Group finally launched a trade paper for advertising – *Campaign* – and the industry had arrived.

Campaign was designed by Swiss typographer Roland Schenk, who had moved to London in 1966 to work on *Town*, then published by Haymarket's precursor Cornmarket. D&AD was quick to recognize the gesture and in 1969 *Campaign* was featured in the annual. It would, however, be another 18 years before graphic designers, so vibrant and prolific in the sixties, would get their own dedicated trade magazine, *Design Week*, but by then London's creative landscape would have changed beyond all recognition. What had begun as a loose alliance of professionals in the communication business had already been transformed by the sixties experience into vigorous and more organized strands of activity. The decade that followed would build upon that achievement even as it strove to deal with a very different cultural and creative climate.

campaign

The newspaper of the communications business
Incorporating WPN
2s 6d
16 July 1968

Bookstall rush likely but subscribers will get copies, says circulation chief

Launch set for new paper

Thomson talks about King, raps agencies, speaks out on women's magazines: exclusive 'Campaign' interview

News starts here

Press

Agencies

Creation

Television

Public Relations

Marketing

Fleet Street men head team

Last word on the 1960s
Alan Fletcher

Thanks to the memories of David Bernstein, Derek Birdsall, Bob Brooks, John Commander, Colin Forbes, Bob Geers, David Hillman, David Kingsley, Peter Mayle, John McConnell, Arnold Schwartzman and Ridley Scott.

Once upon a time ... the 'swinging sixties' was a term heading an article about London in *Time* magazine. They weren't, at least not until well into the decade. 1960 was only a few days older than 1959 and the fifties were indescribably dreary. The average light bulb was 40 watts, with Lyons Corner Houses and ABC teashops, a half-pint bottle of brown the ticket to a party, and the best opportunity for a close encounter with the opposite sex the Saturday night bash at St Martins School of Art.

It was hard graft. Grey. The new decade could only get better. It did. The spirit of a period owes much to the past and the sixties were largely created by the figures of the thirties and forties. The movers and shakers who emerged in the sixties had not inherited a previous generation (the war excluded that). The creative legacy was carried forward by a golden few such as Ashley Havindon, Arped Elfer, Abram Games, Hans Schleger, Tom Eckersley, Henrion, George Him, Misha Black and Milner Gray.

Jesse Collins, head of 'book production and commercial design' at the Central School of Art and Craft in the fifties, brought in Anthony Froshaug and Herbert Spencer whose students – Harold Bartram, Desmond Jeffries, Peter Wildbur, Derek Birdsall, Ken Garland, Colin Forbes, Richard Hollis, Robin Fior – spread the typographic gospel.

A similar visionary was John Gillard at the London College of Printing, alma mater of John Hegarty, Michael Peters, David Hillman and many others. Hillman recalls that Tom Eckersley informed the students that they weren't studying 'Commercial Art' – but 'Graphic Design'.

This was the decade when London became a cauldron for the advertising and design energies emanating from New York, Swiss typographic stances, trends and styles from Milan – a concoction shaken and stirred right here.

It all took place on a broad canvas: The Beatles, The Rolling Stones, Carnaby Street, Granny Takes A Trip, The Smithsons, Design Research Unit, Harold Pinter, Arnold Wesker, Marshal McLuhan, Hugh Hefner, Dick Lester, Ken Russell, ICA, TIT, CPV, CND. *Blow Up*, Sean Kenny, Felix Topolski, Paul Hogarth, Archigram, Olivetti, *A Hard Day's Night*, John Berger, Edward Wright, Victor Papanek, The Royal Court, colour TV, Paul Hamlyn, Christine Keeler and/or Mandy Rice Davis.

Peter Blakes's *Sergeant Pepper's* record sleeve, Heinz Edelman's *The Yellow Submarine*, Marcello Minale, Len Deighton, *The Naked Ape*, *Small is Beautiful*, Pop art, Dieter Rot's books, Munari's books, Sandberg's books. Letraset screens, Helvetica, photosetting, Gerstner & Kutter, Total Design, Pushpin, Chermayeff & Geismar, Ken Garland's manifesto, 1968 student agitation, Oliver Mourgue. Hille, Knoll, Miller, The Portal Gallery, Pauline Boty, Paolozzi, Richard Hamilton, Vidal Sassoon, Allen Jones, David Hockney's gold lamé jacket. Bridget Riley. The Mini, Lycra, Flower Power, the Establishment, the Pill, Hula Hoops, bells, flowers, mini skirts, lottsa long hair. And what happened to Billy Apple?

Then there was the 'Bob syndrome', an influx of Americans: Bob Brooks, Bob Gill, Bob Geers, Bob Gross, Robert Brownjohn. And Lou Klein, Tony Palladino, Mike Savino. And photographers: Don Silverstein and Lester Bookbinder.

Advertising was not strong on consistency or fidelity. Agency names changed in a blink of the eye and staff interchange put swingers to shame. Anyway, at certain points in the decade, Colin Millward and John Salmon reigned at Collet Dickinson and Pearce (CDP), David Bernstein and Ronnie Kirkwood at McCann Erickson, Jeremy Bullmore and Willy Landels at J Walter Thompson, Bob Brooks at Benton & Bowles, Bob Gill at Charles Hobsons, Norman Berry at Davidson Pierce Berry and Tuck, Bob Pethick and Malcolm Hart at Ogilvy & Mather, Denis Auton at Young & Rubicam (Y&R), Peter Mayle with Tony Palladino at the new imported PKL and David Abbott at Doyle Dane Bernbach (DDB).

Names and enterprises switched around continuously. Trying to record this era has been like trying to contain jelly with a rubber band. CDP began on April Fool's Day in 1960. Energetic Kingsley Manton & Palmer (KMP) was the first advertising agency to go public – Brian Palmer wrote the first commercial on UK television. Theo Crosby designed their offices (as well as Geers Gross, BMP, French Gold Abbot). Agencies born in the sixties along with KMP included Geers Gross, BMP and Allen Brady & Marsh.

Young Frank Lowe worked at Benton & Bowles and Geers Gross had a young media manager named Tim Bell. Ken Grange had his studio in Hampstead. Rodney Fitch was helping Terence Conran. John McConnell shared space in Covent Garden (still a market) with John Gorham, Arthur Robins, David Pocknell and others. Marcello Minale left Y&R to team up with Brian Tattersfield. Ridley Scott was at BBC Television and moonlighting doing commercials. In 1963 Alan Parker applied to Bob Gross for a job, but when he asked for £25,000 a year the sky lit up.

BDMW, acronym for Birdsall, Daulby, Mayhew, Wildbur (assisted by Mervyn Kurlansky), was a new design office ensconced at Balding & Mansell's attic in Bloomsbury. Derek Forsyth (advertising manager of British Pirelli) produced the first Pirelli Calendar in 1964 with Beatles photographer Robert Freeman and Derek Birdsall. Germano Facetti and Romek Marber restyled Penguin Books, followed by Alan Aldridge and David Pelham into the Penguin art direction seat.

Other flashbacks: Jock Kinnear and Margaret Calvert signing Britain's roads; Bernard Lodge's TV titles for *Dr Who*; Arnold Schwartzman's *Ready, Steady, Go!*; Brownjohn's film titles for *Goldfinger*. Saul Bass doing the titles for Preminger and Maurice Binder doing the leftovers. Terence Conran and Habitat. Pop group street posters by Michael English. Willy de Majo creating Icograda. Fletcher/Forbes/Gill starting 'The Graphics Workshop' weekly evenings in the basement at Hobsons. The General Trading Company (graphics by Klaus Friedeberger), Carnaby Street, Kings Road, Portobello Market, Elizabeth David's shop, Lawrence Corner.

Campden Hill Tower, Notting Hill. The first residential tower (1961) in London: Mies chairs in the reception, £9 a week rent – me the second guy in. In the lift one met Shirley Conran, John Stevenson, Ray Hawkey, Bob Gill, Dennis Cannon, Lou Klein, Brownjohn, Rose Evansky, Derek Forsyth, as well as proto-celebrities such as Tom Jones, Lionel Blair, Bamber Gascoigne. Don't call him up, but Ray is the only one still there.

On the corner of Goodge Street and Tottenham Court Road was a fast food dispensary. On the floor above was a vague operation called Cramer & Saatchi, overseen by David Puttnam in-between agenting for photographers. Charlie Saatchi sat in one corner writing copy, in another was Alan Parker, Ross Cramer was in the third. I can't remember who was in the fourth – probably Maurice. And above them was Michael Peters in partnership with Lou Klein (who thought up the yellow D&AD pencil in 1966). Over the road was Ambrose Heal's store. Down the road Michael Wolff and Wally Olins were converting design into a serious business.

The watering holes: the French Pub in Dean Street (hangout for artists in the fifties) and Mario & Franco's Terrazza (designed by Enzo Apicella) in Romilly Street. The creative aura, service and food attracted showbiz stars and moguls. When the suits arrived, the ambience changed. Alvaro, a waiter, won the football pools, and opened up a restaurant in the Kings Road (opposite Zeev Aram). The rest of us followed. Then the culinary focus centred on new venues – Trattoo, Aretusa, Meridiano, San Lorenzo, San Frediano and Mr Chow.

The magazines: *Typographica* (1949–1967), edited and designed by Herbert Spencer; *Graphis*; *Oz*; *Private Eye*; *Town* (edited by Jocelyn Stevens) with art directors Tom Wolsey, Dennis Bailey, Keith Godard; *Queen* with Mark Boxer; *Nova* with Dennis Hackett, Harri Peccinotti, Derek Birdsall and David Hillman; *Twen* with Willy Fleckhaus; Ray Hawkey (and Michael Rand) changing the face of *The Daily Express* as well as designing the jackets for Len Deighton's thrillers. Later there would be Michael Rand art directing (Roger Law and David King pasting up) *The Sunday Times colour supplement* with Arnold Schwartzman regularly contributing illustrations. And Harry Evans at *The Times*.

In the fifties Alexanders on Shaftesbury Avenue was the only place in London you could get kitted out in Ivy League suits. In the sixties Mr Major (and Mr Shine) and Doug Hayward took over, dressing up aspiring individuals with sharp suits. I recollect (in 1962) a stunning looking girl walking down Baker Street in a sack, just around the corner from Fletcher/Forbes/Gill. Our studio was next to Victor Sylvester's mews house. Fashion action was emerging with Mary Quant at Bizarre, Zandra Rhodes, Biba, Vivienne Westwood, Twiggy, Tuffin & Foale, Ossie Clark.

Then there was the photography. John French (assistant David Bailey). The trio of Terence Donovan, Brian Duffy and David Bailey. Tony Armstrong-Jones (lived by the Thames in the East End – then foreign territory), John Cole, Barry Lategan, Don McCullin, David Montgomery, Clive Arrowsmith, John Hedgecoe, Adrian Flowers. Television commercials: James Garrett, Ridley Scott, Baker/Brooks/Fulford, Cammell, Hudson and Brownjohn.

Starting in 1959, a group of designers met once a month at a Soho or Charlotte Street restaurant. The habitués included Mark Boxer, Tom Wolsey, Sidney King (he designed the menus), Derek Birdsall, Barry Trengove and George Mayhew. We decided to form the 'Association of Graphic Designers, London' with the notion of holding an annual exhibition. At the time I freelanced for Time Life who had their European headquarters on the corner of Bond and Bruton Streets. A Henry Moore sat in the courtyard and Moore abstracts topped one of the facades. The latter still do.

Anyway, in 1960 the 'Association' held an exhibition in the foyer. Among the exhibitors were Colin Forbes, Dennis Bailey, George Daulby, George Mayhew, Derek Birdsall, Peter Wildbur, Tom Wolsey, Romek Marber, Paul Peter Peich, Arnold Schwartzman, David Collins and myself.

Back in 1961: 'Two things really got up my nose,' Bob Brooks wrote me, 'one was the Layton Awards and the other was the title "visualiser" given to the person who was actually an art director. Layton was a printing and block making company that serviced the major advertising agencies. There was an unwritten agreement between Layton and these agencies that entries be submitted as "designed (or created) on a group basis". To solve both problems it seemed best to start from scratch and form an art directors club in London and hold our own annual show. This would officially do away with "visualiser" and no entry would be accepted unless the creative team was given full credit. Names would be named!' (You may have noticed that I have followed Bob's principle in drafting this historical document.)

Bob Brooks' irritation was shared with others in the advertising community. Notably Bob Geers, Colin Millward and Malcolm Hart. At the time, London was a small place, we all sort of knew each other, and the design and advertising activities were somewhat interchangeable. On behalf of the design faction I contacted Brooks. We all met and the two groups decided to merge plans. Actually, it wasn't quite that simple as 'getting those designers and those art directors to agree on anything', recollects Bob Geers. 'It rates with the United States Constitution as an example of compromise under fire.' Maybe so, but it happened.

D&AD was born in 1962. John Commander (art director at printers Balding & Mansell) was elected chairman. Janet Donovan was the administrative secretary. I copied an entry form from the New York Art Directors Club into English format. The D&AD emblem was designed by Colin Forbes. He found a cube of wood, stuck the four characters on adjacent sides and photographed the angulation. Wolf Spoerl (maestro artworker) cleaned up the fuzzy edges. We got mail lists.

The first show was held in June 1963 and mounted by Bob Gill and students overnight on the mezzanine of the new Hilton Hotel. Lord Snowdon (by then) opened the enterprise. 403 items of print and 38 films were selected from approximately 3,500 entries by the judging panel, which included Robert Brownjohn, Bob Brooks, John Pearce, Barry Trengove, Germano Facetti, Tom Wolsey, Bob Gross, Bob Geers, Malcolm Hart, Colin Forbes, Derek Birdsall, Romek Marber, David Collins, Ian Bradbery and Jock Kinneir.

Arnie Schwartzman, who had three pieces in the show, recollects that 'I really thought, I've arrived'. And Bob Geers confided to me that he paid 'Bob Gross a fiver to get one of my ads in'. Without any luck. The climate changed. The sun shone. Everyone could see what everyone else was doing. Standards were established. The clients became engaged. From then on, creativity acquired value.

At the annual D&AD 1965 general meeting in the gloomy Russell Hotel in Bloomsbury John Commander said he was resigning. The 30-odd attendees were nonplussed. Bob Brooks remembers he nominated an art director at J Walter Thompson called Edward Booth-Clibbon. My recollection is that a young guy (EBC) stood up at the back and said 'I'll do it', and that we were all so relieved we voted him on. Actually, Edward tells me it wasn't like that at all and I've got it all wrong. Maybe he's right. Anyway, he took the helm and ran the organization in his idiosyncratic fashion for the next 25 years.

The sixties were revolutionary because of a dramatic social change, and an explosion of energy and vitality. A period of effervescent optimism and amazing possibilities – some of which were even realized. I know, I was there.

197

70s

The years 1970–9, like most decades when viewed in retrospect, are often depicted as being self-contained and easily summarized. Thus, the seventies is popularly seen as a period that profited from a radically liberated cultural atmosphere once the sixties had kicked down the door and let in the fresh air. In fact, until the 1973 crisis when OPEC triggered high inflation and recession throughout the Western world by quadrupling the price of oil, the sixties simply merged into the seventies with no obvious watershed. Change would take time to filter through. The most resonant popular culture shift was perhaps the break-up of The Beatles, an event which effectively took place in April 1970 when Paul McCartney finally quit, although the split had been on the cards for some time. For many people there was a certain wistful sense of loss inherent in the spectacle of the four uniformed sixties moptops turning into disenchanted seventies individuals, each now with his own dress sense, hairstyle, ambition and agenda. Was diversity and fragmentation going to be the theme of the new decade? Perhaps, but The Beatles, when together, had provided comforting proof that the London-generated, sixties popular culture revolution was no flash in the pan but an ongoing and influential insurgency.

Even if the influences emanating from home-grown design and advertising were little understood by the general public at the time, pretty well everybody knew that The Beatles had made historic inroads in the US pop charts. They had even been showcased in two movies (*Hard Day's Night* and *Help!*) that had at last broken the seemingly unbreakable curse of the pop idol movie by being more than halfway decent films. Both had been directed by D&AD award winner Richard Lester.

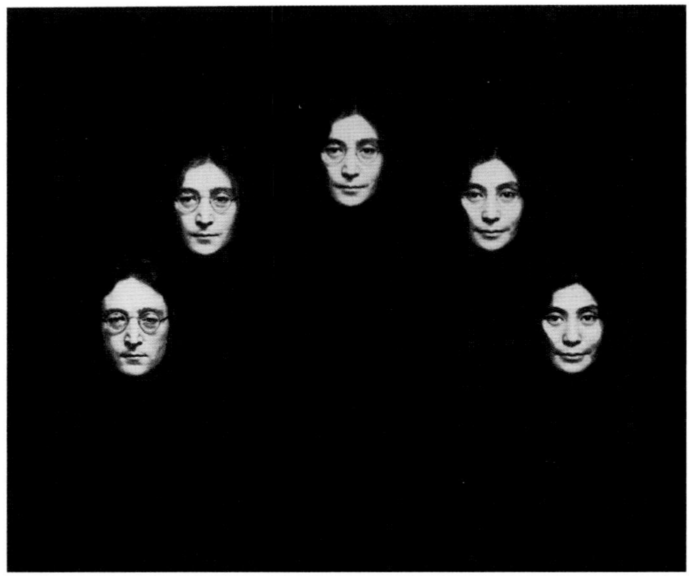

1972.01
Art director: **Ian Macmillan**
Client: **Apple Records**
'Happy Christmas (War Is Over)' sang John Lennon, and along with the anthem came the inevitable message of self-absorption: John and Yoko morphing into a single being. What would become a facile trick in the computer age was here anticipated using laborious photo techniques.

1970.01
Designer: **John McConnell**
Client: **Biba**
John McConnell's definitive Biba look was created in the days before he joined Pentagram. This piece of direct mail marked both a move of premises and an expansion of ambition for the retailer, from boutique to department store.

In design and fashion, the first three or four years of the seventies were also largely a continuation of what had been happening in the previous decade. An exception was the sudden expansion of a small sixties boutique called Biba into something altogether more ambitious. Biba, along with Bus Stop, had been one of the two small but definitive fashion boutiques in London's Kensington Church Street. Mary Quant's sixties fashion revolution had been the inspiration for a number of such highly theatrical boutiques where the ambience, music and decor were as important as the merchandise and clientele, but Biba was the ambitious one. It was the brainchild of fashion designer Barbara Hulanicki, who now sought to encourage youth-oriented fashion retailing to take a giant step. At the end of 1969, the store had expanded and moved into part of the premises of the old Derry & Toms department store (famous for its roof garden) in nearby Kensington High Street. John McConnell's design group produced the D&AD Award-winning literature for the move, complete with Art Nouveau revival logotype and pseudo-Victorian waifs. However, Biba's ambitious retail venture was ultimately doomed to fail. Its large, theatrically lit department store housed a heady synthesis of camp and nostalgic styles, but on the way it lost the mystique and intimacy of its small boutique beginnings. Yet, in its early recognition of shopping as an entertainment activity, Biba earned its place in the history of UK retailing, even if Hulanicki's grasp of business never matched her sense of theatre. When Biba finally closed in 1975 it was another signal that, in many areas, the spirit of the sixties was running out of steam and the seventies was still waiting for a big idea.

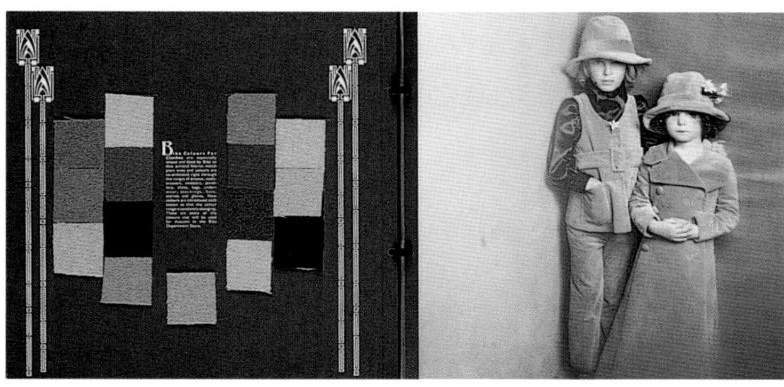

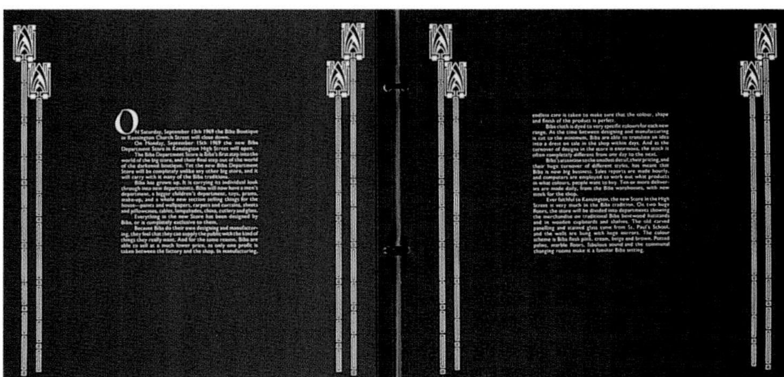

In contrast, the world of advertising was about to explode into a golden age of extraordinary self-confidence, commercial success and global influence.

The ability to match strong ideas with arresting images had been a key feature of late sixties advertising and 1970 saw an immediate endorsement of the trend with Cramer Saatchi's Silver Award-winning poster of a pregnant man. Created for The Health Education Council, it offered definitive proof that as long as the central idea was strong, you did not need shocking realism or a quirky photomontage to create an eye-catching image. All you needed was a cushion stuffed up a man's jumper and a trenchant copy line ('Would you be more careful if it was you that got pregnant?'). The grammar was poor but the idea was powerful. This poster ad was to be the last winner for the agency under that name. It would become Saatchi & Saatchi in September of 1970, marking the start of a 16-year acquisition spree for the Saatchi brothers Charles and Maurice.

The following year's D&AD Gold for outstanding copy ('Why Your First Cigarette Made You Feel Giddy') was credited to Saatchi & Saatchi and Company, and written by Charles Saatchi himself.

1971.01
Agency: **Saatchi & Saatchi**
Client: **The Health Education Council**
John Hegarty, at start-up Saatchi & Saatchi, here resorted to shock tactics. The additional shock is that this is an anti-smoking ad.

1975.01
Agency: **Saatchi & Saatchi**
Client: **The Health Education Council**
By leaving the reader to construe the deliberately misleading headline, the classic *double entendre* adds involvement to impact in this poster.

opposite

1970.02
Agency: **Cramer Saatchi**
Client: **The Health Education Council**
This is the memorable ad that preceded the launch of the Saatchi & Saatchi empire and marked the start of a long relationship with this particular client. At the time *Campaign* reported that many believed the ad 'overstepped the boundaries of good taste'.

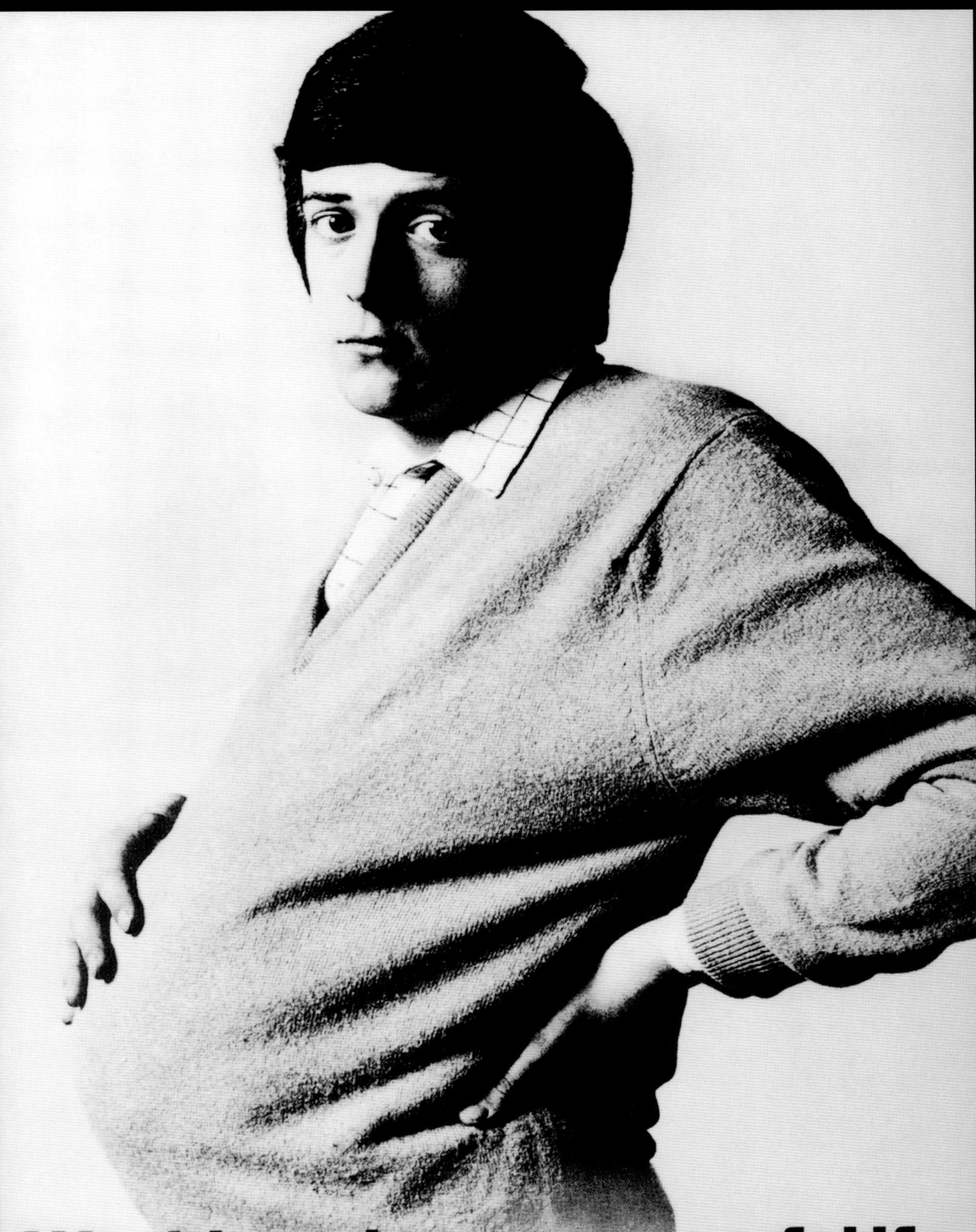
Would you be more careful if
it was you that got pregnant?
Anyone married or single can get advice on contraception from the Family Planning Association.
Margaret Pyke House, 27-35 Mortimer Street, London W1 N 8BQ. Tel. 01-636 9135.
The Health Education Council

Why your first cigarette made you feel giddy.

Cigarettes contain tiny quantities of nicotine, a nerve poison.

The symptoms of mild nicotine poisoning are dizziness, rapid pulse, cold clammy skin, nausea and vomiting.

Smokers experience some of these symptoms with their first few cigarettes.

But once smoking becomes a regular habit, these side effects soon disappear.

Unfortunately, there are other side effects that don't disappear.

The tiny particles of nicotine, and other chemicals that are inhaled, cling to the tubes inside your lungs or enter the blood.

These chemicals gradually form a coating of oily, liquid tar that irritates the tubes, forcing them to produce a thick clogging phlegm.

Heavy smoking increases the irritation in the tubes. When they become infected they start to swell with pus, and sometimes this mixture of infected tar, pus and phlegm rises up in the throat and is swallowed.

But the rest of it slithers deep into the lungs where it congeals and festers.

And that's why smokers cough, are short of wind, have bad breath, and are more susceptible to crippling incurable diseases.

The Health Education Council

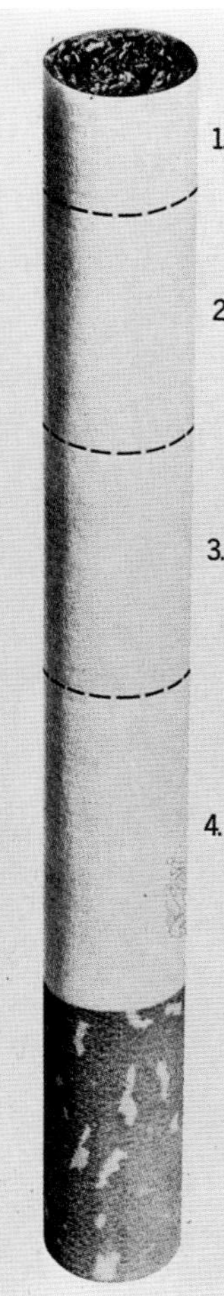

1. The first few draws you take on a cigarette are relatively harmless. The smoke travels through the length of the cigarette, so that most of the tar and nicotine is absorbed by the tobacco and filter.

2. After three or four lungfuls of smoke, tiny particles of nicotine and other chemicals start to irritate the delicate tubes inside your lungs.

3. As more smoke is inhaled these chemicals start to coat the tubes with an oily tar, forcing them to produce a thick clinging phlegm.
When this mixture of tar and phlegm becomes infected it begins to slither deep into your lungs, where it congeals and festers.

4. The tobacco smoke you are now inhaling is so saturated with nicotine and chemicals that it coats your lungs with more liquid tar, causes more irritation to the tubes and produces more clogging phlegm than the other three parts of the cigarette put together.

If you feel you should cut down on your smoking remember it's the last third of the cigarette that does most damage.

The Health Education Council

Tar and discharge collects in the lungs of cigarette smokers.

Every time you inhale a cigarette tiny particles of nicotine and other chemicals are left inside your lungs.

These particles gradually build up into an oily tar, that irritates your lungs till they become clogged or infected with phlegm and pus.

Then, as more of this septic discharge forms, the mixture of tar phlegm and pus sometimes rises up into the throat and is swallowed.

But the rest of it slithers deep into the lungs, where it congeals and festers.

It's not surprising that smokers cough, are short of wind, have bad breath, and are more susceptible to crippling incurable diseases.

The Health Education Council

What makes a cigarette so enjoyable?

Hydrogen Cyanide. The potentially harmful gases in cigarette smoke include Hydrogen Cyanide in a concentration 160 times the amount considered safe in industry. Hydrogen Cyanide is a powerful poison.

Ammonia is commonly used as a household cleansing agent, and in the manufacture of explosives.

Carbon Monoxide, the same deadly gas that is emitted from car exhausts, combines with haemoglobin in red blood cells, thereby reducing the oxygen-carrying capacity of the blood. Since Carbon Monoxide has a much greater affinity for haemoglobin than does oxygen, it literally drives oxygen from the blood.

Nicotine is a colourless oily compound, which in concentrated form is one of the most powerful poisons known. It is marketed as a lethal insecticide (Black leaf 40) and injection of one drop, 70 milligrams, will cause the death of a man of average weight within a few minutes.

Nicotine is probably the addictive agent in cigarette tobacco. When you smoke, it temporarily stimulates the nervous system, and causes the craving for tobacco.

Butane, the gas used in camping stoves and cigarette lighters. Apart from cigarette smoke, it's also found in natural gas and crude petroleum.

Tar. Tobacco tar contains more than 200 compounds, many of them toxic. Among these are at least 10 hydrocarbons that have produced cancer when administered to animals.

As you inhale a cigarette the smoke coats your lungs with this liquid tobacco tar. The further down you smoke your cigarette, the more tar and nicotine it produces. In fact, the last third of the cigarette produces more tar and nicotine than the other two thirds put together.

Phenol has not been proved to cause cancer on its own. However, it does destroy the protective action of the cilia, the small hairlike projections that line the respiratory tract. It is a corrosive poison, and a severe irritant. Used to make glue, paint, plastic and explosives.

Fortunately the poisons in tobacco smoke are counteracted and discharged by the natural defences of the body.

However, the accumulative effects of many years smoking often breaks these defences down.

If you feel you should cut down on your smoking remember it's the last third of the cigarette that does most damage.

The Health Education Council

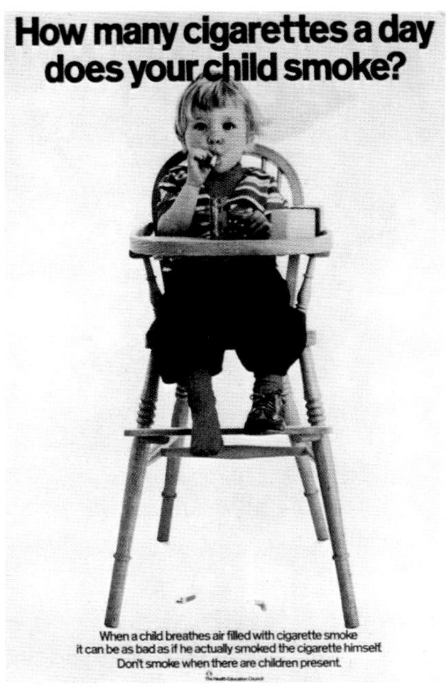

How many cigarettes a day does your child smoke?
When a child breathes air filled with cigarette smoke it can be as bad as if he actually smoked the cigarette himself.
Don't smoke when there are children present.

This is what happens when a fly lands on your food.

Flies can't eat solid food, so to soften it up they vomit on it.

Then they stamp the vomit in until it's a liquid, usually stamping in a few germs for good measure.

Then when it's good and runny they suck it all back again, probably dropping some excrement at the same time.

And then, when they've finished eating, it's your turn.

Cover food. Cover eating and drinking utensils. Cover dustbins.

The Health Education Council

1971.02
Agency: **Saatchi & Saatchi**
Client: **The Health Education Council**
The first stage of The Cigarette Horror Story. A stark white-on-black catalogue of poisons set the tone. A less persuasive bid to get smokers to abandon each cigarette two-thirds of the way through obviously reflected a medical wisdom of the time.

1971.03
Agency: **Saatchi & Saatchi**
Client: **The Health Education Council**
More revolting descriptions of what happens in the smoker's lungs are followed by the introduction of dark irony: what makes a cigarette so enjoyable? What indeed.

this page

1974.01
Agency: **Saatchi & Saatchi**
Client: **The Health Education Council**
Passive smoking is here presented as a shockingly literal idea. Arguably, this is overkill, since with the image of the smoking child you do not really need the headline, and with the headline you do not really need the image of the smoking child.

1970.03
Agency: **Cramer Saatchi**
Client: **The Health Education Council**
A great ad that unsettled many a stomach. Again, an unflinching tell-it-like-it-is approach finds suitably stark expression in the white-on-black type – harder to read but harder still to ignore.

Doyle Dane Bernbach (DDB) was another agency enjoying considerable success with its anglicized version of the US approach to selling products in witty and unexpected ways, and was widely seen as one of the British advertising industry's leaders. It was at DDB that art director Neil Godfrey, who would later play a pivotal part at Collett Dickenson Pearce (CDP), came up with some groundbreaking ads for the German national airline Lufthansa. In a classic example of a press ad fearlessly grasping the nettle, he depicted an aircraft as a sardine can with the copy line 'You can't solve a problem until you admit you've got one.' The theme was repeated in ads that made thinly veiled references to the empty promises made by increasingly busy and oversubscribed airlines. The payoff was always that Lufthansa's investment in superior facilities on the ground was what set them apart. By putting the emphasis on a negative, Godfrey and DDB were simultaneously grabbing attention and mocking the empty hyperbole of the competition. DDB was in London's Baker Street, but the new pretenders to UK advertising's throne were less than a mile away in Howland Street.

1972.02
Agency: **Doyle Dane Bernbach**
Client: **Volkswagen**
Subverting a familiar phrase with an incongruous image was a lesson that, by the early seventies, DDB London had learned very well from its New York office.

1971.04
Agency: **Doyle Dane Bernbach**
Client: **Volkswagen**
DDB offer an elegant solution to the problem of not being able to badmouth the competition in so many words.

opposite

1971.05
Agency: **Doyle Dane Bernbach**
Client: **Lufthansa Airlines**
Neil Godfrey's layout for this artfully persuasive ad dramatically dislocated the body copy from the headline and reversed their familiar positions on the page, adding to the visual drama of the improbably long red carpet.

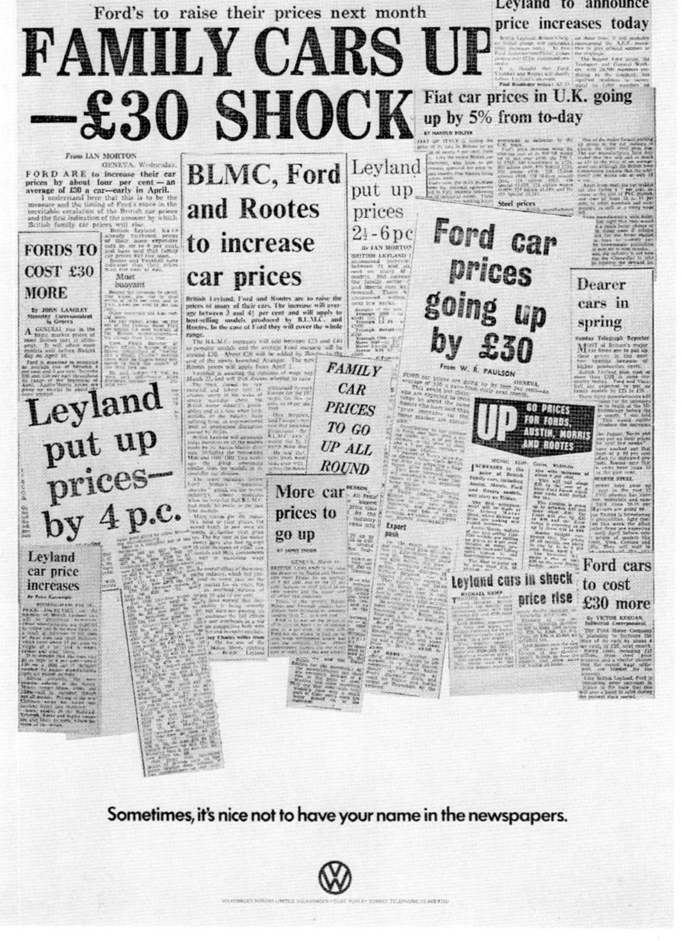

THE TIMES

You can be forgiven for thinking that an airline ticket entitles you to V.I.P. treatment.

With promises of personal service, five-course meals and cloud-soft comfort, it's an illusion the airlines like to nurture.

Like all illusions though, its connection with reality is frail.

Nearer the truth is that airlines today have less and less time to treat you as someone special.

In fact, unless you're flying first class, you have to make do with some pretty basic service.

The problem is how to make this basic service tolerable.

At Lufthansa, we think the answer lies not so much in the air as on the ground.

In the air, there are some things we can do to relieve the irritations of a long-haul flight. But even our 747s won't totally overcome it.

Rather, we figure that if we can keep you happy till the plane takes off, you'll feel better about the whole journey.

Which is why we've spent so much time looking into ground handling.

And even taken it so far as to design new airports.

Airports with completely fresh layouts. (Including plenty of kerb side space, parking facilities and shorter walking distance.)

With shorter check-in times.

With a block-booking plan for the 747 that allows you to embark without the usual jostle.

And a comprehensive ground hostess system.

All of which helps to cope with the ever growing business and tourist traffic.

Naturally we can't force every airport and every airline to take us up on our ideas.

But already some have in one degree or other. (Dallas airport, for one.)

And we hope more will as time shows they should have done so earlier.

Until then, we want you to understand that we understand your frustrations, and that your travel agent does too.

And that, like us, he'll do all he can to smooth them over.

That's a promise.

Lufthansa

We'll do all we can.

Promises. Promises.

At the end of the sixties, the ten-year-old agency CDP had long been showing signs of unusual promise. If it had not yet started to dominate UK advertising completely, it had certainly been consistent in attracting key talents and laying the foundations for a memorable decade of creativity that would be repeatedly honoured by D&AD. During the seventies alone, CDP would win some 56 awards. Hard to analyse in conventional terms of style, CDP's success was rooted in its corporate culture rather than in any easily labelled approach.

John Pearce and Ronnie Dickenson were both in middle-age when they founded CDP by buying an ailing agency, Pictorial Publicity, from John Collett. Seeking to create ads that were more entertaining and effective than the bulk of existing ones (which, by following established strategic guidelines, were predominantly formulaic and predictable), they hired Colin Millward as creative director. Millward, a no-nonsense Yorkshireman, would come to oversee an astonishingly creative ensemble of maverick – and occasionally shambolic – talents who were allowed, encouraged and indeed required to produce stimulating and original advertising.

1977.01
Agency: **Collett Dickenson Pearce**
Client: **Wall's Meat Company**
The reference was to a contemporary airline ad ('I'm Margie. Fly me.') that sought to sexualize the drab experience of air travel. Other punning taglines in a series that CDP claimed revived the 48-sheet poster were 'Porky and Best' and 'Pinky and Porky'.

1971.06
Agency: **Collett Dickenson Pearce**
Client: **Pretty Polly**
Pretty Polly's bid to banish separate items of female underwear was not destined to revolutionize the sector. However, CDP made a virtue out of minimalism and Marilyn Monroe photographer Eve Arnold shot a model who did not seem to be in need of much support in the first place.

opposite

1971.07
Agency: **Collett Dickenson Pearce**
Client: **Hovis**
The poster precursor to Ridley Scott's famous Hovis TV commercials established the same psychology: crusty wholesomeness expressed by subject, surroundings and product ... plus a touch of religiosity in the headline.

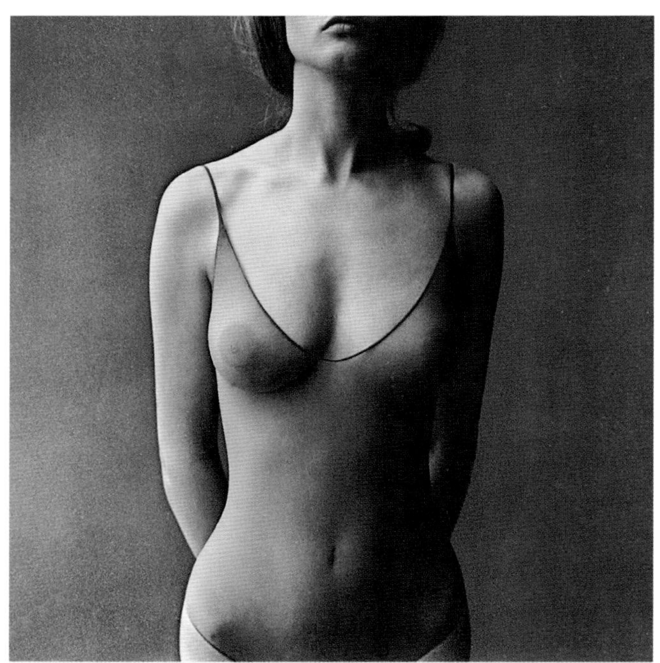

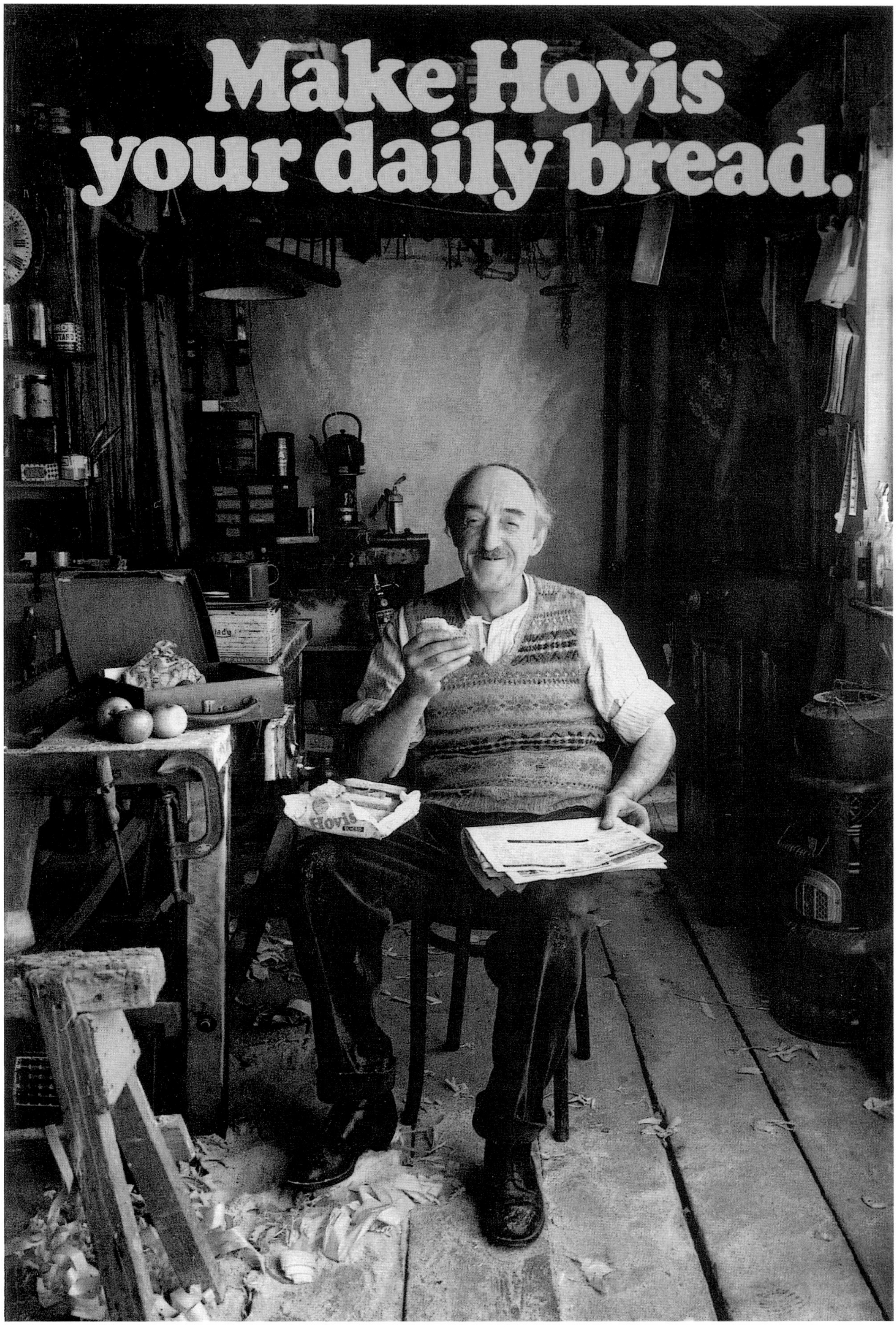
Make Hovis
your daily bread.
Hovis

One of the few strictly enforced corporate rules proved to be a positive one and took the form of a directive that copywriters and art directors had to work together as a team (another was that every job had to be signed off by the upper echelons before the client ever saw it). Creative pairings had worked for DDB but the practice was unfamiliar in most other UK agencies, where copywriter and art director traditionally worked separately. Perhaps the most famous CDP team of all was that of art director Neil Godfrey and copywriter Tony Brignull. Brignull was something of a serial employee at CDP, having worked there on and off in the sixties, seventies and eighties. He confirms that the seventies were the agency's golden years: 'I can't imagine that any agency ever won more awards,' he says. 'As we sat in the basement doing our pitch we knew that upstairs [Alan] Waldie was doing yet more wonderful Benson & Hedges posters, David Brown's group was writing Birds Eye scripts [with June Whitfield] and the famous Hovis campaign, a young Paul Weiland was working on new Hamlet ideas and Terry Lovelock was shooting Heineken commercials. Other groups were working on sensational campaigns for Barclaycard, Army Officer and Metropolitan Police recruitment and Mary Quant cosmetics.'

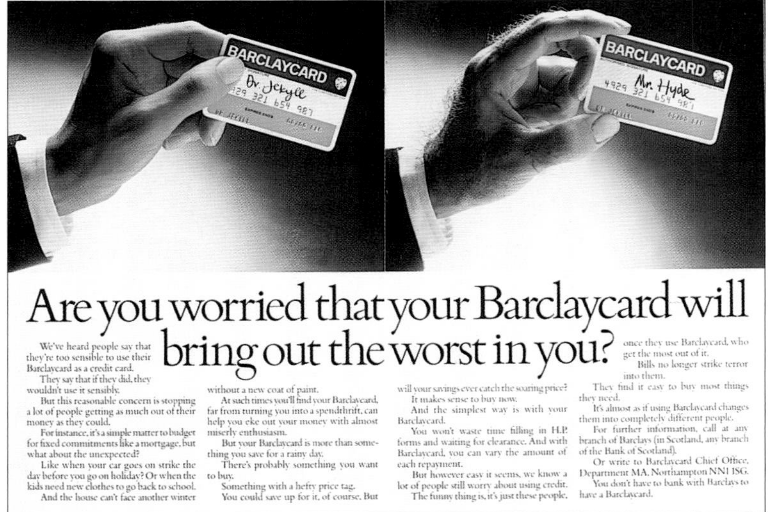

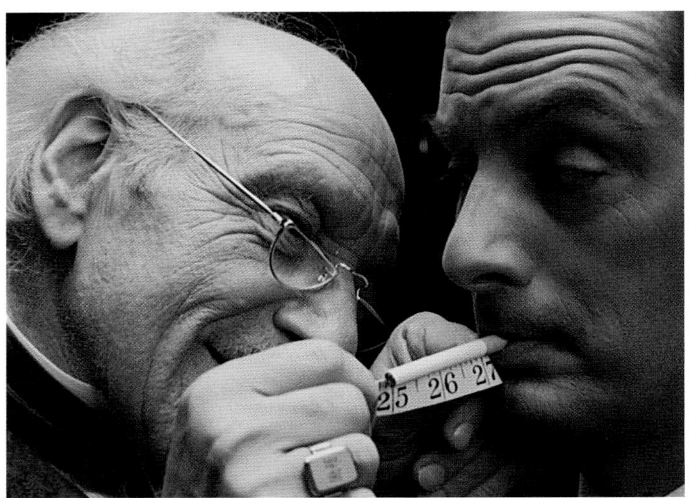

1976.01
Agency: **Collett Dickenson Pearce**
Client: **Pretty Polly**
CDP illustrated another stage in Pretty Polly's continuing campaign to contain the female form in a single, taut, seamless integument.

1970.04
Agency: **Collett Dickenson Pearce**
Client: **Gallaher**
Bob Brooks directed this commercial for Senior Service Extra cigarettes and Michael Seresin lit it. Seresin would later go on to work for CDP colleague Alan Parker on many of his feature films, notably *Angel Heart*.

1977.02
Agency: **Collett Dickenson Pearce**
Client: **Whitbread**
The durable Heineken campaign here referenced a contemporary furore caused by artist Carl Andre's work entitled *Equivalent VII* – a pile of bricks scattered on a gallery floor. The Tate Gallery's purchase of this piece prompted tabloid outrage.

1977.03
Agency: **Collett Dickenson Pearce**
Client: **Barclaycard**
When credit cards first became popular in Britain what hampered their take-up was fear of overspending from prudent consumers. This ad seriously addressed a fear that today no longer needs addressing at all.

this page

1975.02
Agency: **Collett Dickenson Pearce**
Client: **Metropolitan Police**
Part of one of CDP's strongest campaigns, this Metropolitan Police recruitment ad is still hard-hitting. The art direction may look dated but John Salmon's muscular copywriting is timeless.

WHAT WOULD YOU DO IN THESE SITUATIONS?

You answer a call from a neighbour who is disturbed by a domestic shouting match. When you get there the flat is wrecked, a woman is stretched out on the floor and the neighbours are crowding in. What's your first move?

You answer a call to the scene of an accident. A car has run into a petrol tanker at a junction. The driver and passenger of the car are covered in blood and are very still. The tanker driver is in a state of shock. A heavy flow of traffic is moving past at a good clip. Petrol is spreading over the road. A man is lighting a cigarette. Over to you.

PANIC ☐ TICK HERE

VOMIT ☐ TICK HERE

COPE ☐ TICK HERE

RUN ☐ TICK HERE

RIGHT now you may be hesitant to claim that you know how to cope with situations like these.

But after only six months with us in the Metropolitan Police you could be handling even trickier problems with confidence.

How can we be so sure?

We're careful who we take on.

You have to be British, at least 5′ 8″ tall if you're a man (5′ 4″ if you're a woman) intelligent and fit before we'll consider you.

You also have to have a "good character," which means we can't take a chance on you if you've been in serious trouble with the police.

We will bring out the worst in you.

Then you go to Hendon for 15 weeks of intensive training.

Quite a bit of the time is spent in classrooms, learning about law; about police procedures and about the powers of a Police Constable.

You'll do social studies. And you'll learn how to give evidence in court.

And you get practical police training from instructors who are all very experienced police officers. They set up crime and traffic incidents that would make a Chief Superintendent think twice. And then they act the part of awkward members of the public. If you've got a quick temper or a sarcastic tongue they'll find it.

You'll learn how to control yourself under stress. And you'll learn where the pitfalls are for a young Police Constable, and how to avoid them.

Then if you pass your exam, you'll be posted to one of the Metropolitan Police districts.

During the first few weeks at a police station, you'll go out on patrol with an experienced police officer.

Then you learn what it's really all about.

Very quickly you'll realise the difference between being at Hendon and being on the ground in London.

An instructor pretending to bleed to death isn't the same as someone actually doing so outside the local bank.

On the other hand, the criminals you meet may not be quite as awkward as some of the instructors acting the part.

Just like in any other occupation, you get to know when to apply the rules and when to use your common sense.

And then, all of a sudden you're on your own. And we guarantee that by then you won't panic, run, or vomit whatever you encounter. (Well, you won't vomit where anybody can see you anyway.)

But you are still on probation until you've been in the Force for two years.

During which time you'll go on various courses. You'll learn the basics of criminal investigation and you'll probably learn to drive.

And you'll learn more every day you're on street duty.

When the two years are nearly up and you're through your exam, you're all set to apply for promotion or specialisation if that's what you've decided you want.

How far you go is up to you.

The never-ending variety of things that you have to deal with as a Police Constable will keep you involved and interested for years.

A lot of constables spend their whole time in the police on street duty. They feel, quite rightly, that this is where the main police work is done.

In fact, everybody who is in the police who isn't a constable on street duty, is helping the constables on street duty to do their job. You help prevent people injuring one another and robbing one another.

You help them overcome all kinds of difficulties that they can't, won't or don't know how to overcome themselves.

And you can only do so if you're there on the ground, in contact with the people. You can't do it from an office.

Nobody does it just for the money.

As a constable just starting out, if you're under 22, your basic pay would be £3,833. If you're over 22, £4,391, including London Allowances totalling £644 in both cases.

After your first 15 weeks training, you'll do some overtime once you get out on the ground, for which you will be paid.

You'll also receive free accommodation or a tax-paid rent allowance up to £1,177 a year.

As from next September, police pay will go up again, and will keep pace with average earnings elsewhere.

So, excluding overtime, officers who are married and living in their own houses with two years' service will then be receiving over £6,000. If they are single and living in police accommodation, it could be over £5,500.

Promotion is by examination.

Once you've proved yourself as a Police Officer, there's nothing to stop you going for promotion if you want to.

You simply have to qualify through the promotion exam.

After five years' service (less in some cases) you become a Sergeant.

After another four years you may move up to Inspector.

If you do exceptionally well in your exam for Sergeant, you can apply to go to the Police Staff College at Bramshill, for a one year course.

A year after successfully finishing the course you'll almost certainly be an Inspector. (And this is possible before your 25th birthday.)

From an Inspector upwards promotion is by selection.

Along the way, you may decide you want to specialise. You may apply to go into the CID or the Traffic Division, the Mounted Branch or become a Dog Handler. You might fancy the River Police.

As a member of the Metropolitan Police you are automatically a member of all the many sports and social clubs run by the Force. No matter what your favourite sports or hobbies are we cater for them. And our facilities are probably as good or better than you'll find anywhere.

Now, here's a challenge you've got to face right now.

The dreaded coupon.

Have you got what it takes to fill it in and send it to us?

We'd like to think we can depend on you.

THE METROPOLITAN POLICE

METROPOLITAN EIIR POLICE

To join us you should be British, aged 18½ or over and be at least 172 cms (5′ 8″) tall if you're a man; at least 162 cms (5′ 4″) tall if you're a woman.

If you're under 18½ but over 16 you can still join the Metropolitan Police, as a Cadet.

For more information call at our Careers Information Centre at New Scotland Yard, Victoria Street, SW1, or send this coupon to the Chief Inspector, Metropolitan Police Careers Centre, Dept. MD102, 6 Harrow Road, London W2 1XH. Or 'phone us on 01-725 4237.

Name (Mr/Mrs/Miss) ____________________

Address ____________________

____________________ Age ________

LONDON'S 7,000,000 PEOPLE TAKE A LOT OF LOOKING AFTER. COME AND GIVE US A HAND.

Any young man who says he wants to be an Army Officer should have his motives examined.

Don't worry, we'll go into your motives very thoroughly before accepting you. But it might save us all a lot of bother if you read this advertisement. It's intended to discourage people with the wrong motivations from applying at all.

Are you a patriot?

These days it's not very trendy to declare that you're a patriot. And considering the interpretation often put on the word, small wonder.

To many people 'patriotism' is the same as 'jingoism', 'chauvinism' or 'rabid nationalism'.

And since they find the hostility implied by these terms distasteful they might well, if asked suddenly, declare that they aren't patriots.

Take you for instance, do you love your country?

In your heart very likely you do. But that doesn't mean you aren't a touch embarrassed by the question, does it? In smart company you might possibly deny it.

And what does loving your country mean anyway? Loving the political party in power? The system of government? The countryside? The people? The lot?

As far as we're concerned it means, are you prepared to fight if necessary to prevent people taking control of this country by force or other unconstitutional means?

If you can answer yes to that question, read on.

Do you think John Bull is a world beater?

Do you believe that this country could win a war with one of the super-powers?

If you do you're out of touch with reality.

But if we can't win a war, what's the point of armed forces?

For one thing, a country that shows no inclination to protect itself can hardly expect other countries to take the job on.

And a country that's unprotected is very likely to be influenced by the wishes of any big power that exerts a little pressure.

In short, it can lose its freedom little by little, without necessarily being overrun.

And of course it can very easily be overrun if it suits anybody's book to do so.

With the world as it is today we need to make the price of attacking us high enough to cause a potential aggressor to think more than twice.

And our participation in the NATO alliance helps us do this.

So if your reason for wanting to become an Officer is that you want to set about recovering the British Empire, forget it, and go into some other field of endeavour.

But if you can understand the real reasons it's necessary to maintain a professional and highly efficient army you may be one of the people we're looking for.

Will people look up to you in your uniform?

Can't you just imagine it? Smart as a whip in your brand new barathea, marching out there, watched by everybody to inspect your platoon.

If the idea doesn't give you just a little thrill maybe you're not cut out to be an Officer.

Mind you, some people can't see past the uniform. They think that getting togged up in the gear is the beginning and end of the whole business. Well, it is for the Household Cavalry while they're on duty at Horse Guards Parade, but it plays very little part in their life on the streets of Belfast or on patrol in Cyprus.

But even under active service conditions uniform is important. It is visible evidence that you are part of an organized body rather than an uncontrolled mob. And you can see at a glance who your friends are. Which can be very reassuring when things are coming at you from all sides.

However, wearing an Officer's uniform won't make you into an Officer.

The training at Sandhurst won't do it either.

All we can do is bring out and develop qualities that you already have within you.

You have to be brave, energetic, intelligent, enterprising, resourceful, physically competent and able to lead.

If you have these qualities people will respect you regardless of whether you're wearing an Officer's uniform or a pair of bathing trunks.

What's the next move?

Your next move depends on where you are at the moment.

If you're at school studying for your O-levels you don't need any distractions. But if you want to write and discuss your plans for the future we'd be pleased to hear from you.

Looking ahead you might like to consider applying for an Army Scholarship to help you get your A-levels. We grant 60 a year, each worth £260 towards tuition fees and £125 maintenance grant.

If you're hoping to get five O-levels including Maths, Physics and English Language, you can apply for Welbeck College, a boarding school run by the Army which takes boys between the ages of 15 years 9 months and 17 years 2 months. (Acceptance will be conditional on getting your five O-levels.)

If you've got your A-levels and have been accepted by a university you might be eligible for a University Cadetship. Under this scheme there are no fees and you will be paid £1,473 p.a. while you get your degree. When you graduate you do a course of up to 5 months at Sandhurst, after which you're made a Lieutenant with a salary of £2,750.

We send up to 130 serving Officers to read for degrees each year. Up to 90 read Engineering and Science at the Army University, Shrivenham, and the rest go to outside universities.

Of course, if you already have a degree or a professional qualification you can apply for an immediate commission. In which case your seniority would be backdated to bring you into line with those who joined the Army straight from school.

Lastly, if you have a couple of the appropriate A-levels you can apply for Sandhurst and get straight on learning to be an Officer.

If you think we could help you, drop a line to Major J. R. Drew, Army Officer Entry, Department 00, Lansdowne House, Berkeley Square, London, W1X 6AA. Tell him your age and your educational qualifications. Tell him what you'd like to do and ask his advice.

Any young man who has read this far deserves all the help we can give him.

1975.03
Agency: **Collett Dickenson Pearce**
Client: **Central Office of Information**

CDP seemed capable of striking the right note effortlessly, even when dealing with something as unsexy as army officer recruitment. The ad on the left explicitly states that it is intended to discourage people with the wrong motives, the gung-ho illustration ironically reinforcing the irrelevance of outdated preconceptions.

A bid to equate officer training with a university education takes the form of a letter signed by real captains of industry.

Meanwhile, the ad on the right with the copy line 'One day, my boy, all this could be yours' was initially rejected for fear of offending Princess Anne, who had just acquired an army husband in the shape of Captain Mark Phillips. Happily the ad, unlike the marriage, survived.

One day, my boy, all this could be yours.

Joining the Army doesn't mean disappearing into an anonymous khaki mass.

What you join is a regiment, which can be a relatively compact unit such as the one you see here.

This happens to be The Queen's Own Hussars.

At a glance, it looks like any other armoured regiment.

But to the men who belong to it no other regiment is remotely similar.

It is their family and their home.

If you join it as a young officer you will learn its history and legends. And you'll be introduced to its customs and foibles. Before you know it, you'll be living with both, in easy familiarity.

During your career you'll leave it to go on training courses. You could even serve with another army altogether, within Nato or in the Commonwealth.

But between times you'll return to the bosom of your regiment; to your friends and to the familiar customs and traditions.

The concept of the regiment has taken a knocking over the years. It has been the butt of a good deal of television wit. On top of which economic necessity has forced the amalgamation of many historic regiments and corps.

Perhaps surprisingly, a recent research programme carried out among young officers indicated that the feeling of belonging to a regiment was one of the things they valued most highly about being in the Army.

This was true of many Short Service Officers who having completed their three year engagement were about to pursue civilian careers.

As for officers who have decided to make the Army their career, getting command of their regiment was the goal of them all.

So what would be your chance of taking command of your regiment? Well, just about as good as your chances of getting the same amount of responsibility in civilian life.

By the time you're 37 or so, will you be capable of taking full responsibility for about 700 men and their families, plus equipment worth over £12,000,000?

Will you develop the extraordinary powers of leadership that are needed to attune your men to any set of circumstances from active duty in Belfast to patient vigilance in Cyprus?

If you've got the potential the Army will bring it out. You can be sure of that.

It is not easy finding enough men who are good enough.

We hope that you're one of them and that you'll give us the chance of putting you to the test.

Write to Major J. R. Drew, Army Officer Entry, Dept. A20, Lansdowne House, Berkeley Square, London, W1X 6AA. Tell him about your experience and educational attainments at school or university. He'll tell you about the next step.

"So far as we are concerned, three years as an Army Officer can equal three years at university."

Punch, October 20 1976

The attraction of some gold pens soon wears off.

A plated gold pen after one year.

Parker believe that if you buy a gold pen it shouldn't turn into a brass one.

Not a year later. Not 10 years later.

To ensure this never happens with a Parker pen we roll the gold on, in a layer thick enough not to wear off.

In fact, there is as much gold on the Parker Insignia at the bottom of the page, as there is on 10 of the plated pens at the top.

Admittedly, our pen does cost more. But nowhere near 10 times more.

The plated gold pen sells for £4.95*, the Parker Insignia for £8.90*.

If that is a little more than you intended to pay, ask yourself, in the end what kind of pen do you really want?

A brass one or a rolled gold one?

PARKER

A rolled gold Parker after 10 years.

THE PLATED GOLD PEN BELONGS TO MRS SULLIVAN OF BELVEDERE, KENT. THE ROLLED GOLD PARKER TO MR. COOKSEY OF STAFFORD, STAFFS. *RECOMMENDED RETAIL PRICES INCLUDING VAT.

Punch, June 9 1976

Hopefully a Parker Cirrus will last a lifetime. It takes long enough to make.

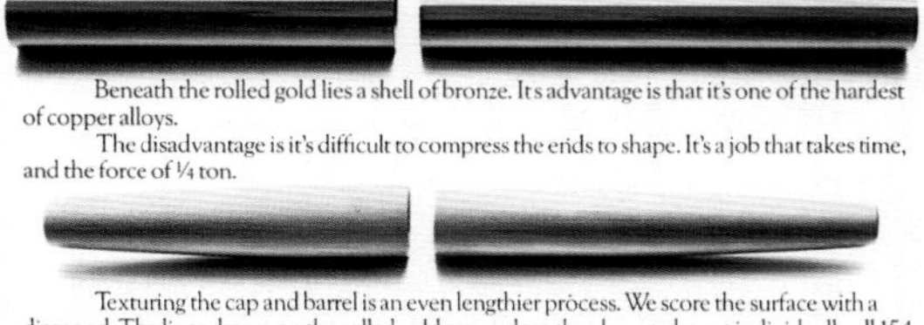

Beneath the rolled gold lies a shell of bronze. It's advantage is that it's one of the hardest of copper alloys.

The disadvantage is it's difficult to compress the ends to shape. It's a job that takes time, and the force of ¼ ton.

Texturing the cap and barrel is an even lengthier process. We score the surface with a diamond. The lines drawn on the rolled gold are so close they have to be cut individually, all 154 of them.

It may be slow, but it's the only method we know that gives such a silken lustre.

Next, we put a shine on the clip and end studs. Which isn't as easy as it sounds, working up a high finish like this takes all of 14 hours.

The barrel band and gold arrow inset get precisely the same treatment.

Once the arrow is inlaid and baked we show it the buff once more to bring up the highlights.

We take just as much trouble over the parts you don't see.

Above, is the ink-collector. Overall it measures no more than ¾" yet it is made of 26 fins, each a different thickness and each set a different distance apart.

Their job is to stop the pen blotting or drying by ensuring an even flow of ink, no matter whether you're writing in the arctic cold, tropical heat or the reduced pressure of an aircraft at 40,000 ft.

The nib is of 14 carat gold, and although it may be the smallest part, more time is spent on it than any other.

It takes no fewer than 15 operations to turn the blank, above, into one of the eight nib styles below.

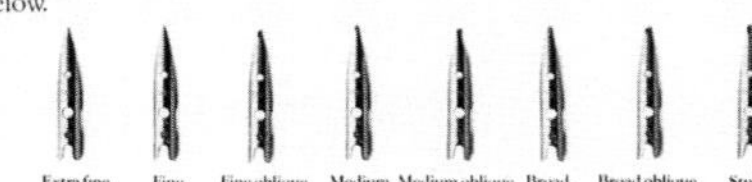

After being stamped, trimmed and worked into shape, the nib's tipped with ruthenium, an alloy four times harder than steel and ten times as smooth.

Then the most delicate task; splitting the nib to conduct the ink. It's cut by hand, with a blade no thicker than a human hair.

More polishing follows, 18 hours this time. Unfortunately, there are no short cuts when burnishing gold.

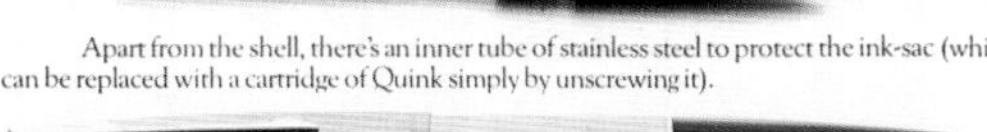

Apart from the shell, there's an inner tube of stainless steel to protect the ink-sac (which can be replaced with a cartridge of Quink simply by unscrewing it).

At long last, the finished pen. It has been filled, written with, cleaned and given a final inspection.

While we know that nothing in this world can ever be perfect, we feel the Parker Cirrus comes very, very close.

PARKER

THE PARKER CIRRUS COSTS £18. THERE IS ALSO A MATCHING CIRRUS BALL PEN AND PENCIL £9 EACH. RECOMMENDED RETAIL PRICES INCLUDING VAT.

1977.04
Agency: **Collett Dickenson Pearce**
Client: **The Parker Pen Company**
A formidable array of CDP talent came together for this series: Bob Isherwood, Tony Brignull, Neil Godfrey and Maggie Lewis.

1977.05
Agency: **Collett Dickenson Pearce**
Client: **The Parker Pen Company**
This ad was based on the idea of putting a disassembled pen on a layout pad and writing around it.

1977.06
Agency: **Collett Dickenson Pearce**
Client: **The Parker Pen Company**
This inspired idea combined the mild thrill of reading other people's correspondence with snippets where both content and handwriting technique are nicely varied.

1977.04
Agency: **Collett Dickenson Pearce**
Client: **The Parker Pen Company**
A CDP object lesson in investing a familiar object with added value contrived to make the rather ordinary Parker Cirrus sound like a highly complex – and therefore precious – piece of light engineering.

Who said no Englishman can write a love letter?

and what a coincidence! You are a cellist and me a pianist. What music we will make together, my little kitten, my love, my dear one! Do you know a Sonata by Galuppi that I transcribed?
Come to my room at Seven.

Extra fine.

The leaves are falling now in the park where we used to meet so often.
I loved you then, I love you now and I will love you always.
Will I see you again before winter sets in and the fountain freezes over? Come today, please come today at 3 o'clock. I'll be there, waiting for you my darling.

Broad oblique.

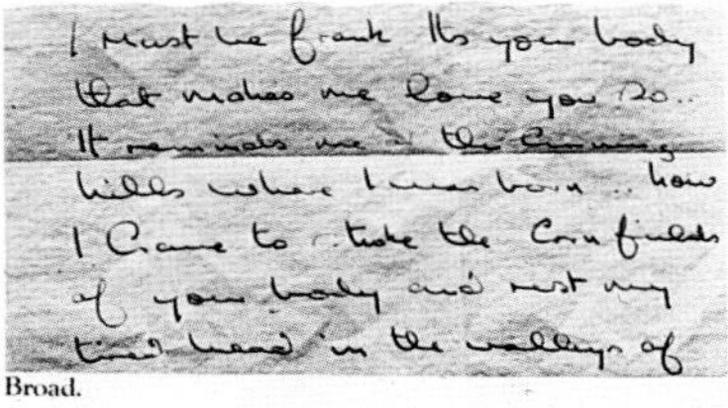

Broad.

and like the man in the short story I walked outside your window all last night hoping I might catch a glimpse of you at the window. Once I thought I heard your dog bark, but perhaps it was only my imagination. Oh, my dearest, when will that brute of a husband release you?

Fine oblique.

My dearest,
The climate is filthy, the food is filthy, the natives are filthy. I miss you very much. Are you pruning the roses as I asked?
Your own Freddie.

Medium oblique.

The enemy artillery is giving us a real towsing. As I crouch here on the trench I know it is not my life I fear to lose but you, my angel!
I can bear death but not separation

Fine.

In any case the doctors may yet be wrong. And if they're right, so what?
Their knives may cut off parts of my body but they can't cut off my love!
Chin up old girl.

Medium.

What! You let an Italian stroke your thighs in the cinema because you were sorry for him?
Am I made of wood? Don't you know you're driving me insane with jealousy?

Stub.

Each of the letters on these pages was written with a new Parker Pen, the Cirrus.

And each was written with a different nib so you can choose the one that best suits your man's style.

Always remembering that if it's the wrong one we'll change it free of charge, if you return it undamaged within a month.

But wait a minute.

Are we suggesting that a rolled gold pen will suddenly turn a man into a writer of passionate love letters?

Not at all. But look at it this way.

When you give him a pen that doesn't blot, scratch, dry-up or leak how can he resist the urge to write something with it?

Whether or not it's a love letter, madam, is frankly up to you.

But we think we can guarantee a thank-you letter.

PARKER

Even when we've sold a pen we still like to look after it.

Our pens have a reputation for being expensive.

They are.

Buy a Parker Cirrus and you'll have to part with £19.80.

In return you'll have a pen that has taken us 6 days to make. Much of it by hand.

We use 14 carat gold for the nib and brushed rolled gold for the casing.

We think the pen is beautiful, but more importantly we know it will last you a lifetime.

If the baby digs the lawn with it, stabs the furniture or tries it as a screwdriver, we will repair it.

Post the pen direct to us, at Newhaven Sussex, and within a few days it'll be returned as near new as we can possibly make it.

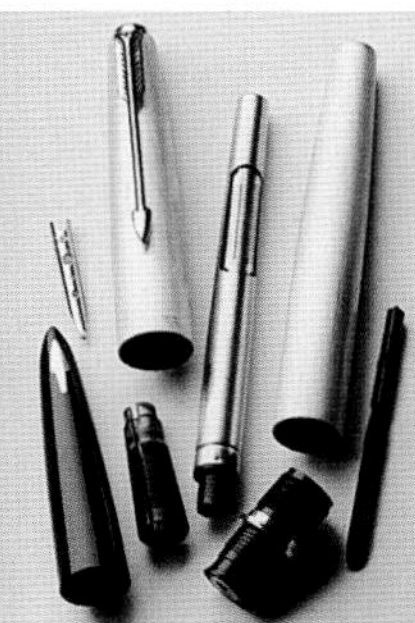

Before we service a pen we pull it to pieces.

Every nib goes under the microscope.

No pen leaves the factory before we've tested it.

We soak the nib in solvent. Twice.

Of the pens sent back to us, happily, few have suffered such fates.

The rest have stood the test of time, often 20, 30 and even 40 years of it. Yet they are in need of nothing more serious than a standard service and a shine.

First we clean the nibs. Then polish them like new pins.

We check the tips of the nibs under a microscope, even though they're unlikely to be damaged (for many years now, we've made them from plathenium, an alloy 4 times stronger than steel).

Any pieces inside the pen we can't clean like new, we drop in the bin and replace with parts fresh from the factory.

A spot of grease or perspiration will upset the ink flow therefore none of these new parts is ever touched by human hand.

Every morning our service ladies find new, white gloves waiting on their work-bench. Brand new gloves, not just clean.

If there are repairs to the pen, the cost will naturally depend on the extent of the damage. For a standard service and clean the cost is a token 65p. (Plus postage and packing).

We can honestly say it's the only cheap thing about any of our pens.

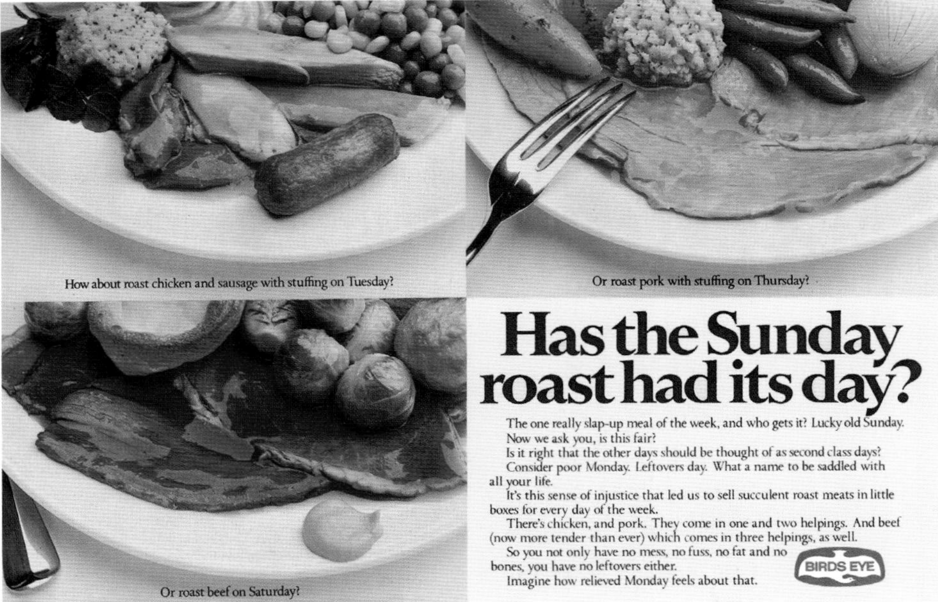

How about roast chicken and sausage with stuffing on Tuesday?
Or roast pork with stuffing on Thursday?
Or roast beef on Saturday?
Has the Sunday roast had its day?
The one really slap-up meal of the week, and who gets it? Lucky old Sunday.
Now we ask you, is this fair?
Is it right that the other days should be thought of as second class days?
Consider poor Monday. Leftovers day. What a name to be saddled with all your life.
It's this sense of injustice that led us to sell succulent roast meats in little boxes for every day of the week.
There's chicken, and pork. They come in one and two helpings. And beef (now more tender than ever) which comes in three helpings, as well.
So you not only have no mess, no fuss, no fat and no bones, you have no leftovers either.
Imagine how relieved Monday feels about that.
BIRDS EYE

We're the first to admit that nothing tastes as good as the pie you bake yourself.

For this reason we never bake Birds Eye Pies. You do.
And there's no point in hiding the fact that they take half an hour in the oven.
Equally we can hardly conceal that they have a competitor: pre-cooked pies.
They only need a few minutes under the grill.
However, they do have a rather serious drawback. The gravy soaks into the pastry and makes it soggy.
This, of course, can't happen with a Birds Eye pie because the pastry isn't cooked until you cook it.
So whether it's shortcrust or puff pastry (some of our pies come in one, some in the other) it's always crisp and light.
Every bit as good, in fact, as the home-baked pie.
Which it is.

Our thanks to Ben Godfrey age seven for the use of his favourite dishes.

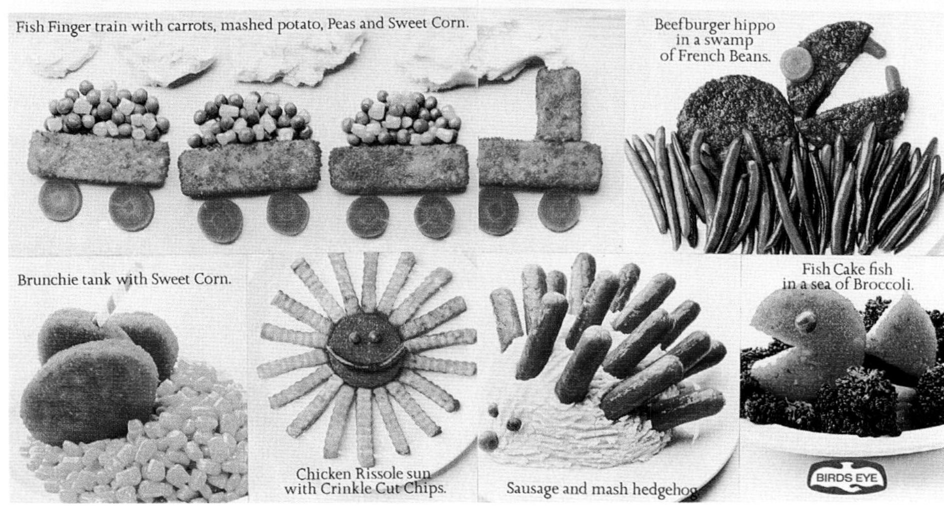

Fish Finger train with carrots, mashed potato, Peas and Sweet Corn.
Beefburger hippo in a swamp of French Beans.
Brunchie tank with Sweet Corn.
Fish Cake fish in a sea of Broccoli.
Chicken Rissole sun with Crinkle Cut Chips.
Sausage and mash hedgehog
BIRDS EYE

1974.02
Agency: **Collett Dickenson Pearce**
Client: **Birds Eye Foods**
These three inspired bids sought to give convenience food more appeal. The first questioned the die-hard British notion of a roast lunch being confined to Sundays. The second tried to woo the housewife who was conditioned to feel that serving ready-made meals was somehow dishonourable. And the third (citing art director Godfrey's son Ben) attempted to make those pallid slabs of meat and veg look like fun.

1972.03
Design group:
Michael Peters & Partners
Client: **Birds Eye Foods**
This award-winning Michael Peters packaging echoed the sixties Wolff Olins work for Bowyers, even using the same illustrator, Tony Meeuwissen.

1974.03
Agency: **Collett Dickenson Pearce**
Client: **G A Dunn**
Proving that ads are very much of their time, this CDP bid to show Dunn & Co as the outfitter who could help disguise a businessman's declining physique would simply not work now.

1976.02
Agency: **Collett Dickenson Pearce**
Client: **Whitbread**
In an early 'Heineken refreshes…' ad, *Star Trek's* Mr Spock is shown with wilting ears that are only restored to pointed perfection by a glass of Heineken. Tony Brignull and Terry Lovelock worked with art director Paul Smith on this one.

With such diversity at play, it is hardly surprising that the CDP house style, if there could be said to be such a thing, resided in the working environment and a certain authentic home-grown feeling that permeated all the work. Where DDB had put a quintessentially New York Jewish humour spin on UK advertising, CDP developed a drier British equivalent, in which the wit and the reference points were rooted in the home culture while the overriding objective remained the universal one of creating advertising that was innovative, relevant and memorable.

Tony Brignull's copywriting talent spanned everything from punchy copy for frozen food to a virtual mini-novel for Dunn & Company's tailoring services. It only worked because of Brignull's professional relationship with Neil Godfrey – and that only worked because CDP nurtured it. Among the duo's many successes were their contributions to the long-running 'Heineken refreshes the parts other beers cannot reach' campaign.

Success doesn't always go to your head.

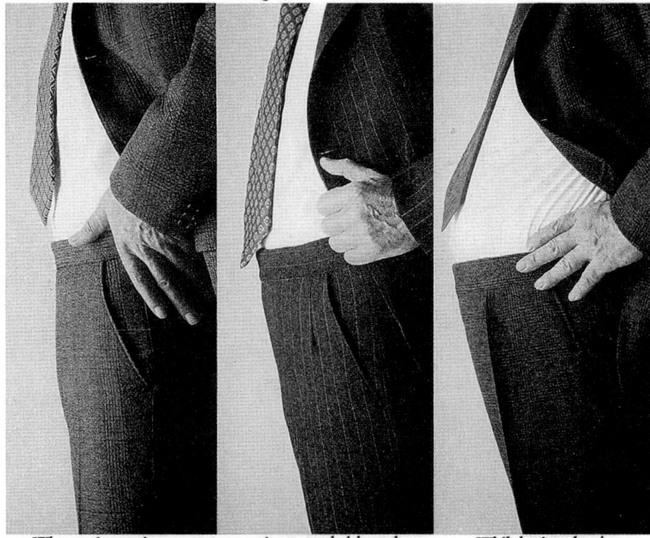

When you're starting out you can probably wear our suits with flat-fronted trousers.

As you get desk bound you might need a couple of darts at the waist.

While business lunches usually mean you need two pleats.

A gentleman's waistline is nobody's business but his own.

For this reason we thought long and seriously about publishing the above photographs.

Are they indiscreet? we asked ourselves. Are we in the slightest way opening our customers to such smirking remarks as:

"You don't need a couple of darts at the waist, old man, you need a grapefruit diet."

But consider our predicament.

There are still some men who just won't believe a ready-to-wear suit will ever fit them.

Even though we have related countless times that we have different fittings for slim, portly, short portly, stout and short stout men.

Not to mention how many times we've mentioned that we also cater for men with long arms or short arms, and men with long legs or short legs.

So we decided to release our waistband secrets and tell the world how we can soften the ravages of time and the business lunch.

Hoping that you will be persuaded to walk into Dunns and try on every suit in the shop.

Safe in the knowledge that even if you hate them all, it won't have cost you a penny.

Dunn & Co

Barclaycard and Access welcome. Or ask about our own fast and confidential credit scheme.

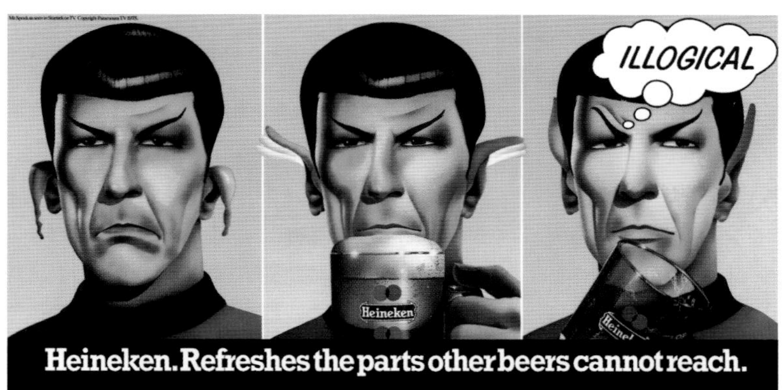

In fact, the idea was dreamed up by another CDP writer, Terry Lovelock, who found Heineken an intractable product to sell until he had one of those inexplicable nocturnal inspirations that, he maintains, caused him to awake from a dreamless sleep in a hotel in Marrakech and jot down the two phrases 'Heineken is now refreshing all parts' and 'Heineken refreshes the parts other beers cannot reach'. Next morning he wrote two scripts: one featured a bored group of people sitting around a pool who were only enlivened when the waiter removed their drinks-with-umbrellas and replaced them with Heineken; the other featured a Charleston competition 'where the knees weren't working due to lack of refreshment'. Alan Parker was slated to direct but his first feature, *Bugsy Malone*, diverted him and so Lovelock and Vernon Howe directed and wrote.

Soon it proved that Lovelock's little conceit offered an inexhaustible number of possibilities for a campaign. Later, many were shot by The Alan Parker Film Company, including one with policemen on the beat whose aching feet and toes needed to be refreshed. The voiceover was by Victor Borge, who also did the same honours for the piano tuner whose ears needed reviving, Frankenstein's monster who needed something more than a charge of electricity to come to life and another *Star Trek* spoof in which bad wigs and rubber monsters posed less serious threat than 'impaired beamability', which of course could be rectified only by imbibing the product. It was a classic advertising idea still being used in the twenty-first century.

Many now famous names would pass through CDP's creative environment, including David Puttnam, Gray Jolliffe, Derrick Hass, Graham Fink, Frank Lowe, David Horry and Bob Isherwood. It did not happen by accident as CDP's rise involved aggressively attracting talent from other agencies. Bob Isherwood recalls: 'I remember when I was at Collett's in the seventies, one of the reasons it was such a great agency was because they had the best people. The policy was, if anybody was great you just got 'em. Put those people together and the creativity is unstoppable.' Soon CDP would find that poaching talent worked both ways and there were many people who came and went with equal rapidity.

1976.03
Agency: **Collett Dickenson Pearce**
Client: **Whitbread**
These two TV commercials took the 'Heineken Refreshes' concept into the professions of piano tuning and law enforcement. Alan Parker's film company was responsible for both.

1976.04
Agency: **Collett Dickenson Pearce**
Client: **The Parker Pen Company**
Paul Weiland and David Brown wrote this witty miniature in which Penelope Keith exhorts the girls at a finishing school to spend 'daddy's lovely money' by signing cheques with Parker Pens, not ballpoints. Alan Parker directed.

this page

1974.04
Agency: **Collett Dickenson Pearce**
Client: **John Harvey & Son**
Another Alan Parker commercial. Here, shipwreck survivors brought a full set of patrician values to marine disaster, passing round the Cockburn's Special Reserve and wondering if anyone thought to bring the *petit fours*.

1972.04
Agency: **Collett Dickenson Pearce**
Client: **Birds Eye Foods**
Alan Parker once more, this time harnessing his feature film success *Bugsy Malone* to help sell the client's beefburgers.

1976.05
Agency: **Collett Dickenson Pearce**
Client: **Birds Eye Foods**
Created by Tony Brignull and Neil Godfrey, this commercial used Scottish comedian Stanley Baxter as a teacher instructing his class how to order Birds Eye dishes in the local dialect.

Alan Parker wrote copy there, as well as trying his hand at some in-house directing in the agency's basement, where he dragooned many of the staff as ad hoc actors. Parker was consultant director on CDP's 1970 Silver Award-winning TV campaign for the Post Office ('Please, Get a TV Licence'). Soon, at the behest of Pearce, Dickenson and Millward, he would leave to form his own commercials film company (his former employers underwrote the bank loan and promised to give him 'a lot of work') and in 1972 he would win D&AD Silvers with commercials for Birds Eye Beefburgers (with CDP) and Heinz Spaghetti (with Dorlands). These were examples of the new, more 'realistic' style of TV commercials; engaging mini-dramas that brought a touch of wit and credibility to even the most contrived scenarios. Here was a touch of cinema style combined with something of the feel of *Coronation Street*, a well-written soap opera that was already enjoying its own golden age. It is perhaps no coincidence that some of the actors featured in Parker's commercials would go on to have soap opera careers later.

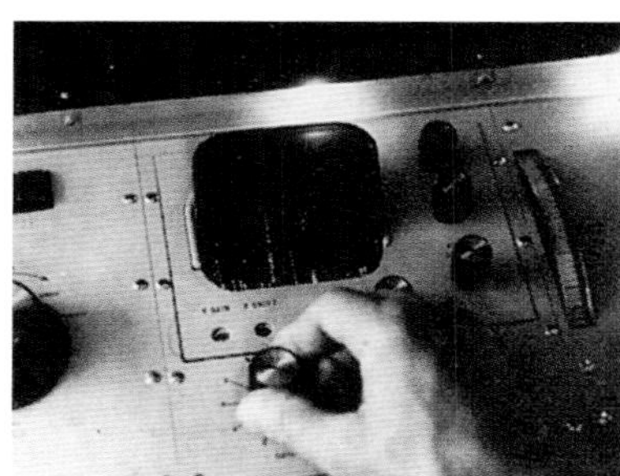

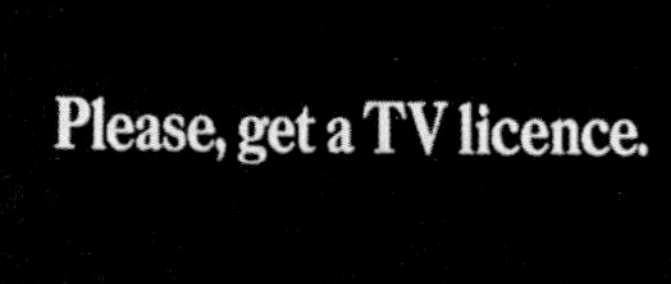

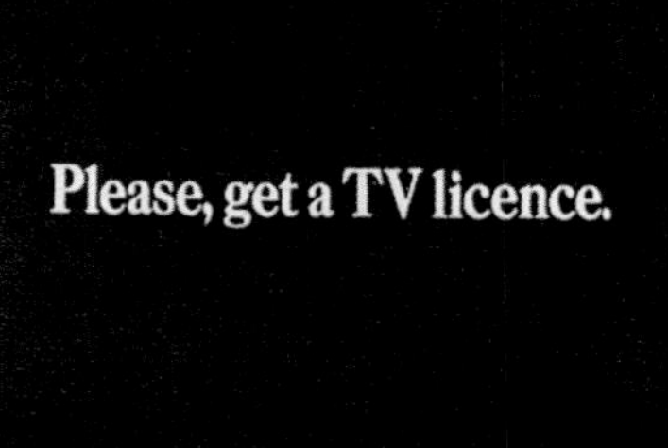

1970.05
Agency: **Collett Dickenson Pearce**
Client: **General Post Office**
Alan Parker's first D&AD win showed TV licence evaders being brought to book in an Orwellian miniature drama. In 1970 the General Post Office was still the custodian of broadcast and telecommunications activities, as well as mail. Margaret Thatcher would eventually break it up.

opposite

1972.05
Agency: **Dorland Advertising**
Client: **H J Heinz**
One of four Gold-winning commercials from Alan Parker for Heinz. This one had a returning cub scout tucking into a plate of Heinz tinned spaghetti that gives his father a Proustian flashback to his own days under canvas.

1978.01
Agency: **Collett Dickenson Pearce**
Client: **Olympus Optical Company**
'Who do you think you are – David Bailey?' was the catchphrase and the running gag was that the amateurs were burdened with cumbersome gear while the professional who they failed to recognize (Bailey) used only the Olympus Trip. Here Bryan Pringle is the amateur. Later, more memorably, George Cole would take over the role.

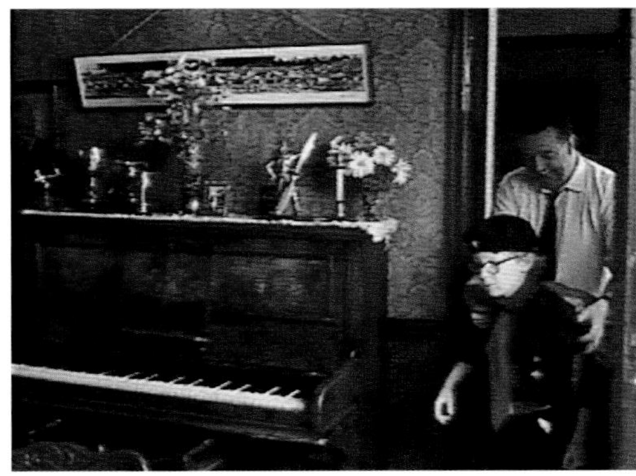

HEINZ
Spaghetti
with
tomato & cheese
sauce
Is someone you love
a Heinz Spaghetti lover?

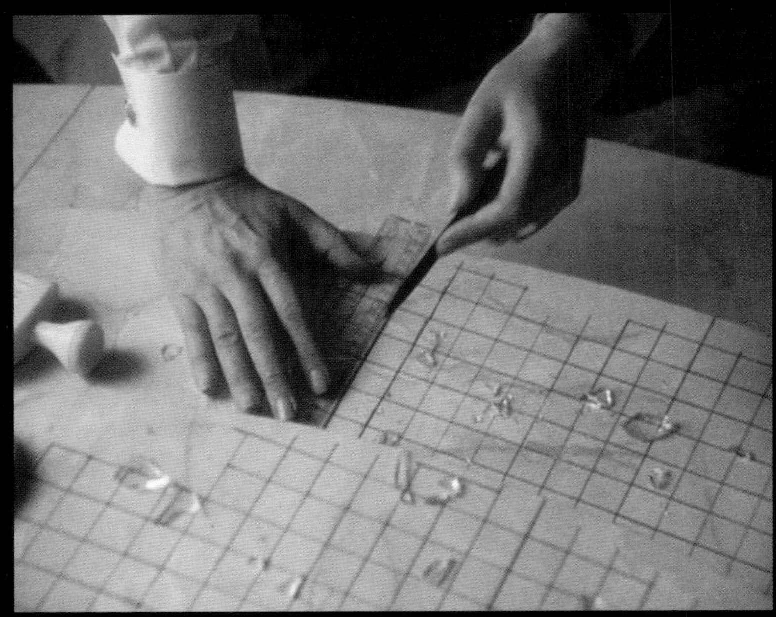

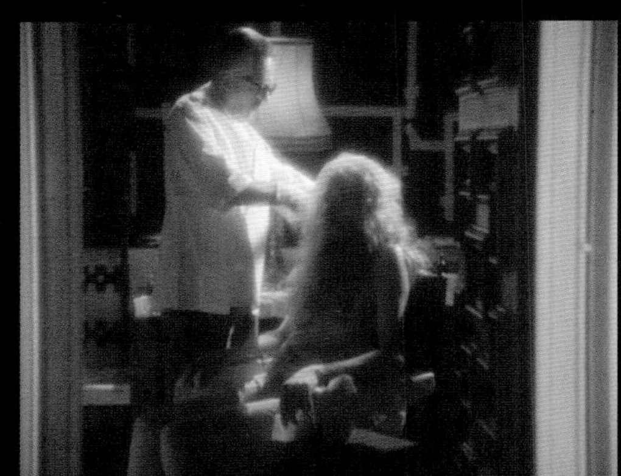

1977.07
Agency: **Collett Dickenson Pearce**
Client: **Daily Express**
These stills are from Alan Parker's documentary-style commercials for serializations of blockbuster books in the *Daily Express*. The paper was at the time adopting a tabloid format and seeking a new and bigger readership.

this page

1972.06
Agency: **Collett Dickenson Pearce**
Client: **Gallaher**
A little Ridley Scott-directed drama about smuggling something more valuable than gold – the client's small cigars.

1975.04
Agency: **Collett Dickenson Pearce**
Client: **Hovis**
Once, the youthful Ridley Scott had made a black and white short film called *Boy & Bicycle*, featuring his brother Tony exploring a rather less idealized northern town than this one in a television ad for Hovis bread.

If there was usually a touch of humour in Parker's work, then Ridley Scott – another CDP collaborator who would later launch a movie career – generally seemed more interested in evocative production values than wit. His 1975 Silver Award-winning Hovis campaign is a legendary piece of fake nostalgia, evoking a fictional sun-dappled Northern England village in which Hovis is fulsomely depicted as a civic mainstay of health and wholesomeness.

Future features director Hugh Hudson (*Greystoke*, *Chariots of Fire* and *Revolution*) was also championed by CDP's Frank Lowe in the early seventies. From the bizarre Benson & Hedges commercials (a swimming pool, iguanas, and a helicopter airlifting a giant cigarette pack across the desert) and the Rossini-scored Fiat 'Strada' ads ('hand-built by robots') to the celebrated Leonard Rossiter/Joan Collins Cinzano mini-sitcoms, Hudson provided the moving images for the bright ideas of CDP's Mike Cozens and Alan Waldie, Paul Weiland and David Horry, Tony Brignull and Neil Godfrey amongst others.

The Benson & Hedges commercials are most usually described as surreal, although they were not so in any strict sense. Surrealism, evolving in the twenties as an artistic movement, had a political agenda and sought to challenge the contemporary way of looking at things through visual dislocations and impossible juxtapositions. But when, in the mid-seventies, CDP produced a poster showing a trio of wall-mounted cigarette packs whose reflected image was a flock of ducks, what we are witnessing is a clever party trick involving little more than the techniques of Surrealism.

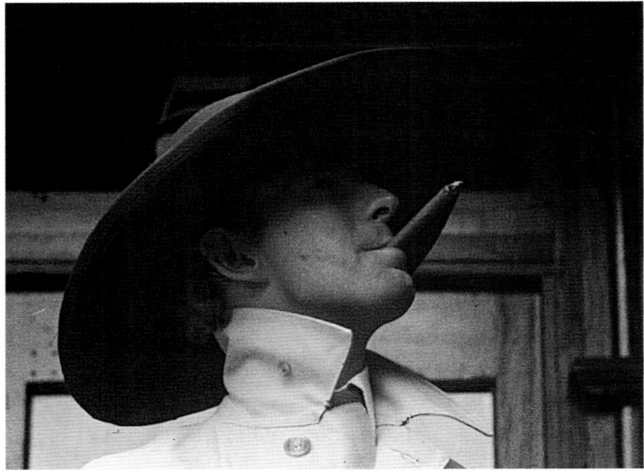

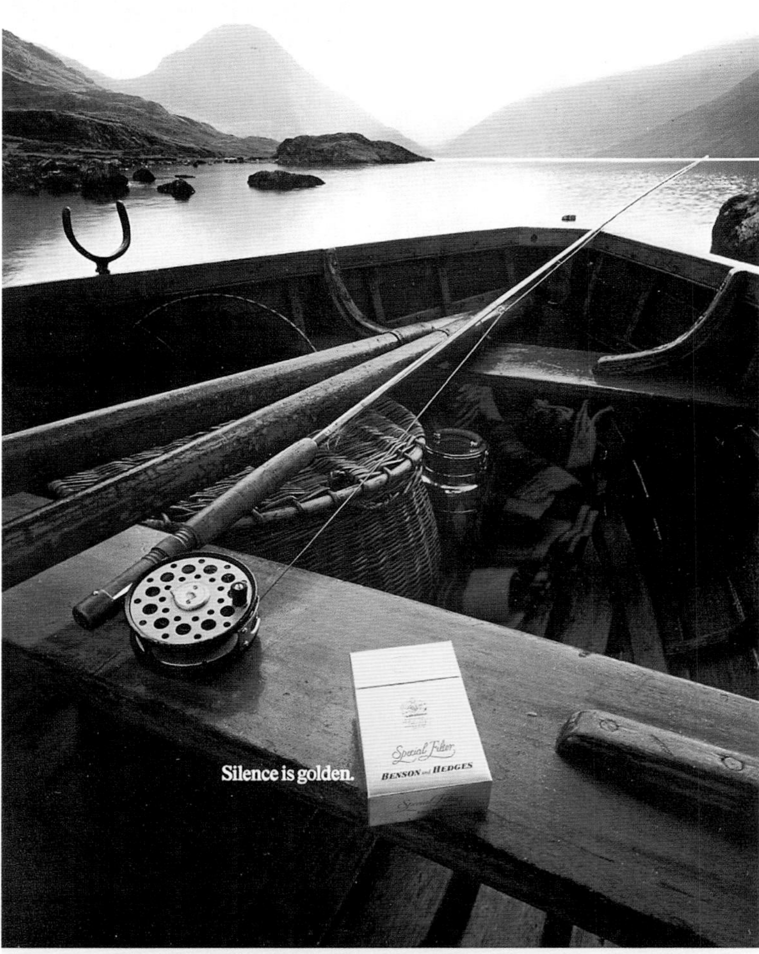

Silence is golden.
Special Filter
BENSON and HEDGES
MIDDLE TAR As defined by H M Government
EVERY PACKET CARRIES A GOVERNMENT HEALTH WARNING

1974.05
Agency: **Collett Dickenson Pearce**
Client: **Gallaher**
Alan Parker directed this story of a man going to be fitted for a hat in a campaign for Benson & Hedges. The wide-brimmed model is intended to allow its wearer to smoke a cigar in the rain.

1975.05
Agency: **Collett Dickenson Pearce**
Client: **Gallaher**
Bob Brooks directed this pastiche of a Graham Greene-style meeting between two spies in Istanbul for Benson & Hedges cigarettes. The presence of George Cole signalled a comic misunderstanding involving the product as part of the recognition protocol.

1973.01
Agency: **Collett Dickenson Pearce**
Client: **Gallaher**
A 'lifestyle' Benson & Hedges ad from the time before advertising's version of Surrealism took over.

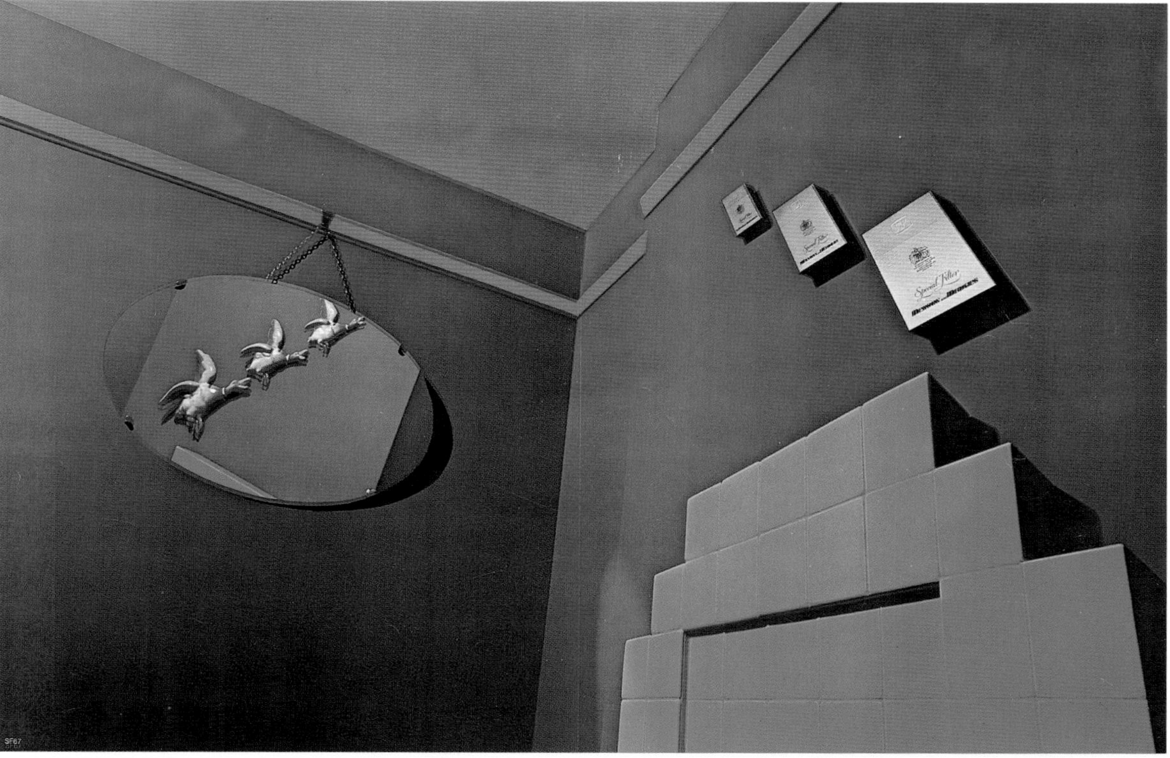

MIDDLE TAR As defined by H.M. Government H.M. Government Health Departments' WARNING: CIGARETTES CAN SERIOUSLY DAMAGE YOUR HEALTH

1978.02
Agency: **Collett Dickenson Pearce**
Client: **Gallaher**
These pre-computer visions of a world built on twisted logic were achieved by photographing specially constructed sets. The mirrored ducks, for example, were part of a second set built behind a hole in the wall.

MIDDLE TAR As defined by H.M. Government
H.M. Government Health Departments' WARNING: CIGARETTES CAN SERIOUSLY DAMAGE YOUR HEALTH

1979.01
Agency: **Collett Dickenson Pearce**
Client: **Gallaher**
This Benson & Hedges poster turned the 'surreal' theme into a 'spot the product' game. Among those who failed to do so was the Egyptian Tourist Office, which requested copies, not realizing it was anything more than a bona fide landscape.

1979.02
Agency: **Collett Dickenson Pearce**
Client: **Gallaher**
Director Hugh Hudson shot 'Swimming Pool' (a Benson & Hedges advert) for the Alan Parker Film Company and it was reputedly the UK's most expensive ever commercial at the time.

opposite

1978.03
Agency: **Collett Dickenson Pearce**
Client: **Fiat Motor Company**
There was no car in this classic CDP poster, and even the unmistakeable figure of speech is rendered without the use of words. A new model, an image and the manufacturer's name did the entire job.

1978.04
Agency: **Collett Dickenson Pearce**
Client: **Fiat Motor Company**
This poster bounced off the traditional threat posed by the Italians in the FIFA World Cup. In the event, Argentina won the 1978 competition on its home turf.

The new Fiat 132.

FIAT

Let's hope the Italian footballers aren't in such good shape.

FIAT

LOZENGES

1979.03
Agency: **Boase Massimi Pollitt Univas**
Client: **Barker & Dobson**
Dave Trott and Derrick Hass' notion that Victory-V pastilles might blow your head off remains an entirely logical one, if a little exaggerated.

this page

1972.07
Agency: **Young & Rubicam**
Client: **International Distillers & Vintners**
Hans Feurer took the picture, John Bacon wrote the copy and the rest, as they say, is history.

Similarly, when Boase Massimi Pollitt Univas' (BMP) Derrick Hass and Dave Trott produced their memorable headless man poster for Victory-V, they simply took the idea of an overpowering taste blowing your head off and then used Magritte's iconic man in a suit to make the image more arresting. In fact, Magritte's services to advertising are considerable, particularly in the many variants of the image of the suited man in bowler hat and collar and tie. In the end, despite the seventies vogue for imaginative tricks of scale and visual non-sequiturs, very few 'surreal' ads matched up to what many would have claimed was their initial inspiration. When DDB's US ad for Volkswagen used a piece of steak shaped like the profile of a Volkswagen, the copy carried through the visual pun ('Can you still get prime quality for $1.26 a pound?'). In contrast, the CDP-led seventies brand of'surrealism' is best seen as part of a broader strand of exotic, attention-grabbing imagery that only adds to the historical perception that this was a decade that was 'all over the place' – a mix of styles and influences without any obvious unifying strand.

There was certainly a clear contrast between the developing 'naturalistic' style typified by many commercials and a more bizarre style of presentation that can be traced back to the first magazine ads for a famous brand of vodka. Young & Rubicam's (Y&R) bid to make Smirnoff seem mysteriously glamorous began with an ad showing a stylish metropolitan fellow in a Panama hat declaring that accountancy had been his life until he discovered Smirnoff. His well-groomed appearance discouraged any misreading that a promising professional career had been blighted by alcoholism, and instead set the tone for a long-running and stylish campaign that rather outrageously identified Smirnoff as a catalyst of desirable lifestyle change.

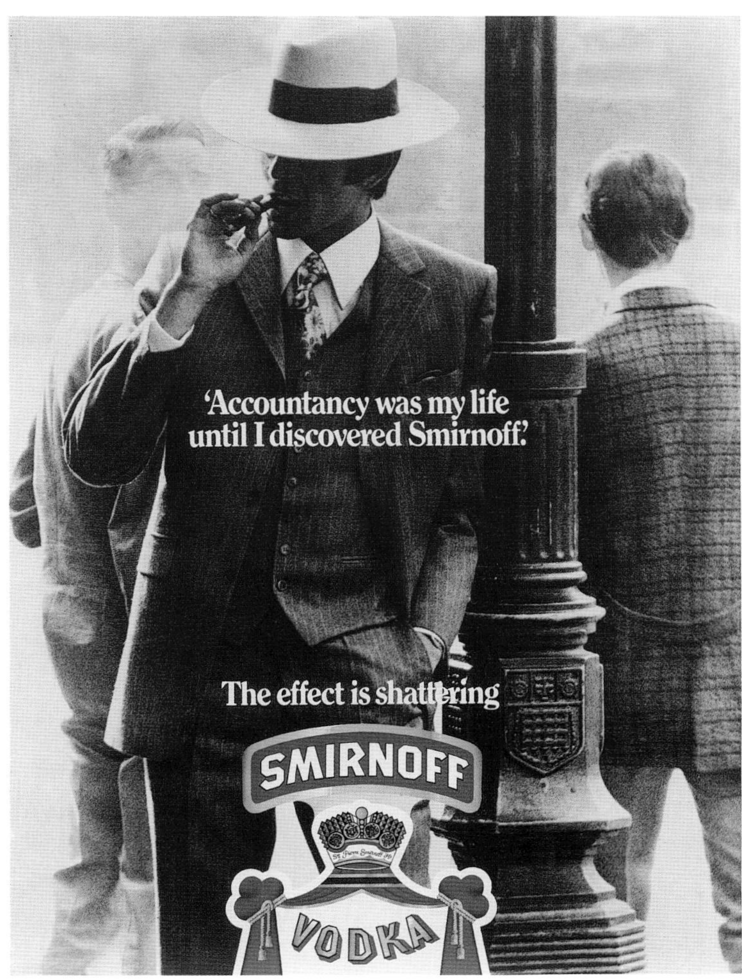

Advertising alcoholic drinks in the seventies explored various strategies, of which the promise of a better lifestyle was just one. Under Bensons, Guinness had moved away from the simple animation of its posters and postcards and instead started to celebrate the idea of 'the reparative drinker' – a decent bloke and family man whose reward was a quiet drink, alone or with his friends at the end of the day. When J Walter Thompson (JWT) took over the account, it developed this idea within a broader campaign to show the many different facets of Guinness, often using the camera to point up the photogenic qualities of the stout with the dark-coloured body and light-coloured head.

Dorland Advertising, meanwhile, literally pushed out the boat to underscore Dubonnet's lifestyle appeal in 1973. If you said 'Dubonnet s'il vous plaît' you could, the commercial suggested, get considerably more than an aromatic bottle of booze – you could acquire an entry to a more attractive world than the one you currently inhabited, with beautiful friends, *al fresco* meals and lazy afternoons spent punting on the river.

By 1979, French Cruttenden Osborn rose above all that with a famous campaign for White Horse Whisky that placed a strikingly real white horse in a series of punning scenarios, of which the best known was 'Scotch and American' where a stars-and-stripes-wearing black basketball player stood next to the horse, matching it in height.

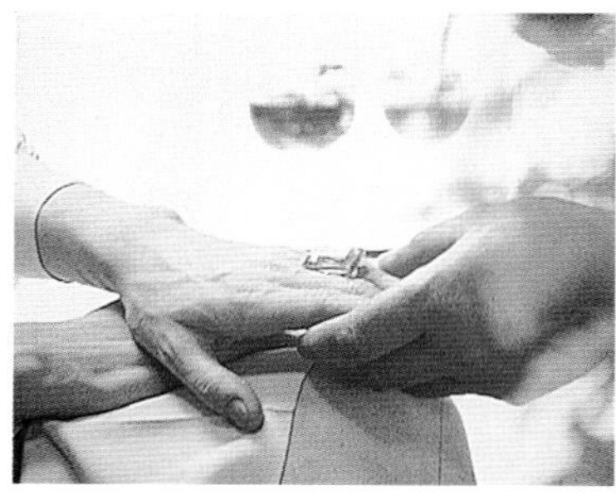

1973.02
Agency: **J Walter Thompson**
Client: **FS Matta**
This television ad for Campari was titled 'Film Director' and was directed by Karel Reisz, film director of *Saturday Night and Sunday Morning* in 1960 and *The French Lieutenant's Woman* in 1981.

1973.03
Agency: **Dorland Advertising**
Client: **Cadbury Schweppes**
Soft-focus lifestyle promises like these for Dubonnet worked at first but were easily lampooned. Eventually, aspirational leisure-time drinking behaviour had to be shown to be rooted in reality not Post-Impressionism.

this page

1970.06
Agency: **J Walter Thompson**
Client: **Guinness**
Terence Donovan directed 'The Ages of Man' which showed the progression from baby bottle to Guinness bottle.

1972.08
Agency: **J Walter Thompson**
Client: **Guinness**
In 'First Taste' a man who thinks he doesn't like Guinness was tricked into trying it by a friend, 'Guinness, but I don't like Guinness'.

1972.09
Agency: **J Walter Thompson**
Client: **Guinness**
In this television commercial, the discovery of the British pub phrase 'the usual' brought eventual liquid relief to thirsty French men who had problems pronouncing 'Guinness'.

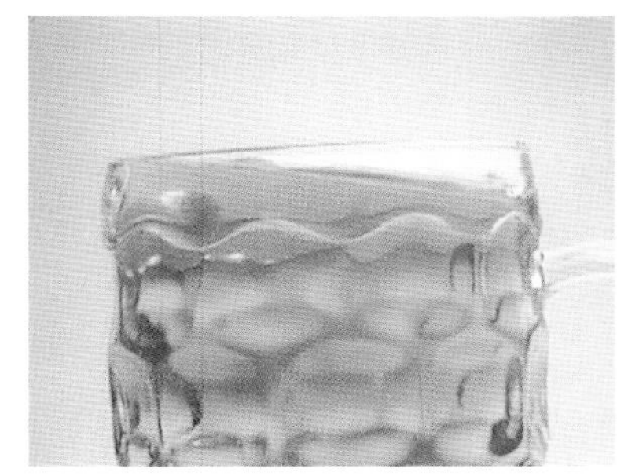

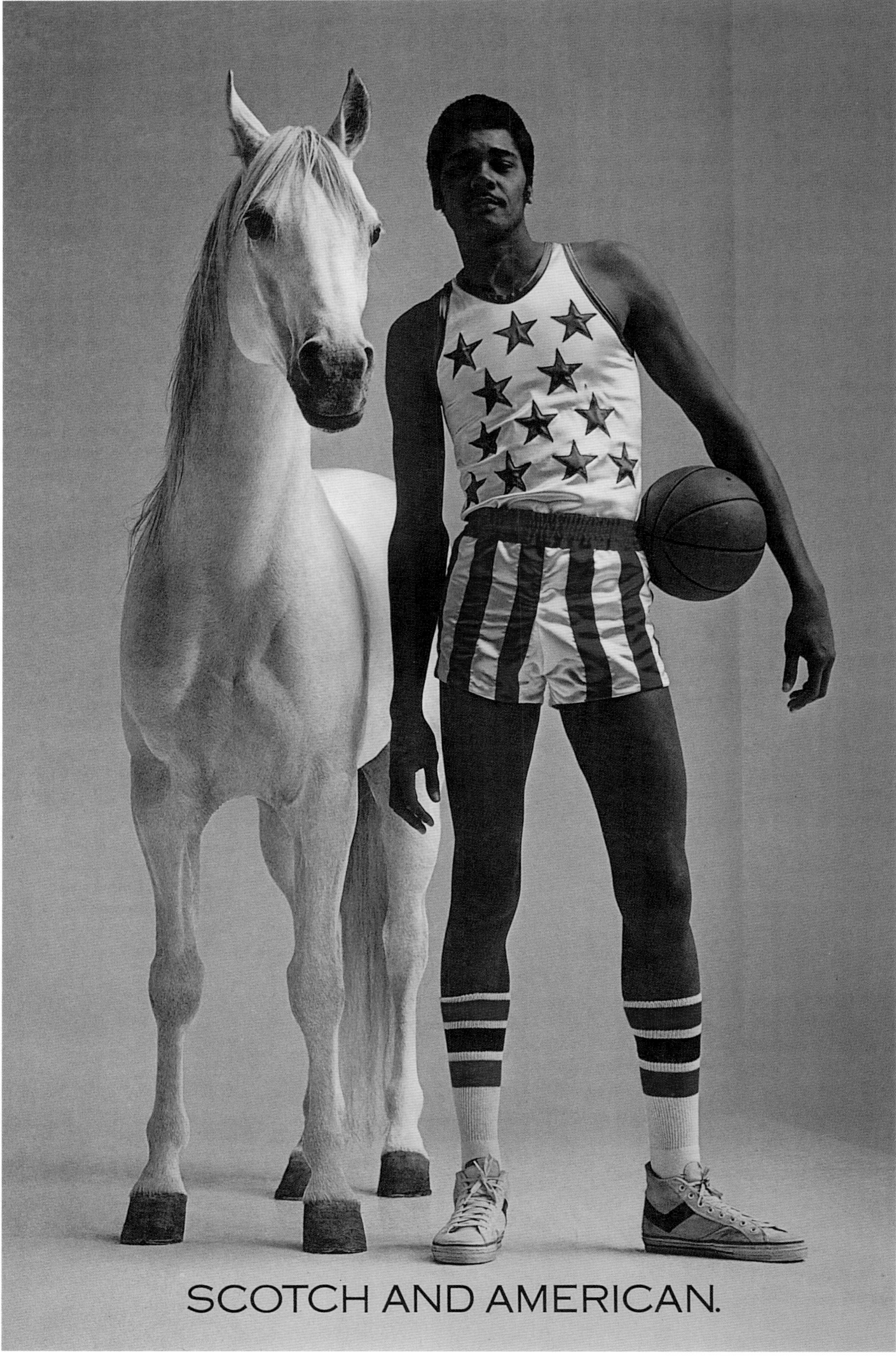

1979.04
Agency: **French Cruttenden Osborn**
Client: **White Horse Distillers**
FCO was a small agency just around the corner from DDB's London office in Baker Street. From there came a number of smart campaigns in the seventies, but none more famous than this series of posters for White Horse whisky. Lester Bookbinder took the shots, Graeme Norways was the art director and Nick Hazzard the copywriter.

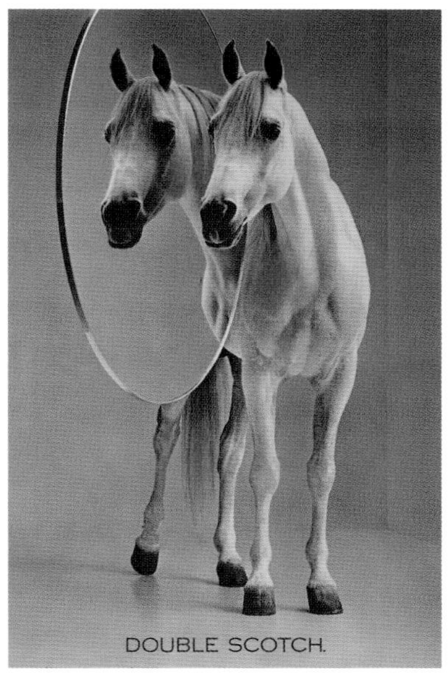
DOUBLE SCOTCH.

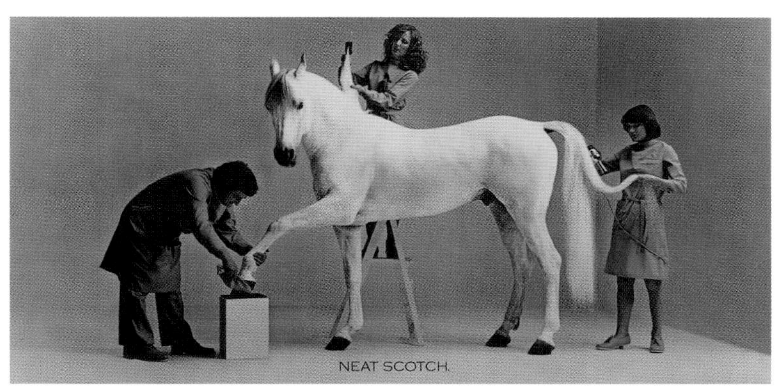
NEAT SCOTCH.

SCOTCH ON THE ROCKS.

SCOTCH AND GINGER.

In a more hedonistic spirit, and just to show that the radical feminists of the sixties still had a long row to harrow, the Pirelli tyre company recruited The Derek Forsyth Partnership, aided and abetted by photographers like Donald Silverstein and Sarah Moon, to help exploit the perennial male fantasy associations involving women's bodies and motor cars. The Pirelli Calendar became an institution that would seek to find ever more unpredictable ways to explore this fantasy. Here was graphic evidence that the perception of the decade as the definitive modern age of sexual libertarianism is misplaced. Sexual rebellion in the sixties was usually a series of isolated gestures staged against a still-powerful establishment (for example the troubled publication of *Lady Chatterley's Lover*, the Profumo scandal, The Rolling Stones' ever-newsworthy country

● 1972.10
Art director: **David Hillman**
Client: **Nova**
Born Marielle Hadengue in England in 1940, photographer Sarah Moon reinvented herself as the chronicler of a fey province upon which the real world rarely intruded. This fashion spread for *Nova* (January 1971 issue) is unusual in that most of her images are sharp.

opposite

● 1972.11
Design group:
The Derek Forsyth Partnership
Client: **Pirelli**
Classic Sarah Moon images for an early Pirelli calendar, soft-focus lace and frills with just a twist of the Pre-Raphaelite. Pirelli and Forsyth would soon be looking for raunchier photographers.

house orgies) but Derek Forsyth's Pirelli images for the award-winning calendar of 1973, created with artist Allen Jones, included images that ranged from the fetishistic to the almost gynaecological, reinforcing the truth that it was actually in the seventies when daring sexual material reached the mainstream. Despite all of which, Pirelli sold no more tyres because of its increasingly hardcore calendar. In fact, in 1974 the company decided to discontinue it after receiving marketing advice that the Pirelli name was now synonymous with the wrong product: it was advised to sell the calendars and give away their tyres. But the floodgates were open and by the seventies even *Nova* magazine was calling in glamour photographer Helmut Newton to provide editorial pictures for a less than academic article about women's underwear.

1973.04
Design group:
The Derek Forsyth Partnership
Client: **Pirelli**
Allen Jones was a godsend to the Pirelli calendar. The pop artist who had made a table out of a life-size female figure on all fours was not going to err on the side of good taste when it came to illustrating a soft-porn calendar.

FEBRUARY PIRELLI
Thursday Friday Saturday Sunday Monday Tuesday Wednesday Thursday Friday Saturday Sunday Monday Tuesday Wednesday Thursday Friday
1 2 3 4 5 6 7 8 9 10 11 12 13 14 15 16
Saturday Sunday Monday Tuesday Wednesday Thursday Friday Saturday Sunday Monday Tuesday Wednesday
17 18 19 20 21 22 23 24 25 26 27 28

Packaging design revealed few clear trends and D&AD rewarded relatively few practitioners. Minale Tattersfield Provinciali began the decade with a Silver Award for its Harrods range of oils and canned goods. Combining a clean graphic treatment with the famous Harrods script, the designs seemed to take Robert Brownjohn's sixties canned food packaging approach for Pickerings one stage further, projecting value rather than just labelling. Six years later the consultancy won another Silver for the same client, this time with smoked salmon packs, part of the meat department range, which was based on the blue and white stripes of a butcher's apron.

1976.06
Design group:
Minale Tattersfield Provinciali
Client: **Harrods**
Packaging in blue and white for Harrods meat department; other products in the range included ox tongue and stewed steak in gravy.

1970.07
Design group:
Minale Tattersfield Provinciali
Client: **Harrods**
The elegant images on the canned fruit and the wine bottle-shaped packaging of the cooking oils demonstrated that Minale Tattersfield Provinciali had a firm understanding of how to add the perception of value to routine provisions.

opposite

1977.08
Design group:
Michael Peters & Partners
Client: **Penhaligon's**
This range of packaging for old-established English perfumers, Penhaligon's, perfectly interpreted a sense of tradition for a contemporary marketplace. Madeleine Bennett and Howard Milton worked on type and images.

1973.05
Design group:
Michael Peters & Partners
Client: **Winsor and Newton**
An imaginative range of packaging for Winsor & Newton ink came from Michael Peters with the help of a range of top illustrators.

1977.09
Design group:
Michael Peters & Partners
Client: **Winsor and Newton**
The 1976 launch of Winsor & Newton's Alkyd oil paint came in response to artists' demands for a pigment that did not dry as fast as acrylics. The paint came in tubes decorated with details from famous paintings that used a relevant palette.

Michael Peters was a creative force who had worked for CDP in the late sixties while developing his own style and business, Michael Peters & Partners. In 1973 he won a Silver for the Most Outstanding Design Programme with packaging for Winsor & Newton Ink. (In 1977 Peters would win again for the same client's tubes of artists' paint.) Using a range of illustrators and artists to show what could be done with the product, Peters created a charmingly eccentric range of images to adorn the boxes, many of them featuring animals and birds. But if Peters' programme contained echoes of Michael Wolffs's fondness for co-opting members of the animal kingdom to make people feel good about products, this campaign was still rather far removed from yet another famous bid to let the fauna do the talking; John Webster, doyen of British advertising, was responsible for both the Cresta Bear and Honey Monster.

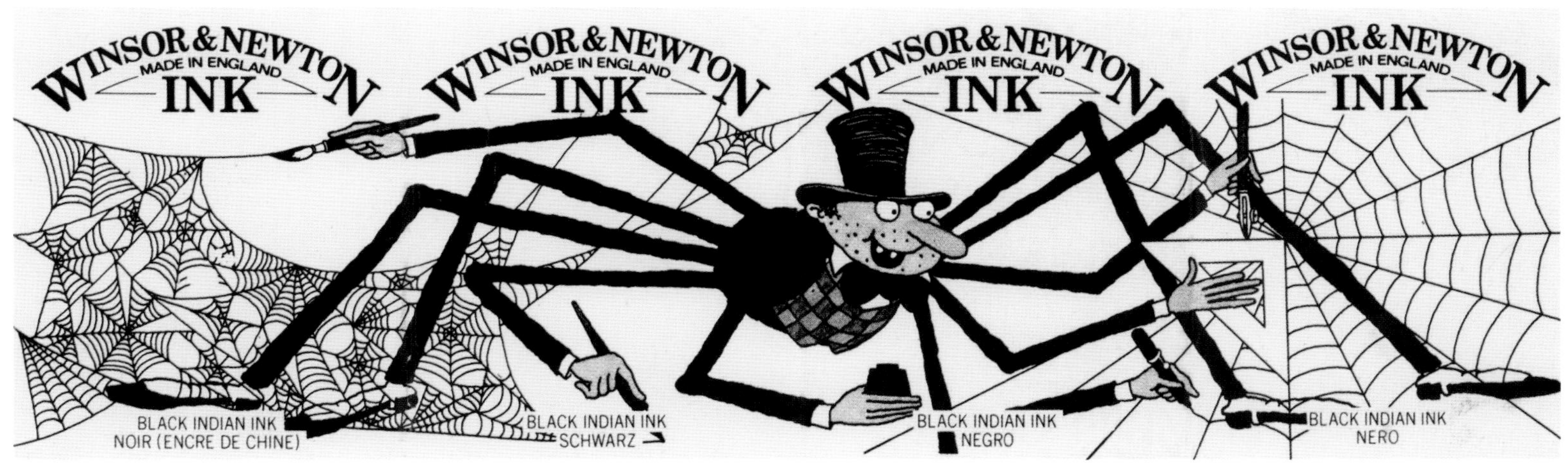

Working for BMP, Webster called in animator Richard Williams (who would eventually strike it big with his animation work on *Who Framed Roger Rabbit?*) to create a hip, shades-wearing polar bear that would catch the public's imagination. The clean line drawing of the white bear who liked Schweppes' Cresta soft drink and talked like a refugee from Haight Ashbury combined graphic minimalism with the dry humour that was to be the trademark of Webster's long career. Webster was always a great fan of creating original characters, animal or otherwise. 'CDP might use Leonard Rossiter and Joan Collins', he says, 'but if you create your own characters as we did, people associate them with the product … they don't say it's a Leonard Rossiter ad for … what is it?'.

Webster and BMP had really arrived with the Cadbury's Smash Martians in 1972. The comic commercial called 'Serious Rival' (where the tiresome business of mashing up a real potato was presented as a no-hope challenge to Cadbury's instant product) was allegedly held up as an example of great advertising at CDP's regular Monday review of new advertising. Webster and BMP went on to create a long-running series of Martians commercials for Cadbury's Smash, which Webster uncharitably recalls as 'a lousy product. There was another one called Yeoman that was much better, but Cadbury's outsold it. It must have been the advertising.'

1974.06
Agency: **Boase Massimi Pollitt**
Client: **Ferrero**
Animator Richard Williams collaborated with John Webster on this stylized little drama about the novelty mints, Tic Tacs.

1973.06
Agency: **Boase Massimi Pollitt**
Client: **Schweppes**
Richard Williams again, this time working with animals. Legend has it that when the Cresta Bear shuddered, the mannerism was based on Jack Nicholson's response to drinking whisky in *Easy Rider*.

this page

1977.10
Agency: **Boase Massimi Pollitt**
Client: **Quaker Oats**
Another Webster creation, the long-running Honey Monster campaign for Sugar Puffs proved a staggering success.

1974.07
Agency: **Boase Massimi Pollitt**
Client: **Cadbury Typhoo Foods**
One of the greatest and most fondly remembered campaigns ever. The Smash Martians' infectiously derisive response to the Earthling method of creating mashed potato was utterly irresistible, although their trademark tinny laughter was apparently an afterthought in the studio.

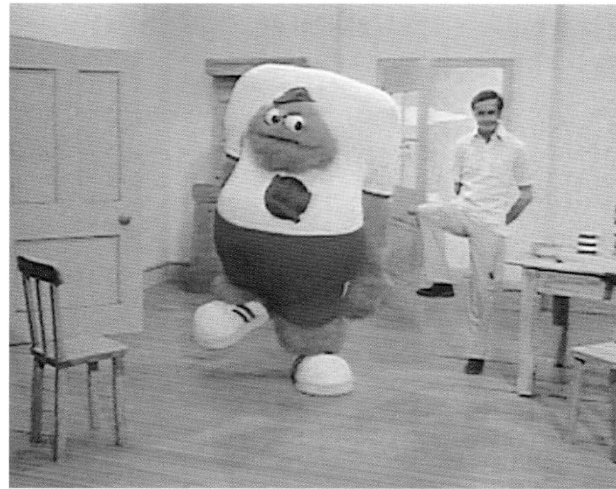

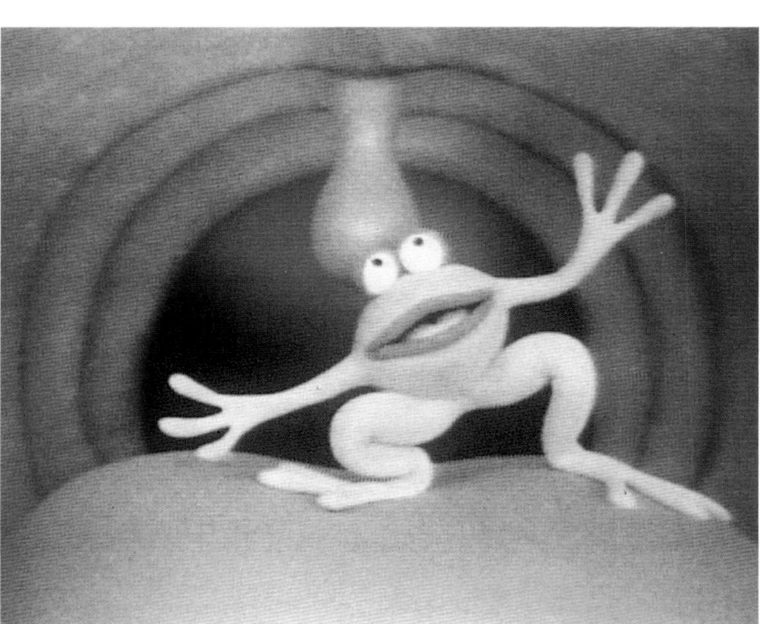

 1975.06
Agency: **Boase Massimi Pollitt**
Client: **Unigate Dairies**
BMP's sure touch was never surer than when it was inventing silly characters or memorable catchphrases. The Humphreys stole milk – even Muhammad Ali's milk. Graham Collis and John Webster were the copywriters.

1979.05
Agency: **Boase Massimi Pollitt Univas**
Client: **Barker & Dobson**
The frog in the throat stands no chance against the Hacks pastille in this commercial. Derrick Hass art directed, David Trott wrote the copy and illustrator Larry Learmont created the singing frog.

opposite

1979.06
Agency: **Boase Massimi Pollitt Univas**
Client: **L'Oréal**
Tony Scott, the man who would later direct *Top Gun* and *True Romance,* helmed this little paean to the tenacity of Ambre Solaire sunblock.

1979.07
Agency: **Boase Massimi Pollitt Univas**
Client: **Courage Brewing**
Actor Gordon Rollings was the memorable incarnation of Arkwright, a character who seemed to inhabit a rather more down-to-earth fictional northern town than Ridley Scott's Hovis-land. John Webster always believed in the value of product-identifiable fictional characters over celebrities who could overshadow the product, in this case John Smith's Yorkshire Bitter.

1974.08
Agency: **Boase Massimi Pollitt**
Client: **Schweppes**
Without the aid of a Michael Jackson or a Britney Spears, Pepsi became instantly hip in the mid-seventies thanks to this pre-rap commercial.

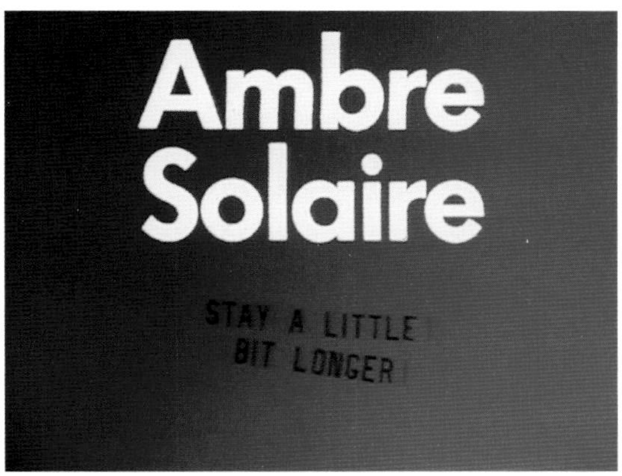

The Honey Monster was another Webster creation for BMP, launching in 1976 to promote Quaker Oats' Sugar Puffs cereal. Less sophisticated than the Cresta Bear, the Honey Monster (man-in-a-furry-suit) may have looked like the product of an underfunded children's TV programme, but his catchphrase-filled double act with actor Henry McGhee would prove a phenomenally popular campaign.

Also for BMP, this time the product of writers Dave Trott and Chris Wilkins and art director Judy Cross, came another youth-oriented commercial with a difference. In what now looks like a tentative stab at a rap video some years before its time, the percussive syllables of Lipsmackin thirstquenchin acetastin motivatin goodbuzzin cooltalkin highwalkin fastlivin evergivin coolfizzin Pepsi were intoned by then-popular DJ Emperor Rosko as the product appeared to fizzy accompaniment. Ridley Scott Associates (RSA) shot it and it became Pepsi's most memorable commercial until an alliance with Michael Jackson became even more memorable for all the wrong reasons.

Lipsmackinthirstquench
inacetastinmotivatin
goodbuzzincooltalkin
highwalkinfastlivin
evergivincoolfizzin...

Prize yogurt's success
as explained to a Raspberry.
Raspberry: My friends have been telling me I've got a couple of pips loose.
Us: You mean screws loose.
Raspberry: Screws to you, pips to me.
Us: Pips aside, what makes you say this?
Raspberry: Basically it's the yogurts I've been seen with.
You know, thin unimaginative yogurts. They say I should be with Prize. That's why I came to you – for the facts.
Us: Well basically the facts are simple.
Prize yogurt's brand share has grown from 14% to 25% representing a sales increase of 64% in a market which grew by only 11% last year.
Raspberry: Hey, hey, hey, higher mathematics was never my strong point. Explain it simply so even a banana could understand.
Us: What it all means simply is that St. Ivel is the fastest growing brand on the market.
Raspberry: Put like that I've only got one thing to say to other yogurts then: (sound of peculiar noise).
St Ivel
Us: Was that a "raspberry"?
Raspberry: What else would you expect?

St. Ivel Salads' success as
explained to a very green salad.
Very Green Salad: I'm a little worried about these new St. Ivel salads.
Don't think I'm colour prejudiced but, they're nothing like me, not a bit green.
St. Ivel: It's nothing to worry about, people just seem to like to have them to make you green salads a bit more interesting.
Very Green Salad: Oh, come on, we're not that dull.
Well, I suppose new St. Ivel Potato Salad and new St. Ivel Vegetable Salad are OK. – you know British.
But the other chap Coleslaw – sounds a bit, how shall I put it, foreign! I mean it's just not cricket.
St. Ivel: Cricket or not, it seems to be what people want, it's brand leader in Coleslaws.
Very Green Salad: Yes, exactly, some of the older chaps are losing sleep over it – see it as us very green salads being eased out, you know greens under the bed and all that.
St. Ivel: Not at all, there's no reason why there shouldn't be room for all of you.
Very Green Salad: What under the bed? I say!
St Ivel

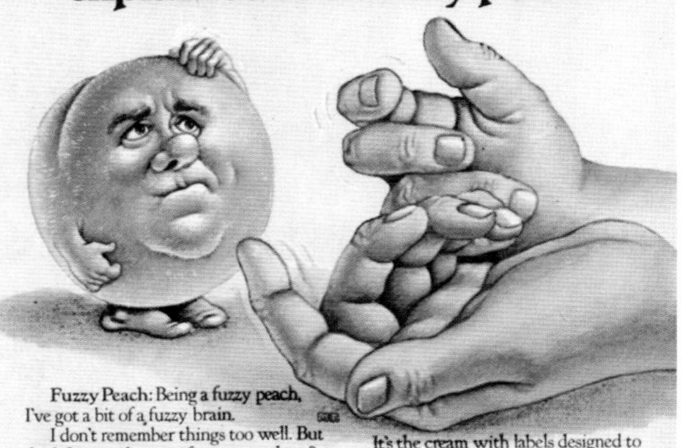

St. Ivel Devon Cream's success as
explained to a fuzzy peach.
Fuzzy Peach: Being a fuzzy peach, I've got a bit of a fuzzy brain.
I don't remember things too well. But don't I remember you from somewhere?
Us: You should do, you shared a plate with one of our products only yesterday.
Fuzzy Peach: Now don't tell me. It was St. Devon Ivel cream.
Us: Close. It's St. Ivel Devon Cream actually.
Fuzzy Peach: That's right. It's delicious. It's the stuff that's made in Scunthorpe and only lasts for a few days.
Us: Wrong again. It's only made in Devon and lasts for weeks.
So housewives can have cream at home whenever they want.
And shops need never be out of stock.
Fuzzy Peach: I remember, I remember.
It's the cream with labels designed to confuse a grapefruit like me.
Us: You're talking about the old label.
We've now got new labels designed especially to be clear and simple.
And, by the way, you're a peach, remember?
St Ivel

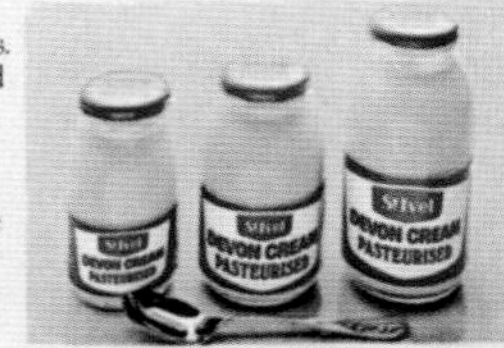

1976.07
Agency: **Boase Massimi Pollitt**
Client: **Unigate Foods**
This wordy campaign for St Ivel products seems to lack BMP's usual sure touch. However, these conversations with fruit and veg were deemed effective enough to win a Silver Award.

opposite

1979.08
Agency: **Boase Massimi Pollitt Univas**
Client: **Renault**

1978.05
Agency: **Boase Massimi Pollitt Univas**
Client: **Renault**

The dense text on the ad about the Renault's four wheels is an exemplary instance of where plenty of information works for the product. The bid to get star football names into a Renault ad looks a bit more contrived but was no doubt partly prompted by the relative novelty of high transfer fees in the late seventies.

1974.09
Agency: **Boase Massimi Pollitt**
Client: **The Labour Party**
A quiet and reasoned appeal to the voter from the Labour Party. In retrospect, it looks a little tame, but it helped to get Labour back into power, where they stayed until an altogether more influential poster for the Conservatives was devised by Saatchi & Saatchi Garland-Compton at the end of the decade.

Why doesn't the Renault 14 have a wheel at each corner?

The back wheels of a Renault 14 are further apart than the front ones.

And one of the back wheels is further forward than the other.

Why?

Simply, because that's the way the car works best. Like everything else in a Renault 14, the wheelbases weren't arrived at by copying other cars. They're the way they are to carry out their functions in the most efficient way.

What functions caused the wheels to be positioned in such odd places?

The designers of the 14 set out to build a car that would carry four people and their luggage in comfort. It sounds easy enough, but it's difficult to make cars very comfortable without also making them very expensive.

It was this concern with comfort that led to the positioning of the wheels.

Putting the back wheels further apart than the front is a blindingly obvious way to make more room where you need it, in the back of the car for passengers and luggage.

Placing the back wheels out of line is a less obvious solution to a problem.

Moving one of the back wheels forward an inch creates enough space to allow the installation of an independent rear suspension system called transverse torsion bars.

You'd think that having the wheels like this would affect the handling of the car, but it doesn't.

Most of the motoring journalists who've tested the Renault 14 have praised its roadholding and handling.

The real benefit of this system though, is superb comfort.

Unless you've ridden in a French car over a rough road, or a Rolls-Royce over a smooth one, it's difficult to describe how comfortable a Renault 14 is.

Of course, comfort doesn't come from just ironing out the bumps in the road. It's as much a state of mind as body and many people who own Renault 14's mention an almost curious feeling of security when they drive their cars. (They really do say that, we've asked lots of them.)

Why do they feel like this?

As usual with feelings of well being, a strong sound body is essential.

And the Renault 14 has probably the strongest body of any hatchback in its class. It's a problem designing strong hatchbacks, because instead of the strengthening box of a boot at the back, there's a great big hole.

Renault overcame this by careful computer-assisted design.

One visible result is the unusual flying buttress shapes over the back wheels.

A less obvious result is that the Renault 14 easily meets all national and international standards for crash resistance.

But Renault went further than government standards.

They found from their own long and careful study of real accidents that these regulations have had the effect of ensuring the survival of the car, rather than its occupants.

They also found that slightly different methods of strengthening the bodyshell ought to be adopted to ensure the safety of the passengers as well as the car.

It may be a relief to know that the Renault 14 also meets these somewhat subtler requirements.

Again, all this is just the external form of the car being shaped by Renault's concern with your comfort and peace of mind.

Even the engine is designed to make the passengers more comfortable.

It's a remarkable design, quite unlike any other car engine.

It takes up very little room, it's smooth and economical, and so efficient that even when it's old it shouldn't cost a lot to run.

This obsession with comfort shows in the smallest details.

Instead of plastic, the rooflining is thick basket-weave material, because that's better at soaking up noise.

Instead of steel, the bumpers are polyester, because that's better at soaking up bumps.

But nothing we could say can tell you as much as driving a Renault 14.

Any Renault dealer will be pleased to arrange that for you, and answer your questions about this interesting car.

If you're thinking of buying a car of this type, give the Renault 14 some consideration. It's only a machine, but it might be able to do the same for you.

The Renault 14 TL (featured here) costs £2871.18. Black paint special order only at no extra charge.

Prices, correct at time of going to press, include Car Tax, 8% VAT and inertia reel front seat belts. Delivery and number plates are extra.

Ask your Renault dealer about other Renault 14 models available and their prices.

The Renault 14 produced these petrol consumption figures for the Department of Energy tests: simulated urban driving, 31 mpg, constant speed driving: at 56 mph, 44.1 mpg; at 75 mph, 31.7 mpg. The top speed of the Renault 14 TL is 89 mph. Acceleration 0-60 mph, 15.3 seconds. (Autocar.)

Luggage capacity: 12 cubic feet. With the rear seat folded, 33.5 cubic feet. (Autocar.)

There are 400 Renault dealers throughout the UK. West End showroom: 77 St. Martin's Lane, London, W.C.2.

Details of low cost Renault Loan and Insurance Plans are available at any Renault dealer. For tax free export facilities write to Renault Ltd., Western Ave., London, W3 ORZ. Renault recommend elf lubricants

RENAULT 14

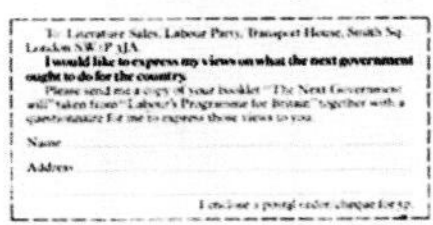

This government won't listen to you. But the next one will.

What the people want and what the government does are rapidly becoming two very different things.

For instance, if you asked the people of this country if the government ought to have been fair with their freeze, most of them will say yes.

But the government has held wages down without doing anything to prevent food prices shooting up.

The trouble is, of course, that the government has never actually bothered to ask you for an opinion.

So we're asking instead. The Labour Party wants to hear your views and hear them now, before the next election, so your ideas can help shape our policies.

We've got some firm ideas of our own, of course, put forward by Party members up and down the country.

We've put these ideas in a booklet which we'll send you when you fill in the coupon on this page.

Ideas like proper government control of key food prices. Does that sound a good idea? We'd like you to tell us.

Or how would you feel about a wealth tax?

Would you agree that if taxes are going to be used to help out companies in trouble, then you should get a share in that company's profits when it gets on its feet?

These are just a few of the things we want you to tell us.

And there's a questionnaire in the back of each booklet for you to record your views and send them in to us here at Transport House.

It is your country and you should have a chance to decide its future.

We think that a government that does what you want is better than a government which does just what it likes.

Which is not a new idea. In fact, it's a very old one.

It's called democracy and the Labour Party thinks this country could do with a bit more of it.

Get a Renault 5 for 1/214th the cost of Kenny Dalglish.

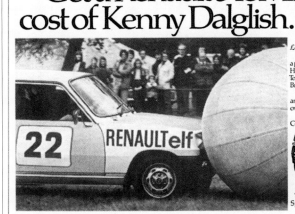

You may not have £440,000 in the transfer kitty.

But you can still afford a player that's faster than Steve Heighway, tougher than Tommy Smith and quieter than Brian Clough.

And the Renault 5 has another distinct advantage over Liverpool's latest signing.

You won't have to go to Celtic to get it.

RENAULT 5

Victor Horsman Limited, Speke Hall Road, Liverpool.

1978.06
Agency: **McCann-Erickson**
Client: **Levi Strauss**

1977.11
Agency: **Young & Rubicam**
Client: **Levi Strauss**

1973.07
Agency: **Young & Rubicam Benelux**
Client: **Levi Strauss**

A trio of ads for Levi's using British directors now synonymous with feature films – Adrian Lyne, Hugh Hudson and Ridley Scott.

1977.12
Agency:
Saatchi & Saatchi Garland-Compton
Client: **Brutus**
David Dundas wrote advertising jingles in the seventies and had a surprise hit in 1976 when 'Jeans On', derived from his composition for this Brutus ad, spent three weeks in the top five of the UK charts. He later wrote the film scores to *Withnail and I* and *How to Get Ahead in Advertising.*

1978.07
Agency: **Zetland Advertising**
Client: **Berlei**
This TV advert for underwear won a Silver Award for its direction by Tony Scott, and was edited by Pamela Power, who was later film editor for both Scott brothers.

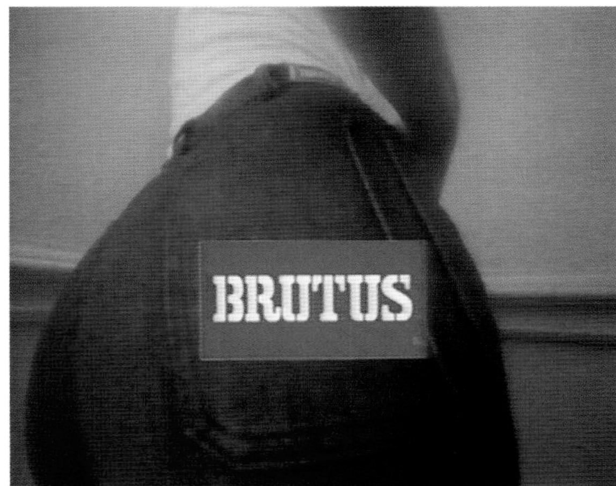

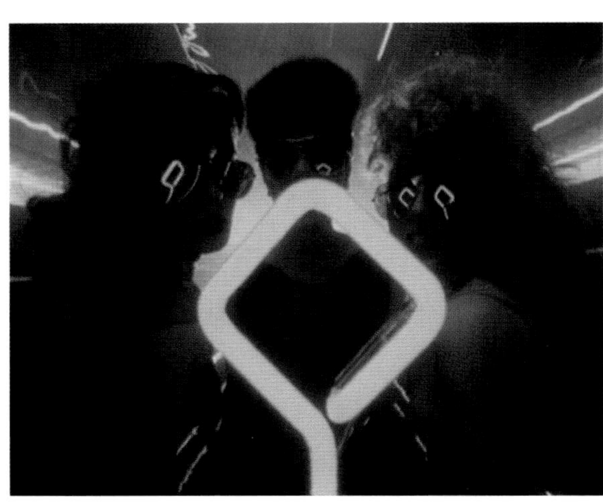

One thing was clear: if the sixties had seen design lead the field of communications, the seventies seemed to be heavily dominated by the advertising industry. However, designers and illustrators were still much in evidence and often making inventive contributions to advertising campaigns. Illustrator George Hardie created an award-winning poster for a new restaurant launched by the then-fashionable clothing chain Mr Freedom. Now transformed into 'Mr Feed'em', the new outlet was celebrated with a Hardie illustration combining a host of cartoon characters in a single tableau – no mean feat considering the different graphic traditions to which Dick Tracy, Popeye, Pluto and the rest all belonged ... not to mention, one would have thought, the risk of complex litigation.

Illustration in the seventies seemed to thrive on cunning quotes from the past and a sense of post-modernism crept in, although in the seventies it was rarely used outside of the world of architecture. Distinctive Penguin covers for novels by Evelyn Waugh and Vladimir Nabokov all hinted at the illustrative and typographical styles of yesterday. John Gorham's famous logo for *Bugsy Malone* was a striking period confection and, of course, a strong piece of branding for the first feature film by an ex-advertising man. Gorham's famous mid-seventies design for the Rowntree's 'Lion' chocolate bar also showed that he could turn his hand to anything.

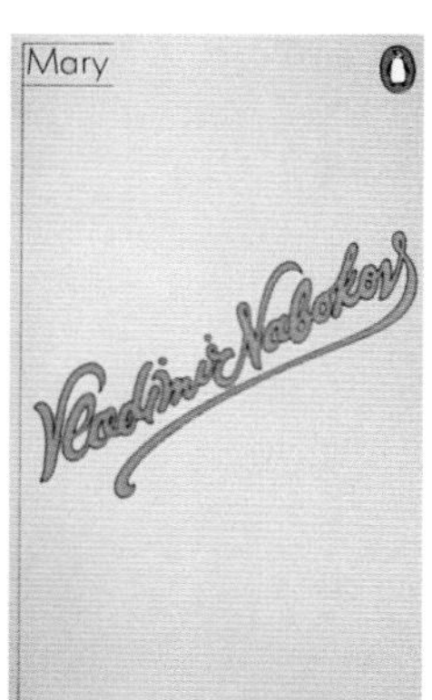

1972.12
Design group:
Nicholas Thirkell Associates
Client: **Mr Freedom**
This menu cover for a new restaurant was largely a George Hardie production as he was the art director, artist and illustrator.

1977.13
Designer: **John Gorham**
Client: **Bugsy Malone Productions**
The late John Gorham was a multi-talented man and not easily categorized. His mock period-piece identity for Alan Parker's *Bugsy Malone* is a very elegant little idea.

1975.07
Designer: **John Gorham**
Client: **Penguin Books**
Gorham designed a series of 'signature' covers for four novels by Vladimir Nabokov, *Mary*, *Glory*, *Bend Sinister* and *Pale Fire*.

1978.08
Designer: **John Gorham**
Client: **Rowntree Mackintosh**
Gorham's wrapper design for this piece of confectionery gave it the look of something far more expensive than it was. The basic principles of his design are still in use today.

opposite

1970.08
Design group:
Bentley/Farrell/Burnett
Client: **Penguin Books**
Six Evelyn Waugh novels are positioned in time according to the prevailing view of nostalgia in the early seventies. David Pelham was the art director.

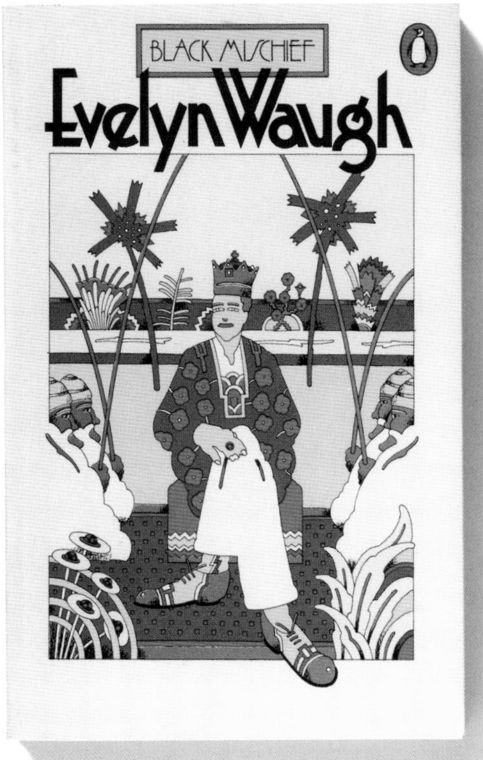
BLACK MISCHIEF
Evelyn Waugh

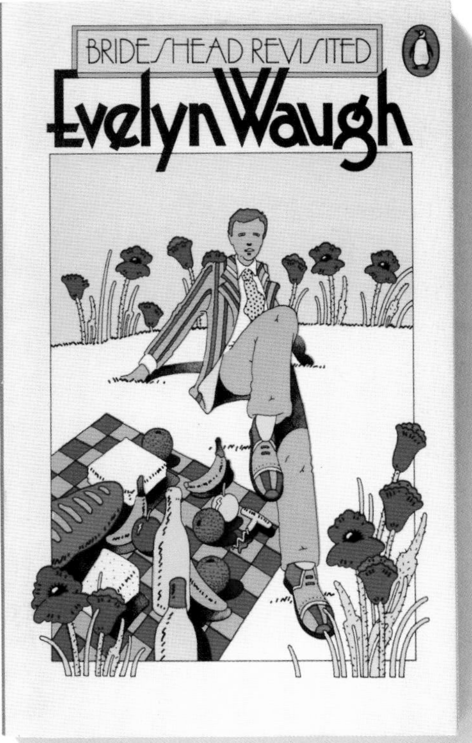
BRIDESHEAD REVISITED
Evelyn Waugh

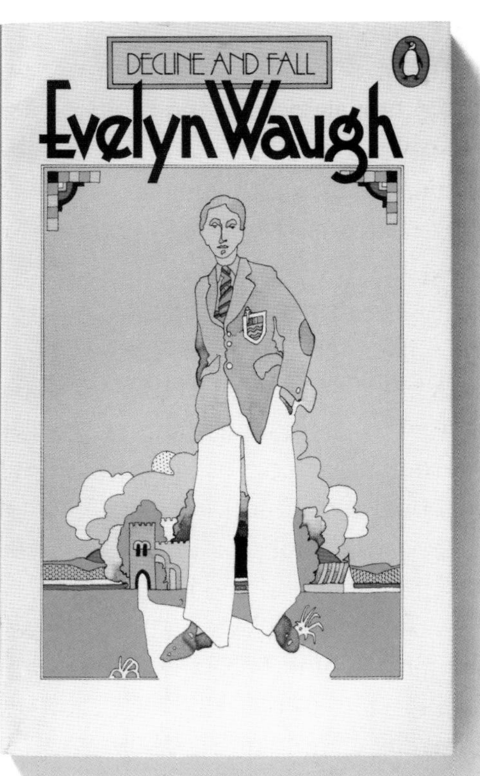
DECLINE AND FALL
Evelyn Waugh

PUT OUT MORE FLAGS
Evelyn Waugh

A HANDFUL OF DUST
Evelyn Waugh

SCOOP
Evelyn Waugh

Gorham had also been an influential design consultant on the Michael Peters' Winsor & Newton packaging work and had created one of the seventies' most memorable promotional calendars for the London photosetting company Face.

David Pelham, too, exerted influence on the seventies and in various guises. He was art director and designer for Penguin's *The Joys of Yiddish* cover. His famous Silver Award-winning Penguin book *Kites* saw him billed as both designer and author of a book that combined technical drawing with exuberant designs and practical advice on kite construction and flying.

1972.13
Design group: **John McConnell**
Client: **Face**
Photosetting was a relatively new thing in the early seventies when John McConnell became a part owner of Face, a groundbreaking house just off London's Oxford Street. McConnell encouraged the production of Face calendars that became collector's items.

1972.14
Designer: **David Pelham**
Client: **Penguin Books**
The Yiddish phrase Oy Vey! (Oh Woe!) is ironically referenced in David Pelham's artful subversion of the book's title. Pelham was a Penguin art director but achieved wider fame with his books of kites.

opposite

1977.14
Designer: **David Pelham**
Client: **Penguin Books**
Pelham wrote and designed one of those magical books that everyone of a certain age seems to own. *Kites* was a happy marriage of personal obsession, practical instruction and enjoyable design in a unique square-format Penguin paperback.

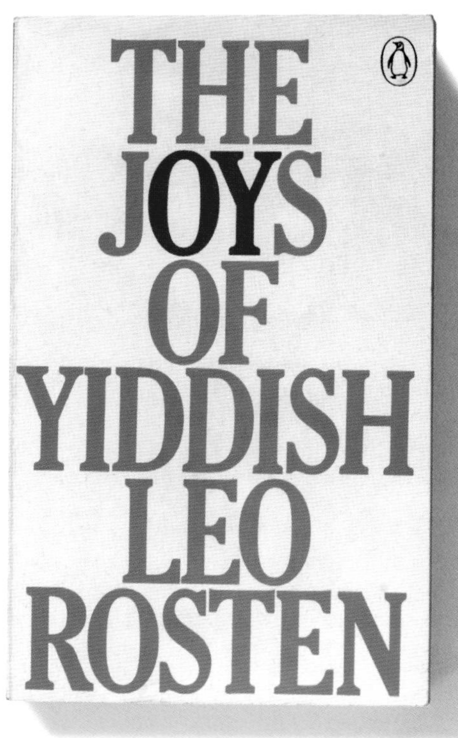

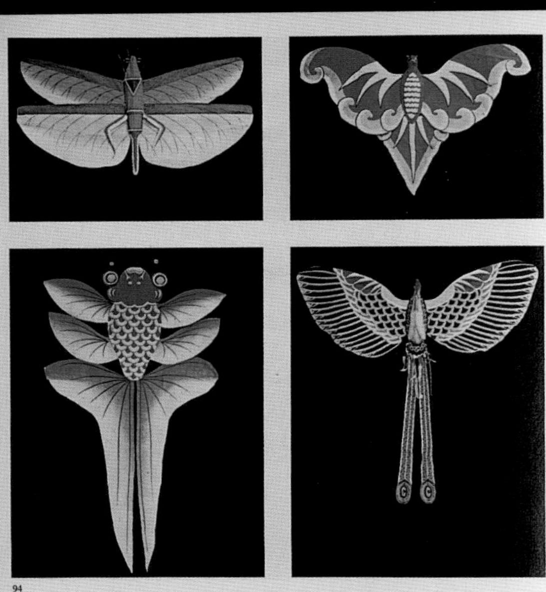

94

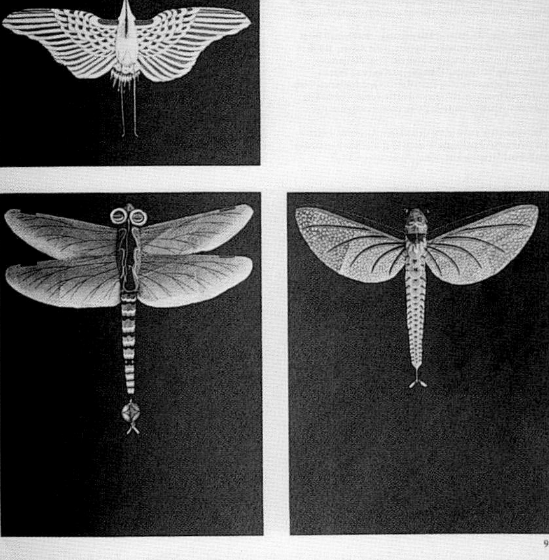

A selection of modern paper kites from the People's Republic of China.

95

A fine example of the Edo kite. Edo was the old name for Tokyo. By Teizo Hashimoto, Tokyo.

106

A Suruga kite, bearing the traditional warrior motif. By Tatsusaburo Kato, Shizuoka.

107

Chinese Centipede

Cover: paper.
Frame: split bamboo or rattan.
Bridle: two-leg.
Tail: paper streamers.
Wind: moderate.

In the classic Chinese version of the Centipede the head tends to be larger and stronger than the discs of the body. While some kite makers favour discs of uniform diameter, others tend to decrease the size through the length of the kite. Though the Centipede becomes progressively more difficult to fly as its length is increased, the longer the body the more striking the kite appears in flight. Individual discs should be balanced before assembly. To do this, place the vertical overlaps at the top and bottom of each disc onto two chair-backs, allowing a see-saw motion to occur in the horizontal plane. Trim the broom straws projecting from the horizontal stays until a good balance is achieved. Though sizes of the Centipede vary considerably, an average diameter for the leading disc is 40 cm (1 ft 3¾ ins.). Tie the discs at their tops and their sides, leaving 30 cm (1 ft) of line between the first two discs. This space should then successively be diminished by decrements of 1 cm (½ in) throughout the kite body. The Centipede kite is more spectacular than efficient.

150

Thai Serpent

Cover: silk.
Frame: split bamboo or rattan.
Bridle: two-leg.
Wind: light to moderate.

Traditionally made from silk, the Thai Serpent is extremely effective when covered with a fine gauge Mylar, though paper and plastic versions fly very successfully. The tail length is arbitrary, though the longer it is the more effective the spectacle.

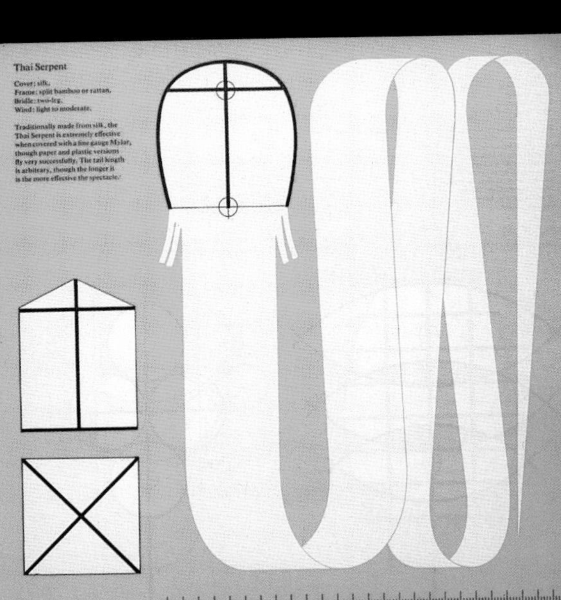

Alternate head-shapes for the Serpent.

'73 '74
Geldig van 3 juni '73–25 mei '74
Prijs inclusief btw f 2,45
Nederlandse Spoorwegen
spoorboekje
Den H

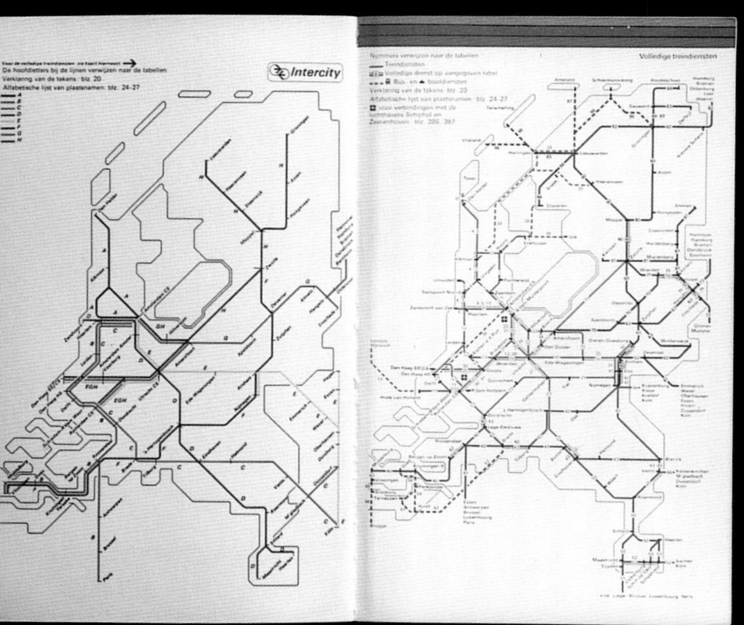
Intercity
Volledige treindiensten

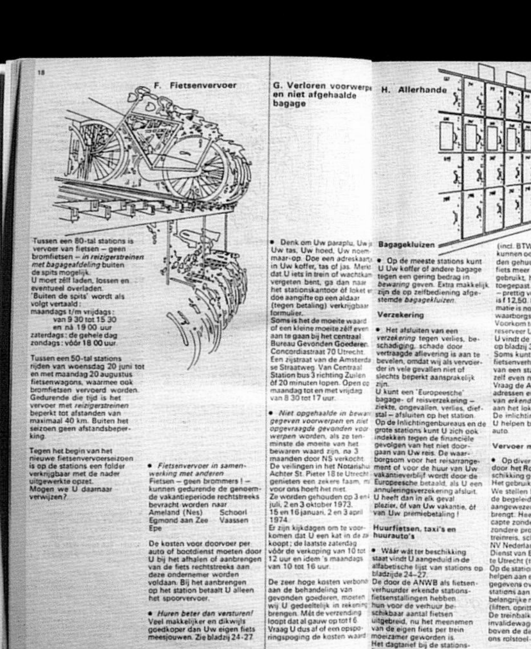
18
F. Fietsenvervoer
G. Verloren voorwerpen en niet afgehaalde bagage
H. Allerhande
19
Bagagekluizen
Verzekering
Huurfietsen, taxi's en huurauto's
Vervoer mindervaliden
Kruiers
Witkar
Giro en cheques

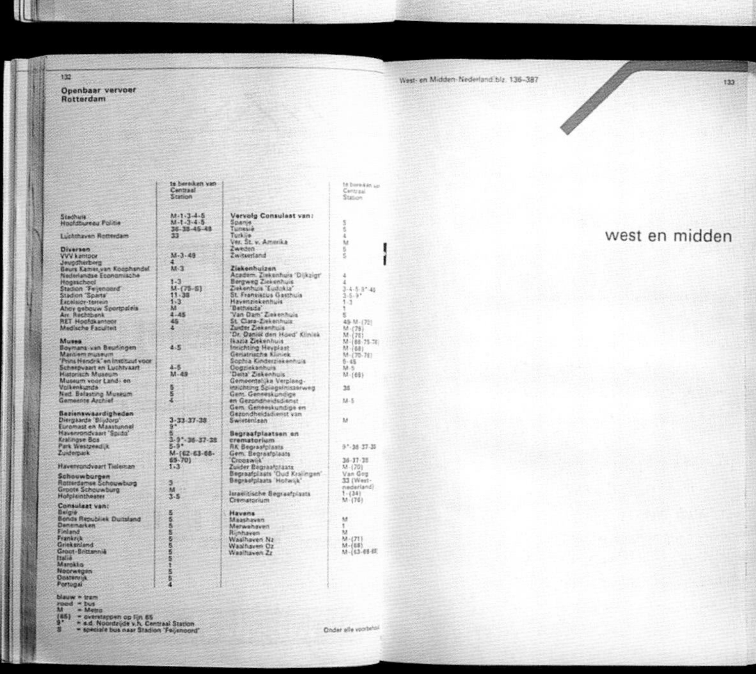
132
Openbaar vervoer Rotterdam
West- en Midden-Nederland blz. 136–387
133
west en midden

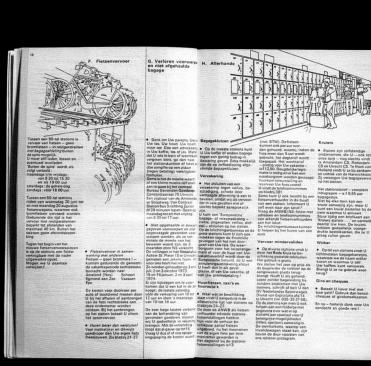

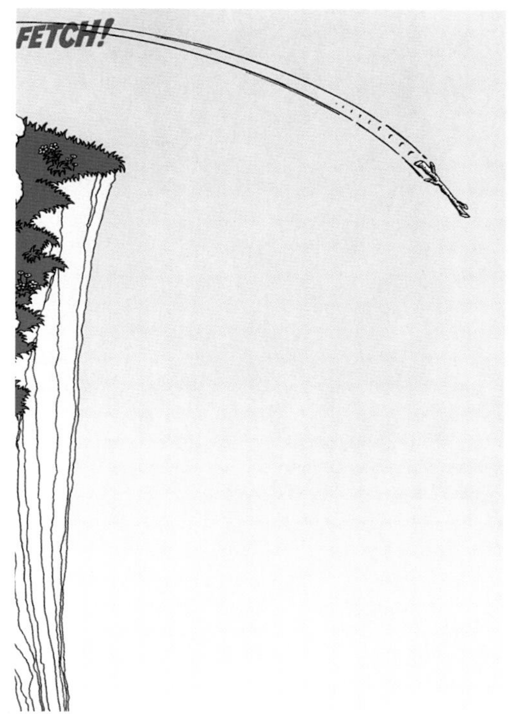

Gert Dumbar, who had been a student at the Royal College of Art (RCA) in London during the sixties, set up Studio Dumbar in Holland in 1977 after some groundbreaking graphic and corporate design work with the consultancy TEL. His contribution to TEL's identity for the Dutch Railway, Nederlandse Spoorwegen, typified the clarity and appeal of the Dumbar approach, which would also be applied to signage for The Rijksmuseum and corporate identities for the Dutch Post Office PTT and the Dutch Automobile Association ANWB.

Another RCA student, Nicholas Wurr, showed early promise with his D&AD Silver Award-winning poster for Fetch!, created for the college in 1977. Wurr would go on to become a founding member of The Partners and was renowned as a designer endowed with an exceptionally dry sense of humour. Following his early death in 1994, the RCA instigated a Nick Wurr Memorial Award for the best use of wit in students' work.

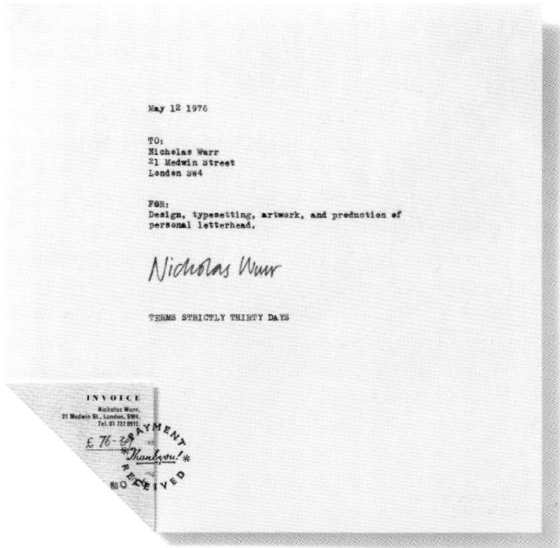
May 12 1976

TO:
Nicholas Wurr
21 Medwin Street
London SW4

FOR:
Design, typesetting, artwork, and production of personal letterhead.

Nicholas Wurr

TERMS STRICTLY THIRTY DAYS

INVOICE
Nicholas Wurr,
21 Medwin St., London, SW4.
Tel. 01 737 0912.
£ 76-39
PAYMENT RECEIVED
Thankyou!

June 4 1976

My Dearest Marlene,
I feel fate must have brought us together – You an injection moulder in a plastics factory and I a graphic designer... Just think what we will create together. Till now our lives have been meaningless: an uphill journey, ~~but~~ without purpose or destination. A winter desolation melted at last by a spring of hope and vigour. How soon before the heat and passion of summer overtake us?
I long to smell again that scent that is only yours: that subtle blend of machine oil and carbolic. I crave the touch of your hands. Was it not their sensitivity that won you the title of "Injection Moulder of the Week" for your outstanding hose nozzles? But most of all I desire your body. It is this that makes me love you so. Somehow it reminds me of home... the soft undulating curves of your ear lobes, the nobbly peaks of your elbows, and that fount of all pleasure, the little well of your belly button. Oh my darling – I can bear anything but separation. How long must I wait before you come off night shift work?
Yours forever
Nicholas.
XXXXXXXXx

Nicholas Wurr
21 Medwin Street
London SW4
01 737 0912

1974.10
Design group:
TEL Design Associated
Client: **Nederlandse Spoorwegen**
Gert Dumbar's work with TEL included this elegant publication complete with a sinuous variant of British Rail's logo for Nederlandse Spoorwegen. It was an early warning of what was to come. In the eighties Dutch design would carry off many D&AD awards.

this page

1977.15
Designer: **Nick Wurr**
Client: **Royal College of Art**
Nick Wurr's precocious Silver Award for this poster, produced while still a student at the Royal College of Art, was a feat only occasionally emulated. Inviting a dog to retrieve an object thrown into a fatal void is an idea revisited more than once in TV commercials since.

1979.09
Design group: **Wurr & Wurr**
Client: **Nick Wurr**
Nick Wurr's personal stationery allowed him to choose the category of communication by folding over the appropriate corner for personal letter, business letter, compliments slip or invoice.

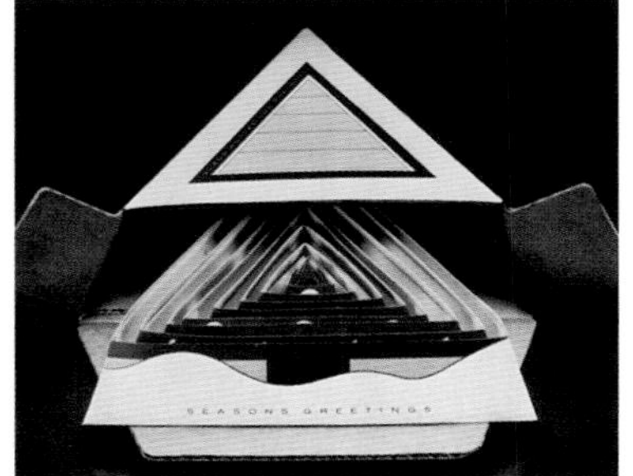

1973.08
Design group: **Shirt Sleeve Studio**
Client: **General Post Office**
This is an effective poster even if the notion that an unprotected egg might not survive the rigours of the national postal service does not come as much of a surprise. Thirty years on, the main shock value of the poster resides in the modest price of the stamp.

1976.08
Agency: **Davidson Pearce Berry and Spottiswoode**
Client: **International Wool Secretariat**
This brilliant inversion of a familiar phrase (promoting flameproof wool) must count as one of the best pieces of direct mail of all time.

1977.16
Designers:
Klaus Wuttke, John George
Client: **Klaus Wuttke & Partners**
An attention-grabbing piece of self-assembly direct mail for the festive season.

opposite

1978.09
Design group:
Rod Springett & Associates
Client: **Ruck Ryan Linsell**
Just west of London's Soho the street layout is anthropomorphized to create this playful set of maps and motifs publicizing a client move.

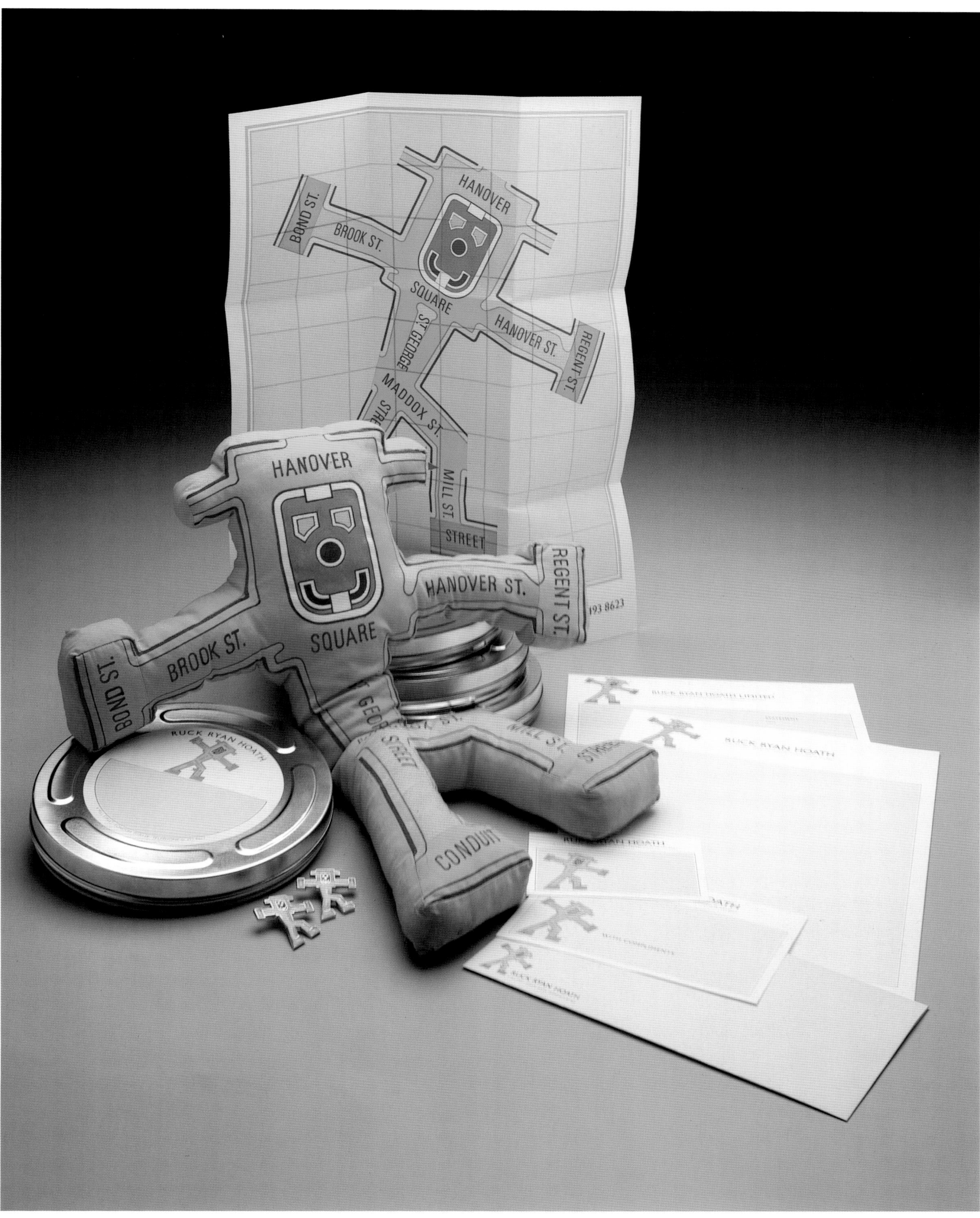
HANOVER
BOND ST.
BROOK ST.
SQUARE
HANOVER ST.
REGENT ST.
ST GEORGE
MADDOX ST.
MILL ST.
STREET
HANOVER
BROOK ST.
SQUARE
HANOVER ST.
REGENT ST.
BOND ST.
MILL ST.
STREET
RUCK RYAN HOATH

Meanwhile, photographers in the seventies seemed willing to mix and match imagery as never before. They were prepared to try anything to catch attention; from photomontage (still being achieved mechanically in the darkroom) to shots charged with a degree of sexuality that would simply not have been possible in the mainstream of the 'liberated' sixties. This, combined with the ongoing appeal of photo reportage, usually in grim locales of violence, may have contributed to the visual richness of the seventies, but also added to the feeling that the decade had no rallying cry and no unifying cause.

On the design front a new and influential design company organized along rather idealistic lines was created in 1972. Its rapid collapse was confidently predicted by many design industry watchers, but in 2002 it is bigger than ever and still thriving. Pentagram grew out of what had once been Fletcher/Forbes/Gill and what became Crosby/Fletcher/Forbes after architect Theo Crosby replaced Bob Gill. Before the transition was made a classic piece of award-winning graphic design was created by Alan Fletcher. His design programme for client Brooks Baker & Fulford featured a memorable portrait of the three principals dressed in white shirts that bled into the white mass of a table top. This stylized image provided the most dramatic – and literal – of letterheads: three heads at the top of a letter. Another award came to Alan Fletcher in 1974; by this time Pentagram was up and running but Fletcher alone is credited with the memorable identity for Reuters. Elegant and understated, it simply borrowed the hole-punched paper tape communication system of the time to depict the characters of the client's name.

In both cases, Fletcher characteristically claimed to have hit upon the solutions almost by accident, recalling how the fading light in the Brooks Baker & Fulford boardroom presented him with the unified white expanse of shirt and table, and how a bit of punched tape he picked up at Reuters suggested that particular solution.

Brooks Baker & Fulford Limited, 3 Princes Street, London W1. 01-629 7916. J. Baker (Managing), R. Brooks (USA), L. Fulford, J. McKeand

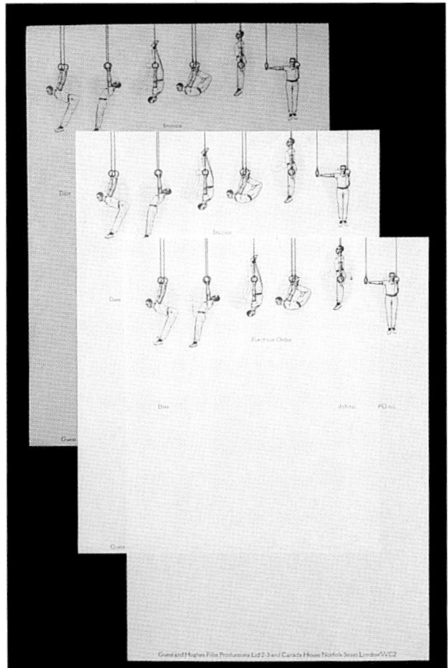

1970.09
Design group: **Crosby/Fletcher/Forbes**
Client: **Brooks Baker & Fulford**
Alan Fletcher recalls that a certain amount of wine also came to the aid of inspiration for this letterhead design.

1974.11
Designer: **Alan Fletcher**
Client: **Reuters**
Thirty years after Fletcher devised this identity Reuters still use a logo that retains the dot motifs although they are now part of a roundel at the end of the name.

this page

1970.10
Design group: **Crosby/Fletcher/Forbes**
Client: **Guest & Hughes**
From a total of four Silver Awards won by Crosby/Fletcher/Forbes in 1970, two were for stationery. This one was for film production company Guest & Hughes.

1970.11
Design group: **Crosby/Fletcher/Forbes**
Client: **Mears Caldwell Hacker**
This poster was a bold attempt to get the British public thinking in metric rather than imperial terms by 'translating' the sizes of everyday objects.

1970.12
Design group: **Crosby/Fletcher/Forbes**
Client: **Crosby/Fletcher/Forbes**
Designers who complain about lack of vision by the client can hardly do so when they are working for themselves. This is an early example of award-winning self promotion by Crosby/Fletcher/Forbes.

1972
designed by
Bentley & Farrell
Derek Birdsall
Mel Calman
Crosby Fletcher Forbes
Michael Foreman
Bob Gill
John Gorham
Lou Klein
John McConnell
Enzo Ragazzini
Herbert Spencer
Arnold Schwartzman

Proceeds for charities in the graphic arts. Printed in England by Thompson & Tompkins. Paper by Wiggins Teape

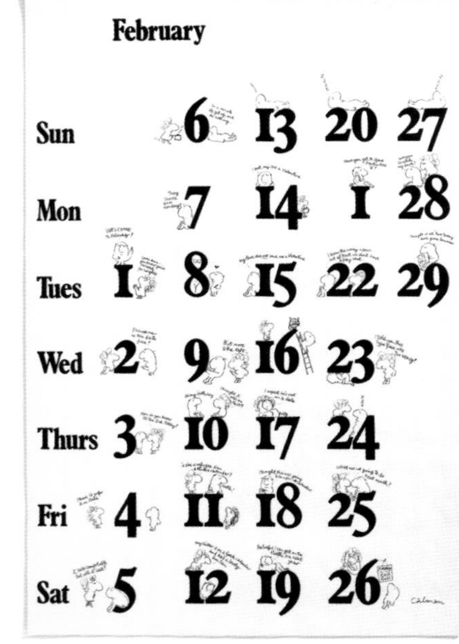

may[1] (mā), *v., pres. sing. 1st pers.* **may,** *2nd* **may** or (*Archaic*) **may-est** or **mayst,** *3rd* **may;** *pres. pl.* **may;** *past* **might. 1.** (used to express wish or prayer): *May you live long.* **2.** (used to express contingency, esp. in clauses indicating condition, concession, purpose, result, etc.): *I may be wrong, but I think you would be wise to go. Times may change, but human nature stays the same.* **3.** (used to express possibility, opportunity, or permission): *It may rain. You may enter.* **4.** *Archaic.* (used to express ability or power.) [OE *mæg,* 1st and 3rd pers. sing. pres. ind. of *magan,* c. G *mögen*]
—Syn. 3. See **can**[1].
may[2] (mā), *n. Archaic.* a maiden.
May (mā), *n.* **1.** the fifth month of the year, containing 31 days. **2.** the early part of one's life, esp. the prime: *a young woman in her May.* **3.** the festivities of May Day. **4.** (*l.c.*) *Brit.* the hawthorn. **5.** Also, **Mae, Mai.** a girl's given name. **—v.i. 6.** (*l.c.*) to gather flowers in the spring: *when we were maying.* [ME; OE *Maius* < L, short for *Maius mensis* Maia's month]

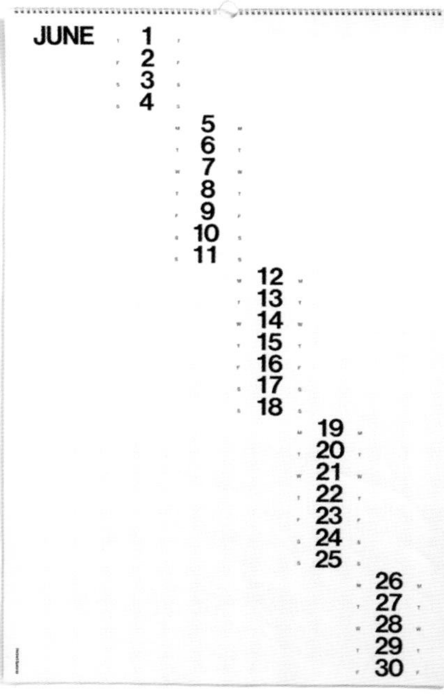

1972.15
Design group: **Pentagram Design**
Client: **Robert Norton**
A dozen seventies design stars were recruited by Pentagram to produce this calendar, ensuring a rare degree of graphic variety spanning January to December.

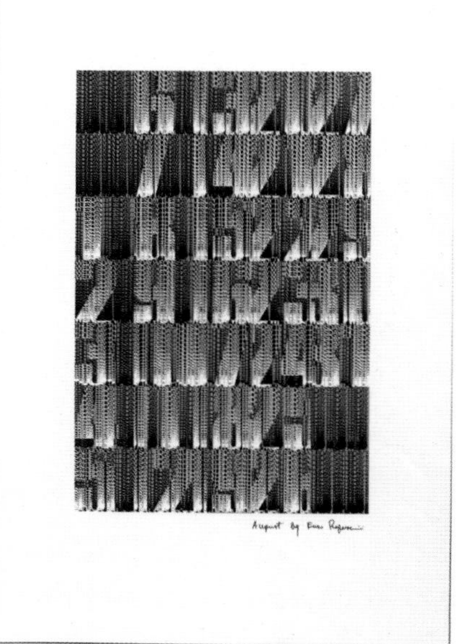

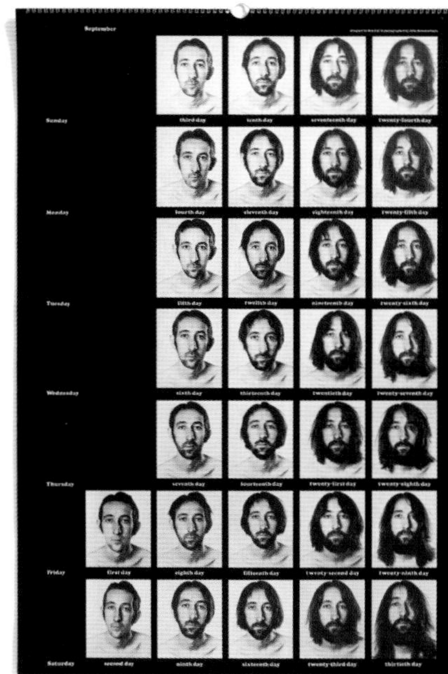

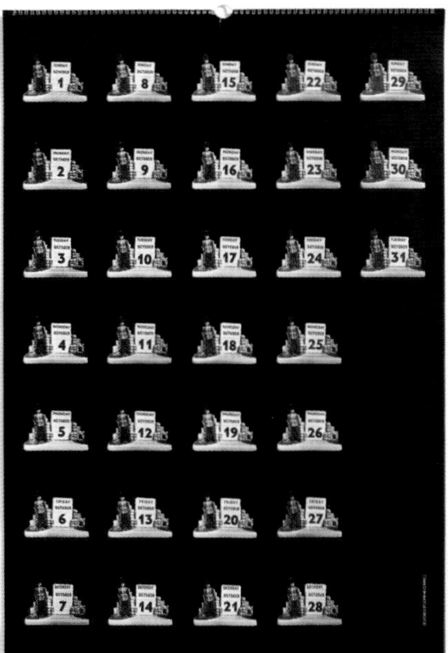

The origins of Pentagram go back to the Central School of Art where Alan Fletcher first met Colin Forbes. When Fletcher graduated and went off on his American adventures, ending up in New York and working for *Time*, Forbes stayed in Britain and embarked upon the teaching route and a stint in advertising before returning to the Central as head of graphics and then setting up his own graphics shop. A three-way alliance with the American Bob Gill lasted for three years before Gill went solo and Theo Crosby joined. Mervyn Kurlansky came on board at the end of the sixties, and in 1972, when Kenneth Grange brought his independent product design organization to join the other four, Pentagram was born.

John McConnell was one of the next to join; today he likes to point out that it was Martin Sorrell (the ex-Saatchi man who later started the world's largest publicly quoted design and advertising business, WPP) who assured him that Pentagram was a foolish hippie idea that had no chance of success. However, three decades after its founding by an industrial designer, an architect and three graphic designers, Pentagram defies conventional business wisdom and operates on an equal ownership basis and with the unshakeable belief that its owners must also be practitioners.

1972.16
Designer: **Mervyn Kurlansky**
Client: **Zinc Development Association**
Pre-Pentagram work from South Africa-born Mervyn Kurlansky who trained in London, practising with Knoll International and Crosby/Fletcher/Forbes before co-founding the famous consultancy in 1972. The cover and two spreads from this book are shown.

opposite

1973.09
Designer: **David Hillman**
Client: **Tony Evans, Brian Rice**
The book *The English Sunrise* by Brian Rice and photographer Tony Evans chronicled a recurring decorative motif in English windows, fixtures and furniture.

1973.10
Design group: **Pentagram Design**
Client: **Pirelli**
Here Pentagram's Georg Staehelin reminds us that the original pneumatic Pirelli product was not a pin-up but a tyre.

1973.11
Design group: **Pentagram Design**
Client: **Roche Products**
This Mervyn Kurlansky project for a drug marketed by Roche was won after he joined Pentagram, and typifies a Kurlansky visual style based on information graphics, diagrams and optical devices.

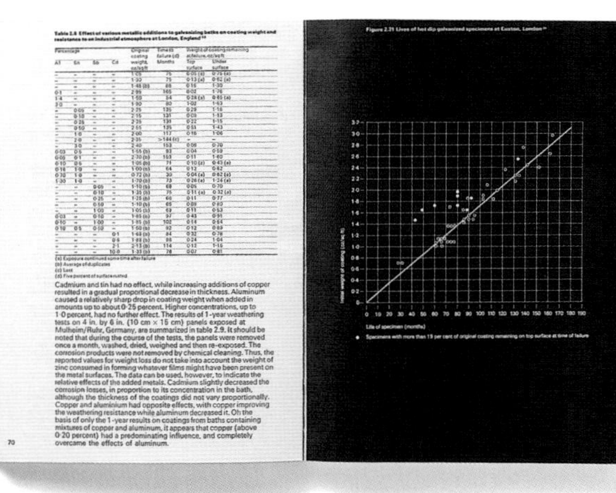

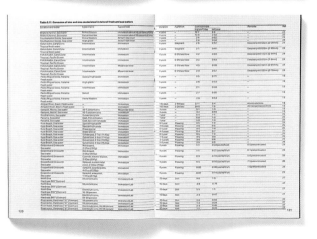

THE ENGLISH SUNRISE

NOBRIUM
GENERAL
PRACTICE
SURVEY

GB
PIRELLI
CINTURATO

GB
EUY

I
PIRELLI
CINTURATO
S
PIRELLI
CINTURATO

CGO
PIRELLI
CINTURATO

'It was always the idea that we should have owners dedicated to their craft and that we wouldn't be a large, formal pyramid,' maintains McConnell, now the elder statesman of the partnership. 'Instead, Pentagram is lots of very small pyramids, each with its own principal. We call ourselves partners, but strictly speaking we're shareholder directors of a privately owned company.' Certainly Pentagram (literally a five-pointed figure once seen as a mystic symbol with magical properties) has multiplied its original number of partners fourfold by the start of the twenty-first century and remains a unique multidisciplinary organization that came together in a decade when other design consultancies formed, divided, reformed and reinvented themselves with bewildering speed.

In 1977, Pentagram won a Silver Award for a particularly inventive design programme for Clarks children's shoes. Clarks had for some time made a point out of appealing to parents' sense of responsibility by using in-store foot gauges to measure both the length and width of children's feet, ensuring non-restrictive fitting. This virtuous approach had no direct appeal to the child, and although back in 1977 today's youth obsession with designer footwear did not exist, it certainly did no harm to engage the interest of the potential wearer as well as the person paying.

The Pentagram programme, designed by John McConnell, Howard Brown and David Pearce, combined a clean graphic presentation of the foot-gauge idea on carriers and display units with 'Guess the Teams' and 'Find the Shoes' picture puzzle panels directly aimed at children. At this time, and perhaps more typically, Pentagram also launched the first two books in its ongoing series of Pentagram Papers. *A Dictionary of Graphic Clichés* was the first, and *The Pessimist Utopia* the second. The occasional series could be called self-promotion only in the most oblique sense, and has over the years built up into a substantial collection of whimsical published curiosities, offering a fitting commentary to a unique consultancy that made a success out of an unlikely business model.

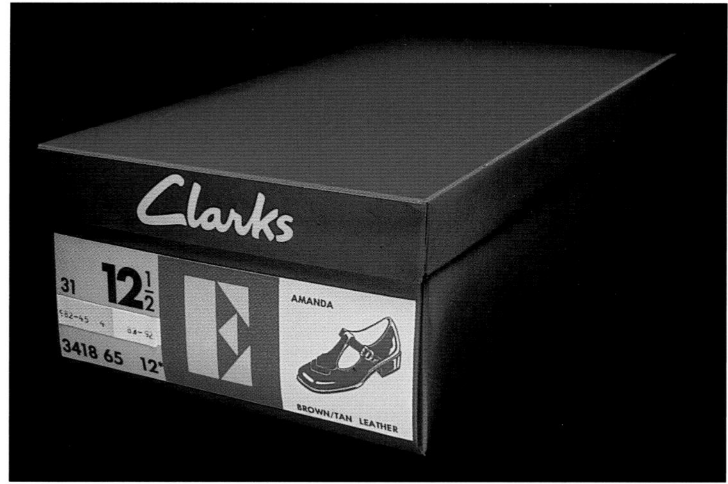

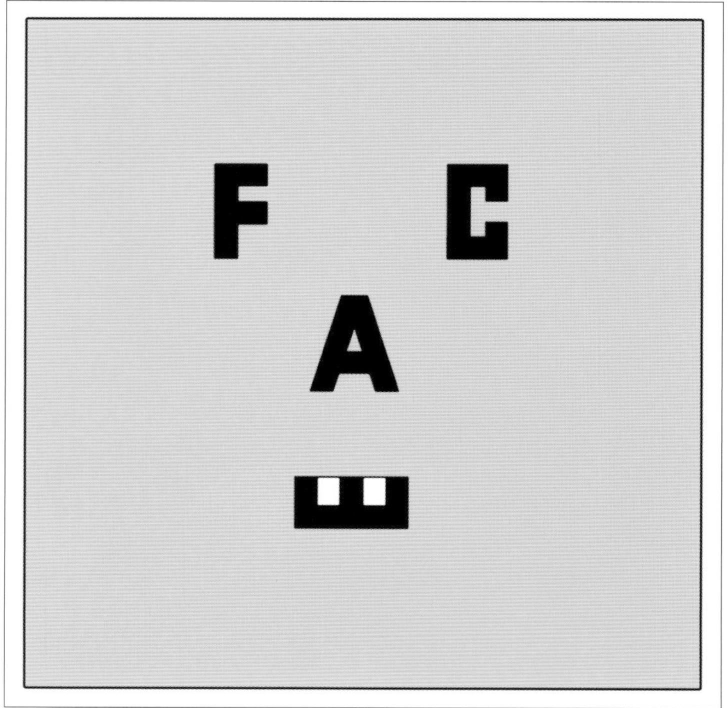

1977.17
Agency: **Pentagram Design**
Client: **Clarks Shoes**
Pentagram produced packaging design for Clarks, who make worthy but sensible shoes for children. The animal footprints device is a bid to interest the child as well as the parent.

1975.08
Designers: **John Gorham, John McConnell**
Client: **Face Photosetting**
One of a series of self-explanatory calendars instigated by Face co-owner John McConnell. Another was a working clock with a friendly face.

this page

1973.12
Designer: **John McConnell**
Client: **Penguin Books**
Titles that look as if they should have been in Penguin's Pelican imprint are given a cerebral treatment by John McConnell.

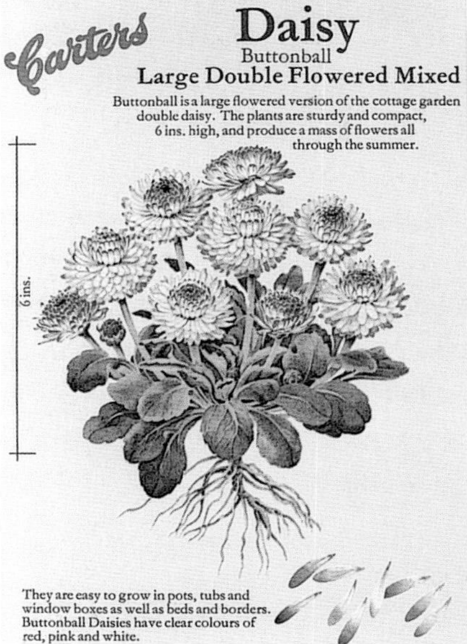

Carters
Daisy
Buttonball
Large Double Flowered Mixed
Buttonball is a large flowered version of the cottage garden double daisy. The plants are sturdy and compact, 6 ins. high, and produce a mass of flowers all through the summer.
6 ins.
They are easy to grow in pots, tubs and window boxes as well as beds and borders. Buttonball Daisies have clear colours of red, pink and white.

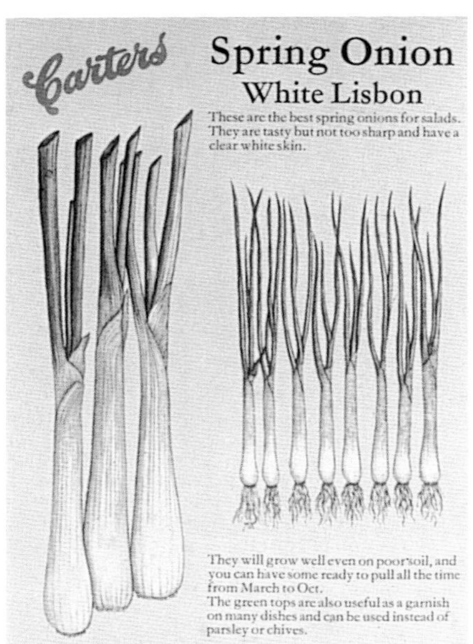

Carters
Spring Onion
White Lisbon
These are the best spring onions for salads. They are tasty but not too sharp and have a clear white skin.
They will grow well even on poor soil, and you can have some ready to pull all the time from March to Oct.
The green tops are also useful as a garnish on many dishes and can be used instead of parsley or chives.

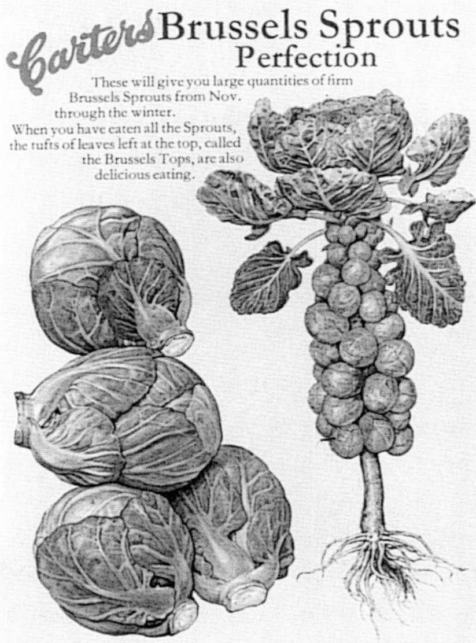

Carters
Brussels Sprouts
Perfection
These will give you large quantities of firm Brussels Sprouts from Nov. through the winter.
When you have eaten all the Sprouts, the tufts of leaves left at the top, called the Brussels Tops, are also delicious eating.

Carters
Forget-Me-Not
Myosotis
Royal Blue
Forget-Me-Nots are very popular and easy to grow. They bloom in late Spring and are lovely either as a solid mass of colour or as companions to wallflowers and tulips which flower at the same time.
6-8 ins.
Forget-Me-Nots are also ideal for window boxes, hanging baskets and tubs.
The flowers are rich blue with distinctive yellow eyes. The plants grow 6-8 ins. tall.

1973.13
Design group: **Wolff Olins**
Client: **R & G Cuthbert**
Some of these beautifully rendered illustrations of what the un-photogenic seeds in the pack might one day become, later lent themselves to an encyclopaedia of flowers and plants.

1975.09
Design group: **Wolff Olins**
Client: **Bovis**
This enduring corporate identity has become legendary, despite the fact that it unaccountably missed out on an award. Ken Lilly's hummingbird could only be shown on a white background, necessitating a white panel to be painted on Bovis' orange equipment.

opposite

1978.10
Design group: **Minale Tattersfield**
Client: **British Airport Authority**
Those long moving walkways at airport terminals almost invite the idea of a crayon held against the gliding wall. Minale Tattersfield harnessed the impulse in a single-line evocation of famous landmarks.

1971.08
Design group:
Minale Tattersfield Provinciali
Client: **Baric Computing Services**
The limitations of early computer printers are imaginatively exploited.

1976.09
Design group:
Minale Tattersfield Provinciali
Client: **Milton Keynes Development Corporation**
Milton Keynes was a conflation of two villages to form the basis of Britain's newest town. Lacking a civic history, its appeal depended heavily on MTP's promotional programme.

1976.10
Design group:
Minale Tattersfield Provinciali
Client: **Hospital Design Partnership**
A Swiss cross is suggested by a shadow motif made from a building with windows.

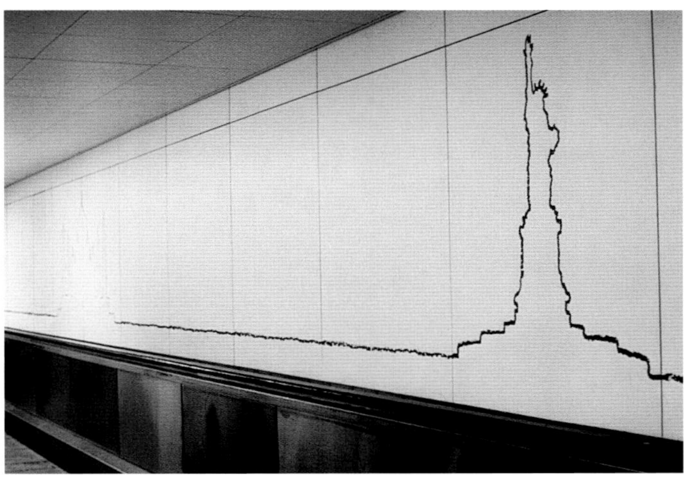

BARIC COMPUTING SERVICES LIMITED

A comparable outfit in terms of seventies prestige was Wolff Olins, which had been established in 1965 by Michael Wolff and Wally Olins. By the seventies it was successfully pursuing a strategy of making corporate identity a recognized and valued part of any major company's list of requirements. In 1975, the Wolff Olins identity solution for Bovis once again took an archetypical Michael Wolff design idea, this time using a hummingbird as the civil engineering company's unexpected but effective identifying image. It was an unlikely solution that became a great success and came at a time when Michael Wolff's distinctive personal style – humane, idealistic and ultimately inimical to a tightly-run business – seemed to belong more to the optimistic sixties than the increasingly purposeful seventies. His departure from the company he co-founded proved inevitable, but Wolff Olins endured and prospered. Sixties trailblazer Minale Tattersfield continued to put a fresh spin on corporate identity programmes that might otherwise have been dull or predictable. For the Milton Keynes Development Corporation it produced a corporate identity and designed promotional material to attract people to this new London overspill town. It also worked with the town's architects to devise and apply information systems. For the Milton Keynes Arts Foundation it created a boldly distinctive hand-and-butterfly symbol. Its work for The Italian Institute of Foreign Trade led to a memorable poster for an Italian knitwear exhibition; instead of taking the obvious Claudia Cardinale-in-a-tight-sweater route, it simply showed a single woollen sock angled to evoke the shape of the Italian mainland.

For Baric Computing Services (an alliance between Barclay's Bank and International Computing Systems) Minale Tattersfield made use of a graphic conceit that echoed the concrete poetry of previous decades: a large image composed of itself in repeated miniature form. Thus, an uppercase *B* is composed of a computer printout matrix of tiny *B*'s. From murals for the British Airports Authority to graphics for a Swiss hospital, Minale Tattersfield, the original design-out-of-advertising consultancy, continued to deliver unexpected and apposite corporate solutions throughout the decade.

By the seventies FHK Henrion could already be considered a past master of graphic design and corporate identity. Born in Nuremberg, he had trained as a textile designer before moving to graphics and, in 1939, emigrating to England, where he immediately found state clients in the form of the General Post Office and the wartime Ministry of Information. His powerful posters of the war years combined some of the techniques of the Surrealists and John Heartfield's photomontages to great propaganda effect. At the start of the fifties he set up Henrion Design Associates, later to become HDA International. With a successful identity for the Dutch airline KLM, alongside work for The National Theatre, Tate & Lyle and Girobank, Henrion won a Silver Award in 1973 for one of the last jobs by Henrion Design Associates before the name and personnel change: it was for British European Airways (BEA) Trident.

In the days when the type of aircraft still held some allure for the travelling public, the Trident name was attached to BEA as a selling point in itself. Henrion's identity was typically clean and clear, testimony to his enthusiasm for the rationalizations of the Swiss School. Soon BEA and British Overseas Airways Corporation (BOAC) would amalgamate under the British Airways banner and Henrion's consultancy would slowly pass into the control of new, younger partners.

On a broader canvas, too, the old order was changing, but whatever new purpose would drive the seventies remained stubbornly unclear. Britain still had Thatcherism to come, with its cult of the entrepreneur and the free market, and the political complexion and public mood of the early-to-mid seventies is best described as uncertain. The oil crisis of 1973 galvanized an uneasy feeling that these insular islanders were all much more susceptible to change, crisis and external forces than they had previously thought. Prime Minister Edward Heath imposed direct British rule on Northern Ireland in 1972, at the same time working to win French acceptance of British entry into the European Economic Community. However, Heath was unable to cope with his own country's mounting economic problems: rising inflation and unemployment, and a series of crippling labour strikes. The first general election of 1974, which Heath called hoping to win a new mandate to lead the country, resulted in lost Conservative seats while Heath's subsequent failure to form a coalition government proved fatal.

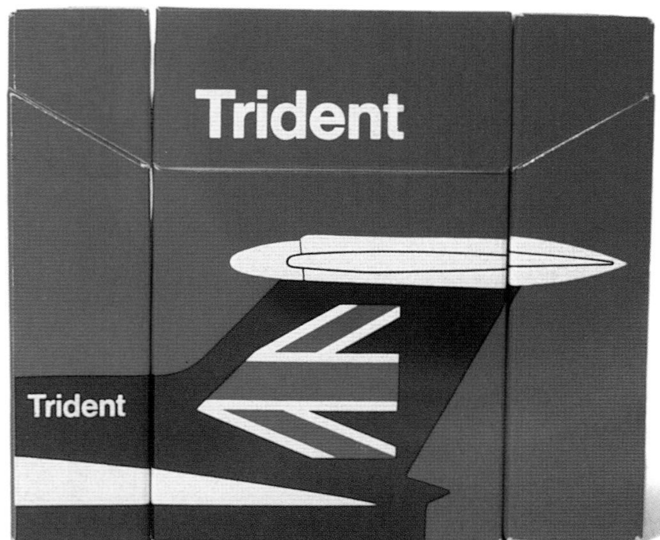

1973.14
Design group:
Henrion Design Associates
Client: **British European Airways**
Considered a pioneer of corporate identity design in Britain, FHK Henrion established his reputation in the UK with his work for the Ministry of Information and the US Office of War Information in London. Henrion Design Associates was established in 1951, renamed in 1973 as HDA International, and later reconfigured as Henrion Ludlow & Schmidt in 1982.

Harold Wilson and the left-wing Labour Party succeeded him on 4 March 1974. A second general election in the same year resulted in another defeat for Heath and the Conservative Party and, as a result, Margaret Thatcher became the party's leader in 1975; she would become Prime Minister in 1979.

Perhaps unsurprisingly, given all this instability, the nation's best-seller lists of the mid-seventies were suddenly featuring a clutch of novels about the devil, disasters and decline. Whereas sixties reading habits had been kick-started by a bracing mix of sex (Penguin's infamous publication of *Lady Chatterley's Lover*), drugs (*The Naked Lunch*) and violence (*Last Exit To Brooklyn*), the seventies began with people reading Erich Segal's *Love Story* but soon turning to *The Exorcist*, *Jaws*, *Carrie* and *Crash*. Increasing vertical integration also meant that the companies which owned the publishers often struck the movie deals too, with the result that most of these books became films (although J G Ballard's *Crash* would have to wait until 1996 and *Love Story* actually started out as a screenplay that was hurriedly novelized by its creator, Erich Segal).

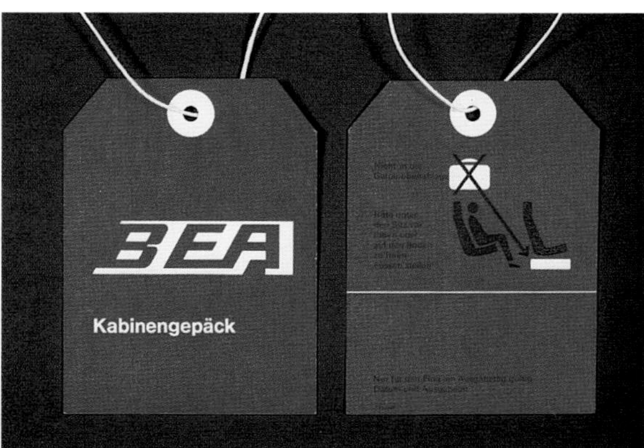

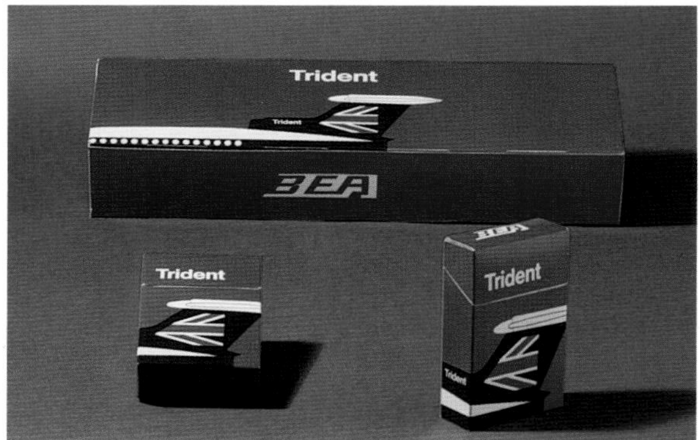

The soundtrack to the decade looked as if it would be provided by the matchless tunes of Abba, but The Sex Pistols and the Punk generation were waiting in the wings with malice aforethought. Jamie Reid's cover for *Never Mind The Bollocks – It's The Sex Pistols* made it clear that 'Dancing Queen' would not be the only song on everyone's lips as the seventies moved into its second phase. Also evident was another album sleeve fashion, this time one that evoked a fey, elfin world apparently located within easy walking distance of Tolkien's Middle-earth and with easy access to some suspect Victorian illustration.

1975.10
Designer: **Vincent McEvoy**
Client: **RSO Records**
McEvoy came up with the ultimate wish-fulfillment cover for English rockers who dreamed of fame and living in America. Having just survived heroin addiction, Clapton for his part was probably glad to be living anywhere.

1971.09
Design group:
Arnold Schwartzman Productions
Client: **Kinney Record Group**
Dandelion Records began in the heady days of flower power as an idealistic venture by British DJ, John Peel. It ran out of steam the year after it won a Silver Award for this album packaging for seventies blues band, Siren. Part of the packaging included a flicker book by Tony Meeuwissen who was to do rather well in the awards the following year too.

1972.17
Designer: **Tony Meeuwissen**
Client: **Transatlantic Records**
Tony Meeuwissen picked up four awards (one Gold and three Silver) in 1972, including one for this label design for Transatlantic Records.

1972.18
Designer: **Tony Meeuwissen**
Client: **Kinney Records**
In retrospect, some award winners are easier to explain than others. This letterhead for Kinney Records hardly conveys brisk corporate efficiency ... but perhaps that was the point.

1972.19
Designer: **Nigel Holmes**
Client: **Island Records**
This Island Records sampler album was designed by Nigel Holmes, who went on to become a guru of information graphics.

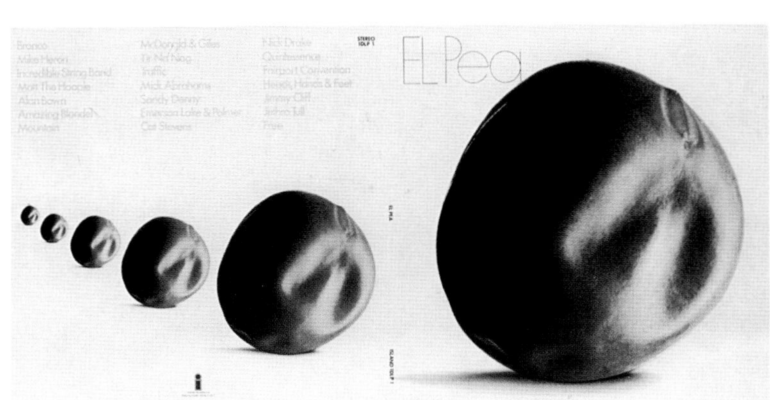

Even so, the music industry in general, and record sleeve design in particular, was to attract some exceptional talents in the seventies. Among the most famous was the Hipgnosis design group, formed in 1968. Hipgnosis specialized in album cover art, most famously with its distinctive Pink Floyd sleeves, the first being *A Saucerful of Secrets* in 1968. Hipgnosis' leading lights were Aubrey Powell, Peter Christopherson and Storm Thorgerson. The team eventually split up in 1983, but Storm Thorgerson remained a design consultant for Pink Floyd. Among the best-known Hipgnosis Pink Floyd album covers are *Animals* (flying pig over Battersea Power Station) and *Dark Side of The Moon* (light/prism/spectrum). However, Hipgnosis was recognized by D&AD in 1977 for covers for two other groups: Black Sabbath and Led Zeppelin. Both featured contributions from designer/illustrator George Hardie (who had drawn but not designed the *Dark Side of The Moon* cover art) and both embodied the Hipgnosis variant of 'surrealism'.

This was usually achieved by a rather stream-of-consciousness chain of creative thought, often kicked off by art director Thorgerson whose quest for metaphors, symbols and visual puns to reflect this or that album title (itself often chosen quite arbitrarily by the group concerned) usually resulted in something that had obscure meaning for the consumer but which, visually speaking, was undeniably stunning and strange. For the cover art of the Pink Floyd album *Nice Pair*, Thorgerson and his team amassed a collection of notes and pencil roughs. 'They were mostly silly jokes and didn't feel sufficiently strong to work on their own,' Thorgerson recalls. 'In the end, we got so attached to them that we decided to use them all.'

1970.13
Designer: **David Juniper**
Client: **Atlantic Records**
David Juniper depicts the early Led Zeppelin in a graphic style somehow suggestive of the band playing at a Hitler Youth Rally.

opposite

1977.18
Design group: **Hipgnosis/NTA Studios**
Clients: **Peter Grant, Swansong**
Seven years on and Hipgnosis is taking Led Zeppelin into very different graphic territory. Now an obelisk is reduced to a trite motif that recurs in a series of banal and arbitrary stock shots on this gatefold cover for the album *Presence*.

¥2,500

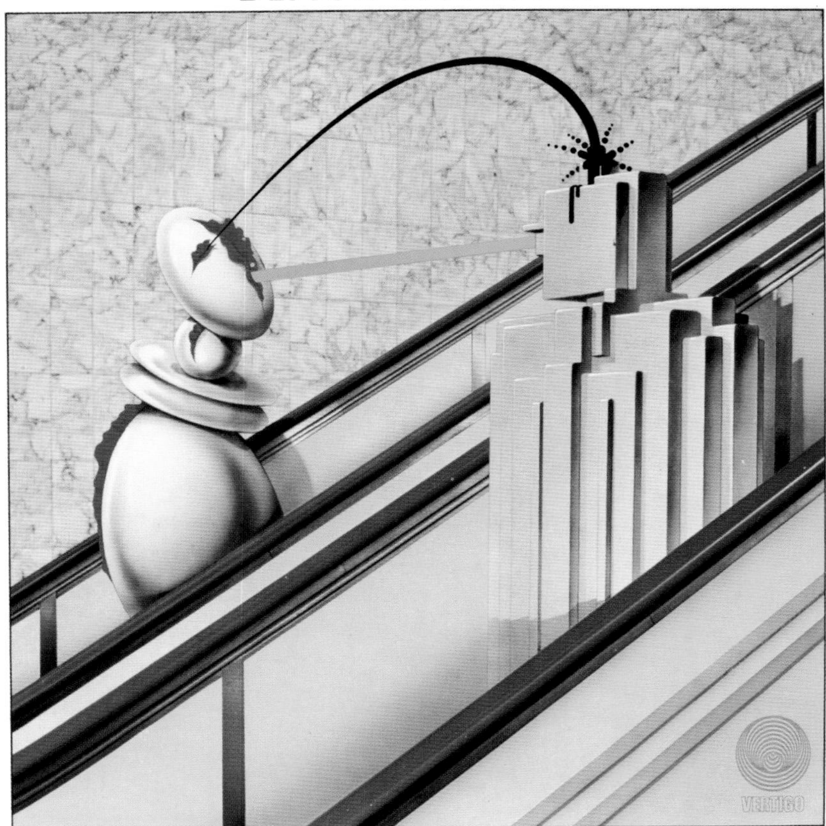

1977.19
Design group: **Hipgnosis**
Client: **Black Sabbath**
George Hardie's distinctive illustrative style dominates this album for the heavy metal group that launched Ozzy Osbourne.

1973.15
Designer: **John Kosh**
Client: **Family**
John Kosh's concept and art told us little about this famous Family album, unless the reference is to Dick Clark's famous *American Bandstand* show that started in the days when TV sets looked like this.

1978.11
Designers: **George Hardie, Storm Thorgerson**
Client: **Thames Television**
The face of pop music as seen by Hardie and Thorgerson, ironic juxtapositions and icons put to new use in *The Beatles Story.*

opposite

1976.11
Designer: **Graham Hughes**
Client: **Goldhawke Records**
The Who's lead singer goes solo and is reincarnated as a pop centaur. Hughes' conceit reflects an increasing enthusiasm for the use of photomontage in the late seventies.

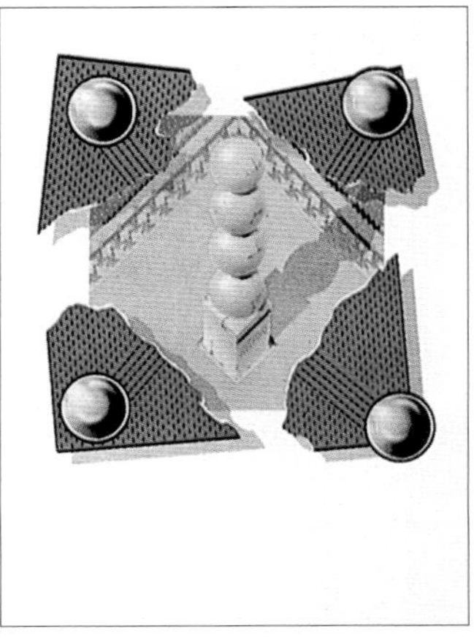

ROGER DALTREY
RIDE A ROCK HORSE
GOLDHAWKE
polydor
ON POLYDOR RECORDS & TAPES

Also prominent in music-related work was graphic designer Pearce Marchbank who, in a long association with Robert Wise, owner of the music publishing company Music Sales, produced many innovative publications, the first of which were recognized by D&AD in 1975 with his three books of John Lennon and Paul McCartney hits. Marchbank had effectively replaced John McConnell at Music Sales when McConnell was thinking of joining Pentagram, and in what was to prove a 25-year association Marchbank did much to make the music publisher's diverse product consistently distinctive.

Marchbank also became famous for his buccaneering art direction of the London listings magazine *Time Out* whose famous glowing masthead he designed and whose consistently inventive seventies front covers he usually created at the last minute in the face of dangerously tight deadlines and not inconsiderable editorial alarm. On one occasion he insisted on making an issue that contained a feature on Surrealism carry a cover which appeared to be burning away from the bottom. The 'exposed' turn page beneath was in fact a genuine facsimile of the page that was traditionally the last to go to press.

1975.11
Designer: **Pearce Marchbank**
Client: **Music Sales**
For a quarter of a century Pearce Marchbank designed innumerable sheet music book covers, folios and related material for the publisher Music Sales. Standards were high and his contribution played a significant part in the company's early success. Marchbank also helped to develop an associated imprint, Omnibus Books, for which he designed many memorable covers.

opposite

1975.12
Designer: **Pearce Marchbank**
Client: **Time Out**
To the London listings magazine *Time Out* Marchbank brought legendary clarity and impact, eschewing multiple copy lines on the cover and delivering simplicity and drama to almost every issue. Note the misspelling of 'antidote', alternative grammar being an indivisible part of the seventies' alternative press.

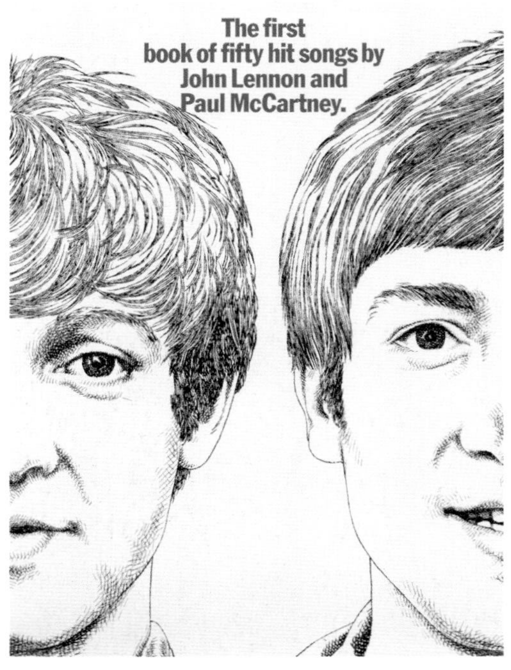

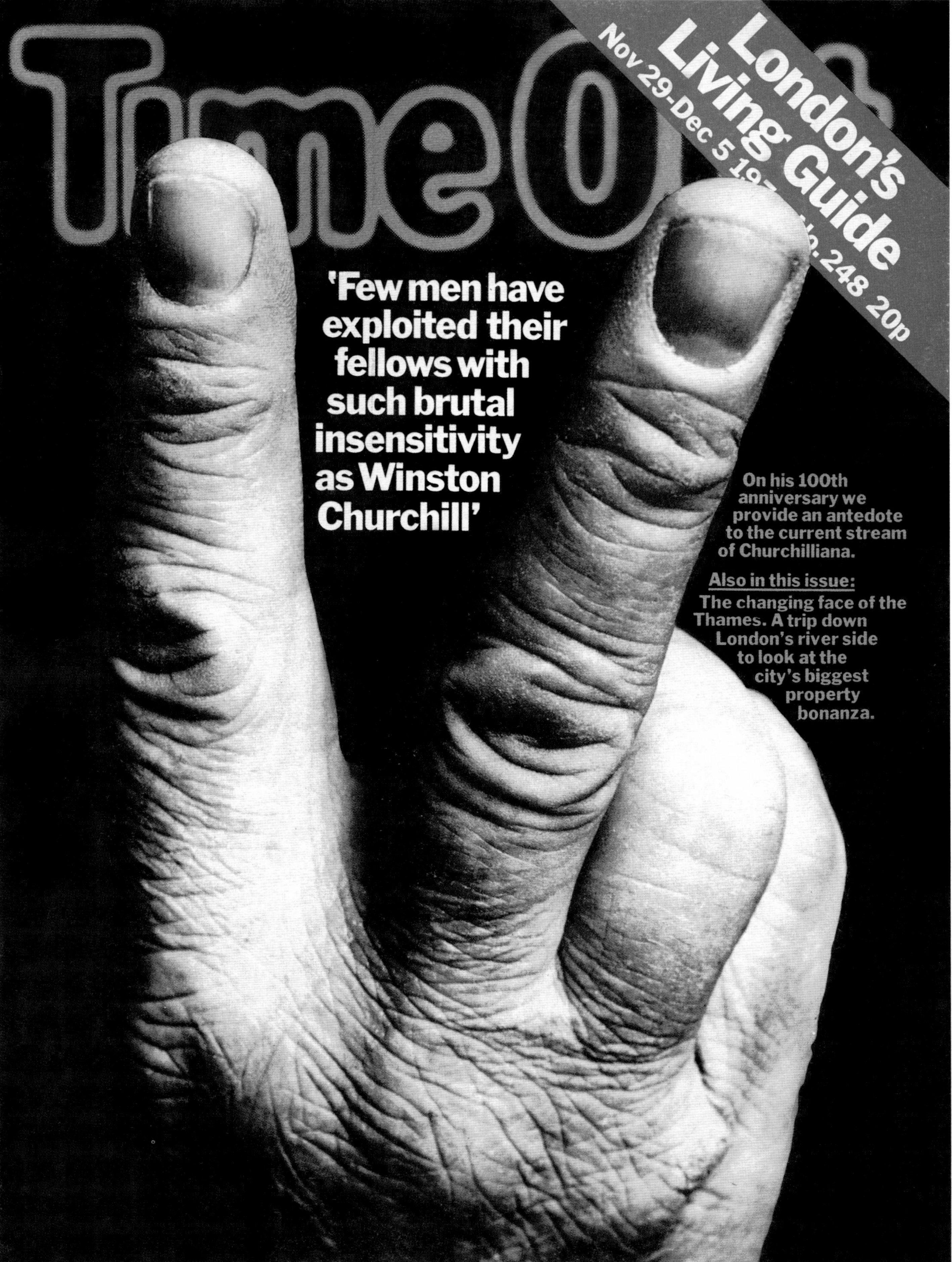
London's Living Guide
20p
'Few men have exploited their fellows with such brutal insensitivity as Winston Churchill'
On his 100th anniversary we provide an antedote to the current stream of Churchilliana.
Also in this issue:
The changing face of the Thames. A trip down London's river side to look at the city's biggest property bonanza.

Another exponent of exceptional seventies editorial design was David Driver, whose tenure at the *Radio Times* is still regarded as one of the creative high points of the magazine's long history. Once the best-selling magazine in the UK by virtue of the fact that almost everyone with a TV or radio in Britain needed to buy it to find out what was being broadcast by the virtual BBC monopoly, the *Radio Times* latterly had to face the challenge of multi-broadcaster listings which also appeared in rival magazines as well as newspapers. Attracting D&AD Awards in 1975, 1976 and 1977, editor Geoffrey Cannon and Driver, variously aided and abetted by Robert Priest and Derek Ungless, guided *Radio Times* from being a rather austere post-Reithian publication into a brisk contemporary magazine that knew it had to compete for its readership but still managed to reflect the BBC's lingering commitment to public education and information. (In fact, *Radio Times* was no longer exclusively concerned with programmes by the BBC, yet its visual character and editorial feel perpetuated the public perception that *RT* was a partisan arm of 'The Beeb'.) A *Radio Times* World Cup special supplement in 1975 won Silver, the magazine

1975.13
Art director: **David Driver**
Client: **Radio Times**
This *Radio Times* special celebrated the 1974 football World Cup with style and panache. The big portraits, strip cartoon pastiche and the newsy shots all combined with a 'listings magazine' layout to add urgency and depth to practical information.

opposite

1976.12
Art editors:
David Driver, Robert Priest
Client: **Radio Times**
Exploring a range of styles, David Driver, Robert Priest and occasionally Nigel Holmes conspired to make the *Radio Times* of the seventies at best brilliant and at worst, lively.

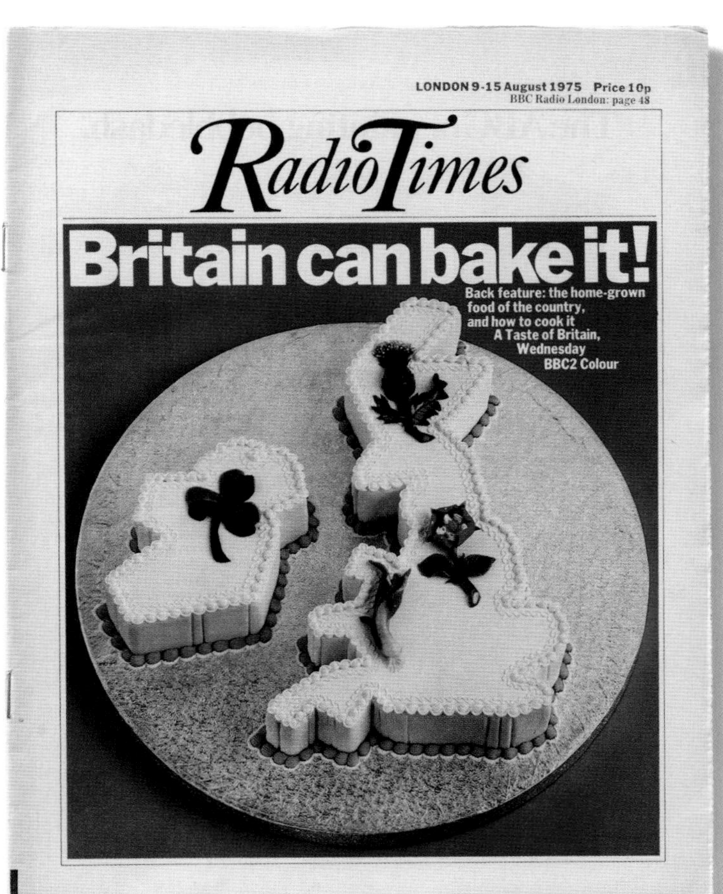
LONDON 9-15 August 1975 Price 10p
BBC Radio London: page 48
Radio Times
Britain can bake it!
Back feature: the home-grown food of the country, and how to cook it
A Taste of Britain, Wednesday
BBC2 Colour

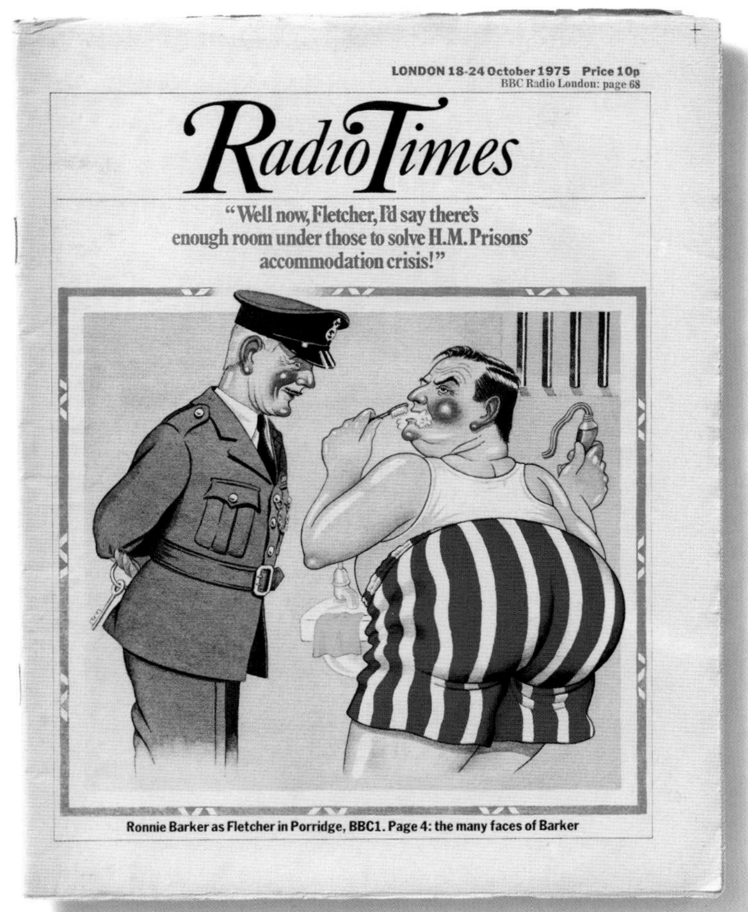
LONDON 18-24 October 1975 Price 10p
BBC Radio London: page 68
Radio Times
"Well now, Fletcher, I'd say there's enough room under those to solve H.M. Prisons' accommodation crisis!"
Ronnie Barker as Fletcher in Porridge, BBC1. Page 4: the many faces of Barker

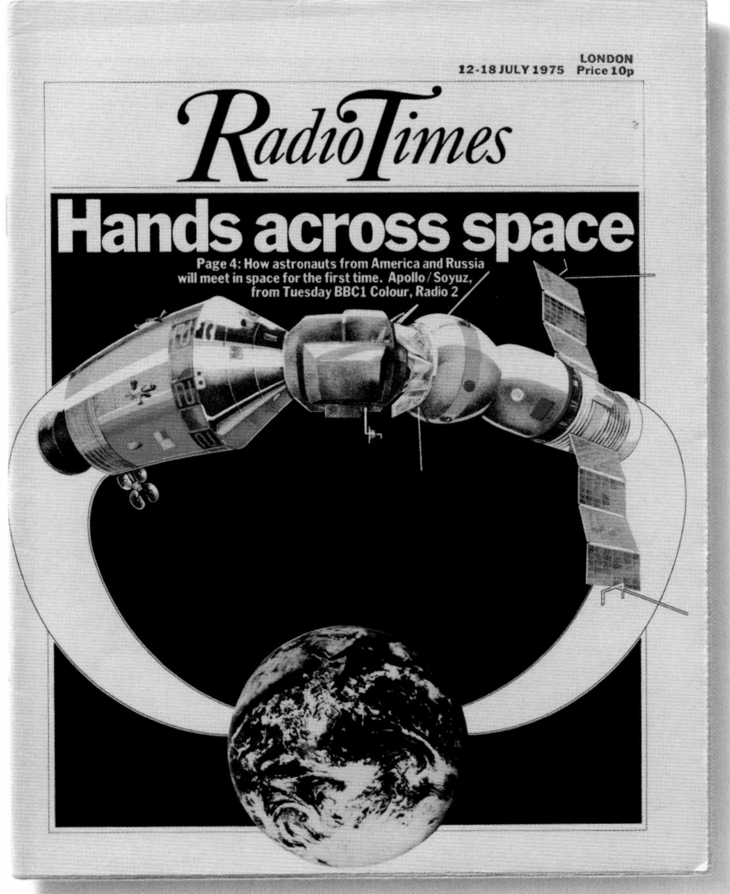
LONDON
12-18 JULY 1975 Price 10p
Radio Times
Hands across space
Page 4: How astronauts from America and Russia will meet in space for the first time. Apollo/Soyuz, from Tuesday BBC1 Colour, Radio 2

NEW YEAR SEASON ON BBC1
LONDON
11-17 January 1975 Price 8p
Radio Times
President of mirth
Back feature: Ken Dodd portrays George Robey—the Prime Minister of Mirth—and other old-time music-hall favourites in The Good Old Days
Friday BBC1 Colour

covers won Gold in 1976 and in 1977 Ralph Steadman's decidedly unheroic illustration of John Wayne for Gavin Millar's *Radio Times* article won Gold. It is some testimony to the vigour of the mid-seventies *Radio Times* that it could attract written contributions not only from Millar and Andy Warhol, but models from Fluck and Law, illustrations from Adrian George and photographs from Carl Fischer. Driver also encouraged the use of diagrammatic magazine illustration to complement television programmes that were often covering space shots and other new topics to do with new technology. For televized topics such as the Apollo/Soyuz linkup in space, Driver got illustrators Peter Brookes and Nigel Holmes to create the kind of explanatory charts that blended the comfortable feel of fifties sci-fi with something of the clarity of the best contemporary car engine maintenance manuals.

In its 70 years of existence the cinema in the United States has paid consistent homage to the Great American Hero. Be he dashing swashbuckler like Flynn's Robin Hood, Wayne's ageing Westerner with True Grit blasting his path to glory across an autumn glade, Warren Beatty's Clyde Barrow, desperate child of the Depression behind the wheel of a battered Ford, or even Tony Perkins's nervous mother-ridden youth in Psycho, the American Movie Hero is essentially an individualist. In Bicentennial week BBCtv is showing a vast line-up of movies that demonstrate this point; Gavin Millar here writes about these heroes, immortalised on celluloid

However, in terms of magazine design perhaps the most consistent talent of the first part of the decade was Michael Rand, who had started his career in 1959 at the *Daily Express* graphics department. He had become a mainstay of *The Sunday Times magazine* in the mid-sixties when the full value of the Sunday newspaper supplement was first being exploited. The possibilities of a magazine that was well-supported by advertisers and enjoyed a circulation of over a million were considerable. Suddenly, here was space and editorial freedom to explore a wide range of pictorially rich subject matter. With Rand as art director and David King as art editor, *The Sunday Times magazine* had created a newspaper-flavoured magazine in which bracing design was put to the service of news, often hard news. Certainly no news was harder than that documented by photojournalist Don McCullin whose bleak adventures made the transition into the early seventies, now offering *The Sunday Times* readers gritty visual commentaries on Northern Ireland in the same spirit as his Vietnamese and Cambodian *verité* essays. Running against the trend elsewhere, it was in the first part of the decade that Rand's vision for *The Sunday Times magazine* was at its most abrasive. It was only when the rest of the media was waking up to the global

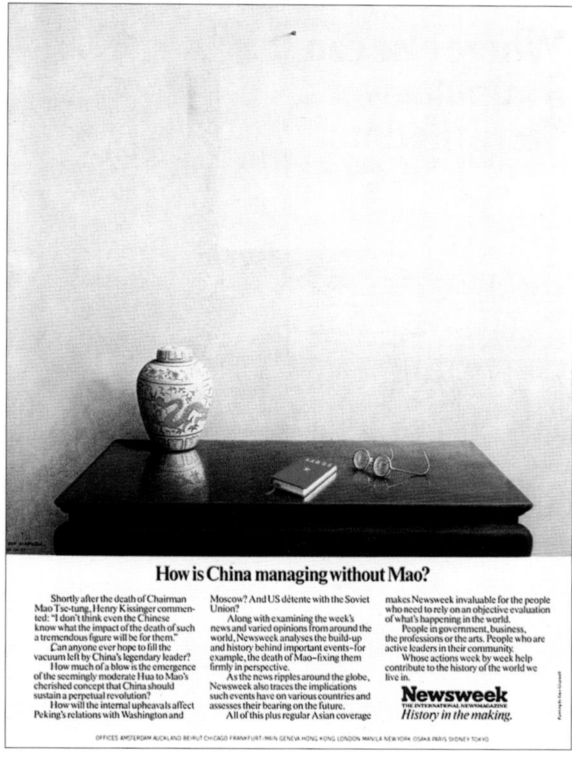

How is China managing without Mao?
Shortly after the death of Chairman Mao Tse-tung, Henry Kissinger commented: "I don't think even the Chinese know what the impact of the death of such a tremendous figure will be for them."
Can anyone ever hope to fill the vacuum left by China's legendary leader?
How much of a blow is the emergence of the seemingly moderate Hua to Mao's cherished concept that China should sustain a perpetual revolution?
How will the internal upheavals affect Peking's relations with Washington and Moscow? And US détente with the Soviet Union?
Along with examining the week's news and varied opinions from around the world, Newsweek analyses the build-up and history behind important events–for example, the death of Mao–fixing them firmly in perspective.
As the news ripples around the globe, Newsweek also traces the implications such events have on various countries and assesses their bearing on the future.
All of this plus regular Asian coverage makes Newsweek invaluable for the people who need to rely on an objective evaluation of what's happening in the world.
People in government, business, the professions or the arts. People who are active leaders in their community.
Whose actions week by week help contribute to the history of the world we live in.
Newsweek
THE INTERNATIONAL NEWSMAGAZINE
History in the making.
OFFICES AMSTERDAM AUCKLAND BEIRUT CHICAGO FRANKFURT/MAIN GENEVA HONG KONG LONDON MANILA NEW YORK OSAKA PARIS SYDNEY TOKYO

uncertainties triggered by the oil crisis in the mid-seventies, that *The Sunday Times* at last softened its approach, finally listening to the dissenting voices that had always maintained that people did not necessarily want bloody images of war as a side dish to their most relaxing breakfast of the week. Editor Magnus Linklater left and *The Sunday Times magazine* increasingly became a 'lifestyle' magazine that flattered its readers rather than unsettling their consciences. There was, however, to be a further legacy of the influence of Rand and Driver. In the heyday of the Sunday magazines (and many others mimicked *The Sunday Times*' formula, at home and abroad) the parent newspapers had remained much the same. Gradually though, they also began to absorb many of the innovative visual ideas of the magazines. *The Sunday Times weekend review* was shaped by Rand and David Hillman while Driver, fresh from the *Radio Times,* was appointed design director of *The Times Saturday review.*

1977.20
Art editors:
David Driver, Robert Priest
Client: **Radio Times**
One of the more memorable *Radio Times* features. Although radical youth had long questioned John Wayne's status, Steadman's hostile caricature was one of the first to display visceral hatred in a mainstream publication.

1978.12
Art director: **David Litchfield**
Client: **Ritz**
Ritz was a fashion and style publication with marked similarities to *Interview*. It bore its principals' names above the masthead and achieved a degree of success that was due more to its visual style than its content.

this page

1978.13
Agency: **TBWA**
Client: **Newsweek International**
This *Newsweek* ad ran to publicize an issue covering the implications of Chairman Mao's death, and was awarded Gold for its illustration by Guy Gladwell.

1970.14
Art director: **Michael Rand**
Client: **The Sunday Times magazine**
The benign father of his country pictured standing on a bit of it. The *faux* naive portrait is all the more unsettling for being transplanted into a sophisticated publication.

THE SUNDAY TIMES *magazine*
DECEMBER 19, 1971
WAR ON THE HOME FRONT
By Donald McCullin

THE SIEGE OF DERRY

Photographs by **Donald McCullin.** Eve since the Great Siege of 1689, Londonderry has been a focal point for Northern Ireland's turbulent history: and it is there that the present complex crisis can be seen in al its tragic intensity. Above: dismayed housewives watch from their Georgian doorways as soldiers of the Royal Anglian Regiment – dressed for battle like Samurai warrior – charge down William Street after an outbreak of stoning. Cover: a boy arrested by a 'snatch-squad' of the Royal Greenjackets

12 13

14 Londonderry Catholics escape over a wall from an attack of CS gas in a burnt-out sorting office at the Little Diamond. Some now have a slight immunity to the gas, and taunt the soldiers: "Give us more, it makes our hair grow!" They have a current joke that the crisis in Bogside is producing Olympic athletes 15

22 Royal Anglian soldiers detain a Catholic boy for searching. Derry is a desolate place littered with broken stones, betting-shops and pubs. Owners of burnt-down property are compensated, so for some people living in Bogside it is almost desirable to be bombed as normal business in the town has more or less ceased● 23

16 A scene of jubilation at the Little Diamond. This and the corner of William and Rossville Streets (known as 'Aggro Corner') are the most lively areas

A sergeant-major of the Anglians, hit in the head during a William Street affray. Missiles include paving-stones, milk-bottles and pieces of slate 17

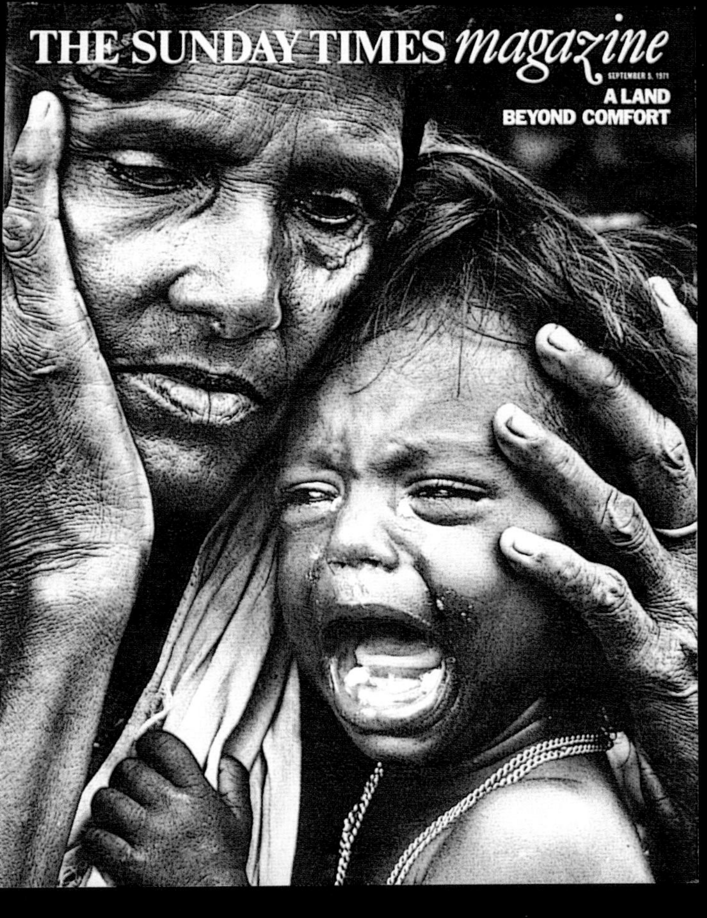
THE SUNDAY TIMES magazine
SEPTEMBER 5, 1971
A LAND
BEYOND COMFORT

AND STILL THEY RUN
The unabated misery of West Bengal photographed by Donald McCullin

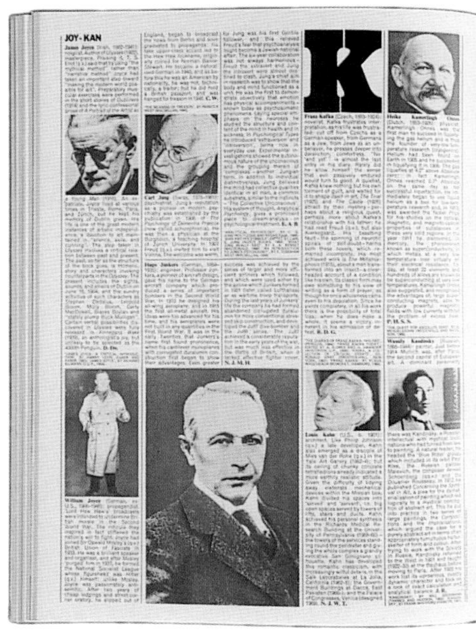

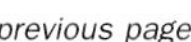

previous page

1972.20
Art director: **Michael Rand**
Client: **The Sunday Times magazine**
Don McCullin had started out shooting pictures of petty violent confrontations on the streets of his home town. Obsessively drawn to conflict, he went on to photograph foreign wars with what seemed like almost suicidal dedication, but in the early seventies he returned to chronicle a shabby war closer to home. His stark pictures of the Northern Ireland 'troubles' at times made a seemingly endless thuggish feud look almost heroic.

opposite

1972.21
Art director: **Michael Rand**
Client: **The Sunday Times magazine**
McCullin went to West Bengal to take the pictures that needed few words, 'A Land Beyond Comfort'. The designer on the article was Gilvrie Misstear.

this page

1970.15
Art director: **Michael Rand**
Client: **The Sunday Times magazine**
One thousand makers of the twentieth century was the ambitious catalogue that Rand commissioned in a classic bid to keep readers buying next week's issue.

As the seventies moved into its final phase, one dazzling piece of television work was honoured with a Silver Award in 1978. Pat Gavin's opening credits for *The South Bank Show*, a London Weekend Television (LWT) arts programme helmed by Melvyn Bragg, were to prove a timely reminder that the BBC's self-appointed monopoly on educating the public was now breached. Admittedly, the ratings-chasing LWT could claim little else in the way of significant arts programming, but *The South Bank Show* and its credits reflected a new and accessible approach to dealing with culture on TV.

Throughout much of the seventies the TV critic Clive James had been using his *Observer* column to publicize his conviction that high and low culture need not – and indeed should not – be seen as separate and mutually exclusive things. Melvyn Bragg took the same view and launched *The South Bank Show* with the express intention of dealing with a serious author one week, a film star the next, then a cartoonist or a sculptor or a film director.

Gavin's opening montage for the programme brilliantly caught this mischievous sense of pluralism in a breathless sequence of drawn images that lingered barely long enough to be recognized before they metamorphosed again (Beethoven, Monroe, Toulouse Lautrec...), all to a suitably eclectic Andrew Lloyd Webber score. Resembling an animated version of Peter Blake's cover for *Sergeant Pepper's Lonely Heart's Club Band* in 1967, this title sequence encapsulated and united the diversity of creative achievement, both serious and playful. The anchoring image was the touching fingers detail from Michelangelo's *Creation of Adam*.

This title sequence has been updated many times (since receiving a Gold Award in 1979), retaining the original logic and always a version of the touching fingers image. An oblique endorsement of this use of the image for a popular arts programme can be found in one of Alan Bennett's *Talking Heads* monologues, 'The Hand of God'. In it, an antique shop owner – a culture snob who loathes the populist *Antiques Road Show* and refuses to watch TV on principle – is gulled into parting with what she believes to be a worthless little drawing in a frame. When it turns out to be a priceless Michelangelo sketch for the touching fingers detail of the *Creation of Adam*, a friend observes that it is a pity she never watched TV 'because they use it on *The South Bank Show* and she might have recognized it'.

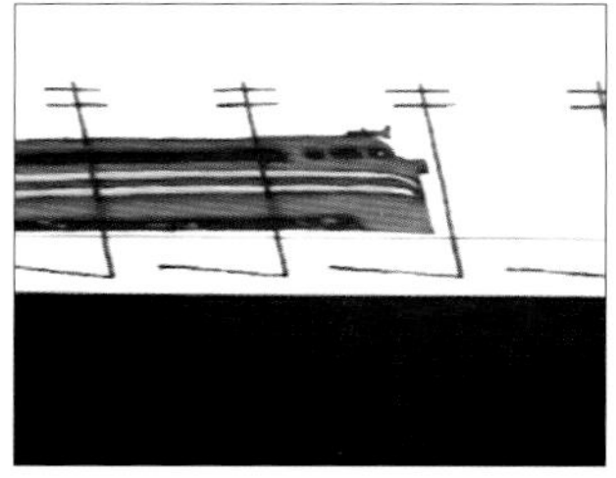

1974.12
Director: **Pat Gavin**
Client: **Amberson Video**
Trouble in Tahiti was a strange and flawed little opera begun by Leonard Bernstein in the early fifties and alleged to be a portrait of his unconvivial parents. Pat Gavin's direction of this animated version won Gold.

this page

1978.14
Director: **Pat Gavin**
Client: **London Weekend Television**
Michelangelo's famous image had already been pressed into service for the opening credits of the 1959 film of *Ben-Hur*. Gavin gave the same detail an irreverent spin that has now defined *The South Bank Show* arts programme for nearly 30 years.

1979.10
Director: **Pat Gavin**
Client: **London Weekend Television**
Following up his Silver Award the previous year, Gavin shared Gold in 1979 with set designer Michael Turney for 'television design and programme identity in which titles, set design and art direction become one unit.'

The South Bank Show's opening sequence of morphing cultural heroes may have changed over the years, but the basic trick is always to make the faces change almost too fast to recognize, and to go for unlikely segues such as Elvis Presley into Leonardo da Vinci.

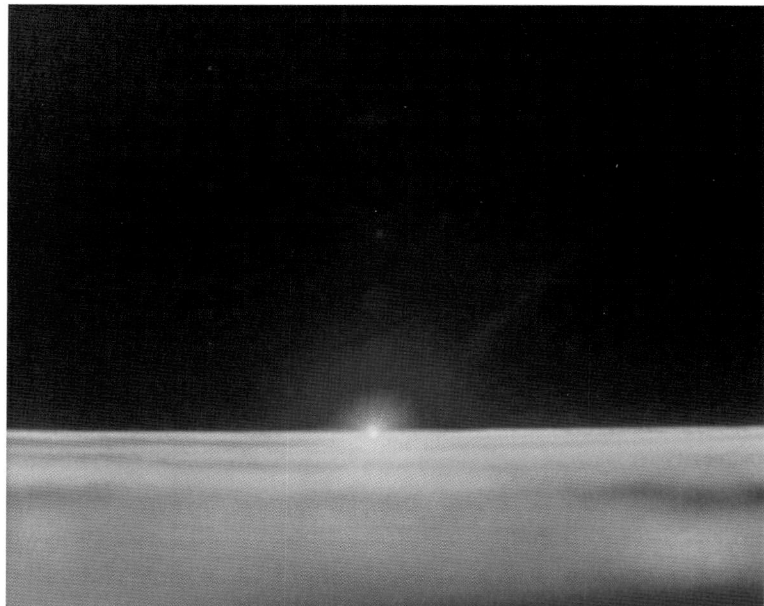

 1979.11
Director: **Roger Kennedy**
Client: **BBC Television**
Horizon has been BBC2's flagship science documentary series for nearly 40 years. Roger Kennedy's rather literal opening titles gave the late seventies season a dramatic start.

1974.13
Director: **George Dunning**
Client: **The Righteous Apple**
Canadian animator and director George Dunning had already directed the film *Yellow Submarine* before winning a Gold for this short animated film.

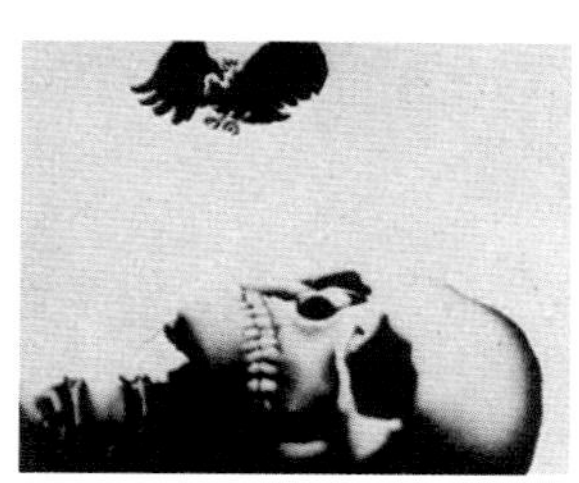

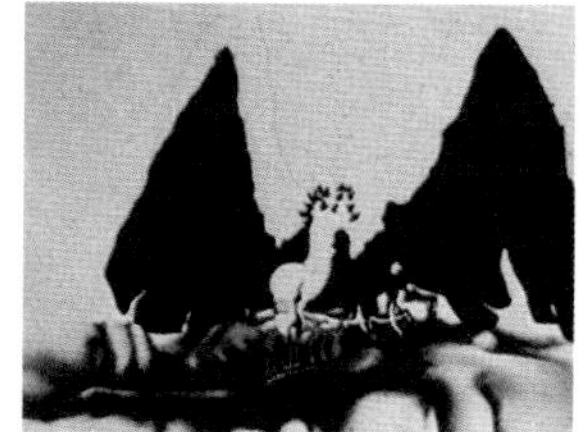

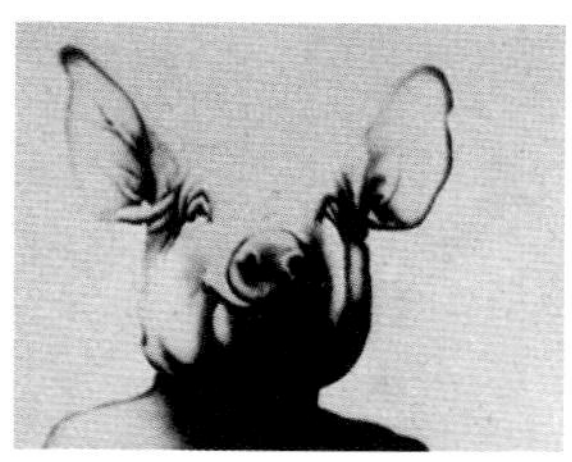

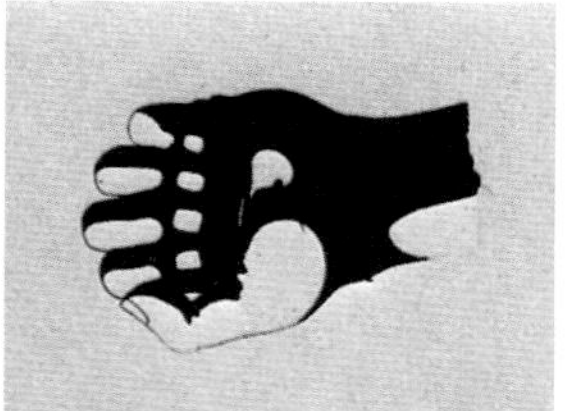

1974.14
Graphic designers:
John Stamp, Ian Kestle
Client: **Thames Television**
Stamp and Kestle produced these inflammable opening titles for producer Jeremy Isaacs' much-acclaimed 26-hour series, *The World at War.* The first programme, *A New Germany*, was transmitted in October 1973.

1978.15
Director: **Pauline Talbot**
Client: **BBC Television Sports Department**
These live-action titles for the BBC's long-running football fixture brought something like big production values to the sort of programme that once had to make do with wobbly Letraset captions.

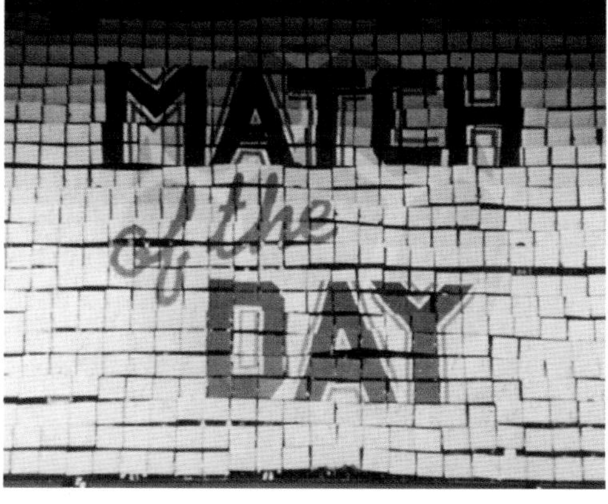

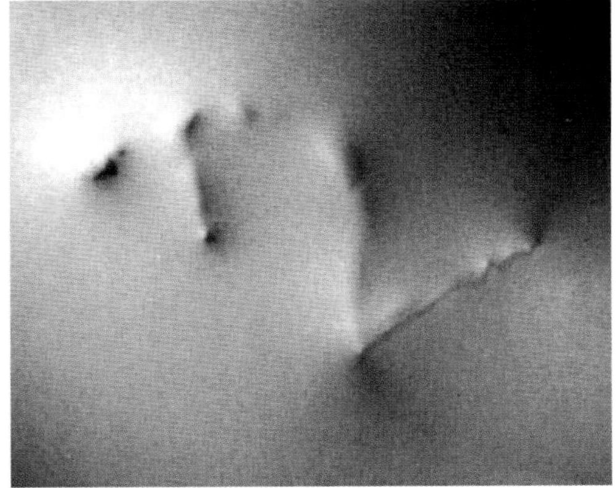

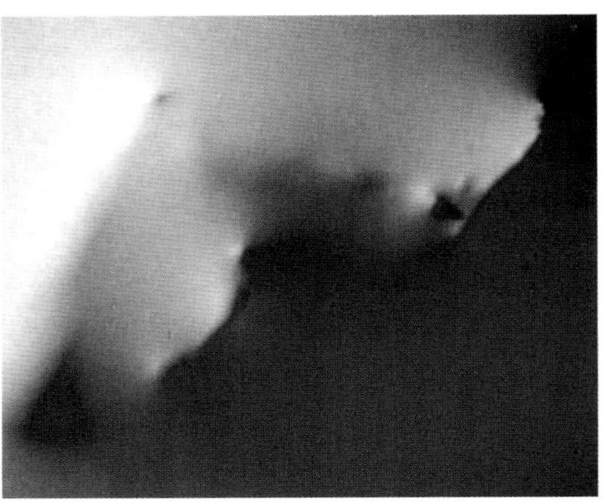

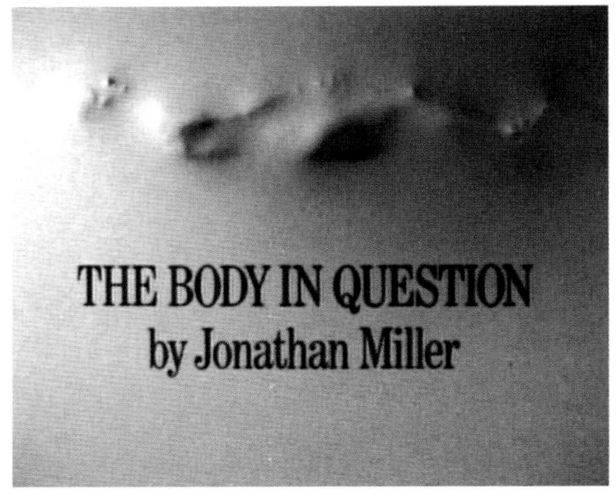

1977.21
Director: **Bernard Lodge**
Client: **BBC Television**
This BBC *Playhouse* series is long forgotten but Lodge's unsettling rostrum images of faces only partially seen retain their impact.

1979.12
Director: **Charles McGhie**
Client: **BBC Television**
Hypnotic viewing at the time, Dr Miller's fearless plunge into human viscera spawned a best-selling book and was heralded each week by eerie images of a human body apparently trapped behind a flexible white membrane.

1978.16
Photographer: **Lord Snowdon**
Client: **The Sunday Times magazine**
Soon after this photo essay, Lord Snowdon set up the Snowdon Award Scheme, providing grants to students with physical disabilities in further and higher education or training.

Also in 1978, and as evidence of how *The Sunday Times magazine* was by now bringing a different sort of photographic feature to the Sunday morning breakfast table, Lord Snowdon's 'Love and Affection' photo essay, subtitled 'A new future for the mentally handicapped' won a D&AD Silver Award. Rand was still art directing, Gilvrie Misstear was the designer and the tone was one of social concern without either sentimentality or discomfort.

In the *Radio Times* satire and edge were surfacing more often via Ralph Steadman's increasingly acerbic drawings of everything from politicians to Australian cricketers. A sublime draughtsman, Steadman, by the end of the seventies, seemed to be taking on more and more subject matter that allowed his cataclysmic trademark blots and pen scratches to suggest blood and laceration. Modelmakers Peter Fluck and Roger Law were also making steady progress – from their witty three-dimensional caricatures usually created for editorial illustration purposes towards the vitriolic puppets that would soon inhabit TV's *Spitting Image*.

LOVE AND AFFECTION
A new future for the mentally handicapped
THE SUNDAY TIMES magazine

UNLOCKING THE DOORS

A round-up of the advertising work featured in the last D&AD Annual of the seventies reveals that DDB was still creating witty ads for Volkswagen, Saatchi's was still trying to help The Health Education Council to raise awareness about unwanted pregnancies, Heineken was still reaching parts inaccessible to others, and while the 'surreal' Benson & Hedges campaign was still flourishing, it was an ironic variation by Hall Advertising for the Scottish Health Education Unit that won a Silver Award in 1979. This time the pack became a coffin laid in a still open grave. The copy line was 'Why do you think every packet carries a government health warning?'

But perhaps the final comment on the seventies came from the advertising agency that began the decade with even more confidence than CDP. By 1979 it was called Saatchi & Saatchi Garland-Compton,

1979.13
Agency: **Hall Advertising**
Client: **Scottish Health Education Unit**
This poster was a double-edged attack on public ignorance about the risks of smoking, and also on the ads that tried to make Benson & Hedges cigarettes seem glamorous.

1979.14
Agency: **Saatchi & Saatchi Garland-Compton**
Client: **The Health Education Council**
And so the decade ended much as it had begun, with a Saatchi team doing their best to help the government stop people from acting irresponsibly.

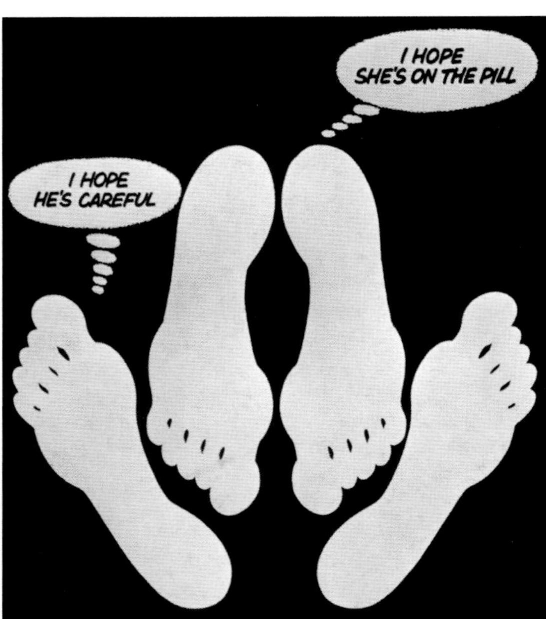

□ 1979.15
Agency: **Saatchi & Saatchi Garland-Compton**
Client: **Conservative Central Office**
The poster that helped sink Old Labour. It would not have been so devastating had it not been rooted in some sort of truth. Certainly the Labour Party that finally regained power under Tony Blair bore little resemblance to the one that Margaret Thatcher vanquished when this image dominated the billboards in 1979.

and what would arguably be its most famous ad ever was created in the form of a poster for the Conservative Party, the party that had lost the nation's trust so badly in the mid-seventies. The poster showed a snaking line of people stretching from an 'unemployment office' to infinity below the headline 'Labour isn't working'. At a stroke, it managed to suggest disappointment in a failed experiment and confirmation of an old prejudice that Labour policies always resulted in unemployment. By personifying the abstract statistics it made the person looking at the poster feel as though he or she might soon be joining that queue. It worked, and it is no exaggeration to say that Margaret Thatcher's victory owed no small debt to Saatchi's brilliantly effective poster. Anyone who might still be resisting the idea that advertising was an important force in society could resist it no longer.

Last word on the 1970s
John Webster

The gate was open. It had been unlocked by The Beatles, The Rolling Stones, Mary Quant, David Hockney, David Bailey, and Michael Caine in the sixties. A new iconoclasm had rejuvenated the theatre and cinema. The old conservative order seemed banished forever. A new breed of working-class hero replaced the old boy network, and a posh accent, previously a guarantee of success, became an object of derision.

It was a time of great optimism compared to today's cynicism and disillusionment. Anything seemed possible. Pop and the young had an unprecedented influence. Good ideas found backers, creativity flourished. Tom Wolfe painted with words. John Lennon was a walrus. Clothes became a mode of expression and exploded in a dandyish myriad of colours, textures and shapes. Hair became big – recorded for posterity in the wonderful D&AD Annual jury photos of the time.

We listened to Abba, The Jackson Five and the Bee Gees. We were scared by *The Godfather*, laughed at *Annie Hall* and flew over The Cuckoo's Nest. Beeching made his rail cuts and Nadia Cominec got a perfect ten.

These were heady times to be in the media and a fresh generation of talent nurtured in the sixties started to change the status quo in agencies, design groups, magazines and film production companies. In advertising, London embarked on what is now recognized as its Golden Age.

Up to that time the British advertising scene had been pretty spineless. All the great stuff had been happening over the pond. Each year we used to pore jealously over the New York Art Directors Annuals – our only access to it – marvelling at the latest exploits of Bill Bernbach, David Ogilvy, Mary Wells and Ed McCabe *et al.* VW's 'The Snowplough', Avis's 'We try Harder', Braniff's 'If you've got it flaunt it', Horn and Hardart's (a chain of cheap New York restaurants with bare décor) 'You can't eat an Atmosphere' and many more. It was brilliant work – on another plane to what was happening in the UK.

Things at last started looking up when Doyle Dane Bernbach opened up a London office, recruited a young and burgeoning writer called David Abbott and started producing witty American-style ads, notably for VW, for the British market. But the revolution was really kick-started by CDP's Colin Millward who gathered a prodigious array of young talent around him with names like Charles Saatchi, Alan Parker and David Puttnam to produce the first great work in the UK that owed nothing to the Americans.

For the next ten years they produced a wonderful series of press and TV ads full of British sensibility and humour that caught the public imagination, won all the awards and changed the face of British advertising. The Hovis delivery lad's epic journey up the hill. Tony Brignull and Neil Godfrey's classic print series for Birds Eye and Parker Pens with erudite copy and art direction, as if done by God. John Salmon's work for Dunns and the Metropolitan Police. Hamlet Cigar's simple formula for happiness that ran for years. The B&H gold box campaign foisting surrealism on an unsuspecting British public. The operatic Fiat robots and Terry Lovelock's infamous 'Refreshes the Parts' for Heineken. It was a thrilling list of work from one source that surely will never be bettered.

Much of the talent that passed through CDP subsequently became famous while Millward, a publicity-shy northerner, remained unknown to the general public. Advertising was still regarded as rather a dishonourable trade in those days and attracted little media interest. Today he would probably be celebrated in tabloid, broadsheet, and on *The South Bank Show*.

Nevertheless, Colin Millward won D&AD's President Award in 1976 and became a legend in the business – the stories abound. One of my favourites is about the young account man who returned to Colin's office to tell him the client had turned down one of his ads and he'd agreed with him. Colin, reading his newspaper, didn't say a word. After an uncomfortable silence the account man enquired what were they going to do? Colin's dour northern tones came from behind his paper, 'You're just going to have to pop back again and tell them you're sorry but you made a mistake.'

Encouraged by CDP, other 'hot shops' sprouted up and started flexing their muscles. BMP entertained the UK with a whole series of TV brand properties. The irresistible Smash Martians, the iconoclastic Cresta Bear, The Humphries who stole your milk, Arkwright and his friend in their flat Yorkshire caps and the ebullient Sugar Puffs Honey Monster.

Charlie Saatchi left his copywriting job at CDP to start first a consultancy then a full agency. His recruits included a young Jeremy Sinclair and a precocious blonde-haired ex-London College of Printing student called John Hegarty. From the moment his audacious launch proclamation hit the national press, Charlie was flying.

I remember being astonished when trying to hire Sinclair and his art director Bill Atherton, at learning how little Charlie was paying them and promptly offered them twice as much to come to BMP. At first they agreed but a few days before their start date Jeremy rang to say they'd changed their minds. Oh well, I thought with satisfaction, at least I made Charlie put his hand in his pocket. I learned later that this was wishful thinking. He'd actually told them he was devastated by their disloyalty and how he'd based the entire future of his company on their talent – producing real tears. The result was they agreed to stay for the same money! I thought, this man will go far.

His agency went on to grow irrepressibly through the decade, creating the iconic 'Pregnant Man' and 'Fly on your food' posters for the Health Education Council plus a whole raft of hard-hitting work for anti-smoking, Jaffa grapefruit, Brutus Jeans and the Conservative Party, culminating in 1979 with Andrew Rutherford's infamous 'Labour isn't Working' that helped gain an election victory for the Tories and launch the country into the Thatcher era.

Charlie's arrogant boast of becoming the largest agency in the world suddenly didn't look so fatuous and indeed he and his brother were to achieve just that in the next decade, turning the company name into an international household word and gaining a knighthood for their original media director Tim Bell.

David Abbott, who'd continued putting his case for the title of Britain's best copywriter with little masterpieces for Chivas Regal, and VW's outrageous Marty Feldman ad, joined Peter Mead and Adrian Vickers to form the fledgling Abbott Mead Vickers. Almost immediately great work for Volvo and Sony gave a foretaste of things to come.

Elsewhere, a pre-Provence Peter Mayle was doing smart stuff for Harrods at PKL, a restless Al Tilby flared wherever he went and writers Tim Delaney, Paul Weiland and Dave Trott cut their teeth at BMP and CDP. This outpouring of talent inevitably shook up the whole advertising scene and had some of the older established agencies with long-standing clients looking enviously over their shoulders. Even the four-square JWT joined in the fun with a memorable TV campaign for Guinness. Its brilliant 'Instant Guinness' press spoof had me and the nation dipping our newspapers fruitlessly into bowls of water on April 1st.

Up to the seventies commercial film production had been appalling in the UK, with crude lighting, cheap sets and dreadful acting, and directed by ex-feature men who were ashamed to be involved in the first place. The only way agency producers could get anything of quality was to bring over the Americans. But that began to change as a new surge of talent infiltrated existing companies or started up on their own. One of the first start-ups was Brooks Baker Fulford, a combo of the two successful stills photographers Bob Brooks and Len Fulford with Jim Baker, an experienced producer. They brought their refined lighting techniques, honed in stills, to the screen in early films for CDP and BMP.

CDP's Alan Parker abandoned copywriting to take up directing. (I remember when he told me I advised him he'd never make a director, he was a writer – how wrong can you be?) Parker brought a new earthiness and humanity to commercials like those for Birds Eye and Heinz and revolutionized casting. His films were full of real people with sticky-out ears and untidy hair as opposed to the prim smiling housewives and male models we'd had up till then. His work developed at a pace through the decade and would eventually lead to Hollywood and international fame.

Ridley Scott, a gruff Geordie, graduated from the Royal College of Art and the BBC to put some electrifying stuff on film. His sweeping camerawork and dramatic visual sense turned CDP's Benson & Hedges scripts into mini-epics for the small screen and his work was never less than spectacular. A workaholic, he revelled in his power behind the camera and vowed to follow his hero Picasso's example – 'when he was eighty he was still smoking, still drinking, still making love and died with a paintbrush in his hand.' Ridley, too, was destined for great things in Hollywood.

Playing Raphael to Ridley's Michelangelo was old Etonian Hugh Hudson. Largely influenced by the classic Italian cinema of Michelangelo Antonioni and Luchino Visconti, his films had a sophistication and an elegance that lifted his commercials into another class. His painterly bucolic pieces for Dubonnet transformed what must have looked very ordinary scripts on the page. CDP was again quick to steal him and, in combination with art director Alan Waldie, Hudson shot in a desert in Arizona what must be one of the most stunning commercials of all time – the hypnotic 'Swimming Pool' for Benson & Hedges.

In photography, Lester Bookbinder snapped majestically at white horses for whisky and Don McCullin crawled along Irish streets to bring us gruelling images of the conflict. *The Sunday Times magazine* consistently provided fresh and irreverent photo-journalism under the influence of Michael Rand. In design, Michael Peters' packaging brought a breath of fresh air to our shelves and Pentagram spread its stylish influence from graphics to architecture.

Yes, things were buzzing. The seventies were confident times, when the atmosphere was right and a plethora of talent was there to take advantage. While the rest of the planet was aghast at Watergate and a newly decimalized Britain struggled under Prime Ministers Edward Heath, Harold Wilson and James Callaghan, in the world of communication we shook our tail feathers to the chimes of Abba and had a ball.

198
POSH

The eighties was a time marked by complexity and contradiction in design and advertising in Britain. The complexity was primarily due to the transformation of the business structure of the communication industry. This was the decade in which British designers lost their commercial virginity while advertising agencies developed international agency networks to match the global aspirations of their clients.

The contradictions owed much to the special cultural climate of the times after Saatchi's 'Labour isn't working' campaign had helped the Conservatives win power in 1979. The monetarist economic policies of Margaret Thatcher's government during the eighties created an environment of raw entrepreneurialism and visible social inequality that was an affront to many of the traditional utopian values of designers and art directors – but it also assisted the rapid expansion of the design and advertising sectors.

The eighties in Britain thus presented a picture of design and advertising revelling in a kind of schizophrenic glory as they grew in commercial power and social influence, completing their journeys from the margins of public acceptability to the heart of popular culture. This was the decade of *Spitting Image*, Next, the Channel 4 logo and Pet Shop Boys album sleeves; of Holsten Pils spoofs, 'Hello Tosh Gotta Toshiba?' and Levi's 'Launderette' in the TV commercial breaks; of *The Face*, *The World of Interiors* and a new national newspaper, *The Independent*, on the newsstands. It was a time of restless innovation and vaulting ambition in all areas of design and advertising.

As British society lurched into conspicuous consumption, replacing punks with yuppies and crèches with cappuccino bars as part of its evolving iconography, brand images, advertising messages and designer shops reflected its decisive changes in increasingly sophisticated ways. From the high street and the workplace to the living room, many things changed forever. The self-styled Big Bang that specifically signalled financial deregulation in the City of London could be applied right across the board.

1985.01
Graphic designer: **Brian Becker**
Client: **Central Independent Television**
Spitting Image, a satirical TV programme featuring the talents of caricaturists Peter Fluck and Roger Law, caught the irreverent social and political mood of eighties Britain right on the button. The opening credits set up the premise of the series superbly with its innovative mix of live action library footage, traditional puppeteering skills, optical and early digital effects.

Spitting Image seeped into people's consciousness and affected political reputations – usually for the worse. Liberal politician David Steele, who was continually portrayed as a tiny and ineffective puppet in the Liberal-Social Democrat alliance, came off badly, although Margaret Thatcher's image as mad, bad and vicious appeared to do her no harm at all.

SPITTING
IMAGE

1988.01
Design group: **Stanton Williams**
Client: **Issey Miyake**
Architects Stanton Williams brought impeccable modernist credentials to this project, a London store for Japan's most famous fashion designer. The result: a flagship of minimalist style which was much publicized and widely imitated in the late eighties as the decorative design excesses of earlier in the decade were forgotten.

opposite

1985.02
Agency: **Boase Massimi Pollitt Univas**
Client: **Greater London Council**
This campaign by Peter Gatley and John Pallant merrily cross-referred newspaper readers to different ads on different pages in a powerful exposition of how maddening bureaucracy would be if Whitehall, rather than Ken Livingstone's Greater London Council, ran London.

1988.02
Photographer: **Sebastião Salgado**
Client: **The Sunday Times magazine**
Shocking and unforgettable photographic imagery from South America offered a throwback to *The Sunday Times magazine* in its consciousness-raising heyday. Also, as western consumer society experienced a boom in the late eighties, it reminded readers over breakfast that working life was very different in other parts of the world.

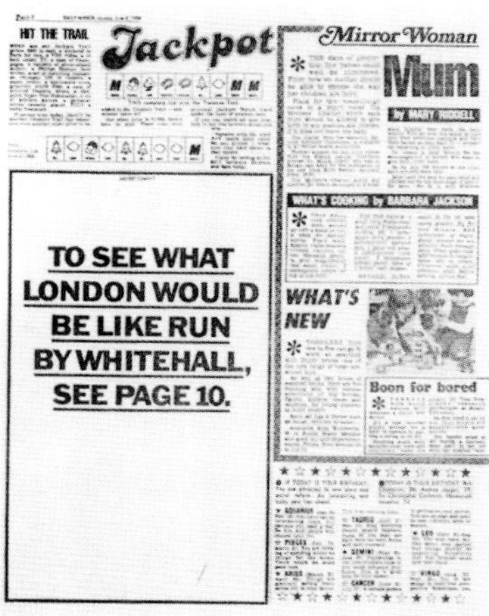

But the eighties was also the decade climaxed by UK tragedies in the form of the King's Cross tube fire, the Hillsborough soccer stadium tragedy and the Townsend Thoreson ferry disaster – a time of stark contrast between private affluence and public squalor, between bond dealers in red braces and rate-capped (and cash-strapped) local authorities. The D&AD Awards of the decade captured the mind-blowing contrariness of it all. In one year – 1985 – Boase Massimi Pollitt's (BMP) brilliantly defiant press and poster campaign to save Ken Livingstone's Greater London Council (GLC) from abolition at the hands of the Thatcher government shared the limelight with an air-headed video animation for Paul McCartney's 'Frog Chorus', hardly the moptop's finest hour.

In 1988, D&AD gave a Gold Award to Issey Miyake's minimalist fashion temple, designed by architects Stanton Williams at the height of chic consumerism, while simultaneously rewarding photographer Sebastião Salgado's harrowing images of the swarms of gold seekers in the Amazon in a *Sunday Times magazine* feature entitled 'In the Hellhole'. From a few expensive designer clothes to thousands of naked slaves scrabbling up a muddy hillside, D&AD was capable of covering the full gamut of emotions in a single awards night.

IN THE HELLHOLE

A great pit lies in the Amazon jungle. Over its sodden floor and walls men swarm in purgatorial torment, laden like beasts and sometimes dying like them. Gold-lust drives them on. Photographs by Sebastião Salgado. Report by Robert Tyrer

It could bite the hand that fed it. David Bailey's famously vicious 'Dumb Animals' cinema commercial for Greenpeace, which won a D&AD Gold in 1986, turned the conventional glamour of the catwalk right on its bloody head ('It takes up to 40 dumb animals to make a fur coat. But only one to wear it'). Indeed, there was a certain paradox in the communication industry advancing image-making techniques to take escapism and fantasy to new heights while simultaneously telling it how it really was. The eighties dealt in ever-more-alluring dreams, hinting at a new sexual landscape that would emerge in the decade that followed, while offering some of the most biting social satire and powerful charity and public service campaigns ever seen in Britain.

Advertising agencies quickly seized the opportunities presented by deregulation, by new competition ushered into all corners of the public realm, by the direct assault of state protectionism and the trade union closed shop. As new magazines, TV channels and other media flourished, the ad industry grew rich and powerful with great speed – to the point at which the financial press in the late eighties could seriously speculate about an advertising agency (Saatchi & Saatchi) buying a high-street financial institution (Midland Bank).

⧫ 1986.01
Agency: **The Yellowhammer Company**
Client: **Greenpeace**
The creative industry turned out in force to offer services for free for Greenpeace's anti-fur campaign. David Bailey was a clever choice to film this vicious piece of work from Yellowhammer's Alan Page and Jeremy Pemberton, having graduated from photography to film. The catwalk set was designed by modelmaker Gerry Judah, who contributed many brilliant sets and special effects in the eighties.

Until this point, Yellowhammer had been regarded as a bit of a design shop by the eighties advertising establishment. The name Yellowhammer pre-dated nineties agency names such as Mother and St Lukes, and in many ways, as this simple but powerful commercial shows, pre-dated their no holds barred sensationalist styles.

It didn't quite happen, but when former Saatchi finance director Martin Sorrell set up the WPP Group in 1986 by taking over a public company shell, Wire and Plastic Products, the world's largest publicly quoted design and advertising conglomerate certainly did. WPP would go on to acquire agency giants J Walter Thompson (JWT) and Ogilvy & Mather (O&M) as well as a clutch of leading design firms, as the British communication industry marched triumphantly down Madison Avenue where once it had simply looked up in awe.

Meanwhile, British design, a fragmented and craft-based cottage industry throughout the seventies, enjoyed unprecedented political and business patronage. If design consultants had entered the eighties hanging on the coat tails of the business world, by a thread in some cases, they found themselves wearing the trousers as the decade progressed. Before the eighties, big manufacturers – the Kodaks, IBMs and Olivettis of this world – were the prime clients of design. But the service economy revolution of the period meant that suddenly everyone was in the market for design skills (or at least a new logo) – fast food chains, theme park owners, even trade unions got in on the act.

1989.01
Agency: **J Walter Thompson**
Client: **US Sprint**
After dominating TV advertising and marching down Madison Avenue on a buying spree during the eighties, British agencies received a wake-up call at the end of the decade in the shape of Chicago-based director Joe Sedelmaier, who suddenly took D&AD by storm. His US Sprint films for J Walter Thompson consisted of distinctive little slices of American office life. Unprepossessing executives were shot close up and ugly. Quickfire repeating dialogue matched the rapid cutting.

The first design group to acquire a Stock Market listing, Allied International Designers in 1980, was swiftly followed by many others, including D&AD winners Rodney Fitch and Michael Peters, as designers became the publicly quoted darlings of the City. Many designers who had worked in public sector employment in the seventies found themselves out on their ears in Thatcher's Britain. They had no option but to step up their own businesses – and they proved surprisingly adept at doing so. By the end of the decade, British designers had their own trade association, their own weekly newspaper, even their own Design Museum (courtesy of Terence Conran). In addition, they had been as internationally acquisitive as their advertising counterparts, having spent a staggering and ill-advised £70 million on purchasing design firms in America.

If all this seemed like an incredible mirage – especially in the light of the severe recession which would brutally cut the design sector down to size in the early nineties – then at least it was in keeping with an age dubbed the 'designer decade', in which style typically triumphed over substance and cosmetic makeovers were there to paper over the cracks. Indeed, much of the design and communication of the period was as superficially alluring and ultimately phoney as that ephemeral eighties creation Max Headroom, a seemingly computer-generated TV presenter on Channel 4 who achieved cult stardom in the middle of the decade.

0 1987.01
Design Group: **Fitch & Company Design Consultants**
Client: **Thresher Wine Merchants**
The local wine merchants given the complete style makeover by the design firm that expanded rapidly and became a large publicly quoted company on the back of giant high street chain projects. Incidentally, Paul Jarvis, one of the designers on Thresher, would later work on the D&AD selected revamp of the RAC (Royal Automobile Club).

Max Headroom (created by directors Annabel Jankel and Rocky Morton) was inspired by new developments in computer graphics and turned many people in design and advertising onto the potential of fractals and raytracing. But Max wasn't a virtual robot at all. Max, star of a Collett Dickenson Pearce (CDP) television commercial for Radio Rentals which featured in the 1986 D&AD Annual ('Hi there televisionists. I'm here to warn you about video nasties … and what could be nastier than your video going on the blink, blink, blink, blink?'), was an actor wearing a bathing cap and plastic suit, with high-tech tricks used to robotize his voice and enhance the colours. He was no more what he seemed than the Next fashion store, which was launched by George Davies in 1982, offering to recreate the pre-war civility of the English clothes shop.

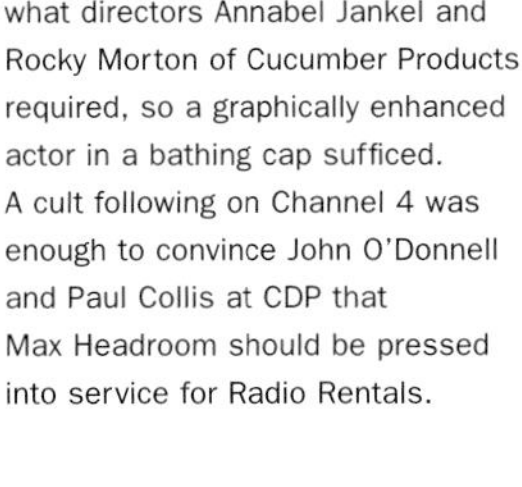

☐ 1986.02
Agency: **Collett Dickenson Pearce**
Client: **Radio Rentals**
The prophet of the digital age arrived a decade too early. Computers in the mid-eighties couldn't achieve what directors Annabel Jankel and Rocky Morton of Cucumber Products required, so a graphically enhanced actor in a bathing cap sufficed.
A cult following on Channel 4 was enough to convince John O'Donnell and Paul Collis at CDP that Max Headroom should be pressed into service for Radio Rentals.

1986.03
Design group:
David Davies Associates
Client: **Next**
The flagship retail project of the designer decade. Fresh, fragrant and well-detailed, Next stores redefined English style. David Davies and collaborator Stuart Baron experienced the pride of winning a D&AD Silver before the fall; by the end of the decade, most retail design firms were facing collapse. David Davies Associates eventually became Davies Baron, then became subsumed into the FutureBrand empire.

While Max Headroom faked the future, which was unusual for design in the eighties, Next and its many competitors – most of them owned by Terence Conran, who had branched out from interiors store Habitat to build a high street empire called Storehouse – faked the past. A pseudo-authentic image of English retro retailing was created by mile upon mile of wrought iron merchandizing units, polished wooden floors and low-voltage lighting up and down the high street. Next was one of the defining design projects of the eighties. By the time its designer David Davies Associates was awarded a D&AD Silver for interior design in 1986 (D&AD juries having found their way to creating a retail environments category via retail graphics), Next was the accepted template for the entire genre – cool, fashionable, uncluttered and contemporary in a very backward-looking way.

In its skilful editing of historical reference, Next captured the *zeitgeist*. The influential graphic designer Tibor Kalman observed, in an essay published in *Design Review*, the magazine of the Chartered Society of Designers, that if designers did away with history in the sixties and saw what the world looked like without it in the seventies, they welcomed it back in the eighties with a vengeance. Today, we can see just how true this was. Designers in the eighties were as determined to stripmine the artistic styles and decorations of the past as their counterparts of the previous 20 years had been to ignore them in favour of the forward-looking doctrine of modernism.

Whether in graphic, product or environmental design, the decade was a golden age of self-knowing historical reference. Advertisers, too, plundered the past with relish, ironically using new technologies to do so. Black-and-white movie legends were pressed into service alongside comedian Griff Rhys Jones in that memorable Holsten Pils TV campaign [page 247]; stills of celluloid heroes like Clark Gable were given Swan matchboxes to hold in a Doyle Dane Bernbach (DDB) campaign for Bryant & May.

The process of welcoming back history in design and art direction at the start of the decade was triggered by a number of things. The improbable publishing success of *The Country Diary of an Edwardian Lady* was one factor. The launch of the garishly colourful Memphis collection of objects by the Italian architect Ettore Sottsass at the 1981 Milan Furniture Fair was another. Memphis was a deliberate affront to designer good taste – to form following function – and it generated massive publicity worldwide. It drew its inspiration from Egyptology, from rock'n'roll and from fifties coffee bars. Memphis suddenly made it okay to decorate products and interiors again. The age of square black boxes and white walls was over. Ornament was no longer a crime and, as in Victorian times, it enjoyed a revival.

The Memphis look washed through and out of British design fairly quickly – but its point was always ideological rather than simply aesthetic. After Memphis, anything was permissible for British designers in the eighties. Rapid technological change, which saw the computer dramatically reshape the way art directors worked, meant that anything was possible.

1986.04
Agency: **Doyle Dane Bernbach**
Client: **Bryant & May**
The creatives on this project – Warren Brown and Bruce Crouch – quite rightly credited the original Hollywood photographers who included George Hurrell and Bert Six. This campaign for Swan Vestas matches was a simple idea brilliantly executed, sending the message that the past was a place that could be pillaged for future campaigns.

SWAN
VESTAS
The Smoker's Match
VESTAS
Britain's favourite old flame.

In 1981, the launch of the Quantel Paintbox revolutionized things for television designers and three years later, the introduction of the Apple Macintosh (with its user-friendly interface and powerful modelling capability) was destined to do the same for creatives in all disciplines. The Apple Macintosh was launched by a famous TV commercial, '1984', directed by Ridley Scott, which ran only once during the Superbowl. Based on an Orwellian vision of a totalitarian future, this was aimed squarely at Apple employees, promising escape from the dominance of IBM. Fittingly, it won a D&AD Silver Award in 1984.

Post-modernism quickly set a new course for the eighties, just as pop had done in the sixties and punk had in the seventies. The shift was most pronounced in architecture, where the neo-classicists quickly came out of the closet and Quinlan Terry remodelled the Thames Richmond riverfront in eighteenth century style. Only the high-tech priests of building design – principally Sir Norman Foster (with the towering Hong Kong and Shanghai Bank) and Sir Richard Rogers (with the exposed services of the Lloyds Building) – were able to survive the pressure to reconstruct the past, not look to the future.

Less was no longer more, it was a bore, as the post-modern architect Robert Venturi remarked. Architects and interior designers began exploring the pink-brick pick-and-mix vocabulary of classical Greek and Roman styles, at least partly in response to, and retreat from, the 'monstrous carbuncle' agenda set in 1984 by Prince Charles, who hammered modern design in a notorious speech to the Royal Institute of British Architects.

Product designers gave high performance electric shavers and light fittings Art Deco-tinged shapes and names in a phenomenon known as 'yestertech'. Graphic designers began harking back to the informal brushstrokes of Matisse, to the US trademarks around the time of the 1939 World's Fair, and to the 'Aryan art' of the forties to create corporate logos for such newly privatized or refocused businesses as the Prudential, National Power and Southern Electric.

1984.01
Agency: **Chiat/Day**
Client: **Apple Computer**
This Ridley Scott commercial, which launched the Apple Macintosh, set the tone for the David and Goliath battle in the computer industry with enormous panache.

⚱ 1980.01
Design group:
Peter Windett Associates
Client: **Crabtree & Evelyn**
Peter Windett had been refining his highly decorative packaging style in the late seventies around the time of the runaway publishing success of *The Country Diary of An Edwardian Lady*. In a familiar pattern at D&AD, this Gold Award came after Windett had already won Silver, as the packaging jury recognized a major trend was emerging and that it should have been rewarded with the highest prize the first time around.

The infatuation with the past was an international phenomenon. When the novelist Tom Wolfe addressed the Industrial Designers Society of America in 1988, he spoke of designers everywhere entering the 'great closet of historical styles' to don the garb of different periods. But it was a game at which British designers and art directors would prove to be masters during the eighties.

In the D&AD Awards, this approach could be seen immediately in packaging and graphic design. In 1980, the D&AD packaging jury gave a Gold Award to designer Peter Windett for the finely detailed nostalgia of his Crabtree & Evelyn range in 1980. Windett, a former assistant to art director Tom Wolsey at *Vogue*, had worked in the early seventies as the sole designer among five illustrators before forming Peter Windett & Associates in 1974.

Making illustration and typography work together to produce memorable packaging designs became Windett's trademark – and Cy Harvey, Crabtree & Evelyn's owner, became his most prominent client. Windett's understanding of the need to be less restricted by the technicalities which beset the photographer – as he explained it – was important in kindling his passion for evocatively illustrated packs.

This passion was quickly shared by others, most notably the design team at Michael Peters & Partners where designer and typographer Madeleine Bennett won Silver Awards in 1981 for Elsenham Quality Foods and in 1982 for Penhaligon's. Both projects were exquisitely executed, repackaging Victorian imagery for a contemporary audience in an artistic way which went beyond mere pastiche, or so its supporters claimed. In a review of eighties packaging published in *Creative Review* in 1989, the designer John Blackburn commented on the trend to recycle the past: 'Clearly there has been some "borrowing" of late nineteenth century and early twentieth century visual imagery – but it has been highly selective. It is less a plagiarism of Victorian design and more a use of style to evoke perceptions of age and tradition where they are product-relevant.'

Aside from physical manifestations of what the Marxist historian Eric Hobsbawn has termed 'the invention of tradition', the other big story in British packaging design in the early eighties was the rise of retailer own-label packaging programmes to compete directly with manufacturer brands. This trend produced a flow of commissions from price-conscious supermarket chains to newly formed design consultancies willing to work for low rates – and anyway regarded as too inexperienced to be let loose on big brand imagery. It also introduced an innovative new packaging vocabulary.

1986.05
Design group: **The Partners**
Client: **The Royal Shakespeare Company**
This theatre programme was art directed by Nick Wurr with great wit and clarity for The Royal Shakespeare Company's production of *The Merry Wives of Windsor.*

1982.01
Design group: **Michael Peters & Partners**
Client: **Penhaligon's**

1981.01
Design group: **Michael Peters & Partners**
Client: **Elsenham Quality Foods**

Two projects which captured *faux* Victorian packaging in the early eighties. As the Michael Peters team demonstrated, modernity was much less appealing than convincingly rebranded nostalgia.

1981.02
Design group:
John Blackburn & Partners
Client: **Gallaher**
Designer John Blackburn took the essence of the Benson & Hedges Gold campaign to create point-of-sale material for newsagents. Another creative idea bubbling up in the late seventies earns its spurs at D&AD in the new decade.

Up until the eighties, the most visible supermarket own-label programme belonged to Sainsbury's, under head of design Peter Dixon. With its clear, modern, no-nonsense Helvetica lettering, Sainbury's packaging signalled quality at reasonable prices – and never remotely sought to compete with more elaborately designed brands. While Sainsbury's ruled supreme in the seventies, UK homegrown Tesco stayed resolutely downmarket, trading on price alone and handing out Green Shield stamps.

But in the early eighties, Tesco changed its design strategy. According to packaging designer Richard Williams, who worked at Sainsbury's under Dixon in the seventies before joining Allied International Designers, 'Tesco was first among a number of retailers who stole a march on the brand owners by discovering the power of packaging design. At that time, most brand manufacturers didn't really understand the medium

1987.02
Design group:
Michael Peters & Partners
Client: **Fine Fare**
The own-label packaging revolution set sail with a project that persuaded supermarkets that they, too, could 'acquire' instant heritage with the nifty deployment of flags and sailing prints straight out of the designer's scrapbook.

1989.02
Design group:
CYB Design Consultants
Client: **Tesco Packaging Design Studio**
Design purists seethed at their success but these cheap and cheerful own-label cereals for Tesco didn't even pretend to compete on the same playing field as the big-brand rivals around them on the shelf.

1987.03
Design group:
Michael Thierens Design
Client: **Waitrose**
This Michael Thierens project for Waitrose was notable not just for its sheer class and elegance but for the designers who worked on it: Dominic Lippa and Harry Pearce, who went on to set up Lippa Pearce, and Lucilla Scrimgeour who went to Lewis Moberly. Brand owners looked at the olive oil bottles in particular and recognized the creative threat.

and just put ads on the side of their packs. Tesco, then other chains, all recognized that packaging could do a lot more. It could take over from the shop assistant on the supermarket floor and give the store credibility. From that moment on, packaging design became a lot more interesting.'

Retailers had none of the constraining influence of visual brand equity stretching back decades to worry about. They were free to invent new styles and categories – and they gave their design consultants plenty of scope to be inventive. Their trust was rewarded. Designers of the period struck a rich vein of form, as reflected in the D&AD Silvers awarded to Michael Thierens Design for elegant designs for the upmarket supermarket Waitrose, Glenn Tutsell at Michael Peters & Partners for more low-key Fine Fare's Dark Rum, and CYB Design Consultants for lively Tesco cereal packs.

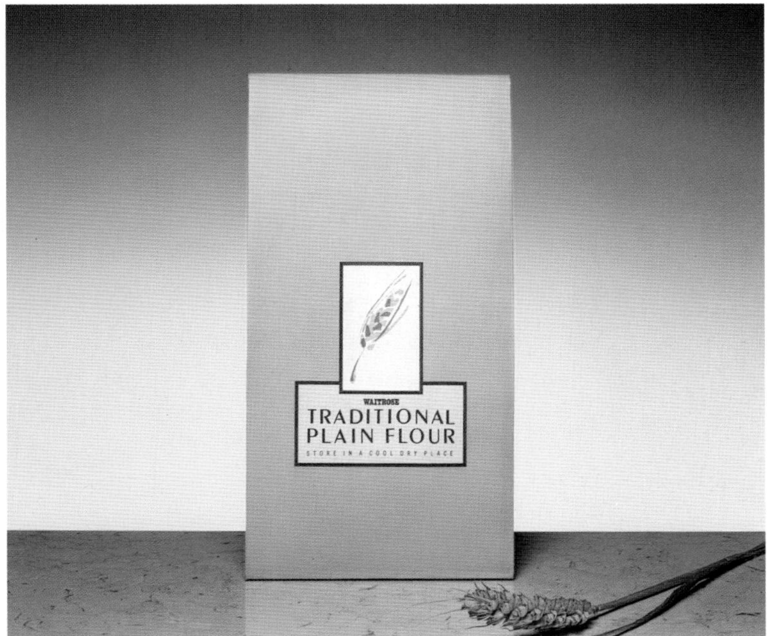

The crowning glory of the supermarket own-label movement was the Gold Award given to Lewis Moberly for an Asda own-label range of alcoholic drinks in 1988. The accolade signalled the arrival of art director Mary Lewis as an unusual talent and major player on the British design scene. The daughter of a Shropshire farmer who rarely came into contact with packaged goods as a child, Lewis had worked her way around UK art schools as a tutor and fine art printmaker before setting up her own design firm in 1983 with her husband Robert Moberly, a former advertising man.

The Asda collection Lewis created, with the help of illustrator Dan Fern, was typical of her bold mix of ideas and style. It featured high-quality own-label versions of Scotch whiskies, fine wines and premium vodkas so accurate and compelling in their imagery that famous brand owners must have been disconcerted; would the average Asda customer be bothered with such an abstract thing as brand heritage, or just reach for the cleverly observed and dependable-looking retailer copy?

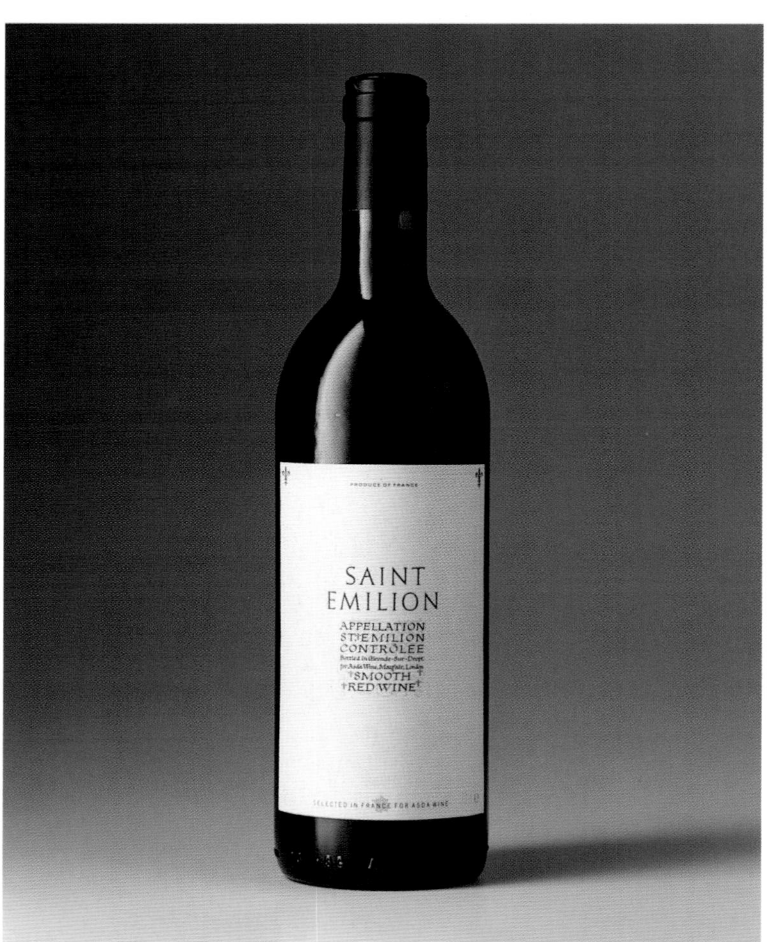

1988.03
Design group: **Lewis Moberly**
Client: **Asda Stores**
The exquisite execution of these wines and spirits for Asda was achieved by illustrator Dan Fern working closely with the Lewis Moberly team. Fern went on to become head of the School of Communication at the Royal College of Art. Mary Lewis never lost her flair for British retailing, later doing projects with Boots, Jaeger, Marks & Spencer and Harrods.

GENUINE
VODKA
QUALITY SPIRIT
PURE DISTILLED
BLEND
PRODUCED IN THE
UNITED KINGDOM

JOSEPH
PARFUM
DE JOUR
JOSEPH
PARFUM
DE JOUR

1986.06
Design group:
Michael Peters & Partners
Client: **Penhaligon's**
A hip-flask filled with scent was art director Madeleine Bennett's way of giving perfume packaging a less fussy interpretation of English style.

this page

1983.01
Design group: **Robinson Lambie-Nairn**
Client: **Readymix Drypack**
A down-to-earth job amid much mannered work from designer Brett Haggerty.

1984.02
Design group:
Pearce Marchbank Studio
Client: **Le Nez Rouge Wine Club**
Pearce Marchbank's riposte to the historicists.

1989.03
Design group: **Carter Wong**
Client: **Katsouris Brothers**
Carter Wong's italic 'O' was a simple and straightforward idea for olive packaging – and it worked.

The impact of popular own-label packaging triggered an immediate response from the more savvy brand manufacturers during the eighties, who recognized that they, too, needed to change their creative game. D&AD juries identified some of these more adventurous brand designs, showing a penchant for selecting those packs that exhibited a cool, simple modernism in reaction to the highly decorative phase of the early eighties.

Carter Wong's olive packaging for the Katsouris Brothers, Pearce Marchbank's Le Nez Rouge wine label and the Joseph Parfum de Jour pack by Madeleine Bennett (another classically elegant piece of work by Michael Peters & Partners for Penhaligon's) all reflected the gradual move away from complicated decoration towards design simplicity as the decade wore on. There seemed to be a consensus that people no longer had time to study packs in any detail. Robinson Lambie-Nairn's Readymix Drypack packaging, a Silver winner in 1983, art directed by Brett Haggerty with Habitat-style line drawings, even proved to be a forerunner of the still popular Ronseal 'it does exactly what it says on the tin' school of directness.

But perhaps the most radical of the brand owner responses to own-label packaging belonged to a Cuisine Française label for Sharwood's, designed by Smith & Milton and chosen for the D&AD Annual in 1985. With its white background, Matisse-style brushstroke illustration by Brian Grimwood, and absence of standard food packshot, here was a brand breaking the rules and behaving like an own-label product. In fact, Sharwood's packaging was linked to a broader trend in graphic design: a loose, hand-drawn, brushstroke style that spread like wildfire among corporate designers wearied by all those relentlessly geometric logos of the sixties and seventies.

Minale Tattersfield's trademark scribble logo, with which the design firm launched itself in the early sixties, was the forerunner to the trend. In the early eighties, Minale Tattersfield returned to the theme with a direct mail campaign for its own Cubic Metre furniture venture, winning a D&AD Silver in 1983. One of Cubic Metre's most iconic products, a table light with a dome on top, inspired by the image of a Franciscan monk, was expressed in a loose, hand-drawn style. Illustration quickly became the thing in all areas of graphic design – from annual reports and book jackets to retail graphics and posters – just as it had blossomed under the patronage of Peter Windett and Madeleine Bennett in packaging.

1982.02
Design group: **Design Magazine**
Client: **Design Council**
This Donna Muir cover for the Design Council's magazine *Design* set the tone for illustration in the eighties – loose, gestural, scribbled and seemingly done in a matter of minutes.

1983.02
Design group:
Minale Tattersfield & Partners
Client: **Cubic Metre Furniture**
Minale Tattersfield nearly lost its shirt diversifying into furniture but their loosely drawn direct mailer for Cubic Metre set an informal illustrative trend in design.

opposite

1985.03
Design group: **Smith & Milton**
Client: **JA Sharwood & Company**
It may not have won at D&AD but this pack opened a huge can of worms. Designer Howard Milton always cites this project as 'the one that started it all' as designers began to emulate artists.

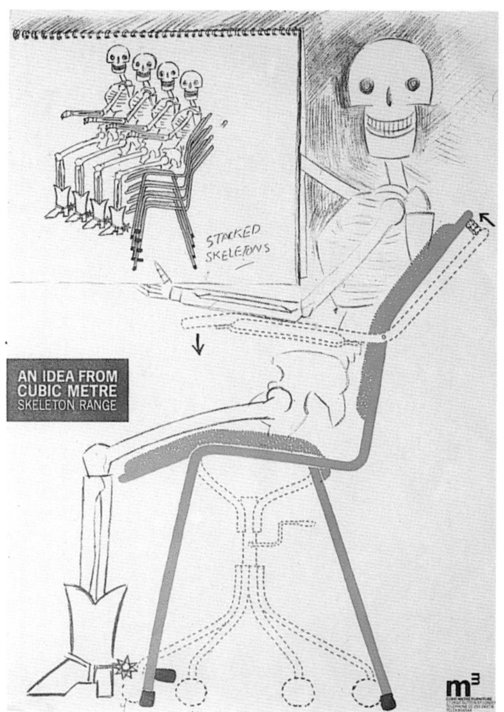

Sharwood's
cuisine française
Sauce Citron
lemon and tarragon sauce for
over fish or poultry

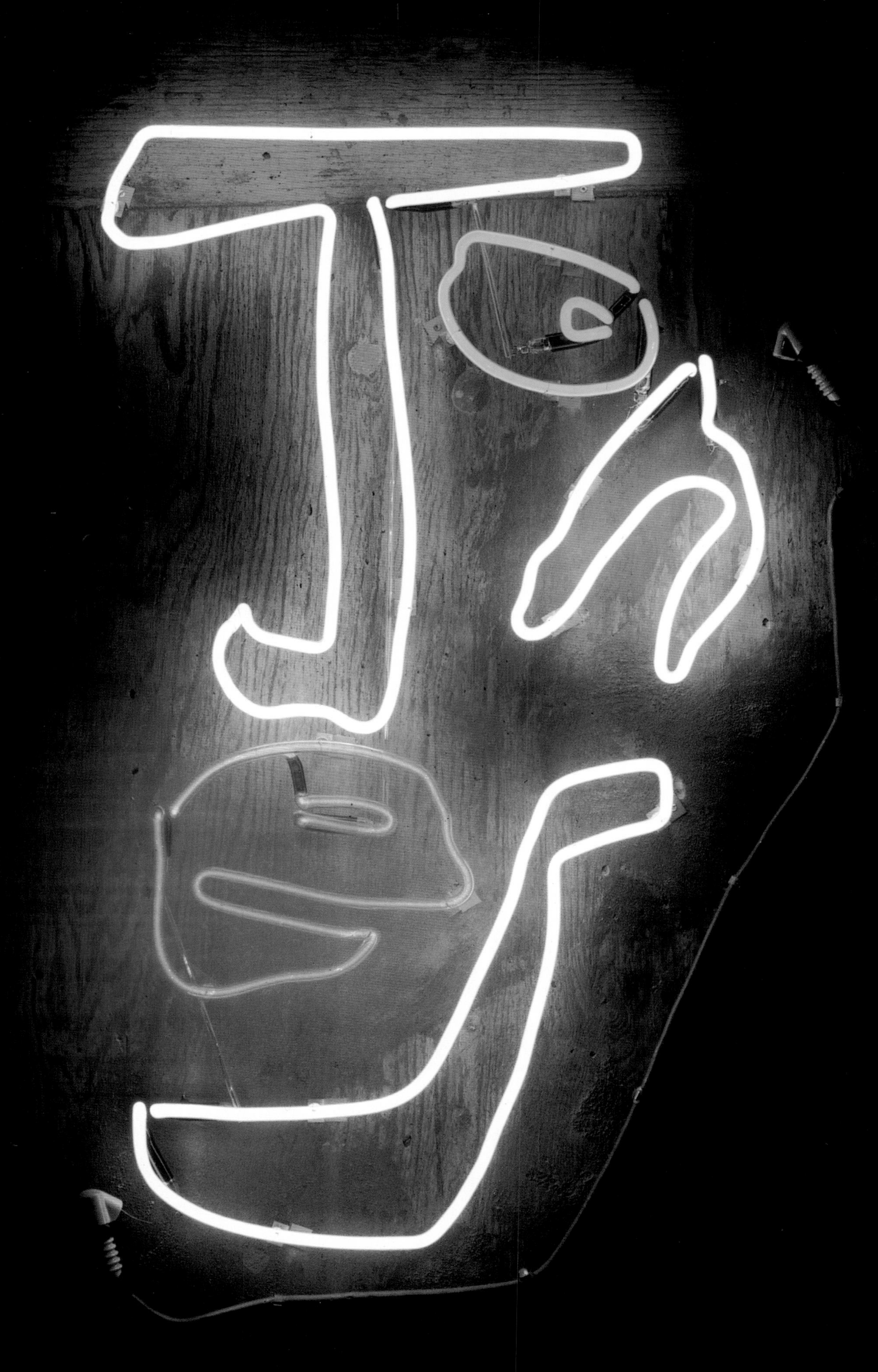

1986.07
Design group:
Autograph Design Partnership
Client: **Jones**
Like the Sharwood pack, the logo for retailer Jones didn't win at D&AD either. But this seemingly small and insignificant project went on to have a huge impact in the design industry. Logos had been hard-edged, abstract and geometric for generations. Now, Jones suggested a new way of writing company names. In a sense, it was a return to the signwriting roots of the commercial artist, albeit with a certain sophistication.

The Matisse-inspired look of the Sharwood's label was mirrored by a broad brushstroked logo for the Jones retail store, created by the Autograph Design Partnership with illustrator Richard Rockwood (and featured by D&AD in 1986). Together, these two designs set the template for a trio of famous identities executed later in the eighties by Wolff Olins: the Prudential, 3i and, finally, BT, the piper figure representing the high watermark of the trend. Rockwood, it was rumoured, even did some early drawings for the Prudential logo, a project which confirmed how corporate identity was softening its edges. According to designer Michael Johnson, 'Everyone started doing stuff with chalks and gouaches and then put some type to it. A lot of designers seriously thought they could be artists.'

Only the very best could get away with it. Alan Fletcher, in the mature phase of his Pentagram career, did so with a set of 'Art' posters for IBM. These skilful compositions seemingly undermined Fletcher's own observation that 'artists solve their own problems, designers solve other people's'. Clearly, by the mid-eighties, designers were interested in behaving more like artists.

In fact, this period was a golden age for illustrators like Donna Muir, Dan Fern, Bush Hollyhead, Brian Grimwood and Jeff Fisher, who were able to provide the

1984.03
Design group: **Pentagram Design**
Client: **IBM Europe**
Alan Fletcher's posters were arguably more interesting than the art that eventually replaced them in the IBM foyer that they were designed as placeholders for.

1985.04
Agency: **Boase Massimi Pollitt Univas**
Client: **Greater London Council**
Bush Hollyhead led the charge of the illustration light brigade right into this poster promoting events for the GLC.

1980.02
Designer: **Dan Fern**
Client: **Liberty's of London**
Design and illustration merge into one entity in this poster for Liberty's.

1988.04
Designer: **Kate Stephens**
Client: **Association for Business Sponsorship of the Arts**
Nobody did the Matisse-style brushstroke better in the eighties than the illustrator Brian Grimwood.

1989.04
Designer: **Jeff Fisher**
Client: **Minneapolis College of Art, Minnesota**
Among the most original of the illustration gang, Jeff Fisher won widespread acclaim for this poster for an exhibition of British illustrators, which showed his witty and allusive style to good effect.

loose artistic imagery with which graphic designers and art directors less technically gifted than Fletcher had become so enamoured. The D&AD Annuals of the period resonate with some great work by these names. Hollyhead won a Silver in 1985 for his work on a GLC Thamesday poster by BMP for the Greater London Council, as did Grimwood in 1988 for an ABSA annual report designed by Kate Stephens. Fisher, an expatriate Australian living in London, won a Silver for illustration in 1989 with his 'Unusually good haircuts' piece for the Minneapolis College of Art in Minnesota.

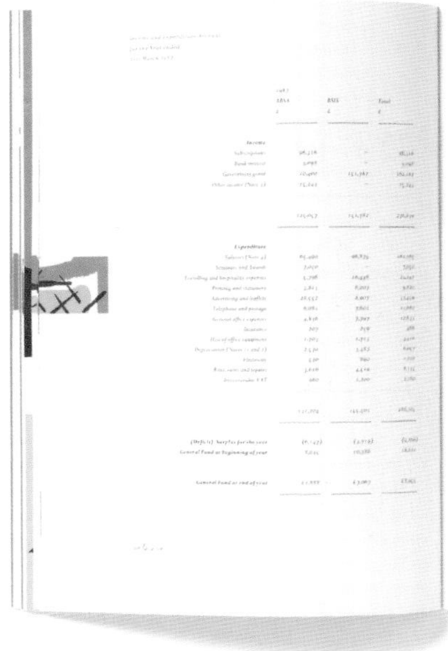

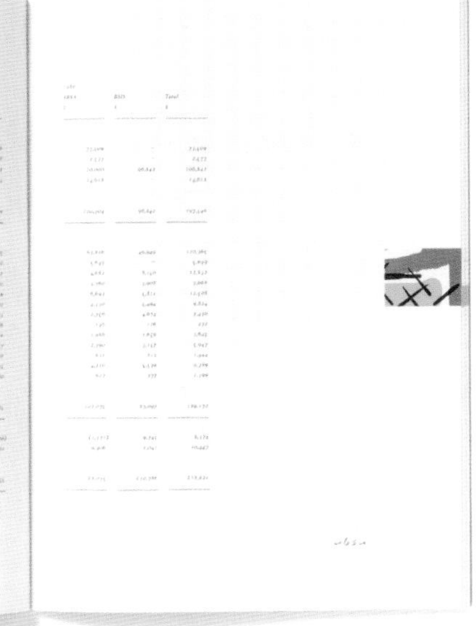

By the end of the eighties, as Fisher's piece proved, the slightly whimsical brushstroke illustrative style had become an international commodity. There were some notable attempts to cling onto geometry in graphic design and not abandon it entirely. Minale Tattersfield's corporate identity for the famous London department store Heal's, a Silver winner in 1982, was an elegant solution using a recognizable kit of engineered visual parts that could be assembled by a graphic mechanic rather than a fully paid-up artist.

Later, in 1988, Roundel Design Group's Railfreight identity marshalled geometric elements into badges to evoke the pioneering locomotive shed spirit of the British railways. But for all its formal composition, Railfreight's identity, like Glenn Tutsel's Fine Fare wine bottle, explored decorative aspects of English heraldry and could be said to belong to the *faux* historicism that swept through design in the eighties as art directors eagerly plundered the back-catalogue of British visual culture.

1988.05
Design group: **Roundel Design Group**
Client: **BR Railfreight**

1982.03
Design group: **Minale Tattersfield**
Client: **Heal & Son**

Two projects which retained a formal geometry while the edges softened everywhere else in design. These identities were shortlived as Heal's and Railfreight were taken over amid the acquisition and privatization mania of the eighties.

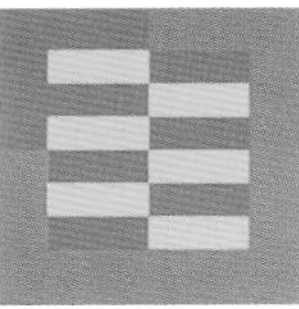

1985.05
Design group: **Carroll & Dempsey**
Client: **The Post Office**

1985.06
Design group: **Cooper Thirkell**
Client: **Penguin Books**

1986.08
Design group: **Cooper Thirkell**
Client: **Victoria and Albert Museum**

It is hard to believe today that these two design groups, that were to form Carroll Dempsey Thirkell when Nick Thirkell joined Ken Carroll and Mike Dempsey in 1986, could have annexed mid-eighties print design so completely. But the Gold Awards tell their own story, reflecting the awe in which such craft skills were held. What is intriguing is that Mike Dempsey, a designer trained in the modernist sixties, should have become the king of historicist craft in the eighties.

The hallmarks of the *faux* historical look were established in a 1984 D&AD Silver-winning book jacket by Carroll & Dempsey for Faber & Faber, with its effete, spindly, widely spaced serif capital letters. Awards the following year – including Cooper Thirkell's book jacket series for Penguin, with illustrations by Lawrence Mynott, and another Carroll & Dempsey project, a beautifully researched and designed book on Royal Mail Special Stamps – confirmed the trend. By 1986, the D&AD Awards were awash with historical pastiche: Faber & Faber again, with an illustrated book cover for *The Iron Man* by Ted Hughes, as well as projects for the Victoria and Albert Museum and the Royal Shakespeare Company.

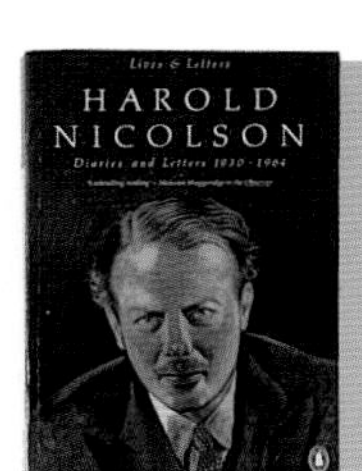

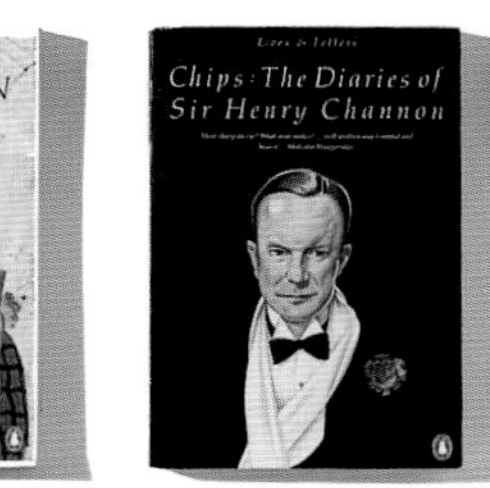

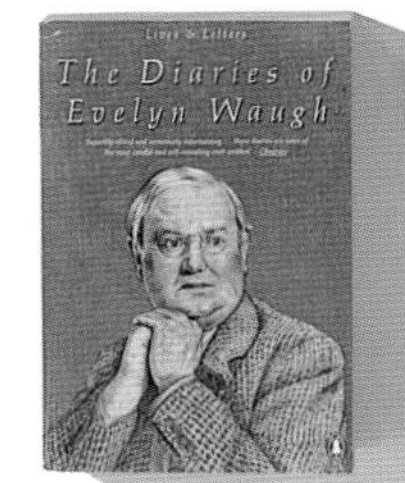

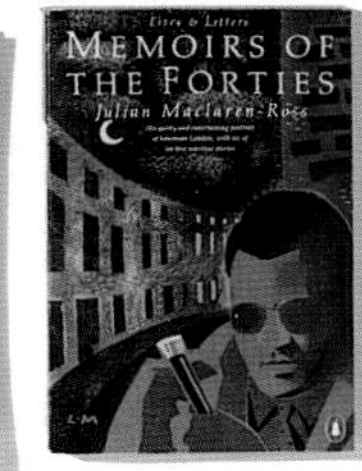

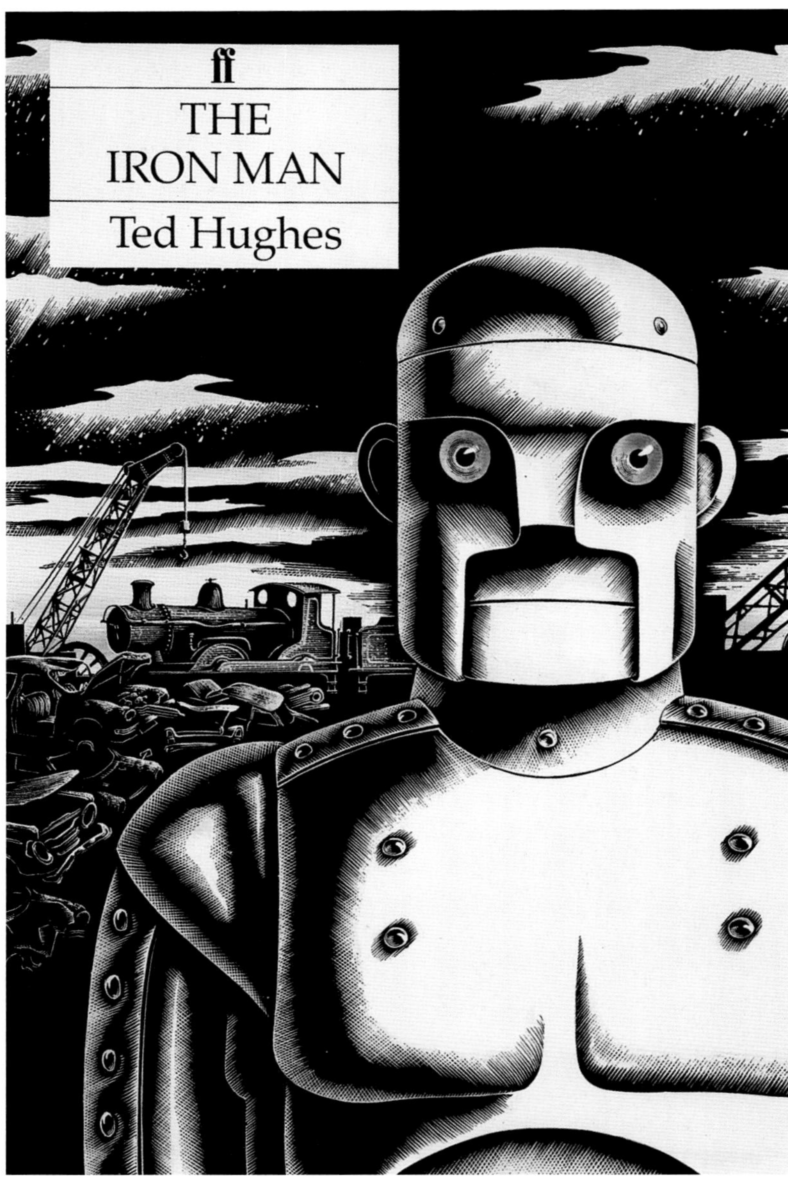

1986.09
Illustrator: **Andrew Davidson**
Client: **Faber & Faber**

1983.03
Design group: **Pentagram Design**
Client: **Faber & Faber**

1984.04
Design group: **Carroll & Dempsey**
Client: **Faber & Faber**

A trio of projects for Faber & Faber reveal art director John McConnell of Pentagram as a leading player in setting the tone for soft, decorative graphics in the mid-eighties. McConnell's collaboration with Mike Dempsey and Ken Carroll was especially influential, defining a look in which justified retro-serif capitals work with tiny little pictures within a forced rectangular grid. Clearly, Arnold, Schoenberg, Wassily and Kandinsky are words of different lengths, but that didn't stop designers in the eighties from justifying any piece of type they felt like.

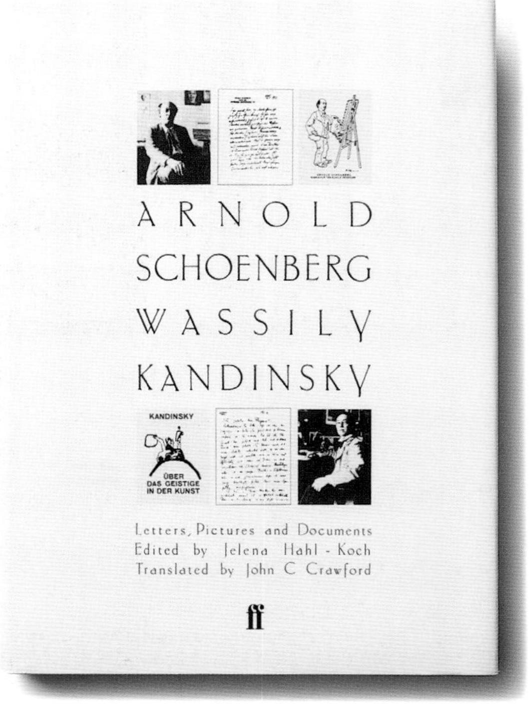

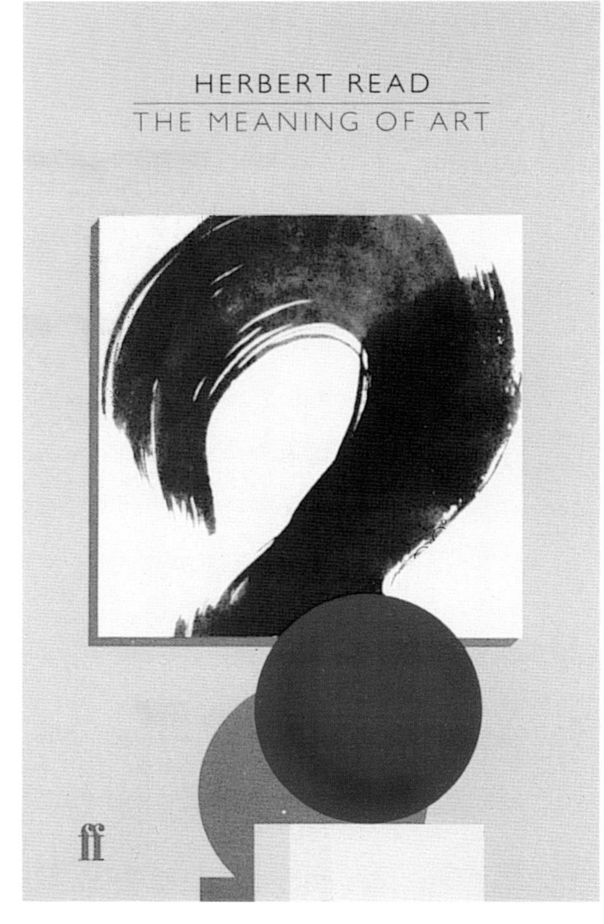

1987.04
Design group: **The Partners**
Client: **Wood & Wood International Signs for Courage**
Faced with an enormous number of signs to produce for Courage pubs, David Stuart and Brigid McMullen hit upon a realistic solution. By imposing silhouettes as a linking style, they could commission a series of illustrators (six in total, including Mick Brownfield and John Gorham) to work on the project, so enabling a coherent house style to come through in the work.

Much of this work was about as authentic as the ploughman's lunch. (This was an adman's invention which lent its name to the 1983 film directed by Richard Eyre, starring Jonathan Pryce and written by Ian McEwan, which coolly studied the falseness and artifice of British society through the prism of a morally bankrupt journalist attending a Conservative Party Conference.) A 1987 D&AD Silver-winning series of pub signs designed by The Partners for the Courage pub chain was all 'ploughman's lunch' – evoking a Britain of warm beer, craft skills and rural charm that had long disappeared, if it ever existed at all.

The movement to recreate the past even had its own house magazine – *The World of Interiors*. Under Wendy Harrop's inspired art direction, this publication was launched in 1981 and reintroduced swags, *trompe d'œil* and rag-rolling to British homes stripped bare by the Habitat modernism of the seventies. Each page was a treat, its formal, delicate serif typography accompanying images of domestic elegance and gilded ornament. By the time *The World of Interiors* won a D&AD Silver in 1984, its look was already mirrored in another D&AD winning project – a Saatchi photographic campaign for Alexon & Company, art directed by Paul Arden.

1984.05
Art director: **Wendy Harrop**
Client: **The World of Interiors**
Remember when you decided to rag-roll your walls and fit flowing drapes in the bedroom? Wendy Harrop, inspired art director of *The World of Interiors*, was probably responsible.

1984.06
Agency: **Saatchi & Saatchi**
Client: **Alexon & Company**
Alexon were expecting a much more standard shot but, inspired by Carol Beckwith's book, *Nomads of Niger*, photographer Richard Avedon and art director Paul Arden told Iman to wrap the dress she was supposed to be wearing around her head.

1984.07
Agency: **Saatchi & Saatchi**
Client: **Alexon & Company**
Shot in a small anteroom next to the dining room at The Ritz, art director Tim Mellors had to keep the door shut with his foot to spare diners the embarrassment of a full frontal.

Yee hoo!, the old woman cries, as she butts the dancer gently in the belly. The dancer has been approved. The dancer is outstanding. The eye popping, limb contorting swirl of magic and colour that is the tribal dance of the Nomads of the Niger has reached its mesmeric climax. In a great white egg of a studio somewhere on New York's East Side, Richard Avedon the photographer who Truman Capote has called "The man with gifted eyes," breathes the tingling magic of the Wodaabe tribe into Alexon's African collection. Colours and primitive pattern woven into cloth, woven into clothes bring Alexon screeching into the now.

1982.04
Photographer: **Barry Lategan**
Client: **Condé Nast**

1982.05
Photographer: **Barry Lategan**
Client: **Olympus Optical Company**

Two projects reflecting the rise of fashion photographer Barry Lategan in the early eighties. Lategan made his name – as he put it – 'photographing beautiful women beautifully'. It is a sign of a great photographer that he even managed to make a dodgy early eighties haircut look great for Condé Nast.

As well as shooting women, another Lategan obsession was shooting trees, as shown in the Olympus campaign. He has remained one of the advertising community's snappers of choice for two decades and tells a story against the fashion industry's blinkered vision. Once, he was shooting on a hill in Santorini in Greece. A bystander approached his group, peered at the horizon and asked what they were photographing. The art editor replied, 'The February issue.'

The fragile *faux* historicist style invited a backlash and it duly emerged from the mid-eighties onwards. The new design trend was as hard and robust as Faber & Faber book jackets or *The World of Interiors* editorial spreads had been soft and effete. Pearce Marchbank's aggressive *Skinhead* book jacket, which won a D&AD Silver in 1985, signalled the march towards what was termed in some quarters 'the new brutalism'.

Suddenly, D&AD juries welcomed a different graphic design approach: massive black sans type accompanying in-your-face imagery. Two Silver-winning projects by typographer Peter Davenport (a magazine to market the Broadgate property development in 1988 and a promotional book for photographer Brian Griffin in 1989) loomed large over the design landscape. It wasn't exactly a return to year zero – traces of Soviet constructivism could be seen in the heroic compositions – but the tone had undeniably changed.

1985.07
Design group:
Pearce Marchbank Studio
Client: **Omnibus Press**
The ever-present Pearce Marchbank led the backlash against the fragile historicist look with this project featuring the talents of photographer Nick Knight. A robust solution that could have come from any period in D&AD's history.

1981.03
Design group: **Carroll & Dempsey**
Client: **Manpower Services Commission**
Before they got tangled up in effete imagery, Ken Carroll and Mike Dempsey showed that they, too, could be tough and to the point in these leaflets for Manpower Services Commission.

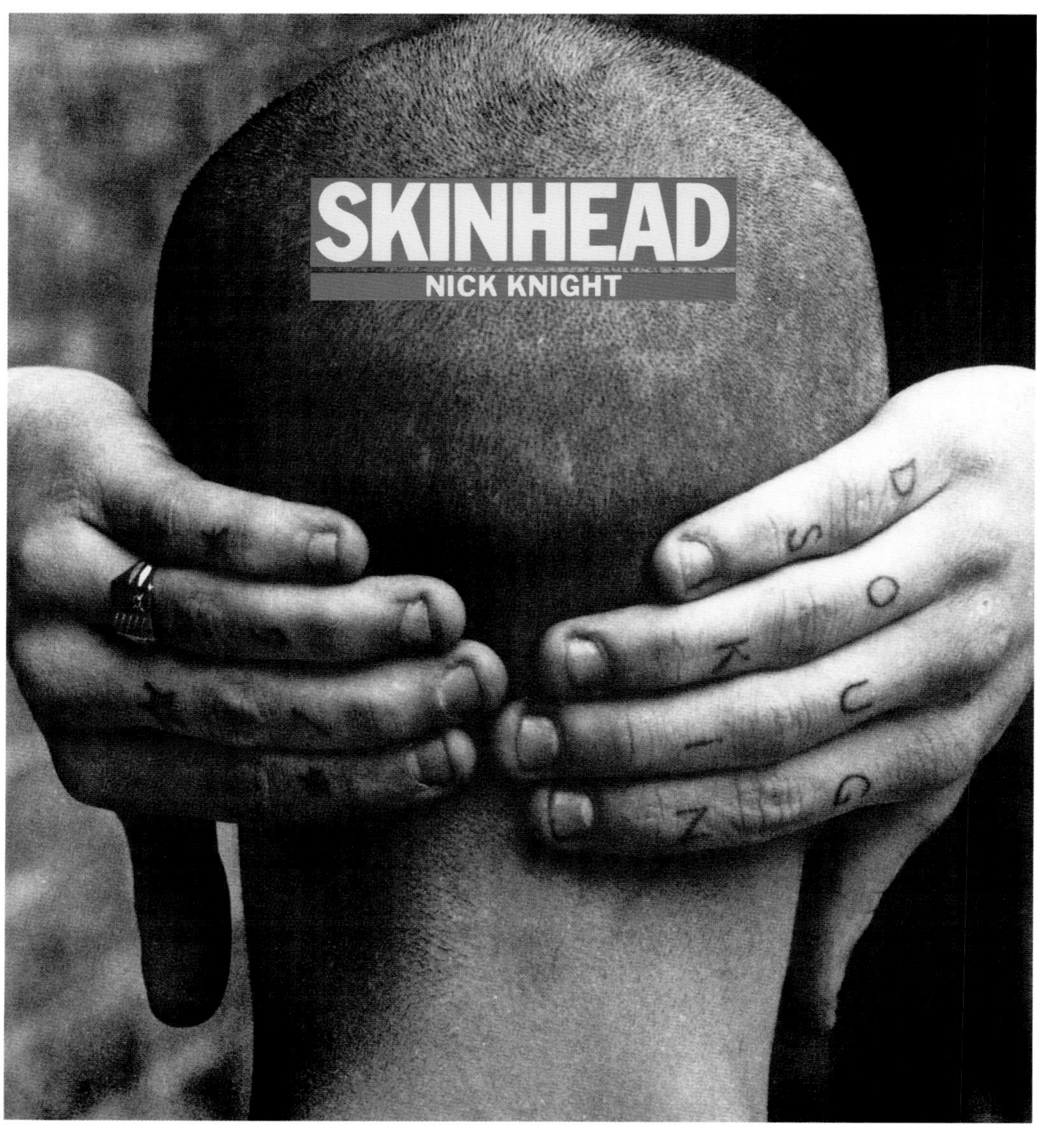

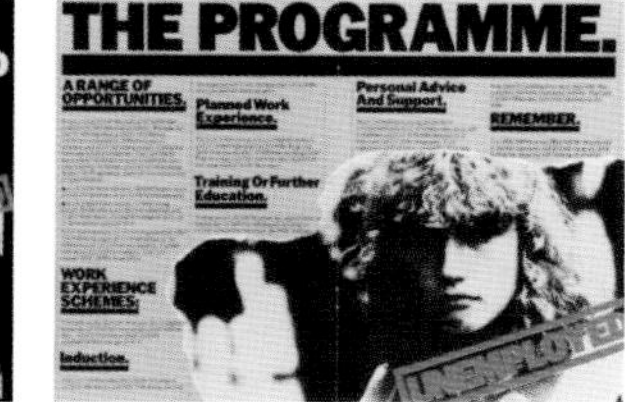

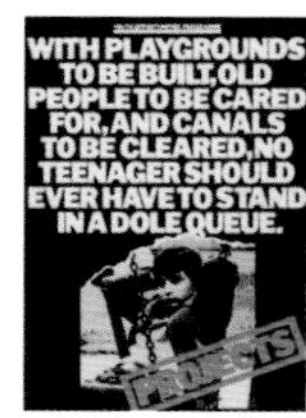

1988.06
Design group: **Davenport Designs**
Client: **Rosehaugh Stanhope Developments**

1989.05
Designer: **Peter Davenport**
Client: **Brian Griffin**

Two strong-minded projects by Peter Davenport that helped to put the skids under all those intricate woodcuts and serif-dominated layouts. The single heroic image and thick black headlines were back big-time at D&AD, used here on a promotional magazine and a book of photographer Brian Griffin's work, called *Work*.

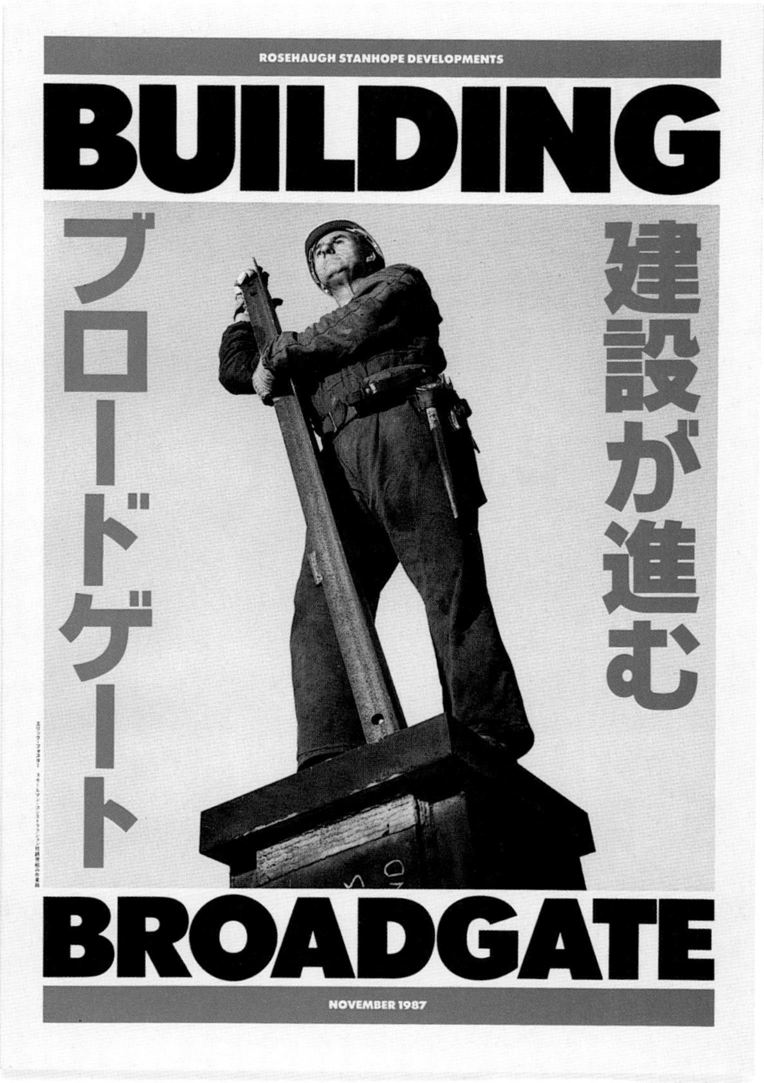

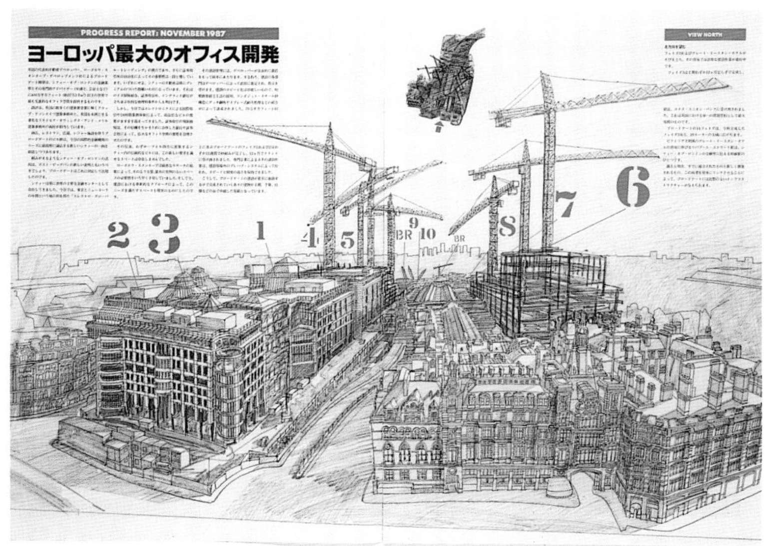

Editorial design led the way. Art director Simon Esterson's powerful design for the architectural magazine *Blueprint* was as influential in putting some iron back into the prevailing current of graphic design as *The World of Interiors* had been in softening it up. With its strict grids, large format, disciplined white space and brilliant interrelationship of black headlines and architectural imagery, *Blueprint* won Silver at D&AD for most outstanding complete magazine twice, first in 1986 and then in 1989, when it shared the spotlight with another famously bold editorial redesign of the decade – *The Guardian*.

The story of how Pentagram's David Hillman gave *The Guardian* a completely new look can be read as an ultimately successful attempt to make Britain's best known left-of-centre broadsheet appear less British and backward-looking and more continental and forward-looking. *The Guardian*'s circulation had been hit by the launch of *The Independent* with its carefully cultivated 'fogey' serif image designed by Cooper & Thirkell in 1986. The paper also hadn't been properly redesigned since 1969 and was renowned for its poor printing and constant misprints.

Hillman, a former design assistant on *The Sunday Times magazine* and art director at *Nova*, responded to editor Peter Preston's call for a 'slightly continental air' with a total facelift emphasizing crispness and aggression. Helvetica headlines and Nimrod body text gave the paper a new urgency and modernity. Toughness was back after a decade in which British graphic designers had all but exhausted the classical good manners of typographic traditions.

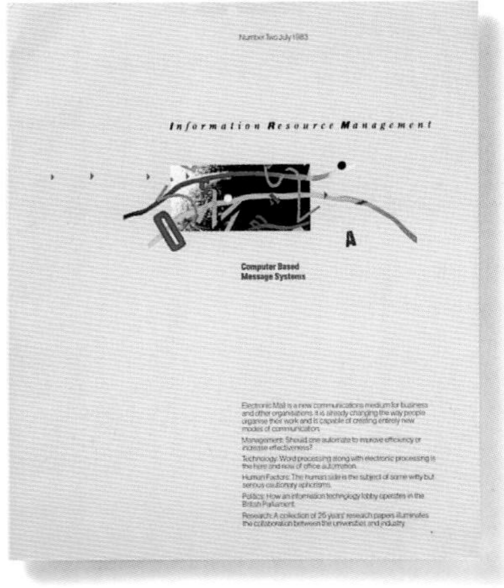

1986.10
Art director: **Simon Esterson**
Client: **Blueprint Magazine**
A powerful collaboration between editor Deyan Sudjic and art director Simon Esterson gave the British design and architectural communities an exciting new visual platform for their work in the eighties. Journalism and imagery became seamless as *Blueprint* aggressively promoted a new generation of emerging architects and furniture designers. Sudjic and Esterson would later go on to revive the famous Italian design magazine *Domus*, once edited by Gio Ponti, in much the same spirit. Meanwhile, Esterson's assistant designer at *Blueprint*, Stephen Coates, would go on to design *Eye* magazine for editor Rick Poynor at the turn of the nineties.

1984.08
Design group: **Pentagram Design**
Client: **Ericsson Information Systems**
David Hillman and Bruce Mau won a Silver Award for this magazine for Ericsson Information Systems, which employed the work of seven illustrators including Wolf Spoerl and Ralph Steadman.

this page

1989.06
Design group: **Pentagram Design**
Client: **The Guardian Newspaper**
When *The Guardian* first unveiled its slightly brutalist, European-influenced redesign, the rest of Fleet Street thought that editor Peter Preston had committed an enormous folly. Rival editor Max Hastings at the *Daily Telegraph*, when invited to comment publicly on the new look, replied, 'I do not wish to intrude on private grief.' A lot of other people also criticized the design initially but it has stood the test of time now for 15 years, albeit with regular tweaks and improvements, many of them, incidentally, orchestrated by Simon Esterson.

Home news, page 4
Reginald Harraden: packaging Manchester

Analysis, page 23
Lord Carrington's end of term report on Nato

Movie, page 34
Holly Hunter's Berlin broadcast

Sport, page 18
Norman Whiteside: old head on young feet

25p
Thursday
February 18
1988
Published in London and Manchester

The Guardian

Top officers face fresh RUC inquiry

David Hearst, John Carvel and Joe Joyce

Unanswered questions, page 3
Day in politics, page 6

Righteous indignation. . . Police try persuasion with a Christian CND supporter

Photograph: Martin Argles

Solicitor charged with submitting false forms

Scotland Yard queries legal aid claims

Exclusive

Clare Dyer
Legal Correspondent

Soldiers of Christ arise and put armour on

Ed Vulliamy

Legal history made, page 4

US colonel kidnapped

Julie Flint in Beirut

Kinnock sees Palestinian tragedy, page 24

Aids warnings 'ignored'

Angella Johnson

News in brief

Kinnock in Israel attack

Page 24

Nuclear crash admission

Wrong number

Helicopter shooting

Page 2

Thatcher weapons call

Page 24

Waldheim support drops

Page 10

Inside today's Guardian

Arts, Reviews	21
Financial News	14-16
Cartoons	26
Computer Guardian	25-33
Crosswords	26,28
Entertainments	33
Grassroots	36
Guardian Women	20
Home News	2-4,6,24
International News	10-13
Letters	22
Listings	35
Movie Guardian	34
Personal/Law Report	37
Politics	6
Sports News	17-19

Of course, not all the graphic design work featured at D&AD in the eighties fell into recognizable camps. Some projects were so unusual and distinctive that they resisted easy categorization. Overwhelmingly though, the impression was of an obsession with visual style swamping ideas. Problem-solving went out of fashion. Why communicate when you could simply decorate? All of this made those ideas-led projects strong enough to swim against the tide all the more commendable – and those one-off talents who defied pigeonholing all the more remarkable.

Madeleine Bennett's logo for the International Coffee Organisation (1983), Howard Brown and John Gorham's *Red Monarch* poster for Goldcrest Films (a Silver winner in 1984) and The Fine White Line's Tate Gallery poster for London Underground (a Silver winner in 1988 which used paints to create an exquisite Tube map) kept the flag flying for an ideas-based approach. David Pelham, winner of two awards in 1982 and 1984 for his books *Kites* and *The Human Body*, which pushed the boundaries of paper engineering, showed there was still a place for the graphic maverick in an increasingly corporate design world.

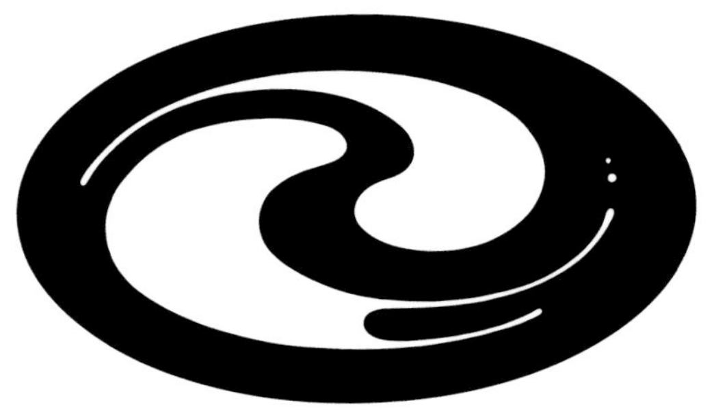

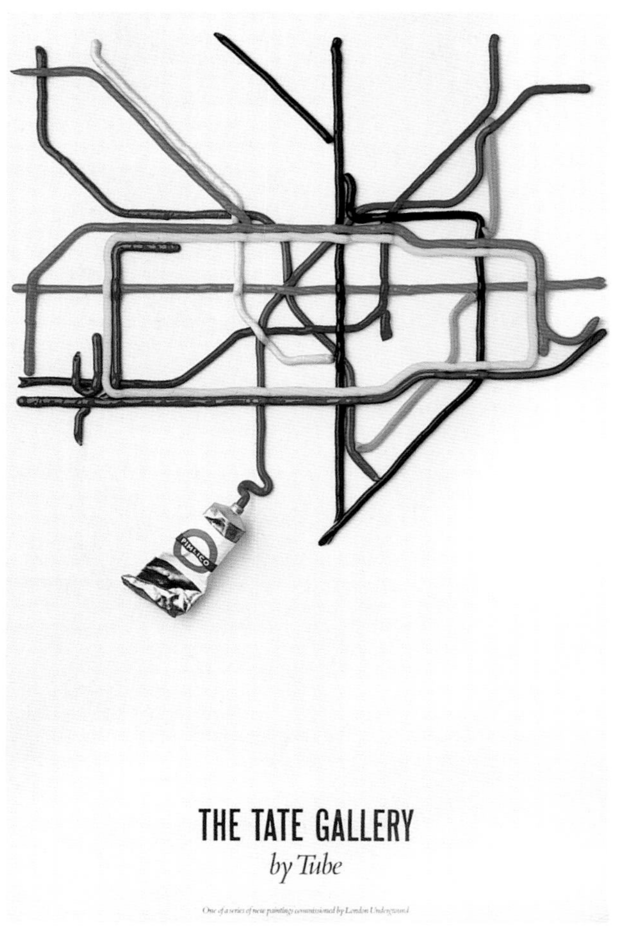

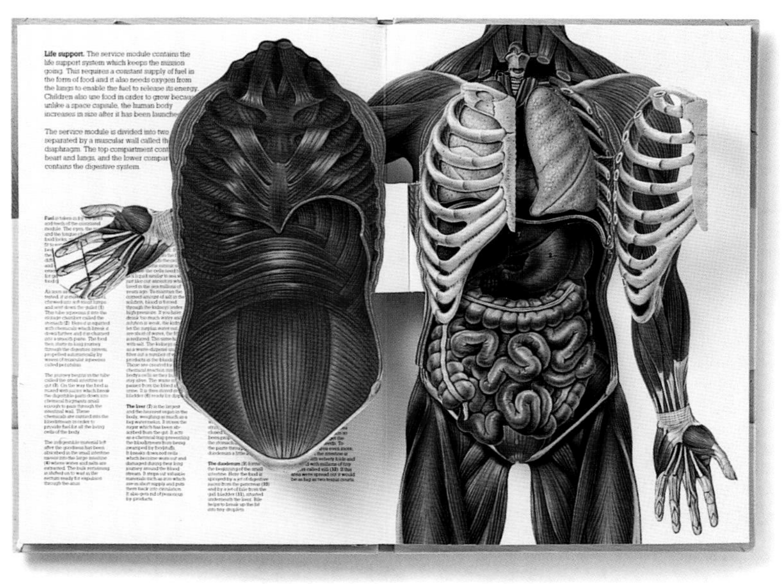

1983.04
Design group:
Michael Peters & Partners
Client: **International Coffee Organisation**
In retrospect, these solutions look obvious. But they are classic ideas brilliantly executed.

1984.09
Design group: **Pentagram Design**
Client: **Jonathan Cape**
The Human Body pop-up book dates from David Pelham's stint at Pentagram. It sold close to three million copies.

1988.07
Agency: **The Fine White Line Communications Company**
Client: **London Underground**
The Fine White Line was a trailblazing group that, unusually at the time, worked on both advertising and design projects.

this page

1984.10
Art directors: **Howard Brown & John Gorham**
Client: **Goldcrest Films & Television**
The idea for this poster allegedly came as the two designers walked through Soho. Gorham saw a tomato on the pavement and suggested it make the hated despot's nose.

1982.06
Designer: **David Pelham**
Client: **Pan Books**

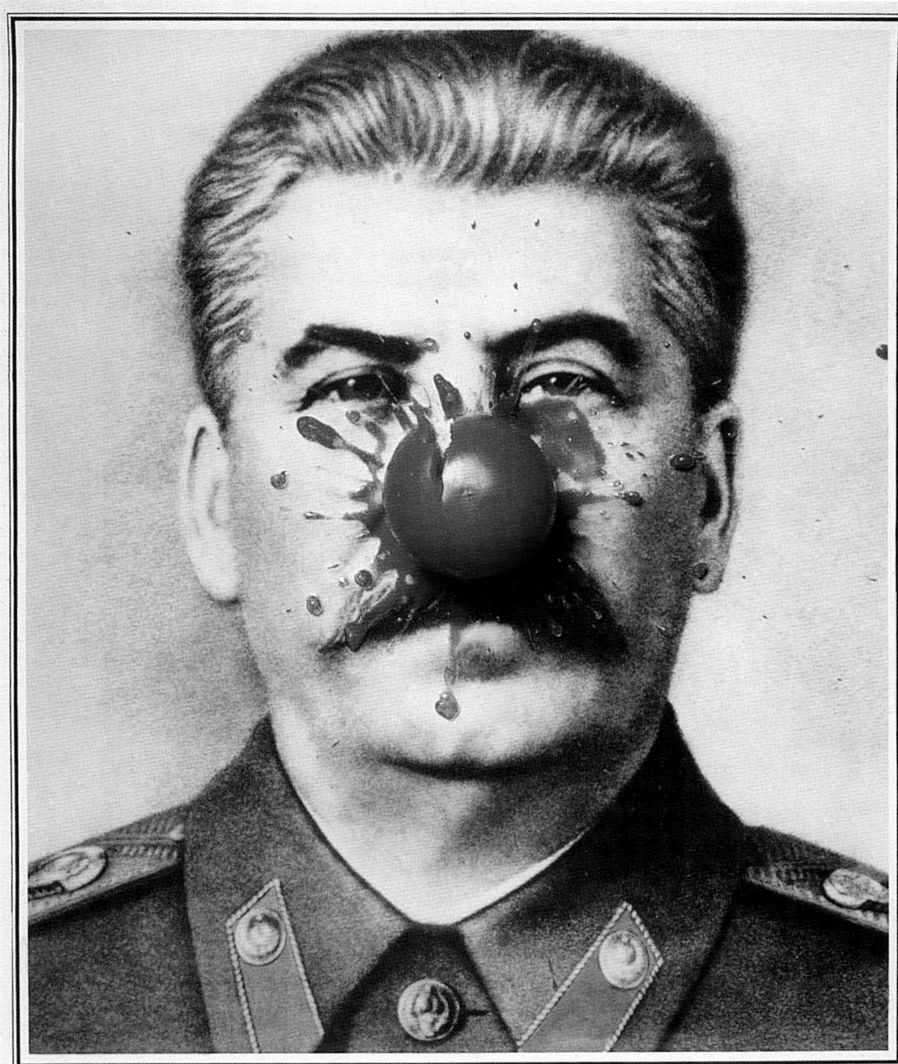

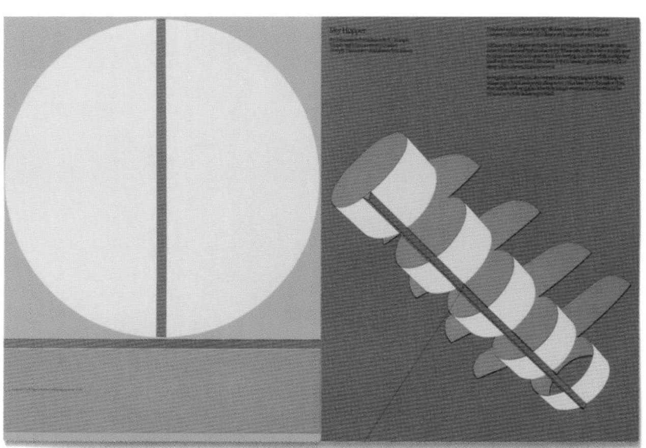

The outstanding individual graphic designer of the eighties was a similarly free spirit who belonged to no particular camp and wasn't even based in the UK. Dutchman Gert Dumbar, based in The Hague, emerged as D&AD's most prolific performer with a string of award-winning projects that spanned the decade (from a Studio Dumbar stationery range in 1981 to a set of posters for the Holland Festival in 1988).

Dumbar had studied in Britain at the Royal College of Art in the sixties and joined D&AD as a student in 1967. His early career was spent with TEL Design in the Hague before he founded Studio Dumbar in 1977 with the avowed aim not to sacrifice his often whimsical and idealistic creative ideas on the altar of commerce.

Many of Studio Dumbar's clients were public bodies, such as the Westeinde Hospital in The Hague and the Rijksmuseum in Amsterdam, for which the firm designed functional and witty identity and signage programmes. These projects won Gold Awards in 1982 and 1987 respectively, and anticipated Studio Dumbar's milestone public sector design programmes in the nineties for the Dutch post office PTT and Police. Meanwhile, Dumbar's earlier poster campaign for the Rijksmuseum, winner of a Silver Award in 1982, introduced a quirky mixed new typographic language which appeared to prefigure the new Californian graphics of April Greiman and others of the American new wave.

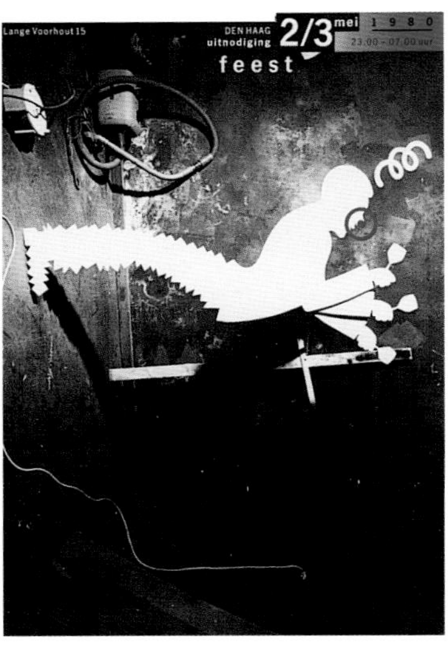

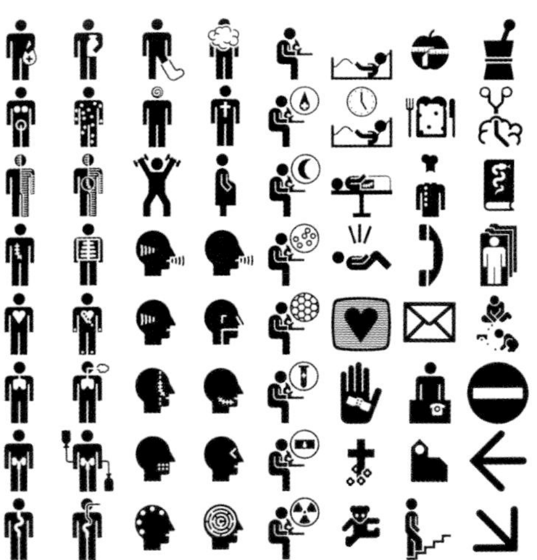

1981.04
Design group: **Studio Dumbar**
Client: **Studio Dumbar**
Although Gert Dumbar had experimented with sculptural and staged photography throughout the seventies, this design (a card to announce the studio opening) with Ko Sliggers for his own studio pushed the concept further than ever before. Dumbar had a photographic studio permanently installed in his studio to help with experimentation.

1982.07
Design group: **Studio Dumbar**
Client: **Westeinde Hospital**
Dumbar built on his creative position at the end of the seventies – functional information graphics with a playful twist – to create this immensely flexible scheme for a Dutch hospital. The design firm even handed the symbols over free of charge. The yellow ball flies around the signage, in case you're wondering.

this page

1982.08
Design group: **Studio Dumbar**
Client: **Rijksmuseum**
This is where Dumbar's 'new' thinking excels – four posters from one year for the stuffy old Rijksmuseum in Amsterdam featuring letter-spaced capitals, a seemingly evolving house style that emanates from the top left of the posters, immediately portraying the museum as more contemporary. The project created a more-or-less instant benchmark in graphics for the world's cultural institutions.

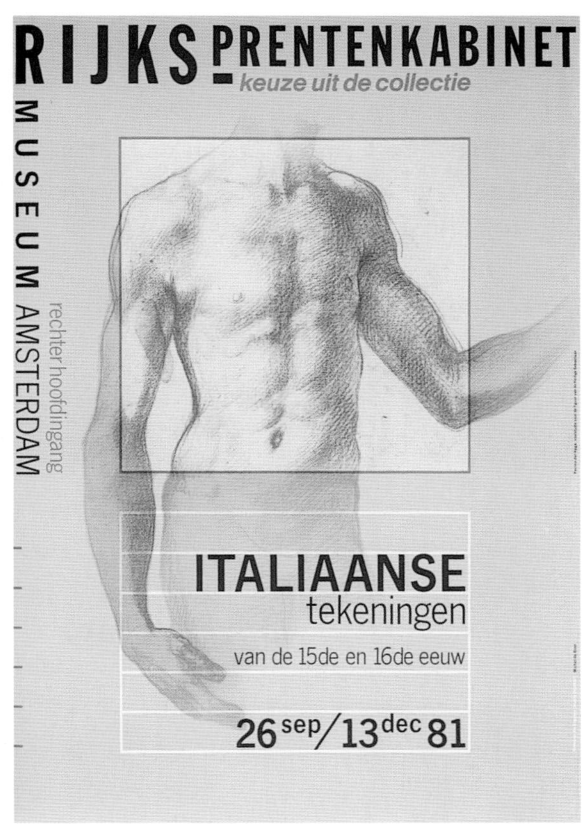

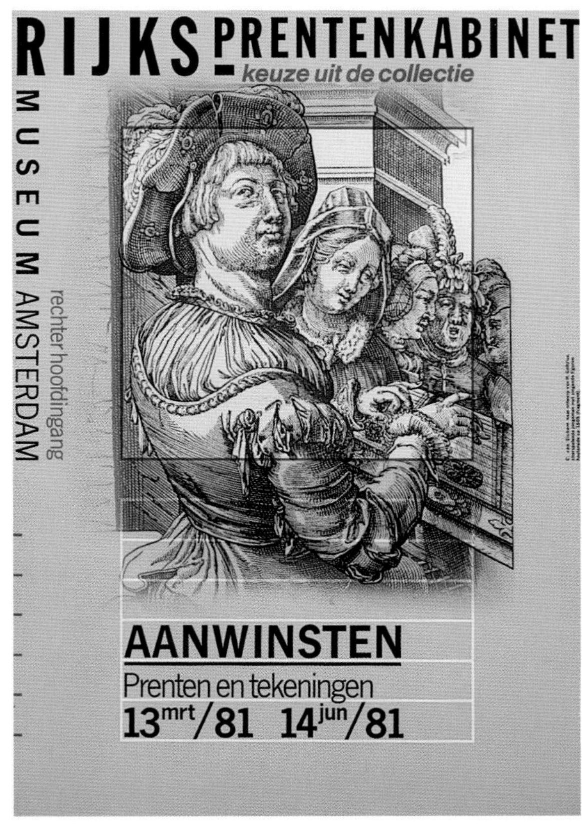

WC
WC

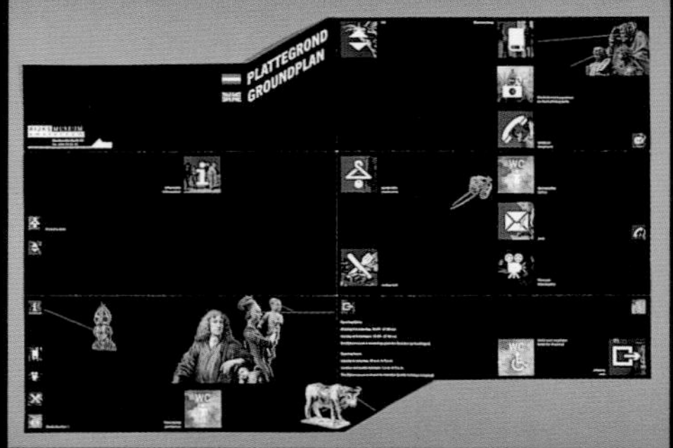
PLATTEGROND
GROUNDPLAN

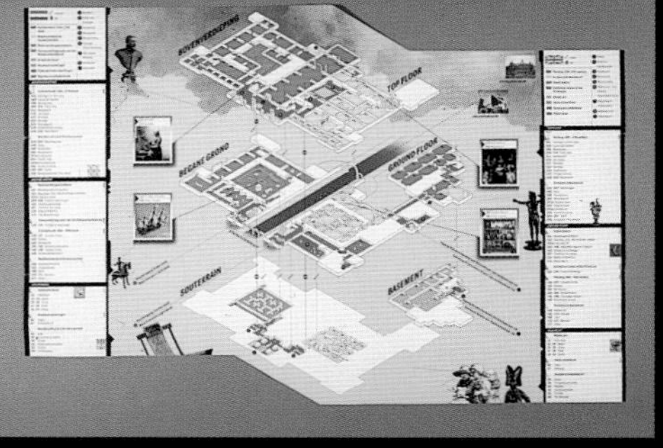

1987.05
Design group: **Studio Dumbar**
Client: **Rijksmuseum**
Dumbar and Michel de Boer worked on this scheme which managed to inject interest and personality into the Rijksmuseum identity by using pictorial elements of the collection as backgrounds for the signage system and icons. The innovatively shaped signage was also classic Dumbarism. Studio Dumbar worked closely with public sector and cultural clients in the eighties who were receptive to its more experimental visual ideas.

this page

1988.08
Design group: **Studio Dumbar**
Client: **Holland Festival**
Robert Nakata's art direction is possibly the peak of the Dumbar style of this period: 3D letters cascade in and around the layouts, shadows and gels play across surfaces. In the end, it becomes difficult to ascertain what is type and what is within the picture. The layout has become one seamless whole rather than two related but separate elements.

Gert Dumbar also pioneered a new technique called stage photography in which models were made and photographed (by collaborator Lex van Pieterson) as a form of 3D sculptural illustration. The final image would then be retouched. Best seen in Dumbar's Holland Festival posters, this complex technique was highly original in pushing the boundaries of where graphics, illustration and photography meet.

Dumbar's presidency of D&AD in 1988 gave him a platform from which to reach the widest audience with his approach. His appointment as a visiting professor of graphic design at the Royal College of Art during the eighties (a role cut short when he was controversially sacked by the college's rector Jocelyn Stevens) also enabled him to influence a new generation of graphic designers which would carry his ideas forward into the nineties.

If Dumbar made a big splash in corporate graphics in the early eighties, uniting design and advertising perspectives behind his singular vision, then Martin Lambie-Nairn did the same in television graphics. The project that did the trick was his computer-animated on-screen identity for Channel 4, launched in November 1982. Channel 4 was the first new British terrestrial television channel since BBC2 started in 1964. It caused a stir because it had a new remit – to take risks, to be alternative and to appeal to minority interests – and it had a new modus operandi. Channel 4 set out to commission programmes from independent programme-makers rather than make everything in-house, as the BBC had traditionally done.

This central idea of different elements being dynamically pulled together from a variety of sources formed the basis of a design idea which Lambie-Nairn presented to Channel 4. Coloured bars would fly around before forming a figure 4. It was a groundbreaking concept capable of giving Channel 4 a flexible identity with a strong core personality. The trouble was that the computer graphics technology that existed in the UK at the time was too feeble and unsophisticated to give the flying elements any drama and authority. Just two months before Channel 4's launch, Lambie-Nairn was forced to fly out to Hollywood and seek help from a Los Angeles special effects company which had worked on the movie *Tron*. The eventual result was spectacularly successful.

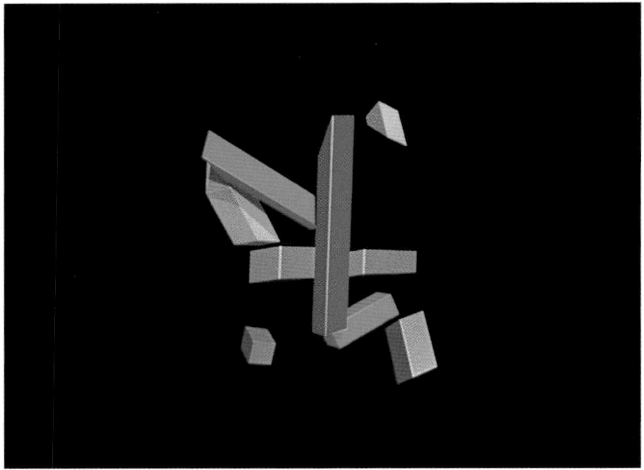

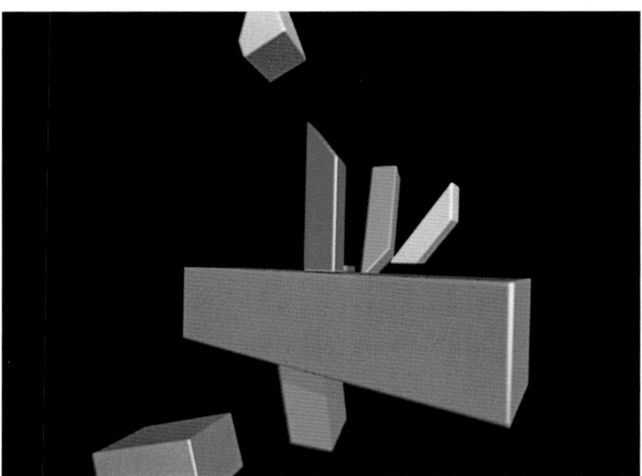

● 1983.05
Design group: **Robinson Lambie-Nairn**
Client: **Channel Four Television**
Martin Lambie-Nairn's television design experience enabled him to beat Wolff Olins to win the career-defining Channel 4 job. But the project nearly ended in disaster when one senior C4 executive insisted that the logo should be silver-chromed and another argued that there was no such thing in the history of typography as a figure 4 with a base serif. Lambie-Nairn won the arguments. The rest is history.

● 1985.08
Agency: **Collett Dickenson Pearce**
Client: **Gallaher**
An affectionate spoof for Hamlet which Lambie-Nairn directed himself.

Despite a shaky start to its programming, Channel 4's on-screen identity was much talked about and set a trend in computerized graphic identities, winning a D&AD Gold Award in 1983. Channel 4 also received an affectionate parody in a Hamlet cigar TV commercial made by CDP. In the commercial conceived by Rod Waskett and Paul Weinberger, the coloured blocks come together but mistakenly form a '5'. Then they try again but make nothing in particular; finally they make a face, give up and light a cigar. Lambie-Nairn himself directed the ad with Anna Hart, having first sought permission for the spoof from Channel 4's then-head Jeremy Isaacs. A D&AD Silver for Animation in 1985 was his reward.

Due to the pulling power of Channel 4, Lambie-Nairn was swamped with offers from advertising agencies to design computer-animated commercials in the mid-eighties. He made a series of Smarties commercials for JWT, with the tagline 'Only Smarties have the answer', but quickly tired of technology for its own sake. By the end of the decade, he had forsaken pixels altogether and was busy creating the quirky on-screen '2' figure for BBC2 as a balsa wood model with paint thrown at it and shot using live-action.

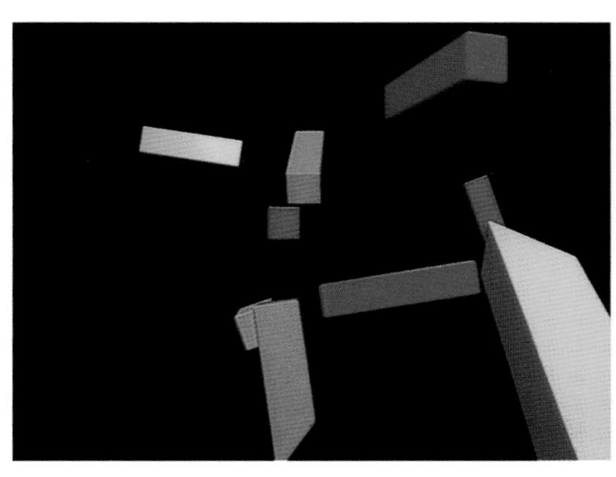

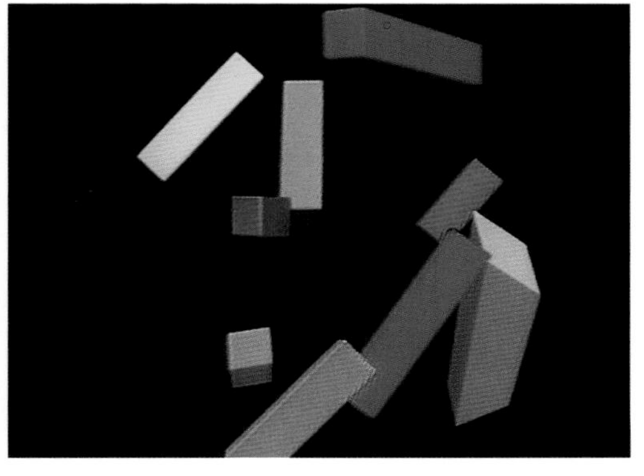

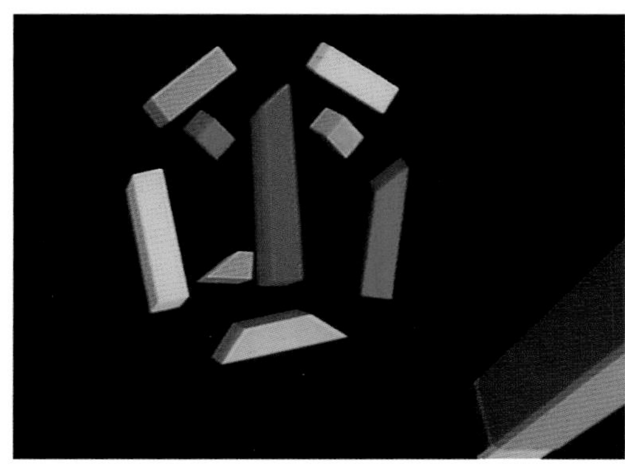

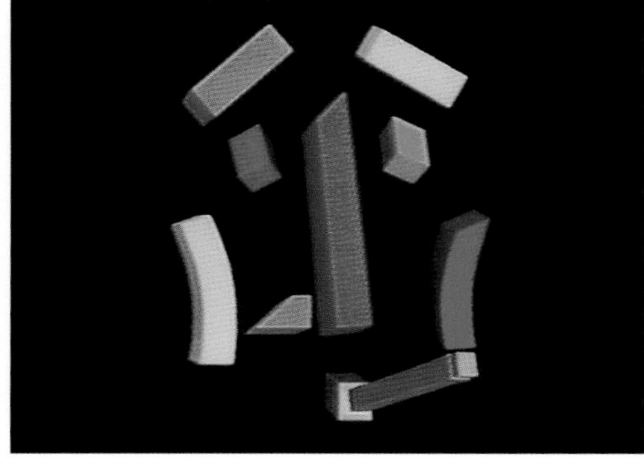

Channel 4 generated the high-tech computer graphics craze of the eighties just as the low-tech BBC2 identity would later revive live action and modelmaking in the early nineties. But Lambie-Nairn was also responsible for another television design classic of the decade, as the originator of *Spitting Image*. This weekly programme by Central Independent TV, featuring the puppetmaster skills of caricaturists Peter Fluck and Roger Law, rewrote the rules of political satire in the eighties.

Fluck and Law had been around in the sixties and seventies as illustrators and cartoonists. Now they created what they described as 'the first caricature factory in history', bringing in an army of talented craftsmen, artists and mechanics to draw, model, paint, sculpt and shoot to tight weekly deadlines.

Spitting Image, which won two D&AD Silvers in 1985 for television graphics and best design of a comedy programme, became renowned for the savagery of its humour. Its venomous puppets targeted everyone from pompous rock stars and manic politicians like Margaret Thatcher and Ronald Reagan to the Royal family. Some victims even asked Fluck and Law if they could buy their puppet after particular episodes of *Spitting Image* were screened, including Michael Heseltine, then Defence Minister in Thatcher's government. Law apparently told a Ministry of Defence flunky, 'Tell him if he sends Cruise [US missiles based on UK soil] back he can have his puppet for nothing.'

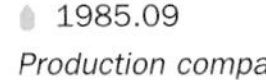

1985.09
Production company:
Spitting Image Productions
Client: **Central Independent Television**
While celebrities and politicians queued up to buy their puppets and were often refused, agencies queued up to use the *Spitting Image* style in advertising campaigns. But Fluck and Law, true to their radical sixties roots, resisted the lure of adland, as *Campaign* 'Diary' items from the period reveal.

1980.03
Production company:
Caravel Film Services
Client: **BBC Television**

1981.05
Graphic designer: **Stewart Austin**
Client: **BBC Television**

1983.06
Set designer:
David Myerscough-Jones
Client: **BBC Television**

Three successful BBC productions reflecting the Corporation's high design standards in the early eighties. Set designer David Myerscough-Jones won Gold for his work on *Therese Raquin*. The classic sequence for the John Le Carré thriller, *Tinker Tailor Soldier Spy*, was directed by Douglas Burd.

Lambie-Nairn found his status as *Spitting Image* originator occasionally uncomfortable. When he pitched for Anglia Television's identity, he encountered Anglia board member Mary Archer, whose husband Jeffrey Archer, then a Conservative Party MP, was always top of Fluck and Law's hit list. Nevertheless, *Spitting Image* was a triumph, its opening credits inventively mixing library footage, traditional puppeteering skills and digital and optical effects in a groundbreaking way. There was nothing quite like it in British television graphics at the time, although D&AD juries took a shine to plenty of TV projects in the eighties, starting with a Silver Award in 1980 for Douglas Burd's drama titles for a BBC production of John Le Carré's *Tinker Tailor Soldier Spy*, in which a sequence of Russian dolls open up to reveal the identity of a faceless spy.

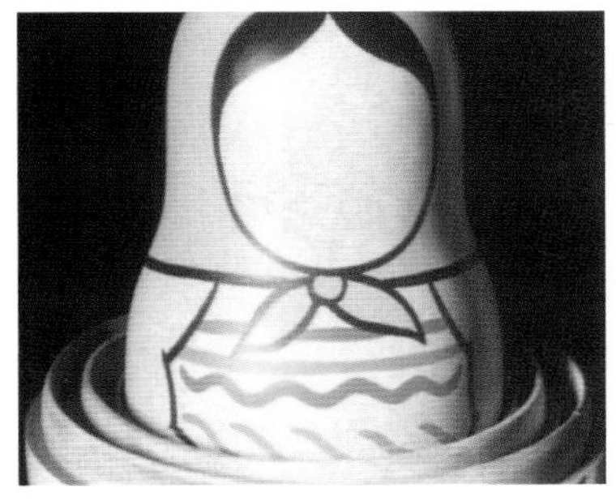

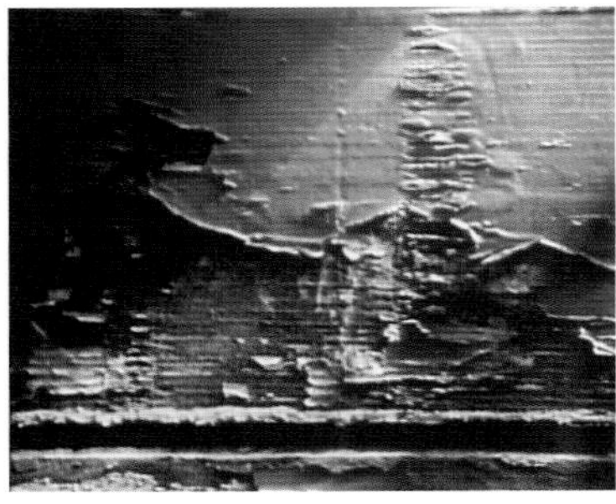

Burd won again in 1981 with graphic inserts of the 'Babel Fish' for the BBC production of *The Hitchhiker's Guide to the Galaxy* written by Douglas Adams, while Raymond Briggs' animation classic *The Snowman*, commissioned by Channel 4, earned a D&AD Silver in 1983. Many of the seasoned talents who had guided Lambie-Nairn's TV design career in the seventies were still on song, including Bernard Lodge (Gold winner in 1983 with the graphics for a TV documentary on spices) and Pat Gavin (Silver winner in 1984 with the titles for a London Weekend Television series on the industrial arts).

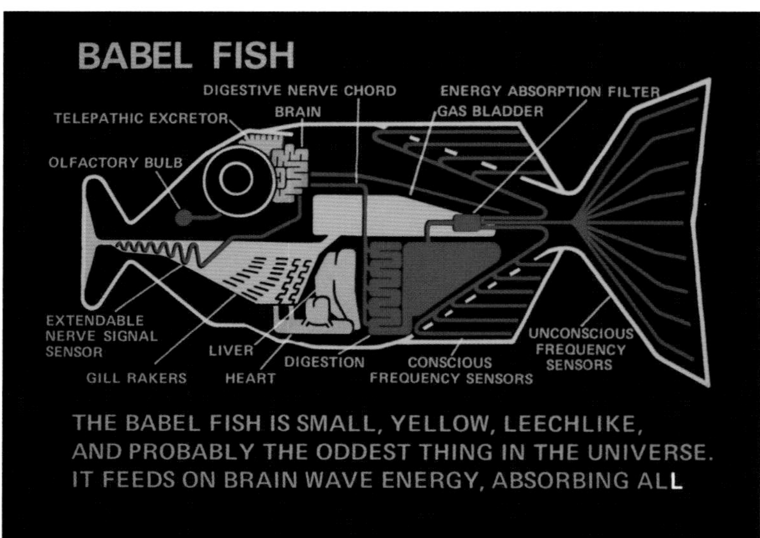

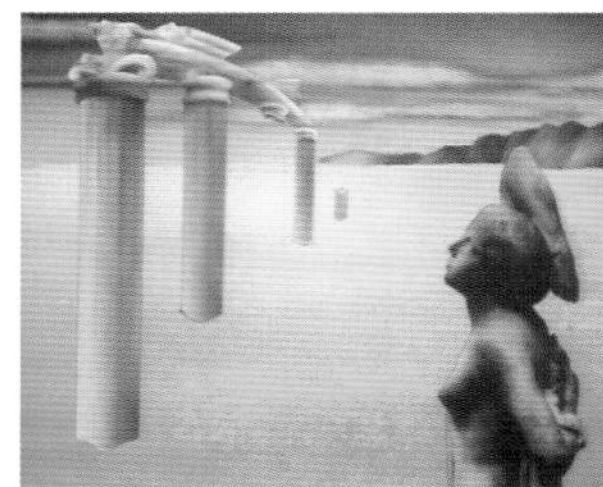

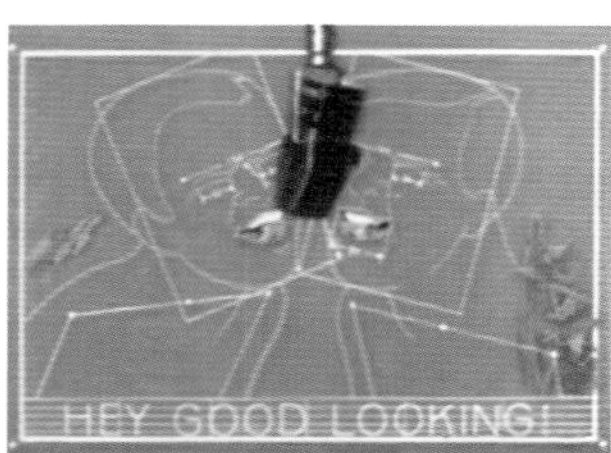

1981.06
Graphic designers: **Douglas Burd & Rod Lord**
Client: **BBC Television**

1983.07
Graphic designer: **Darrell Pockett**
Client: **BBC Television**

1984.11
Graphic designer: **Pat Gavin**
Client: **London Weekend Television**

1983.08
Graphic designer: **Bernard Lodge**
Client: **Blackrod**

This selection of D&AD-winning TV titles and graphic interjections from the early eighties shows the skill of practitioners who were required to address diverse subject matter and create a modern and futuristic appeal within the tightest of budgets. This was the era in which a 'computer graphics' look was simulated before computers were really available. Running clockwise from top left they are, 'Babel Fish', *Omnibus*, *Hey Good Looking* and *Spice of Life*.

opposite

1983.09
Production company: **Snowman Enterprises**
Client: **Channel Four Television**
This half-hour animated film was commissioned as a Christmas special and became a children's favourite. It propelled animators Raymond Briggs and Jill Brooks into the limelight and also did its bit for boy soprano Aled Jones' career.

However, from the mid-eighties onwards, there was new competition for Lambie-Nairn in the form of English Markell Pockett (EMP), which won the contract to rebrand ITV while Lambie-Nairn handled the identities for BBC1 and 2. Darrell Pockett directed the 1983 D&AD Silver-winning credits for BBC arts programme *Omnibus* before leaving BBC Television to team up with Bob English and Richard Markell. By 1986, the trio's new television design firm was a D&AD winner with the programme graphics for *Ghosts in the Machine*, a six-part series on experimental video art. EMP's opening sequence featured standard video colour bars being broken and distorted to symbolize the way experimental video artists disturb convention.

A fertile decade for television graphics ended with a 1989 Silver Award for Matt Forrest's head-banging opening credits for a Channel 4 magazine programme called *Wired*. In the sequence, a skeletal automaton named Mad Bastard crashes through a ghost town to raise hell in a kind of mutant *mardi-gras*. In its combination of live action and computer animation, *Wired* reflected the decade's debt to Channel 4's computerized flying girders – but also hinted at the more sophisticated characterizations that would emerge in the ninieties.

1986.11
Graphic designer: **Richard Markell**
Client: **Illumination**
Designed for a series of programmes on video art, the title sequence for *Ghosts in the Machine* borrowed heavily from the experimental techniques of video artists themselves, as TV graphics in the mid-eighties explored a widening array of cultural sources.

opposite

1989.07
Graphic designer: **Matt Forrest**
Client: **Initial Film and Television**
'Mad Bastard', the animated character who stars in the *Wired* title sequence, caused enough mayhem to make its creator Matt Forrest a sought-after pop promo director in the nineties. Forrest claimed at the time that he produced the storyboard for the 50-second title sequence in seven minutes flat – 'but I thought about it for a whole two weeks before that,' he added.

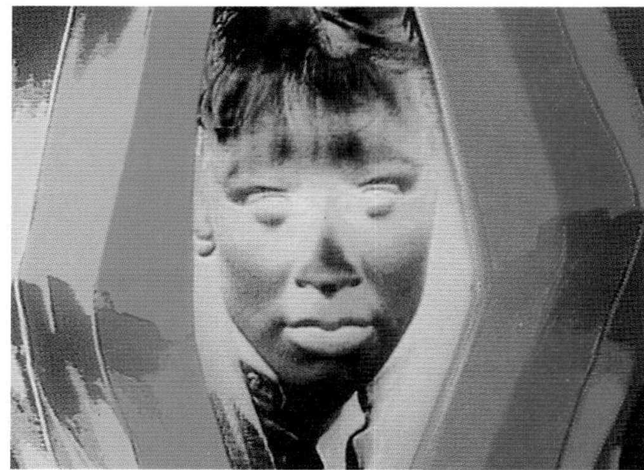

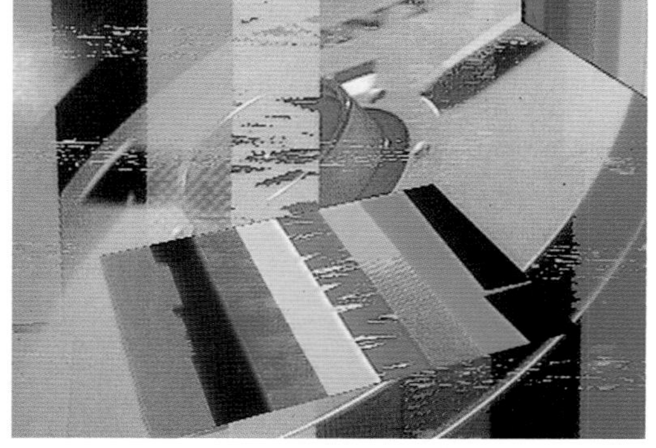

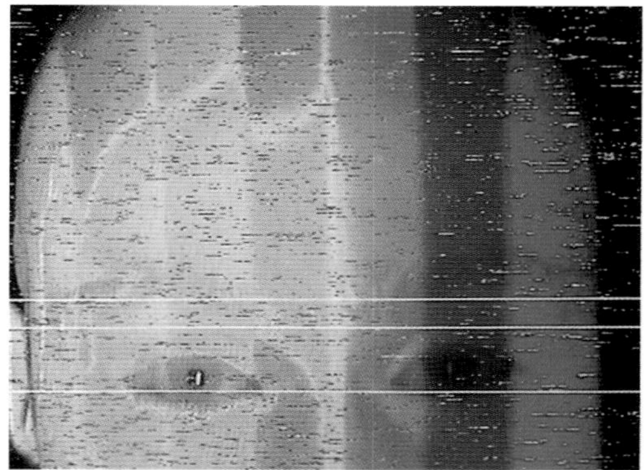

WIRED

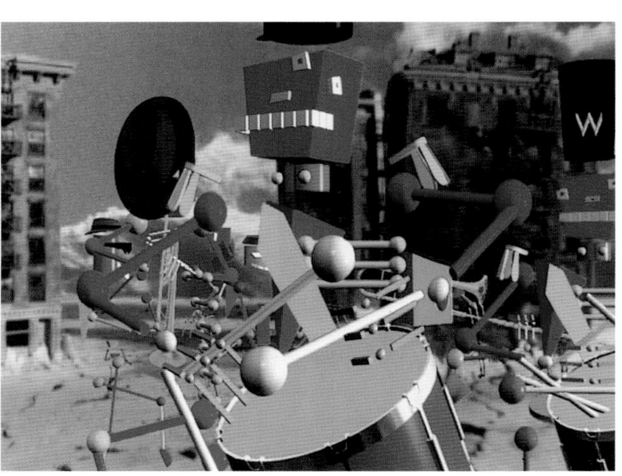
W

While television graphics responded to the varied programme content of the decade with a kaleidescope of different styles and techniques, the music industry graphics highlighted by the D&AD Awards in the eighties increasingly packaged contemporary music in an archly minimal fashion. The trend towards a bleak techno-modern look was set early on by art director Peter Saville with album sleeve work for such bands as Orchestral Manoeuvres in the Dark (OMD) and Joy Division. Tony Wilson at Factory Records in Manchester was a willing client, and Saville's work dominated much of the eighties.

This was before the mantle passed to Mark Farrow, whose collaboration with former art school students Neil Tennant and Chris Lowe of the Pet Shop Boys produced the memorably minimal 'Suburbia' record sleeve, a Silver winner in 1987. One page of the 1989 D&AD Annual caught the final handover between the two: a Saville sleeve for Factory Records on top, a Farrow limited edition cover for the Pet Shop Boys below. Saville never entered the D&AD Awards again.

1981.07
Design group: **Peter Saville**
Client: **Dindisc Records**
Peter Saville's collaborator on this record sleeve for OMD was none other than Ben Kelly, before he decided he wanted to be an interior designer. Kelly would later feature at D&AD for environments and architecture.

1989.08
Design group: **Three Associates**
Client: **Parlophone Records & Pet Shop Boys**
While still with design firm Three Associates (better known as 3a), Mark Farrow had begun his Pet Shop Boys relationship which was consolidated by album designs such as this. The six coloured bars presented a kind of minimalist TV test screen to the record-buying public.

1981.08
Design group: **Peter Saville**
Client: **Factory Records**
This came from a period when Saville's work for Joy Division, the Manchester-based new wave band with suicidal lead singer Ian Curtis, was highly classical in its approach. On this album cover we see austere forest scenes and a subtle line of capitals.

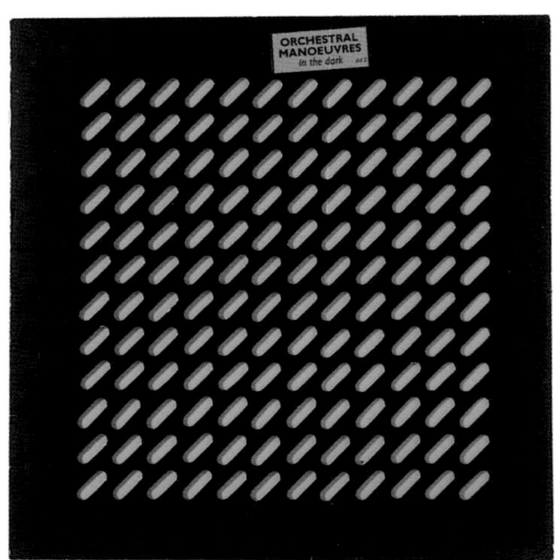

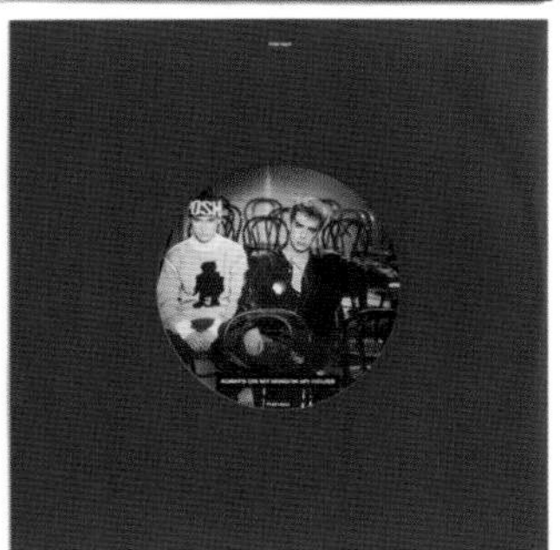

1989.09
Design group:
Peter Saville Associates
Client: **Factory Communications**
A record sleeve from the height of Peter Saville's eighties relationship with New Order, the band that grew from Joy Division. By now, Saville was working regularly with Brett Wickens and the late Trevor Key, a photographer around whose processing experiments much of the work of this period revolves entirely. The approach emulated Man Ray's Rayographs from the thirties – in particular Man Ray's 1931 series for a Paris electricity company (La Compagnie Parisienne de Distribution de l'Éléctricité). But Saville did so in a high-colour environment. While this style looks easy to accomplish now, it was still achieved pre-computer and pre-Photoshop.

1987.06
Design group: **Three Associates**
Client: **Parlophone Records & Pet Shop Boys**
Three Associates and Mark Farrow really announced their arrival with this 1987 D&AD Silver winner, which, in Saville-esque style, rejected typographic accompaniment almost completely, apart from the embroidered 'poshboy' on Chris Lowe's T-shirt. Incidentally, Farrow still cites Saville's *Unknown Pleasures* sleeve for Joy Divison as the design that made him realize the power of the medium (and the design advances that could be made within the genre).

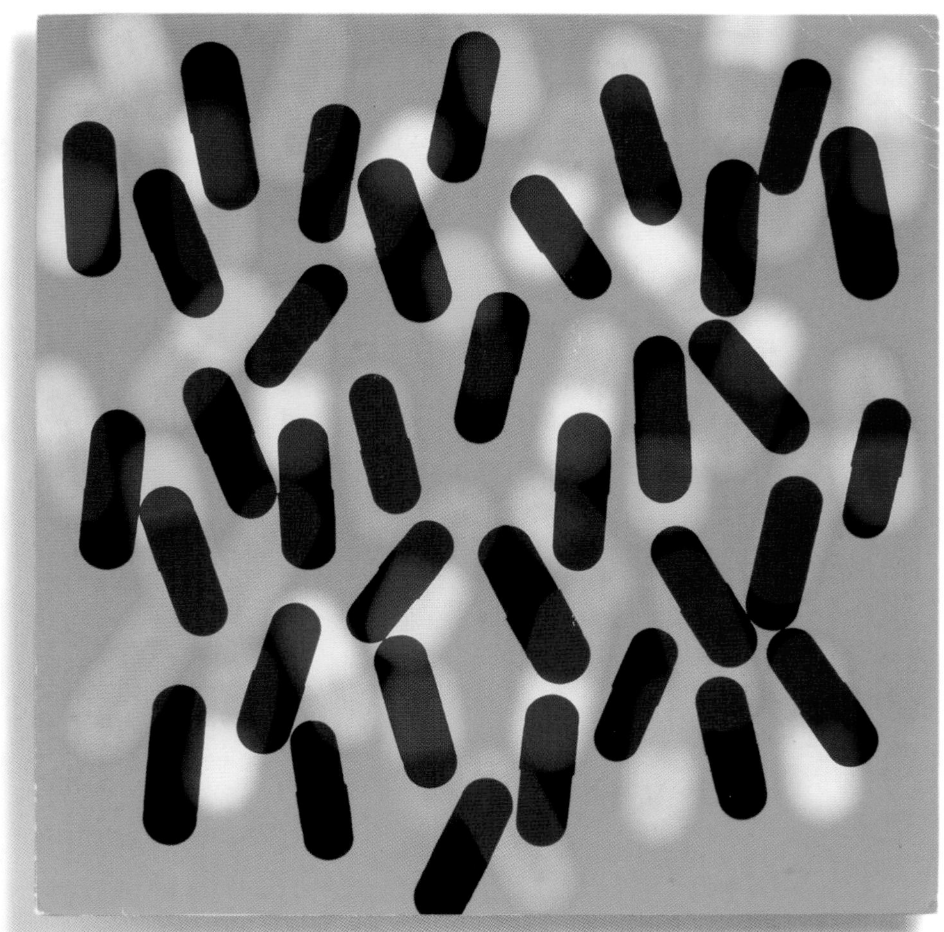

There were stylistic interruptions to the Saville-Farrow axis. Kate Hepburn's odd Chinese cultural pastiche for a Jean-Michel Jarre record promotion won a Silver Award in 1983 and Mike Dempsey's elegantly simple London Chamber Orchestra sleeves did the same in 1989. (Dempsey and his design team at Carroll Dempsey & Thirkell (CDT) used the project to explore a Studio Dumbar-influenced style that they would refine in the nineties in posters for English National Opera.) Jean-Paul Goude, the French stylist behind the rise of Grace Jones, was responsible in 1983 for one of the defining music biz images of the eighties – the angular Grace Jones *Living My Life* album cover.

1983.10
Art director: **Kate Hepburn**
Client: **Francis Dreyfus Music**

1983.11
Art director: **Jean-Paul Goude**
Client: **Island Records**

The French connection in early eighties record promotion; Jean-Michel Jarre art directed by Kate Hepburn, and Jean-Paul Goude art directed Grace Jones in one of the more memorable sleeves of the period.

opposite

1989.10
Design group:
Carroll Dempsey & Thirkell
Client: **Virgin Records & the London Chamber Orchestra**
A critical project for Mike Dempsey. Having spent much of the seventies and eighties working in a craft-based style, he approached this set of CD covers with a decorative mindset and regular collaborator Andy Seymour. But this time his antennae were alert to the changing styles around him. As London revived sans serif typefaces and began to rediscover modernism at the end of the eighties, he turned back to Helvetica and re-invented his design approach to something much more akin to that which he studied in the sixties. It was on the back of this project that CDT was appointed to work on the milestone identity project for English National Opera in the nineties.

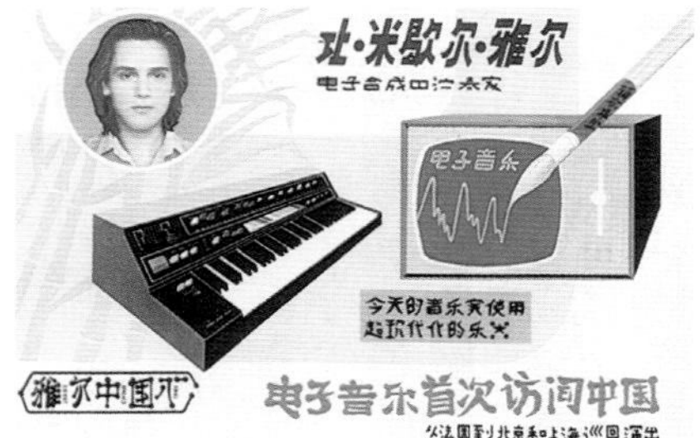

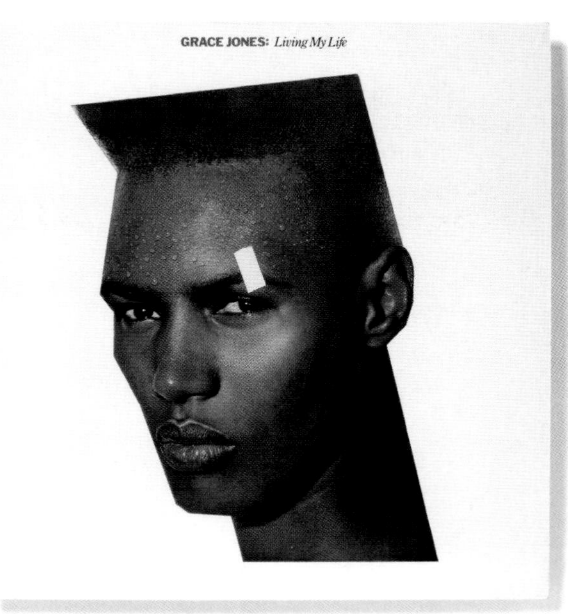

Mozart
LCO1
London
Chamber
Orchestra
Mozart
Sinfonia Concertante
for violin & viola
Sinfonia Concertante
for wind

Vaughan Williams/Elgar
LCO2
London
Chamber
Orchestra
Vaughan Williams
The Lark Ascending
Fantasia
on a theme
by Thomas Tallis
Fantasia
on Greensleeves
Elgar
Introduction
& Allegro
Serenade
for Strings

Vivaldi/Pachelbel/Albinoni
LCO3
London
Chamber
Orchestra
Vivaldi
The Four Seasons
Pachelbel
Canon
Albinoni
Adagio

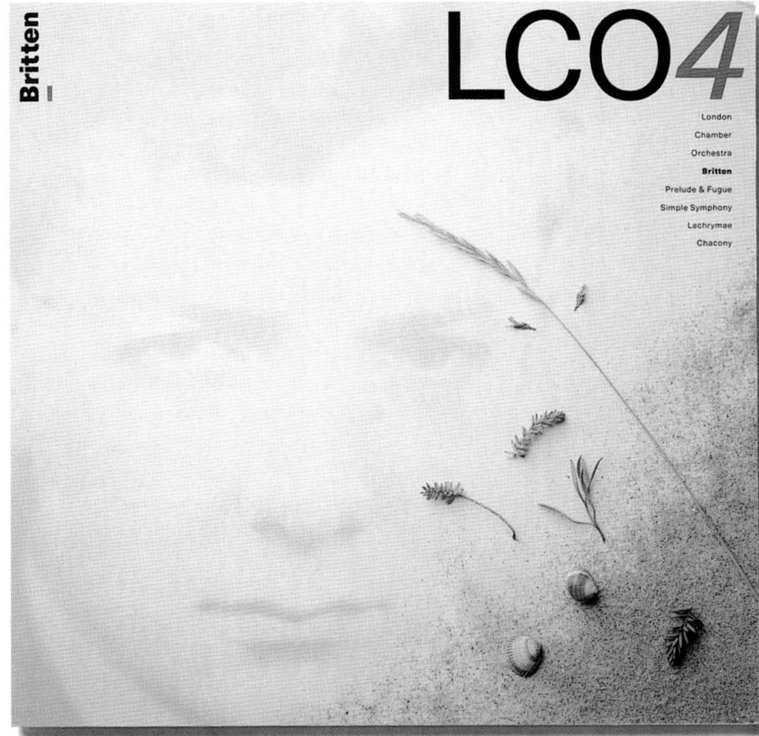
Britten
LCO4
London
Chamber
Orchestra
Britten
Prelude & Fugue
Simple Symphony
Lachrymae
Chacony

D&AD's record sleeve category even featured, for the one and only time in 1982, a project by Neville Brody, arguably the most important of the new graphic designers operating in the vanguard of pop culture. This was a self-illustrated sleeve for Fetish Records. Brody cut his teeth as a designer at independent label Stiff Records in the seventies before becoming the art director of *The Face*, which was launched in 1980 by publishing whizzkid Nick Logan with his own savings and which became the first and best of the style magazines of that period. 1980 was a big year for magazines, with the launch of *Creative Review* (the first magazine for design and advertising creatives) and *i-D* magazine (a self-styled 'worldwide manual of style' edited and art directed by Terry Jones) among the new titles.

In this climate of creative opportunity, as art directors everywhere re-engaged with design history, Brody, an unknown talent at the time, quickly caught the eye. His layouts for *The Face* reflected his own fascination with earlier eras of graphic innovation, in particular the Soviet constructivist and Dutch De Stijl movements. *The Face*'s influence on fashion, advertising and communications was enormous. By the end of the eighties, this publishing outsider was owned by Condé Nast, Logan was a rich man and Brody a famous designer, courtesy of a one-man show at the Victoria and Albert Museum, of all places.

But if Saville, Farrow and Brody all stamped their mark on music and style graphics in the eighties, the inescapable feeling was that the art of the record sleeve belonged to the sixties and seventies and that the real creative action was in directing pop promos. Was the music video a bastard cousin of the TV commercial, an animated record sleeve or a much-shrunken *Jailhouse Rock* or *Summer Holiday*? Nobody was sure. But as MTV, the first 24-hour TV station devoted to plugging the music industry, quickly established itself, one thing was for certain: every self-respecting artist needed to make a promotional video just as much as they needed to produce the song.

1982.09
Art director: **Neville Brody**
Client: **Fetish Records**
The only D&AD example of work by Neville Brody, whose approach to design was deemed so original that the Victoria and Albert Museum awarded him a major retrospective exhibition in 1988 while still relatively young and inexperienced.

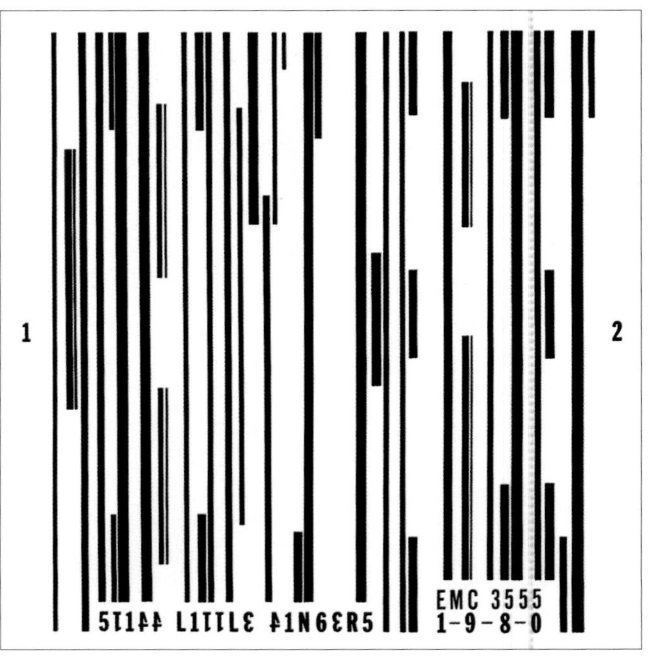

1981.09
Art director: **Peter Wagg**
Client: **Chrysalis Records**
This album cover featured the illustrative talents of Geoff Halpin, a designer later to work with Michael Peters at the Identica Partnership.

□ 1982.10
Production company:
Stewart-Hardy Films
Client: **BBC Television**
The programme that never dies. Despite hovering permanently on the edge of naffness, *TOTP*, as it is affectionately known by BBC insiders, has always managed to escape the axe with regular personnel changes and visual updates. This title revamp prepared the programme for the techno-tinged glamour of the eighties pop business.

That old BBC TV warhorse *Top of the Pops* was given a new title sequence by director Marc Ortman, a project which featured in the 1982 D&AD Annual and included a musical arrangement by Ultravox's Midge Ure and Thin Lizzy's Phil Lynott. Meanwhile, a host of other late night rock shows and early morning children's TV programmes lined up to screen pop promos. The audience was ready, but it took one half of the seventies rock band 10cc – Kevin Godley and Lol Creme – to really get to grips with this emerging creative medium.

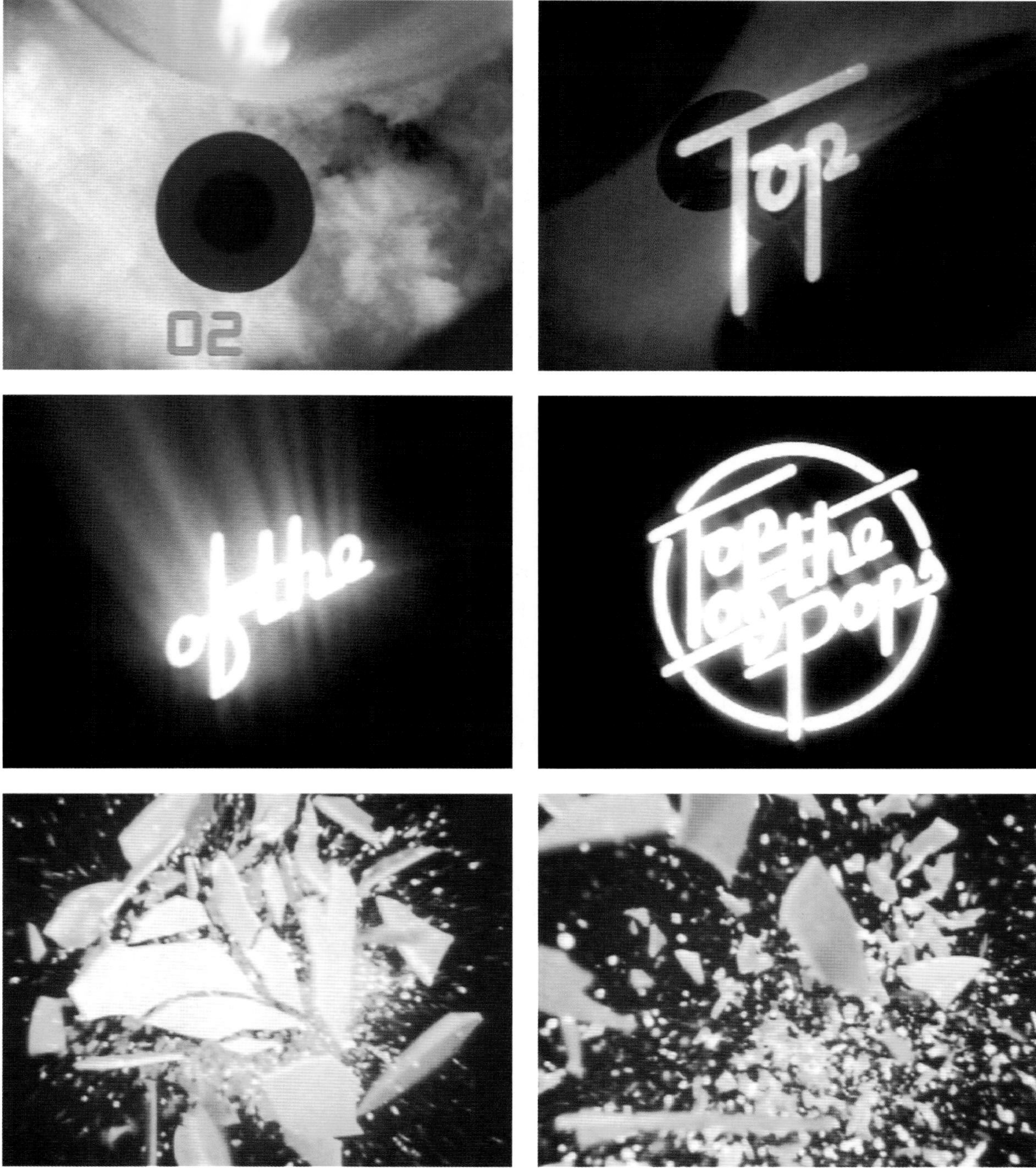

The first music video Godley and Creme jointly directed was for their own song 'An Englishman in New York', taken from their 1979 album *Freeze Frame*. Soon they were being courted by the advertising industry and contributed the soundtracks to several notable commercials, including the D&AD winning Benson & Hedges 'Swimming Pool' extravaganza directed by Hugh Hudson.

The pop promo business really took off for Godley and Creme with the 'Two Tribes' video for Frankie Goes to Hollywood, featured in the 1985 D&AD Annual. As art school graduates, Godley and Creme worked to meticulously detailed storyboards to make the actual shooting more of a formality and to manage the difficult art of co-direction more successfully. The pair also handled the off-line editing themselves. This approach was in contrast to the more freewheeling, improvisational methods of less experienced pop promo wonderkids.

1983.12
Directors: **Kevin Godley & Lol Creme**
Client: **Bluebell Apparel**
'Wrangler, that's what going on' was repeated *ad nauseum* throughout and it looks pretty dated now. But Godley and Creme's work on this jeans ad for CDP was revolutionary at the time, as it was still two years ahead of the big jeans breakthrough by Bartle Bogle Hegarty for Levi's.

opposite

1985.10
Directors: **Kevin Godley & Lol Creme**
Client: **Frankie Goes to Hollywood**
Behind the liberated and seemingly improvised success of Frankie Goes to Hollywood, Godley and Creme's pop promo work was meticulously planned and storyboarded right down to the last frame.

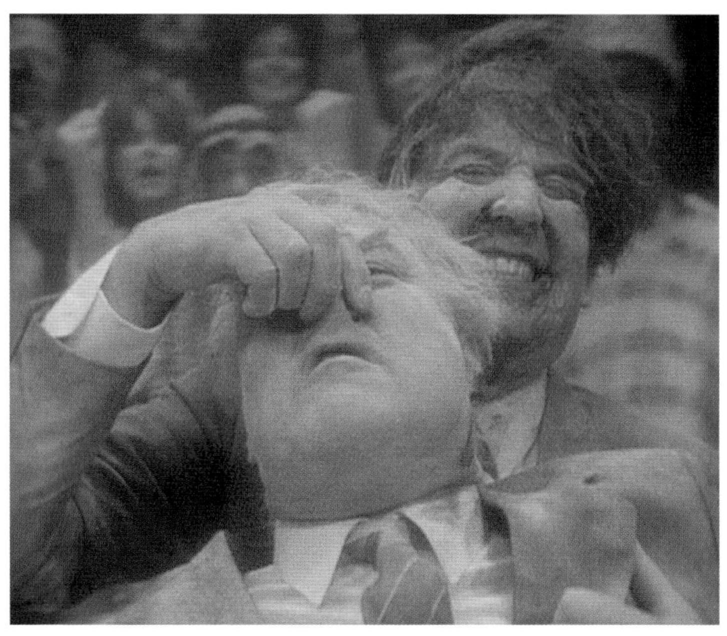

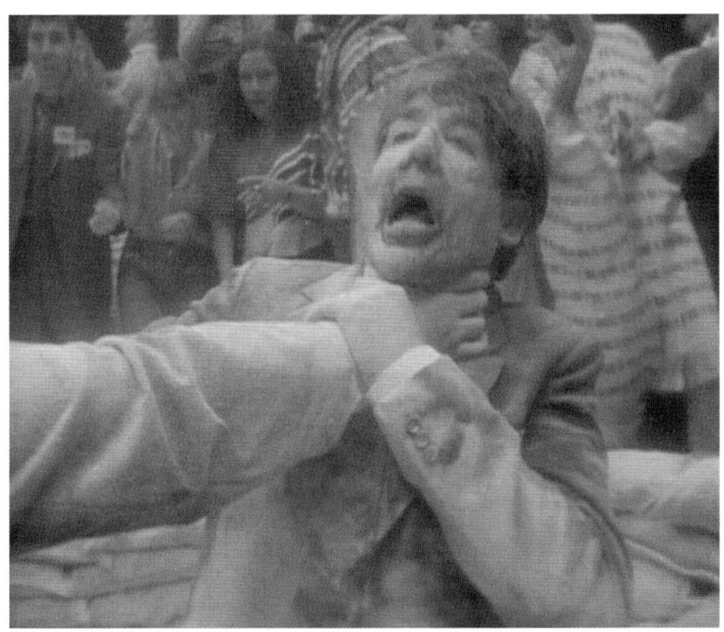

Godley and Creme's highly stylized and surrealistic approach was best appreciated with 'Cry', a video for their own song, which was based on a simple idea. A series of close-ups of intriguing human faces (including those of the artists themselves) dissolved into each other as they sang the lines of the song. The effect was brilliant and emotional – and much imitated by other directors. In fact, the video's technically expert dissolves, achieved by Godley and Creme's production company Media Lab, prefigured human morphing techniques on computer by more than a decade. 'Cry' won a D&AD Silver in 1986.

The only other real pretenders to Godley and Creme's pop promo crown were Julien Temple, who made the music videos for the Rolling Stones and David Bowie before going on to direct the movie musical *Absolute Beginners*, and Russell Mulcahy, who directed Elton John before similarly heading for the silver screen to make a big-budget Sean Connery film called *Highlander*. While Temple's style was moodily filmic, as seen in the 'Undercover of the Night' promo for the Stones, Mulcahy's approach was far more graphic and his feelgood 'I'm Still Standing' promo for a white-suited Elton John won a D&AD Silver in 1984.

1984.12
Director: **Russell Mulcahy**
Client: **Elton John**
Russell Mulcahy turned to the big musical heritage of the straight-up song-and-dance man for Elton John's 'I'm Still Standing'. Choreography on this video was by Arlene Philips, once of dance troupe Hot Gossip on *Top of the Pops*. Philips also choreographed the long-running Andrew Lloyd Webber musical *Cats*.

opposite

1986.12
Directors: **Kevin Godley & Lol Creme**
Client: **Polydor**
Eerily reminiscent of a John and Yoko label for Apple from the early seventies (even Beatles record sleeves from a decade before in the Hamburg period), 'Cry' shot human faces full-on out of black. But what made the video new and different were the morphing techniques which anticipated *Terminator 2* by some distance. A far cry for Kevin and Lol from 10cc and 'I'm a Neanderthal man...' Or was it?

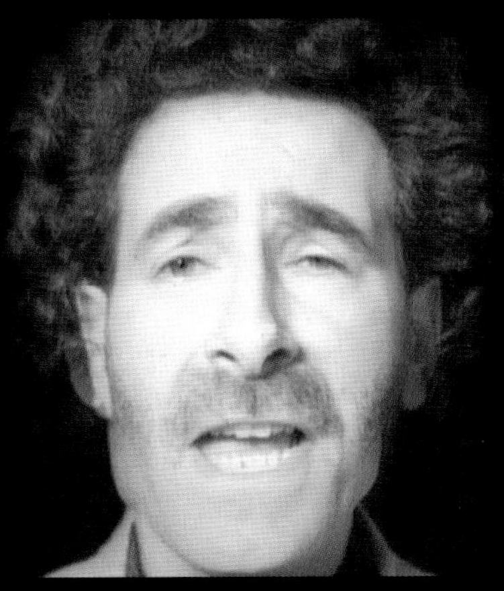

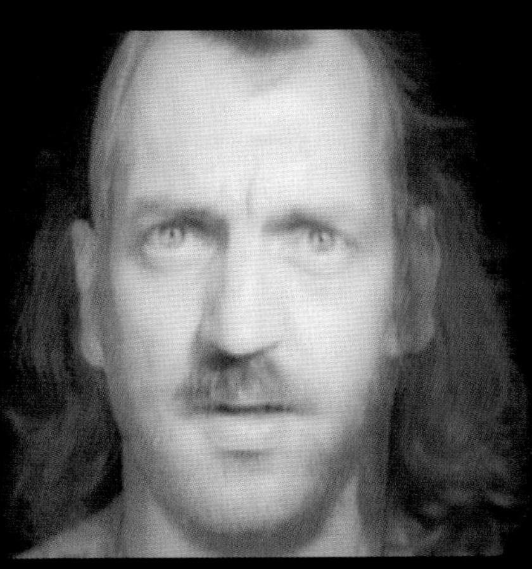

Elsewhere, pop promos were proving as emphemeral as the manufactured eighties pop bands which acted badly in them. However, a video for Peter Gabriel's 'Sledgehammer', directed by Stephen Johnson and featuring animation by Bristol-based Aardman Animations and the Brothers Quay, proved an exception to the rule that pop promos should be instantly forgettable. This used various stop-frame animation techniques to 'pixillate' trains, tools, fruit and dead chickens around Gabriel's head during a marathon 300 hours of shooting. 'Sledgehammer' won a D&AD Silver in 1987.

1987.07
Director: **Stephen Johnson**
Client: **Virgin Records**
Aardman Animations and the Brothers Quay featured on this animated Peter Gabriel promo.

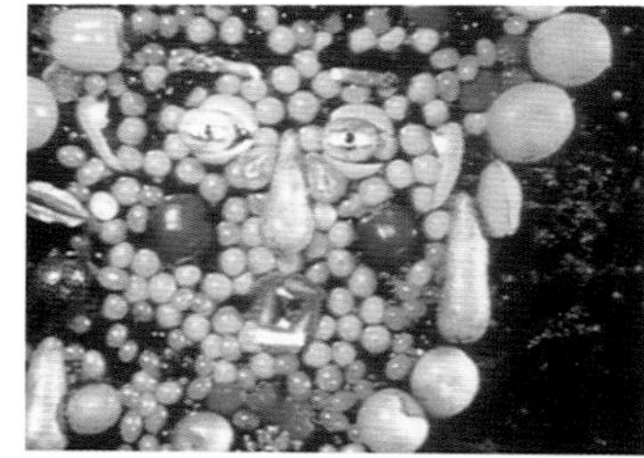

1981.10
Agency: **Boase Massimi Pollitt Univas Partnership**
Client: **Courage Brewing**
'Rabbit, Rabbit' by Cockney pub rockers Chas 'n' Dave featured in this TV ad for Courage Best Bitter.

opposite

1982.11
Agency: **Boase Massimi Pollitt Univas Partnership**
Client: **Courage Brewing**
One of the classic 'Arkwright' ads by BMP, courtesy of John Webster. This campaign ran for over nine years and the death of the actor who played Arkwright was the first time a character from a commercial was mourned by public and press.

1983.13
Agency: **Boase Massimi Pollitt Univas Partnership**
Client: **Courage Brewing**
More dry Webster humour to make punters wet their whistle with John Smith's lager.

While pop promos were a testing ground for eye-popping new computer animation techniques, bigger-budget TV and cinema commercials in the eighties used such frills and thrills more sparingly. Great ideas, good acting, strong direction – these were still the staples of the discipline (as in DDB's campaign for Commercial Union, which won a D&AD Silver in 1980).

However, in tune with the tenor of the times, adland also went in for its own pastiche of the past by spoofing the movies. BMP's 1982 Gold-winning commercial for John Smith's Yorkshire Bitter, written by John Webster and directed by Ian McMillan, was part of a campaign which recreated Laurel and Hardy song-and-dance routines step for step in a Yorkshire pub.

More cinematic homage was to follow. When the cult film *Dead Men Don't Wear Plaid* interspersed comedian Steve Martin with old Hollywood footage, a lightbulb lit up in the minds of creative team Steve Henry and Axel Chaldecott at Gold Greenlees Trott (GGT). The result was a classic black-and-white campaign for Holsten Pils, memorably directed by Richard Sloggett, in which comedian Griff Rhys Jones played opposite Humphrey Bogart, James Cagney, George Raft, John Wayne and Barbara Stanwyck. Sloggett spent six months working on the project with Henry and Chaldecott and shot three test films before he coaxed a great performance from Rhys Jones during the final two-day shoot. Footage of comedian Robbie Coltrane had been used for the tests.

The Holsten Pils campaign, which won a D&AD Gold Award in 1984, was commercially successful as well as critically acclaimed. It enabled the brand to grab a two-thirds share of the Pils lager market in the UK and, quipped agency boss Michael Greenlees, the casting of dead stars saved on repeat fees. (Holsten Pils also confirmed Griff Rhys Jones as an advertising star, although he and his partner Mel Smith had already won a D&AD Gold in 1983 with their 'Firips' radio spots for Philips, the only really exceptional radio advertising campaign of the eighties.)

1983.14
Agency:
The Leagas Delaney Partnership
Client: **Philips Video Division**
The high point of eighties radio advertising. Tim Delaney created the memorable concept about the consumer obsession with all electronic things Japanese; Griff Rhys Jones and Mel Smith, fast approaching the peak of their celebrity, wrote the 'Firips' scripts.

opposite

1984.13
Agency: **Gold Greenlees Trott**
Client: **Holsten Distributors**
Hollywood history pillaged to promote Pils. Whilst cleverly done, these Holsten ads just reinforced for many people the belief that the adman's job was an easy one – just watch lots of movies and rip off the best ideas – the inspiration here being the Steve Martin film *Dead Men Don't Wear Plaid.* But, at the time, the sheer artistic conviction and technical skill of the whole campaign made it a Gold Award winner and a talking point in the pub and at work.

FIRIPS'

CUSTOMER: Morning Squire.
SALESMAN: Morning Sir.
CUSTOMER: I'd like a video caster please.
SALESMAN: A video recorder, any one in particular.
CUSTOMER: Well I'd like to have some specifications.
SALESMAN: Yes.
CUSTOMER: And functions. I must have some functions.
SALESMAN: I see did you have any model in mind.
CUSTOMER: Well a friend mentioned the Harry-keri-caboogie casoonni-whatchamacallit you know the Japanese one the 2000 'cause I'm very technically minded you see.
SALESMAN: I can see that Sir.
CUSTOMER: So I want one with all the bits on it, all the Japanese bits you know the 2000.
SALESMAN: What system?
CUSTOMER: Oh aah well electrical I think 'cause I'd like to be able to plug it in to the television you see I've got a Japanese television.
SALESMAN: Have you?
CUSTOMER: Yeah, I thought you'd be impressed, yeah the 2000 the Hoki-Koki 2000.
SALESMAN: Well Sir there is this model.
CUSTOMER: It looks smart.
SALESMAN: Eight hours per cassette all the functions that the others have and I know this will be of interest a lot of scientific research has gone in to making it easy to operate even by a complete idiot like you.
CUSTOMER: Pardon?
SALESMAN: It's a Philips.
CUSTOMER: Doesn't sound very Japanese.
SALESMAN: No a Firips, I mean a Firips, it's a Firips.
CUSTOMER: Well, aah it is a 2000 is it?
SALESMAN: Well, in fact it's the 2022.
CUSTOMER: Mmmm, no, no, it hasn't got enough knobs on it, no. What's that one over there?
SALESMAN: That's a washing machine.
CUSTOMER: What sort Japanese?...
MVO: The VR2022 video you can understand from Firips

John Webster wasn't entirely happy with what he described as 'the time of the great piss take' in TV advertising. In 1985, he wrote despairingly in *Creative Review*: 'Perhaps it's inevitable that things become cynical in a once-great country now in decline with massive unemployment, widening class differences, and sitting on a sediment of broken promises.' But cynical or not, commercials like Holsten Pils and John Smith's Yorkshire Bitter helped advertising to achieve a kind of popular breakthrough in the eighties. These campaigns were talked about in the same way and on the same cultural wavelength as pop songs or paintings or new film releases.

Other TV commercials confirmed this new status by seeping into popular consciousness, leaping from the ad breaks into people's daily conversations and catchphrases. 'Hello Tosh, gotta Toshiba?' signalled another outstanding GGT campaign, again directed by Richard Sloggett; this featured the irrepressible Alexei Sayle, then part of the hit eighties TV comedy series *The Young Ones*.

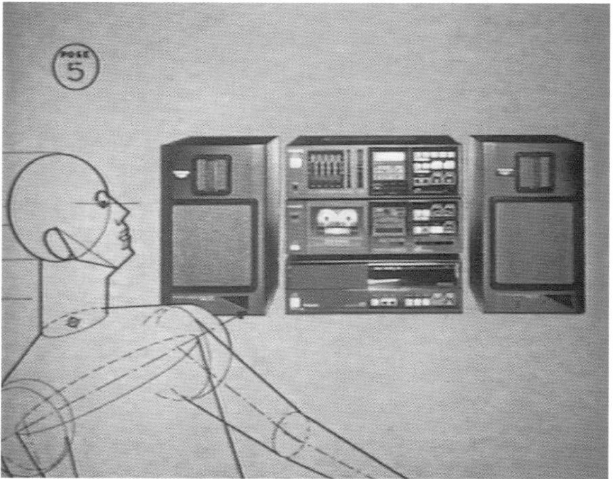

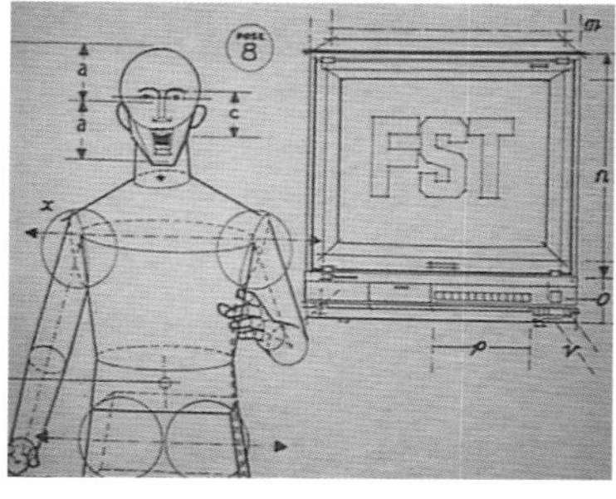

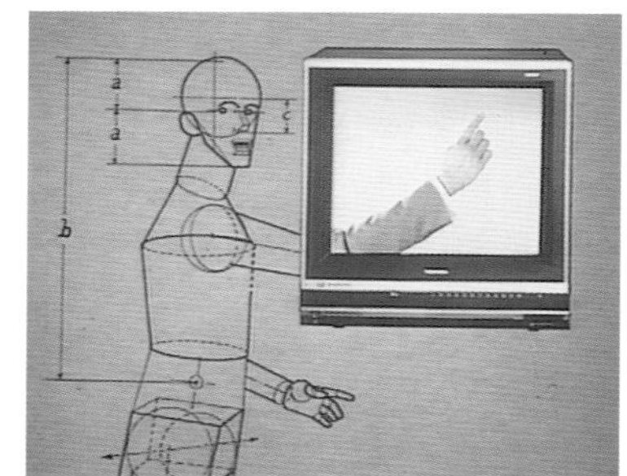

1985.11
Agency: **Gold Greenlees Trott**
Client: **Toshiba**
Inspired by Alexei Sayle's 'Ullo John...', this was classic Dave Trott, an archetypal ad from the man that put the 'oi' into British advertising. Famously brutal with his creative teams, Trott still built a fantastic team of loyal creatives who worked for him for low salaries. Trott was so difficult to present to (for a job) that he even wrote a paper on 'How to get your first job in advertising'; this would be simply handed out to hapless job candidates.

this page

1983.15
Agency: **Gold Greenlees Trott**
Client: **William Levene**
More from the Trott hit factory, written by Steve Henry and Axel Chaldecott and directed by Paul Weiland. The ad starred Bert Kwok, most famous for his role as Inspector Clouseau's ninja manservant Kato.

1983.16
Agency: **Doyle Dane Bernbach**
Client: **Corona Soft Drinks**
Tango orange drink makes its first appearance at D&AD in this DDB ad directed by Graham Rose. This commercial is largely forgotten today, eclipsed by the brand's spectacular re-emergence in the nineties backed by the controversial 'Orange man' advertising of Howell Henry Chaldecott Lury.

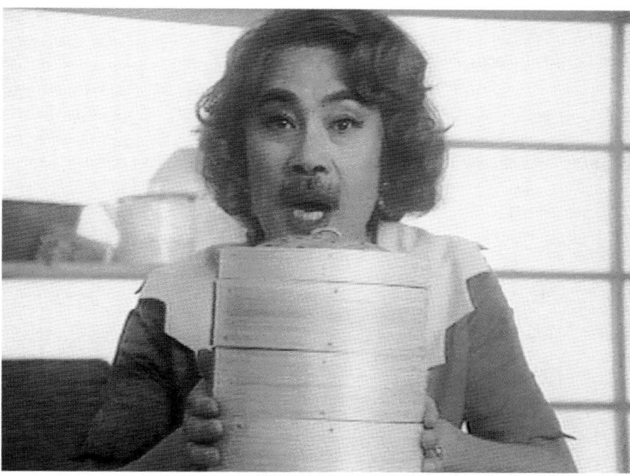

'Water in Majorca' was another hugely popular line from a Lowe-Howard Spink Marschalk commercial for Heineken, brilliantly directed by Paul Weiland, in which comedy actor Bryan Pringle hilariously gave reverse elocution lessons to a Sloane Ranger. And women all over Britain practised stomping out of the house to abandon everything but the car keys after DDB Needham's 'Changes' commercial for Volkswagen was directed by David Bailey over an Alan Price soundtrack. Interestingly, none of these landmark campaigns won an award, although they all made it into the D&AD Annual.

At least some of TV advertising's newfound cut-through appeal was due to Dave Trott, the brilliant and autocratic creative director at GGT, an agency which had the hottest of hot streaks in the mid-eighties. Trott had worked with John Webster at BMP in the seventies before co-founding the agency in 1980 (the same year that he won a D&AD Silver for writing a BMP commercial for brewers Courage, directed by Hugh Hudson).

Trott had studied in America and observed the golden age of Madison Avenue, the era of Bill Bernbach, and he brought a tough-minded approach to the business of creating ads. At GGT, his methods quickly became folklore: a creative department staffed with eager young guns; all the work out in the open; creative teams within the agency competing ferociously with one another; jobs switched from one to another after one week if there was insufficient progress. It was a formula which worked.

1988.09
Agency: **DDB Needham Worldwide**
Client: **VAG UK**
This commercial is often cited as the ultimate eighties ad. Model Paula Hamilton plays a material girl newly split from her (we presume) bastard husband. She chucks the earrings, the pearl necklace, the fur coat and the brooch into the gutter but can't bear to throw away the keys to her Sloane-mobile, the VW Golf. She drives off in defiance, proving the old adage that 'If only everything in life was as reliable as a Volkswagen.' This is 'I will survive' with a smart eighties consumerist twist.

1986.13
Agency:
Lowe Howard-Spink Marschalk
Client: **Whitbread & Company**
A memorable pastiche of the 'rain in Spain' scene in *My Fair Lady* by Adrian Holmes and Alan Waldie. Eventually, after sipping a can of Heineken, the latterday Eliza Doolittle turns from Sloane to Cockney, with 'The worta in Majorka don't taste like wot it oughta.'

1980.04
Agency: **Boase Massimi Pollitt Univas Partnership**
Client: **Courage Brewing**
The talents of John Webster, Hugh Hudson and Dave Trott all featured in this flat-cap, black-and-white celebration of the East End pub and Courage Best Bitter. The soundtrack was 'Gertcha' by Chas 'n' Dave, which reached the charts in 1979.

But while some television commercials, like 'Hello Tosh', crossed over because they seized the public imagination, others were cherished by industry insiders as simply outstanding examples of the craft. A TBWA commercial for Lego, 'Kipper', created by Mike Cozens and Graham Watson, won a D&AD Gold in 1981 for its faultless approach. An evocative Bob Brooks-directed ad for Yellow Pages, 'Fly Fishing by J R Hartley', demonstrated to everyone's satisfaction that David Abbott's writing skills extended to television. And Trott's mentor, John Webster, produced one of the decade's more memorable speeded-up sequences in a TV spot for Sony. This showed the life of a viewer on the sofa from a baby to an old man and then death, with the line 'Sony Triniton. Designed to Last'; it won a D&AD Silver in 1985.

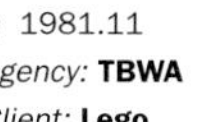

1981.11
Agency: **TBWA**
Client: **Lego**
A beautifully executed cat-and-mouse game of Lego in which the combatants at the mousehole are metamorphosized into all sorts of Lego brick creatures (and then back into a cat and mouse). Apparently, when asked about the complicated ideas for the background set, art director Graham Watson simply suggested a glass floor and one single mousehole, rather than the big set number planned.

1985.12
Agency: **Boase Massimi Pollitt Univas Partnership**
Client: **Sony**
John Webster had to rework this ad to make the elderly viewer's eventual demise acceptable. All that is left on the sofa is the pipe and slippers.

opposite

1984.14
Agency: **Abbott Mead Vickers/SMS**
Client: **Yellow Pages**
Still one of the best-remembered Yellow Pages ads, this commercial was so successful that the fictional fly-fisherman J R Hartley (played by actor Norman Lumsden) even launched his own book on fly-fishing in response to public demand.

BOOKS & PRINTS
BOUGHT & SOLD

YELLOW PAGES
LONDON SOUTH WEST 1991/92

YELLOW PAGES

И
ЭТО
«LEVI'S»

1986.14
Agency: **Bartle Bogle Hegarty**
Client: **Levi Strauss**
Within three years the Berlin Wall would fall and this commercial would be consigned to the historical curio bin. But at the time, 'Airport' caught the bleak Soviet style of the Cold War era in memorable monochrome. (The only colour is the red Levi's tab.) The music was specially composed for the commercial by Karl Jenkins and Mike Ratledge, two former members of the band Soft Machine.

this page

1985.13
Agency: **Bartle Bogle Hegarty**
Client: **Levi Strauss**
Tony Scott shoots a mini-epic on a boat with a simple message. If Levi's stitching can hook a big marlin then it can keep your trousers up. Another D&AD winner written by Mike Cozens and Graham Watson.

In the mid-eighties, Bartle Bogle Hegarty (BBH) embarked on a trio of D&AD-nominated TV ads which aimed to resurrect the fortunes of Levi's jeans. The first, 'Stitching' directed by Tony Scott with more than passing reference to Steven Spielberg's *Jaws*, was shot in the Gulf of Mexico and featured a tussle with a large marlin. The inference – that Levi's thread is strong enough to hook a big fish ('There's stitching and there's Levi's stitching') – followed an earlier campaign directed by Nick Lewin called 'Rivets' ('There's rivets and there's Levi's rivets').

But having majored on product quality and durability with 'Rivets' and 'Stitching', the agency's creative director John Hegarty explained the need to show how desirable the jeans were – desirable enough to take the risk of smuggling them behind the Iron Curtain. The result was 'Airport', set in Soviet Russia and full of classic Cold War imagery but actually shot in black and white by director Roger Woodburn in Newbury Park Bus Station in London.

'Airport' was powerful stuff but the last of the BBH ad trio was even more memorable. 'Launderette', directed by Roger Lyons, returned Levi Strauss to the familiar territory of late fifties America and a small-town launderette in which a young man calmly strips to the astonishment of onlookers and chucks his jeans in the machine together with a bagful of stones, to the accompaniment of Marvin Gaye's 'I Heard it Through the Grapevine' (viewers are told Levi's 501 jeans are now available stone-washed).

This much-imitated spot – simultaneously sexy and nostalgic – not only triggered a major Motown revival in the charts and made model Nick Kamen a star, but catapulted Levi's jeans back to the frontline of popular culture. The D&AD jury failed to give it an award, although it made the book in 1986.

Away from selling jeans, the business of flogging cars supplied some of the more arresting moving pictures in the early eighties – from the 1980 Gold Award-winning Fiat Strada robot sequence (directed by Hugh Hudson to the accompaniment of Rossini's 'Figaro' from *The Barber of Seville*) to the eerily effective 'Dead Cars' commercial by Wight Collins Rutherford Scott (WCRS) which launched the BMW 7 series in 1983.

1980.05
Agency: **Collett Dickenson Pearce**
Client: **Fiat Motor Company**
Directed by Hugh Hudson, this Gold Award-winner for the Fiat Strada was created by Paul Weiland and David Horry. The car was called the Fiat Ritmo elsewhere in Europe and it is said that the music, Rossini's 'Figaro', was originally chosen because it rhymed with Ritmo. Inspired by the balletic use of synchronized Minis in the film *The Italian Job*, the ad, filmed on the famous rooftop test track of Fiat's Turin factory, was only broadcast three times in the UK but was highly popular – much more so than the car itself.

1983.17
Agency:
Wight Collins Rutherford Scott
Client: **BMW**
Although it didn't win at D&AD, this 'Dead Cars' commercial, which persuaded BMW to go back into TV advertising, was highly influential. Art director Ken Hoggins recalls that BMW was so nervous about the car graveyard idea that the creative team had to build a scale model with toys in a sandpit to demonstrate it.

1986.15
Agency: **Bartle Bogle Hegarty**
Client: **Levi Strauss Europe**
A defining moment in TV advertising in the eighties, art directed by John Hegarty and written by Barbara Nokes, yet it missed out on a major award at D&AD. As Nick Kamen took his jeans off, sales of Levi 501s reversed their downturn to record a huge increase in sales of jeans and the death of the tanga brief. Roger Lyons directed the blueprint for a winning combination – good-looking models and Motown soul – that would be repeated across adland over the next few years.

Alcohol and cigars were also prominent subjects for TV campaigns, including an early showing for Aussie actor Paul Hogan in a Foster's commercial and two classic CDP spots for Hamlet ('Photobooth' directed by Graham Rose and 'Crash of 87' directed by Bernard Lodge, in which a downward-sliding business graph takes a break to light up). As the style decade wore on, slick commercials for such lifestyle brands as Speedo (by BBH) and Brylcreem (by Grey) came to the fore.

1983.18
Agency: **Hedger Mitchell Stark**
Client: **Watney Mann & Truman Brewers**
Paul Hogan was already famous in his native Australia for his down-to-earth character in a cigarette campaign. By making him shrewder and more cosmopolitan in the long-running Foster's campaign, HMS laid the ground for Hogan's casting as the eponymous hero in the world-widebox office hit *Crocodile Dundee.*

1987.08
Agency: **Collett Dickenson Pearce**
Client: **Gallaher**
The 'Happiness is a cigar called Hamlet' campaign worked wonders in tandem with the sound of Bach's 'Air on a G String.' The bald man in the photo booth, featuring a pre-*Rab C Nesbitt* Gregor Fisher struggling with his locks, is one of the best remembered.

this page

1981.12
Agency: **Collett Dickenson Pearce**
Client: **Whitbread & Company**
Early commercial take on the arcade game craze that followed the availability of home game kits. The technology may have been primitive but the idea was spot on as Heineken once more refreshed the parts… giving the player a far better chance of winning.

1988.10
Agency: **Collett Dickenson Pearce**
Client: **Gallaher**
Another classic Hamlet commercial for a brand built almost entirely by TV ads. (Hamlet attained a 40 per cent market share of cigars prior to the TV advertising ban introduced by government legislation in 1991.) The falling graph ad was conceived the morning after the October 1987 Stock Market crash and aired 31 hours later. Broadsheets contacted the agency to see if some sort of insider trading had taken place.

1980.06
Agency: **Collett Dickenson Pearce**
Client: **Gallaher**
This was Paul Weiland's directorial debut for the Alan Parker Film Company, and was a commercial for Hamlet cigar based on a news story about a Japanese golfer who got stuck in a bunker in a major tournament.

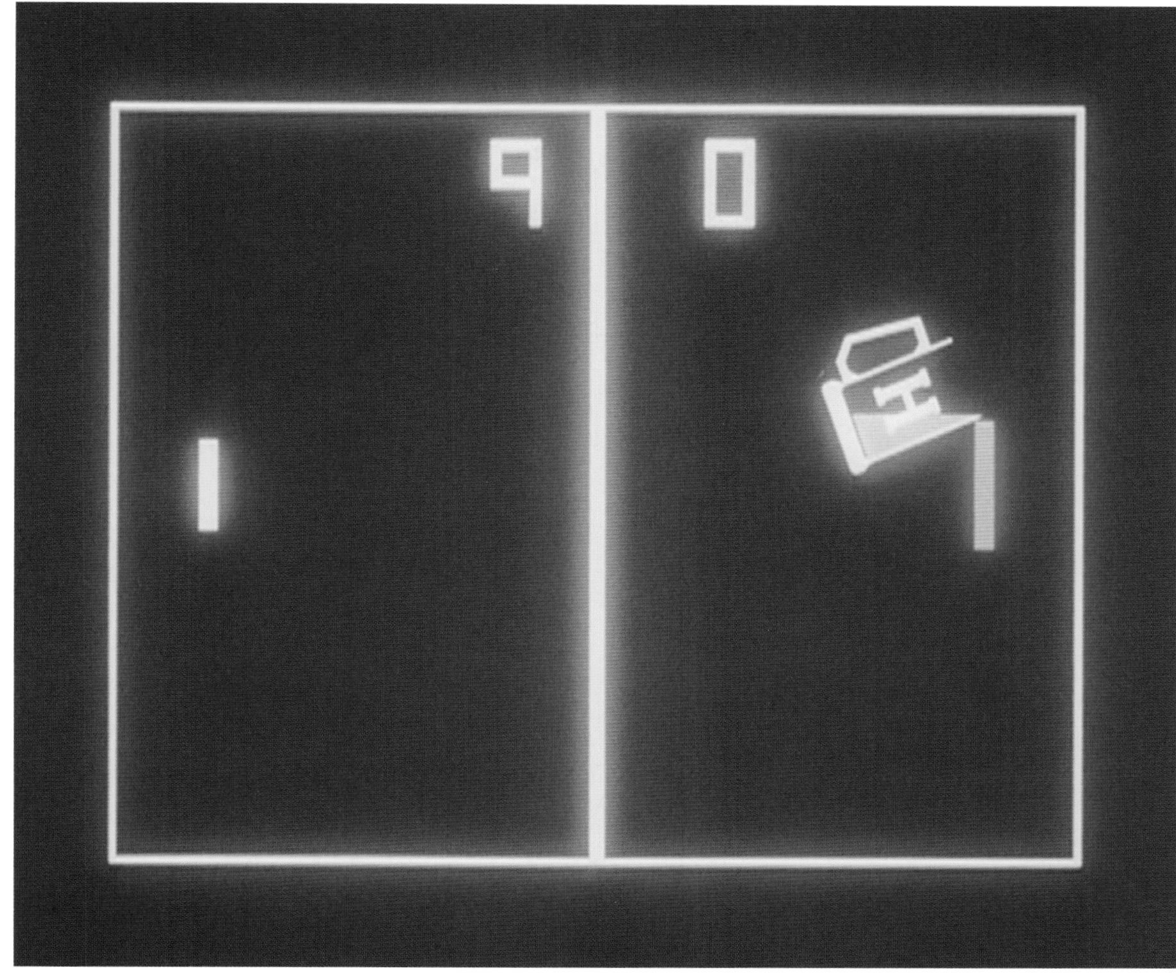

1989.11
Agency: **Bartle Bogle Hegarty**
Client: **Speedo Europe**
From the creative team of Chris Herring and Graham Watson, this commercial for Speedo swimwear at the end of the eighties anticipated some of the cinematic preoccupations and filmic values of TV advertising in the following decade, when dialogue and characterization would become subservient to imagery and style.

below & opposite

1986.16
Agency: **Grey**
Client: **Beecham Proprietaries**
Like so many other revivalist trends of the eighties – from retro high- street retailing with Next to the marketing of the Filofax – the repositioning of Brylcreem as a style accessory was an attempt to evoke a vanished era of English civility. Smothering your hair with a greasy gel last popular in the austere fifties was presented as the height of fashion. D&AD juries were convinced enough to give the campaign a Silver Award.

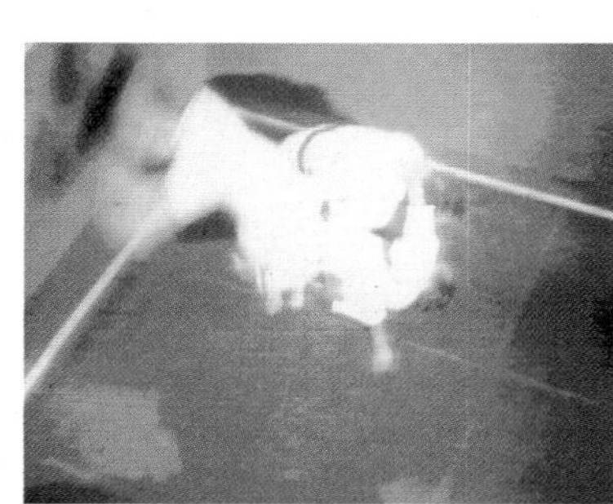

BRYLCREEM

FOR THE SMART
MODERN LOOK

BRYLCREEM
for
HANDSOME VITAL HAIR

BRYLCREEM
MAN'S FAVOURITE
HAIRDRESSING

But, amid the usual suspects, the eighties also produced a good number of commercials which showed the other, more socially conscious side of adland. In 1986, Saatchi & Saatchi won a Silver Award with a brilliant cinema spot for the counselling charity The Samaritans, in which a face and hands try to push through a sinister grey wall to the sound of electronic screams and Pink Floyd's 'Is There Anybody Out There?'.

The same year, the tradition of powerful anti-smoking ads was proudly maintained by FCO's 'First Natural Born Smoker', directed by Barry Myers. Aimed at teenagers, this commercial showed a grotesque future smoker with every body function and feature distorted to absorb nicotine. Chairman of the Health Education Council, Richard French, explained the strategy, 'Our advertising solution is a world-first. We're telling teenagers: smoke your heart out ... just understand what it means.'

1986.17
Agency: **Saatchi & Saatchi**
Client: **The Samaritans**

1986.18
Agency: **FCO**
Client: **Central Office of Information**

Two award-winning commercials from the mid-eighties address social issues with creative flair and conviction. The Samaritans spot, directed by Barney Edwards, owed something to a TV title sequence for Jonathan Miller's *Human Body* series from the late 1970s in the way the face and hands struggle to break out. The anti-smoking ad directed by Barry Myers owed something to Ridley Scott's *Bladerunner* in the atmospheric imagery of the mutated future smoker. Myers followed a well-worn path of UK commercials directors heading for Hollywood but, unlike Ridley Scott, it all ended in tears as he was fired from his first big movie.

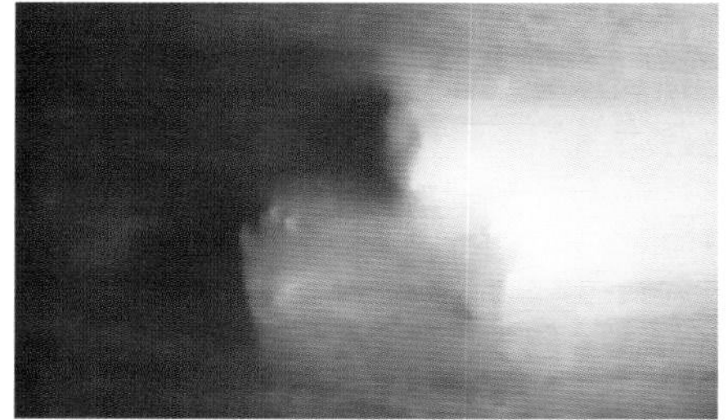

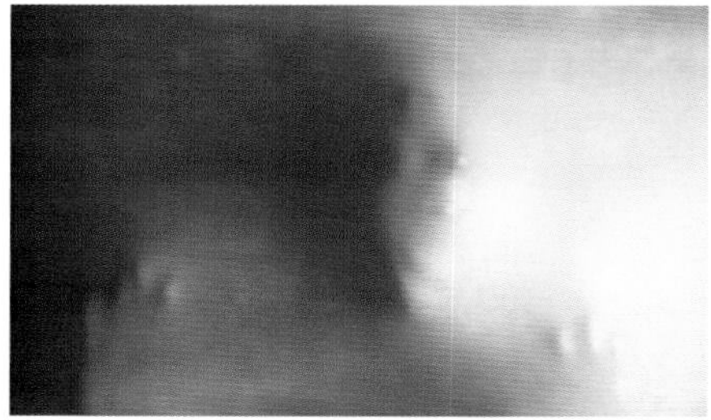

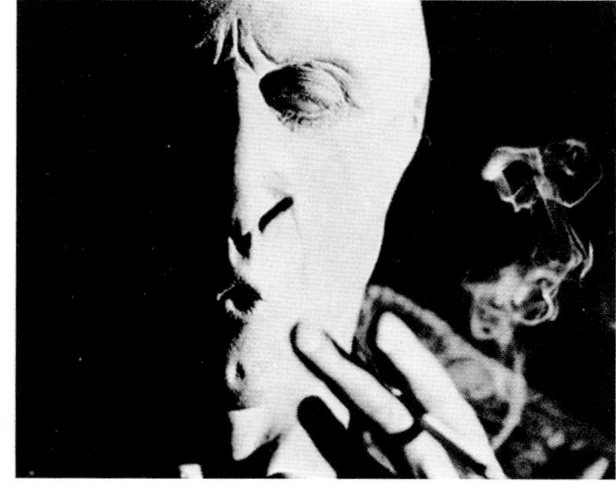

MIDDLE TAR
H.M. Government Health Departments' WARNING: CIGARETTES CAN SERIOUSLY DAMAGE YOUR HEALTH

1981.13
Agency: **Collett Dickenson Pearce**
Client: **Gallaher**
A classic piece of work by Neil Godfrey and Tony Brignull for Benson & Hedges maintaining the surreal campaign established in the seventies. Jimmy Wormser was again the photographer. Given work of this calibre, the anti-smoking lobby had much to do to fight creative fire with fire.

1988.11
Agency: **Saatchi & Saatchi**
Client: **Gallaher**

overleaf

1988.12
Agency: **Saatchi & Saatchi**
Client: **Gallaher**

Cigarette advertising hangs on by a thread. These Silk Cut ads were both art directed by Alexandra Taylor. Despite loud and frequent calls to equal up the gender balance, female creatives remained very much in the minority in agencies in the eighties.

MACHINE TWIST
SILK
THREAD
MADE IN GREAT BRITAIN
LOW TAR As defined by H.M. Government
Warning: MORE THAN 30,000 PEOPLE DIE EACH YEAR IN THE UK FROM LUNG CANCER
Health Departments' Chief Medical Officers

LOW TAR

Warning: MORE THAN 30,000 PEOPLE DI
Health Departments

by H.M. Government

CH YEAR IN THE UK FROM LUNG CANCER
ief Medical Officers

Two commercials directed by Paul Weiland for BMP – 'Magpies' which addressed crime prevention for the government, and 'Points of View' which cleverly showed how *The Guardian* covers things from both sides – also provided a thoughtful counterbalance to the decade's rampant consumerism. But by the late eighties, there were winds of change for TV and cinema advertising.

Many of the familiar names in direction were being lost to Hollywood like Alan Parker and Ridley Scott before them. A void was emerging. In 1988, D&AD opened up its award scheme to international entries (the same year that it also welcomed product design) and immediately an International Gold went to Ogilvy & Mather (O&M) in New York for a Drug Free America film campaign.

1988.13
Agency: **Ogilvy & Mather**
Client: **Media Advertising Partnership for a Drug Free America**
A wake-up call for complacent UK agencies as an American anti-drugs campaign wins Gold at D&AD.

1985.14
Agency: **Boase Massimi Pollitt Univas Partnership**
Client: **Central Office of Information**
Characteristically bold direction by Paul Weiland addresses the issue of house burglaries in this TV ad.

1987.09
Agency: **Boase Massimi Pollitt Partnership**
Client: **The Guardian**
The 'Points of View' commerical for *The Guardian* ran to counter the launch of its rival, *The Independent*.

opposite

1989.12
Agency: **Saatchi & Saatchi**
Client: **British Rail**
A totally unrealistic, sepia-tinted view of British Rail, but it signalled Tony Kaye's arrival as a star director.

1989.13
Agency: **Cliff Freeman & Partners**
Client: **Little Caesars Enterprises**
Enter Joe Sedelmaier from Chicago, forerunner to the 'real life/cast ugly' school of TV advertising.

1989.14
Agency: **Saatchi & Saatchi**
Client: **Chamber of Coal Traders**

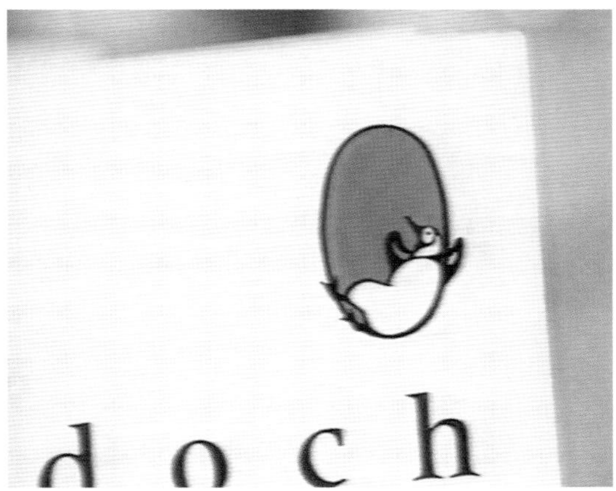

In 1989, however, two original new directing talents emerged simultaneously at D&AD to fill the void: one was British (Tony Kaye), the other American (Joe Sedelmaier). Kaye took some time to break through from one-to-watch to major player. Many in the industry were nervous of his reputation as an *enfant terrible* who was rumoured to do crazy things like fight on the set, conduct all-night shoots and refuse to show the client the rushes. But Kaye's left-field talent was undeniable and he won two Silvers in 1989 with commercials for Saatchi & Saatchi: the first promoted the warmth of a real fire for the Chamber of Coal Traders, the second basked British Rail travellers in an unfamiliarly relaxing glow as the world sped by.

While Kaye filled the screen with seductive and highly personal imagery (such as scenes showing a Hasidic Jew playing chess with a young boy in the British Rail ad), Chicago-based Joe Sedelmaier brought something different altogether. His rapid-cut slices of life for such clients as US Sprint and Little Caesars Enterprises, with their quickfire repeating dialogue and ugly casting, introduced a new vocabulary of real people squaring up to the camera. The effect was galvanizing on the hitherto glossy commercials scene in the UK and helped set a new direction for the nineties. Generally, by 1989, there was a feeling that the discipline had grown too flabby and self-conscious and badly needed a shot in the arm. Sedelmaier provided that shot.

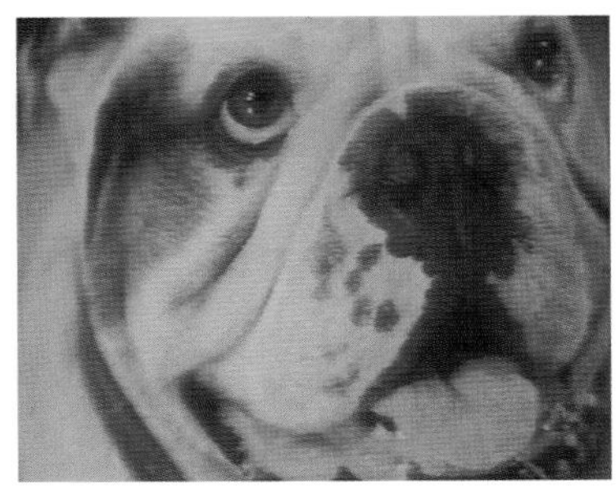

If the D&AD Awards for commercials had been a closed shop in the seventies, dominated largely by CDP and BMP, one thing the eighties did was widen the field. At the start of the decade, many in adland complained that the same names won at D&AD every year, recalling the old *Frost Report* line from the sixties, 'Someone broke into the Kremlin last night and stole next year's election results.' But newcomers learnt quickly at the feet of the masters; WCRS, BBH, GGT and others in a second agency wave soon grabbed their share of the glory.

The same democratic process of widening the skillbase of the industry was evident in press and poster advertising. In posters, for example, the eighties started where the seventies had left off. Classic work by BMP for Volkswagen earned a Silver in 1980 (although Barbara Nokes, who wrote the great line 'You're in this

1980.07
Agency: **Doyle Dane Bernbach**
Client: **Volkswagen**
Classic work from copywriter Barbara Nokes prior to her high-profile departure from BMP to team up with John Hegarty at BBH. VW gets away from those famous Helmut Krone layouts, finally.

1981.14
Agency: **Collett Dickenson Pearce**
Client: **Parker Pen Company**
The eighties started off in much the same way the seventies finished, with a Gold Award for CDP. The late typographer Maggie Lewis became a type legend in the eighties for her work on Parker Pens and other accounts.

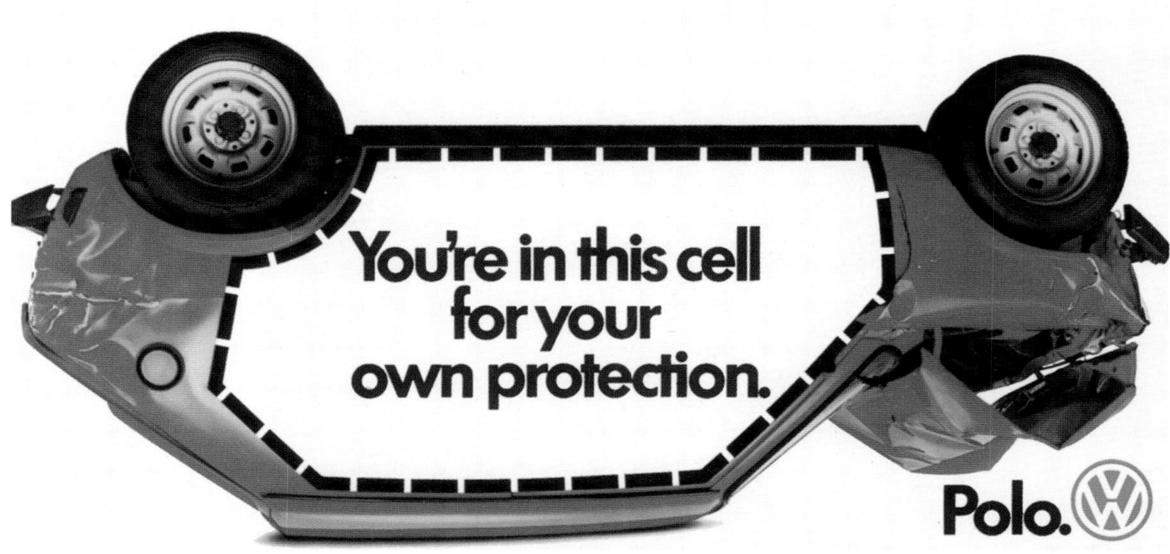

1985.15
Agency: **Boase Massimi Pollitt Univas Partnership**
Client: **Greater London Council**

1986.19
Agency:
Lowe Howard-Spink Marschalk
Client: **Whitbread & Company**

Two of the best uses of poster sites as an outdoor medium in the eighties. BMP wrapped red tape around a giant billboard to show how Whitehall bureaucracy would strangle London without the GLC. Lowe Howard-Spink Marschalk based its Heineken prison bars poster on a tri-wonder to reveal the three scenes.

cell for your own protection', would soon defect to BBH to work with John Hegarty). CDP won a Gold for Parker Pens and a Silver for Benson & Hedges in 1981.

But then different and exciting things started to happen. In fact, D&AD in the eighties showcased three of the truly outstanding examples of posters being used as an outdoor medium: FCO's campaign for Araldite glue, in which a car was glued to a Cromwell Road billboard in London; BMP's campaign to save the Greater London Council, which wrapped a giant poster in red tape to show what London would be like if run by Whitehall; and Lowe Howard-Spink Marschalk's tri-vision poster for Heineken, which removed the bars of a prisoner's cell in three image changes to demonstrate that 'Heineken refreshes the bars other beers cannot reach'.

The original brief for Araldite, which won at D&AD two years running in 1983 and 1984, started out as a black-and-white trade press ad. But the agency (FCO Univas, later just FCO) convinced the client that even with a small budget it could become famous – and that a London poster campaign was better than burying an ad in an ironmongery journal. So Araldite's boffins went to work to find a way to stick a car to a hoarding. With lines like 'It also sticks handles to teapots', 'The tension mounts', and – when the car was removed to reveal a nasty hole – 'How did we pull it off?', the Araldite campaign brilliantly prefigured Ambient Media, a new D&AD category that would be introduced nearly 20 years later.

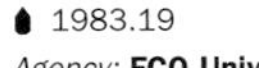
1983.19
Agency: **FCO Univas**
Client: **Ciba Geigy**

1984.15
Agency: **FCO**
Client: **Ciba Ceigy**

The first Araldite poster had all eyes glued to the billboard instead of the road. Better than a trade press ad, argued the agency. One year later, and the three part Araldite follow-up work cleverly built on the massive media interest in the campaign.

opposite

1985.16
Agency: **Boase Massimi Pollitt Univas Partnership**
Client: **Greater London Council**
Not even BMP's creative skills could save Ken Livingstone from Margaret Thatcher's axe in the mid-eighties. The Greater London Council leader would fare better in his battle with Tony Blair over London 15 years later.

1981.15
Agency:
Wight Collins Rutherford Scott
Client: **Chefaro Proprietaries**

1985.17
Agency: **Lowe Howard-Spink Campbell-Ewald**
Client: **Whitbread & Company**

This classic Bergasol ad was created by Ron Collins and Andrew Rutherford in 1981. The Heineken spoof was nominated for a Silver Award at D&AD four years later.

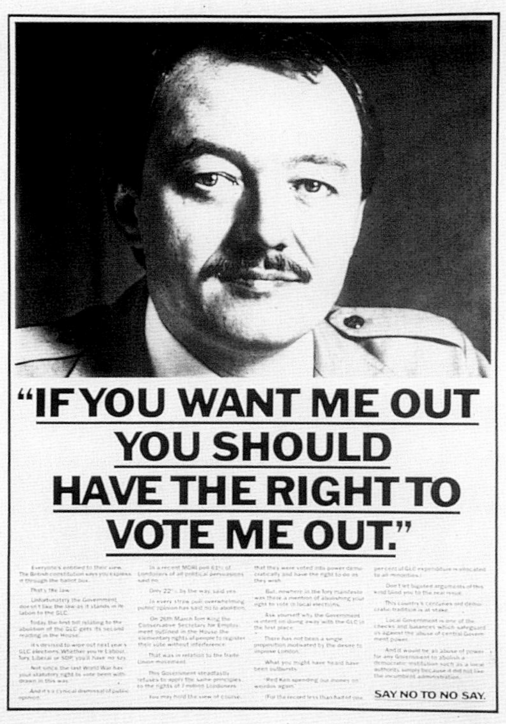

The spirit of the red-tape GLC poster, which won a Silver in 1985, was extended into a press campaign featuring one of the hottest political lines of the age beneath a deliberately low-key shot of the Council's leader Ken Livingstone: 'If you want me out you should have the right to vote me out.' Many creative directors had benefitted hugely from Thatcherism and feared Red Ken (later to return as London's independent Mayor), but nevertheless admired BMP's campaign.

As for Heineken, the prison bar poster (a Silver Award-winner in 1986) belonged to a rollicking campaign by Lowe Howard-Spink. This drew on several British cultural icons of the age (such as Frank Muir's bowtie and *Hi-de-Hi*) and showed the new-found confidence of advertising in self-referentially spoofing another ad – a WCRS press campaign for suntan lotion Bergasol, showing the light and dark backs of two sunbathers, which had already been recognized by D&AD in 1981.

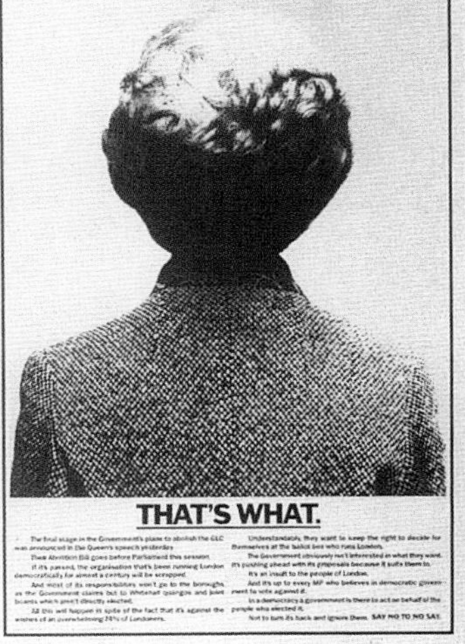

Dave Trott brought his customary energy to bear on a memorable GGT poster campaign for London Weekend Television (LWT), which earned a D&AD Silver Award in 1982 and eventually ran to well over 100 posters. Designed to be produced quickly so as to be fresh and controversial, and tied into upcoming programmes, the work caught the topical mood in the same way as political satire magazine *Private Eye* covers of the period. One of the most arresting LWT posters to run was for a *Victims of Revolution* special on Ayatollah Khomenei, showing an image of a hanged victim dangling behind the despot's head under the headline 'He's saving people from choosing the wrong religion'. (Like John Webster's Sony Triniton campaign, Trott proved that even death could sell in the eighties.)

But some ideas put forward by the agency were just too strong even for LWT to run, like Churchill posing with an exploding cigar under the headline 'For 10 years nobody took him seriously' (a poster to promote *Churchill: the Wilderness Years*). Then there were the canned concepts for a poster for a Steven Spielberg special on *The South Bank Show* – 'He's lonely. He's scared. He's two feet from Melvyn Bragg', and 'He's made more people go to the cinema than the BBC has'.

1982.12
Agency: **Gold Greenlees Trott**
Client: **London Weekend Television**
Advertising as satirical journalism. In the spirit of *Private Eye*, some of the strongest ideas for LWT didn't run.

opposite

1985.18
Agency: **Ogilvy & Mather**
Client: **Bovril**
Advertising's penchant for surrealism combined with the current vogue for illustration in this mid-eighties poster campaign.

1983.20
Agency: **Gold Greenlees Trott**
Client: **Time Out**
Steve Henry and Axel Chaldecott worked on both LWT and *Time Out*, a partnership that eventually led to the formation of Howell Henry Chaldecott Lury.

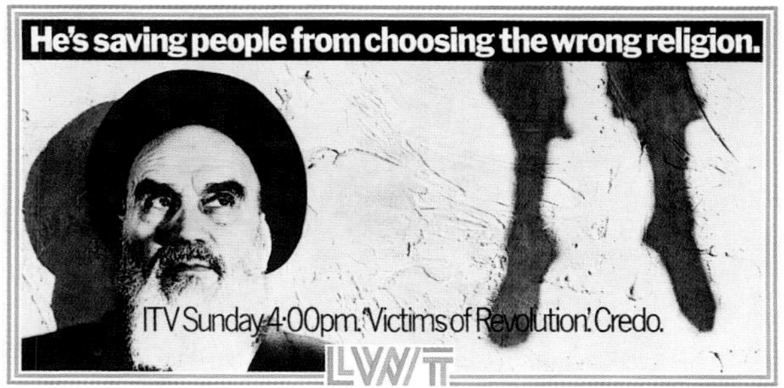

At 12 noon on Sunday, Margaret Thatcher talks about her policy on money. (You remember money.)

ITV Weekend World. Sunday 1st. Feb.

LWT

For all its topical drive, the LWT campaign conformed visually to what a traditional image-and-headline poster advertising campaign should look like. But new ideas about posters were also emerging at D&AD, such as the singular image concept which needs no copyline. This was symbolized by a *Time Out* poster showing the candle being burnt at both ends, by Axel Chaldecott and Steve Henry of GGT (Silver in 1983), and by O&M's surreal campaign for Bovril cubes, art directed by Martyn Walsh (Silver in 1985). The Bovril work featured illustrations by Mick Brownfield; at precisely the moment graphic designers went overboard on illustration, many advertising art directors did the same.

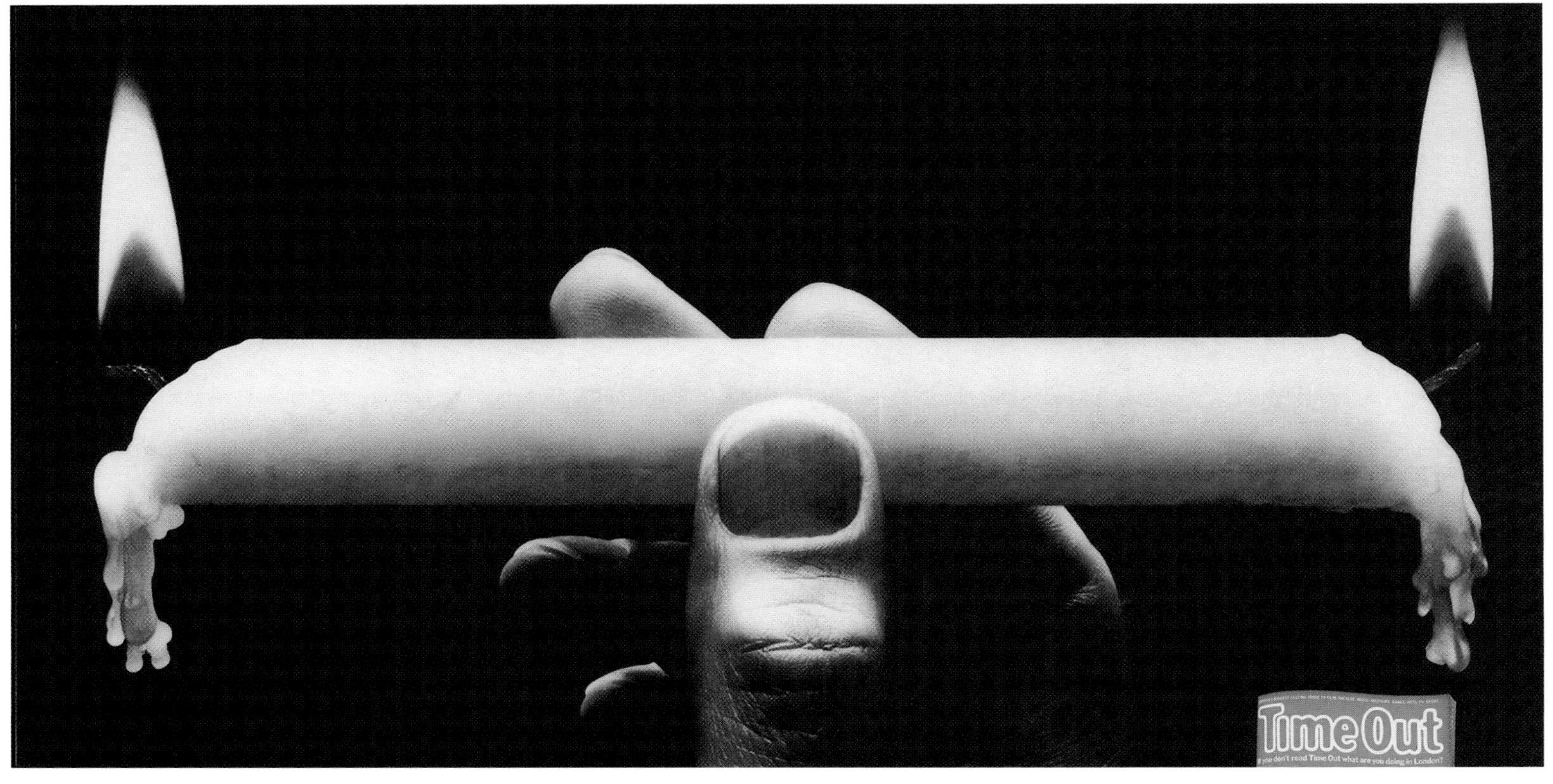

Perhaps the greatest departure from a conventional poster ad format was BMP's quirkily post-modern John Smith's Yorkshire Bitter campaign for Courage, which won a D&AD Silver Award in 1989. This cut-and-paste approach to type and imagery showed a wit and a willingness to mess with the medium, unlike most other campaigns. But it was quickly over-shadowed by the emergence of one of the greatest poster campaigns in D&AD's history, Abbott Mead Vickers' (AMV) work on *The Economist*, which surfaced in the D&AD Annual in 1989 with the memorable line 'I never read *The Economist* – Management trainee. Aged 42'.

1989.15
Agency: **BMP Davidson Pearce**
Client: **Courage**
What a difference a decade makes. John Smith's Yorkshire Bitter started the eighties with all that hardline East End pub promotion but ended it with this decidedly post-modern poster campaign extolling the virtues of a beer 'all the way from sun-kissed Tadcaster'.

1989.16
Agency: **Abbott Mead Vickers/SMS**
Client: **The Economist**
Another one that got away from D&AD juries. No major award but this was the poster that really set the benchmark for the entire seminal *Economist* campaign. It was chosen by John Hegarty to feature in a major exhibition, *The Power of the Poster*, at the Victoria and Albert Museum in the late nineties.

1984.16
Agency: **Bartle Bogle Hegarty**
Client: **James Robertson & Sons**
A brilliantly simple piece of art direction that political correctness has since consigned to curio corner. Art directed by John Hegarty and written by Barbara Nokes, you can almost feel the taste of inferior marmalades on your tongue.

When the agency won the account in the late eighties, *The Economist* enjoyed a strong readership in the economic and financial worlds, but not beyond. Its circulation hovering below 100,000 reflected a view that this was a magazine for big business only – not for the broader reader interested in how the world works.

Over the next decade and more, AMV would radically and permanently change perceptions of the magazine to reposition it as essential reading for the smart and well-informed, whatever field they worked in. It would do so using two short bursts of poster advertising – in spring and autumn, for just four weeks a year. And its posters would all share the same pared-down style (one colour, one typeface). *The Economist* posters of 1989 heralded the obsessive focus in the nineties on building the brand.

Press advertising in the eighties fought an increasingly sophisticated battle against editorial in newspapers and magazines for the reader's attention. One tactic was to be topical: to tie campaigns into the political issues of the day. Thus, D&AD Award-winning press ads for Lego and Olympus expertly caught the mood of feuding heavyweights Michael Foot, Tony Benn and Denis Healey fighting for the Labour Party leadership in the early eighties.

In seeking to match the power of journalism, another approach was good writing of long-copy ads, as demonstrated by a classic DDB campaign for Commercial Union ('We won't make a drama out of a crisis') which won a D&AD Silver in 1980. David Abbott's beautifully crafted work for Sainsbury's quickly showed itself to be a cut above the rest in this area, winning a D&AD Silver in 1982. (When the supermarket chain decided to sell cosmetics, for example, Abbott sold the idea with the line 'Pick up a peaches and cream complexion where you pick up your peaches and cream'.)

They obviously felt like shooting each other.

Who can blame them?

They've got their hands on an Olympus XA. Automatic exposure control and a coupled range-finder ensure a perfect seaside snap.

A great help, whether you are an accomplished photographer, like the gentleman on the right. Or a less experienced one, like the gentleman on the far left.

It's nice they're seeing eye to eye over something.

THE OLYMPUS XA.

Olympus XA shown actual size. For further details write to: Olympus Optical Company (UK) Limited, 2-8 Honduras Street, London EC1Y 0TX. Tel: 01-253 2772.

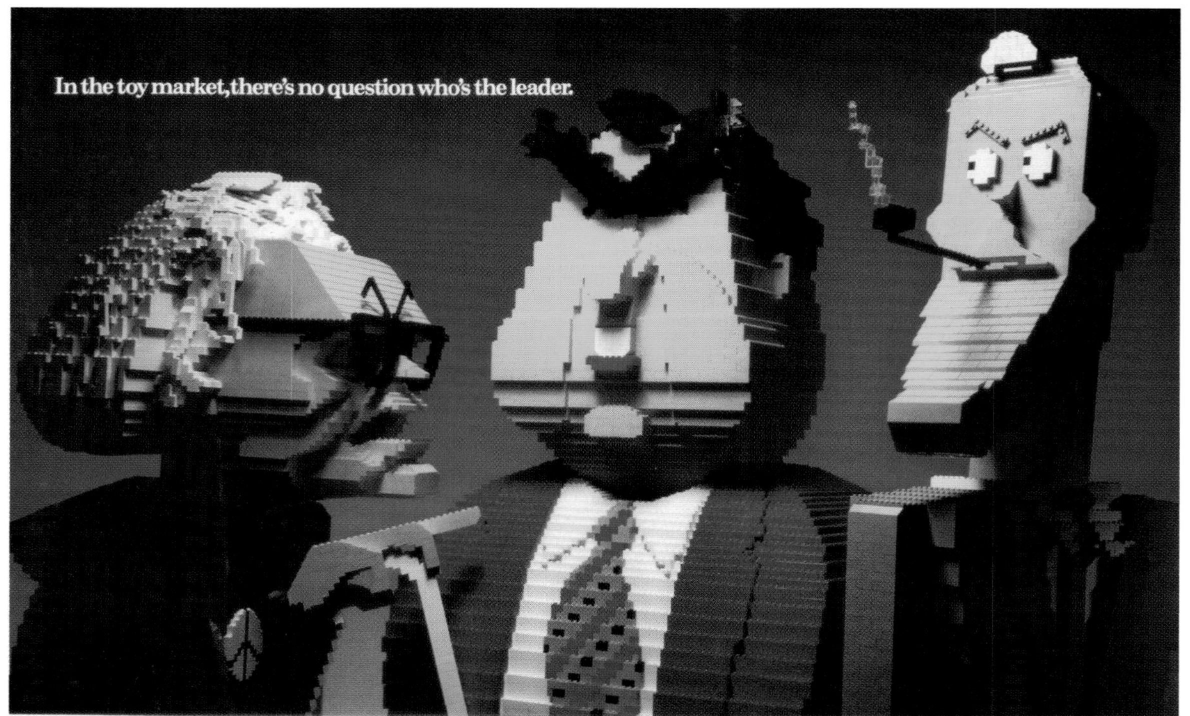

In the toy market, there's no question who's the leader.

Let the opposition look left and right for a new direction.

We're standing by the policies that have kept us leaders through a year of recession.

More investment in the railways. Increased support for the space programme. More to improve and encourage development of our towns.

All backed by new ideas, new initiative.

And to make interest rates soar, a higher level of spending in the public sector than ever before.

Lastly, to get the country back to work, let us remind you that we are committed to a National Building Competition.

This is the way ahead. This is the road to a higher standard of living.

And, you know, this can only be achieved by U-turning.

You turning LEGO bricks into prosperity.

LEGO

The world's most popular toy.

1981.16
Agency: **Collett Dickenson Pearce**
Client: **Olympus Optical Company**
Denis Healey snaps Tony Benn, Tony Benn snaps Denis Healey, sharp-eyed CDP spotted the camera was an Olympus and a great ad was created in a flash.

1982.13
Agency: **TBWA**
Client: **Lego**
Another topical press ad which caught the rancid mood of the Labour leadership battle in the early eighties, following the disastrous defeat of Jim Callaghan in the 1979 General Election. While press ads in the eighties jostled with editorial for attention, they continued to be consciously styled as advertising. The trend towards visually disguising press ads would come a decade later.

Financial Times

Seven days later, we bought a brand new red Volkswagen for the man who'd just bought a brand new red Volkswagen.

On 2nd April 1973, the morning weather forecast happened to mention there would be gusty showers around the South East.

For once, the clairvoyants at the Met Office were right.

But while other people were simply getting blown about, one man was getting more than he bargained for from the elements.

Though modesty prevents him from lending his name to our story, we can reveal that he was a school teacher in Guildford at the time. And the proud owner of a new Volkswagen Beetle.

No sooner had he parked it, locked it and turned his back on it than a ton and a half of tree trunk crashed down onto the bonnet.

With the result that his new red Volkswagen was effectively a new red write-off.

The teacher called his local branch of Commercial Union.

As his insurance company, we of course needed to see the damage for ourselves.

By late morning we had the claim form signed, sealed and on its way to head office for final approval.

This we received within two days, on 4th April.

Then came the tricky part.

We told the teacher that we'd be happy to replace his Volkswagen immediately with a new one, whereupon he told us he had this thing about red.

Then red it is, we said. But it may take a little time.

As it turned out, very little time indeed. On 9th April, just 7 days (not to mention scores of phone calls) later, our learned friend took delivery of a brand new Volkswagen.

And, we're happy to say, the colour was such you'd be hard put to spot a ripe tomato on the bonnet.

Of course, we can't always promise to deal with every claim with such speed and so little fuss. But we'll do our level best.

Whether you suddenly find yourself without a car or a colour television, your home or your health: armed with the right policy, you'll find us more than willing to help.

And if that means a cheque within days, rather than weeks, we'll be the first with a first class stamp.

CU ASSURANCE

We won't make a drama out of a crisis.

Financial Times

When Mrs Marion Gibson first planned the evening's meal, nothing could have been further from her mind than hot-plate flambé.

In fact, the family dinner that night had started life as steak and chips.

But, by 6.20, there had been a dramatic change in the menu.

Moments earlier, the oil in the chip pan had been bubbling away quite merrily: so it was with every confidence that Mrs Gibson turned her back to lay the table.

It was then that the oil reached boiling point and instantly caught light.

Within seconds the entire cooker was ablaze.

Thankfully though, the fire brigade arrived in time to drown the kitchen, before the flames had a chance to take hold in the rest of the house.

The following morning, with the gloomy prospect of weeks of Chinese takeaways ahead of them, the Gibsons took little comfort from the fact they were insured.

After all, as everyone knows, it takes more than a completed claims form to restore life to some sort of normality after a serious fire.

The following day, we gave Mrs Gibson another chance to burn the dinner.

It takes people who are prepared to put themselves out.

At Commercial Union, we pride ourselves in the knowledge that we have these sort of people working in our midst. As the Gibsons were soon to discover for themselves.

Barely an hour after reporting the fire to our local branch office, Mr Gibson found himself opening his front door to one of our claims inspectors.

No sooner had he assessed the damage, than he agreed to a settlement. On the spot.

That afternoon a second surprise appeared on the Gibsons' doorstep.

Quite simply, a brand new cooker. Identical in every way to their original.

Courtesy of Commercial Union.

In the normal course of events, we would replace a cooker with a cheque. Not a cooker.

But then, there are always exceptions to the rule.

Being down to earth insurance folk, we would never claim to work miracles.

CU ASSURANCE

Though Mrs Gibson would doubtless disagree with us.

We won't make a drama out of a crisis.

1980.08
Agency: **Doyle Dane Bernbach**
Client: **Commercial Union Assurance**

1980.09
Agency: **Doyle Dane Bernbach**
Client: **Commercial Union Assurance**

DDB's 'We won't make a drama out of a crisis' for Commercial Union won Silver Awards in both the press and TV advertising categories in 1980. The campaign was created by copywriter Suzie Henry and art director Bill Thompson. Max Forsythe photographed the press work; Peter Webb, later to shoot the ill-fated *Give My Regards to Broad Street* movie for Paul McCartney, directed the commercials.

'J' Moisturiser.
'J' Foundation.

It's called 'J' Cosmetics and sparing the blushes of our beauty experts we think it's a remarkable range.
First we look after your skin.
We started on the basis that a healthy skin is the basis of good looks.
So our beauty system begins with a collection of seven cleansers, toners and moisturisers.
As you'd expect, the formulae are of the highest quality.
Our 'J' Enriched Moisture Cream, for example, is rich in emollients, vitamin E and valuable wheat germ oil.
It helps give the skin a youthful freshness, smoothness and glow.
A process that's helped further by our creamy smooth foundations, powders and soft-toned blushers. (We're particularly pleased with our 'J' All-In-One Foundation.
All three shades give a soft matt finish and the special oil-free formulation and sun-screen really protect the skin.)
Then we take care of your looks.
We haven't neglected your eyes, either.
Our mascaras are smudge proof, our eye pencils double ended (a kohl at one end, a fine liner at the other) and there's a glistening range of eye shadows.
For lips and nails we offer a selection of ten fashionable shades – some to match, some to tone in.
As for the colours themselves you really have to visit our stores to appreciate them.
But you can probably guess at one or two shades.
Having sold you peaches and cream we're not likely to forget plum and apricot.
New 'J' Cosmetics. Exclusive to Sainsbury's.

1982.14
Agency: **Abbott Mead Vickers/SMS**
Client: **J Sainsbury**
Who else could put 'fickle fungus' in a headline but David Abbott? One of the great press advertising campaigns from the early eighties. In fact, this distinctive Sainsbury's style ran for 16 years. It set the template for how a press ad should be done in the eighties, with its formal composition, superb imagery and typographic rigour.

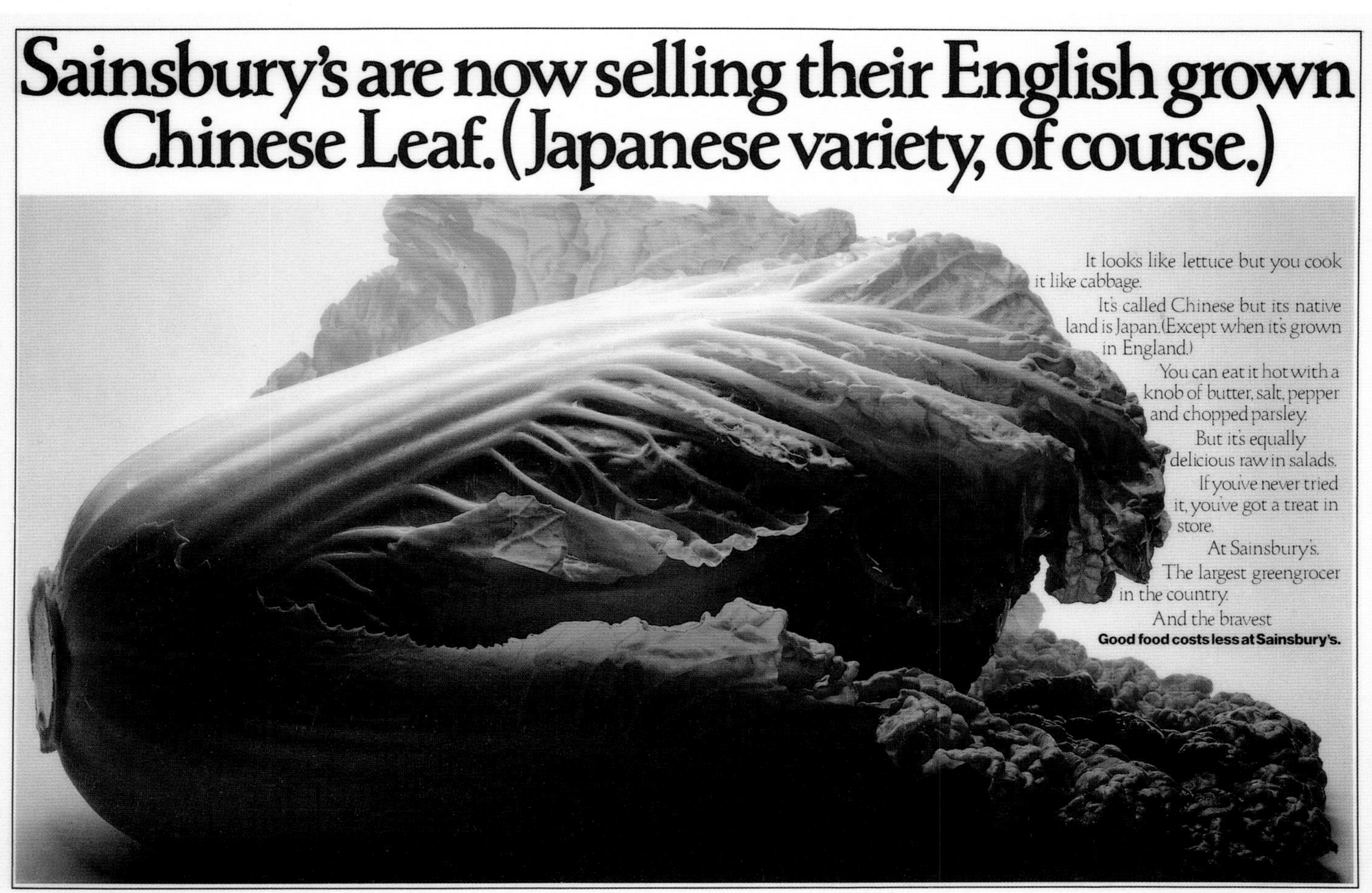

Sainsbury's are now selling their English grown Chinese Leaf. (Japanese variety, of course.)
It looks like lettuce but you cook it like cabbage.
It's called Chinese but its native land is Japan. (Except when it's grown in England.)
You can eat it hot with a knob of butter, salt, pepper and chopped parsley.
But it's equally delicious raw in salads.
If you've never tried it, you've got a treat in store.
At Sainsbury's.
The largest greengrocer in the country.
And the bravest.
Good food costs less at Sainsbury's.

Sainsbury's announce sandwich courses in Dutch, Hungarian, Polish, Belgian, French, Italian, Greek, German and Danish.

If you've never thought of Sainsbury's as a delicatessen, think again.

We sell 115 kinds of cooked meats and delicatessen products.

(Even the smallest Sainsbury's stocks around 40.)

If you like salami, for instance, many of our stores can offer you Italian, Danish, German, or Hungarian – even a salami flavoured with rum.

We sell Taramosalata and the Greek bread to go with it, and if your fancy runs to Bierwurst or Extrawurst you can do a lot worse than buy them from us.

(As you'd expect few delicatessens can match us for value.)

Our French brawn has just the right mix between meat and jelly.

Our Smokie Frankfurters are firm and plump.

(Not surprising when you learn they contain 85% meat.)

And if Bavarian Ham Sausage, Polish Krajana, and Pâté Ardenne sound a little strange, you'll find their quality reassuringly familiar.

Whichever you choose, the lesson is clear.

If you want to put something more interesting on your bread, try putting Sainsbury's on your shopping list.

Good food costs less at Sainsbury's.

Dutch smoked sausage.

Italian mortadella with peppers.

Danish salami.

Belgian liver sausage.

A fickle fungus makes these wines remarkable. A fickle public keeps them reasonable.

In certain parts of Bordeaux the humid autumn weather encourages a particular kind of fungus to attack the grapes.

What might appear to be a catastrophe is, in fact, a blessing.

The fungus is called by the locals 'la pourriture noble' (the noble rot) and they watch its progress through the vineyard like anxious parents.

Anxious lest it should stop.

For the bizarre fact is, the fungus causes a wonderful concentration of the grapes' juices that gives the wines of Sauternes and Barsac a unique rich texture and aroma.

Unfortunately, the fungus is fickle and doesn't attack all the grapes in the vineyard at the same time.

Some grapes may be ready for picking in September, others may not be graced with the 'noble rot' until October or even November.

In a long fine autumn it can take as many as seven pickings to complete the harvest. In a severe autumn, the grapes can be ruined before the fungus does its work.

Small wonder that the production of these sweet Bordeaux wines is a hazardous and costly business.

Why then can you find Appellation Contrôlée wines from these regions sitting on Sainsbury's shelves for around £2 or £3 a bottle?

We'd like to claim it's because of our excellent buying powers – and that's largely true – but it's also due to the fickleness of public taste.

Many people still think it unsophisticated to enjoy a sweet wine.

Others don't quite know when to drink a Sauternes and consequently ignore it.

In the face of such prejudice the wines haven't yet been able to command the prices they deserve; but the picture is changing.

More and more wine experts are writing about these neglected wines.

Some recommend you drink your Sauternes with fruit – perhaps a fresh peach, strawberries or nectarine.

Others favour it accompanied by a biscuit or a bowl of nuts.

Many believe you should enjoy it on its own. All believe you should drink it chilled.

As for Sainsbury's, we merely suggest you buy in a bottle or two while prices are still something of a bargain.

After all, with publicity such as this, the public could be fickle once more and cause quite a demand.

Good wine costs less at Sainsbury's.

AMV was also behind other well-written campaigns for Volvo and Cow & Gate (which won a D&AD Gold in 1984). Up until Cow & Gate, babyfood ads in magazines were full of platitudes, recalls Chris O'Shea, copywriter on the Cow & Gate campaign: 'We recognized that mothers wanted lots of information. Suddenly press ads were telling it like it really was.'

Being candid about the subject, in a way not seen before, was a feature of Lowe Howard-Spink's 1983 Silver Award-winning campaign for Albany Life, which talked about life insurance in a refreshingly honest and humorous way. (One ad in the series featured Ronald Reagan in his B-movie days beneath the headline 'Will you be as fortunate finding a second career?') This approach also defined BBH's press work for Dr White's Tampons, with copywriter Barbara Nokes again on great form with 'Have you ever wondered how men would carry on if they had periods?'

1984.17
Agency: **Abbott Mead Vickers/SMS**
Client: **Cow & Gate**
The idea that a baby food campaign, and a press campaign at that, could beguile a cynical bunch like the D&AD Gold Jury would have been unthinkable – until Cow & Gate.

opposite

1984.18
Agency: **Abbott Mead Vickers/SMS**
Client: **Volvo Concessionaires**
The most amazing typography story ever told. This Volvo ad was done by typographer Joe Hoza in an age before computers – painstakingly set to fit then re-set and re-set again.

1986.20
Agency: **Boase Massimi Pollitt Partnership**
Client: **Fisher Price**
A classic uh? aaah! ad from BMP for the toy manufacturer Fisher Price.

1986.21
Agency: **Bartle Bogle Hegarty**
Client: **Smith & Nephew Consumer Products**
More classic press work from Barbara Nokes and John Hegarty.

May we recommend the liver and bacon to follow?

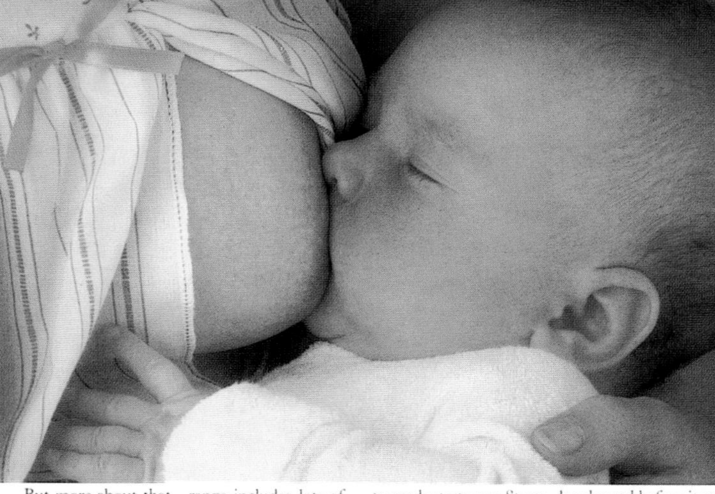

During the first few months of life, breast milk is the perfect baby food.

Then, at around 3 or 4 months, something a little more substantial is called, or even cried, for.

But liver and bacon?

Are we mad?

On the contrary. We're one of the country's longest-established makers of baby food.

Experience has taught us that most mothers prefer their babies to move from the breast or bottle to real grown-up food as naturally and smoothly as possible.

So our babymeals are designed to help you do just that.

Learning to eat in easy stages.

Cow & Gate baby meals aren't simply little glass jars of babyfood.

They're a two-stage training programme that gently paves the way to adult food.

Stage 1 meals are for babies starting out on solids, and still getting much of their nourishment from breast or baby milk.

Since your baby will only be able to suck and swallow, they're finely sieved or puréed.

Then, about 3 months later, it'll be time to move onto our Stage 2 meals.

But more about that later on.

The first step.

If you're still troubled by the thought of a young baby tucking into liver and bacon, let us explain.

Sooner or later your baby will have to get used to adult food tastes.

And there's really no reason why it shouldn't be sooner rather than later.

That's why our Stage 1 range includes lots of grown-up tastes.

There are cereals, meats, vegetables, puddings, fruits and even artificial additive-free yogurt desserts.

So during those first few months of weaning, your baby's palate will be in for quite an education.

After 2 or 3 months, it'll be complete. And your baby will be ready to graduate to our Stage 2 meals.

Grown-up tastes. Grown-up textures.

The next stage is to develop your baby's ability to chew.

For this reason, our Stage 2 meals are thicker, and have either meaty or fruity pieces in them.

With a little practice your baby will soon realise that food needs to be chewed before it can be swallowed.

(And knowing that babies don't like coping with too many changes at once, most of our Stage 2 meals are available in the same varieties as Stage 1.)

The 55 meal menu.

You wouldn't take too kindly to eating the same food day in day out.

And neither do babies.

That's one reason why we make 23 different Stage 1 varieties, 23 Stage 2 varieties and 9 yogurt desserts.

But it isn't the only reason.

Perhaps more importantly, your baby grows so fast in the early months that a varied and well-balanced diet is essential.

What's more, it should help you avoid trouble in the years to come.

By educating your baby's palate to accept all sorts of different tastes and textures you should forestall 'food fads' later on.

The best for your baby.

When it comes to feeding young babies, you can't be too careful.

That's something that we at Cow & Gate never, ever forget.

So we buy only the best foods.

All our suppliers must meet the rigorous standards we set.

Every item of food that comes in is checked by our inspectors.

Then our chemists carry out checks of their own.

And the same thing happens all through the cooking process.

In fact, over 20% of our staff do nothing else.

It tastes like adult food…

If you think all babymeals are bland and flavourless, you've obviously not tasted ours.

We've recently altered our recipes so our meals now taste much more akin to grown-up food.

The fact is, we've found that babies prefer them that way.

And so do mothers.

Because when the time comes to move onto adult food, the switch will be that much gentler because your baby will already be used to its taste.

…but it isn't adult food.

Compared to adult food, our babymeals have some very important differences.

We add a little extra vitamin C to some of our desserts to replace the amount lost in cooking.

But we don't add any salt whatsoever to any of our meals.

And none of them contain any artificial colourings, flavourings or preservatives.

But we do, however, make sure they supply protein, vitamins and minerals a growing baby needs.

Gently does it.

We hope we've shown you how our babymeals make the journey to adult food in short, gentle steps.

If you have any queries, have a word with your Health Visitor.

Or by all means write to us at Cow & Gate, Trowbridge, Wilts BA14 8YX.

But it's worth remembering that no two babies are the same.

While you can encourage progress, never force the pace.

And be prepared for some little dramas and setbacks on the way.

But don't lose heart.

If it's a Cow & Gate meal now, it shouldn't be too long before it's real home cooking with the rest of the family.

Two short steps to grown-up food.

THE MOST AMAZING TURNING-CIRCLE STORY EVER TOLD.

When is a 15-foot 8-inch Volvo 240 Estate smaller than a 12-foot 6-inch VW Golf? When it's turning round. Although over three feet longer than the Golf, the Volvo's turning circle is seven inches smaller. A dizzy 32 feet 2 inches, between kerbs. Parking a Volvo 240 Estate is like getting a quart into a pint pot. Only without the struggle. Its power-assisted steering makes the car as light to drive as the Golf.

But we don't want to pick on the Golf.

The Ford Escort, Talbot Horizon and Fiat Strada all have a bigger turning circle than the Volvo.

And when you compare the car with other big estates, there's no comparison. The Peugeot 505 Estate, for instance, needs 2 feet 7 inches more to turn round in. The Mercedes 200 Estate, 3 feet 6 inches more. The Ford Granada Estate, 4 feet 2 inches more. Of course, it's not just feet you're interested in, it's cubic feet. And the Volvo 240 Estate has seventy five of them, with the rear seat folded down. Both your cargo and your passengers travel in carpeted comfort.

You, the driver, have the additional benefit of an automatically heated seat. (It switches itself on as soon as the temperature drops below 14° Centigrade.) The construction of the car is equally comforting. Like all Volvos, the 240 Estate is built around a rigid safety cage of welded box steel pillars. Each weld is strong enough to support the weight of the entire car. There are impact-absorbing crumple zones front and rear, and steel bars in the doors.

The 240 Estate protects your investment, as well as your life. It goes through a 19-stage painting and rustproofing process. A PVC coating is applied not only to the underbody, but to the sills and sidepanels too. All vulnerable and inaccessible parts of the body are made of double-sided, hot-dipped zinc plate. And the exposed parts of the exhaust system have a special rust-resisting aluminium finish.

Happily, the Volvo 240 Estate is not as expensive as it sounds. It can be yours for just £7,998, including car tax and VAT. (Not to mention central locking, rear seat belts and internally adjustable door mirrors.)

Any way you look at it, that's not a lot of money for an estate car. Especially an estate car that can turn on a sixpence. **THE VOLVO 240 SERIES ESTATES. FROM £7998.**

PRICE INCLUDES CAR TAX & VAT (DELIVERY & NUMBER PLATES EXTRA) CORRECT AT TIME OF GOING TO PRESS. SALES TELEPHONE: HIGH WYCOMBE (0494) 33444. OR WRITE TO DEPT TSM4, VOLVO CUSTOMER INFORMATION, HIGH WYCOMBE, BUCKS HP12 3PN

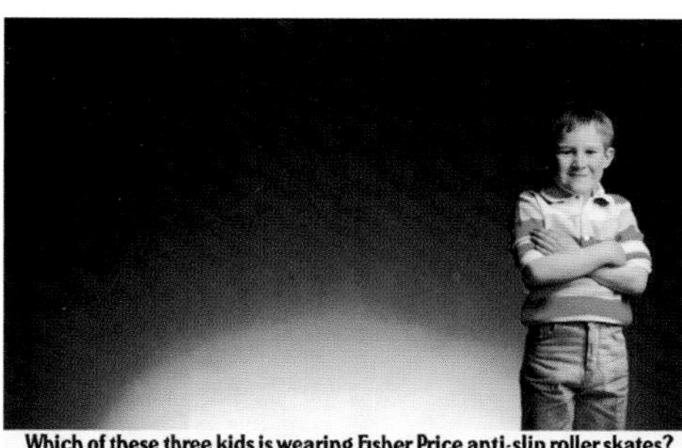

Which of these three kids is wearing Fisher Price anti-slip roller skates?
Fisher-Price

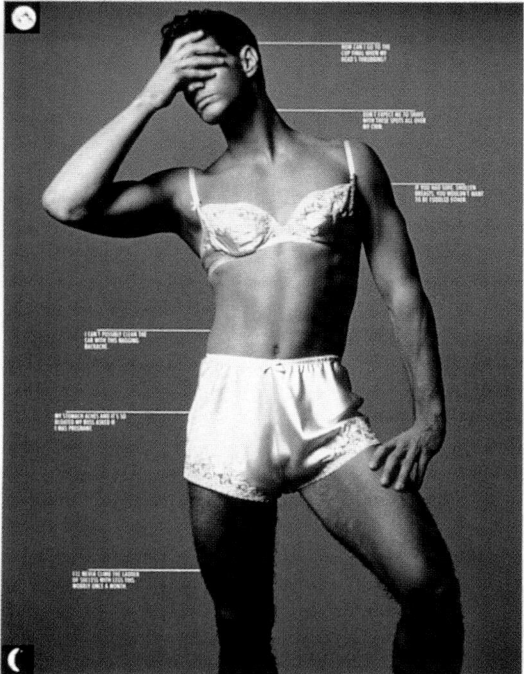

Have you ever wondered how men would carry on if they had periods?

Dr White's Towels and Tampons.

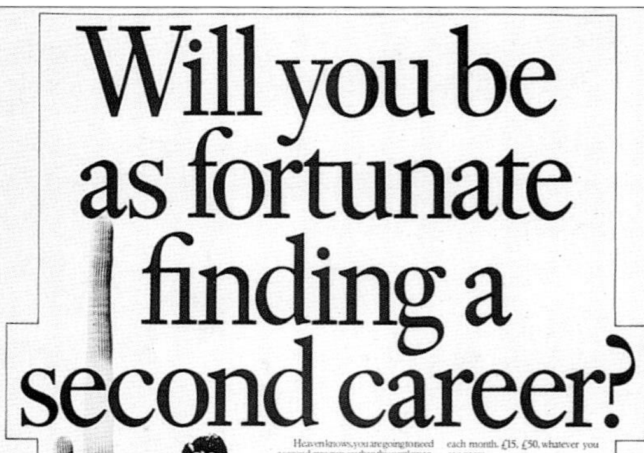

above & opposite

1981.17
Agency: **Advertising and Marketing Services**
Client: **Albany Life Assurance**

bottom left

1983.21
Agency: **Lowe & Howard-Spink**
Client: **Albany Life Assurance**

No campaign had ever talked about life insurance in such direct terms ('answer these ten questions and work out the date of your own death'). A classic example of eighties press work cutting to the chase. Tony Brignull and Neil Godfrey created the initial campaign, photographed by Jimmy Wormser. Alfredo Marcantonio and David Christensen of Lowe Howard-Spink moved it forward in 1983.

If they ever give me
the push I will...

TICK YOUR FAVOURITE FANTASY.
Become a monk.
Run an antique shop.
Go on the dole.
Leave this crazy country.
Open a restaurant.
Start a consultancy.
Albany Life

Answer these
ten questions and
work out the date
of your own death.
Start with the age of 77 for a man and 81 for a woman (assuming you are over twenty years old now) and add or subtract according to your answers.
1. How old are you now?
Up to 50 no score.
51 – 55 add one year.
56 – 60 add two years.
61 – 65 add three years.
66 – 70 add four years.
2. Do you smoke?
Over 40 a day subtract 9 years.
Over 20 a day subtract 6 years.
Up to 20 a day no score.
3. Do you drink?
Heavily (more than 5 drinks a day) subtract 10 years.
Moderately, no score.
Teetotal, subtract 2 years.
4. Sex?
If you enjoy sex once a week, add 1 year.
5. Family History?
If any close relative has died of heart disease before 50, subtract 4 years.
Between ages 51–65, subtract 2 years.
If any close relative has suffered from diabetes or mental disorder, subtract 3 years.
6. Overweight?
If your problem is measured in stones rather than pounds, subtract 6 years.
7. Your job?
Professional, technical or management, add 1 year.
Semi-skilled, subtract 1 year.
Labourer, subtract 4 years.
But: active, add 2 years, desk-bound, subtract 2 years.
8. Exercise?
Proper exercise (heavy breathing) at least twice a week, add 3 years.
9. Life-Style?
Single, living alone, subtract 1 year.
Widow, or separated within past 2 years, subtract 4 years.
10. Health?
If you have an annual check-up, add 2 years.
Any serious illness or disease requiring hospital treatment in the last 5 years subtract 10 years.
Albany Life

Can you afford
to live to
a ripe old age?
IF INFLATION CARRIES ON AT ONLY 10% THIS IS WHAT THINGS WILL COST IN THE YEAR 2001.
£216.00
£5 per lb.
£160 to fill tank
£29,792.00
£3.00
£4.50
£202.00
Albany Life

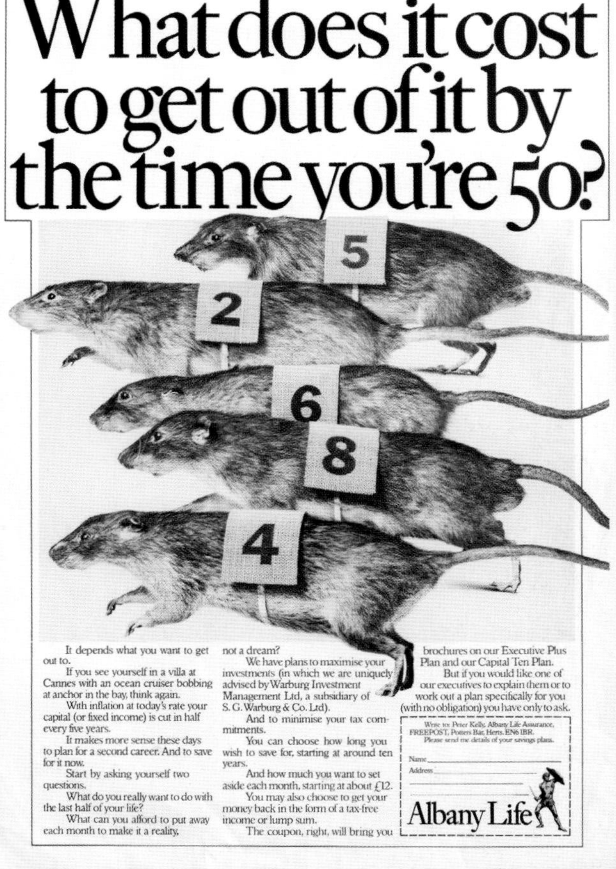
What does it cost
to get out of it by
the time you're 50?
5
2
6
8
4
Albany Life

Not all press campaigns communicated with such directness and clarity. Several in the mid-eighties reflected broader design trends towards the decorative, ephemeral and effeté. Style-driven work for cruise liner company Cunard, Dickens & Jones, Linguaphone and Harrods were selected at D&AD and looked of the moment, but many questioned their effectiveness. A BMP press campaign for Hellmann's Mayonnaise, which won a Silver Award in 1986 for the creative team of Paul Leeves and Alan Tilby, was thoroughly post-modern in its use of spaced out and deconstructed type.

Illustration swept through press advertising at the same time as it did through posters and book jackets. When it worked, it worked brilliantly, as in art director Tony Muranka's 'Temptation Beyond Endurance' campaign for Planters peanuts, featuring illustrator Warren Madill. Agencies TBWA and Minale Tattersfield combined to produce a memorably graphic campaign for Land Rover. A CDP press ad for Beck's Bier recycled the German 'Aryan Art' of the thirties in a collaboration with illustrator Barry Craddock and design firm The Fine White Line.

'A table for two? Certainly you old trout.'

LINGUAPHONE

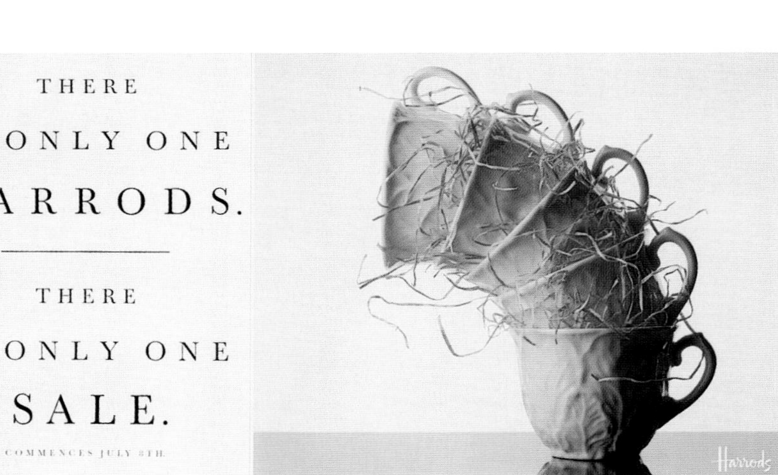

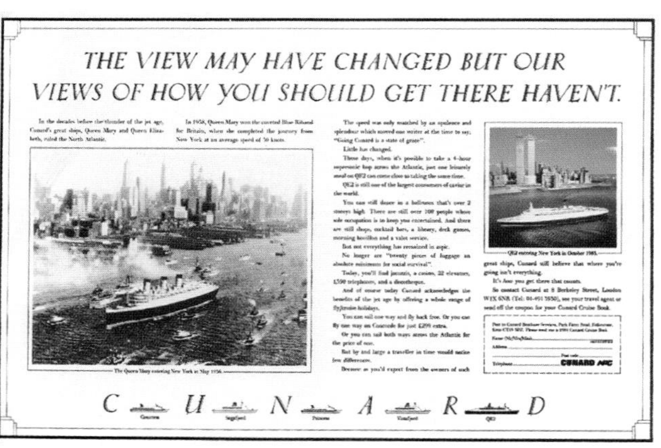

At the end of this sentence there's a full stop. It's about the size of the musket ball that killed Nelson at Trafalgar.

The musket ball that robbed Britain of her greatest ever admiral also made a jagged 18mm blood-stained hole in the shoulder of the blue naval officers' coat he was wearing at the time.

You can see that same coat today. It's standing on display in the National Maritime Museum, at Greenwich.

Nearby is a reconstruction of the sitting room in the house at Merton, where Nelson lived with his mistress, Lady Hamilton.

She's the one historians guardedly refer to as 'stormy' and 'tempestuous.'

Perhaps the lack of vases in the room tells us something about their relationship.

Even the everyday life of the man is revealed, by the all-in-one knife and fork set he had specially made after losing his arm at Tenerife.

Of course, naval history, sexual politics and dismemberment might not be your tot of rum. In which case, you should go to see the pictures.

As you might expect, the museum has the world's finest collection of Dutch and Flemish seascapes.

The great portrait painters are represented by Hogarth, Gainsborough, Reynolds, and Romney. And marking a turning point in the history of art (as well as the history of the world) is Turner's magnificent 'Battle of Trafalgar.'

From the great age of exploration, the Museum has 40,000 charts and a huge collection of navigational instruments.

Look at the beautifully made marine chronometer used by Captain Cook in the Pacific. (As you do, consider this: when Neil Armstrong went to the moon, scientists knew its diameter – even its weight. When Cook set sail, he didn't know New Zealand was an island!)

Both Nelson's and Cook's ships are represented among the collection of over 2,000 intricately detailed ship models.

You can see the great Mauretania, reminiscent of the golden age of transatlantic liners, when even the rats wore dinner jackets after 7pm.

Find 'submarine boat No.1' and ask yourself whether you'd trust it to keep you dry in a thunderstorm, let alone ferry you about a few fathoms down.

The Museum buildings were designed by England's two greatest architects – Sir Christopher Wren and Inigo Jones.

(Bearing in mind your present whereabouts, it's worth pointing out that neither of them ever designed an underground station.)

The best place to appreciate their work is on the hill where Wren's old Royal Observatory stands. Once there, you can stand astride the brass line which marks the Greenwich Meridian – zero degrees longitude.

It's the starting point for the world's measurement of time and Britain's greatest gift to the science of navigation.

If you've never been to the National Maritime Museum, you owe yourself a day there.

There's a good restaurant in the museum and some delightful pubs nearby.

It's probably one of the most enjoyable experiences London has to offer.

Which is a lot more than can be said for hanging round gloomy underground stations, reading the posters.

The coat Nelson wore at Trafalgar.

The National Maritime Museum at Greenwich.

The History of Britain and the Sea. In a Palace by the River.

1988.14
Agency: **Leagas Delaney**
Client: **Linguaphone Institute**
The chortle produced by Tim Delaney's novice linguist's gaffe is made all the more bittersweet by Graham Cornthwaites charming and atmospheric picture.

1985.19
Agency: **Saatchi & Saatchi**
Client: **The National Maritime Museum**
Designed to be read by stranded Underground passengers with nothing better to do, this was one of the few examples of a brilliantly crafted long-copy ad. The idea of the full stop being the size of the musket ball that killed Nelson is a superb use of the medium.

1984.19
Agency: **Saatchi & Saatchi**
Client: **Cunard Line**

1988.15
Agency: **Leagas Delaney**
Client: **Harrods**

A duo of press ads which reflected the broader trends in graphic design of the period, as advertising and editorial began their long march towards a visual coalescence. By the late eighties that merger was more and more on the cards.

this page

1986.22
Agency: **Boase Massimi Pollitt Partnership**
Client: **CPC**
Typographers became type artists in the mid-eighties and David Wakefield's work for Hellmann's Mayonnaise broke new ground in the use of deconstructed post-modern typography. Was this sheer self-indulgence, as those old-timers schooled in the cool modernism of Bill Bernbach argued? Or was it an exciting new departure? Probably a bit of both. Mayonnaise anyone?

1987.10
Agency: **Saatchi & Saatchi**
Client: **Dickens & Jones**
Shot by Clive Arrowsmith, this long-running campaign upped the stakes at the higher end of the fashion retailing market.

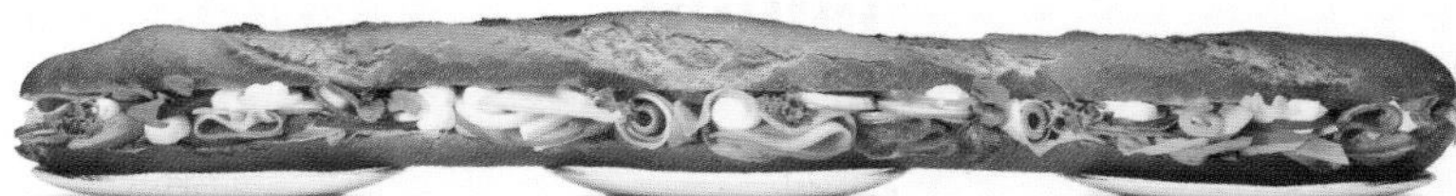

Advanced Sandwich Tecknology (Or Robert Carrier Eat Your Heart Out.)

I had been engrossed in the geometric formation of a cheese butty for some hours when Dad peered up from his copy of the Bugle. "You know what you can do with that infernal sandwich...." Quite by chance he'd stumbled on a brilliant New sandwiching Tecknique :–

My Rolled-Up And Stuffed Sarnie.

Hard way:– Cut all the crusts off a loaf, slice it longways as thin as you Can and flatten slices with Aunt Gerty's rolling pin.

Easy way:– Sometimes I can't be bothered so I just cut all the crusts off a white slice.

Next lay some ham on it. Spread it with shredded Cheddar and diced pimento mixed with Hellmann's and roll it up.

After a few hours in the fridge slice 'em into nice 'n's.

(Look at all the gOod thingies it's got.)

Over the next few months I devised and applied many more Principles of sandwichery.

My BLT Double Decker
(DEGREE OF DIFFICULTY 9)

Sandwich three slices with grilled bacoN, lettuce and tomato mixed with Hellmann's and crumbled blue cheese.

I'm still working on the question of wether to toast or not to toast.

Either way, make lots of double deckers 'cos you'll have Bus loads of scRoungers, worst luck.

The Three Foot Hero.
(DEGREE OF DIFFICULTY 8.4)

Buy a long French stick. (Do not pretend it's Excallabor on the way home). Cut it all the way up the middle end to end, then rest.

You can fill it with all sorts (not liquorice), different salamis & cheeses, slices of tomato and onion with lovely, creAmy Hellmann's spread between each layer. Ooh, Brill.

My FaVouriTe ZeBra.
(DEGREE OF DIFFICULTY 204)

Tons of research and development went into this. Ready? 1. Blend two hard-boiled eggs with some chopped parsley and

Hellmann's. 2. Blend minced onion with cream cheese. 3. Take 4 wholemeal slices and 3 white ones and do this :–

Brown, cheesey mix, white, Hellmann's mix, brown, cheesey mix, etc. Wrap it in clingy plastic and put it in the fridge. Slice it into 5 fingers when famished.

If you like you can write for my B.Sc. (butty science) sandwich course.

You Can Sandwich Anything In Hellmann's MaYoNnaise.

Diddley dum, didley dum, diddley dum.

I sat transfixed by my BriTish Rail cheese 'n' Pickalilly sarnie.

As it curled at each corner I fell into a swoon and was transported to exotic

places and faraway sandwiches.

Le 'Ellmann's Sarnie
a La Parisienne
(aVec Toast FrAnSaIs.)

Premier:– take a leetle slice of le cooked chicken or le turkey and le ham.

Zen put some cheese cheddar through le grater.

Stir ever-re-things into 3 (trois) spoons of 'ellmann's Mayonnaise. Bon. Next:– beat le egg in milk. Dip le sarnie all over and grill (sur le derrier aussi).

Hoo, say manyfeek!

A Culinary Tour De France (Also Italy, Denmark And Solihull).

HOwTa-MAka-Pizza-WiTha-BiTsaNDpiZzaS.

Take-a some-a Mozzarella chese-a. Ora some-a cheddar chees-a. Choppa chese-a anda-mixitupa-witha-Hellmann's Adda slice-a tomato. Grilla on-a halfa Crumpit. Mumma mia.

(CAn'T SpeAK Danish So I'LL Do This One Normal.)

N.B. Danish open sarnies are 'triff' if

you're short of bread 'cos you only need one slice.

Try these :–

a) Prawn, tomato sauce and It.
b) Chicken roll with orange pieces stuffed with It.
c) Chopped roast beef with horseradish and It.

All these go a treat with all the good things in It.

P.S. One Mrs Patel Showed Me.

1/2 cup diced chicken, 1/2 cup chopped celery and apple, 1/4 cup diced green Pepper, 1/4 teaspoon curry powder, 1/2 dash Pepper

and paprika all mixed up with Hellmann's in a plain nan.

Bet that makes your ~~mouth~~ eyes water!

Au revois, ariva dertchi, (thingy) sat sri akal.

You Can Sandwich Anything In Hellmann's MaYoNnaise.

1980.10
Agency: **Cherry Hedger & Seymour**
Client: **Standard Brands**

1982.15
Agency: **Carter Hedger Mitchell & Partners**
Client: **Romix Foods**

A brilliant use of illustration in a memorable campaign from the early eighties. The idea that your own shadow would not be able to resist stealing your nuts was not controversial, but the thieving intervention of the Hand of God certainly was. It was the execution by art director Tony Muranka and illustrator Warren Madill that enabled such a blasphemous proposition to work so effectively. The composition of the ad drew heavily on classical art.

THIS LAND ROVER IS IN REVERSE GEAR.

THIS LAND ROVER IS IN FORWARD GEAR.

 1986.23
Agency: **Collett Dickenson Pearce**
Client: **Scottish & Newcastle Breweries**
Created by The Fine White Line, then an offshoot of CDP, this ad for Beck's Bier was very influential at the time because it cued into the 'Aryan Art' movement then sweeping through British design. In the search for novelty, designers even began stripmining the morally-suspect visual archive of the thirties and forties. Barry Craddock's illustrations were actually based on a set of thirties German stamps showing the reconstruction of the Fatherland. Very dubious.

1981.18
Agency: **TBWA**
Client: **Land Rover**
Malcolm Gaskin and Neil Patterson created this classic ad for TBWA, with symbol design by Minale Tattersfield. The reader was instantly engaged by having to turn the page to get the point.

Occasionally, press advertising seemed in danger of disappearing up a design cul-de-sac, but the no-bullshit approach wasn't forgotten and late in the decade it was back with a vengeance in press work for charity and public sector clients. Hard-hitting campaigns by Saatchi & Saatchi for the National Society for the Prevention of Cruelty to Children, The Samaritans and Guide Dogs for the Blind, by BMP for War on Want, and by CDP for Great Ormond Street Hospital and the Metropolitan Police (a series featuring work by veteran war photographer Don McCullin) featured strongly at D&AD.

1987.11
Agency: **Boase Massimi Pollitt Partnership**
Client: **War on Want**

1988.16
Agency: **Collett Dickenson Pearce**
Client: **Great Ormond Street Hospital**

1986.24
Agency: **Saatchi & Saatchi**
Client: **NSPCC**

1983.22
Agency: **Saatchi & Saatchi**
Client: **NSPCC**

A selection of hard-hitting charity and pubic service press advertising from the eighties. At a time when Bob Geldof's Live Aid campaign, one of the defining social conscience moments of the decade, had drawn attention to famine in Africa, BMP's War on Want campaign focused on why people were starving in Ethiopia. The ads ran in *The Spectator* and the music press. Meanwhile, Saatchi's brilliant press ad for Great Ormond Street Hospital, solicited support from an entirely new perspective.

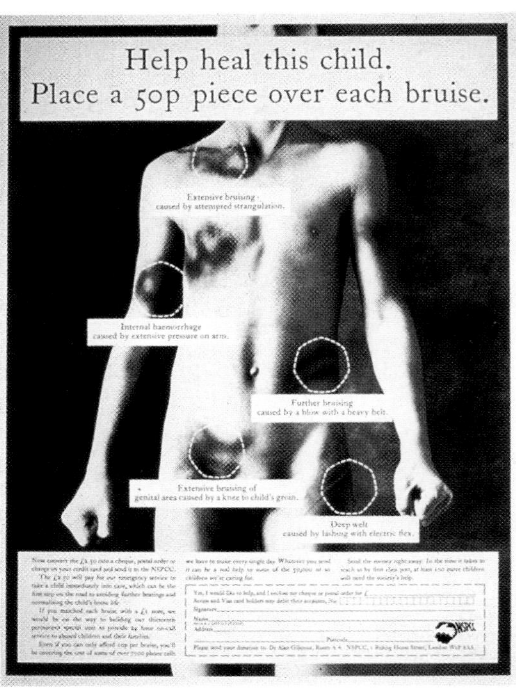

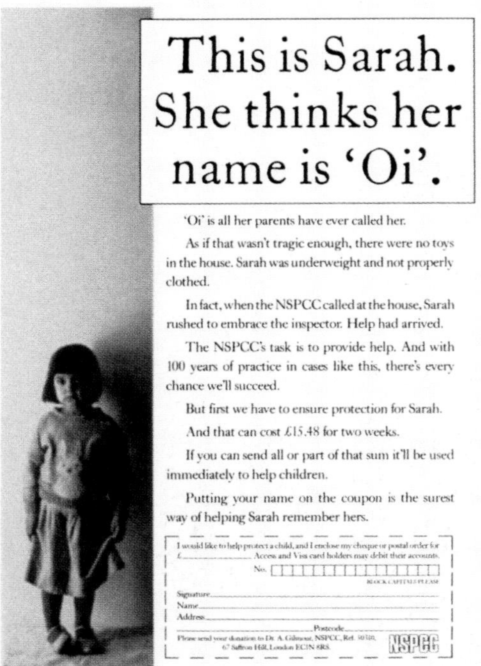

COULD YOU TURN THE OTHER CHEEK?

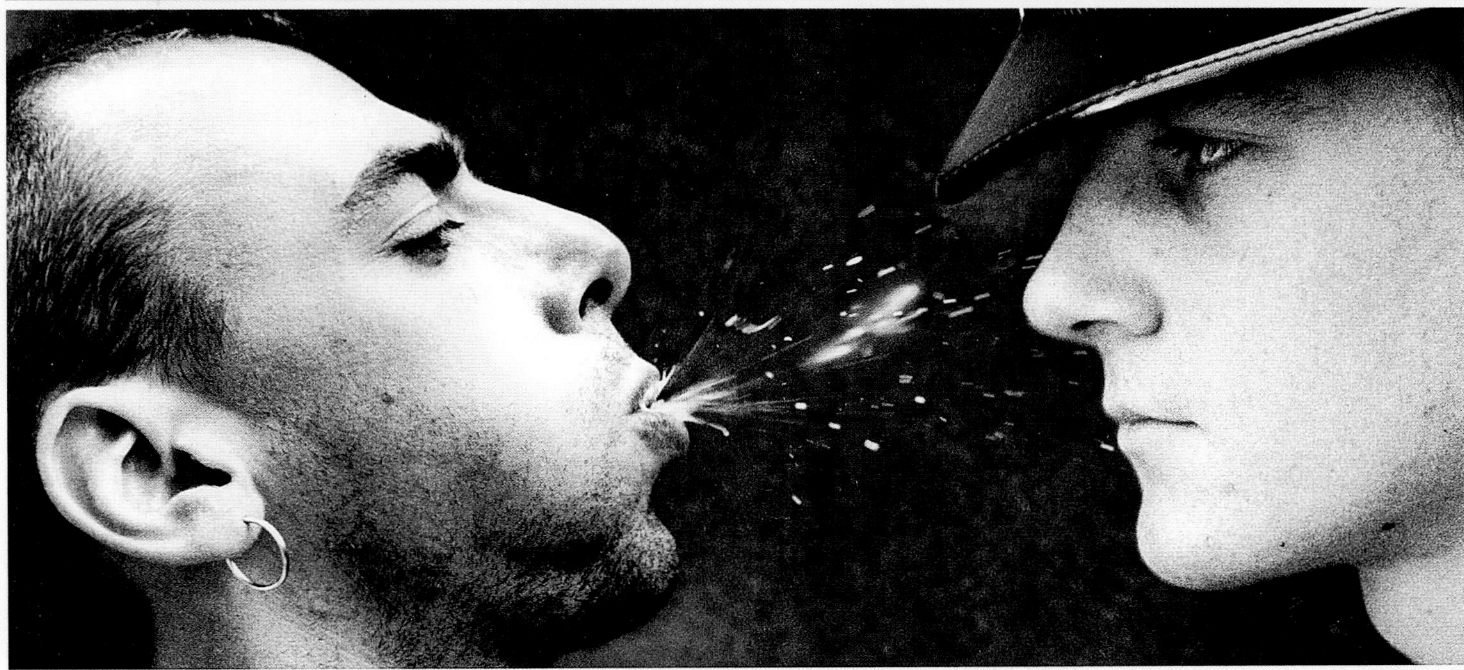

COOL CUSTOMER, are you? Okay, let's see how far you can get before you blow your stack.

As a police officer, sooner or later you're bound to encounter abuse, threats, provocation, even physical violence. Be careful how you respond. Lose your temper and you could lose your job. **Photograph by Don McCullin**

You are walking down a street. Some youths start jeering at you: "'Ello, 'ello, 'ello." Smile. You've heard it all before, every name a copper can be called: rozzer, old bill, pig, fuzz, peeler, flatfoot, the filth. And some less complimentary. Shrug it off.

You're out in the patrol car when you see a car without lights weaving through the traffic. You flash your headlights at him to stop. Instead, he accelerates away.

Siren on. Ahead your target, still without lights, narrowly misses a woman on a pedestrian crossing and then goes the wrong way round a roundabout, while a youth leaning out of the passenger window showers you with empty beer cans and two-finger salutes.

The car skids round another corner and slides into a brick wall, but the youths inside are out and running. You chase, abandoning your car with its engine still on and door left wide open. As you grab the driver, he mouths obscenities at you.

"You can't go on the attack, whatever the provocation."

Still in control of your temper? Okay, try this.

A demonstration is turning into a riot. You're bussed in, nervous and not sure what to expect. It's frightening. The crowd, in ugly mood, surges against the frail police line.

Suddenly a lone voice calls your number "EF203, EF203." The others take it up. "EF203, EF203." They're all staring at you, trying to psyche you out. Why you?

It gets worse. Bottles are down and burst in showers of flame. Stones and half bricks drop out of the air and threaten to brain you. You cannot leave the line.

At last the crowd starts drifting away. As the tension ebbs, you see a man step forward and deliberately stub out his cigarette on the flank of a police horse.

This all sounds a bit melodramatic, but we've made none of it up. Each of the details we've described really happened.

How would you have reacted?

Strangely, people often find that in a real emergency they stay calm. But stress builds up in the body like static and can earth itself without warning.

Three days after a riot like the one above you may arrest a well dressed drunk. "Look here," he drawls, "do you realise who you're talking to?" And jabs you in the chest.

Careful. This trivial annoyance may become the lightning rod for all that pent up stress and rage.

If, in any of the situations we have described above, you were to lose your temper, you might also lose your job.

It doesn't seem fair, does it? But then being a police officer is no ordinary job. As someone sworn to uphold the law, you of all people cannot break it.

And the law says that you may use no more than reasonable force. You can't go on the attack. No matter what the provocation.

So what should you do? Should you say: "Are you going to come quietly or do I have to use earplugs?" In fact, a bit of humour can often defuse a potentially ugly situation. As can tact, restraint and good common sense.

Of course, it's a strain being on best behaviour 24 hours a day. Never switching off. With the very highest standards to set and live up to. Sometimes, all that bottled up stress can make us difficult to live with.

An officer on motorway patrol raced to an accident. A car was on fire. The heat was ferocious. He had to watch, helpless, as a child the same age as his own daughter burned to death before his eyes.

When he got home, his wife produced supper. Without a word, he picked up his plate of food and flung it through the window. Until then he had kept control of his emotions. But that night of all nights he could not face a cooked meal.

As a police officer you will inevitably endure your share of unpleasantness and you'll have to evolve your own way of dealing with it.

But why are we dwelling on these traumatic subjects? Isn't this supposed to be a recruitment advertisement? Are we trying to put you off?

Actually, yes.

If you're put off by an advertisement, you'd never be able to cope with the reality.

"It gets worse. Bottles arc down and burst in showers of flame."

And we need people who can cope. People who are tough, tender, sensitive, strong and disciplined, all at the same time. They aren't easy to find. At present we take only one in five applicants. We'd rather look at fewer, better candidates.

Seeing you've got this far, we'll now admit that a career in the Met isn't all grief. Few jobs are as rewarding.

Ask the much loved Streatham home beat officer who, helmet under arm, cigar stuck firmly in mouth in flagrant disregard of regulations, can tell you the name of every child in his manor.

Ask the constable who, while patiently unravelling the intricacies of gang warfare in, of all places, Southall, has been invited to six Indian weddings in the last year.

Ask the sergeant who now runs what is virtually a Bengali advice centre in Whitechapel.

We can offer 28,000 more examples. If you don't believe us, stop any police officer in the street and ask.

When you've learned what they get out of the job, ask how they got in.

They'll tell you about our twenty week basic training course at Hendon. And life on the beat at one of London's 187 police stations where, under the tutelage of a sergeant, you will learn the art of handling people. And yourself.

Right now, your next step is to fill in and post the coupon below.

We're looking for mature, fit people aged between 18½ and 45, especially from the ethnic minorities. You should be at least 172cms tall if you're a man, 162cms if you're a woman.

Ideally, you'll have some 'O' level passes or their equivalents, but we value your personal qualities more.

To find out more please telephone: 01-725 4492 (Ansaphone: 01-725 4575) or fill in the coupon or write to: The Recruiting Officer, The Metropolitan Police Selection Centre, Department MD 960, Freepost, London W2 1BR.

Name

Address

Postcode *Age*

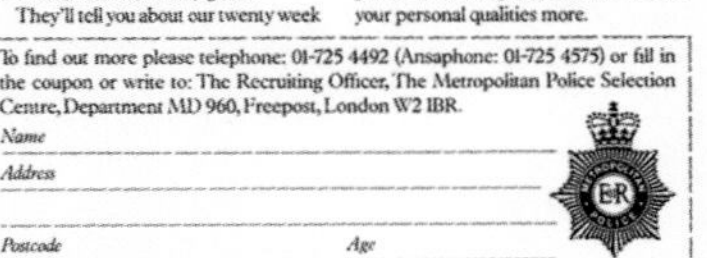
ER

COULD YOU DISARM HIM?
Unlike officers in the New York Police Department, a copper in the Met, when confronted with a gunman pointing a sawn-off shotgun at him, has to disarm him using only his hands and, more importantly his head. Photographs by Don McCullin

Open 24 hours a day.
The Samaritans

above & centre

1989.17
Agency: **Collett Dickenson Pearce**
Client: **Metropolitan Police**

1988.17
Agency: **Collett Dickenson Pearce**
Client: **Metropolitan Police**

The work of veteran war photographer Don McCullin and typography by Len Cheeseman were used to good effect on this editorial-style campaign for police recruitment. The campaign (art directed by Graham Fink and then Neil Godfrey at CDP) certainly put its point across in a must-read way.

far right

1989.18
Agency: **Saatchi & Saatchi**
Client: **The Samaritans**
Simple, sound and surprisingly memorable work art directed by Fergus Fleming and Judyth Greenburgh.

Dave Trott was among those in the industry who were cynical about charity accounts, saying, 'A lot of agencies just do charity ads for the parrot protection society to win awards.' But few doubted the worthiness of the causes or the effectiveness of the communication. O&M's mixed media campaign for the Royal National Institute for the Deaf, which won a Silver Award in 1988, was a case in point. This set out to raise awareness, not money, and to give deaf and hearing-impaired people a positive image. It featured brilliant work by the creative team of Derrick Hass and Howard Fletcher, including a poster showing two ears with a copyline between reading, 'Just because we're deaf, it doesn't mean we've nothing between our ears.'

But while such charity campaigns were full of empathy and compelling social commentary, the advertising industry itself had become bloated and hedonistic. In 1983, there had been rumours that the Albany Life press ad featuring Ronald Reagan had necessitated several trips to America to source the cactus. The following year, leading adman Jay Chiat told an Advertising Association conference that the financial responsibilities of newly public agencies were beginning to weigh heavily.

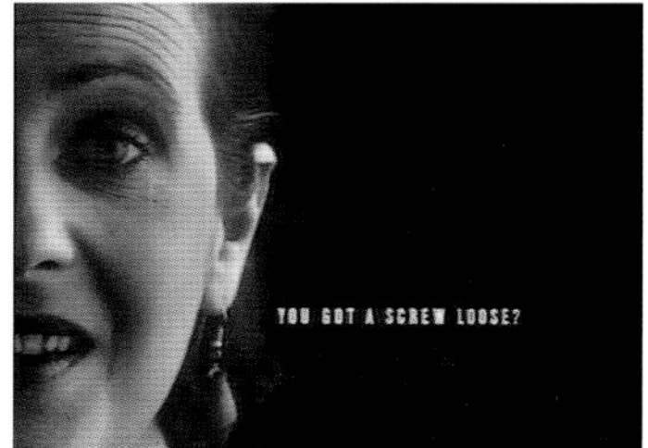

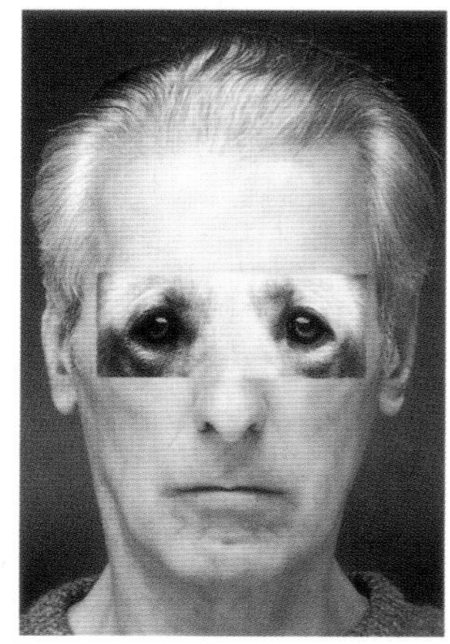

bottom left

1987.12
Agency: **Saatchi & Saatchi**
Client: **Guide Dogs for the Blind Association**
Jeff Stark and Mike Shafron's Guide Dogs for the Blind ad is a subtle and haunting piece of collage.

opposite & this page

1988.18
Agency: **Ogilvy & Mather**
Client: **Royal National Institute for the Deaf**
In researching this campaign, the creative team of Derrick Hass and Howard Fletcher learnt from the client how deaf people are misunderstood in society. The creative task was simply to draw attention to the problem, to challenge existing attitudes and to create an understanding for how the deaf feel.

The line 'She's going deaf, not daft' summed up the creative approach. With next to no budget, the agency begged favours from all and sundry. Photographer John Claridge donated the 'Granny' shot, and the TV commercial was directed by David Brown for minimal cost, the total production budget coming in at just £5,000. 'Sign Language' was not only the first charity commercial on TV, it was also the first silent 60-second commercial. The commercial also ran in cinemas, where it silenced audiences everywhere.

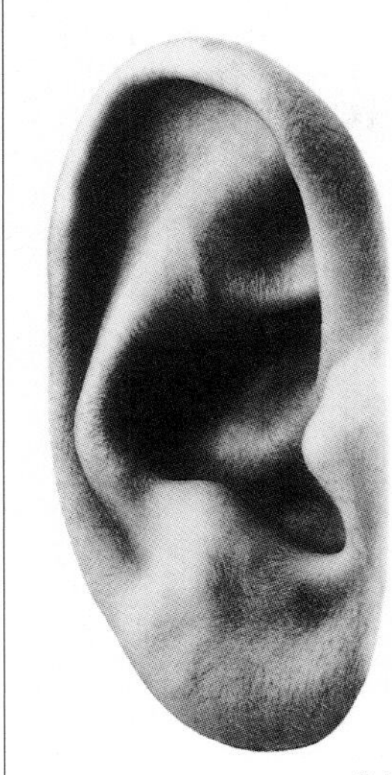

JUST BECAUSE WE'RE DEAF,

IT DOESN'T MEAN WE'VE NOTHING

BETWEEN OUR EARS.

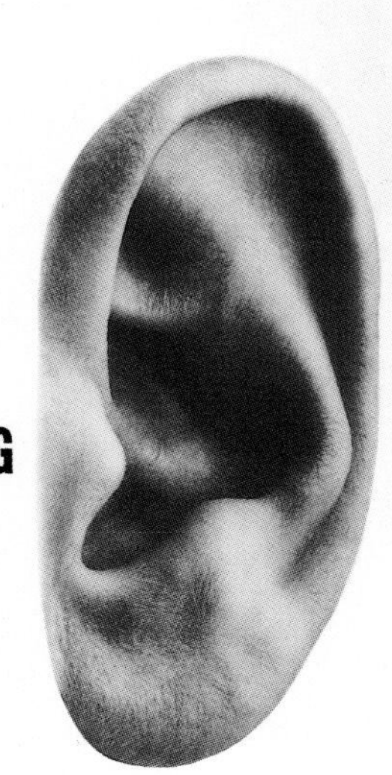

THE ROYAL NATIONAL INSTITUTE FOR THE DEAF.

SHE'S ONLY LOSING HER HEARING. NOT HER MARBLES.

"Don't take any notice of gran. She's deaf as a post, and a bit batty." No, please don't ignore her. If you do, she'll just opt out of the world, feeling rejected and isolated. And don't shout at the old dear. Loud sounds can actually cause the deaf physical pain. Talk to her, clearly and slowly, in a moderately loud voice. Apart from that, treat her like any other sane human being. She's going deaf, not daft.

THE ROYAL NATIONAL INSTITUTE FOR THE DEAF.

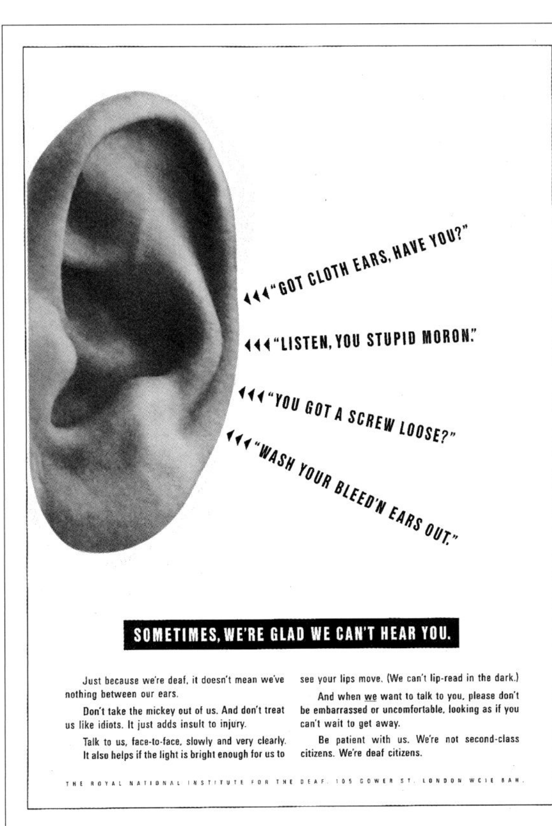

When Saatchi & Saatchi acquired an entire agency just to recruit one creative director (Jeff Stark), many openly questioned where the industry was heading. Budgets and costs soared as British advertising entertained grandiose schemes on a global scale – but the high fliers were heading for a fall. The same pattern was repeated in design, where no less a figure than Sir Terence Conran warned of the industry overheating. 'There's so much movement, so much turmoil, so many people thinking they're going to rush off and make their million, that the design business is a dangerous place to be at the moment,' he told *Creative Review* in 1985. 'Good design ... is not to be done in the middle of a maelstrom.' Much of the heat was emanating from the high-street boom in retail design, which transformed some small graphic design firms into larger multi-disciplinary ones, offering environmental and product design alongside their traditional services. D&AD expanded its categories accordingly, to accommodate this extension of design services. Pentagram's inventive retail graphics for travel agency Wakefield Fortune, a winner in 1983, was followed by the first D&AD Silver Award for retail design in 1985. This was won by Michael Peters & Partners for hairdresser Dar Salons.

Minimalist fashion interiors intertwining commerce and culture quickly caught the eye at D&AD, among them schemes for Next, Issey Miyake and Anna Federici (by architect Eva Jiricna). All of this prompted the Dutch cultural historian Frederique Huygens to comment that British shops started to look like museums in the eighties and the museums like shops. (A Saatchi & Saatchi campaign controversially reinvented the V&A as 'an ace caff' with museum attached.)

But the milestone environmental design programme of the period – Fitch & Co's revamp of Midland Bank on the high street (a Silver winner in 1987) – wasn't a clothes store at all. It just looked like one. The redesign of a solid financial institution to resemble a trendy boutique with low-voltage lighting and wooden floors must have seemed like a good idea at the time. But as Midland Bank's performance dipped, many saw the Fitch scheme as symptomatic of design being all promise and no delivery, and all style and no substance.

1989.19
Design group: **Eva Jiricna Architects**
Client: **Anna Federici**
Minimalist upmarket fashion retailing is rewarded at D&AD, ignoring the mass of overblown and over-hyped design on the high street.

1985.20
Design group: **Michael Peters & Partners**
Client: **Dar Salons**
The first retail interior to win at D&AD, designed by a group with a rich pedigree in winning awards. Branching out from retail packaging and graphics into environments was seen as a natural commercial move in the expansionist eighties.

1987.13
Design group: **Fitch & Co Design Consultants**
Client: **Midland Bank**
The scheme which tried to turn a bank into a trendy youth destination. As all high-street outlets increasingly looked alike, customers didn't know whether to order an overdraft or a cappuccino.

this page

1983.23
Design group: **Pentagram Design**
Client: **Wakefield Fortune**

1981.19
Design group: **Pentagram Design**
Client: **Fios**

Point-of-sale graphics in retail spaces provided the bridge between 2D projects and full-blown architectural schemes. These two projects are by Pentagram (winning a Gold Award for this sales promotion duvet for Slumberdown) which would later branch out into retail interiors for Swatch and others. The point-of-sale giant postcards with 'testimonials' written by satisfied customers on the reverse were art directed by David Hillman for a chain of travel agents, reflected the illustration fever of the early eighties.

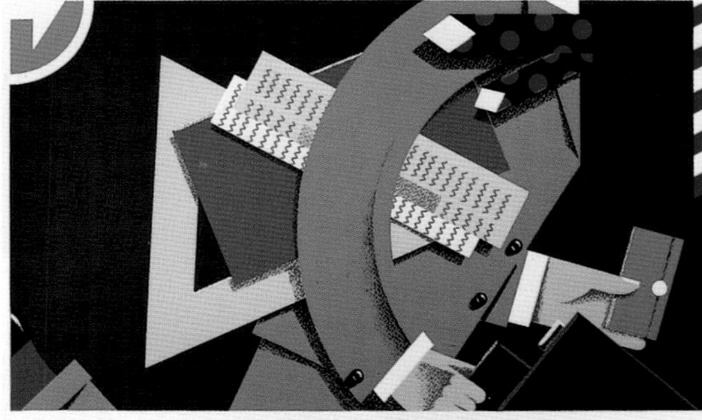

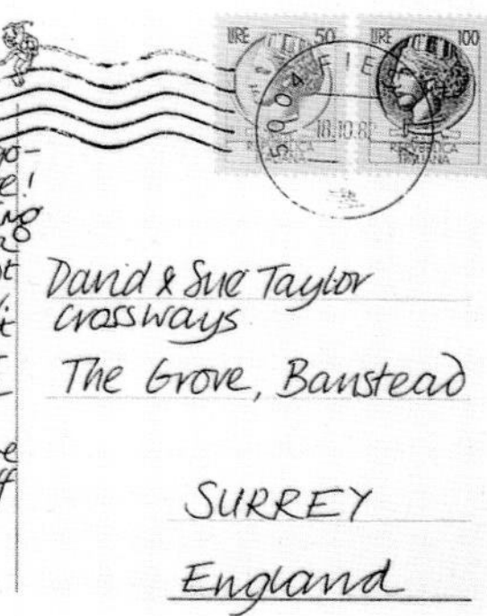

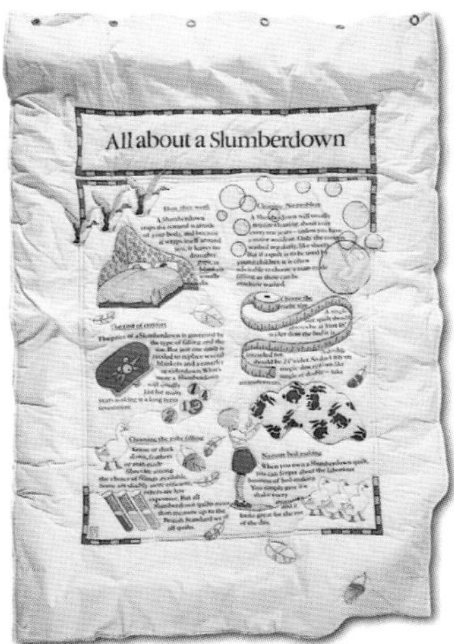

By the end of the eighties, the commercial thoroughfares of Britain's most distinctive towns and cities had been homogenized by a few chain stores all bearing the same visual hallmarks. 'Designer' shops and 'designer' goods were already beginning to acquire a negative connotation by the time D&AD opened its doors to product design entries in 1988. The first year saw no product winners, but in 1989 the jury awarded Silvers to a Rodney Kinsman table and a stylish telephone designed by Andy Davey of Wharmby Associates. This was a modest platform on which product designers at D&AD would later build great things.

1989 was the peak year for the British design industry. More than 30,000 people were employed and the 100 largest design firms earned more than £500 million in fees. It coudn't last, of course, and it didn't. The high-street credit and property price booms which fuelled client spending on design were swiftly followed by bust. Much the same thing happened with a slump in advertising. The fallout from social deprivation and disaster at the end of the decade made its own commentary on the darker side of conspicuous consumption.

The early nineties would see the design and advertising industry in Britain mired in recession, its complexity unravelling, its contradictions exposed. But for all of that, the creative achievements of British design and advertising in the eighties stand undiminished. Designers and art directors held up a mirror to a greedy, go-for-it era in which British society expressed a new confidence in many ways – even if the new reality they communicated was often only skin-deep.

1989.20
Design group: **Kinsman Associates**
Client: **OMK Design**
Designer Rodney Kinsman's OMK company did cool Milanese furniture design better than the Italians themselves in the eighties.

1989.21
Design group: **Wharmby Associates**
Client: **Browns Holdings**
A funky phone designed by Andy Davey gave the briefest of glimpses of how product design would emerge at D&AD as a powerful communication discipline ten years later.

Last word on the 1980s
Peter York

'Stop it Nick, you're blinding me.' My friend Nick – committed modernist, Leftist, youth writer, punk supporter – had gone and had his teeth done. Hollywoodized. His snaggly grey grin had been replaced with immaculate dazzling white caps. It came with the two-book contract and the new youth TV presenting job. And the Notting Hill flat – a big move from Archway – that he called an apartment. It was 1985. That's the difference six years makes, and several hundred thousand pounds in his back pocket, and exposure to American publishers and American TV networks.

Money and America were the big themes of the eighties. Getting money and becoming more like Americans. The wisest man I know, a captain of industry, told me the night Thatcher resigned in 1990 that her achievement – like it or not – had been to make us more like America, the country she worshipped. That meant Brits being proper capitalists, not half-hearted ones who dreamt of having tea at Buckingham Palace instead of having a giant equity portfolio.

Serious money – making it and losing it, spending it and showing it – is what I remember about the eighties. I remember the first time I saw a full-tilt Docklands apartment got up with every now-familiar design cliché – the massive arched windows overlooking the river, the bare brick walls of the original wharf it'd been cut out of, the blonde stripped wood floors, the lot. But in 1986 it was all very new. Walking into it was like being on fast-forward. You wanted to touch everything, explore the fittings, gasp at the honed marble bathroom. The Docklands apartment belonged to an adman friend who'd sold his business for what was then considered millions. Cashed in. The only precedent was New York, where the bankers were chucking the artists out of those downtown lofts (convenient for Wall St). Meanwhile, the North was full of empty factories and the evening newscasts had developed a sort of sunspot device to show you how many thousands of jobs had been lost that very day. Talk about a two-tier economy.

The early part of the decade was a sort of phoney boom where some people talked about money, prayed for it and pretended to have it (the New Romantics played at money and glamorous high style while they were still living in squats). But in the second half (and no, I haven't forgotten the miners' strike or any of the other terrible conflicts) Britain really started to polarize, because significant numbers of people in the South were getting serious money. The City post-Big Bang (October 1986) became an amazing fortune-making machine while the domestic property boom made lots of little fortunes.

Many of my friends were in some kind of design racket, designing advertising and magazines, shops and clothes and interiors. In the eighties, after years of having to argue over pennies, they found themselves being sought out as saviours, being written up as The Next Big Thing, getting huge budgets to spend and building big businesses that many of them went on to sell, making themselves some serious money. The business of fixing up shops – what used to be called shopfitting and became 'retail design' in the eighties – was a massive business. This was because the half-dozen conglomerates which owned most of the shops in every high street and mall started to think that shoppers would buy practically anything if it was beautifully presented in a shop with 'aspirational values' – a shop that took you into a different world instead of saying '50% off'.

Think Next. Next brought central London design values and the dress-codes of admen and architects into small-town suburbia. And they were ready for it because, over the decade, newsagents had been transformed by a massive range of new magazine titles in every big-spend area.

The launch ad for *The World of Interiors* (1981) said 'where the other half live.' In a few years, the housey-housey category went from four perfect-bound glossies to something nearer forty. They were following the housing boom. *Country Living*, for instance, was invented for newly rich townies who bought into the dream by buying that cottage, that rectory, that converted mill, with that lovely money.

And new fashion magazines seemed to be launched every month, for more and more precise groups of women. Magazine life – the world of dreams and aspirations and it-could-be-you – was very real to me of course. It provided the material for my first book *Style Wars* in 1980 (good title, huh!) and the platform for Ann Barr's and my *Official Sloane Ranger Handbook* of 1982, a book that came out of *Harper's and Queen* and went on to sell in tons to aspirational people who wanted to spend their eighties money in the proper posh way.

We got a lot of stick about the *Official Sloane Ranger Handbook* from people who said we were making role models of the worst people imaginable. (We thought we were writing an amusing social study.) The issue was class, of course. Sloane Rangers represented traditional upper middle-class values and styles reasserting themselves in a rather surreal way. The Princess of Wales was our cover model. It helped sales no end.

199

90s

The story of design and advertising took a sharp new turn in the nineties as the communication industry in the UK radically adapted its approach to respond to the new challenges of globalization, brand management and digital technology. This was the decade in which creative businesses went off in several different directions at once. Globalization increasingly forced agencies to ditch country-specific work revolving around dialogue or local references in favour of big image-driven 'international' campaigns. The irresistible rise of the brand blurred the borders between design and advertising to the point at which the two disciplines became indivisible, and hitherto unimagined cooperation was required between the separate camps. The epoch-making shift to digital technology meant that designers and art directors had to rethink the very core of their practices.

In Britain, all this was to have a profound effect, although at first design firms and advertising agencies had energy only for a panicked response to the deepest business recession for 60 years – a reflex driven by the realization that the party was over, that the self-indulgence of the eighties could not be continued, that costs needed to be brought under strict control and that creative work needed to become more measurable and accountable. Only later in the decade would the communication industry recover some of its customary bounce and emerge as a tougher, tighter, leaner act which recognized that the changes it had been forced to adopt were for the better. The introduction of digital technology proved to be a saviour in this respect, as it provided the streamlined means to do more to meet the newly stringent demands of clients with less people in the studio.

So it was that the communication industry occupied a strange new landscape in the nineties, one in which there was a focus on proving the business effectiveness of creative communication and, initially at least, some sense of denial among agency and design folk who renamed themselves 'brand architects' or 'brand consultants' to avoid the stigma of old-style advertising and design after the champagne went flat and the lights went out. The dreaded d-word, in particular, became outlawed for a time. In an uncanny echo of the ill-fated 'back to basics' movement of the Conservative government of John Major (who replaced Margaret Thatcher in a Tory cabinet coup of 1990), many designers ditched the business suits and corporate strategies and got back to the craft basics of their profession.

1991.01
Agency: **The Martin Agency**
Client: **Bernie's Tattooing**
American agencies came to the fore at D&AD in the nineties, with shockingly direct work that forced UK adland out of its complacency. This tattoo parlour effort by the Texan Martin Agency was an early and impressive sign of things to come from across the Atlantic.

opposite

1999.01
Agency: **Lowe Howard-Spink**
Client: **The Independent**
This gritty and grainy commercial – shot in black and white over four days on location in Liverpool using real people – reflected the 'real life' preoccupations of late nineties advertising. British poet John Cooper-Clark rants over a rapid series of reportage images showing how we are constantly bombarded with instructions on things we shouldn't do. The commercial positions *The Independent* as a newspaper for open-minded people who don't like being told what to do or what to think. But by the time it was aired, *The Independent* had become so symbolic of the era in which it was launched (the eighties) that even this bold and contemporary spot found it hard to shift opinion.

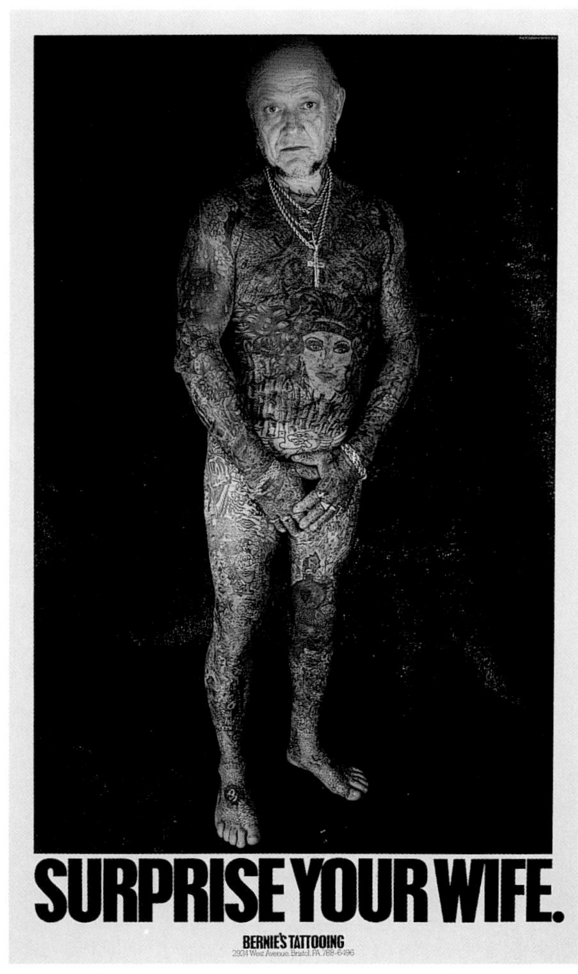
SURPRISE YOUR WIFE.
BERNIE'S TATTOOING

THE INDEPENDENT

This process of 'cold turkey' after the hedonism of the previous decade influenced the style of much of the work. While considerable effort went into reviving craft skills in typography or copywriting, for example, a darker mood also descended, replacing the arbitrary glamour and escapism of the eighties with an approach that might be termed anti-advertising or anti-design. Many commercials cast ugly and shot grainy, abandoning the gorgeous and the glossy to depict real lives in messy and mundane detail. Graphic design, too, eventually turned dark and brutal after the soft, friendly brushstrokes of the previous decade. In this context, photography made a comeback in the nineties, pushing the art of the illustrator back to the margins.

Such pendulum swings in the creative environment were documented by D&AD juries, who gave Silver Awards to photographers Nick Knight and James Cotier for campaigns featuring old and cranky subjects, not young and beautiful models. Both Knight's work on a Bartle Bogle Hegarty (BBH) press campaign for Levi Strauss, and Cotier's own self-promotional essay in a bath house, evoked the changing social and demographic picture of the nineties, as the communication industry was slowly forced to wake up to the consumer power of an ageing population.

1997.01
Agency: **Bartle Bogle Hegarty**
Client: **Levi Strauss**
Nick Knight was the Mondino of the nineties, the photographer who defined which way the lens should be pointing. Who else could have made septuagenarians swing as he did in these Levi ads?

opposite

1993.01
Photographer: **James Cotier**
Client: **James Cotier**
James Cotier, once Terence Donovan's apprentice, finally proved his own photographic mastery in portrait photography of older people that is truly ageless.

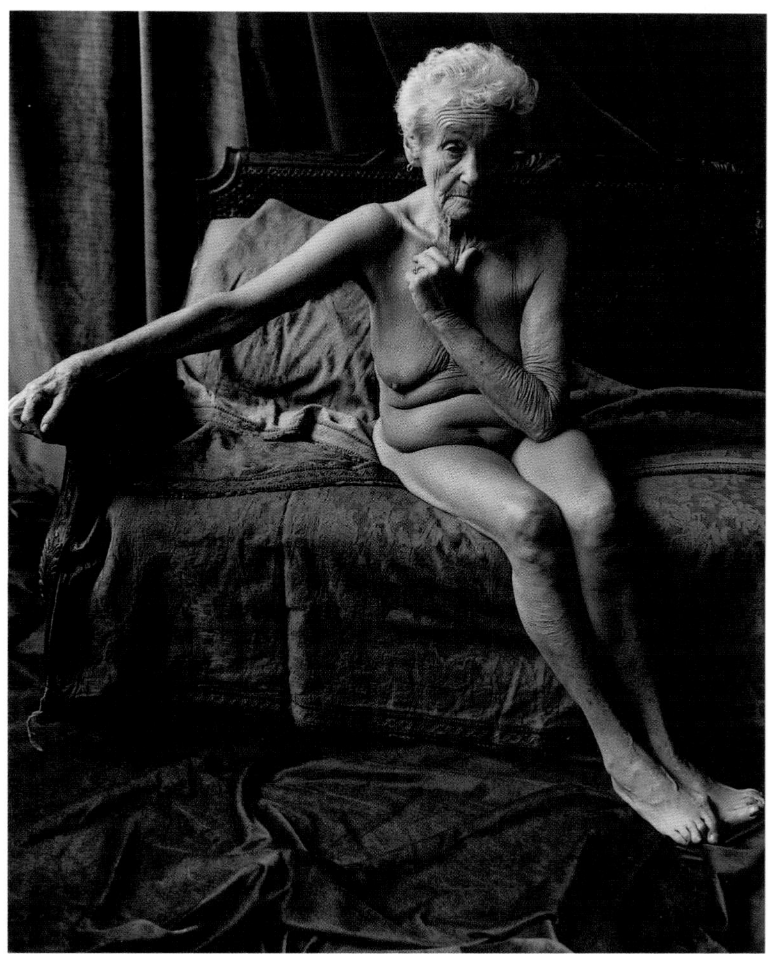

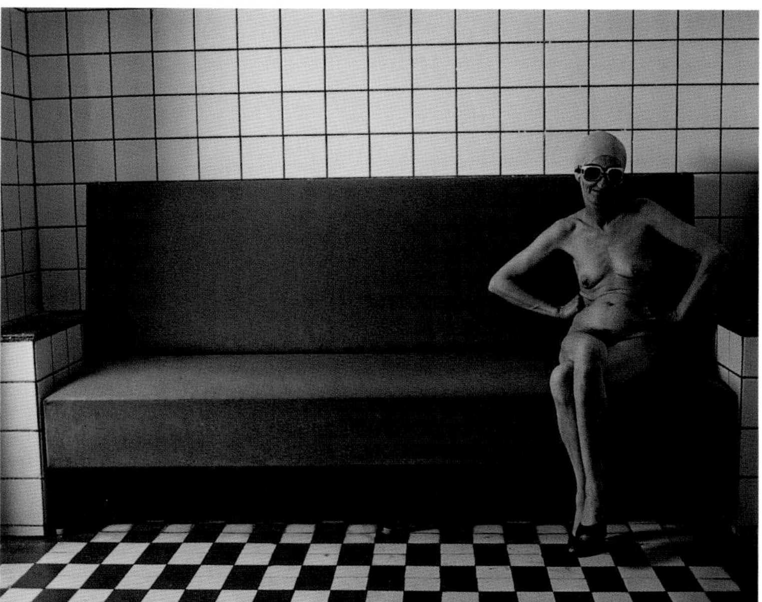

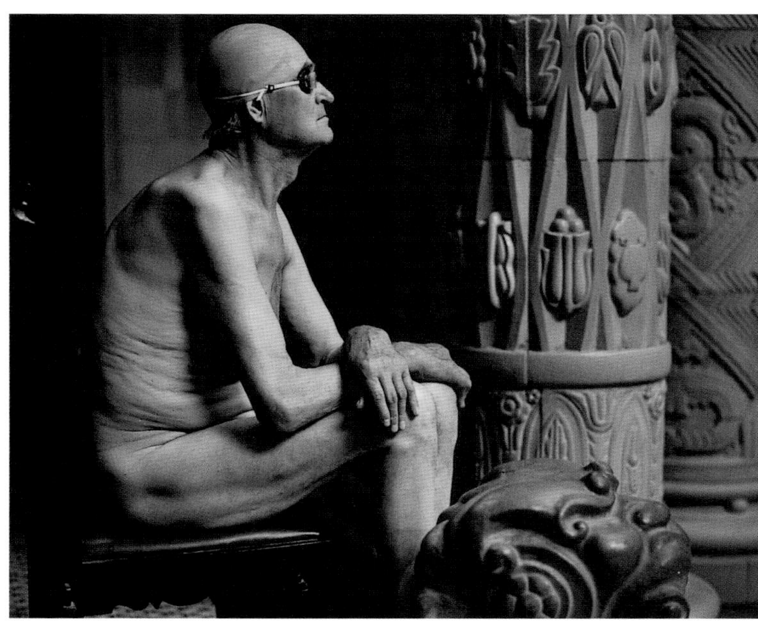

Brands like Levi's and Harley Davidson faced a dilemma in the nineties about whether to stick with the original customer base of baby boomers as they got older and richer, or cut and run with a younger generation. Levi's would eventually cut and run; Harley Davidson would reap the rewards of loyalty to the baby boomers. To complement brand strategy was brand style, encapsulated in the D&AD Awards for such work as Glen Luchford's cool Prada fashion shots and for Nadav Kander's stark, black-and-white imagery for the Dunham boot, a US footwear brand.

As international brand management shot up the communication agenda in the early nineties, all the issues – strategic and stylistic – were seemingly crystallized by the emerging global tussle between a trio of sportswear brands. By 1992, both Nike and Reebok had already appeared on the D&AD winners' roster. Indeed, the dynamic creative competition between Nike, Reebok and Adidas during the nineties helped to encourage innovation in the advertising disciplines. By the time a memorable commercial for Nike called 'Parklife' won a D&AD Silver in 1998, the decade had been punctuated by repeated clashes of the training shoe titans.

1994.01
Agency: **Wieden + Kennedy Amsterdam**
Client: **Nike International**
This Wieden + Kennedy campaign was in the vanguard of the hand-written copy style that became voguish in the nineties. Some observers suggested this trend was a reaction to the then-corporateness of global brands like Nike.

1992.01
Agency: **Doyle Advertising & Design Group**
Client: **The Dunham Company**
Nadav Kander's reductionist approach to photography was cleverly employed by art director John Doyle to tell the story of a boot with almost Zen simplicity. Boston-based Doyle was concerned to keep the Dunham brand a blue-collar working boot – which might also have leisure appeal. He remarks of Kander's work, 'nothing distracts, nothing prettifies. There's a real primal attraction in the picture.'

1998.01
Agency: **TBWA Simons Palmer**
Client: **Nike**
The two great obsessions of late twentieth-century British youth – football and pop music – have never collided more effectively than in this Jonathan Glazer promo dressed up as an ad. The discarded orange segment in the last shot with the Nike logo says it all. The atmosphere of the Sunday soccer leagues is almost tangible. The commercial was made just as Simons Palmer was being subsumed within the TBWA empire.

'Parklife' was directed by Jonathan Glazer, a prominent directing talent in the nineties. In essence, this was a documentary slice of urban life which transported four famous Premier League footballers to Hackney Marshes to play on bumpy Sunday League pitches in cheap, ungainly kits. The soundtrack was a song by Blur, a band in the vanguard of the Britpop movement. Britpop belonged to the 'Cool Britannia' hype engendered by the Labour Party election victory of 1997 and new Prime Minister Tony Blair's subsequent adoption of the creative industries as emblematic of a new, modernized Britain.

In a strange echo of late sixties British art, pop music, film, fashion and graphics all recaptured their edge and their confidence in the late nineties; even *Newsweek* declared that London was swinging again. Product design became hip, as the creative industry re-engaged with the modern after a decade of looking backwards. Apple computers and Audi cars themselves were lauded at D&AD, not just their promotion. But the bigger picture in communication was not confined to a single city or ideology. More broadly, the business world in the nineties managed to achieve what it had failed to do in previous decades. It launched new brands with the potential to become global properties almost overnight.

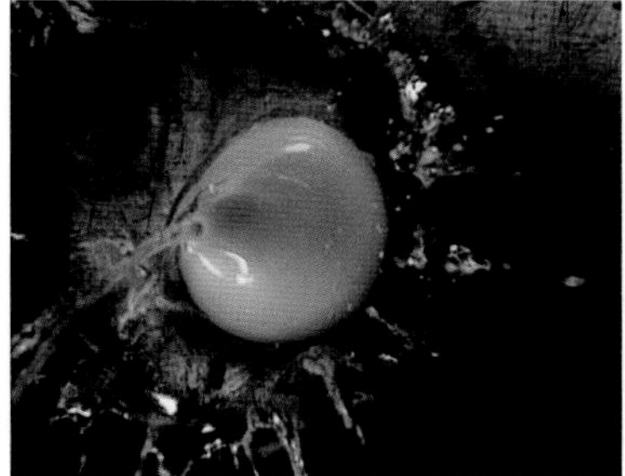

Orange, a mobile telephone network owned by Hutchison Telecom (based in Hong Kong), epitomized the trend. Launched in 1994, Orange managed to build a customer base of half a million UK subscribers and to float on the Stock Exchange with a valuation of £2.5 billion by 1996. Orange's identity was created by Wolff Olins, which worked with a range of other creative agencies to develop a consistent personality for the brand as part of an integrated communication campaign. Within ten weeks of launch, spontaneous awareness of Orange had risen from zero to 45 per cent.

Advertising by WCRS, in the style of the big international cinematic imagery of the era, was part of the equation, but only part. No longer did the advertising have to make sense on its own. The closing line 'The future's bright, the future's Orange' did not sum up what the viewer had just seen but was part of a bigger package of communication which integrated identity, retail frontage, packaging graphics, website and TV advertising to deliver a seamless whole with a distinctive 'brand vocabulary' that would strike a chord in the customer's mind.

The Orange example was influential in determining that ad agencies and design firms would no longer produce advertising and design but contribute complementary elements to a brand's overall tone of voice. By then, the communication industry and its clients had learnt how to embrace a mix of media. But, oddly enough, the decade's outstanding mixed media campaign was not in the service of a mobile phone service or a sports shoe, but for the British Army.

Saatchi & Saatchi's 'Be The Best' campaign for Army recruitment worked across a range of media – from TV and radio to press advertising and even scratchcards – to spectacular effect. The background to the project lay in the recruitment crisis facing the British Army following the fall of the Berlin Wall and the end of the Cold War. As the overall strength of the Army was reduced, people left faster than required and new recruits proved difficult to attract. Based on calculations, the Army worked out that if it didn't manage to keep up its recruitment levels it would face a catastrophic manning shortage of 20,000 soldiers by the year 2000 and be unable to meet its international obligations. In fact, it needed to ramp up recruitment levels, not just hold the line; the recruitment process also needed to become more efficient, with a better calibre of applicant.

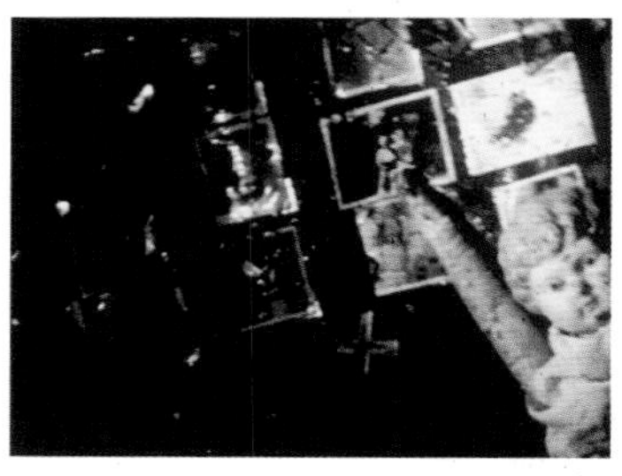

1995.01
Agency: **WCRS**
Client: **Hutchison Telecom**
This was the campaign that finally proved that director Frank Budgen could join the big league. Orange symbolized a new business focus on creating a cohesive advertising and design strategy prior to the product's launch. Based in the Far East, Hutchison Telecom realized that its name meant nothing in the UK, hence the strong brand approach.

1999.02
Agency: **Saatchi & Saatchi**
Client: **COI/The Army**
By tackling the taboo subject of soldier rape in a brave and adult piece of communication, Saatchi & Saatchi's British Army campaign reached even greater maturity. Directed by Alexandra Taylor.

this page

1997.02
Agency: **Saatchi & Saatchi**
Client: **COI/The Army**
Over a decade, the combined intelligence and clarity of the Central Office of Information and Saatchi & Saatchi created an Army recruitment campaign that moved perception from that of thick squaddy to that of a vital job for a better world. The copylines, which suggest a shift from other jobs, are especially clever in this work.

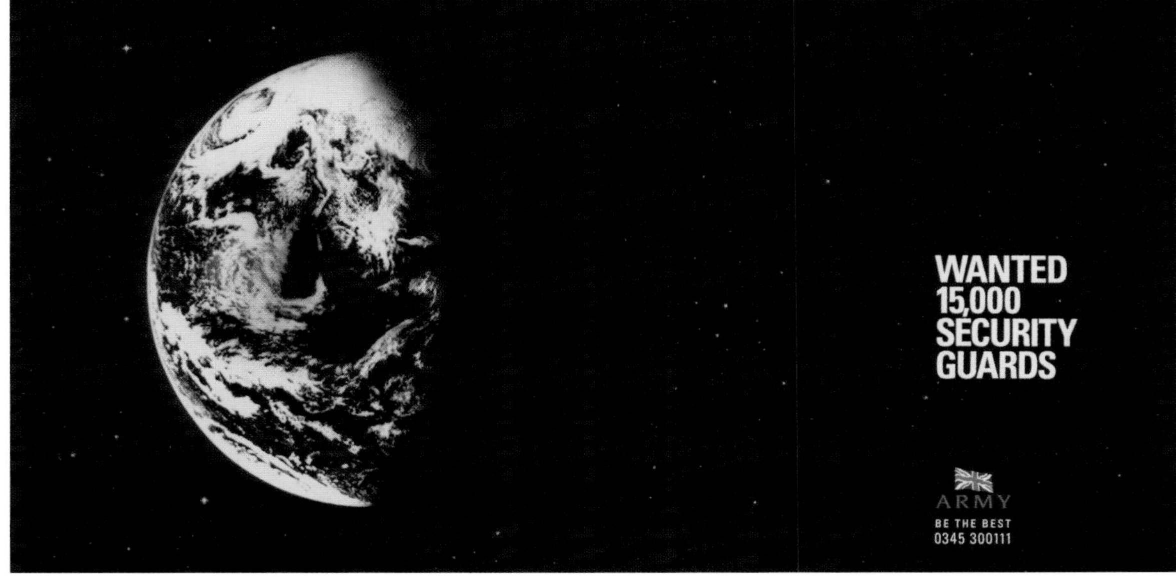

'Be The Best' engaged people by putting them in the shoes of Army personnel and asking them to make life-or-death decisions. But the campaign wasn't just a creative landmark – it shifted the numbers, too. Between 1995 and 1998, Army recruitment increased by more than 60 per cent and the process became twice as efficient as before the campaign started, according to data submitted to the Advertising Effectiveness Awards run by the Institute of Practitioners in Advertising. This increase in efficiency saved the Army (and the UK taxpayer) £16.4 million after subtracting the ad spend.

Saatchi & Saatchi expertly turned the Army into a brand with its own distinctive language of communication – and carefully measured the effectiveness of its creative work. But all the strings on the project were being pulled by an agency that recognizably belonged to the advertising fraternity. Elsewhere in the creative jungle, a new wave of agencies was emerging that belonged to neither the advertising nor the design camps, but drew on the cultures of both in order to create strong brands. Among the hybrid firms was Mother, whose self-promotional English Football Hooligan Set mailer, a D&AD Silver Award-winner in 1999, summed up a number of the decade's key trends in a single project.

The 'Mother Miniatures' mailer was a clever pastiche of a ready-to-assemble Japanese model tank kit, timed to coincide with the 1998 FIFA World Cup Finals in France. With its product instructions ('each social malcontent has been lovingly crafted'), history of the hooligan and helpful chants ('you're going home in a f***ing ambulance – clap, clap, clap'), it caught the current ugly, subversive mood of graphics with telling clarity. The way the model kit was appropriated jackdaw-style reflected the 'sampling' techniques of designers and art directors in the nineties. After the orthodox mining of historical styles in the previous decade, here was a more random, anything-goes approach to sourcing the raw material for communication.

1999.03
Agency: **Mother**
Client: **Mother**
Mother belonged to a new wave of agencies in the nineties that refused to bed down in either the design or advertising camps. And nothing summed up the wanton irreverence of Mother better than the Mother Miniatures – a carefully crafted box of amusing malice.

opposite

1997.03
Agency: **Saatchi & Saatchi**
Client: **COI/The Army**
More from the long-running Army campaign. Adam Kean and Jason Fretwell wrote this documentary-style recruitment ad for the officer class.

1998.02
Agency: **Saatchi & Saatchi**
Client: **Department of Health/COI**
Working the magic they had previously wrought for the Army, Saatchi & Saatchi brought the same harrowing realism to another government department. Photographed by former Saatchi art director Graham Cornthwaite, and once again proving the supremacy of type master Roger Kennedy, this campaign to recruit more nurses turned the daily caseload into a scrapbook-style press ad.

12
IF YOU DON'T INOCULATE THEM THEY'LL DIE IF YOU DO INOCULATE THEM THEY'LL DIE
EASY BEING AN ARMY OFFICER ISN'T IT?
STORY 88
ROLL 67
FRAME 7
ARMY
BE THE BEST

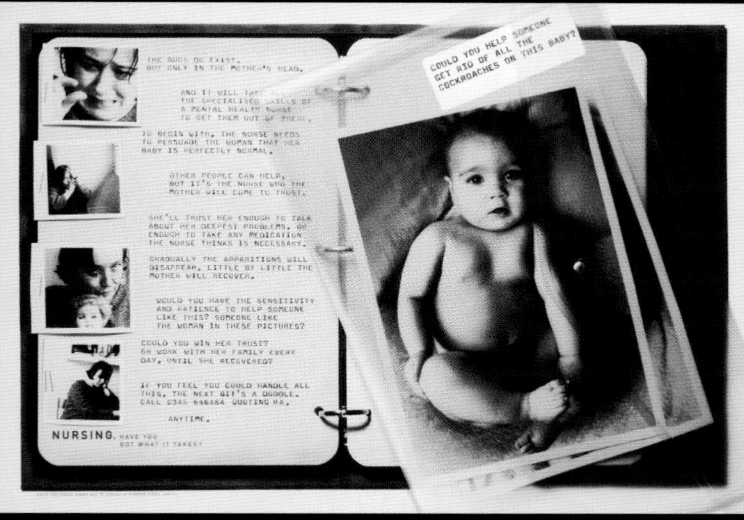
COULD YOU HELP SOMEONE GET RID OF ALL THE COCKROACHES ON THIS BABY?
THE BUGS DO EXIST.
BUT ONLY IN THE MOTHER'S HEAD.
TO BEGIN WITH, THE NURSE NEEDS TO PERSUADE THE WOMAN THAT HER BABY IS PERFECTLY NORMAL.
OTHER PEOPLE CAN HELP, BUT IT'S THE NURSE WHO THE MOTHER WILL COME TO TRUST.
SHE'LL TRUST HER ENOUGH TO TALK ABOUT HER DEEPEST PROBLEMS, OR ENOUGH TO TAKE ANY MEDICATION THE NURSE THINKS IS NECESSARY.
GRADUALLY THE APPARITIONS WILL DISAPPEAR, LITTLE BY LITTLE THE MOTHER WILL RECOVER.
WOULD YOU HAVE THE SENSITIVITY AND PATIENCE TO HELP SOMEONE LIKE THIS? SOMEONE LIKE THE WOMAN IN THESE PICTURES?
COULD YOU WIN HER TRUST? OR WORK WITH HER FAMILY EVERY DAY, UNTIL SHE RECOVERED?
IF YOU FEEL YOU COULD HANDLE ALL THIS, THE NEXT BIT'S A DOODLE. CALL 0345 646464 QUOTING HA.
ANYTIME.
NURSING. HAVE YOU GOT WHAT IT TAKES?

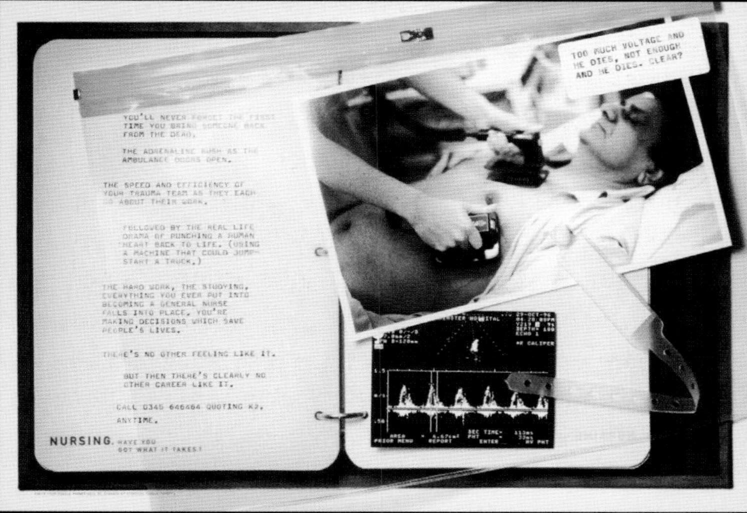
TOO MUCH VOLTAGE AND HE DIES. NOT ENOUGH AND HE DIES. CLEAR?
THE SPEED AND EFFICIENCY OF YOUR TRAUMA TEAM AS THEY EACH GO ABOUT THEIR WORK.
FOLLOWED BY THE REAL LIFE DRAMA OF PUNCHING A HUMAN HEART BACK TO LIFE. (USING A MACHINE THAT COULD JUMP-START A TRUCK.)
THE HARD WORK, THE STUDYING, EVERYTHING YOU EVER PUT INTO BECOMING A GENERAL NURSE FALLS INTO PLACE. YOU'RE MAKING DECISIONS WHICH SAVE PEOPLE'S LIVES.
THERE'S NO OTHER FEELING LIKE IT.
BUT THEN THERE'S CLEARLY NO OTHER CAREER LIKE IT.
CALL 0345 646464 QUOTING K2.
ANYTIME.
NURSING. HAVE YOU GOT WHAT IT TAKES?

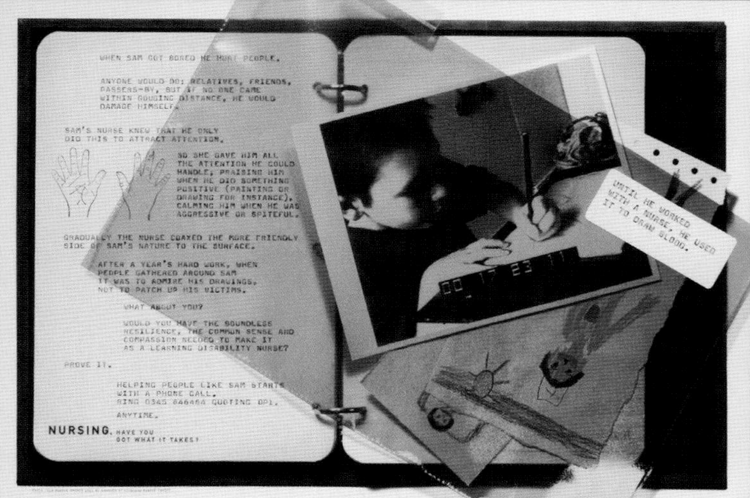
ANYONE WOULD DO: RELATIVES, FRIENDS, PASSERS-BY, BUT IF NO ONE CAME WITHIN GOUGING DISTANCE, HE WOULD DAMAGE HIMSELF.
SAM'S NURSE KNEW THAT HE ONLY DID THIS TO ATTRACT ATTENTION.
SO SHE GAVE HIM ALL THE ATTENTION HE COULD HANDLE, PRAISING HIM WHEN HE DID SOMETHING POSITIVE (PAINTING OR DRAWING FOR INSTANCE), CALMING HIM WHEN HE WAS AGGRESSIVE OR SPITEFUL.
GRADUALLY THE NURSE COAXED THE MORE FRIENDLY SIDE OF SAM'S NATURE TO THE SURFACE.
AFTER A YEAR'S HARD WORK, WHEN PEOPLE GATHERED AROUND SAM IT WAS TO ADMIRE HIS DRAWINGS, NOT TO PATCH UP HIS VICTIMS.
WHAT ABOUT YOU?
WOULD YOU HAVE THE BOUNDLESS RESILIENCE, THE COMMON SENSE AND COMPASSION NEEDED TO MAKE IT AS A LEARNING DISABILITY NURSE?
PROVE IT.
HELPING PEOPLE LIKE SAM STARTS WITH A PHONE CALL.
RING 0345 646464 QUOTING DP1.
ANYTIME.
UNTIL HE WORKED WITH A NURSE, HE USED IT TO DRAW BLOOD.
NURSING. HAVE YOU GOT WHAT IT TAKES?

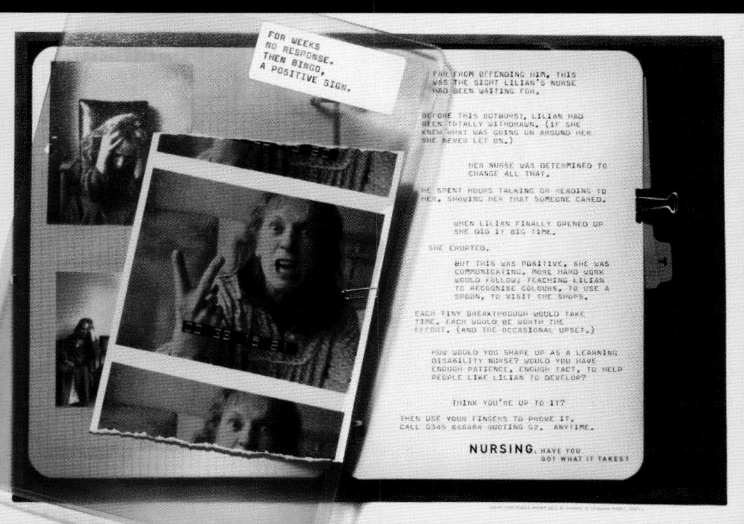
FOR WEEKS NO RESPONSE. THEN BINGO, A POSITIVE SIGN.
FAR FROM OFFENDING HIM, THIS WAS THE SIGHT LILIAN'S NURSE HAD BEEN WAITING FOR.
BEFORE THIS OUTBURST, LILIAN HAD BEEN TOTALLY WITHDRAWN. (IF SHE KNEW WHAT WAS GOING ON AROUND HER SHE NEVER LET ON.)
HER NURSE WAS DETERMINED TO CHANGE ALL THAT.
HE SPENT HOURS TALKING OR READING TO HER, SHOWING HER THAT SOMEONE CARED.
WHEN LILIAN FINALLY OPENED UP SHE DID IT BIG TIME.
SHE ERUPTED.
BUT THIS WAS POSITIVE, SHE WAS COMMUNICATING. MORE HARD WORK WOULD FOLLOW; TEACHING LILIAN TO RECOGNISE COLOURS, TO USE A SPOON, TO VISIT THE SHOPS.
EACH TINY BREAKTHROUGH WOULD TAKE TIME. EACH WOULD BE WORTH THE EFFORT. (AND THE OCCASIONAL UPSET.)
HOW WOULD YOU SHAPE UP AS A LEARNING DISABILITY NURSE? WOULD YOU HAVE ENOUGH PATIENCE, ENOUGH TACT, TO HELP PEOPLE LIKE LILIAN TO DEVELOP?
THINK YOU'RE UP TO IT?
THEN USE YOUR FINGERS TO PROVE IT.
CALL 0345 646464 QUOTING G2. ANYTIME.
NURSING. HAVE YOU GOT WHAT IT TAKES?

The D&AD Awards of the nineties did a good job of reflecting the diversity of creative output that was being encouraged by the availability of digital techniques. These techniques enabled designers and agencies to take ideas and images from any style or period to make a brand or campaign stand out. Where D&AD was slower to catch on was in the area of digital technology itself. This was mainly because its arbiters of taste had little understanding and even less experience of new media.

It was 1997 before an Interactive Media category was introduced at D&AD. One of the Silver-winners that year was the first European in-store interactive kiosk, designed for Levi Strauss by Antirom, which used its experience in CD-ROMs, computer games and internet products to extend the brand into new territory. But by then, the communication industry had already faced up to the obsolescence of its traditional technologies and practices and was fast adapting to a new era.

The portents of this change had been around for some time. The technology guru Nicholas Negroponte set up Media Laboratory at MIT (Massachusetts Institute of Technology) in the US in the mid-eighties because, since 1979, he had been arguing that three discrete areas of communication – broadcast and motion pictures, print and publishing and the computer industry – would have come together by the year 2000. Their coalescence was due to the shift to digital technology which could break down information (visual or textual) into common digital elements capable of being delivered and copied without degradation (via broadcast or reproduction on disc). Most importantly, all of these previously separate media could now talk to one another. This had enormous social and creative implications. Negroponte was just one of the first to see it and the first to set up a major education and research establishment predicated on the trend.

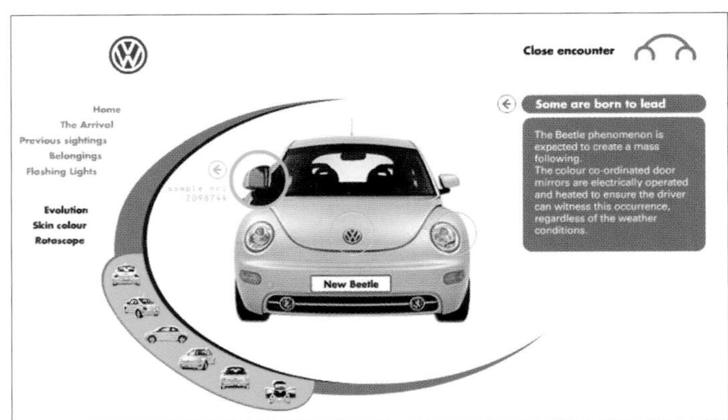

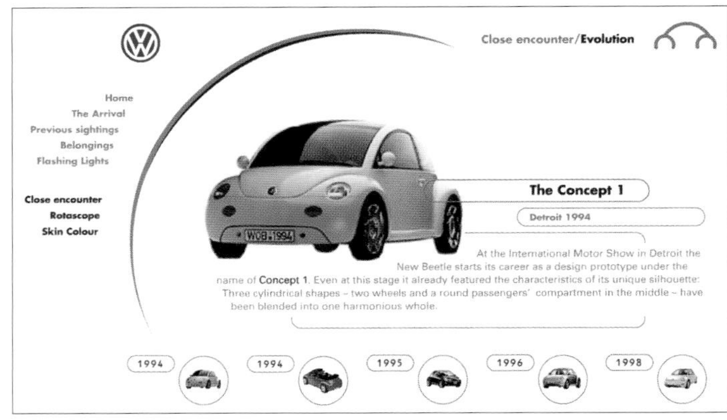

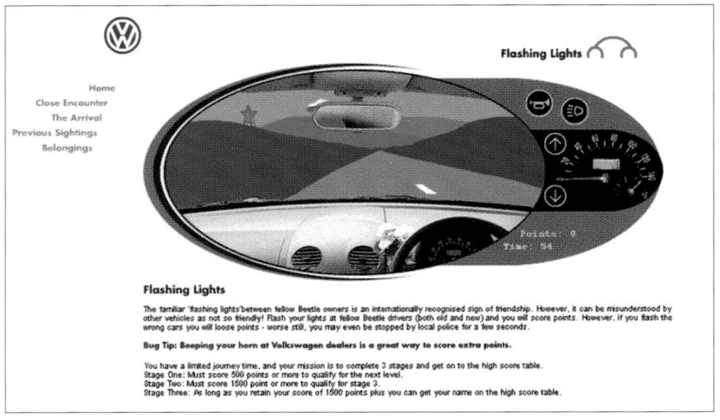

1999.04
Agency: **Deepend**
Client: **Volkswagen**
Deepend's groundbreaking VW Beetle website featured things we now take for granted: conspicuous use of Flash software, multiple rollovers, and embedded sound. At the time, it was quite groundbreaking, which just goes to show how quickly the interactive state of the art matures and moves on.

this page

1997.04
Production company: **Antirom**
Client: **Levi Strauss**
Briefed by Levi's to create the first in-store interactive kiosk across Europe, Antirom used its experience in computer games to extend the brand into exciting new communication territory – and take the visitor through a history of the jeans' production, fit guides and so on. Antirom was based around the brothers Tom and Nick Roope, but eventually folded as Tom took his team into the Tomato collective.

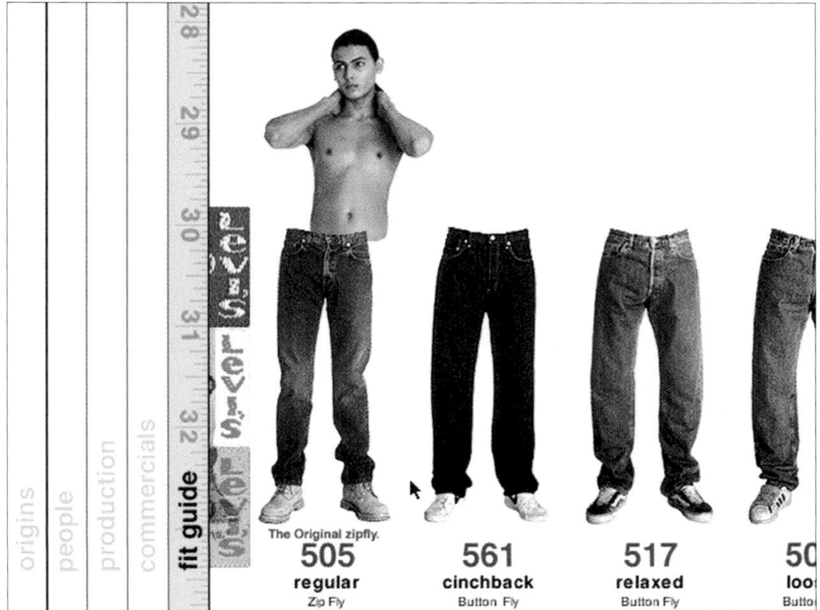

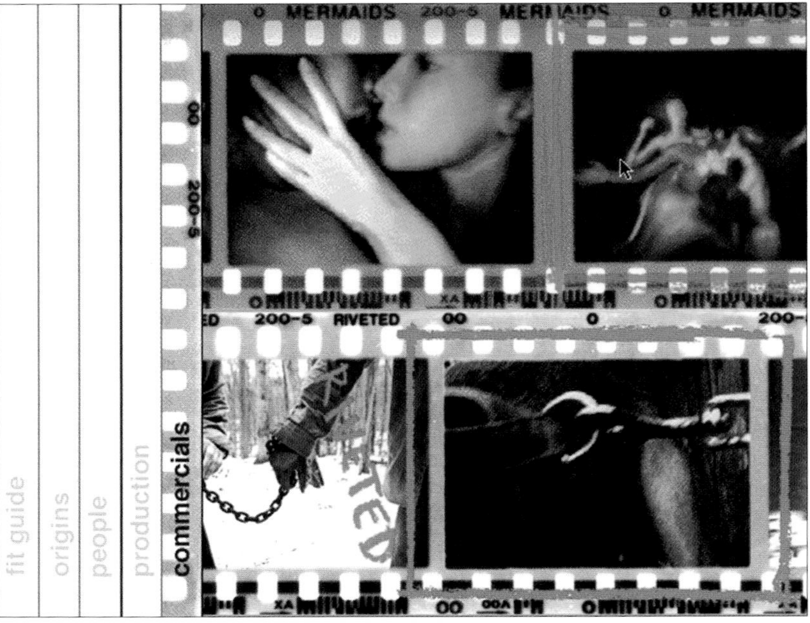

Whereas the communication industry in the eighties had largely play-acted with new technology, using laborious production techniques to ape its effects, now the digital revolution delivered the real thing. The nineties saw the explosion of the world wide web, a user-friendly point-and-click aspect of the internet invented by British scientist Tim Berners-Lee in 1989. The decade also witnessed the first attempts at e-commerce, which involved selling goods without shops. As narrowband communications (such as telephone dial-ups) were replaced by broadband channels (using fast fibre optics), vast amounts of digital information were able to be transferred instantly. Thus, post-production work for special effects could be created in London for Hollywood movies and the rushes viewed in California on the same day. Restrictive practices which had tied the film and newspaper industries in knots for years were swept away.

Suddenly, there was a greater democracy of creation in the communication industry. Once upon a time, it had cost a fortune in equipment, stock, processing and personnel to shoot professional movie footage. Now, everyone could be a movie-maker. Director Graham Fink, who was President of D&AD in 1996, used the first Sony digital handheld camera as a portable sketch book and actually introduced some brief frames he had shot on spec in the street into a broadcast TV commercial.

This instant movie trend led to movie phenomena like *The Blair Witch Project*, which was shot by two novice film-makers in 1999 for virtually nothing and which had no promotional budget. *Blair Witch* was promoted free on the internet and went on to make millions of dollars at the box office. Later, Stephen King would experiment with publishing exclusively on the internet, demonstrating that you did not need a traditional print publisher at all if people wanted your product, and the music industry would become embroiled in a war with Napster to protect its property since the technology now existed for perfect digital copies of CD tracks (pure, digitized music) to be freely circulated and downloaded on the internet.

In adland, the merging of film, video, graphics and computers not only encouraged a new type of hybrid creative company but also a new type of creative product. Digital effects blurred the boundaries between production and post-production, enabling creative firms from a design background like Tomato and Fuel to branch out into making films with a new visual language.

this page & opposite

1995.02
Agency: **Faulds Advertising**
Client: **BBC Radio Scotland**
Featuring art direction by Tomato members and Jonathan Barnbrook, this series for Radio Scotland appeared radical in its use and abuse of technology. Importantly, it signalled that graphic designers were now film-makers in the digital age – and that the once-static discipline of typographic experiment was part of the language of the moving image.

Directing commercials or pop promos no longer required an agency apprenticeship, the long slog through the ranks to gain the trust necessary to control an expensive and laborious production process. All it took was access to an Apple Macintosh computer, a digital video camera and the right software. The development of digital off-line editing suites, particularly Avid, put the creative power back into the hands of small production teams who could now do what it had previously taken huge editing suites and labs to achieve. Meanwhile, website design began to attract a whole generation of design students who would have gone into traditional forms of design in previous decades – and many who would not have become designers at all.

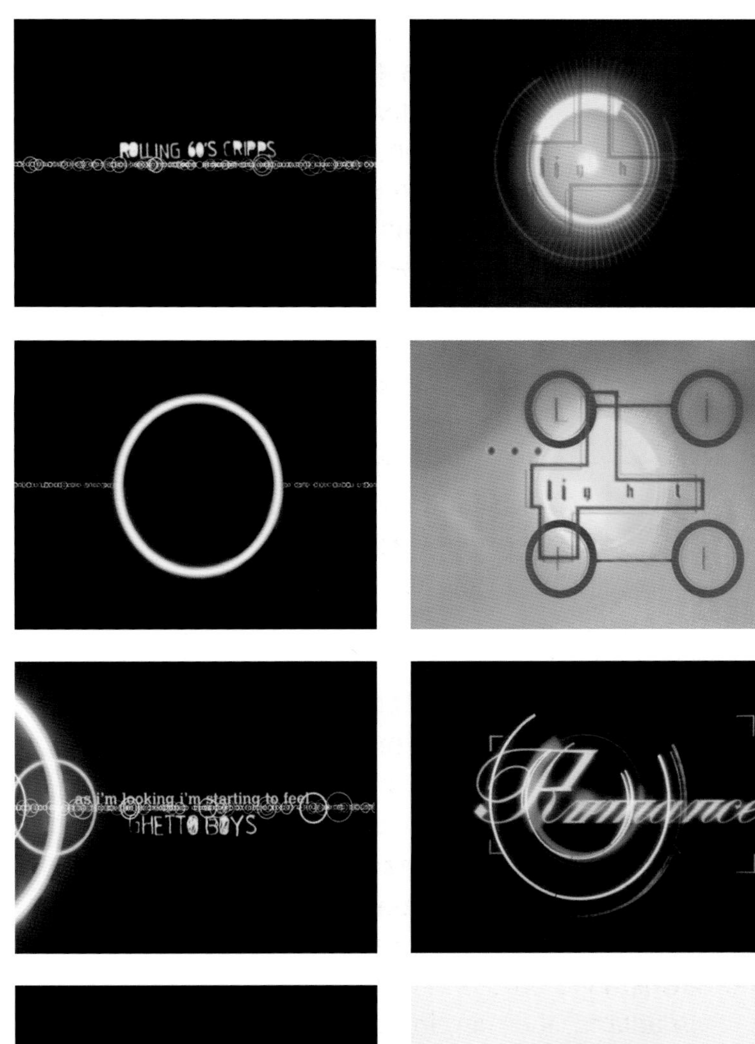

The BBC's 'Perfect Day' promotional film, which won Silver in 1998, was an almost perfect metaphor for the artistic diversity that the digital revolution encouraged. Shot by director Gregory Rood to promote the BBC's breadth of music output across all its TV and radio channels, 'Perfect Day' melded different contributions to the same song (by a wide range of international musical stars, from Lou Reed to opera singer Lesley Garrett) into a single mesmerizing four-minute sequence under skies shot in Richmond Park. (This, incidentally, was the project which induced country singer Tammy Wynette and her entourage to drive 500 miles just to take part – for a fee of £250.)

But, while one might have expected the effects of the digital era to make themselves felt most keenly at D&AD in the Television and Cinema Graphics category, the milestone project in this category in the early nineties – a new on-screen identity for BBC2 – actually marked a retreat by television identity designer Martin Lambie-Nairn from computer graphics back to good old live action, with a balsa wood model splashed with paint and shot by a high-speed camera. And this at a point in time when digital technology had matured to the stage at which it could simulate almost anything.

It was BBC2 controller Alan Yentob who drew attention to the problem with the existing identity when he assumed control of the channel in the late eighties. 'It was obvious that the logo made absolutely no impact,' he said of a bland coloured TWO on a white background, originally designed by Alan Jeapes. 'My BBC2 design of the TWO was part of the last knockings of the BBC as a gentle place where you could put up a painterly idea of elegant shapes in white space,' explained Jeapes. 'It didn't even say BBC. But then the BBC in those days didn't think it was in the advertising business.'

As design consultant to BBC Television, Lambie-Nairn set about turning BBC2 into a more indentifiable, accessible and contemporary brand to reflect the diversity of the channel's output. The figure 2 was hand-drawn with a full body to the point at which it took on its own personality and became a real character. In storyboarded sequences, the 2 character adopted a variety of guises, being splattered with paint, covered with silk, falling like a blade and being illuminated with a copper patina. The effect was sophisticated, witty and, above all, memorable, although Lambie-Nairn fretted initially that the greens, greys and blacks in the first batch of idents made the BBC2 image too cold.

1998.03
Agency: **Leagas Delaney**
Client: **BBC Television**
There was much behind-the-scenes arguing as to who was actually behind the scenes on this BBC epic. Did the agency Leagas Delaney pull the shoot together with the Paul Weiland Film Company or the BBC's internal department? Fortunately at the D&AD Awards ceremony it turned out to be, in Lou Reed's words, a 'Perfect Day'.

this page

1991.02
Agency: **Lambie-Nairn**
Client: **BBC Television**
Once again, Lambie-Nairn opens a decade with a groundbreaking TV project. An initial batch of BBC2 idents introduced the versatile '2' character that would drive the channel's friendly new identity.

A subsequent set of idents warmed the palette with new ideas such as a zebra print 2 and a firework 2. BBC insiders recognized a good thing when they saw it. 'The BBC2 identity was mould-breaking,' recalled former BBC head of graphic design John Aston. 'Everyone warmed to it. It was a six-lane highway that could take you anywhere you wanted to go.'

It was a measure of Lambie-Nairn's success that while he and his co-director Daniel Barber won a D&AD Silver Award in 1991 for the first batch of BBC idents, the coveted Gold went in 1994 to the BBC Graphic Design Department, which had mastered the brand language and produced some truly stunning work with the versatile 2 character. When the Royal Television Society gave its Judges' Award to Lambie-Nairn in 1995, the citation spoke of how 'he lets his artistic imagination soar – he's always pushing the creative frontiers of the genre.'

Other screen projects more overtly reflected the new typographic versatility resulting from the shift to digital. Both 'Letters of Love', directed by Oliver Harrison for the Royal Mail, and 'Poems on the Box', a Gold-winner for BBC Bristol Graphic Design Department, demonstrated the rich potential of animating type.

1990.01
Agency:
D'Arcy Masius Benton & Bowles
Client: **Royal Mail Letters**
This animated ad was based almost entirely on a student project by Oliver Harrison at Saint Martins College of Art & Design in London. After graduation he signed up with a production company which suggested it to the agency for use with Royal Mail.

1994.02
Design group: **BBC Bristol Graphic Design Department**
Client: **BBC Television**
'Dis Poetry' and '40 Love' won a Gold Award in recognition of a particularly accomplished example of a new trend of television content: the digitally composed typographic visual essay.

opposite

1994.03
Agency: **BBC Graphic Design Department**
Client: **BBC Presentation**
The BBC's own designers have fun with the new BBC2 identity, proving that the idea could be taken in-house without any loss of creative energy. Quite the reverse.

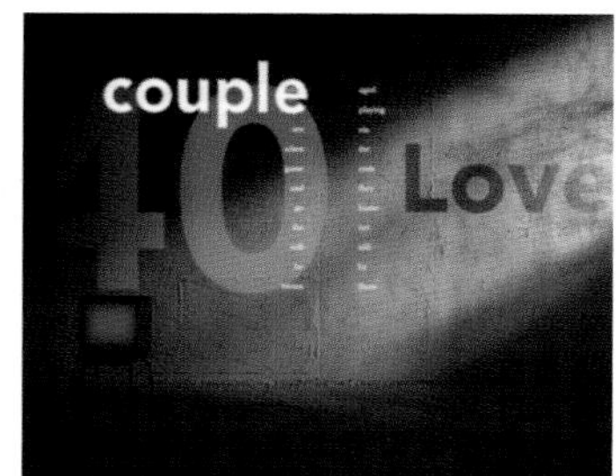

But, although playing with letterforms on computer would become one of the themes of the nineties across many disciplines, such digital manipulation was not the be all and end all. The outstanding individual performer in D&AD's TV and Cinema Graphics category in the nineties was the American designer Kyle Cooper, who won awards in 1996 and 1998 for the title sequences to the movies *SE7EN* and *Gattaca*. True, Cooper enjoyed a close relationship with the production house of digital effects guru Robert Greenberg, a technology pioneer who had predicted with accuracy what the merging of film, video and computers would do to design and advertising. But Cooper's work reflected the belief that technology should be the servant of the idea, not the other way around.

Cooper's celebrated opening titles for David Fincher's *SE7EN* set the dark mood of the film with their jumpy, out-of-register graphics superimposed on fetishistic shots of a serial murderer's grubby paraphernalia. The normal practice of using a pin-register camera to prevent titles from 'weaving' against the background plates was deliberately avoided in order to exaggerate the out-of-kilter sense of menace. Meanwhile, the title sequence for *Gattaca* introduced the story of the film via a masterfully orchestrated, microscopic study of hair and skin falling.

Cooper's double triumph (with work which could have appeared at any period in D&AD's history) served as a potent reminder to UK creatives that they were now competing in a global talent pool, a point reinforced by the 1999 Silver Award given to Cooper's company Imaginary Forces for the titles to an MTV film called *Dead Man on Campus*. This project presented a bleakly humorous animated manual on how to commit suicide, in the style of simple technical illustration, to set the film up. Truly, a dark mood fell over the creative industries at the end of the decade.

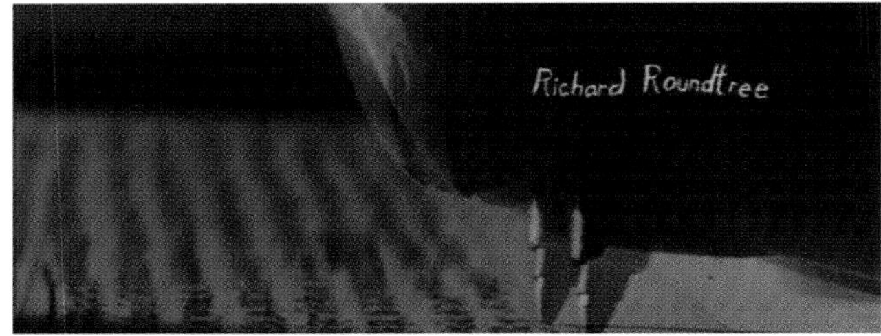

1996.01
Designers: **Kyle Cooper, Jennifer Shainin**
Clients: **New Line Cinema, David Fincher**

this page

1998.04
Design director: **Kyle Cooper**
Clients: **Columbia Pictures, Jersey Films**

1999.05
Designers: **Karin Fong, Adam Bluming**
Clients: **Alan Cohn, MTV Films**

With these projects, Kyle Cooper and Imaginary Forces truly establish themselves as the Saul Bass of their generation. The seminal work is clearly *SE7EN*, still some of the creepiest titles ever, whilst *Gattaca* is altogether cooler in approach. *Dead Man on Campus* shows that doing humorous pastiche properly is a deadly serious business.

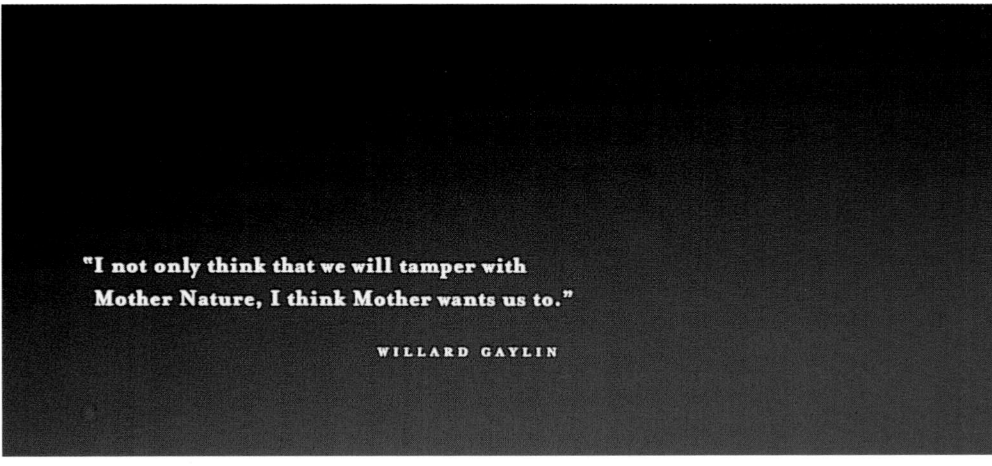

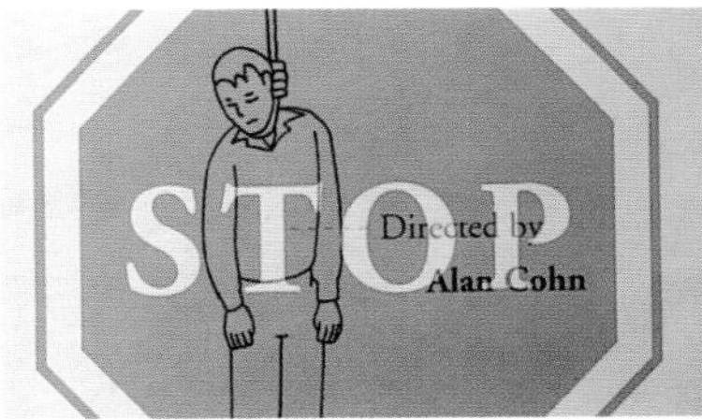

It had all started a lot more brightly, especially in the ice cream sector, where a prominent press campaign for Häagen-Dazs made vanilla and strawberry irresistibly sexy, receiving recognition for typographer Matthew Kemsley in 1992. Despite the industry watchdogs, press advertising in the nineties began to roll back some of the sexual inhibitions of previous decades, resulting in Saatchi & Saatchi's notorious 'Gobble, gobble' campaign for Club 18-30. Lines like 'One swallow doesn't make a summer' ensured a Silver Award in 1997, completing a journey from the slyly disguised *double entrendre* to holiday promotion of the blow job in less than 20 years.

1992.02
Agency: **Bartle Bogle Hegarty**
Client: **Häagen-Dazs**
In its day, this now seemingly gentle evocation of sex and ice cream was the stuff of tabloid headlines. It somehow never found the same level of approval with D&AD Awards juries as it did with the press, robbing the creative team of Rooney Carruthers and Larry Barker of a deserved gong. It ironically went into the D&AD Annual for typography. Was anyone looking at the type?

this page

1997.05
Agency: **Saatchi & Saatchi**
Client: **Flying Colours**
'As subtle as an air raid' was one juror's comment on this landmark campaign from Saatchi. Loud, flashy, vulgar and preposterously 'in yer face' – just like a Club 18-30 holidaymaker, really.

Holiday forecast: Damp, followed by wet patches.

Club 18-30

Spain, Greece, Turkey.

When the Government killed the dog licence they left us to kill the dogs.

One thousand dogs are killed in Britain every day.

For the most part, healthy dogs and puppies with years of life left in them.

The killings take place at local vets, in RSPCA centres and other animal charities throughout the country.

The dogs are given an overdose of anaesthetic and die within seconds.

A van makes regular collections and the dead dogs are taken to the local incinerator.

It doesn't take long to turn a Jock, Spot or Sandy into a small pile of ashes.

This daily slaughter is strange work for a society founded to prevent cruelty to animals.

We hate the killing.

We are sick of doing the Government's dirty work behind closed doors.

We want you to help us force through a dog registration scheme.

The dogs we kill are homeless dogs. Unwanted, or strays left to roam the streets and parks, often in packs.

There are at least 500,000 of them out there right now.

Left to themselves, the figure would be close to 4 million in ten years' time.

Homeless dogs cause road accidents, attack livestock and foul our parks and pavements.

And yet we can't blame the dogs, for we live in a society that makes it more difficult to own a television than a living, breathing creature.

There is no licence required. The Government abolished the licence last year and we are now seeing the consequences.

The RSPCA want to see a dog registration scheme introduced.

And so it seems do most of you. In a recent poll, 92% of you said "yes" to registration.

If there was a registration fee it would encourage responsible dog-ownership.

Each dog could be identified with a number so that its owner could be traced and held responsible for the dog's actions.

The money raised would finance a national dog warden scheme, more efficient clean-up operations and more education for dog-owners.

These measures seem so sensible you wonder why they haven't been tried before.

Well, many of them have.

Sweden, America, Germany, Australia, Russia, France and Ireland all have a more enlightened policy than Britain.

Help us catch up.

Write to your MP and press for dog registration.

If you're not sure how to go about it, call free on 0800 400478 and we'll give you an action-pack and add your name to our petition.

Do it now, for every day that goes by sees another 1,000 dogs put down.

And what kind of society kills healthy dogs?

Registration, not extermination.

How does it feel to have a mental age of thirty and a physical age of one?

IF YOU'D LIKE TO MAKE A DONATION WRITE TO: THE MULTIPLE SCLEROSIS SOCIETY, EFFIE ROAD, FULHAM, LONDON SW6 1EE. TELEPHONE

Press advertising proved to be a pivotal discipline in the nineties in shaping and describing how the communication industry was changing. For the first 30 years of the D&AD Awards, press ads had looked recognizably like press ads. There was, in fact, an optimum way to create them, encapsulated by the writing of David Abbott and the art direction of Ron Brown at Abbott Mead Vickers (AMV). Their press campaign for the RSPCA, a Silver winner in 1990, was a perfect example of their craft: a great headline ('When the Government killed the dog licence they left us to kill the dogs'); a classic layout; a compelling image; superb typography. But it marked the end of an era, not just for the long copy specialist but for press ads that conformed to the reader's expectations.

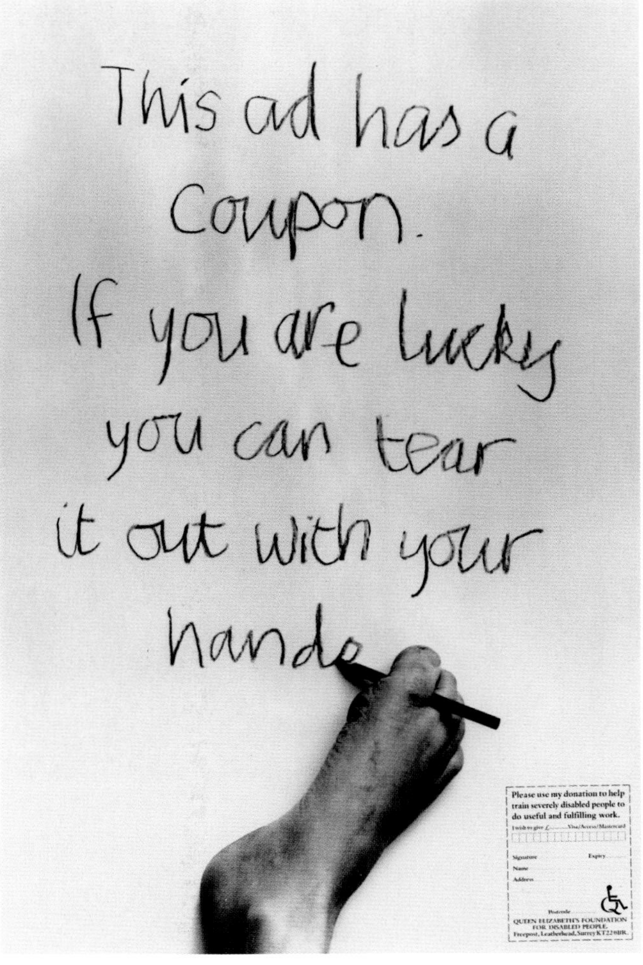

1990.02
Agency: **Abbott Mead Vickers.SMS**
Client: **RSPCA**
David Abbott and Ron Brown again switching effortlessly from the sure-handed soft sell for Sainsbury's to rapier-like irony and blistering visuals for the RSPCA.

1991.03
Agency: **BMP DDB Needham**
Client: **Multiple Sclerosis Society**
Unusually restrained art direction for Mark Reddy, the eclectic designer who would later create the symbol for the Millennium celebrations in the UK.

this page

1995.03
Agency: **Abbott Mead Vickers.BBDO**
Client: **Queen Elizabeth's Foundation for Disabled People**
Paired with a multi award-winning TV commercial, this was another sign of early promise by the future creative director of AMV, Peter Souter, and his art director Paul Brazier.

1992.03
Agency: **Saatchi & Saatchi**
Client: **NSPCC**
Of all the contentious NSPCC ads, this is perhaps the most contentious of all. But Mike Boles' sensitive and intelligent writing made its point with truth and discretion.

What's it like to be raped as a 3 year old? A victim explains.

I FIRST remember being sexually abused by my father when I was about 3. It may have happened before, I don't know.

I can see it now, me lying in bed, with that big face coming towards me. He'd kiss me good-night, but he didn't stop at kissing.

He used to tell me it was our secret. And if I ever told anyone about it I'd be sent away.

But even as a child I knew something wasn't right. It was those words, "I'll protect you". How could he be protecting me? He was bloody hurting me.

It's strange really, he was my enemy, but at the same time my only friend in the world. He made me depend on him. He controlled me. My body was his toy for more than 9 years.

At school I found it hard to mix. I felt different. I'd never let anyone get close to me. In the changing rooms after P.E. I hated people seeing my naked body. I was so ashamed, thought they might be able to tell what had been happening to me and call me a poofter.

Even when I managed to find a girlfriend I still wasn't sure if I was heterosexual. I was terribly rough with her. I suppose I wanted to be in control of someone, like my father was with me.

Sex terrified me. Having an orgasm just made me think of what my father did inside of me. And that big smiling face.

I met someone else eventually. We got married. After 2 years she left me. She said I was cold and didn't understand her.

But that's how I was. I just wasn't aware of causing or feeling mental or physical pain. Something inside me had been switched off long ago. There were times when I could actually cut myself with a knife and not feel a thing.

After the divorce, I turned to drink. It was a way of escaping. But I still suffered deep depressions.

Last year, my father finally died. I think that's what made me contact the NSPCC. I was 53 years old, and it was the first time I'd ever told anyone about my childhood.

Once a week for 6 months a Child Protection Officer worked with me. He got me to tell him everything about my experience. Talking about it was very painful. For over 40 years I guess I'd been trying not to think about it.

Eventually though, it started to work. He made me realise that what happened wasn't my fault.

For the first time I can ever remember I actually began to feel good about myself. It was just like being let out of a dark and lonely cell.

I'll never forget what happened to me. But at least I can start to live my life.

For further information on the work of the NSPCC, or to make a donation, please write to: NSPCC, 67 Saffron Hill, London, EC1N 8RS or call 071 242 1626.

To report a suspected case of child abuse, call the NSPCC Child Protection Helpline on 0800 800 500.

NSPCC
Act Now For Children.

In the early nineties, the rules changed abruptly. Agencies began to try anything, borrow any style, pull any trick, so long as the result didn't look like a piece of advertising. The whole idea was to stop readers simply turning the page. The editorial-style illustrations of Janet Woolley defined a BBH campaign for Murphy's Bitter; the brillliant editorial lens of photographer Sebastião Salgado, a previous winner with documentary work for *The Sunday Times magazine*, was pressed into action to sell Le Creuset kitchenware.

A scrapbook collage with typed notes featured in a Saatchi & Saatchi campaign to promote nursing as a profession. A similarly random assembly of images characterized a Lowe Howard-Spink series for Olympus cameras, while a Levi's 501 jeans press campaign no longer showed the product but presented a Warhol-esque art collage of rows of washing machines ('torture them') and washing powders ('the more you wash them, the better they get'). All these campaigns won Silver Awards at D&AD in the nineties.

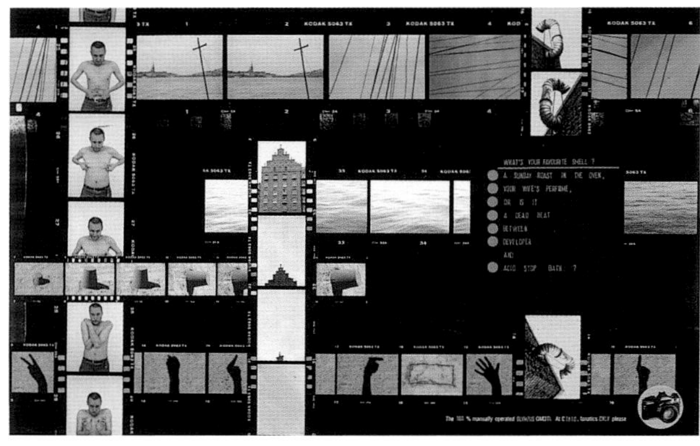

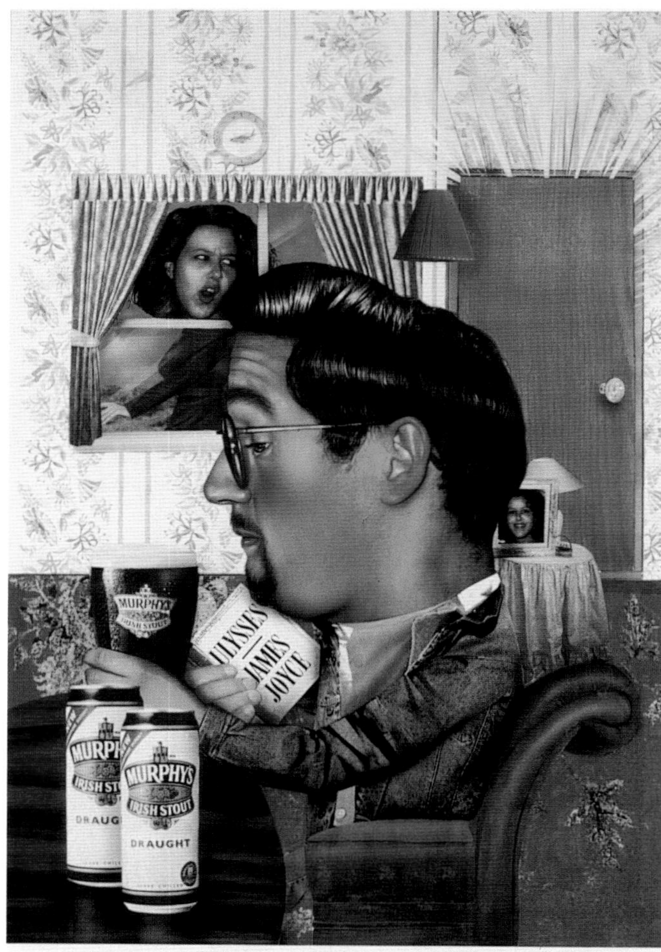

Maguire ended up with Joyce instead of Kate,
but like the Murphy's he wasn't bitter.

Eamon's team lost 84-0,
but like the Murphy's he wasn't bitter.

1996.02
Agency: **Lowe Howard-Spink**
Client: **Olympus Cameras**
Head of art Steve Dunn created a more contemporary style of art direction at Lowe's, as evidenced in this Olympus campaign.

1994.04
Agency: **Bartle Bogle Hegarty**
Client: **The Whitbread Beer Company**
The rumour that photos of BBH personnel were used as the basis for these illustrations made each new ad the subject of industry gossip.

this page

1993.02
Agency: **Bartle Bogle & Hegarty**
Client: **Levi Strauss**
Art director John Gorse and his copywriter partner Nick Worthington took the pictures themselves for this campaign for Levi's 501 jeans.

1990.03
Agency: **Saatchi & Saatchi**
Client: **Kitchenware Merchants**
This studiedly unglamorous series of photographs by Sebastião Salgado created a cool and effective image for Le Creuset.

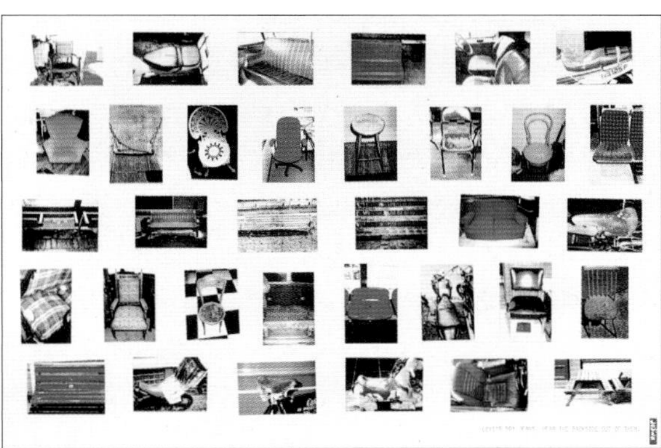

Press ads didn't just imitate art or editorial in their direct emotional appeal. A clever series for Waterstone's booksellers by the creative team of Nigel Roberts and Paul Belford at TBWA presented the main communication messages of the campaign within a series of beautifully crafted mock book covers. The same creative team was also responsible for a Tate Gallery press campaign aimed at people known by the Tate as 'cuspers' – potential visitors who are interested in art but can never quite get round to attending a gallery. Roberts and Belford adopted the view that the Tate should not patronize its visitors, that art is subjective and that individuals must be allowed to form their own opinions. So their campaign (with the line 'Minds open from 10am') focused on found objects; mundane everyday things such as rocks, conkers, apples and pieces of wood that could take on another meaning or a more profound beauty in the eye of the beholder after a visit to the Tate Gallery.

Campaigns like the Tate's showed how press and poster advertising were becoming almost interchangeable in the nineties. In a speeded-up media world, the need to get to the communication message more quickly than ever before meant that press ads had to behave more like posters. Thus, D&AD-commended press campaigns for Pirelli ('Power is nothing without control'), Volkswagen ('Surprisingly ordinary prices'), Boddingtons Bitter ('The Cream of Manchester') and *The Economist* could just as easily have been posters.

1998.05
Agency: **BDDP.GGT**
Client: **Waterstone's Booksellers**
The birth of this famously minimalist press ad campaign for Waterstone's booksellers received a D&AD nomination when it first appeared from agency BDDP.

opposite

1999.06
Agency: **TBWA**
Client: **Waterstone's Booksellers**
A year later – and now from TBWA – better work or a kinder jury rewarded Paul Belford and Nigel Roberts' efforts with a full Silver Award. This was one press campaign that really did ask Waterstone's customers to judge a book by its cover.

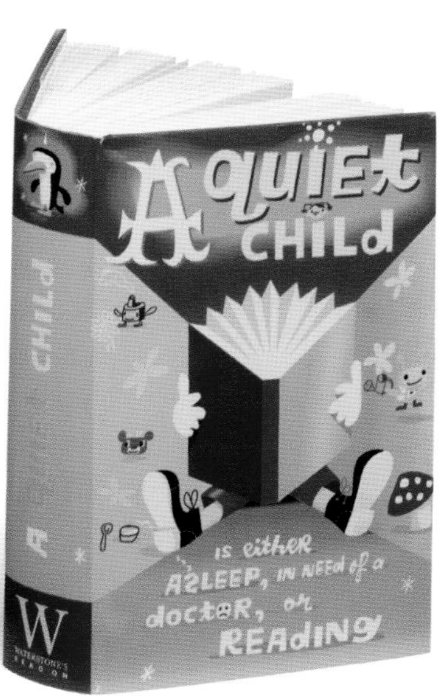
A quiet child
is either asleep, in need of a doctor, or reading
A QUIET CHILD
W
WATERSTONE'S
READ ON

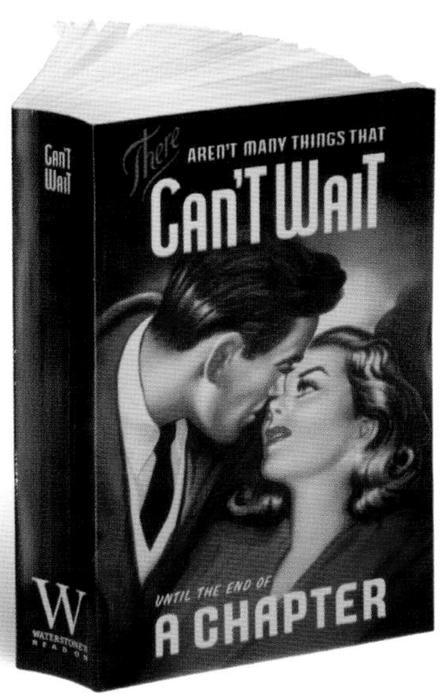
There aren't many things that
CAN'T WAIT
until the end of
A CHAPTER
CAN'T WAIT
W
WATERSTONE'S
READ ON

There is one thing
the
BRITISH
like to do
WITH THE BEDROOM LIGHT ON
BEDROOM LIGHT
W
WATERSTONE'S
READ ON

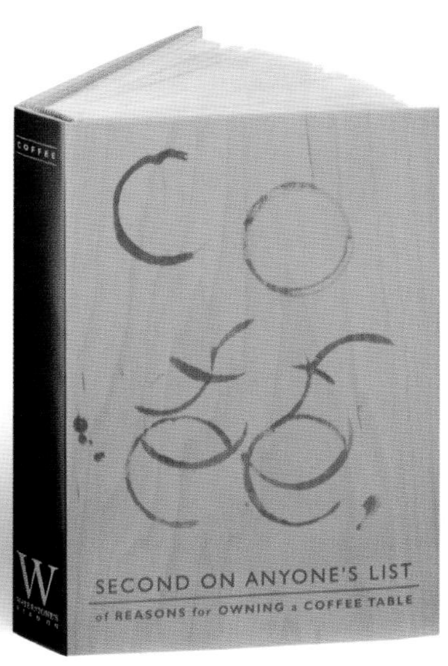
COFFEE
SECOND ON ANYONE'S LIST
of REASONS for OWNING a COFFEE TABLE
W

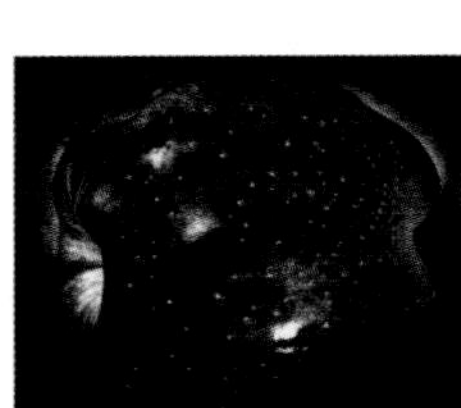

An apple, noticed after
a visit to the Tate.
Minds open from 10am.
TateGallery

A conker, noticed after
a visit to the Tate.
Minds open from 10am.
TateGallery

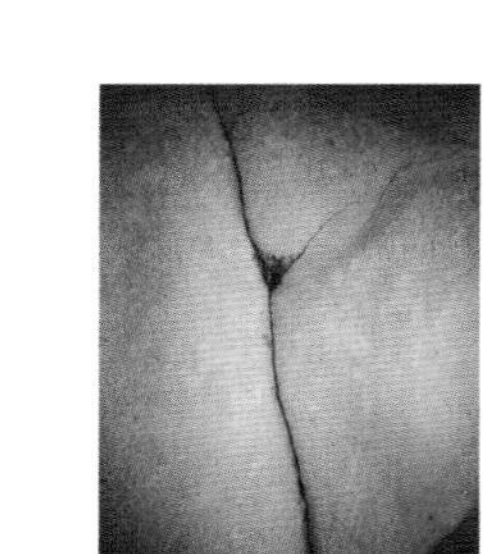

A rock, noticed after
a visit to the Tate.
Minds open from 10am.
TateGallery

A piece of wood, noticed
after a visit to the Tate.
Minds open from 10am.
TateGallery

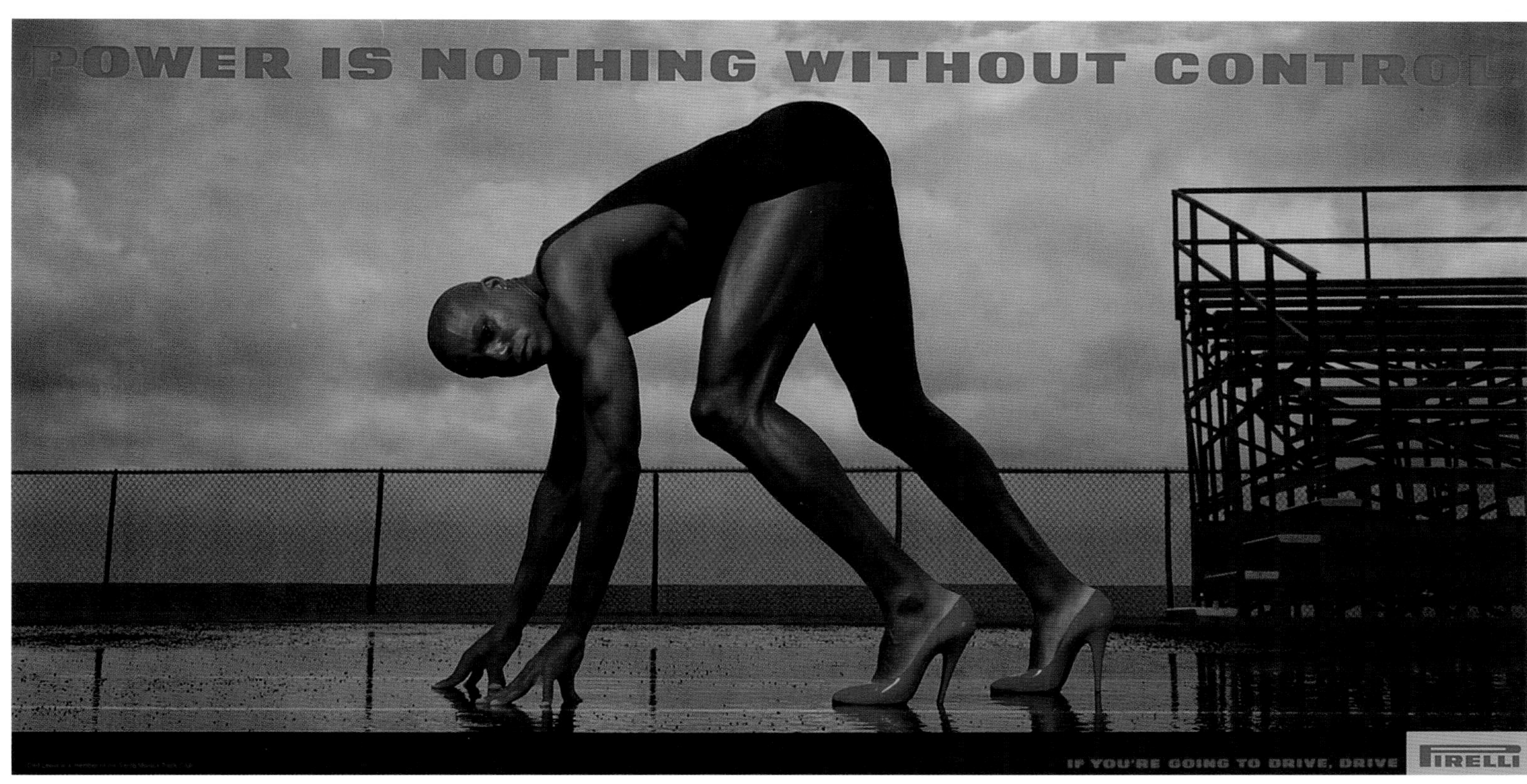

1999.07
Agency: **TBWA**
Client: **Tate Gallery**
More evidence of the increasing blurring of the boundaries between advertising and design in the nineties. Paul Belford and Nigel Roberts of TBWA turn on the taste for the Tate Gallery in this series of posters.

this page

1995.04
Agency: **Young & Rubicam**
Client: **Pirelli**
Art director Graeme Norways wisely commissioned Annie Leibovitz to take this exceptional shot of Carl Lewis, perhaps thinking of her remarkable work with celebrities in *Esquire*.

1992.04
Agency: **Bartle Bogle Hegarty**
Client: **The Whitbread Beer Company**
'The Cream of Manchester' was reportedly based on the slogan painted on the old brewery in Manchester.

In fact, one classic idea in the long-running AMV campaign for *The Economist*, featuring a simple white keyhole on the familar red background, won D&AD Silvers in both press and poster categories. Meanwhile, Volkswagen's out of focus bride-and-groom press shot (the photographer zooms instead onto a bus advertising the Polo for just £8,290) reflected the edgy, grainy style of communication – unsentimental almost to the point of viciousness – that emerged in the late nineties.

Much earlier in the decade, BBH developed a landmark press campaign for the Whitbread-owned Boddingtons beer brand, with simple orange and black art direction designed to stand out poster-like on the back covers of publications. The work was enormously effective. When Whitbread bought the Boddingtons brewery in Manchester in 1989, Boddingtons bitter was a declining regional brand. By the mid-nineties, it had risen to become the UK's fourth largest bitter brand and the market leader in cans.

BBH's advertising strategy flew in the face of conventional wisdom, which said mainstream beers should lead with TV advertising and focus on images of drinkers in pubs. Boddingtons led with press advertising and focused on aspirational and surreal images of the product itself, which has a creamy head. The 'cream of Manchester' idea enabled Boddingtons to remain true to its Northern roots while broadening its appeal nationally, although initially it caused some confusion inside the creative industry. As Jim Thornton, a copywriter at J Walter Thomson (JWT), wrote in *Campaign* in September 1991 after an ad appeared with a foaming pint next to a cut-throat razor, 'I'm not sure I'll ever be able to raise a pint of this brew to my lips again without anticipating the taste of shaving cream. Or maybe I'm completely missing the pint [sic], and it is actually saying that real Mancunian men shave with Boddingtons.'

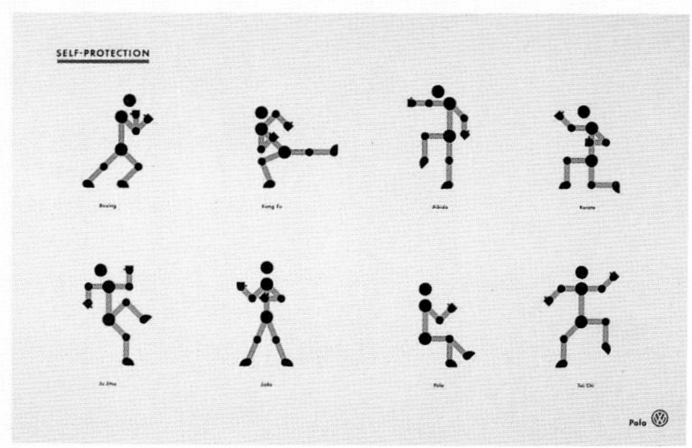

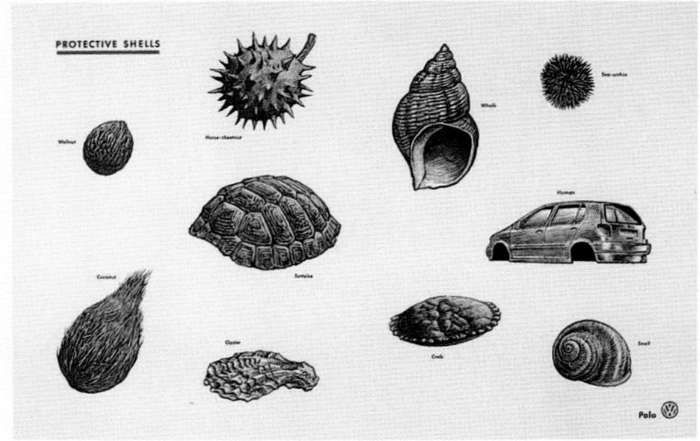

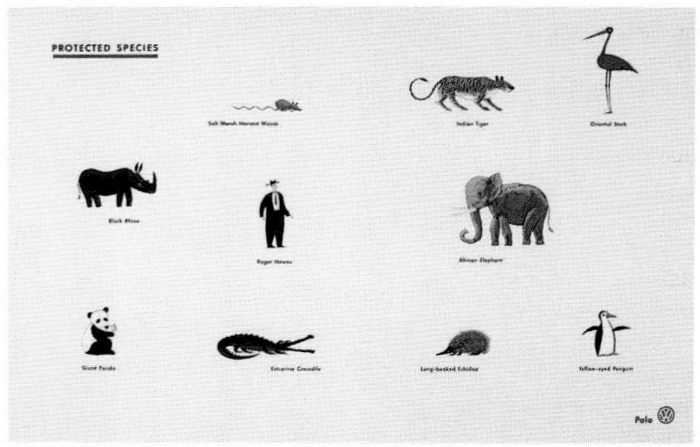

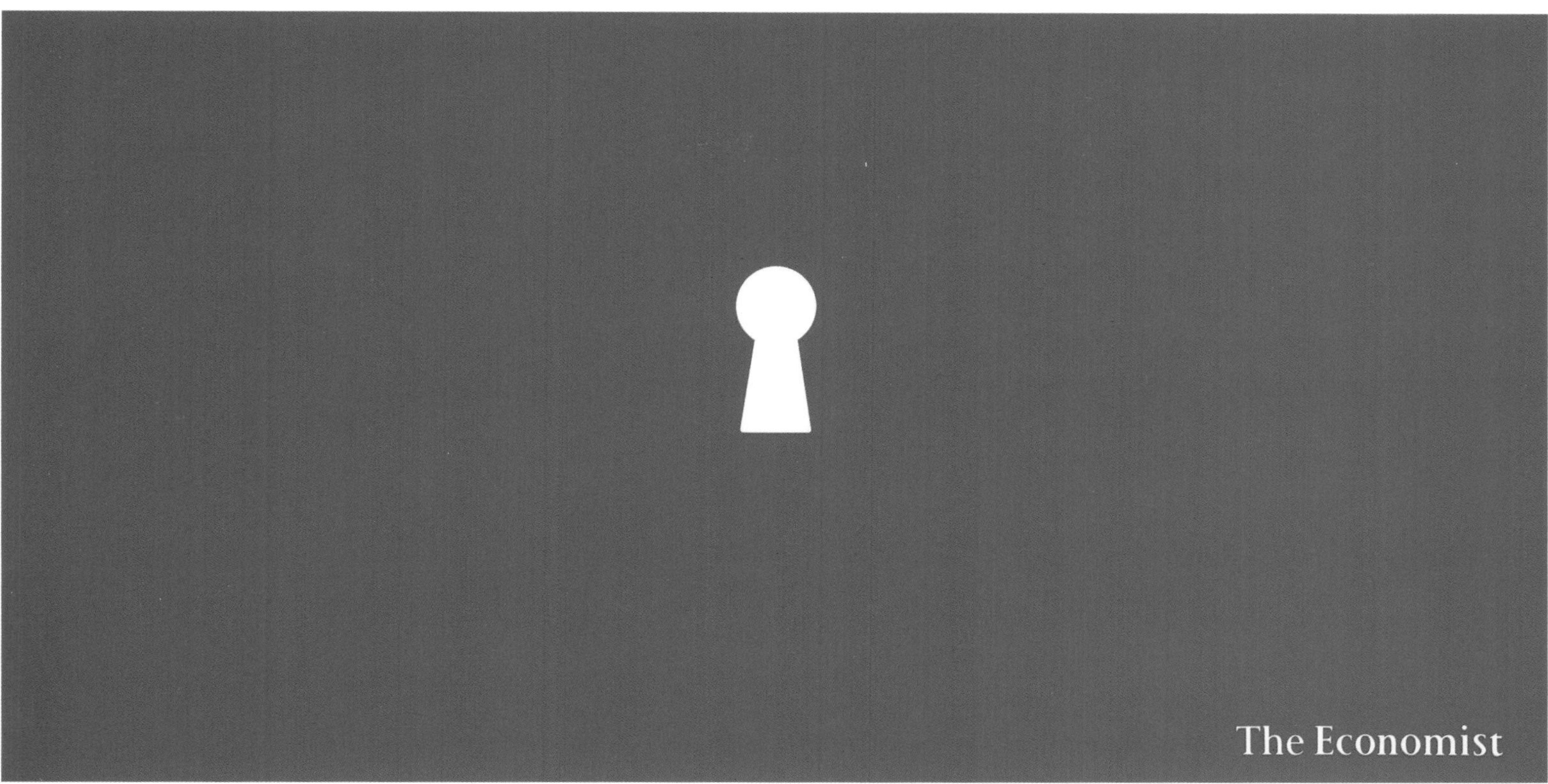
The Economist

● 1999.08
Agency: **BMP DDB**
Client: **Volkswagen**
In the nineties VW really capitalized on three decades of familiar and popular advertising and relied on its reputation to carry the message. Here, cool and quirky illustrations tell the reliability story.

● 1999.09
Agency: **BMP DDB**
Client: **Volkswagen**
No ad encapsulates the spirit of the no-nonsense nineties better than the VW 'Wedding' ad. No car, no driver. Even the brand name is obscured by a telegraph pole. No other advertiser could get away with such a confident statement.

this page

● 1992.05
Agency: **Abbott Mead Vickers.BBDO**
Client: **The Economist**
One of the most understated posters of the decade. Art director John Horton reportedly considered omitting the logo and allowing the familiar *Economist* red and white to brand what surely would have been the minimalist ad of the century.

● 1994.05
Agency: **Abbott Mead Vickers.BBDO**
Client: **The Economist**
Economist ads look deceptively simple and easy, but the longer the campaign runs, the harder it gets to come up with fresh thinking. This unusual execution, based on sifting through the shredder bin, kept up the standard in 1994.

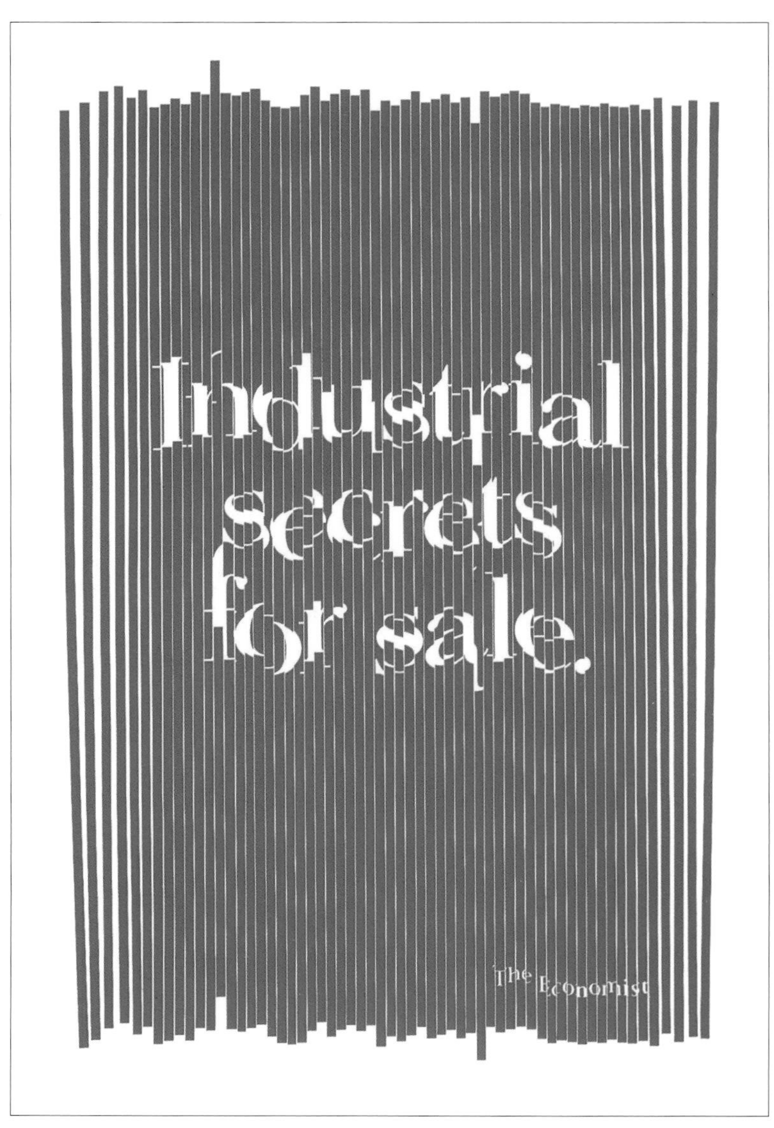
Industrial secrets for sale.
The Economist

Elsewhere in press advertising, there were the by-now obligatory mood swings at D&AD between the stylish and silly (a faintly ridiculous Silver-winning Saatchi campaign in 1992 showed tribal influences on a new Habitat collection) and the socially hard-hitting (cut-through work for such charities as the NSPCC, the Bhopal medical appeal and ASH in Scotland). A couple of projects even combined both sides of the coin – style and social conscience – in one creative campaign. A series for homeless aid charity Crisis by SP Lintas presented homeless people as fashion models under the heading 'Winter Warmers'; BMP's page-turning press campaign for the Health Education Authority demonstrated what happens to a beautiful woman with the AIDs virus over a few years (precisely nothing).

No campaigns, however, occupied the crossover between press and poster advertising quite like those for the global sportswear brands. Reebok offered 'The Edge' (courtesy of Lowe Howard-Spink) and Adidas appealed to the runner in everyone in a campaign by Leagas Delaney. But it was Nike, in particular, which started to lead the British market in the nineties, supported by a vigorous campaign devised by Simons Palmer Denton Clemmow & Johnson which accurately reflected changing attitudes to sport and sportsmen.

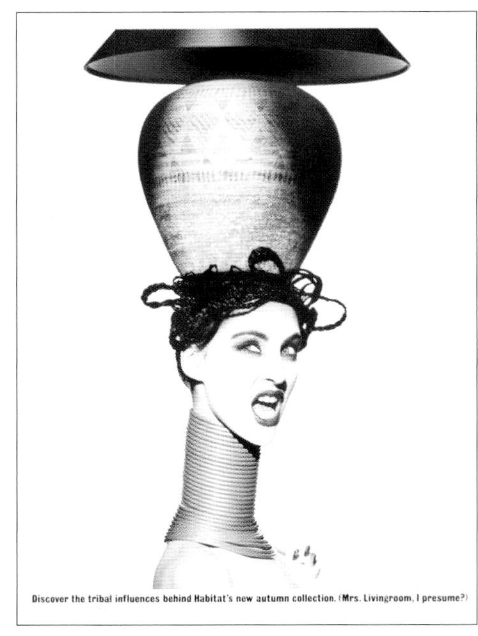

Discover the tribal influences behind Habitat's new autumn collection. (Mrs. Livingroom, I presume?)

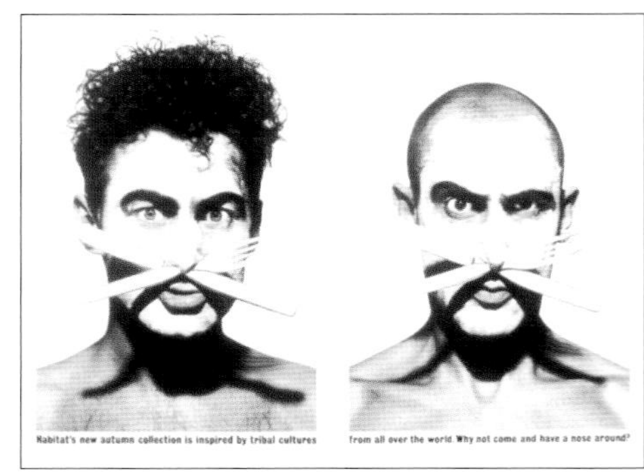

Habitat's new autumn collection is inspired by tribal cultures
from all over the world. Why not come and have a nose around?

"THOUSANDS OF OUR CHILDREN WERE NOT SO LUCKY. THEY SURVIVED."
THE INTERNATIONAL MEDICAL APPEAL FOR BHOPAL

1992.06
Agency: **Saatchi & Saatchi**
Client: **The Habitat Group**
A long way from Terence Conran's original Provençal inspiration for Habitat, these outlandish ads by Saatchi gave the ailing store a quick kick up the flameproof chicken brick.

1995.05
Agency: **Collett Dickenson Pearce**
Client: **Satinath Sarangi**
Agencies have frequently been accused of cynicism in creating charity ads to win awards. That's something that could never be leveled against Indra Sinha, whose commitment to combating corruption, bigotry and poverty in his native India have led to some of the finest writing ever seen in English language advertising. This was his last ad for CDP.

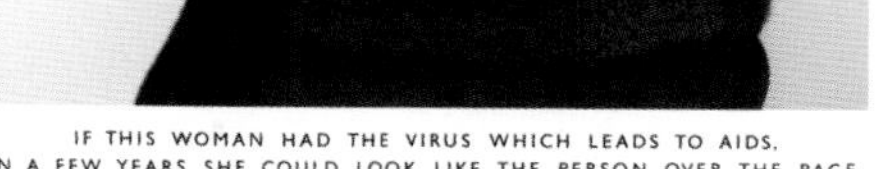

IF THIS WOMAN HAD THE VIRUS WHICH LEADS TO AIDS.
IN A FEW YEARS SHE COULD LOOK LIKE THE PERSON OVER THE PAGE.

WORRYING ISN'T IT.
AIDS. YOU'RE AS SAFE AS YOU WANT TO BE.

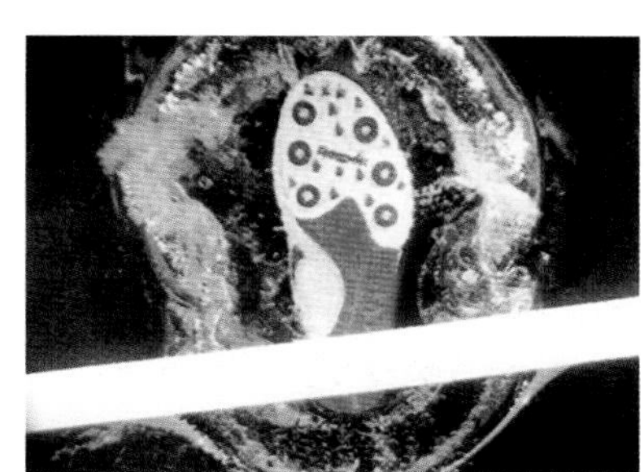

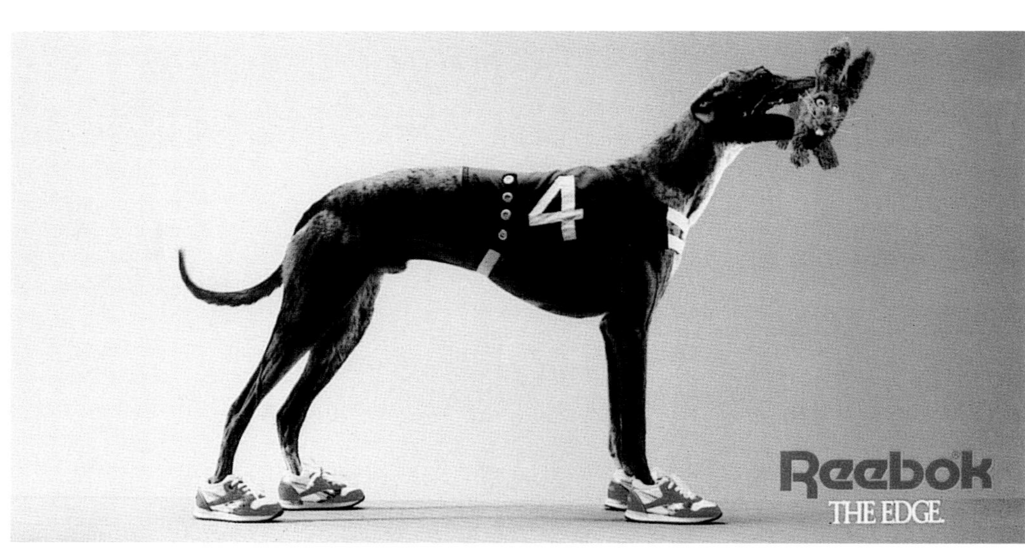

Reebok
THE EDGE.

1990.04
Agency:
BMP DDB Needham Worldwide
Client: **Health Education Authority**
Watching the D&AD jury trying to spot the difference between the girl who has AIDS and the one who doesn't in David Bailey's photographs, really proved Frank Budgen and Peter Gatley's point in this press ad which ran on consecutive right-hand pages of newspapers.

1992.07
Agency: **Lowe Howard-Spink**
Client: **Reebok**
Though always in the running with press and posters, Reebok was usually in the bronze medal position on TV until David Garfath created the most technically superior spot of its time.

1990.05
Agency: **Lowe Howard-Spink**
Client: **Reebok**
Eschewing the glamorous athlete route favoured by competitors like Nike and Adidas, there's something quintessentially English about Lowe's simple witty poster for Reebok.

SPANISH AIR TRAFFIC CONTROL
HAS BEEN NOTIFIED.

YOU'VE JUST PASSED MICHAEL JOHNSON.
MORE THAN MOST
ATHLETES WILL DO THIS SUMMER.

EVER HEARD THE
ALGERIAN NATIONAL ANTHEM?
YOU WILL.

1993.03
Agency: **Simons Palmer Denton Clemmow & Johnson**
Client: **Nike**

opposite

1994.06
Agency: **Simons Palmer Denton Clemmow & Johnson**
Client: **Nike**

Not surprisingly, these Nike posters came from the agency that also handled *The Sun*. The newspaper-style headlines for Nike became so famous, they appeared as news items. Simons Palmer Denton Clemmow & Johnson at its absolute peak – celebrity endorsement combined with challenging copy. Many of London's future creative directors learnt their trade on this campaign.

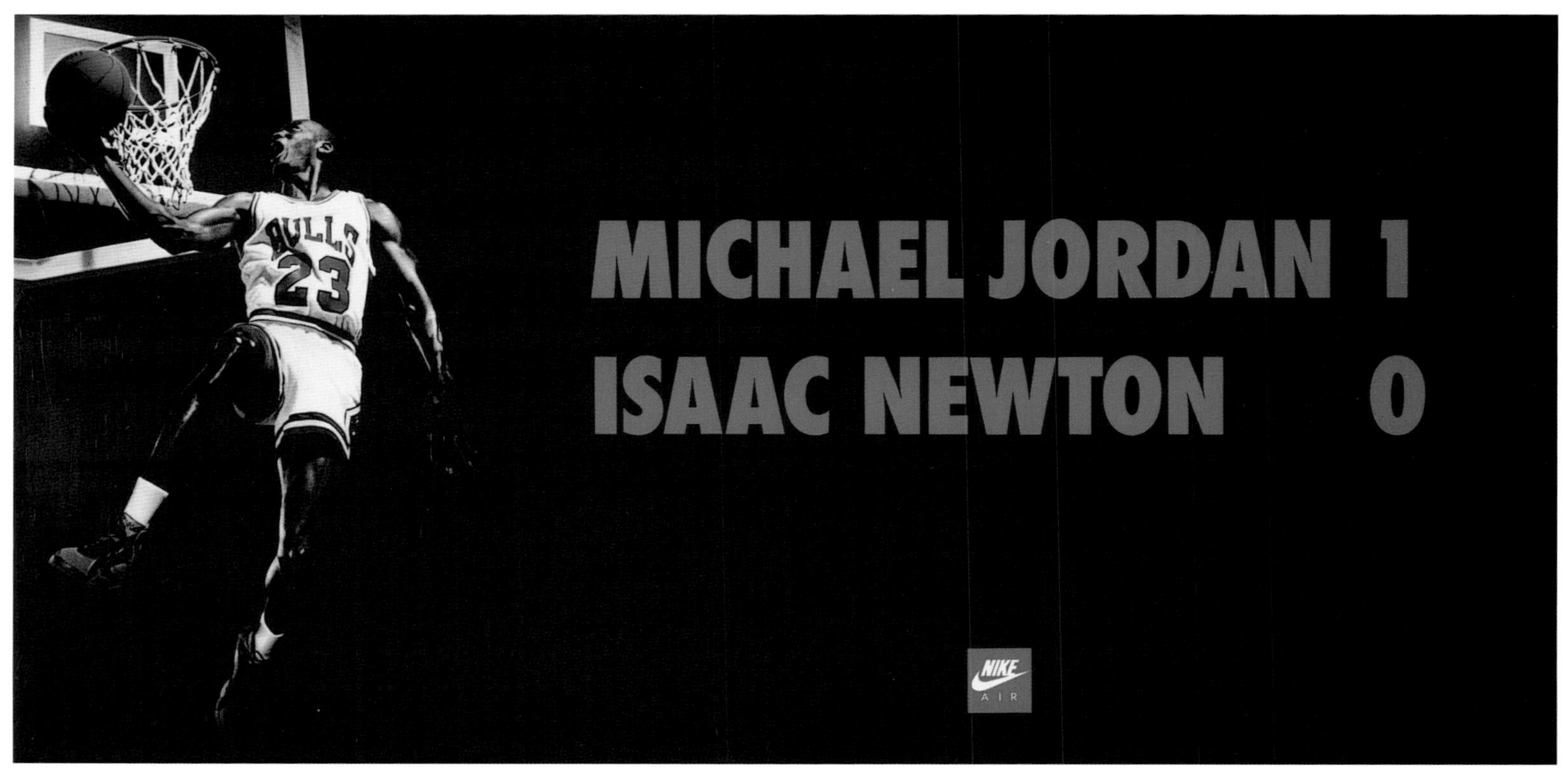

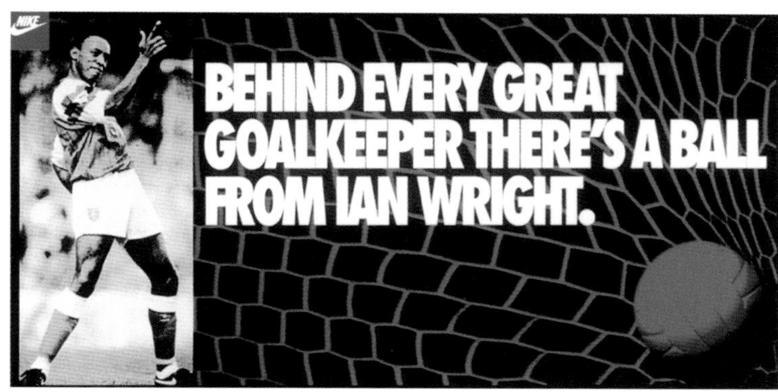

Simons Palmer was a leading member of the 'third wave' of agencies which emerged following the business fall-out at the end of the eighties. (Names like JWT, Ogilvy & Mather (O&M) and Collett Dickenson Pearce (CDP) were in the first wave and BBH, Gold Greenlees Trott (GGT) and Wight Collins Rutherford Scott (WCRS) were in the second.) Its early work for Nike ('Beat your opponent not your feet' and 'There's only one thing more painful than carrying on. Giving up') was promising but pretty tame compared to what would follow. After its initial efforts, the agency suddenly found a way to give the emotional directness of Nike's best US advertising an authentic English accent. The synthesis of North American can-do spirit and more self-deprecating British wit created a powerful voice, best seen in press and poster work featuring footballers Ian Wright ('Behind every great goalkeeper there's a ball from Ian Wright') and Eric Cantona (''66 was a great year for English football. Eric was born').

Nike increased sales revenues five-fold over a seven-year period in the nineties and estimated that incremental sales generated above the overall market trend paid for its advertising 13 times over. If the Nike campaign paid off commercially, it also wasn't afraid to ring the creative changes to keep things fresh. Its 'Flower Power' press work in the mid-nineties ('Make War Not Love') reflected the same capacity for nostalgic pastiche that Levi's showed at the same time with its 'Cut in the Sixties' press and poster campaign for its White Tab range. Art directed by Tiger Savage of BBH, the Levi's campaign won Silver in 1996. Icons such as Henry Cooper were used to cash in on the Mod revival that was gathering pace at the time.

1996.03
Agency: **Bartle Bogle Hegarty**
Client: **Levi Strauss**
Tiger Savage's daring and probably extremely expensive idea of printing sixties icons on metallic board was a subtle and extremely clever nod to another great sixties icon, Andy Warhol.

overleaf

1995.06
Agency: **Simons Palmer Denton Clemmow & Johnson**
Client: **Nike**
From art director Andy McKay and copywriter Giles Montgomery, this classic Nike poster caught the mid-nineties peak of French footballer Eric Cantona's popularity in the UK during his time at Manchester United.

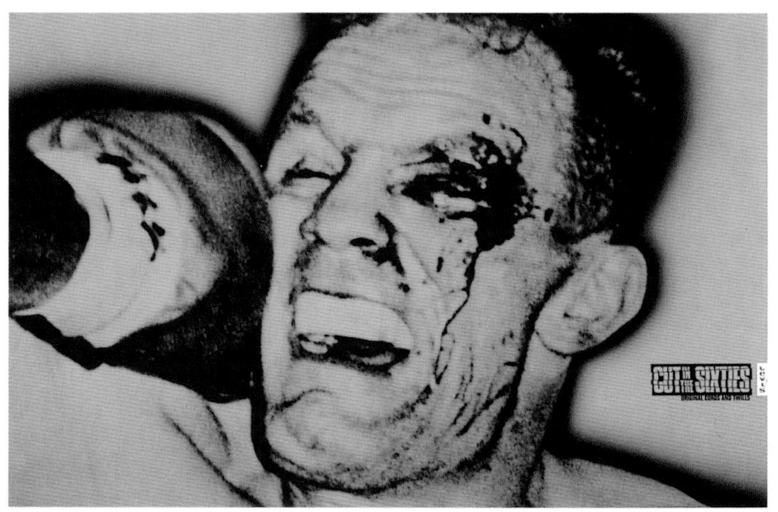

NIKE
ER

'66 WAS A
GREAT YEAR
OR ENGLISH
FOOTBALL.
C WAS BORN.

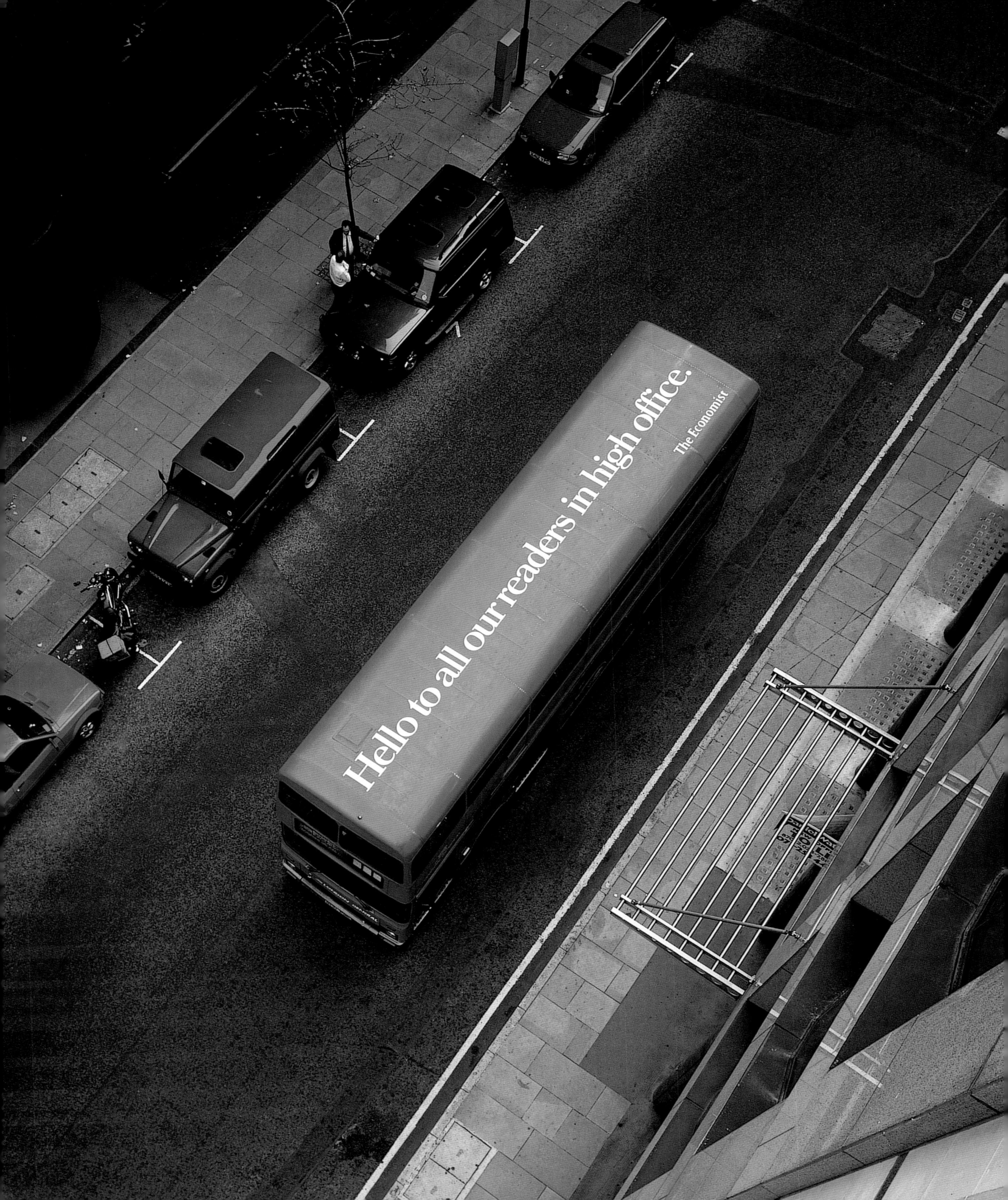
Hello to all our readers in high office.
The Economist

opposite

1994.07
Agency: **Abbott Mead Vickers.BBDO**
Client: **The Economist**
Questions as to whether the *Economist* campaign could travel were cheekily answered by this bus-top winner, a daring forerunner to later ambient media work at D&AD.

this page

1991.04
Agency: **McCann Erickson**
Client: **Friends of the Earth**
The genius of this poster is its directness, literally an acid test for the thousands of column inches written about acid rain. It saw the McCann Erickson agency on the winners' podium at D&AD for the first time in many years.

overleaf

1995.07
Agency: **TBWA**
Client: **Playtex**
Whilst public controversy raged over the sexism in this Playtex poster, a similar furore raged in the advertising industry as to who actually wrote it. Trevor Beattie later admitted the author and art director were both Nigel Rose. While this proved to be the most memorable poster in the entire campaign, its *double entendre* is unclear – is she calling her breasts boys, are there a gaggle of men on her doorstep or is she addressing passers-by on the street?

As an outdoor medium, poster advertising in the nineties did not quite reach the heights set in the previous decade by Araldite's glued-on car or the GLC red tape billboard, but the D&AD Awards, nevertheless, produced a couple of ambient classics. A Friends of the Earth poster made of litmus paper promised to turn red when acid rain was falling, while another idea from *The Economist*, a poster on the top of buses travelling past City skyscrapers, said, 'Hello to all our readers in high office.'

The decade's most talked-about poster series stood out for very different reasons. This was an aggressive pan-European campaign for the Playtex Wonderbra by TBWA, which took a product usually confined to the prim pages of women's magazines and blazoned it across giant billboards with provocative lines like 'Hello Boys' and 'Or are you just pleased to see me?' (Copywriter Trevor Beattie, who worked on the Wonderbra campaign, would later go on to even greater infamy with his FCUK campaign for French Connection UK.) The Playtex Wonderbra posters instantly divided public opinion, making the question of sexism something very much in the eye of the beholder. But nobody doubted the impact of the campaign in generating an enormous amount of publicity – valued at more than £18 million – despite a relatively small advertising spend (just £330,000).

The background to the project was a business saga dubbed by the media as the 'Bra Wars'. When the Sara Lee Corporation acquired the licence of Canadian lingerie maker Candelle and awarded it to its UK subsidiary Playtex, rival Courtaulds retaliated with the launch of the Gossard Ultrabra. So the scene was set in the early nineties for a showdown between two products designed to enhance the fuller figure. The Playtex Wonderbra faced the prospect of sagging sales as the new and glamorous Gossard Ultrabra surged ahead. But TBWA's work more than doubled Playtex Wonderbra sales after the campaign began in 1992.

H

THE

ELLO
BOYS.

AL PUSH-UP PLUNGE BRA. AVAILABLE IN SIZES 32-38ABC.

More subtle in approach was a 1992 Silver-winning poster campaign for Heinz by BSB Dorland. This deployed the skills of illustrator Robin Heighway-Bury to make a range of products once synonymous with the artificial preservatives of mass production look more natural and organic in flavour. The Heinz series quietly demonstrated the drive for simplicity and immediacy in UK advertising in the nineties by enclosing all the messages within a single illustration, without recourse to logo or packshot.

More noisily controversial was Lowe Howard-Spink's Regal Cigarettes poster campaign for Imperial Tobacco, a Silver-winner in 1993 featuring a fat, balding character called Reg. The agency circumvented the rules about cigarettes not appealing to the young by successfully arguing that Reg was repulsive and 'uncool'. But in the more satirical social climate of the early nineties, when comics like *Viz* were attracting millions of readers to the gross antics of their characters, Reg quickly became a cult figure. The only antidote at D&AD was a Silver Award given in 1991 to a poster by Smith-Dennison saying simply 'Thank you for smoking. Smiden & Son. Undertakers.'

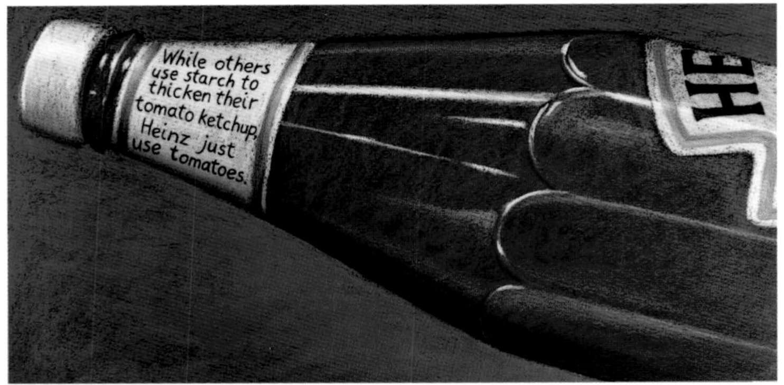

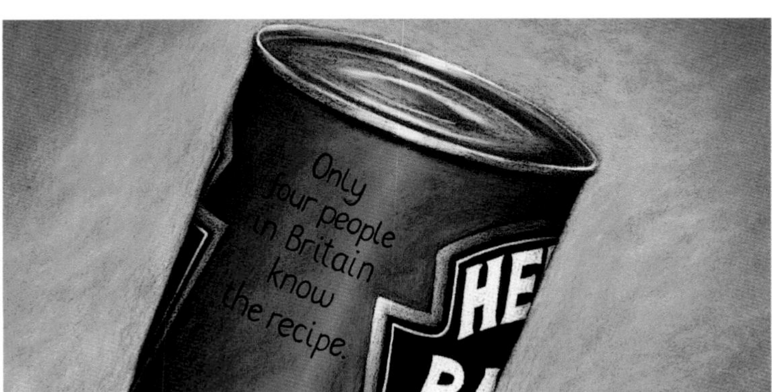

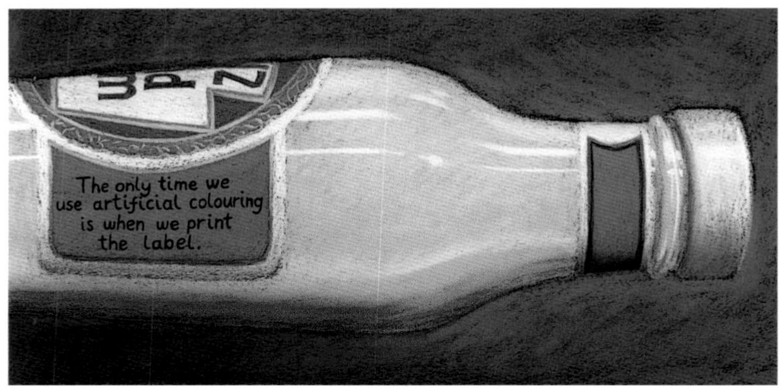

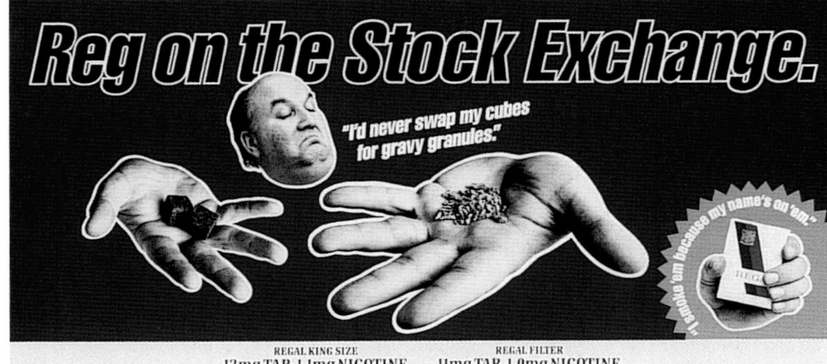

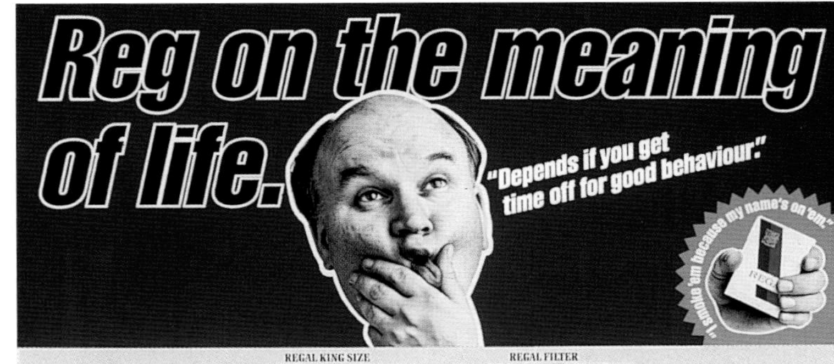

Reg's twin brother Al smokes Mild.
"I smoke 'em because my name's on 'em."
8mg TAR 0.8mg NICOTINE
SMOKING CAUSES CANCER
Health Departments' Chief Medical Officers

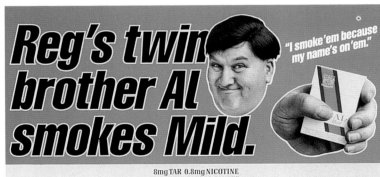

1992.08
Agency: **BSB Dorland**
Client: **HJ Heinz Company**
At first glance it seems like the client said 'let's just run with the layout'. But in reality the confidence and subtlety of these posters reeks of quality for Heinz. They looked then (and still do) completely unlike anything else, especially huge on a 48-sheet site.

1991.05
Agency: **Smith-Dennison**
Client: **North West Ash**
Created by the founders of the small agency Smith-Dennison, their names also seem to combine in Smiden, the name of the undertakers in the ad. A subsidiary?

1991.06
Agency: **Marr Associates**
Client: **Action on Smoking & Health**
Scottish agencies have a long history of powerful charity and public sector work. This ad by Marr Associates is no exception.

this page

1993.04
Agency: **Lowe Howard-Spink**
Client: **Imperial Tobacco**
Reg (and his twin brother Al) were creations formed by holding your thumb over the REGAL brand name to create new monikers (the famous line being 'I smoke 'em coz my names on 'em') and Reg became something of a working class hero.

Some poster campaigns of the early nineties featured mini-plots and stories, for example, the 'I want to...' series for Prudential by WCRS and the 'Australians wouldn't give a XXXX for anything else' work by Saatchi for Allied Breweries. But as the decade wore on, such narratives were pared down. Two BMP DDB posters of the late nineties caught the new mood. The first, art directed by Jerry Hollens for the Volkswagen Sharan in 1997, showed how the new model was a direct descendant of the much loved VW camper van by having it emerge from a jelly-mould of the old vehicle. No copyline needed. The second, art directed by Richard Flintham in 1998, suggested how London Transport was 'making London simple' by showing an image of an eerily depopulated capital with only one house, the Thames and Eros in view.

The focus on big brand imagery for international markets in the nineties also levered a change of approach in TV commercials. Many campaigns moved away from story-led narrative and dialogue towards the filmic blockbuster full of glossy cinematography, which needed less viewer attention and got there faster. Where once British campaigns like the Cinzano ads or 'Water in Majorca' had been so carefully crafted and wittily distinctive, now there was a shift towards the melodramatic, big-budget image fest, each frame beautifully set up and shot in the manner of an MTV music video. According to the TBWA creative team of James Sinclair and Ed Morris, who worked around several London agencies during the decade, 'The sitcom died in TV advertising in the nineties and the pop promo took over.'

1998.06
Agency: **BMP DDB**
Client: **London Transport**
London Transport has been creating artistic posters since the thirties. Viewed in the context of such a history, this eerie and surrealistic Tube poster is part of a great creative tradition. A great idea, beautifully delivered by rising star lensman Giles Revell. From your home to Eros – how simple is that?

1993.05
Agency: **WCRS**
Client: **Prudential**
The 'I want to be' poster and TV campaign for Prudential tapped into the spirit of anything's possible that characterized nineties optimism.

1992.09
Agency: **Saatchi & Saatchi**
Client: **Allied Breweries Brands Marketing**
With more than an echo of Larsen's 'The Far Side' series, Alexandra Taylor's art direction strikes just the right cartoon posture for another poster in this long running campaign for Castlemaine XXXX.

1997.06
Agency: **BMP DDB**
Client: **Volkswagen**
Not simply because it features an early VW camper, but in its photography and the lean economy of the idea, this Sharan ad could sit easily alongside Helmut Krone's classic VW ads of the sixties.

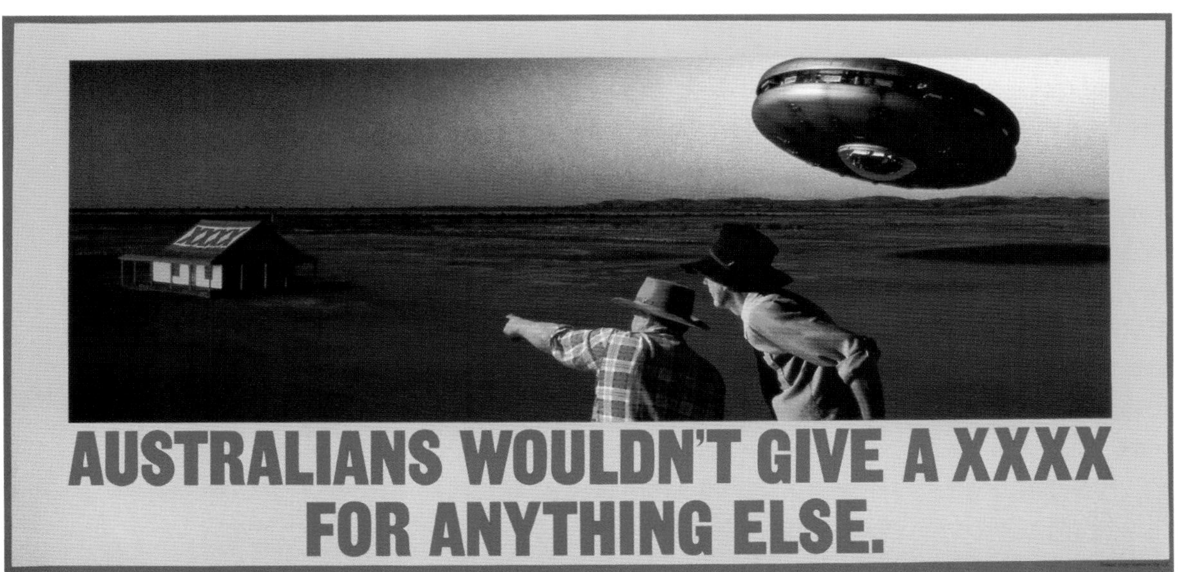

First up was Saatchi & Saatchi's 'Global' commercial for British Airways, which was directed by Hugh Hudson to give the airline a warmer global image. This cost a reported £1 million to shoot and starred 3,000 American high school kids grouped in the Utah desert to form an enormous smiling face. Set to a racy Malcolm MacLaren version of the music from the opera *Lakme* and featuring the easily translated voice-over 'Every year British Airways brings 24 million people together', the 'Global' commercial featured in the 1991 D&AD Annual. It set a template of visual extravaganza for the nineties TV commercial that was swiftly noted and emulated by clients as diverse as British Telecom (with its Saatchi epic starring Professor Stephen Hawkins) and Tesco (with a highly choreographed Lowe Howard-Spink film called 'Baby').

Very quickly, the market was cornered by AMV, an agency not previously famous for television work. Copywriter Tom Carty and art director Walter Campbell at AMV began working closely with controversial director Tony Kaye, who had emerged so dramatically in the late eighties. Kaye's big filmic vision suited the new image-driven demands of the age. The collaboration produced award-winning TV work for Dunlop Tyres and Volvo (as well as a memorable press series for British Telecom's 'One Phone Day' campaign which earned Kaye a D&AD Silver Award for stills photography in 1995).

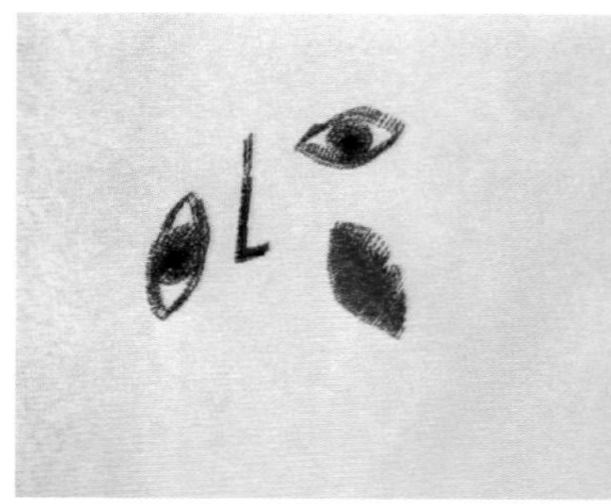

1994.08
Agency: **Lowe Howard-Spink**
Client: **Tesco Stores**
Frank Budgen created each cameo in this high-class album of moving snaps with a photographer's eye. As this 'Baby' commercial showed, pop promo-style imagery increasingly replaced narrative and dialogue in TV advertising of the nineties.

1991.07
Agency: **Saatchi & Saatchi**
Client: **British Airways**
Memorable in many ways, not least of which is that the ear we see moving around in a clearing is never united with the face. Hugh Hudson's film was featured for several years in *The Guinness Book of Records* as the most expensive commercial ever made.

1994.09
Agency: **Saatchi & Saatchi**
Client: **British Telecom**
The notion of an electronic dismembered voice exhorting us to 'keep talking' could have a strange 'Brave New World' quality to it. But Gerard De Thame's beautiful pictures and the sincerity of Stephen Hawkins' delivery lift this BT television ad far out of the ordinary.

1995.08
Agency: **Lowe Howard-Spink**
Client: **British Telecom**
You only have to look at a Tony Kaye commercial to see that he can light and compose a great photograph. But it took lateral thinking by Tom Carty and Walter Campbell to get him to do it.

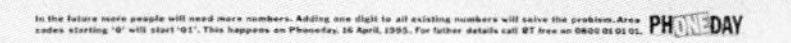

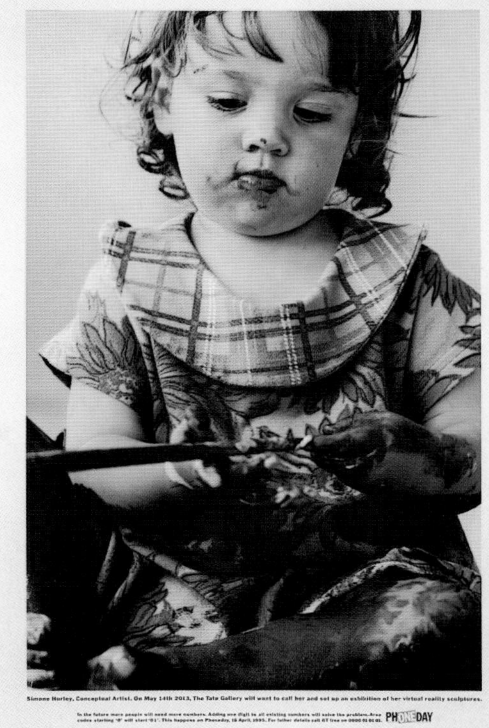

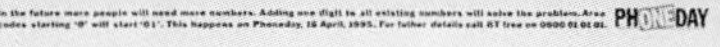

The Dunlop and Volvo commercials reflected a new era in TV advertising in which one-sentence scripts like 'good versus evil' or 'car drives through hurricane' replaced the dialogue-heavy scripts of earlier decades. Dunlop's 'Unexpected' spot was a fantasy in a weirdly coloured landscape set to the strains of the Velvet Underground's sado-masochistic classic 'Venus in Furs'. 'We wanted to get away from all the clichés of tyre advertising,' explained Carty. 'Dark night. It's raining. You've got the family in the back of the car. Truck comes towards you ... we wanted to turn it all on its head, if you like.'

Dunlop's 'Unexpected' was the first television commercial in the UK to feature artificial colour – the film was shot in black and white and 'colourized' electronically in a Los Angeles production house. The idea was that manufactured colour would stand out in the nineties in the way that black-and-white commercials had done in the eighties. Getting noticed in a media-saturated world mattered above everything.

Just as Dunlop tyres were given an intense new glamour which raced ahead of the reality of the product in order to reposition it, so Kaye's Volvo commercials ('The Volvo 850. A car you can believe in') took a safe, solid, unsexy marque and placed it at the heart of a trio of exciting filmic masterpieces featuring a stuntman, a female photographer and a tornado-chasing meteorologist. Equating a car that was previously the vehicle of choice for concerned middle-class parents in the suburbs with such action-hero professionals was a clever piece of advertising strategy. Beyond that, Kaye's overwhelming sense of cinematographic style took over. His super-rich documentary approach required thousands of hours of footage to compile, but the overall effect was thrilling.

1994.10
Agency: **Abbott Mead Vickers.BBDO**
Client: **SP Tyres**
This Dunlop commercial, shot in artificial colour, was reviewed in *Campaign* by adman Tim Mellors as either 'a work of a genius or utter bunkum'. It did wonders for Tom Carty, Walter Campbell and Tony Kaye – and probably sold a few tyres too.

1996.04
Agency: **Abbott Mead Vickers.BBDO**
Client: **Volvo**
'Twister' showed off Kaye's talents as a movie-scale director and was one of the stand-out projects in nineties advertising. In fact, many feel this 60-second epic was better than the movie of the same name that came out a year later. A Gold-winning masterpiece, it encouraged Kaye to campaign for his work to be treated as art and included in major galleries and museums.

'Stuntman' won a D&AD Silver in 1995 but the real *tour de force*, everyone agreed, was 'Twister' (the tornado saga) which won a D&AD Gold in 1996. With its memorable image of the flower against the grimy face of the meteorologist, it was, in Kaye's words, 'more about man against nature' than the earlier commercials that had readdressed the drive qualities of the Volvo.

Before the Volvo commercials, Kaye had already established himself at the top of the directing tree in the nineties with his vibrant 'Can I kick it?' commercial for Nike starring footballer Ian Wright, and a stunning piece of work for the Volkswagen Passat, 'God Bless the Child', set to the Billie Holiday song. But his work with Tom Carty and Walter Campbell defined the style of TV commercials in the nineties – and it was a style that attracted its fair share of critics, despite the many D&AD Awards showered on it. Industry veterans asked if it really was great advertising or self-indulgent visual anarchy that only said 'look at me'. Eminent copywriter Tony Brignull told *Creative Review* that Kaye's work smacked of 'MTV time'. John Webster, meanwhile, spoke more broadly of a communication industry that 'has fallen in love with technology and become dominated by it'. Webster added, 'MTV has exerted an enormous influence on young people. They come in here with no idea and the first thing they do is show me a technique. Technique is fine if it is the servant of the idea, but so often the content is just not there.'

The cosy catchphrases, characters and vignettes that formed the TV advertising heartland for Webster and his peers in the seventies and eighties were fast receding by the late nineties, as the international cinematographic sweep of commercials continued its hold. Part of the new influence was dictated by the need to appeal to the growing Sky Television audiences watching football on big screens in pubs. In this context, any complexity or subtlety went out of the window. Wieden + Kennedy's 'Good versus Evil' commercial for Nike, a D&AD Silver winner in 1997 directed by Tarsem in which soccer heroes are literally confronted by demons on a fiery pitch, was ideal for the medium.

1995.09
Agency: **Abbott Mead Vickers.BBDO**
Client: **Volvo**
Tony Kaye's 'Stuntman' commerical for Volvo attributed daredevil exploits to a car once synonymous with suburban safety. One of the bystanders on this shoot, when hearing someone say 'Have you seen that stuntman, he must be crazy', is reported to have replied 'You should see the director!'

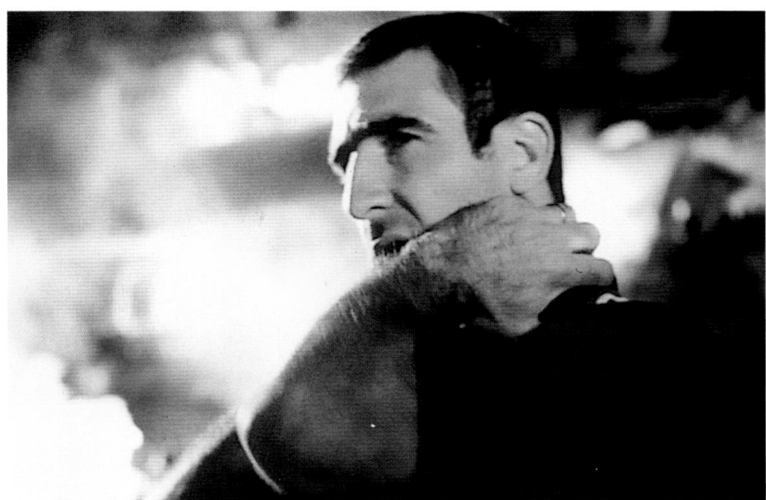

1997.07
Agency: **Wieden + Kennedy**
Client: **Nike**
While the UK agency TBWA Simons Palmer gave its Nike ads 'street credibility' [page 303], Wieden + Kennedy (in the US) created much darker grand-scale epics that appealed to the other side of the PlayStation generation. This was the epitomy of the global ad – global agency, global stars, just one line of copy spoken, in French, by a worldwide soccer celebrity.

1990.06
Agency:
BMP DDB Needham Worldwide
Client: **VAG**
Tony Kaye shot most of this film at the eyeline height of the little girl in the big city it portrayed. Combined with Billie Holiday's plaintive singing, 'God Bless the Child', he created an unusually vulnerable piece of film-making in this commercial for Volkswagen's Passat car.

Campbell and Carty, meanwhile, went on from their collaboration with Kaye to work with director Jonathan Glazer on 'Swimblack' for Guinness, after AMV famously wrested the account away from O&M. Set in a beautiful Italian village, the commercial tells the story of two brothers, Marco and Franco. Marco is the local hero, a former Olympic swimmer who every year swims a bizarre race against the pulling of the perfect pint of Guinness in his brother Franco's bar. Franco narrates the film.

'Swimblack' is full of brilliant artistry, a mini epic which builds suspense in order to deliver the new Guinness proposition 'Good things come to those who wait', updating the original line 'Guinness is good for you' for a new generation of drinkers. In keeping with the 'real-life' feel of advertising in the late nineties, the creative team avoided models and actors, casting a diving instructor and fitness nut they discovered on a beach in Tuscany to play Marco just a week before shooting began. Franco was cast even later in the process; his face was plucked from footage shot in Monopoli's fish market only a day before the shoot.

'Swimblack', which won a Silver Award in 1999, crowned a decade of extravagant commercial-making at D&AD. But many other films shared in the new visual language that emerged in this period, not least an earlier Guinness commercial called 'Chain' directed by Doug Foster for O&M. This took the viewer on a timeless journey through a glass of swirling draught Guinness, across a strange universe, to a mysterious planet. Was this 'pure genius', as the commercial (which won a D&AD Silver Award in 1995 for its use of music) suggested? At least 'Swimblack' had a discernible story in a 'real' world, of sorts.

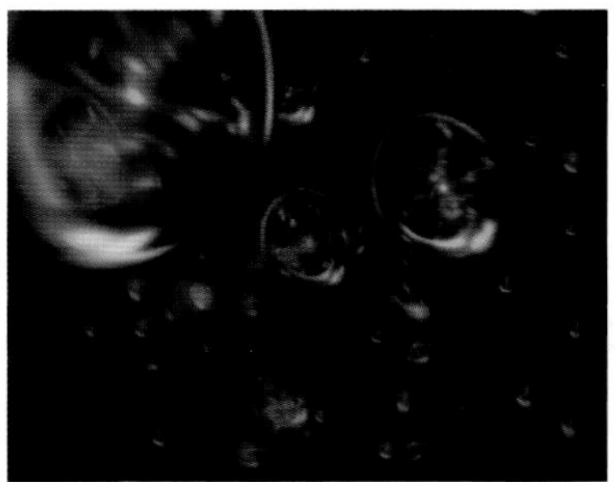

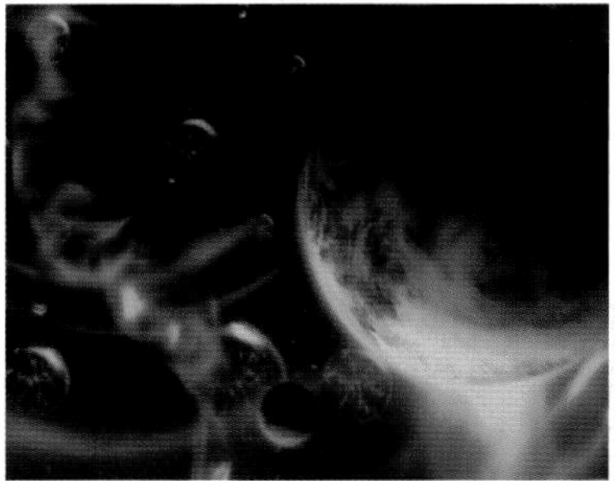

1995.10
Agency: **Ogilvy & Mather**
Client: **Guinness**
'Chain', directed by Doug Foster, featured actor Rutger Hauer who was the face of Guinness in a series of commercials. It also used the classic James Bond theme, 'We Have All the Time in the World', from *On Her Majesty's Secret Service* which was written by John Barry and performed by Louis Armstong.

this page

1999.10
Agency: **Abbott Mead Vickers.BBDO**
Client: **Guinness**
Though nothing like as technically difficult as the later and much praised 'Surfer' spot for Guinness [see page 455], which was also directed by Jonathan Glazer, this was the most run Guinness ad of the series, perhaps because it so vigorously captured the 'waiting' strategy in Marco's race against the pulling of a pint of the black stuff.

BBH's commercials for Levi Strauss in the nineties sought to balance a continuing reliance on storylines and characters with the heightened filmic vocabulary demanded in the MTV age. The results included two outstanding films. 'Swimmer', directed by Tarsem and written by a future D&AD President Larry Barker, features a boy from the wrong side of the tracks who swims across several swimming pools in an affluent suburb to get to his girlfriend. 'Creek', directed by the directing duo Vaughan and Anthea, tells a tale of two prim pioneer girls in the mid-nineteenth century on an excursion in a horse-drawn cart, who spy on a cowboy in a creek shrinking his jeans to fit.

In the best tradition of Levi's commercials, both spots made expert use of music. The swimmer makes waves to the soundtrack of Dinah Washington's 'Mad About the Boy'; the pioneer girls look on to the accompaniment of a music track by Peter Lawlor. Originally, 'Creek' was shot to a track by US indie band The Smashing Pumpkins, but the band decided that they would rather have ideological credibility than oodles of cash and refused to allow their song to be used.

1992.10
Agency: **Bartle Bogle Hegarty**
Client: **Levi Strauss**
An inspired choice of a previously unremarkable Dinah Washington track and a crisp piece of pre-*American Beauty* observation of middle-class suburban America (lifted from the movie *The Swimmer* starring Burt Lancaster), made this Tarsem-directed film a classic. Again, it was by the creative team of Rooney Carruthers and Larry Barker; again, it didn't win at D&AD.

opposite

1994.11
Agency: **Bartle Bogle Hegarty**
Client: **Levi Strauss**
For many people the ultimate Levi's commercial, this project by Vaughan Arnell and Anthea Benton, known professionally as Vaughan and Anthea, (one of a growing number of directing duos in commercials in the nineties) took the campaign in a different direction, just when it seemed to be getting tired. At the same time, it also spawned another round of black and white spots.

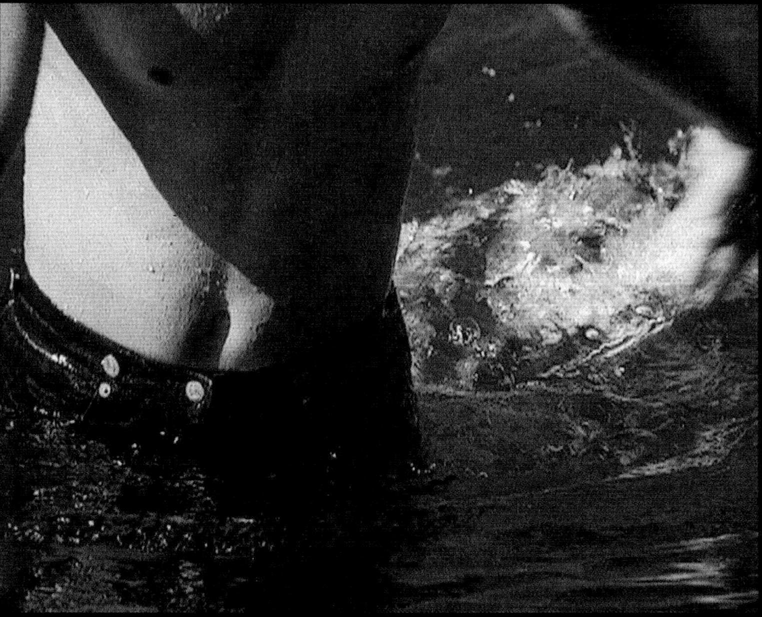

Big budget cinematography in TV commercials was always likely to face a backlash in the nineties, and it did. The backlash took two forms. One was a kind of DIY, low-budget approach. The other was anti-glamour, making commercials as real, gritty, edgy and ugly as possible. Volkswagen, which had already gone the glossy route with Kaye's 'God Bless the Child', won a Silver Award in 1996 for a dealership campaign called 'Exotic Locations' which the creative team at BMP DDB claimed cost nothing to make. Model cars, hand-drawn captions and a toilet seat featured in a commercial shot on a camcorder in director Mick Rudman's home.

'Exotic Locations' was the polar opposite of 'Twister', and Volkswagen followed up this *cinéma verité* approach with its 'Surprisingly Low Prices' campaign in which ordinary people walk into lamp posts or are cured of hiccups when they see how cheap a Polo is to buy. Directed by Paul Gay, these new VW commercials were very visually flat, with no tricks and few production values. The subliminal down-to-earth message was that by saving on the commercial, the brand gives you better value for money. Much the same thinking was behind an earlier campaign for Maxell tapes by Howell Henry Chaldecott Lury (HHCL), which featured a man on a busy road discarding a series of hand-drawn placards on which the (incorrect) lyrics to a Skids song are written.

1990.07
Agency:
Howell Henry Chaldecott Lury
Client: **Maxell**
A classic early HHCL commercial, with Tim Ashton as art director. Although the misheard lyrics in this commercial were the work of punk band The Skids, an even greater influence was Bob Dylan who used this idea of discarding the lyrics of the song as you go along in 'Subterranean Homesick Blues', one of the earliest promos in the late sixties.

1996.05
Agency: **BMP DDB Needham**
Client: **Volkswagen**
Director Mick Rudman excelled in the deadpan observational style he brought to Nick Gill and Tony Davidson's scripts for this VW commercial.

opposite

1998.07
Agency: **BMP DDB**
Client: **Volkswagen**
The flatness of this campaign, directed by Paul Gray, provided a clear point of difference from the cinematic gloss of much of the TV advertising that preceded it.

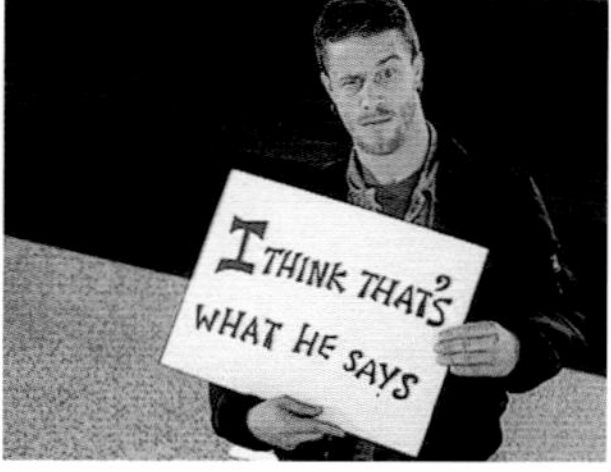

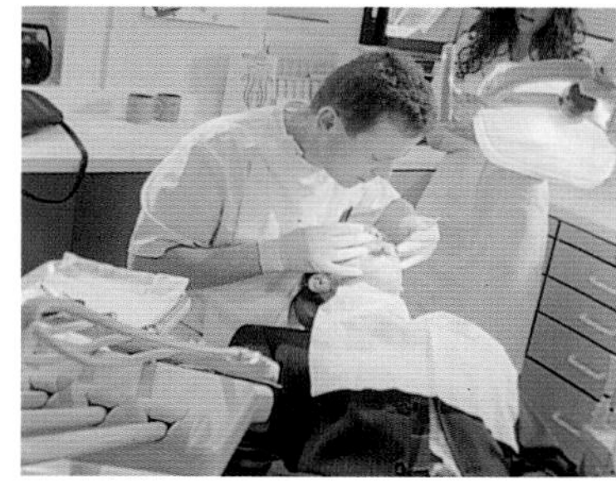

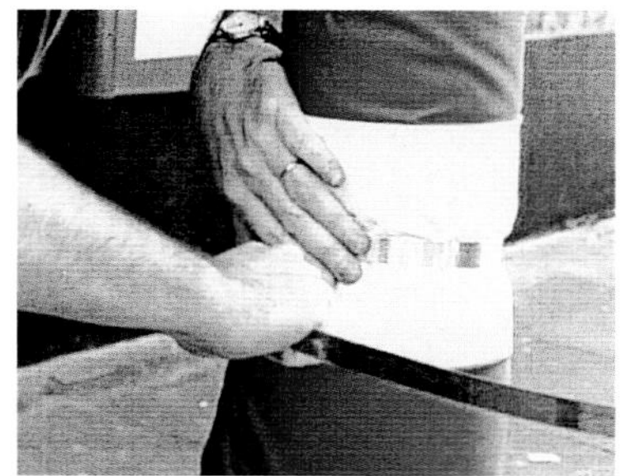

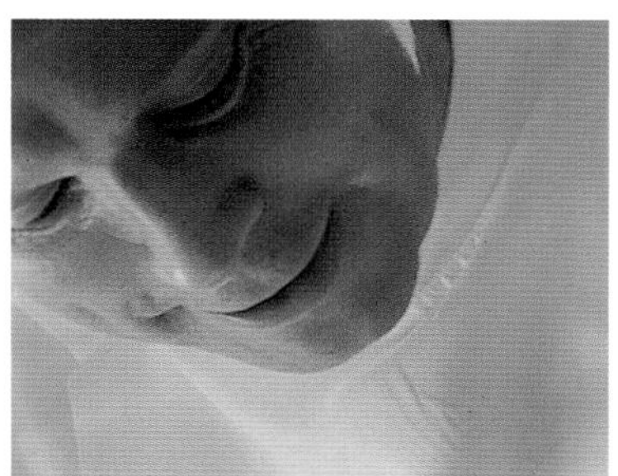

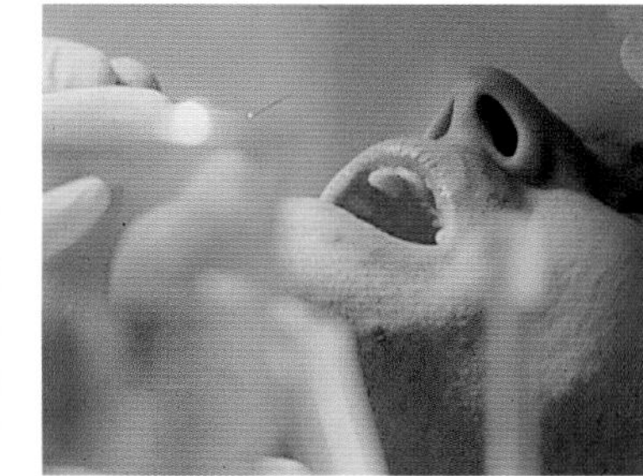

WEST PARK
ROAD
Polo L,
only
£8145.

Surprisingly ordinary prices.
www.volkswagen.co.uk

Polo,
from only
£7,990.

Surprisingly ordinary prices.
www.volkswagen.co.uk

Polo,
from only
£7,990.
Polo L

Surprisingly ordinary prices.
www.volkswagen.co.uk

Surprisingly ordinary prices.
www.volkswagen.co.uk

HHCL – a prominent member of the group of 'third wave' agencies – was also behind the school of ugly-edgy TV advertising in the nineties. The stand-out campaign that defined this approach was for Tango, in which a fat, bald 'Orange Man' slaps a guy in the street about the face to illustrate 'the bite and buzz of real oranges' in the Tango soft drink. The commercial, directed by Matt Forrest (whose Mad Bastard character for *Wired* had electrified TV credits in the late eighties), won a D&AD Silver in 1992 but ran into a storm of controversy from parents, teachers and doctors amid a craze of copycat face-slapping in playgrounds all over the UK.

The agency was forced to remake the ad, replacing the slap with a kiss from the orange genie. Critics argued that this lessened the impact of the 'hit' of oranges which was integral to the brand's message, but Tango was already on the same wavelength as its target audience. A later D&AD Award-winning commercial for Blackcurrant Tango – 'St George', in which a fat, ugly Tango executive takes issue with a French exchange student and bizarrely marches out to fight him in a boxing ring on the white cliffs of Dover – only served to reinforce the brand's cult appeal.

Other ugly-edgy TV work included a BBH commercial for Polaroid, in which a young Japanese salaryman photographs his bum (we presume) and sends it to his boss as a resignation note, and an AMV spot for Alka Seltzer addressing the subject of cannibalism in a film about two shipwrecked sailors ('Alka Seltzer, when you've eaten something you shouldn't have'). The darker side also defined D&AD-winning commercials for Taunton Cider (featuring the antics of an extremely rude Machiavellian duke), Golden Wonder (showing a cranky old walker pouring crisps down his pants), and Sony PlayStation (with its gallery of oddballs).

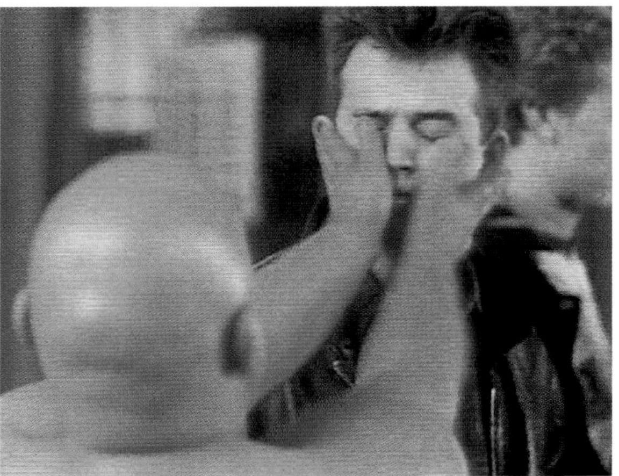

1992.11
Agency:
Howell Henry Chaldecott Lury
Client: **Britvic Soft Drinks**
Matt Forrest trained as an animator before he got into directing. Nowhere does the unique sense of exaggerated casting and comic timing it gave him come more into play than in this controversial and high-profile commercial introducing the Tango Orange Man.

1997.08
Agency:
Howell Henry Chaldecott Lury
Client: **Britvic Soft Drinks**
An amazingly jingoistic and chauvinistic piece of hoax communication, this commercial directed by Colin Gregg immediately caught on as a cult ad, like so many other Tango spots. The phoney exec also turned up on the D&AD Awards night to take the prize.

this page

1997.09
Agency: **Bartle Bogle Hegarty**
Client: **Polaroid**
Director Michel Gondry took John Gorse and Nick Worthington's deliberately low key idea of a Japanese salaryman having a sly poke at his female boss with a dodgy Polaroid, and makes you feel you've witnessed a slice of a Japanese-style Claude Chabrol film.

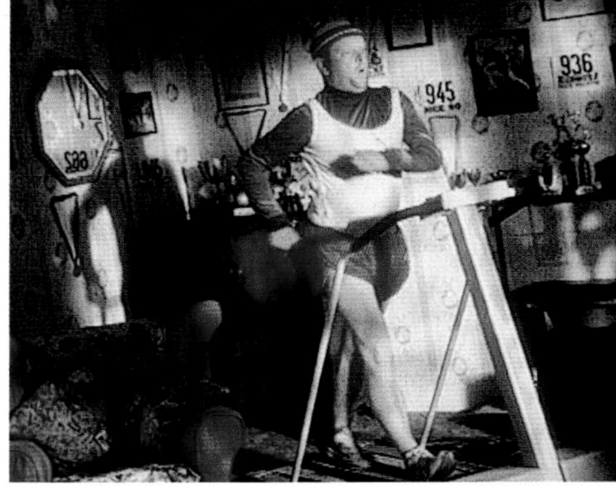

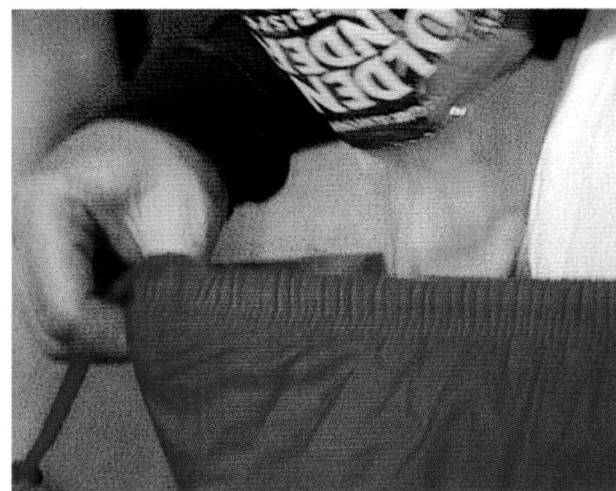

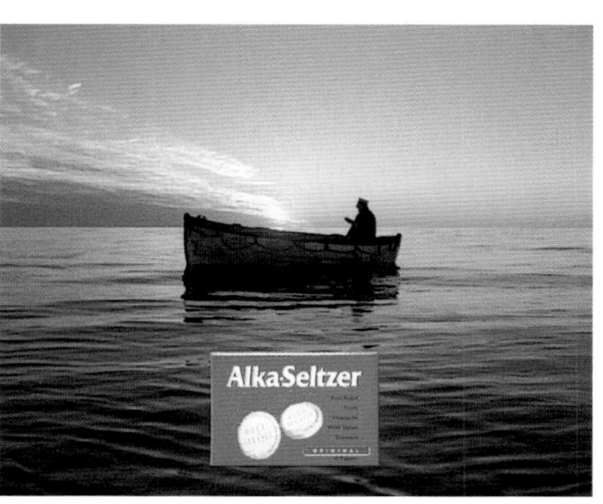

1996.06
Agency: **Ogilvy & Mather**
Client: **Golden Wonder**
The antidote to a thousand commercials for sports companies featuring perfect pecs, this O&M spoof for Golden Wonder crisps was ably directed by Chris Palmer who also had a fair hand in a number of the ads this spot parodies.

1997.10
Agency: **Abbott Mead Vickers.BBDO**
Client: **Bayer**
A locked off camera, a boat, two men and a cannibalism joke. This commercial for Alka Seltzer was simple and perfect for the over-stuffed Christmas TV schedule.

opposite

1995.11
Agency: **Cowan Kemsley Taylor**
Client: **Taunton Cider**
Cowan Kemsley Taylor scooped a Silver Award with this mesmerizing television commerical for the Taunton Cider Company.

1999.11
Agency: **TBWA**
Client: **Sony Computer Entertainment**
Clips of this commercial for the Sony PlayStation give the strangely haunting feel of obsession that Frank Budgen's portraits and Gabriel Faure's music conjure up. But, despite its length and inter-cutting from one disconcerting character to the next, the single image that lodges in the memory is of a freaky young Scottish boy saying just three words, 'and conquered wirrrlds...'.

That weirdness and bad manners in commercials could be commercially effective merely reflected the changing social attitudes of the time – even if moral guardians on BBC Radio 4 began complaining that society was going to the dogs. A manic, animated TV campaign by Still Price Lintas for Pepperami, a meat-based snack bar, presented the product as mischievous, anarchic and badly behaved, with the pay-off-line 'It's a bit of an animal'. Sales leapt immediately – up 42 per cent on existing patterns within weeks of the commercials breaking. So strong was the campaign that two leading supermarket chains – Sainsbury's and Tesco – withdrew their own-brand salami sticks from the shelves.

1994.12
Agency: **Still Price Lintas**
Client: **Van den Berghs & Jurgens**
The Pepperami 'Animal' campaign, directed by Ken Lidster and featuring the skills of modelmaker Andy Baker, not only revolutionized grocery advertising for Van den Berghs but showed that rudeness could sell.

1998.08
Agency: **Cliff Freeman & Partners**
Client: **Fox Network**
Cliff Freeman & Partners' savagely funny campaign for Fox Sports consistently scored at D&AD since the Awards opened its doors to work by agencies outside Britain. The pay-off in the Fox ads was that they show hockey-style violence in other sports and end with the lines like 'Billiards would be better if it were hockey.'

this page

1999.12
Agency: **Cliff Freeman & Partners**
Client: **outpost.com**
A hilariously funny campaign for an internet electronics retailer fronted by an avuncular, not-to-be-trusted figure in a leather chair, familiar from US TV series from the sixties.

However, it was American agencies, growing steadily in status and success at D&AD during the nineties, which began to define the genre of cruelty. Some UK agencies argued that this was because the American ad scene faced far fewer watchdogs and restrictions on what could be shown in a TV commercial, complaining that there was not a level playing field in the D&AD Awards. But there was no denying the originality of a US agency like Cliff Freeman & Partners, whose work for Fox Sports and outpost.com took savage humour to a new level.

Outpost.com, a campaign for an internet electronics store, in particular, shocked UK observers, who asked how creative ideas such as shooting unsuspecting gerbils from cannons, setting hungry wolves on marching high-school bands or tattooing children's foreheads in a nursery ever got past the regulators. The Cliff Freeman team argued in its defence that, for all the evident cruelty (one Fox Sports ad has a baseball fan being kicked in the face by a horse), its work was based on strong advertising ideas and not just style.

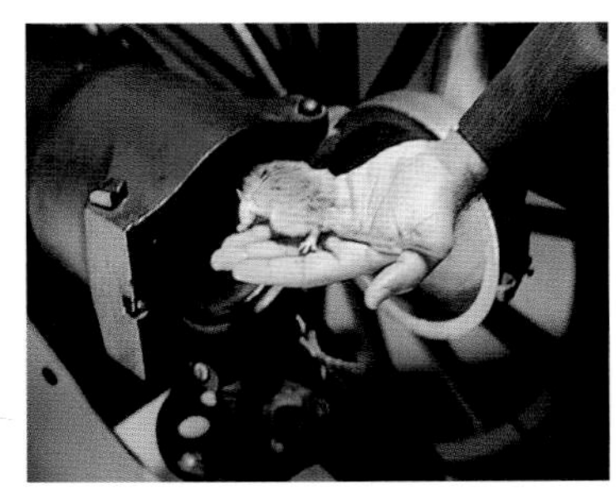

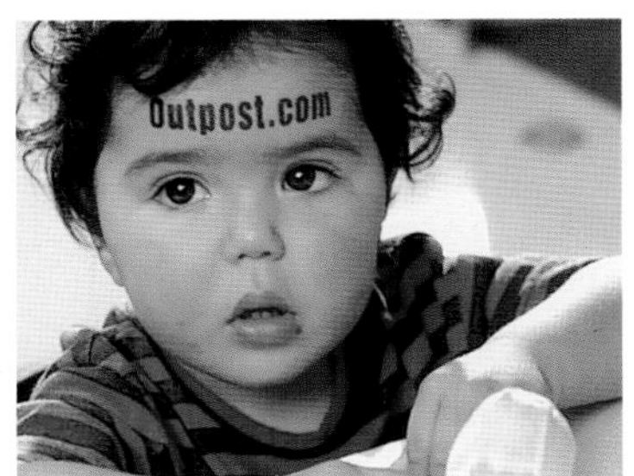

Other US agencies made a more conventional impact at D&AD in the nineties, in particular those contributing to a by now long-running tradition of outstanding public service and charity ads. New York agency Street Smart won a Silver in 1993 with its commercial for the Coalition for the Homeless, featuring homeless people singing lines from 'New York, New York'. The same year, a commercial by Saatchi & Saatchi Singapore produced one of the classic don't-drink-and-drive campaigns of the decade, based on an ultra simple idea – an increasingly blurred image of a city street at night shot through a series of glasses placed one in front of the other.

Social conscience work wasn't just confined to TV commercials. The pick of radio advertising in the nineties included memorable spots for Queen Elizabeth's Foundation for Disabled People ('Tapioca Pudding' by AMV) and Childline (a haunting piece on child abuse by TBWA in which a woman's voice discussing a sexual encounter morphs gradually into that of a young child). Both campaigns exhibited a sombre mood that was at odds with a governing advertising culture determined not to take things too seriously and increasingly reliant on pastiche as a way to communicate.

IT'S UP TO YOU
NEW YORK, NEW YORK.

COALITION FOR THE HOMELESS
695-8700

WOMAN

(Using a technique similar to morphing, the woman's voice slowly changes to that of a child's during the course of the commercial)

FV1: (mature woman) he dimmed the lights and, smiling,led me by the hand to the bedroom. Slowly,

FV2: (slightly younger)...he lay me down on the bed. His eyes pierced my skin. As he caressed my cheek, I could feel his breath...

FV3: (young teenager)...hot on my neck. His hand moved down towards my top, so lightly I could hardly feel it.

FV4: (10 year old girl) I breathed fast as he undid my shirt. He touched me and whispered in my ear...

FV5: (5 year old)...don't tell mommy.

FVO: Sexual abuse can scar you for life. Get help, call Childline on 08000 555555.

1993.06
Agency: **Street Smart**
Client: **Coalition for the Homeless**
Such a simple idea. Take a popular song that extorts the charms of a city. Then get the people who have least access to those charms to sing about them. The resulting paradox creates instant revelation.

1996.07
Agency: **Hunt Lascaris TBWA**
Client: **Childline**
Handled without restraint this radio ad could have turned out at best cartoonish, at worst vulgar and crass. Fortunately, the production matches the subtle idea.

1995.03
Agency: **Abbott Mead Vickers.BBDO**
Client: **Queen Elizabeth's Foundation for Disabled People**
In this radio commercial and an equally inspirational television ad, the achievements of severely disabled people were brought home in powerful fashion.

1993.07
Agency:
Saatchi & Saatchi, Singapore
Client: **Traffic Police**
Bill Bernbach's direction 'Keep it Simple' could have no better illustration than this powerful drink drive ad. A Singapore agency winning Gold at D&AD? It just showed how the creative business was becoming truly global in the nineties.

TAPIOCA PUDDING

My name is Andy Dixon and I don't like tapioca pudding. For the first 22 years of my life this was not a problem. I would just tell people.

Then I fell off a motorway bridge.

The fall left me virtually blind, spastic in all my limbs and speechless. In the hospital the nurses did everything they could for me and I was very grateful. Except at lunchtime. That's when they gave me tapioca pudding. A lot of tapioca pudding.

The only thing I could do to let them know I didn't like it was to spit it out. The doctors took my spitting as a sign of behavioural problems and classified me as a difficult patient.

Fortunately, after two years in various hospitals I was given one last chance. I was sent to a centre run by Queen Elizabeth's Foundation for Disabled People for assessment and rehabilitation.

They fixed me up with the specially adapted machine which is allowing me to talk to you now. I am tapping out letters using a pressure pad under my chin. It's a painfully slow process but it means I can do two things.

I can ask you to support QEFDP in any way you can. And I can say I don't like tapioca pudding.

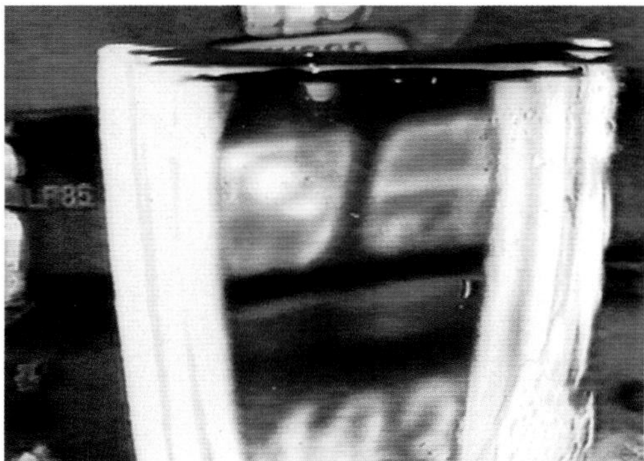

EACH DRINK YOU
HAVE BEFORE DRIVING
IMPAIRS
YOUR JUDGEMENT.

Some of the pastiche on offer was very beautiful and sophisticated indeed, as in a commercial for Guess Jeans by Paul Marciano Advertising, starring Harry Dean Stanton as a Chandleresque private eye in a *film noir* tale of entrapment. Equally compelling was a D&AD Silver winning campaign for Stella Artois by Lowe Howard-Spink based on the Provence setting of the famous French film *Jean de Florette*. In 'Les Nouvelles Chaussures', a charming tale which gives a twist to the cinematic myth of the red shoes, a young man toils to buy a pair for his grandmother, only to be distracted by the pleasures of Belgium's famous lager. A Stella Artois beer mat to patch the sole of her existing shoes must suffice instead.

The decade began with a mildly humorous *Dambusters* spoof for Carling Black Label by WCRS and included a GGT campaign for Red Rock Cider which starred Leslie Nielsen of *Naked Gun* and was in the style of US TV series *Police Squad*, making it in effect a pastiche of a pastiche. Wieden + Kennedy's work for a new American beer, Black Star, went even further by inventing an entirely fictional (and convincing) history of the brew's advertising.

But perhaps the outstanding piece of pastiche in the nineties was a series of Doritos sponsorship credits for ITV's Movie Premieres, which won a D&AD Gold Award in 1997. Written by Andy McLeod and art directed by Richard Flintham of BMP DDB, the idents featured a series of movie star stills, including John Wayne, Charlie Chaplin, Bruce Lee and Lassie the dog, each with a live-action mouth superimposed munching a pack of Doritos. Actor John Thomson from British television sketch show *The Fast Show* supplied the voices. But then this was just one example of the 'cultural crossover' between TV advertising and the adjacent fields of cinema, comedy and computer games in the nineties. As in previous decades, agencies continued to 'sample' anything that might add to the popularity of the product being promoted.

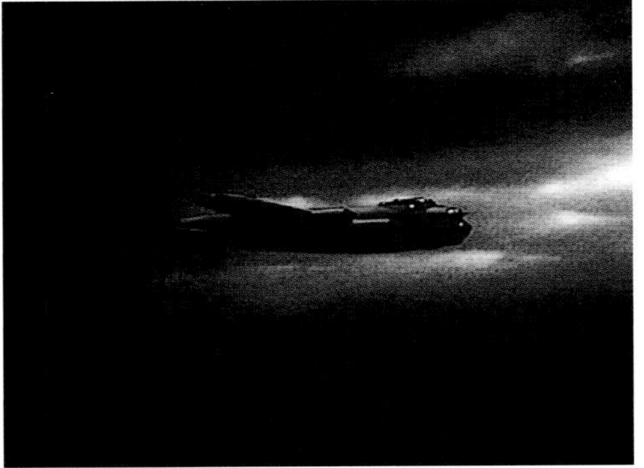

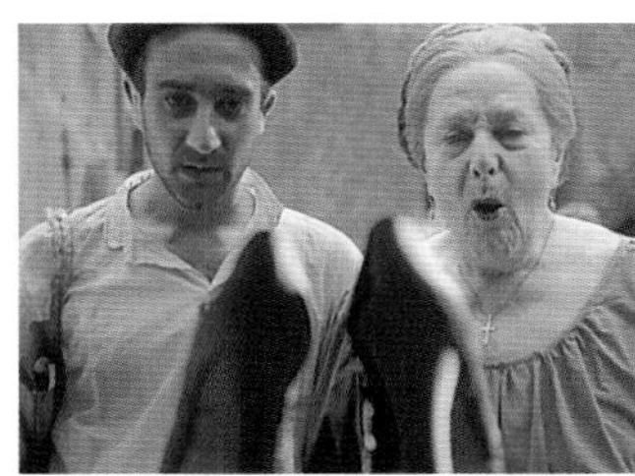

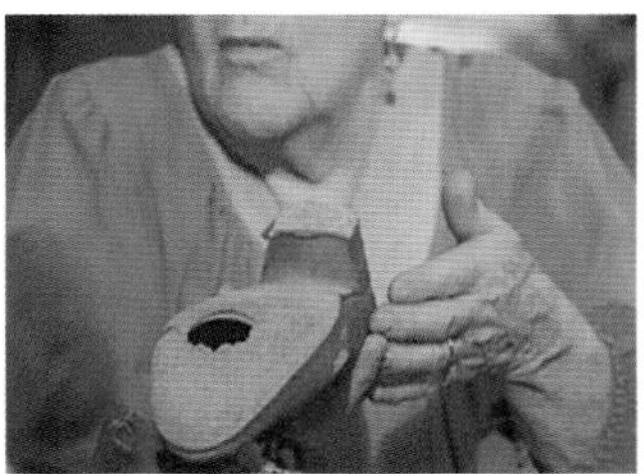

 1990.08
Agency:
WCRS Mathews Marcantonio
Client: **Bass**
Director Roger Woodburn had won many awards working with John Webster over the years. But here, in a *Dambusters* parody written by the creative team of Kes Grey and Jonathan Greenalgh for Carling Black Label lager, he created sets and art direction that surpassed even his best.

this page

1997.11
Agency: **Lowe Howard-Spink**
Client: **Whitbread Beer Company**
When Vaughan and Anthea worked together as directors, it was always difficult to say who did what. But the fantastic eye for fashion detail that came from Anthea Benton's training gave the French costumes in this Stella Artois spot, set in Provence, added authenticity.

1991.08
Agency: **GGT**
Client: **Taunton Cider Company**
Leslie Nielsen's ability to effect a pompous exterior makes his pratfalls so unexpected. On this shoot for Red Rock Cider it apparently took three days to find out that Nielsen was behind the whoopee cushions left all over the set.

1996.08
Agency: **Paul Marciano Advertising**
Client: **Guess?**
Commissioned directly by the owner of Guess Jeans, producer Laura Gregory pulled off the coup of casting Hollywood stars Juliette Lewis and Harry Dean Stanton in this commercial, and Andy Morahan made a slice of celluloid magic that oozed style.

1993.08
Agency: **Wieden + Kennedy**
Client: **McKenzie River Corporation**
Directed by Alex Proyas, this Wieden + Kennedy campaign invented an entirely fictional history for an American beer, thus managing to capture the warmth engendered by newsreel nostalgia while launching something new.

opposite

1997.12
Agency: **BMP DDB**
Client: **Walkers Snack Food**
Sponsorship credits tended to be given to juniors until Richard Flintham and Andy McLeod took these on for Doritos and made them the sexy, fun end of the business.

DORITOS

A BSB Dorland commercial for Woolworths, for example, borrowed from the Super Mario Brothers to create a scenario in which a youth on his way to Woolies to buy a computer game encounters an obstacle course of giant rats, umbrella-wielding grannies and axe-swinging workmen, all intent on blocking his progress. A charity ad for comedy telethon Red Nose Day sampled British comedian Adrian Edmonson, while a BMP DDB campaign for John Smith's Bitter relied on the talents of deadpan comic Jack Dee, a rising star in the early nineties. A Heat Electric campaign by GGK London was based on the Academy Award-winning *Creature Comforts* success of Aardman Animations' Nick Park.

Aardman Animations' trademark soft-modelling animation also featured in a music video for Parlophone Records, with those famous characters Wallace and Gromit making a guest appearance in a likeable promo for a duet between Tina Turner and Barry White. The project, 'Never in Your Wildest Dreams', was one of only a few pop promos which won a D&AD Silver Award in the nineties. Generally, this creative discipline failed to sufficiently define its own identity alongside a TV commercial sector voraciously borrowing not only its visual language but its directors, too.

There was some strong promo work, such as the sci-fi 'Scream' directed by Mark Romanek for Michael and Janet Jackson and a disturbing film by Chris Cunningham for Aphex Twin, featuring demonic kids who all have Aphex Twin (Richard D James) faces, and who terrorize a housing estate. But as the general approach moved away from simply capturing the artist's performance on film and much of the imagery became bigger than the band itself, the entire creative discipline became a kind of training ground for commercial directors either to experiment with digital effects or to make the kind of social comment not permitted in mainstream TV advertising. This explains why award-winning commercials director Jonathan Glazer made a bizarre promo for UNKLE in 1999, in which a defiant pedestrian is repeatedly knocked down, as a metaphor for man overcoming the material world.

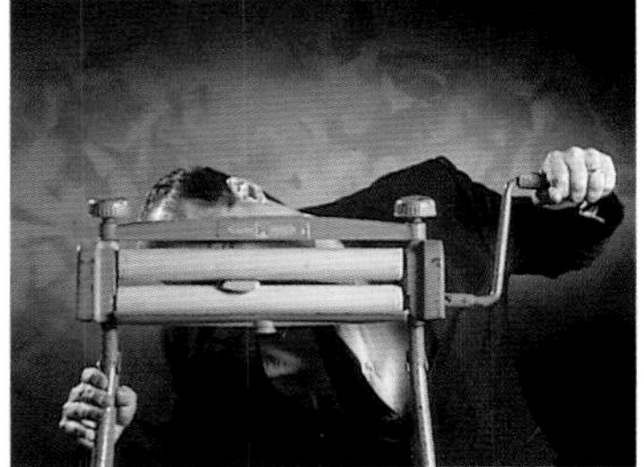

1992.12
Agency: **Paul Weiland Film Company**
Client: **Charity Projects**
Comedian Adrian Edmonson starred in this Paul Weiland spot for the Red Nose Day TV fundraiser.

1994.13
Agency: **BMP DDB Needham**
Client: **Courage**
The unexpected bonus of these ads for John Smith's Bitter was the popularity of the penguins. They eclipsed even Britain's then most popular comic, Jack Dee.

this page

1991.09
Agency: **GGK London**
Client: **Electricity Association**
GGK came from nowhere to top the creative rankings with this one idea. Unfortunately, they disappeared just as quickly when the campaign ended. The ads were made in reverse – the interviewees were taped and the animation created to match the tapes.

1997.13
Production company:
Aardman Animations
Client: **Parlophone Records**
Tina Turner got the Aardman Animations treatment in a lively promo for 'Never in Your Wildest Dreams'.

1993.09
Agency: **BSB Dorland**
Client: **Woolworths**
Richard Dean broke out of the video director's box with this clever pastiche of computer games for Woolworths.

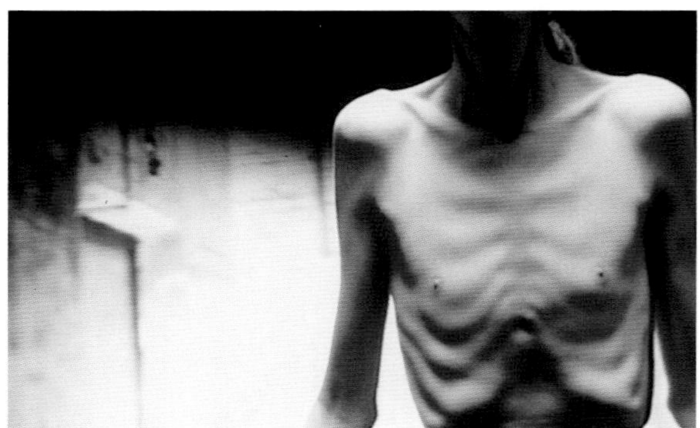

 1998.09
Director: **Chris Cunningham**
Client: **Warp Records**
In Cunningham's promo for Aphex Twin, demonic kids with ageing faces terrorized the inhabitants of a local housing estate. The pop video discipline in the nineties became a platform for (often controversial) social comment and visual experiment that the commercial constraints of TV advertising would not permit.

1996.09
Director: **Mark Romanek**
Client: **Epic**
Mark Romanek's 'Scream' promo for Michael and Janet Jackson was a glossy and polished piece of work for a mainstream global act, designed to be lapped up by the MTV generation.

opposite

1999.13
Director: **Jonathan Glazer**
Client: **Island Records**
Jonathan Glazer's UNKLE video was banned in the UK by MTV, which described 'Rabbit in Your Headlights' as one of the most disturbing films it had seen. MTV demanded that the collisions between the demented pedestrian (French actor Denis Lavant) and the cars be pixillated before the video could be screened. But even after Glazer acceded to these demands, the ban remained, provoking outrage. Glazer argued: 'What they are saying is anyone on the edge of society shouldn't be seen on television. MTV's definition of the real world is four models living together in a luxury flat.'

E897 FPH

The savagery of Glazer and Cunningham's bleak videos was matched in music graphics, especially in a startling poster of a giant bug for Massive Attack by photographer Nick Knight and in a set of grotesquely surreal images for The Beautiful South by illustrator David Cutter. Both won D&AD Silvers. But graphic designers didn't need the excuse of a music industry client to make their own journey to the heart of darkness.

There was a general reaction against the soft-edged decoration of much graphic design of the previous decade, a mood summed up by awards for illustrator David Hughes' edgy work on a large-format picture book of *Othello* designed by The Chase and a business card designed by Studio Myerscough for an architectural historian (featuring a graffiti 'Joe' scrawled on a traffic bollard). When new Pentagram partner Angus Hyland produced a pocket-sized version of the Canons [see page 375], the covers were full of the dark, brooding, end-of-the-world imagery that not only suited the subject matter so well but also reflected the prevailing mood.

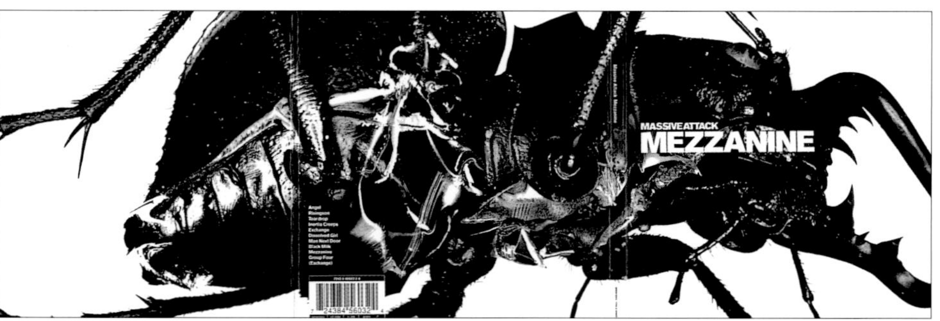

1999.14
Design group: **Tom Hingston Studio**
Clients: **Circa, Virgin Records**
Robert Del Naja and Tom Hingston contacted photographer Nick Knight on the back of some fashion shots Knight had done, where models had bits of insect growing out of their bodies. The result, for Massive Attack's *Mezzanine* album, is one of the most memorable music industry images of the nineties.

opposite

1993.10
Illustrator: **David Cutter**
Clients: **The Beautiful South, Go Discs**
Savage and surreal, David Cutter's stunning illustrations for the album *0898* seem strangely at odds with the soft rock style of the band being promoted, The Beautiful South.

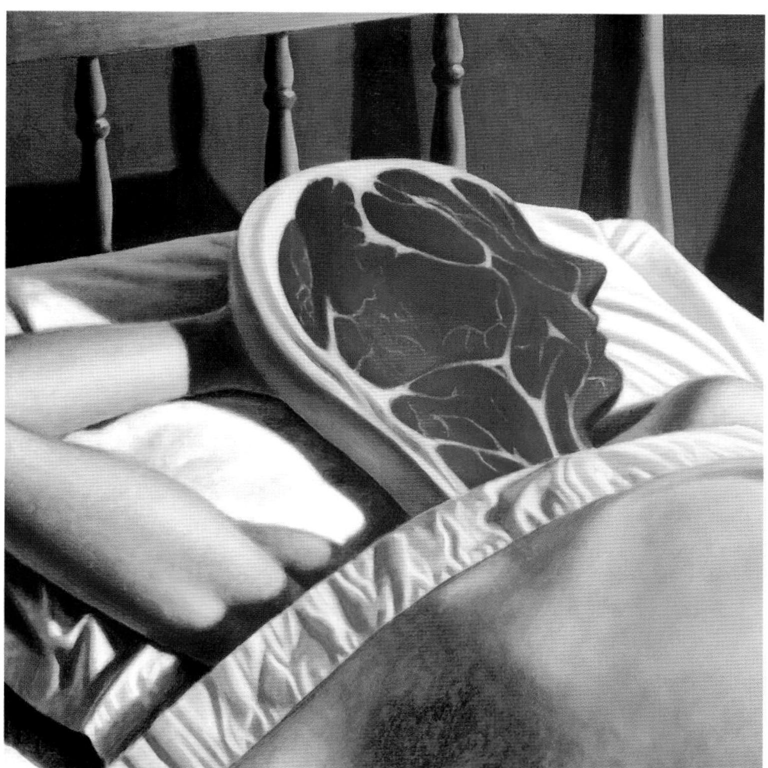

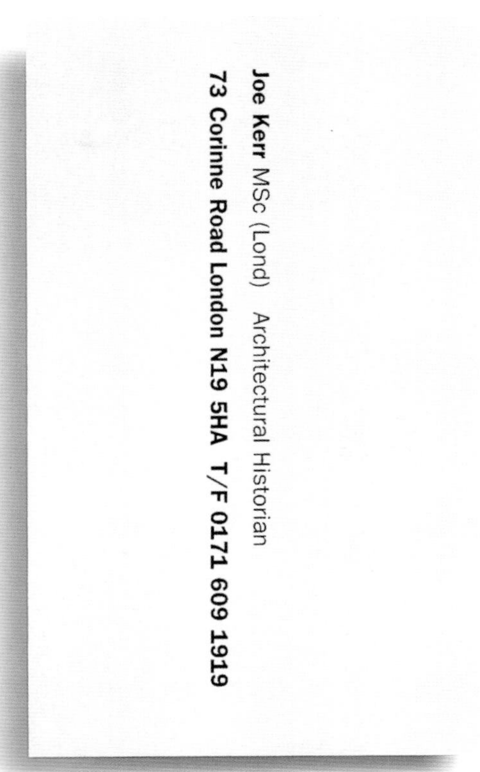

Joe Kerr MSc (Lond) Architectural Historian
73 Corinne Road London N19 5HA T/F 0171 609 1919

1998.10
Design group: **Studio Myerscough**
Client: **Joe Kerr**
Designed for an architectural historian, this business card captured the new gritty mood in graphics at D&AD. 'It was so fresh, so simple, so witty,' observed jury foreman Derek Birdsall. 'We all wished we'd done it.'

1999.15
Design group: **The Chase**
Client: **Alibaba Verlag**
Illustrator David Hughes captured the dark, angry undertones of Shakespeare's *Othello* in this illustrated book, art directed by Ben Casey.

opposite

1999.16
Design group: **Pentagram Design**
Client: **Canongate Books**
Writer and editor Lewis Blackwell once described Angus Hyland as an 'emotional classicist'. Anyone who can put nuclear explosions, winding roads and dead fish on the cover of the Canons deserves that title. When D&AD voted this project in, wags said that at last the Bible was going in the Bible.

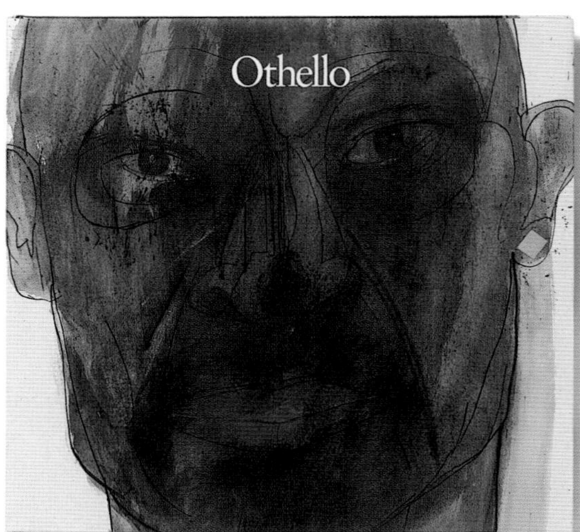

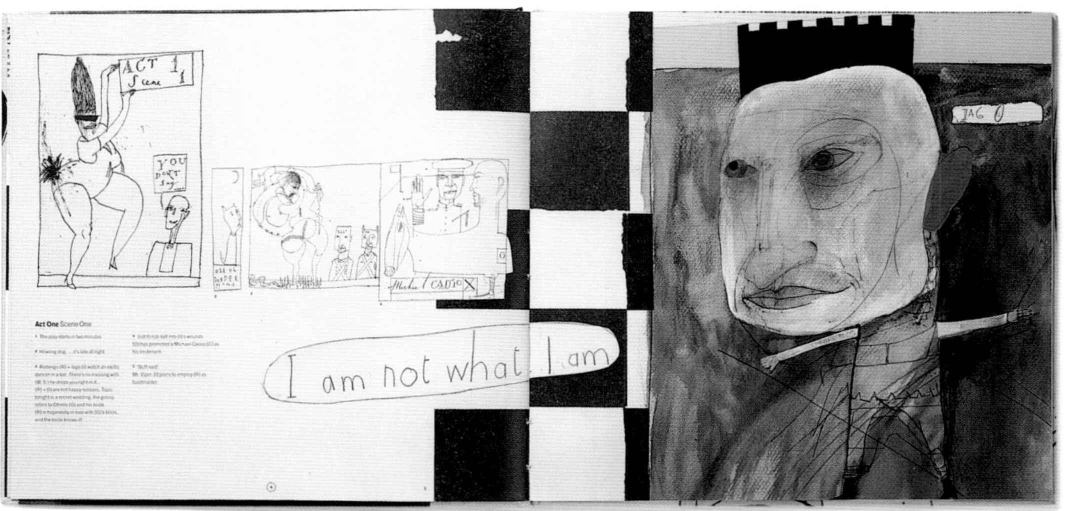

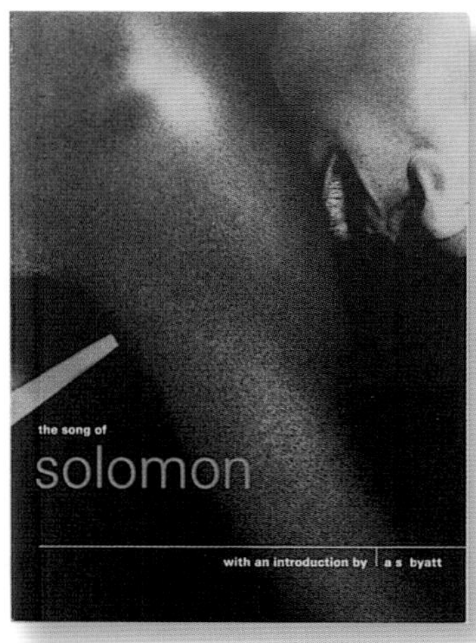
the song of
solomon
with an introduction by | a s byatt

the gospel according to
matthew
with an introduction by | a n wilson

the gospel according to
john
with an introduction by | blake morrison

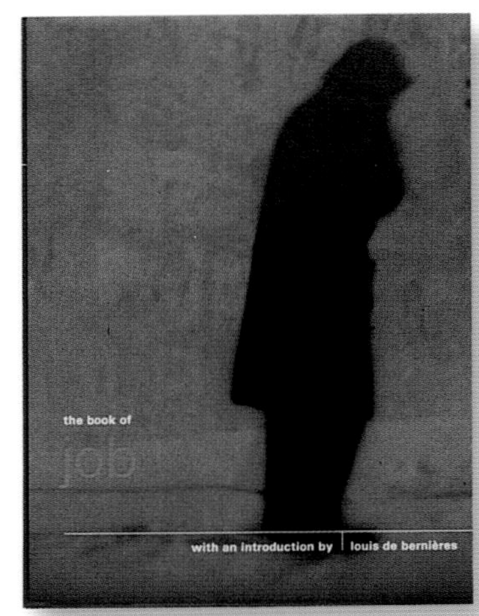
the book of
job
with an introduction by | louis de bernières

the first book of moses, called
genesis
with an introduction by | steven rose

proverbs
with an introduction by | charles johnson

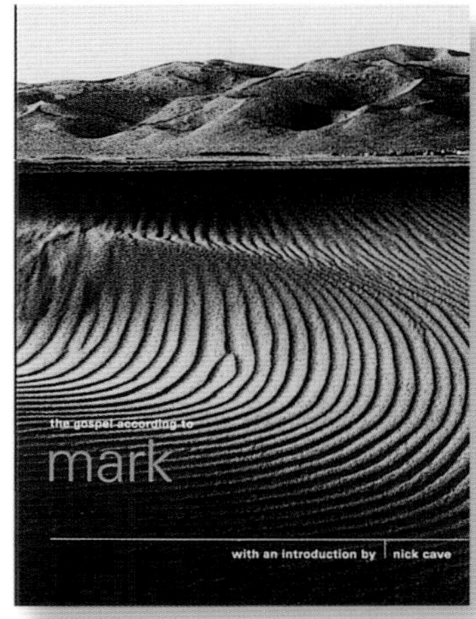
the gospel according to
mark
with an introduction by | nick cave

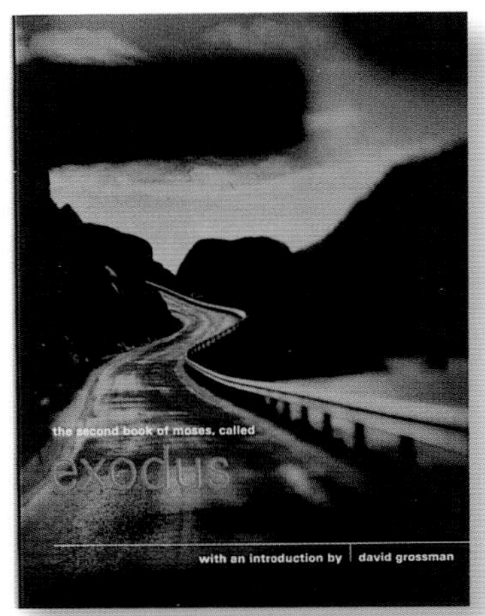
the second book of moses, called
exodus
with an introduction by | david grossman

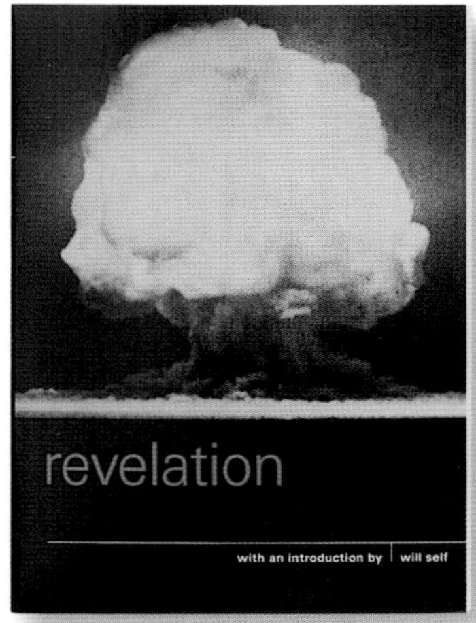
revelation
with an introduction by | will self

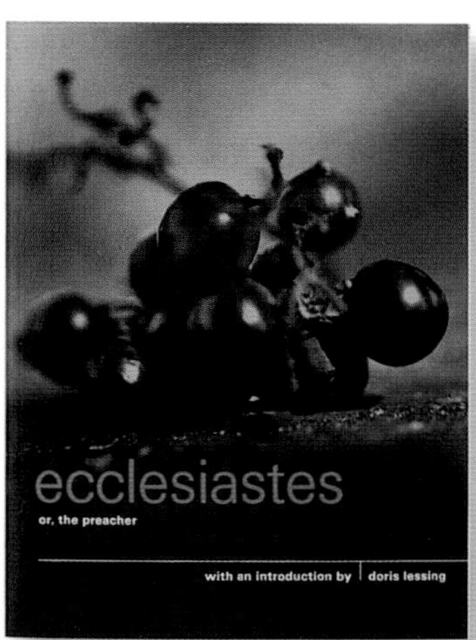
ecclesiastes
or, the preacher
with an introduction by | doris lessing

the gospel according to
with an introduction by | richard holloway

the epistles of paul the apostle to the
corinthians
with an introduction by | fay weldon

The spirit of Dutch graphic designer Gert Dumbar, so dominant in the eighties, lived on in the new decade. Not only did the great man himself immediately win a Silver Award for his corporate identity programme for the Dutch Post Office, the PTT, but other Netherlands firms like Koeweiden-Postma and UNA Amsterdam also got among the prizes as D&AD graphic design juries fell in love with all things from across the North Sea.

Meanwhile, the group of young designers Dumbar trained at the Royal College of Art began to attract attention. Notable Dumbar acolytes to show up strongly at D&AD included Siobhan Keaney, who created stylish projects for product designers Seymour Powell and the API Corporation, and Sean Perkins whose design firm North rebranded the Royal Automobile Club (RAC). The RAC had been losing ground in the competitive arena of motoring services. Its new image required design and advertising to work together, in the same way as Orange had done. North worked closely with agency BDDH to reposition the RAC as modern, dynamic and equipped to face future motoring challenges. The Royal Crown was removed and a modular design introduced, with patrol cars decked out in bright orange.

1990.09
Design group: **Koeweiden-Postma**
Client: **Frascati Theatre**
Koeweiden-Postma arrived at D&AD after Gert Dumbar's trailblazing. This poster advertising a theatre festival was huge and the title was foil blocked which gave it a beautifully rich quality.

1992.13
Design group: **UNA Amsterdam**
Client: **UNA Amsterdam**
The UNA diary was one in a long line of stylish self-promotional diaries produced by the Amsterdam-based group.

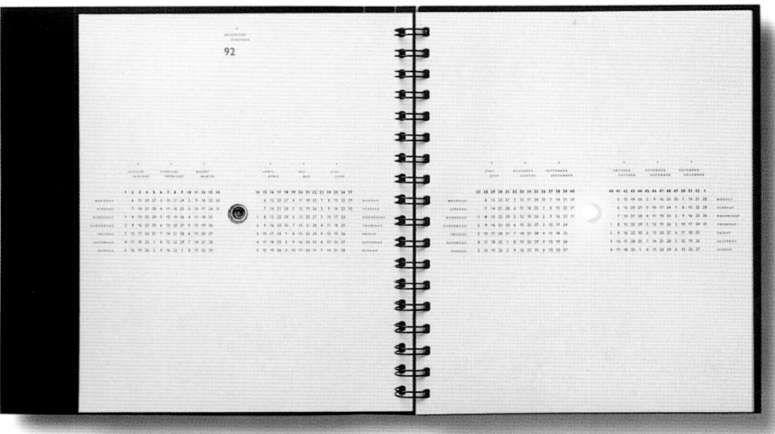

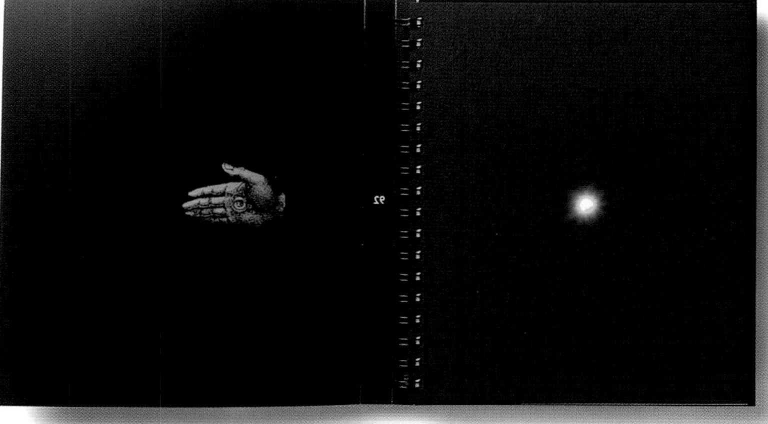

1990.10
Design group: **Studio Dumbar**
Client: **PTT Nederland NV**
From Studio Dumbar's 'mature' period, when the group started to get major jobs from government organizations like the Dutch Post Office and the Dutch Police. As an identity programme, PTT might look revolutionary, but in a country with Piet Zwart in its history, Dumbar's work follows logically within a context of radical public sector graphics.

1998.11
Design group: **North**
Client: **RAC**
Sean Perkins and Simon Browning studied at the RCA during Dumbar's tenure before later starting their own firm. It was quite a big deal for the RAC to give such a prestigious job to a small design group, and the new look repositioned the motoring organization as more contemporary.

1990.11
Designers: **Siobhan Keaney, Karen Wilks**
Client: **API Corporation**
Keaney did a placement at Studio Dumbar in the eighties. On returning to the UK she set about producing her own London take on the Dutch master's style. These are spreads from an annual report for a Japanese pharmaceutical company.

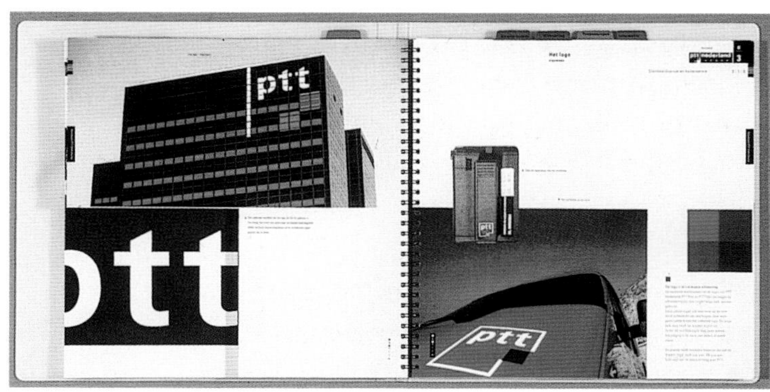

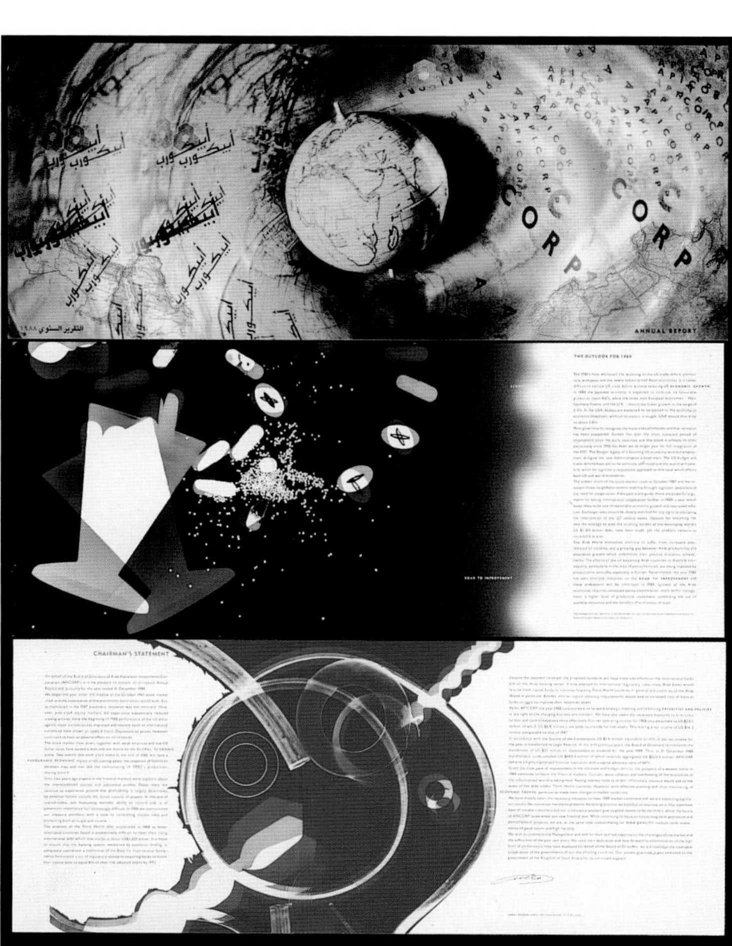

So powerful was Dumbar's presence that even the project that vied with the PTT and RAC as the outstanding corporate identity programme of the decade – Carroll Dempsey & Thirkell's (CDT) work for English National Opera (ENO) – owed something to his influence, especially his technique of modelmaking and stage photography. Design director Mike Dempsey not only created a classic logo for an opera company – the 'O' forms an open mouth – but his series of Dumbar-esque posters for ENO productions, finely balanced between modernity and tradition, generated a new visual language that the company was able to make its own.

The ENO programme won a D&AD Silver Award in 1992, but its quality and impact heralded a false dawn for corporate identity in the new decade. A tabloid newspaper furore over British Telecom's new 'piper' identity by Wolff Olins the previous year, focusing on the seemingly large amounts of money spent on small logo changes, had poisoned the well for other large public companies thinking of rebranding. The corporate design make-over became a hunted species in the nineties, with precious few decent examples to reward. Only new identities for low-cost airline Go (a bright and modern effort by Wolff Olins) and British Airways (a brave but doomed attempt by Newell & Sorrell to turn the pinstriped carrier into a cosmopolitan 'citizen of the world' using a global array of tailfin artists) showed up on D&AD's radar. Neither was deemed worthy of a major award.

Beyond Dumbar's immediate sphere of influence, the British graphic design scene splintered into two distinct camps in the nineties. In one corner were the 'style counsellors' who were very much of the moment and whose creative backgrounds were in music and fashion. In the other corner were the 'problem solvers' whose penchant for witty and timeless ideas could have belonged to any period in D&AD's history. There was a clash of cultures between the two camps.

EN
O

1992.14
Design group:
Carroll Dempsey & Thirkell
Client: **English National Opera**

1999.17
Agency: **Wolff Olins**
Client: **Go Fly**
This identity for low-cost airline Go was nominated for Silver. Within three years Go would be sold to its biggest rival, easyJet.

this page

1992.15
Design group:
Carroll Dempsey & Thirkell
Client: **English National Opera**
Mike Dempsey and his team of recruits from St Martins (including Fernando Gutiérrez and Barbro Ohlson) set about the identity programme for ENO with modernist relish. The new image featured a logo with the 'O' representing an opera singer's open mouth, two typefaces, functionalist grids and staged or reverse processed photography.

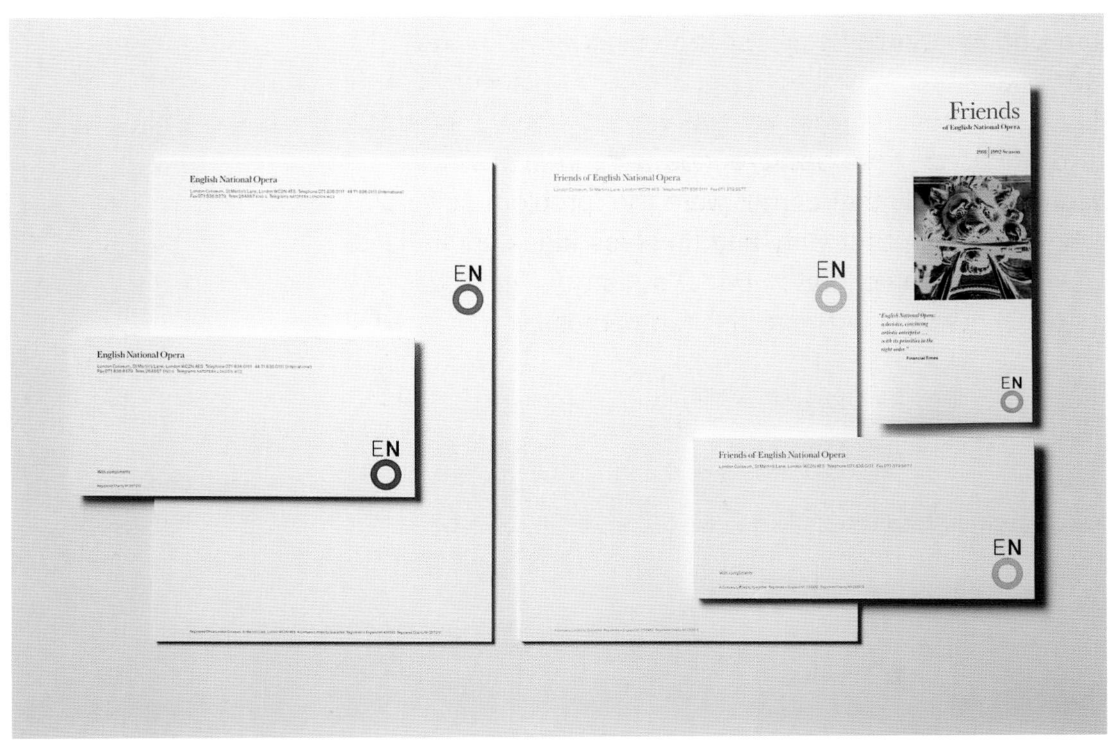

While the 'problem solvers' refined the perfect execution of the clever idea for clients as diverse as the Royal Mail and a toilet cubicle manufacturer, D&AD Award-winning projects by such designers as David James (for Big Life Records), Mark Farrow (for the Cream nightclub), Aboud Sodano (for fashion designer Paul Smith) and Stephanie Nash and Anthony Michael (for Circa Records) showed the stylists hard at work, looking minimal and cool in one crowded corner of the market.

The flagship graphic style project of the decade was a poster designed by Stylorouge for *Trainspotting*, Channel 4's prize-winning 1996 film based on Irvine Welsh's 1993 novel about a nihilistic gang of young Edinburgh villains. *Trainspotting* was much imitated but itself owed plenty to an arch-modernist language defined by Mark Farrow, whose collaboration with the Pet Shop Boys (featuring a beautifully shot straitjacket on 'Yesterday, When I Was Mad') continued to win accolades at D&AD.

1995.12
Design group:
Michael Nash Associates
Client: **Circa Records**
Cool music packaging graphics from a design team destined to shake up packaging design for Harvey Nichols.

1996.10
Designers:
Mark Farrow, Rob Petrie, Phil Sims
Client: **Cream**
Although the designers' relationship ended in acrimony, this CD set they produced stands the test of time.

opposite

1995.13
Design group:
David James Associates
Client: **Big Life Records**
David James recycled conceptual art beautifully in this set of music packaging for dance band System 7.

1995.14
Design group: **Farrow**
Client: **Pet Shop Boys**

1995.15
Design group: **Farrow**
Client: **Pet Shop Boys**

This CD and poster scheme featured the photographic talents of Richard Burbridge.

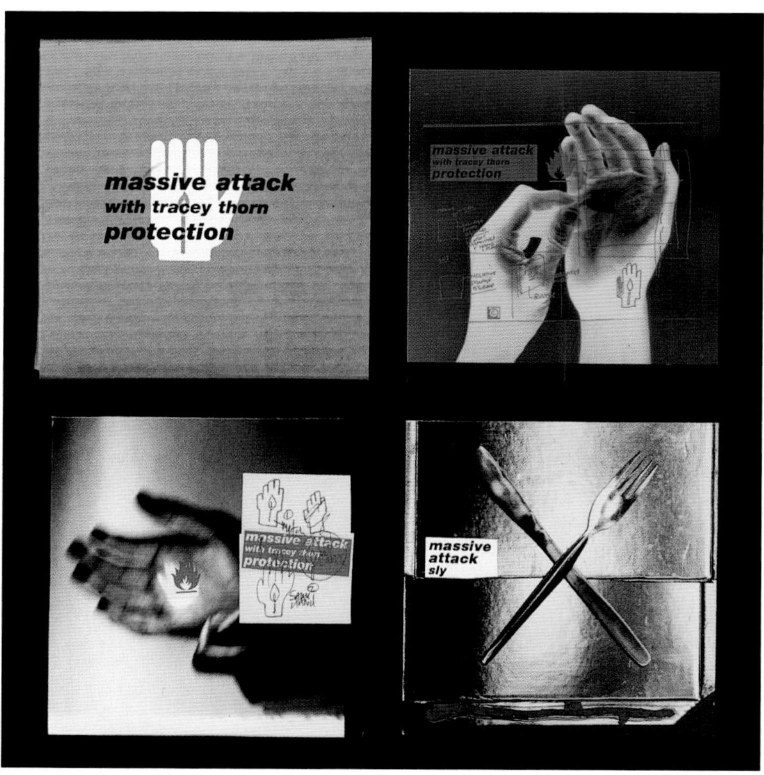

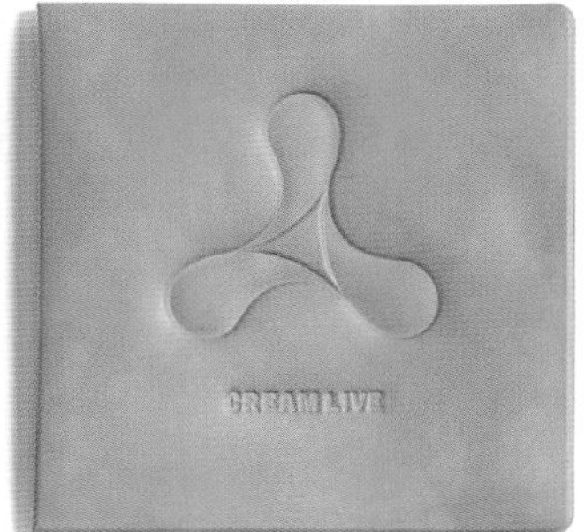

SYSTEM 7 POINT 3 FIRE ALBUM
MYSTERIOUS TRAVELLER
ALPHA WAVE COLTRANE SIRENES
OVERVIEW BATUKAU JUPITER
DR LIVINGSTONE I
RADIATE
GLIDING ON DUO-TONE CURVES

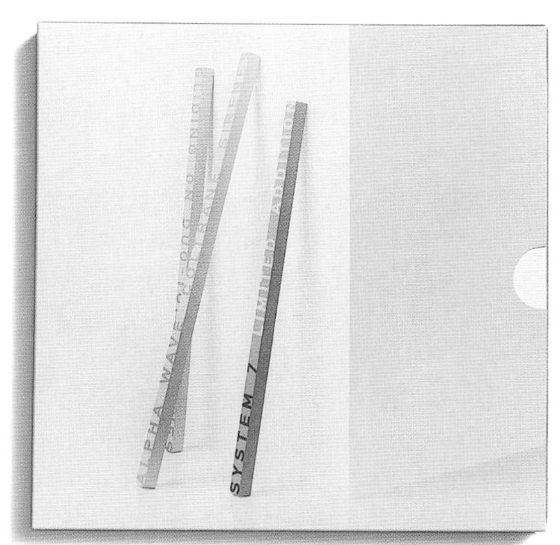
ALPHA WAVE
SYSTEM 7

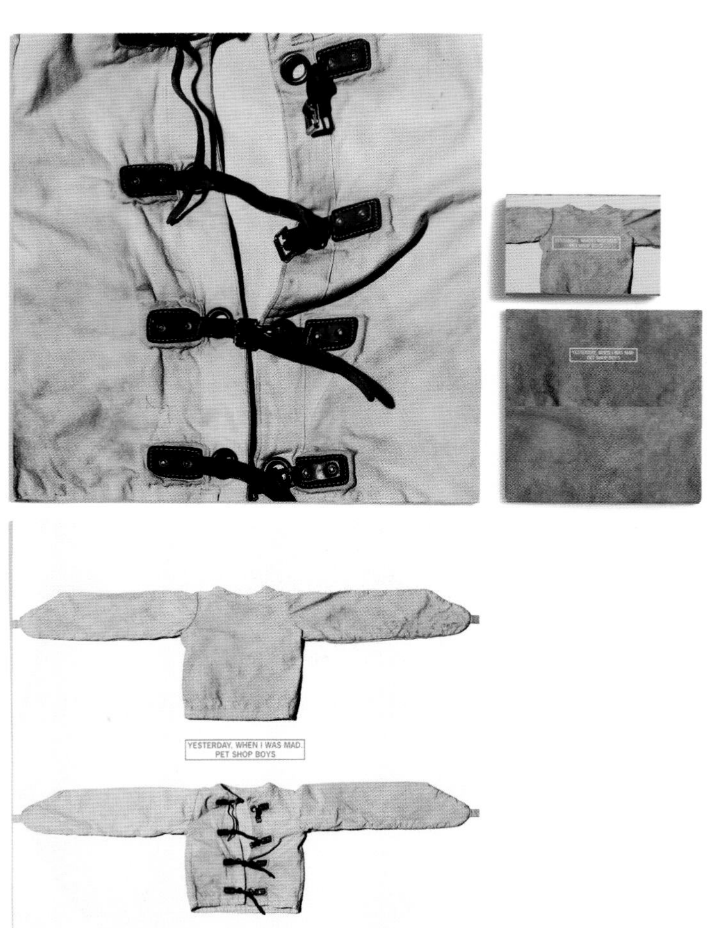
YESTERDAY, WHEN I WAS MAD.
PET SHOP BOYS

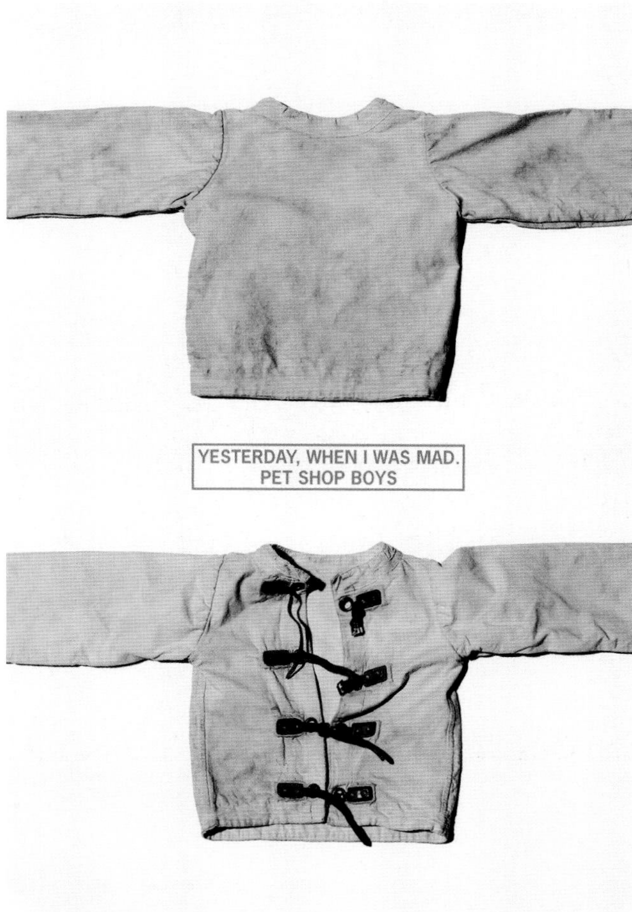
YESTERDAY, WHEN I WAS MAD.
PET SHOP BOYS

Trainspotting 18

THIS FILM IS EXPECTED TO ARRIVE...

23:02:96

From the team that brought you Shallow Grave

1996.11
Design group: **Stylorouge**
Client: **Polygram Filmed Entertainment**
The long-awaited film adaptation of the cult Irving Welsh novel announced itself with a film poster that looked nothing like a film poster. Its fashion editorial style, photography and bright orange graphics gave it the look of a nightclub flyer, and the much-imitated posters soon adorned a million bedroom walls. Stylorouge cleverly recycled all the modern design tics of the era – visible grids, boxed information panels, bold sans serif type, information graphics vernacular. For once, a film and its poster were as good as each other.

opposite

1991.10
Design group: **Cartlidge Levene**
Client: **Wordsearch**
Eye magazine became a forum for the graphic design plurality of the nineties but the look of its promotional poster belonged to one particular camp of communication stylists.

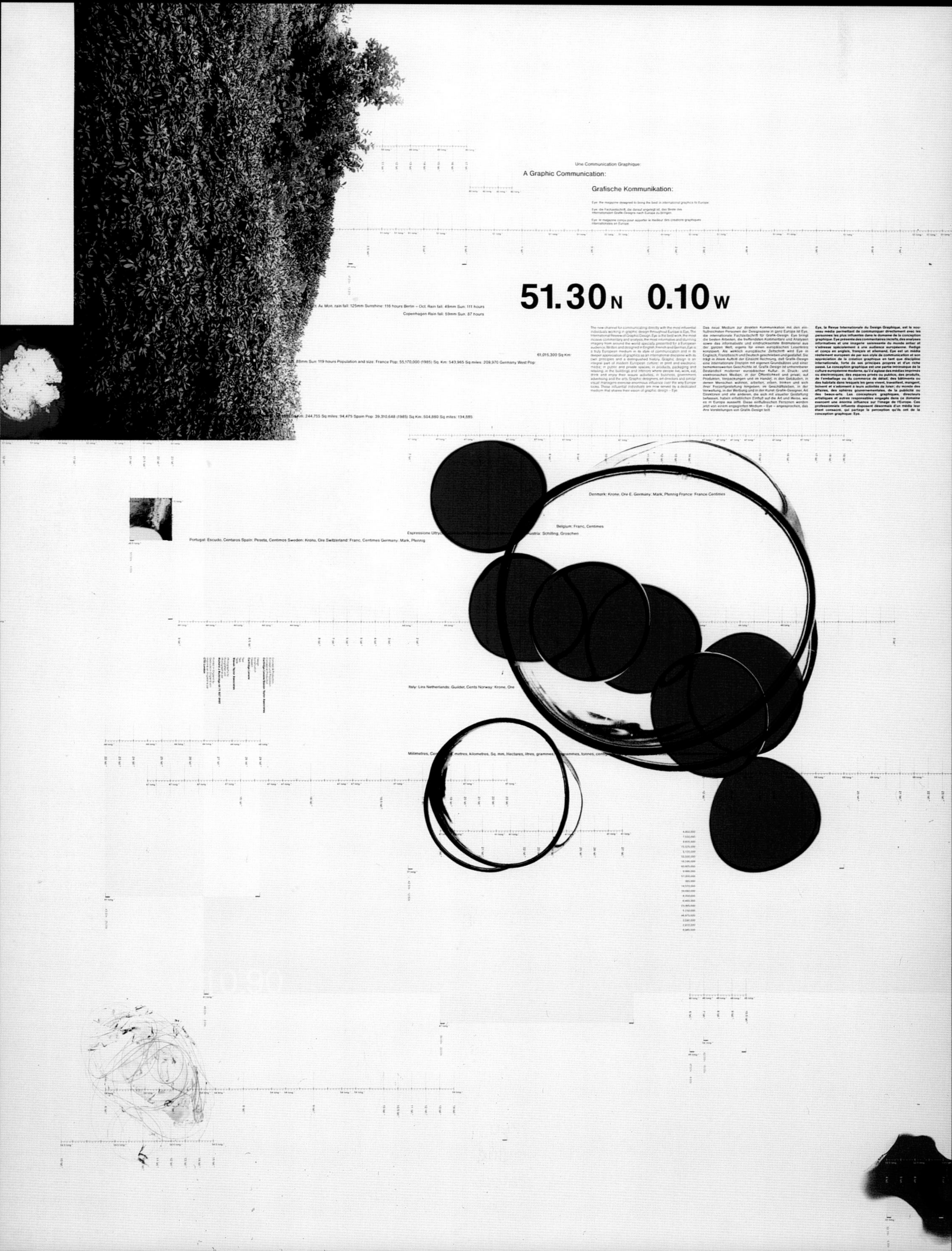

Une Communication Graphique:

A Graphic Communication:

Grafische Kommunikation:

Eye: the magazine designed to bring the best in international graphics to Europe.

Eye: die Fachzeitschrift, die darauf angelegt ist, das Beste des internationalen Grafik-Designs nach Europe zu bringen.

Eye: le magazine conçu pour apporter le meilleur des créations graphiques internationales en Europe.

...Av. Mon. rain fall: 125mm Sunshine: 116 hours Berlin – Oct. Rain fall: 49mm Sun: 111 hours
Copenhagen Rain fall: 59mm Sun: 87 hours

88mm Sun 119 hours Population and size: France Pop: 55,170,000 (1985) Sq. Km: 543,965 Sq miles: 209,970 Germany West Pop: 61,015,300 Sq Km:

Km: 244,755 Sq miles: 94,475 Spain Pop: 39,310,648 (1985) Sq Km: 504,880 Sq miles: 194,885

The new channel for communicating directly with the most influential individuals working in graphic design throughout Europe is Eye, The International Review of Graphic Design. Eye is the best work, the most incisive commentary and analysis, the most informative and stunning imagery from around the world specially presented for a European audience. Written and designed in English, French and German, Eye is a truly European medium in its style of communication and in its deeper appreciation of graphics as an international discipline with its own principles and a distinguished history. Graphic design is an integral part of modern European culture: in print and electronic media; in public and private spaces; in products, packaging and retailing; in the buildings and interiors where people live, work, eat, drink and enjoy their leisure activities; in business, government, advertising and the arts. Graphic designers, art directors and similar visual managers exercise enormous influence over the way Europe looks. These influential individuals are now served by a dedicated medium that shares their vision of graphic design – Eye.

Das neue Medium zur direkten Kommunikation mit den einflußreichsten Personen der Designszene in ganz Europa ist Eye, die internationale Fachzeitschrift für Grafik-Design. Eye bringt die besten Arbeiten, die treffendsten Kommentare und Analysen sowie das informativste und eindrucksvollste Bildmaterial aus der ganzen Welt, eigens für einen europäischen Leserkreis konzipiert. Als wirklich europäische Zeitschrift wird Eye in Englisch, Französisch und Deutsch geschrieben und gestaltet. Sie trägt in ihrem Auftritt der Einsicht Rechnung, daß Grafik-Design eine internationale Disziplin mit eigenen Grundsätzen und einer bemerkenswerten Geschichte ist. Grafik-Design ist untrennbarer Bestandteil moderner europäischer Kultur: in Druck- und elektronischen Medien; in der Öffentlichkeit und privat; auf Produkten, Verpackungen und im Handel; in den Gebäuden, in denen Menschen wohnen, arbeiten, essen, trinken und sich ihrer Freizeitgestaltung hingeben; im Geschäftsleben, in der Verwaltung, in der Werbung und in der Kunst. Grafik-Designer, Art Direktoren und alle anderen, die sich mit visueller Gestaltung befassen, haben erheblichen Einfluß auf die Art und Weise, wie es in Europa aussieht. Diese einflußreichen Personen werden jetzt von einem engagierten Medium – Eye – angesprochen, das ihre Vorstellungen von Grafik-Design teilt.

Eye, la Revue Internationale du Design Graphique, est le nouveau média permettant de communiquer directement avec les personnes les plus influentes dans le domaine de la conception graphique. Eye présente des commentaires incisifs, des analyses informatives et une imagerie saisissante du monde entier et s'adresse spécialement à une audience européenne. Rédigé et conçu en anglais, français et allemand, Eye est un média réellement européen de par son style de communication et son appréciation de la création graphique en tant que discipline internationale, forte de ses principes propres et d'un riche passé. La conception graphique est une partie intrinsèque de la culture européenne moderne, qu'il s'agisse des médias imprimés ou électroniques; des espaces privés ou publics; des produits, de l'emballage ou du commerce de détail; des bâtiments ou des habitats dans lesquels les gens vivent, travaillent, mangent, boivent et s'adonnent à leurs activités de loisir; du monde des affaires, des sphères gouvernementales, de la publicité ou des beaux-arts. Les concepteurs graphiques, directeurs artistiques et autres responsables engagés dans ce domaine exercent une énorme influence sur l'image de l'Europe. Ces professionnels influents disposent désormais d'un média leur étant consacré, qui partage la perception qu'ils ont de la conception graphique: Eye.

Denmark: Krone, Ore E. Germany: Mark, Pfennig France: France Centimes

Belgium: Franc, Centimes

Espressione Ultr... ...ustria: Schilling, Groschen

Portugal: Escudo, Centaros Spain: Peseta, Centimos Sweden: Krona, Ore Switzerland: Franc, Centimes Germany: Mark, Pfennig

Italy: Lira Netherlands: Guilder, Cents Norway: Krone, Ore

Millimetres, Ce... metres, kilometres, Sq. mm, Hectares, litres, grammes, ...grammes, tonnes, cent...

The tribal divisions in UK graphic design in the nineties were faithfully chronicled by *Eye* magazine, a highbrow journal of the graphic arts under the influential editorship of design critic Rick Poyner. *Eye* commissioned a D&AD-winning promotional poster from Cartlidge Levene which recognizably belonged to the 'style counsellor' camp; but as the magazine also won an award for its own intelligent and well-disciplined art direction by Stephen Coates and generally avoided a partisan approach, it deserved to be seen for what it was – a catalyst for the creative plurality of the age.

Aside from *Eye*, few magazines made waves at D&AD in the nineties, inducing jury veterans to get nostalgic about the great days of *Nova* and *The Sunday Times magazine*. D&AD handed out Silvers to Stephen Male's work on *i-D* (a belated recognition for one of the more original titles of the eighties) and Vince Frost's *Big* magazine (which brilliantly exploited a large monochrome format for client Big Location). Frost's former colleagues at Pentagram produced an elegant corporate magazine for Polaroid while Paul Elliman and Peter Miles designed and published a bizarre magazine on strips of fax paper. This was one of the decade's more flimsy and fast-dating print design projects, but such was the thirst for something different at D&AD that it won Gold in 1991.

1993.11
Art director: **Stephen Coates**
Client: **Wordsearch Publishing**
Eye magazine managed a difficult balancing act in showcasing graphic trends by maintaining an authority and readability while being exciting and innovative in design.

opposite

1990.12
Designer: **Stephen Male**
Client: **i-D Magazine**
i-D magazine, one of the more important fashion publishing ideas of the eighties, was given belated recognition at D&AD.

1991.11
Designers: **Paul Elliman, Peter Miles**
Clients: **Paul Elliman & Peter Miles**
It looks a little dated now but printing an entire magazine for themselves and their friends on fax paper strips was highly imaginative at the time.

NO. 76 DECEMBER 1989/JANUARY 1990 £1.80
Queen B
— the future of rock'n'roll?
i-D MAGAZINE
up TIME
INSi-DE
Soul II Soul — the success story continues/ Natural Uppers And Legal Highs/ Street jeans report — what you're wearing now/ John Richmond and his fashion manifesto/ Cyberspace — science fiction becomes science fact/ Goodbye to the '80s — a decade of i-Deas

Ecstasy might have been the designer drug of the '80s, but the drugs of the '90s are going to be
A GU-iDE TO NATURAL HIGHS
up...
healthy, natural and legal. If you believe that you'll believe anything, but have you looked in your local health shop lately? Nowadays people aren't asking "have you got any E?", but "have you got any G?"
i-Directory of Herbal Highs and Natural Uppers

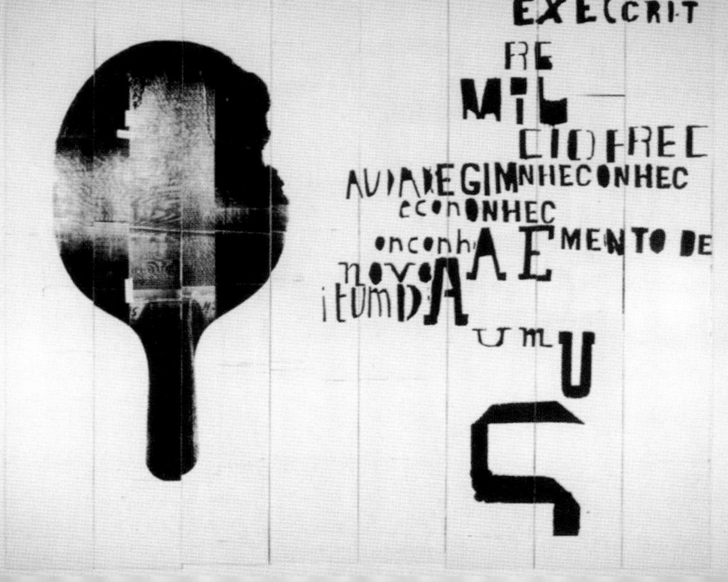
EXECCRIT
RE
MIL
CIOFREC
AUDAREGIMNHECONHEC
econONHEC
onconhAEMENTO DE
novo
itumDA
um
U

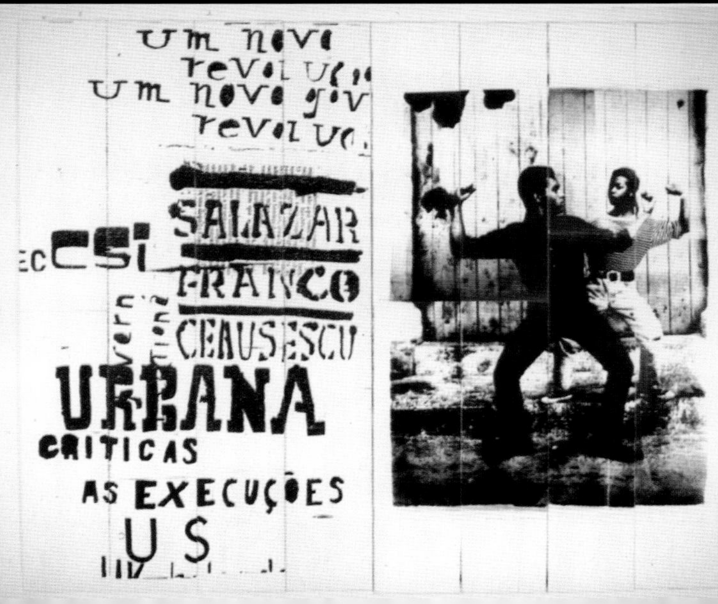
um novo
revoluç
um novo gov
revol uç
SALAZAR
ecCSI
FRANCO
CEAUSESCU
URBANA
CRITICAS
AS EXECUÇÕES
US

open

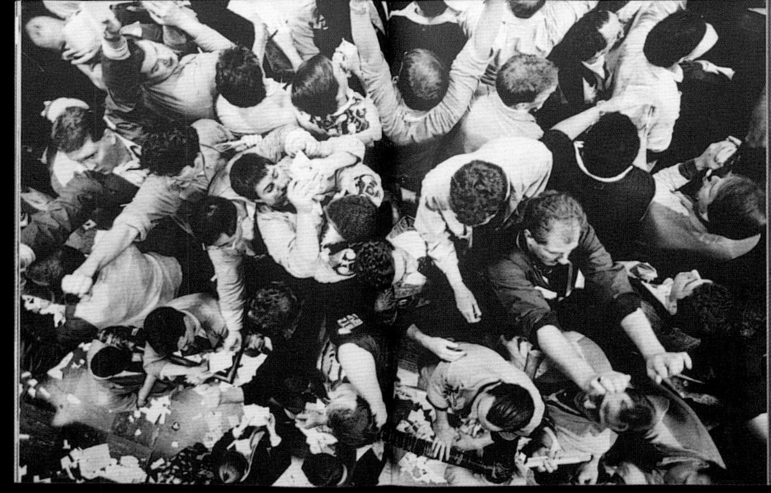

out cry

pump up the vol ume

In 1993, the Chicago Board of Trade exceeded its 1990 world trading record by over 24 million contracts—setting a new world record of 178,773,105 contracts traded. By providing the deepest, most liquid markets at the lowest possible cost for both its members and its customers, the CBOT has established a new level of success. This new volume record demonstrates customer confidence in our markets.

1994.14
Design group: **Frost Design**
Client: **Big Location**
Veteran wood-type artist Alan Kitching worked with art director Vince Frost on this powerful and handsome large-format magazine.

1995.16
Design group: **VSA Partners**
Client: **Chicago Board of Trade**

this page

1994.15
Design group: **Pentagram Design**
Client: **Crafts Council**

The contrast between VSA's direct, aggressive appeal for this Chicago Board of Trade annual report and Pentagram's elegant, well-behaved report for the Crafts Council reflects how the rules changed in annual reports as US designers made their influence felt in the mid-nineties.

1995.17
Design group: **Pentagram Design**
Client: **Polaroid**
Smoothly does it, by Pentagram partner John Rushworth for Polaroid's corporate magazine.

As for corporate annual reports, the growing influence at D&AD of American design entries slowly began to change how things were done. The contrast between the correct and well-mannered UK approach, with measured columns of text balanced against elegant imagery, and the more urgent, aggressive US art direction involving less words and more direct emotion, could be seen in two D&AD Silver winners spaced just a year apart. Pentagram's work for the Crafts Council in 1994 was everything a well-made annual report should be; VSA Partners' report for the Chicago Board of Trade the following year captured the frenetic mood on the trading floor in a powerful visual essay and thus rewrote the best practice rules.

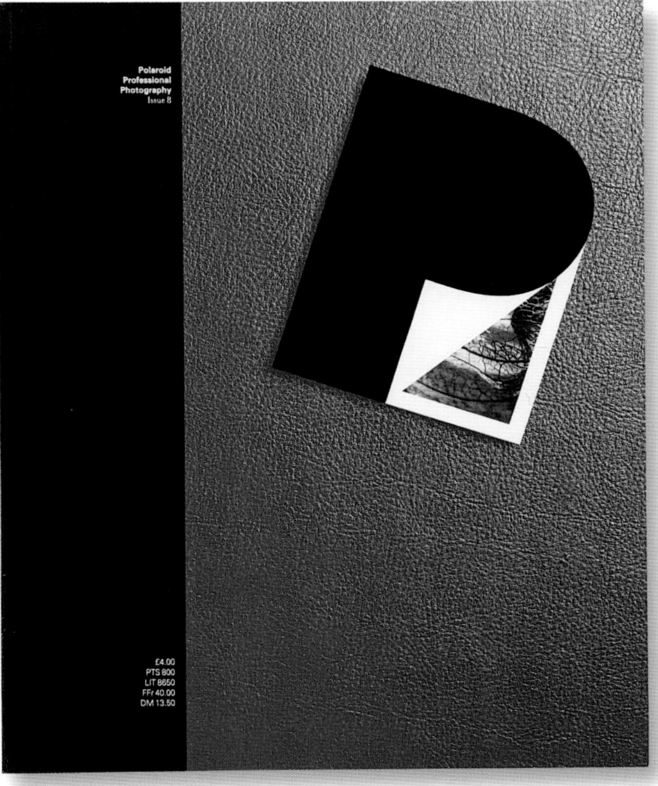

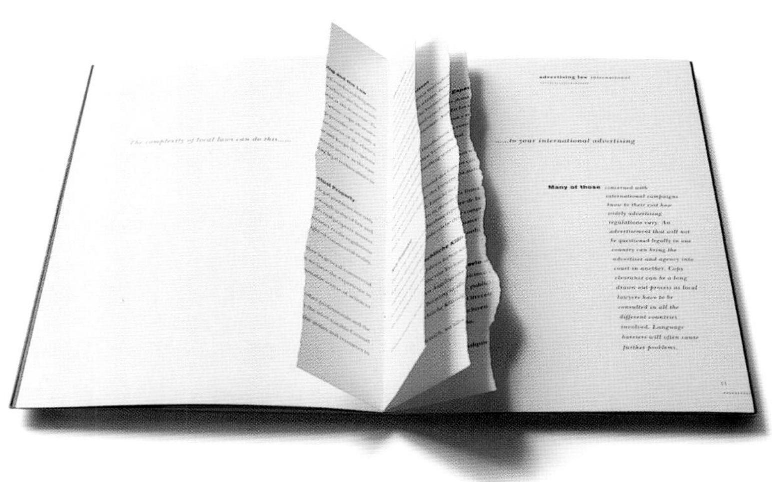

1990.13
Design group:
Michael Peters & Partners
Client: **Royal Mail Stamps**

1995.18
Design group: **Trickett & Webb**
Clients: **The Simkins Partnership, Advertising Law International**

1994.16
Design group: **Pentagram Design**
Client: **Interior Design International**

Three Silver-winning projects from the witty wing of the British graphic design brigade, including a direct mail piece for a firm of advertising law solicitors with the pages half ripped out. Modern clocks and Bauhaus chairs were as much ready-made clichés for an interiors show as smiley clowns and Cheshire Cat grins were for a set of 'smile' stamps. Unfortunately, while the stamps were much licked, Interior Design International folded shortly after David Hillman's posters ran and so the event was cancelled.

1997.14
Design group: **Hughes & Moulton**
Client: **Cow Lane Garage**

1997.15
Design group: **johnson banks**
Client: **Canna Kendall & Co**

Two stationery projects playing with visual metaphor and trickery. Cow Lane Garage, get it? As for Canna Kendall & Co, a recruitment consultancy, the message on the paper is that they can make matches as good as Popeye and Olive, bacon and eggs, dog and bone etc.

Meanwhile, the problem-solving wing of British graphic design got its teeth into all manner of projects, literally so in the case of Michael Peters & Partners, whose 'smile' stamps for the Royal Mail won a Silver Award in 1990. The idea was a simple and witty one – a set of stamps featuring a score of classic smiles (including the Cheshire Cat and Mona Lisa), guaranteed to make posting a letter a nicer experience. When an American designer complained that the concept had been lifted from a project for a dental practice called The Smile Specialists, published in the 1989 US Art Directors Club Annual, Michael Peters' design director Mark Pearce was sanguine in explaining to *Creative Review* that all great ideas had probably been done before and that 'sometimes the best way to communicate is via cliché'.

The 'smile' episode lifted the lid on a whole series of lookalike logo and identical identity arguments that ran in the industry throughout the nineties, as designers used classic images in the same way that musicians sampled classic riffs. Ownership issues were rarely resolved and anyway, became increasingly irrelevant.

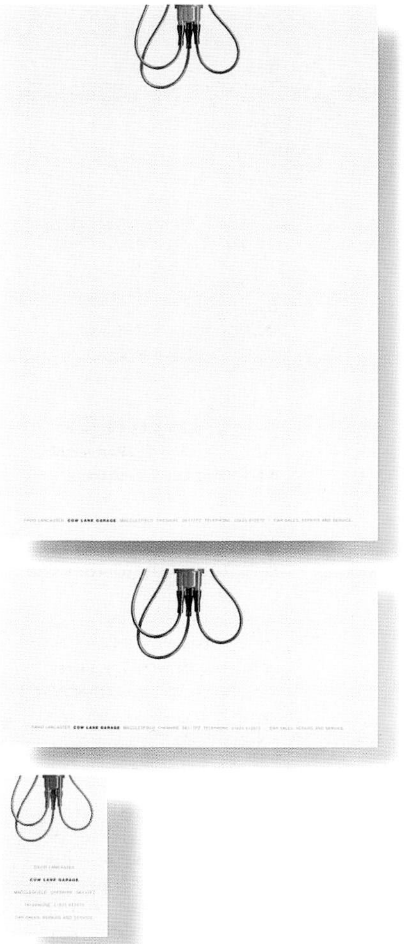

Madeleine Bennett, another art director associated with Michael Peters, worked with Brent Oppenheimer at Addison Design on a commission for a set of official posters for the 1992 Barcelona Olympics. Design briefs didn't come much more prestigious – and difficult – than that. Early concepts included athletes performing in the city, body close-ups and 'essential moments' in sport. The winning idea was a montage of action in different sports, as seen from outer space, so that the athletes (from cyclists to gymnasts) literally perform on the surface of the Earth.

The digital image retouching (by Jones Bloom) was a delicate task to achieve the right effect, but the Barcelona series was rewarded with a D&AD Silver in 1992. A different take on the Olympics was evident in a poster for the AIDS charity Terrence Higgins Trust on the subject of safer sex. This showed the Olympic rings as condoms with the line 'be a good sport'.

1993.12
Agency: **Simons Palmer Denton Clemmow & Johnson**
Client: **The Terrence Higgins Trust**

1991.12
Agency: **Simons Palmer Denton Clemmow & Johnson**
Client: **The Terrence Higgins Trust**

Two projects (a poster and a cinema commerical) for an AIDS charity by Simons Palmer presented a new angle on a famous symbol of sportsmanship and animated the issue of safe sex.

opposite

1992.16
Design group: **Addison Design Consultants**
Client: **COOB '92**
Madeleine Bennett was brought in as a freelancer to work on this landmark project. The work owed much to Addison's strong links with Spain in the nineties and the overall influence of Michael Wolff, who was Addison's creative director at the time.

Be a good sport

For more information about safer sex call our helpline on 071-242 1010.

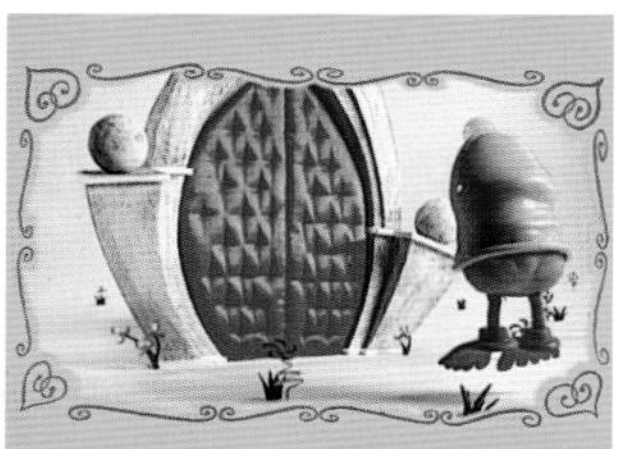

Barcelona'92
Jocs de la XXVa Olimpíada Barcelona 1992
Juegos de la XXV Olimpiada Barcelona 1992
Jeux de la XXVe Olympiade Barcelona 1992
Games of the XXV Olympiad Barcelona 1992

Meanwhile, clients as diverse as a law firm, a garage, a trade exhibition and a manufacturer of toilet cubicles earned recognition from D&AD graphic design juries for ideas-driven creativity. The manufacturer in question, Thrislington Cubicles, made a commendable effort to project a more imaginative image in a sector noted only for downmarket utilitarian design, through a series of calendars and brochures designed by The Partners. A minimalist Thrislington calendar based on the idea of spending a penny, with coin slots for every day of the year, won a D&AD Silver Award in 1994.

Part of the playful wit that was a feature of British graphics in the early nineties concerned typographic experimentation. This manifested itself at D&AD in a number of ways; from Kate Stephens' formal, tightly choreographed typography on an annual report for ABSA, in which type mirrored the shape of images, to a project designed by Michael Johnson while at Smith & Milton, for paper company James McNaughton, presenting a much looser type-fest to show the qualities of the paper.

1994.17
Design group: **The Partners**
Client: **Thrislington Cubicles**
A new design take on the old phrase 'spending a penny' for a maker of toilet cubicles.

opposite

1998.12
Designer: **Kate Stephens**
Client: **Association for Business Sponsorship of the Arts**
Type as the raw material for artistic composition with text pages mirroring the photographed images opposite them in this annual report. Work of this sort requires enormous amounts of skill and patience.

1993.13
Design group: **Smith & Milton**
Client: **James McNaughton Paper**
Typography as a playful form of illustration in this promotion for a paper company.

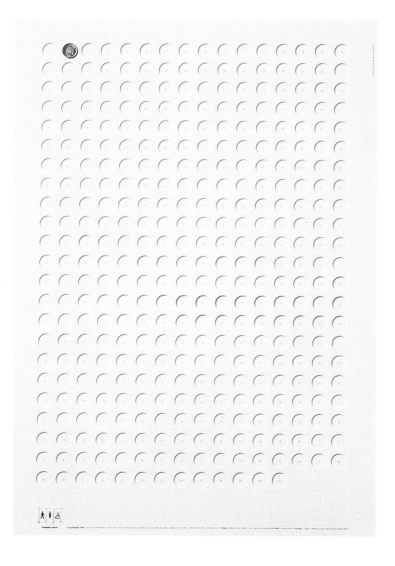

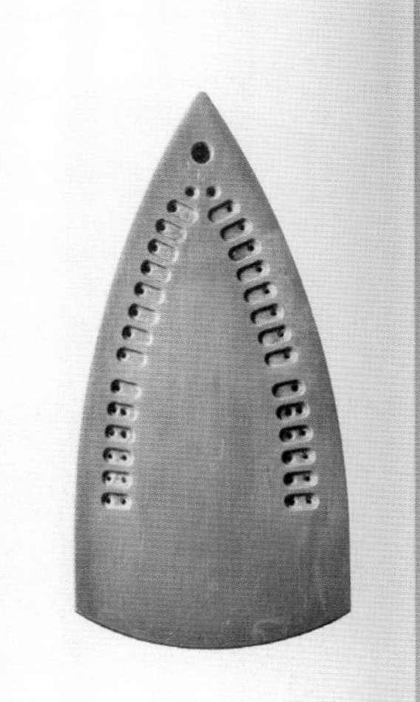

TREASURES OF THE WORLD ON THE SKYE RANGE of paper
Life, the greatest treasure
them all
SKYESILK natural white

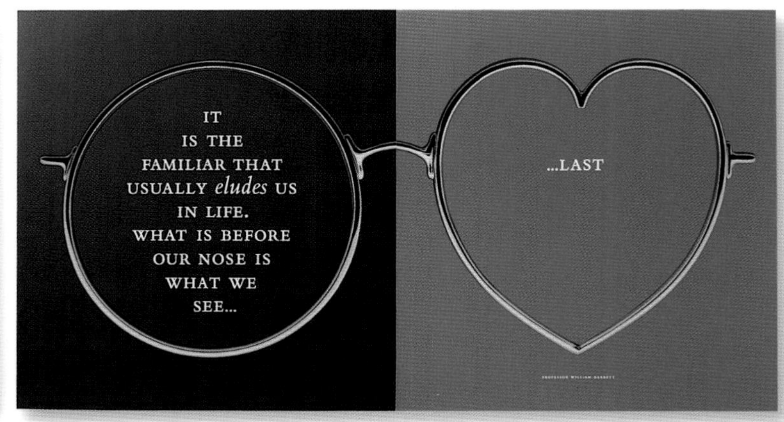
IT IS THE FAMILIAR THAT USUALLY *eludes* US IN LIFE. WHAT IS BEFORE OUR NOSE IS WHAT WE SEE...
...LAST

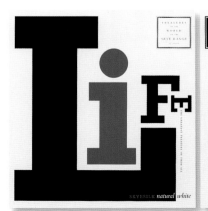

This typeface wasn't designed to be this big

it was designed to be this small

Yellow Regular

ABCDEFGHIJKLMNOPQRSTUVWXYZ
abcdefghijklmnopqrstuvwxyz
0123456789!?,"£$&%@*

1999.18
Design group: **johnson banks**
Client: **Yellow Pages**
Since its launch in 1966, *Yellow Pages* have taken thousands of small businesses and services into every household in the UK. When johnson banks embarked on the directory's first makeover for 15 years, a key part of the project was to create a new layout and a customized typeface to increase legibility and include more information on each page. In the new typeface, ascenders and descenders were reduced to 75 per cent of normal height.

1999.19
Design group: **MetaDesign London**
Client: **Glasgow 1999: UK City of Architecture and Design**
Under the artistic direction of Deyan Sudjic, who won at D&AD in the eighties with *Blueprint* magazine, Glasgow (UK City of Architecture and Design) commissioned its own typeface from MetaDesign, seen here in a web-based film. Tim Fendley's creative direction hints at Glasgow's Charles Rennie Mackintosh heritage while maintaining modernity fit for the Apple Macintosh generation.

1998.13
Production company: **Spin**
Client: **Diesel**
Fashion logs on to the internet revolution with this high-style CD-ROM project commissioned by trendy store Diesel.

1997.16
Design group: **Cleaver et al**
Client: **The Type Museum**
Ever since leaving the Central School of Arts & Crafts where he studied under Anthony Froshaug, Phil Cleaver has maintained a strong reputation as a typographer of the old school. So who better to design a prospectus for The Type Museum?

Later in the decade, johnson banks turned in its own Silver-winning typographic project, this time with a new typeface for *Yellow Pages*, as part of the first makeover for the well-known directory since the early eighties. To achieve a clean new look with more characters per line, johnson banks worked with type experts The Foundry. Phil Cleaver's immaculate hot metal work on a prospectus for The Type Museum won a D&AD Silver in 1997. There was even a type project among the Silver winners in D&AD's new Interactive Media category. MetaDesign London's animated typeface for Glasgow, which was UK City of Architecture and Design in 1999, shared the honours with such cutting-edge interactive work as Spin's CD-ROM for fashion store Diesel and Deepend's website for the VW Beetle.

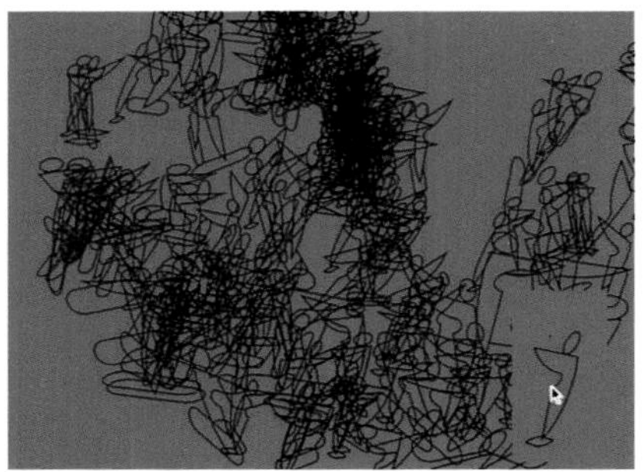

The emphasis on experimenting with typography was, however, part of a much broader obsession with a return to craft-based values in graphic design after the flirtation with corporate power in the late eighties. (The business crash of such design empires as the Michael Peters Group in the recession of the early nineties, which broke down many large design firms into smaller units, further encouraged a back-to-studio-basics approach.) At D&AD, craft finesse and execution came to the fore in many guises – from Tony Meeuwissen's elaborately illustrated book of cards for a Philadelphia publisher to Area's catalogue for a fashion show, 'One Woman's Wardrobe', which folded out from a handbag into a parade of stunning images and typographic forms.

Pentagram's use of photographer Giles Revell's digital spiralling imagery on literature for the Berkeley Hotel reflected the power of the alliance between photography and computers. But although the tide turned decisively against illustration in the nineties, Jeff Fisher's work for Bloomsbury Publishers and Geoff Grandfield's dark drawings for the Folio Society both won the attention of D&AD's craft juries. D&AD also introduced a new craft category, Design Writing, in recognition of the role that words play in creating great graphic design. The first winner in this field was veteran advertising wordsmith Jeremy Bullmore in 1999, writing an introduction to the WPP Group annual report.

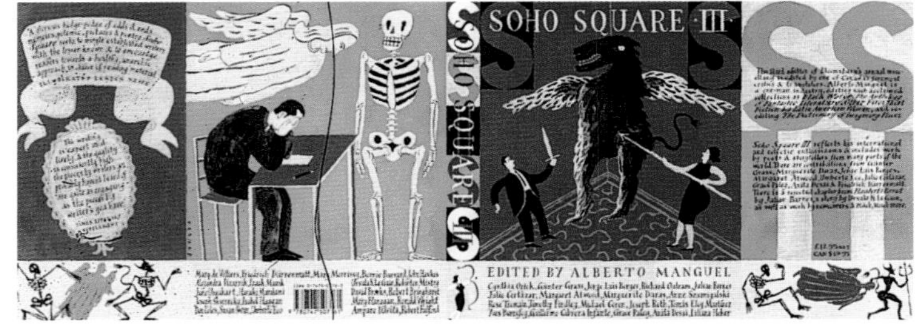

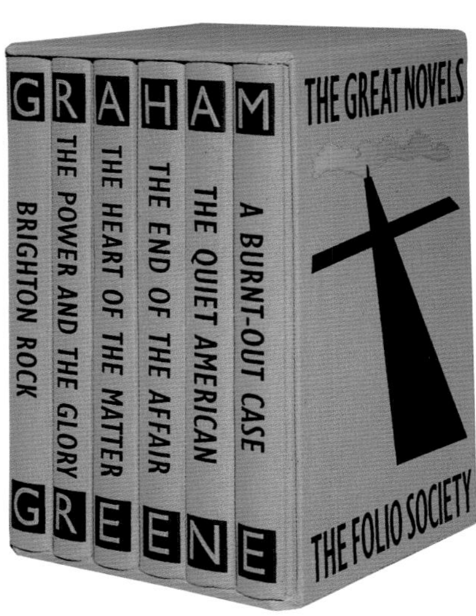

1997.17
Design group: **Pentagram Design**
Client: **The Savoy Group of Hotels & Restaurants**
This directory for The Berkeley Hotel won a Silver for image manipulation.

1991.13
Illustrator: **Jeff Fisher**
Client: **Bloomsbury Publishers**
Jeff Fisher was awarded a Silver for his illustration of this book jacket.

1998.14
Illustrator: **Geoff Grandfield**
Client: **The Folio Society**
Geoff Grandfield's work for the Folio Society's set of Graham Greene novels captured the depth of the writing in a set of urgent, economical illustrations.

opposite

1993.14
Illustrator: **Tony Meeuwissen**
Client: **Philadelphia Pavilion Books**
Originally commissioned by the Victoria and Albert Museum, this stunning set of cards by Tony Meeuwissen is based on traditional nursery rhymes.

Laughing Mouse
CHEESE SPREAD

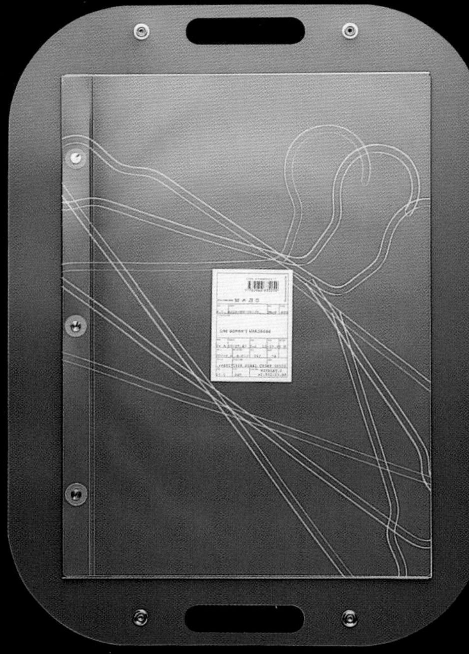

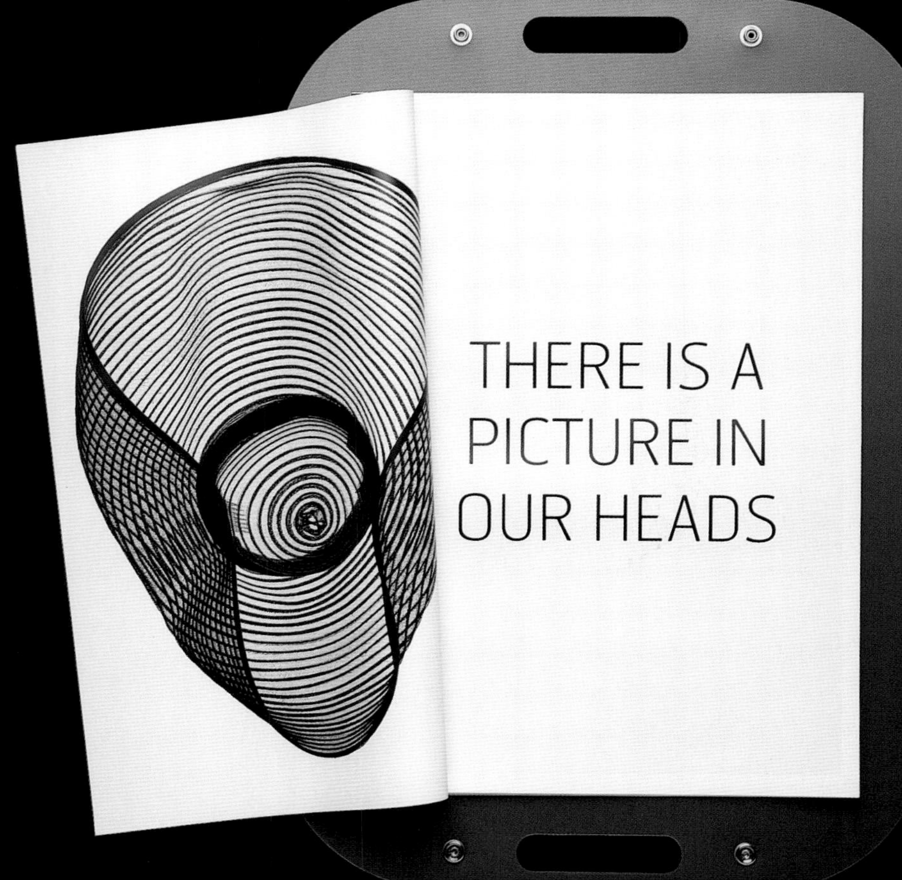
THERE IS A
PICTURE IN
OUR HEADS

1999.20
Design group: **Area**
Client: **Jill Ritblat**
When Jill Ritblatt donated her outstanding collection of women's fashion to the Victoria and Albert Museum, she wanted the catalogue for the exhibition documenting her gift to match the innovative quality of the clothes.

this page

1999.21
Design group: **Addison**
Client: **WPP Group**
Jeremy Bullmore's smoothly persuasive work for the WPP Group won the first Silver Award in the new Design Writing category at D&AD. His quoting of Theodore Levitt, 'people don't want a quarter-inch drill; they want a quarter-inch hole', reminded the creative business of its obligations to clients and consumers, not just to itself.

WPP Group plc

Polishing the Apples

The value of marketing communications
by Jeremy Bullmore

It's always a good question to put to a new client: we all know what you make – but are you as certain what your customers are buying?

Simple as it sounds, it's a constructively difficult question to answer.

You make expensive pens; but that's not what people are buying. What people are buying will be prestige, or personal pleasure, or the hope of gratitude from a recipient.

You make multi-coloured chocolate buttons; but that's not what people are buying. What people are buying is a moment's welcome peace from demanding children.

You make laptop PCs; but that's not what people are buying. What people are buying will be self-sufficiency, self-esteem, efficiency and mobility.

As Theodore Levitt pointed out many years ago: people don't want a quarter-inch drill; they want a quarter-inch hole. And for every product or service, there's an equivalent distinction to be made – though seldom so easily or so elegantly.

So it was time, it seemed to us, to ask exactly the same question of ourselves. We know what we make, all right: what we produce. But what is it exactly that our clients are buying?

2

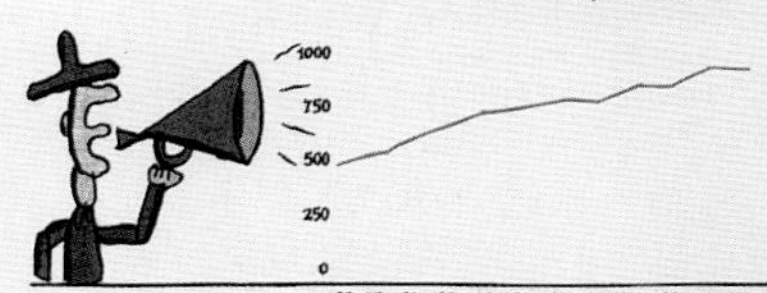

Here are some of the more familiar 'products' of the marketing services industry: advertisements, tracking studies, market analysis, strategic counsel, retail interiors, corporate videos, annual reports, corporate identities and liveries, sales promotions, media, database marketing, pack designs, employee communications, public relations and public affairs advice.

Worldwide expenditure on all marketing services in 1997 was estimated at almost $1 trillion. As the illustration shows, there continues to be a more-or-less steady growth in such expenditure and the figure represents the aggregate of millions of different decisions voluntarily made by millions of individuals in millions of different competitive enterprises. So it can presumably be assumed that marketing companies, with attitudes ranging from cheerful confidence to resigned reluctance, believe their marketing expenditures to be necessary.

But, as with Ted Levitt's drill, nobody wants to buy advertisements or research reports for their own sakes, to be kept proudly behind glass in the corporate lobby. As with Ted Levitt's drill, all these products are bought in the hope that they will do something: to provide the equivalent of Ted Levitt's hole. Precisely what that something is, and how it differs from service to service, is a great deal harder to identify and articulate. To say that they are bought by companies to make themselves more successful is both true and unhelpful. It tells us what these services are expected to achieve but not how.

3

Packaging design pushed craft skills to new heights in the nineties, but the discipline also re-engaged with simple and direct communication after the overwhelming trend towards packs with complicated historical decoration in the previous decade. The own-brand sector was still the place where exciting things were liable to happen, as demonstrated at D&AD by stand-out projects for Boots, Safeway and Harvey Nichols. But the big idea in nineties packaging design was... the big idea.

In 1991, for example, Lewis Moberly was asked by UK high-street retailer Boots to revitalise its flagging own-brand hosiery range. The simple but sophisticated creative solution, revealing the product through the leg cutout, had a dramatic impact. Sales shot up immediately, without additional marketing support. For every 1p spent on design, Boots earned £1 of additional hosiery business. The project consolidated Mary Lewis's reputation as an arch-stylist with great ideas. (The previous year she and her team had skilfully packaged a Safeway range of shortbread biscuits in the vernacular of a tartan blanket.) Later, in 2001, Lewis would win the D&AD President's Award for lifetime achievement in design, earning a description from David Stuart of The Partners as 'a designer out of the top drawer – or maybe the secret compartment just above it'.

1991.13
Design group: **Lewis Moberly**
Client: **The Boots Company**

opposite

1990.14
Design group: **Lewis Moberly**
Client: **Safeway**

Two projects from the Lewis Moberly stable, which demonstrated the return of ideas-based design in own-label packaging at the start of the nineties. The cut-out on the Boots hosiery pack reveals the product in its rightful context; the tartan blanket label on the Safeway shortbread pack lends product authenticity in a different, but equally compelling way.

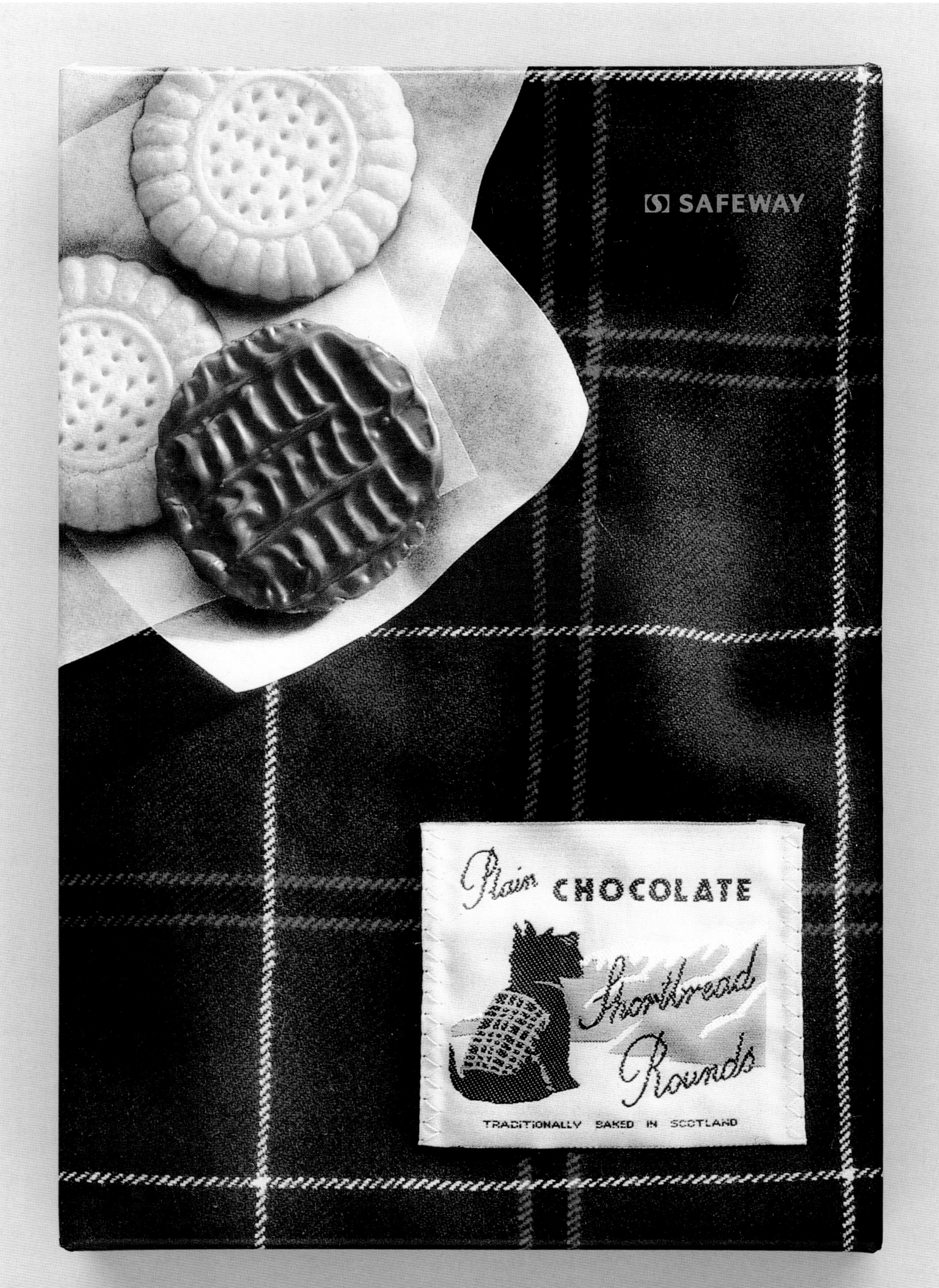
SAFEWAY
Plain CHOCOLATE
Shortbread
Rounds
TRADITIONALLY BAKED IN SCOTLAND

Lewis Moberly helped to open the floodgates on a decade of graphic ideas and wit in packaging design. A frosted vodka bottle for D'Amico & Partners by Glenn Tutssel at Michael Peters & Partners revealed the brand through a scratch in the frost. A pack of own-brand cotton handkerchiefs for the National Portrait Gallery by Four IV Design Consultants featured noses from portraits in the collection. A project by Wickens Tutt Southgate for the Seattle Coffee Company used mood poems on packs to create a brand light years away from the standard coffee bean/cup imagery to sell coffee.

Even in an area as boring as office supplies, wit could still shine through. Newell and Sorrell's black-and-white brand identity for Niceday, an office supplies enterprise formed by WH Smith's acquisition of five independent companies, was based on the idea (unique to the sector) of making people smile. US artist Charles Barsotti was commissioned to create a cartoon worm, bird and dog which were then skilfully applied to 2,000 products, vehicle liveries, stationery, signage and publicity material. The creative packaging approach paid off – handsomely – as market share, sales and profits all rose.

1990.15
Design group:
Michael Peters & Partners
Client: **D'Amico & Partners**
Packaging for Tsaritsa vodka at its icy minimalist best. It takes a brave (or foolhardy) client to have the confidence to put that on the shelf.

1998.15
Design group:
Wickens Tutt Southgate
Client: **Seattle Coffee Company**
Now subsumed by the Starbucks behemoth, the Seattle Coffee Company did the *Friends*-style, pseudo-Greenwich-Village thing better than anyone else in the late nineties, with poetry on the packs and a Seattle spring in its step.

1993.15
Design group: **Newell & Sorrell**
Client: **WH Smith Office & Supplies**
A charming product of Michael Wolff's time working between Newell & Sorrell and WH Smith. American cartoonist Charles Barsotti, a long-time collaborator of Wolff's, worked long distance by fax with the UK-based design team. Apparently, he would start each working day by faxing over a beautiful black-and-white line drawing of bacon and eggs to the Newell & Sorrell designers in London.

this page

1998.16
Design group:
Four IV Design Consultants
Client: **National Portrait Gallery**
In the eighties Gert Dumbar put priceless paintings on gallery signage. Here, Four IV used paintings on cotton handkerchief packaging for the National Portrait Gallery. Some designers just have a nose for that great idea.

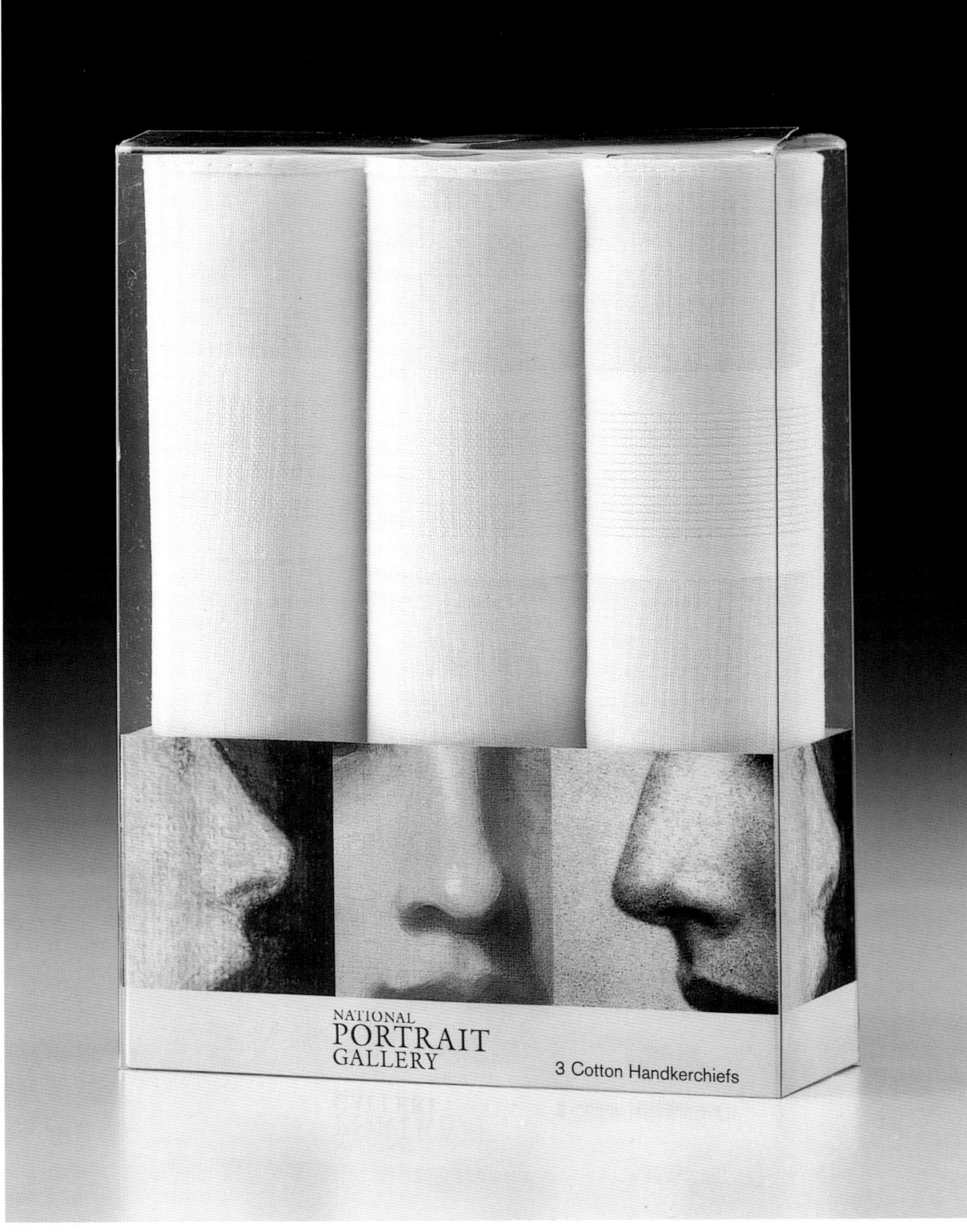

Not all new packaging ideas trumpeted at D&AD were as commercially effective as Niceday's. Wieden + Kennedy, for example, won a D&AD Silver Award in 1995 for its work on a soft drinks range called OK for Coca-Cola. Aimed at a new 'slacker' market sector which generally avoided big brands, this worked on the proposition that if Kurt Cobain of Nirvana had designed a canned drink, it would look like this. The concept bombed.

While experienced and polished performers like John Blackburn continued to win packaging awards at D&AD, the new mood of the nineties was inescapably influenced by an influx of new talent. A gamble in 1993 by Knightsbridge department store Harvey Nichols in recruiting the talents of Stephanie Nash and Anthony Michael from the music industry to design own-label food packaging paid off, with one of the most exquisite projects of the decade.

1995.19
Design group: **Blackburn's**
Client: **Harveys of Bristol**
Classic and understated, Harveys Bristol Cream is in good hands with art director John Blackburn, who, by the mid-nineties, had seen it all before.

1995.20
Designer: **Todd Waterbury**
Client: **The Coca-Cola Company**
Wieden + Kennedy design director Todd Waterbury used the cult comic-book artists Daniel Clowes, Charles Burnes, Calef Brown and David Cowles to attain the appropriate underground look to these cans of the soft drink OK, dreamt up by the same team that invented Fruitopia.

this page

1993.16
Design group:
Michael Nash Associates
Client: **Harvey Nichols**
Designers have always loved simple forms, abstract black-and-white photography and minimalist style. Michael Nash were the first designers to put them all on a range of packs for the food and beverage department of Harvey Nichols, thus earning the envy of the entire graphic design world in one fell swoop. They even managed to make the letter-spaced Futura typeface look good.

Teresa Roviras, who had worked with Michael Nash Associates, then went off to produce stunning perfume packaging for Joseph, overprinted with a girl's nose and lips. This project won a D&AD Silver Award in 1998.

But if retailers borrowed music industry talents and techniques to package their wares, the music industry was still capable of a few tricks of its own. Mark Farrow's limited edition CD for the band Spiritualized placed 12 three-inch CDs – one for each track – in foil-wrapped pill-packs. This brilliant and unexpected pastiche of pharmaceutical packaging won a Silver Award in 1998.

1998.17
Designer: **Teresa Roviras**
Client: **Joseph**
Teresa Roviras worked on the Harvey Nichols scheme with Michael Nash Associates before going freelance. This stunning work for Joseph shows her sureness of creative touch throughout the nineties. But what was it about noses and other facial parts on D&AD winning packs?

opposite

1998.18
Design group: **Farrow Design**
Client: **Dedicated Records**
No one would ever have expected pastiche from Farrow Design, but that's exactly what this is. Of course, it happened to coincide with a vernacular that they wanted to draw on, but that doesn't get away from the fact that this CD packaging is a classic piece of ideas-based design from a one-time minimal stylist.

1992.17
Design group: **The Partners**
Client: **SC Properties**
The big idea here was that the tape measure in the window measured the huge square footage available in this empty and available building. Designed by Janice Davison before she moved to rival designers Turner Duckworth.

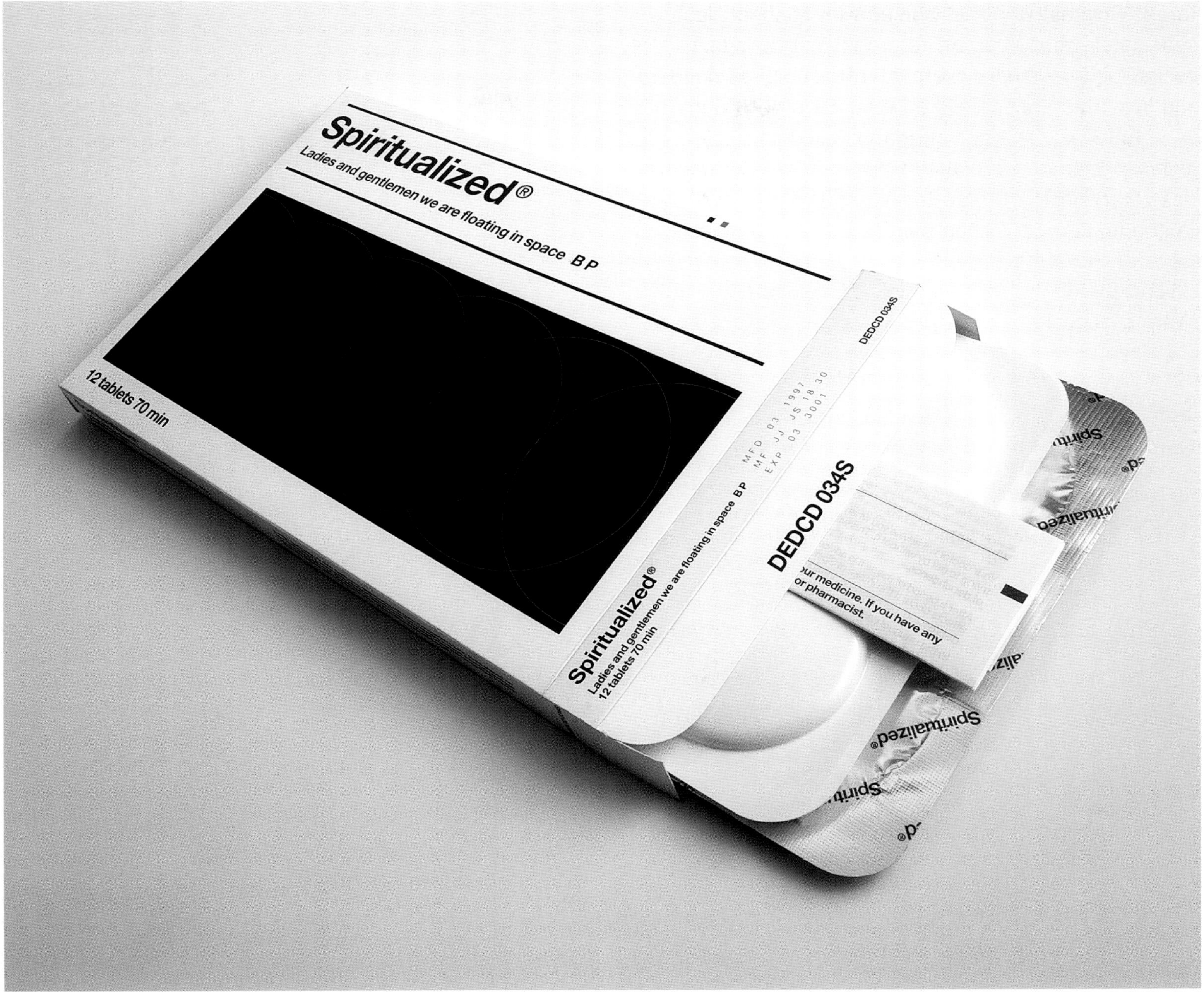

For architects and interior designers who were welcomed into the D&AD fold in the eighties, the retail scene proved to be a wasteland in the early nineties, as large chains cut back on design to focus on such things as pricing, procurement and property location. Environmental design was no longer the panacea that could throng the high street with shoppers and there was widespread suspicion of design schemes that required expensive roll-outs.

D&AD juries of this category concentrated outside the mainstream, focusing instead on high-style boutiques and awarding Nicole Farhi (by Din Associates) and Kenzo (by David Chipperfield Architects). A 1994 Silver Award for Richard Woolf's work on Muji triggered a love affair at D&AD with all things Japanese and minimalist in environmental design, continuing throughout the decade.

Many designers looked for work beyond the retail sector in the nineties and found it in office interiors, as clients increasingly demanded more creative and less automaton-like workplaces. Design firm Buschow Henley produced an imaginative scheme for film company Prospect Pictures, refurbishing a six-storey building on London's Great Portland Street. The building was exposed as a series of simple white volumes inhabited by material and light-emitting installations, with a 'colour wall' of red, green and blue light shielding administrative offices from the street.

1994.18
Design group: **Harper Mackay**
Client: **Mujirushi Ryohin Europe**

1991.15
Designer:
David Chipperfield Architects
Client: **Joseph Ettedgui**

Two environmental design projects from the early nineties. Richard Woolf's design work with architect Harper Mackay for Muji and David Chipperfield's approach to Kenzo (owned by parent company Joseph) are almost graphic in their simplicity.

1990.16
Design group: **Din Associates**
Client: **Nicole Farhi**
Designed by project designer Lesley Batchelor to create a private auditorium for fashion shows and a showroom for buyers, this scheme floods a previously dark space with natural light, thanks to a new glass roof. The oak floor and custom-designed tables enhance the feel of light and space.

1997.18
Design group: **Buschow Henley**
Client: **Prospect Pictures**
Offices go cool and creative with this scheme designed by Ralph Buschow and Simon Henley, formerly of Harper Mackay. A new stone floor and glazed shopfront create a link from Great Portland Street to a courtyard at the rear in this high-style scheme for a London film company.

1994.19
Design group: **Stanton Williams**
Client: **The South Bank Centre**

1995.21
Design group:
First Year Industrial Design Students
Client: **Royal College of Art**

As standards of exhibition design rose rapidly in the UK in the early nineties, so D&AD juries woke up to the potential of the medium. Stanton Williams' work at the South Bank Centre showed minimalist-tendency architects at work with maximum restraint. (Stanton Williams would later go on to remodel aspects of Denys Lasdun's modernist National Theatre on the same site.) The spectacular Industrial Design Show at the Royal College of Art shows the hand of Daniel Weil, then Professor of Industrial Design at the RCA before he left to join Pentagram as a partner.

The public sector, a real no-no for interior design in the eighties, also became more fertile ground for commissions – especially in national museums and galleries, where decades of neglect needed to be addressed. Stanton Williams won a D&AD Silver in 1994 for its exhibition design work at the South Bank Centre, as did Ben Kelly Design in 1996 for its enterprising masterplanning and detailed design for The Basement in the Science Museum. This turned a dull, difficult space into a tactile and technicolour environment which could 'switch children onto science'. Ranged with steps, ramps, screens, walkways and exposed services in a vivid palette of oranges, purples and lime greens, The Basement was instrumental in transforming a dusty national institution, attended under duress on wet weekends, into a vibrant visitor attraction.

 1996.12
Design group: **Ben Kelly Design**
Client: **The National Museum of Science & Industry**
Contemporary design penetrated deep into the vaults of the Science Museum with this scheme, master-planned by Ben Kelly. The original brief to provide a picnic area for school parties was expanded to create a constantly animated central space, which mutated and changed during the course of the day as groups gathered and dispersed. Services and structures were left partially exposed to reveal the workings of construction and encourage enquiry.

⬮ 1998.19
Design group: **Heatherwick Studio**
Client: **Harvey Nichols**
When given the brief by Harvey Nichols to create a window display for London Fashion Week, Thomas Heatherwick decided, in his own words, 'to try to break away from arbitrary picking of window themes, and to come up with something that reacted with its architectural context'. The single weaving element that created this project was 200 metres long. Structural engineer Ron Packman was instrumental in realizing a scheme that introduced the wow factor to Knightsbridge for one week in autumn 1997.

However, the truly outstanding environmental design project of the nineties was back in a familiar place – the high street – and the client was also well known to D&AD. Thomas Heatherwick's Gold-winning 'Autumn Intrusion' didn't just burst from the windows of fashion store Harvey Nichols onto the Knightsbridge street, as part of a London Fashion Week promotion in 1997; as the weaving wooden structure spectacularly wrapped itself in and out of the building facade, attracting crowds and extensive media coverage, it sent a powerful message about the potential of environmental design as a communication medium in its own right. This emphasis on architecture as advertising would be explored at D&AD with greater intensity in the new millennium.

The product design category at D&AD had got off to a fairly quiet, and somewhat confused, start at the end of the eighties, and it took some time to find its feet in the new decade. Faced with such a vast spectrum of goods from across the global field of production, D&AD juries struggled to find the common ground between projects with a high degree of engineering and an association rooted in the communication arts. The struggle showed in a disparate group of initial Silver winners which included a pair of binoculars by Rodd Industrial Design, a pair of spectacle frames by Andy Davey of TKO and a marine device by IDEO. What were the creative criteria that bound these products together? It was hard to tell.

Part of the problem was that UK product design was on its knees in the early nineties. Richard Seymour, a future D&AD President, wrote, 'Any designer working exclusively in the UK was retraining to run a whelk store or reorienting rapidly to serve an international market.' Another factor was that, given the high degree of fast-moving technology involved in the discipline, new products were always going to date more rapidly than, say, a book cover or a poster. This factor made Seymour Powell's 1991 mobile phone for Technophone (the size of a brick and modelled on military field phones) a toe-curling embarrassment within a few years of its launch.

1990.17
Design group:
Rodd Industrial Design
Client: **UAD Company**
Sports binoculars developed as part of a Department of Trade and Industry design initiative. The off-centre hinge allowed for compact folding and the body parts were made from moulded ABS plastic.

1991.16
Design group: **IDEO**
Client: **Qubit**
Marine equipment designed by IDEO whose involvement of end-users in a 'co-design' process would become a key influence on product design in the nineties.

1991.17
Design group: **Seymour Powell**
Client: **Technophone**
A breakthrough back then, but over the next decade, mobile phones would just get smaller and smaller.

this page

1993.17
Design group: **TKO**
Client: **Seiko Corporation**
After his success in the late eighties, another product design award at D&AD for Andy Davey, this time with his own company, TKO.

1996.13
Design group: **Studio X**
Client: **Connolly**
Luxury luggage from designer Ross Lovegrove who explained, 'After 118 years in the leather business, the Connolly family were not looking for mediocrity, they were looking for excellence.' They got it.

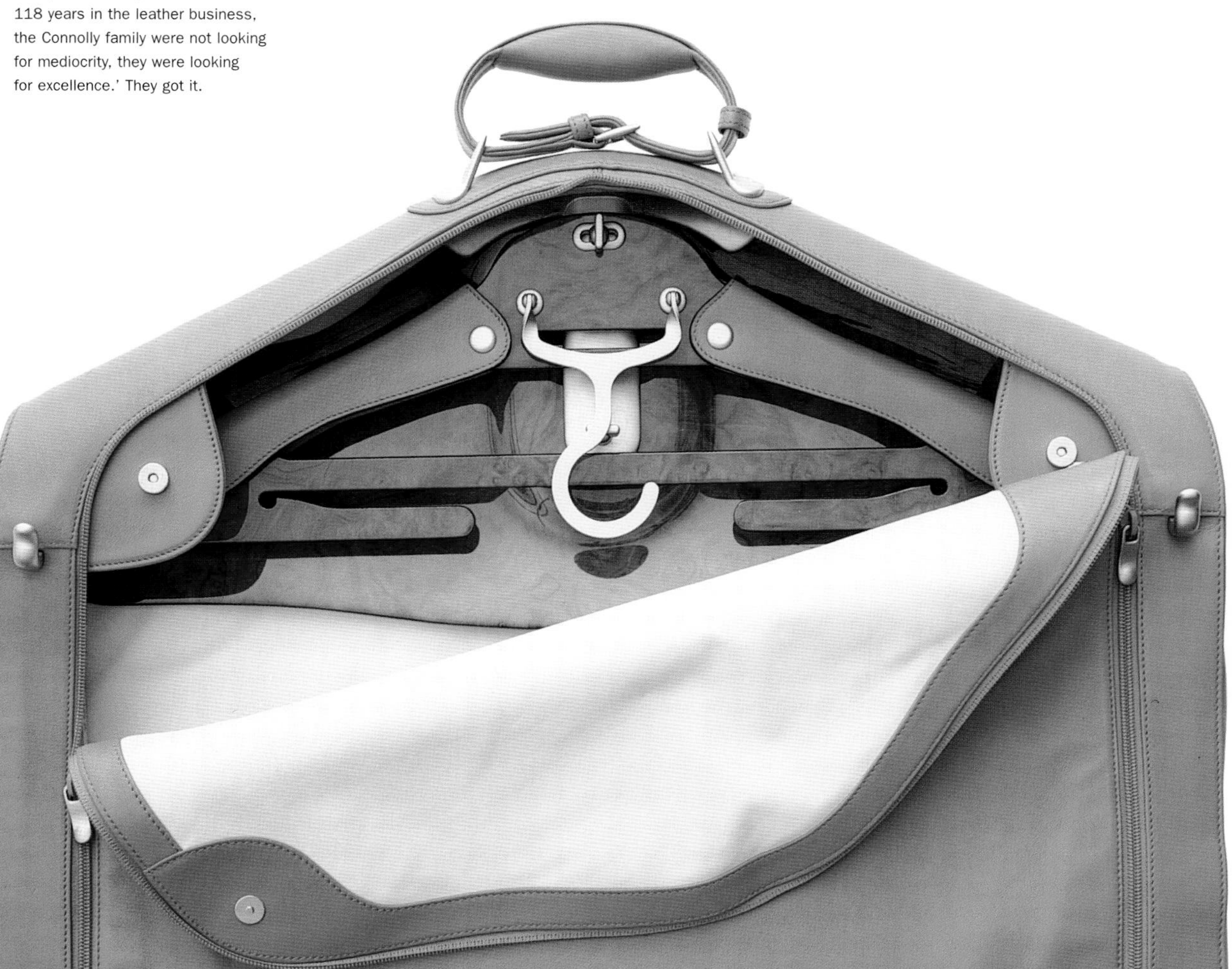

Nevertheless, product design at D&AD eventually got into its stride with projects that began to make sense within the bigger picture of design and advertising creativity. Products showed that they could be wittily communicative – a trend symbolized by Paul Priestman's engaging Cactus radiator for Bisque; a stroke of genius that completely reinvented that type of household equipment. Product ranges demonstrated that they could create a complete visual language; IDEO's design work for NEC computer monitors, for example, introduced a sweeping 'mono-form' back to give the impression of occupying less desk space. And product designers proved that they, too, could be authentic creative heroes, with Richard Seymour and Dick Powell of Seymour Powell leading the charge onto TV with their own series *Better by Design* and James Dyson leading the charge into the marketplace with his own product.

Dyson did what every industrial designer dreams of doing. He had a brilliant idea, manufactured his own product and made millions. His eureka moment was to see the potential of adapting the cyclonic tower principle, used to trap sawdust in sawmills, to the much smaller domestic scale of the vacuum cleaner. It took him five years and more than 5,000 prototypes to refine the dual cyclone technology, and a further decade to manufacture a bagless dual cyclone vacuum cleaner under his own name in the UK. But once the product was launched in 1993, Dyson never looked back. He became Britain's fastest growing manufacturer by grabbing a third of the UK market by volume and more than half by value.

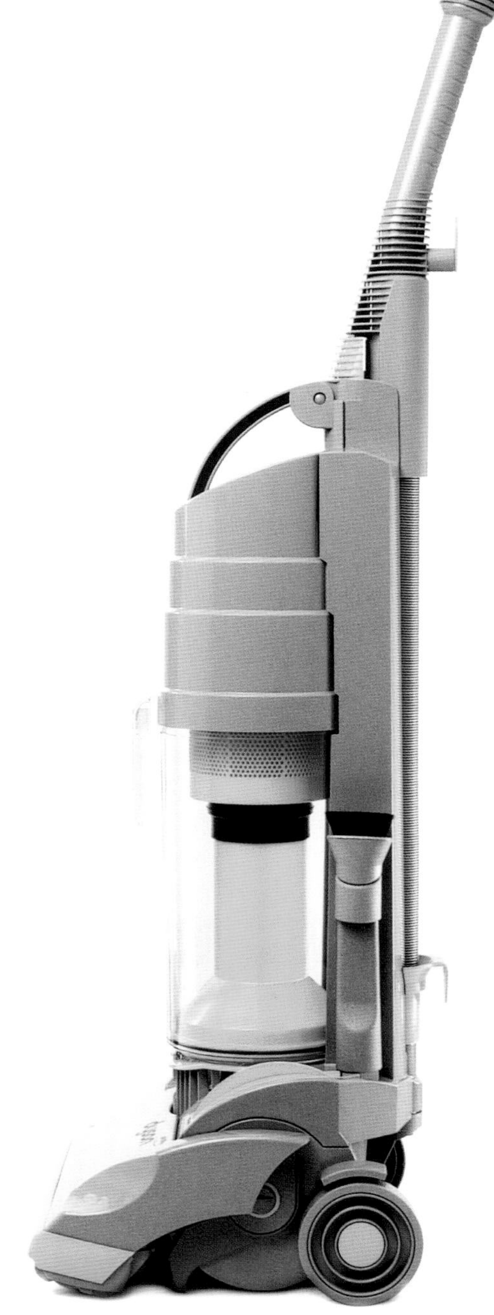

1996.14
Design group: **IDEO Product Development**
Client: **NEC Home Industries**
IDEO's work for NEC showed how product detailing could contribute to a company's overall identity with this computer monitor.

1994.20
Design group: **Dyson Design**
Client: **Dyson Appliances**
The original vacuum cleaner from James Dyson, the DC01.

1993.18
Design group: **Seymour Powell**
Client: **MuZ**
Seymour Powell's famed obsession with motorbike design rode to the rescue of an ailing East German manufacturer.

this page

1995.22
Design group: **Glaxo Research and Development, Device Development Unit**
Client: **Glaxo**
Glaxo's asthma inhaler had a compact shape, ergonomic design and minimal operating steps, and won Silver for Glaxo's in-house research and development team.

1993.19
Design group: **Priestman Associates**
Client: **Bisque Radiators**
Paul Priestman turned the heating coil into a piece of sculpture for Bisque. Truly inspired.

Dyson proved that anyone – not just design experts or style victims – would buy a more expensive 'designer' product if it worked better. The radical technology of the first Dyson Dual Cyclone vacuum cleaner was matched by futuristic looks. The inclusion of a transparent bin to view the dust spinning at 924 mph in the cylonic chambers appealed to a perceived hidden psychological need of householders to see all the dirt being sucked up. Design was integral to Dyson's success and his story, captured in an autobiography entitled *Against the Odds*, turned business heads everywhere.

After Dyson's appearance in 1994, product design at D&AD never looked back. The discipline became sexier and sexier. Seymour and Powell worked hard to raise its profile, not just through their television work but also through such projects as the Skorpion motorbike for German manufacturer MuZ. IDEO, an Anglo-American product design group built on the back of the Silicon Valley boom, worked hard to create a global network and a blue-chip client list to rival that of any advertising agency.

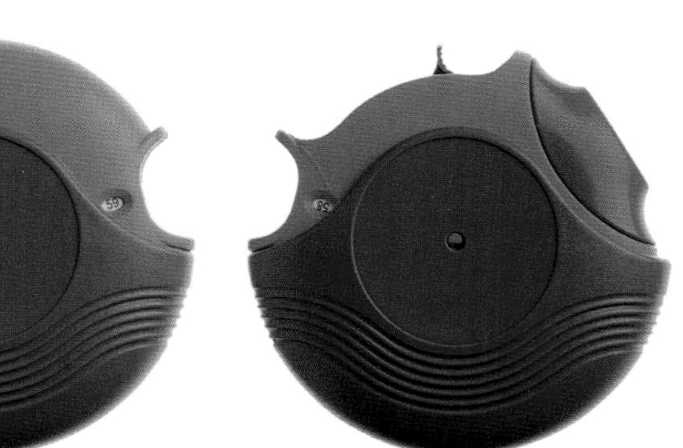

IDEO's collaboration with Nike and leading athletes to create Nike eyewear for the 1996 Atlanta Olympics was indicative of the new vistas in product design. Most sunglasses until then were fashion-oriented and compromised sporting performance, so athletes avoided wearing them. But IDEO's research produced new concepts, including a ventilated nose-bridge, which confronted the crucial environmental and visual demands of road and track running while improving the comfort level and performance of the serious athlete. The Nike V8 and V12 sunglasses won a D&AD Silver Award in 1997.

Towards the end of the decade, momentous product design projects came thick and fast at D&AD. The Eurostar train exterior designed by Jones Garrard created a symbol for an outstanding innovation in transport. The JCB Teletruk, a pioneering development of a counter-balanced forklift truck with a telescopic forward reach arm, cut the time to unload a vehicle by two thirds and improved driver comfort and safety. And the Audi TT Coupé, designed by Peter Schreyer, represented a rare case of a concept car going directly into production. All won D&AD Silver Awards.

1997.19
Design group:
IDEO Product Development
Client: **Nike**
Technical innovation and celebrity input combined to good effect on this high-profile brand extension into Nike eyewear.

1997.20
Design group: **Jones Garrard**
Client: **Eurostar**
The public image of Eurostar, the exterior of the 300 kph train that links the capitals of France, Belgium and Britain via the Channel Tunnel. GEC Alsthom Transport was the contractor.

1998.20
Design group: **JCB Industrial**
Client: **JCB Industrial**
The conventional forklift truck has a vertically extending mast operated by chains. This piece of innovation replaced the mast with a telescoping boom that pivots forwards and upwards, setting new standards in operator visibility.

1999.22
Design group:
Queensberry Hunt Levien
Client: **Ideal Standard**
Product design at D&AD goes down the pan – literally – with this highly innovative space-saving toilet that can be positioned conventionally or at a 45 degree angle in cramped bathrooms.

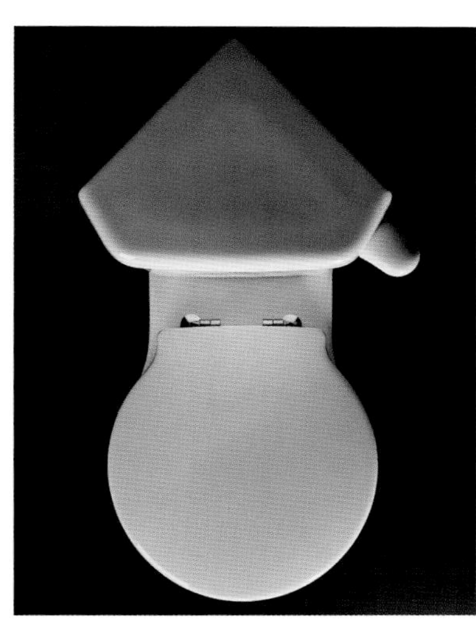

1999.23
Designer: **Peter Schreyer**
Client: **Audi**
This project, led by Royal College of Art graduate Peter Schreyer, turned a concept car, sketched in California and first exhibited at the 1995 Frankfurt Motor Show, into a dramatically designed production roadster. External styling flair was matched by beautiful interior details.

1997.21
Senior designer: **Thomas Meyerhöffer**
Client: **Apple Computer**
Apple signalled its fight back with this boldly designed laptop, the e-Mate.

overleaf

1999.24
Design group: **Apple Design Group**
Client: **Apple Computer**
During the iMac's first 139 days, one was sold every 15 seconds of every minute, of every hour of every day, of every week. Jonathan Ive's visual flair proved a major contributor to the turnaround in Apple's notoriously up and down fortunes, although Apple co-founder Steve Jobs maintained that the real reason for the iMac's success was not how it looked but the fact that it was an all-in-one computer that was easy to plug in and use – and thus went right back to Apple's roots.

But the most significant development in product design was reserved for the very end of the nineties: the emergence of Apple Computer at the creative pinnacle for D&AD. Apple had struggled for much of the decade, chasing market trends and usually getting it wrong, as its vice-president of industrial design Jonathan Ive freely admitted. Ive, an Englishman, had joined Apple from the design firm Tangerine in 1992 and assumed the chief design role in 1996 upon the appointment of a new CEO, Gil Amelio. When Amelio resigned the following year, Apple co-founder Steve Jobs returned to the company after a 12-year absence and forged a strong personal alliance with Ive.

Jobs was determined to return Apple to its pioneering roots as an innovation leader. The signs were encouraging when the Apple e-Mate laptop computer won a D&AD Silver Award in 1997, its translucent, moulded casing and bold form designed by Thomas Meyerhöffer signalling a creative departure from other laptops. But the real breakthrough was in 1999 when the Apple iMac won Gold. This was a superbly engineered all-in-one computer that was friendly and accessible – and available in a range of five candy colours to address home as well as office settings for the computer. Consumers craving simplicity got all they wanted, and more.

The nineties saw design and advertising finally free of all moorings, merging past, present and future in a digital blur. Was it ironic that an example of the computer technology that did so much to encourage the magpie-like tendencies of communication should end the decade among the winners at D&AD? Nobody doubted Apple's right to be up there with the best. The Apple Macintosh liberated designers and art directors in the nineties, and eventually the creative thrust of the decade liberated Apple itself.

Last word on the 1990s
Richard Seymour

Is it March that's supposed to 'come in like a lion and go out like a lamb'? In this same poetic spirit, the nineties (God... that sounds so eighties) came in like a fighter plane with its fuel tanks on fire and went out like a light. As 1989's Father Time stumbled haplessly off into decade heaven, Japan was facing economic meltdown and a cultural shockwave that was to put it onto the commercial back burner for... well, we still don't know, do we?

We were also facing a strange new thing, which we called 'new media', with the internet sprouting little pictures and websites and stuff, the relevance of which we all struggled to understand. Who would have thought, at the beginning of the decade, that this monster would woo so many sensible people into making really stupid business decisions? That 'dotcom' would become a collective noun for fiscal *hari kiri*? That it would spawn a master race of Generation Z practitioners such as Deepend and then flip them into the crapper only a few months into the new millennium?

But the digital dawn, much heralded in the eighties, did happen. We now point three-chip digicams at our family on the beach that pro film-makers would have given their eyeteeth for only ten years earlier. Apple Computer, still trying to find its feet after the launch of the Macintosh in 1984, rose from early nineties uncertainty towards a glorious millennial curtain-call, with Jonny Ive's translucent confections winning hearts and Gold Awards in equal measure.

Mobile phones invaded the planet; shrinking from ungainly, housebrick proportions into delicate, digital jewellery, and our right thumbs became bold, strong appendages from ceaseless text messaging and the occasional *Gran Tourismo*.

We learned to stare into screens in the nineties. Even advertising creatives discovered e-mail eventually – as fax, the business revolution of the eighties, gave way to its computerized, digital nemesis. Analogue pen and paper made their unceremonious exits, leaving only the Post-it Note as their epitaph. The mouse-click replaced the stamp-lick as the terminal guidance for the birthday card. Prose deliquesced into emoticon-laden wordwooze...

From Desert Storm to the Millennium Dome, the nineties will probably be remembered most as the decade where the new World Order became the United States and the Rest of Us. One of the most poignant memories I have of that decade is a discussion with an expensively educated 14-year-old American girl, in 1999, about technology. 'Doesn't it piss you guys off that we invented everything?' she asked me, her stainless-steel orthodontic brace glittering menacingly.

I asked her to give me an example. She cited the automobile. 'So who did invent the automobile?', I enquired lightly. 'Henry Ford, of course' came the indignant answer. When I pointed out that the 'automobile' was invented in Germany 30 years before Ransom Olds and Henry Ford organized the world's first viable vehicle production line, I received the kind of facial expression reserved for Alzheimer's patients by care workers.

History, it suddenly struck me, was being rewritten. But in a particularly dangerous way. The new, editorially liberated Information Stream was haemorrhaging integrity. The hidden, neo-political cant of the dominant search engines could replace even Murdoch in its ability to spin our birthright. It wasn't that this girl had been lied to, it was the fact that the actual truth had been missed out of her education that was so particularly chilling.

Disney's version of the Pocahontas story decided that she stayed with her people (instead of dying wretchedly in England of influenza) and conveniently laid the blame for the extinction of the aboriginal American Indian on our doorstep... yup, it was us naughty Brits, not John Wayne, wot done it. For better or worse, Planet Earth swept across the Millennial Rubicon with Uncle Sam well and truly at the helm. Our diet, our media, our politics... even our history, look west across the Atlantic more than they look to ourselves, all of a sudden.

This cultural ambivalence was demonstrated in the most spectacularly ironic manner at the very moment the nineties disappeared. As the real Millennial celebrations raged outside in pyrotechnic splendour, the Chosen Few elected to watch it, second hand, on large television screens within the Dome.

The commentator's voice-over was drowned out by the fusillade taking place only yards up the Thames. What more fitting an epitaph to round off a thousand years of human endeavour? Political scandal. Hopeless organization. Virtually empty other than the fast-food catering booths and pre-marked queuing lanes. This is really how the decade ended.

Not with a bang... but with a whimper.

200

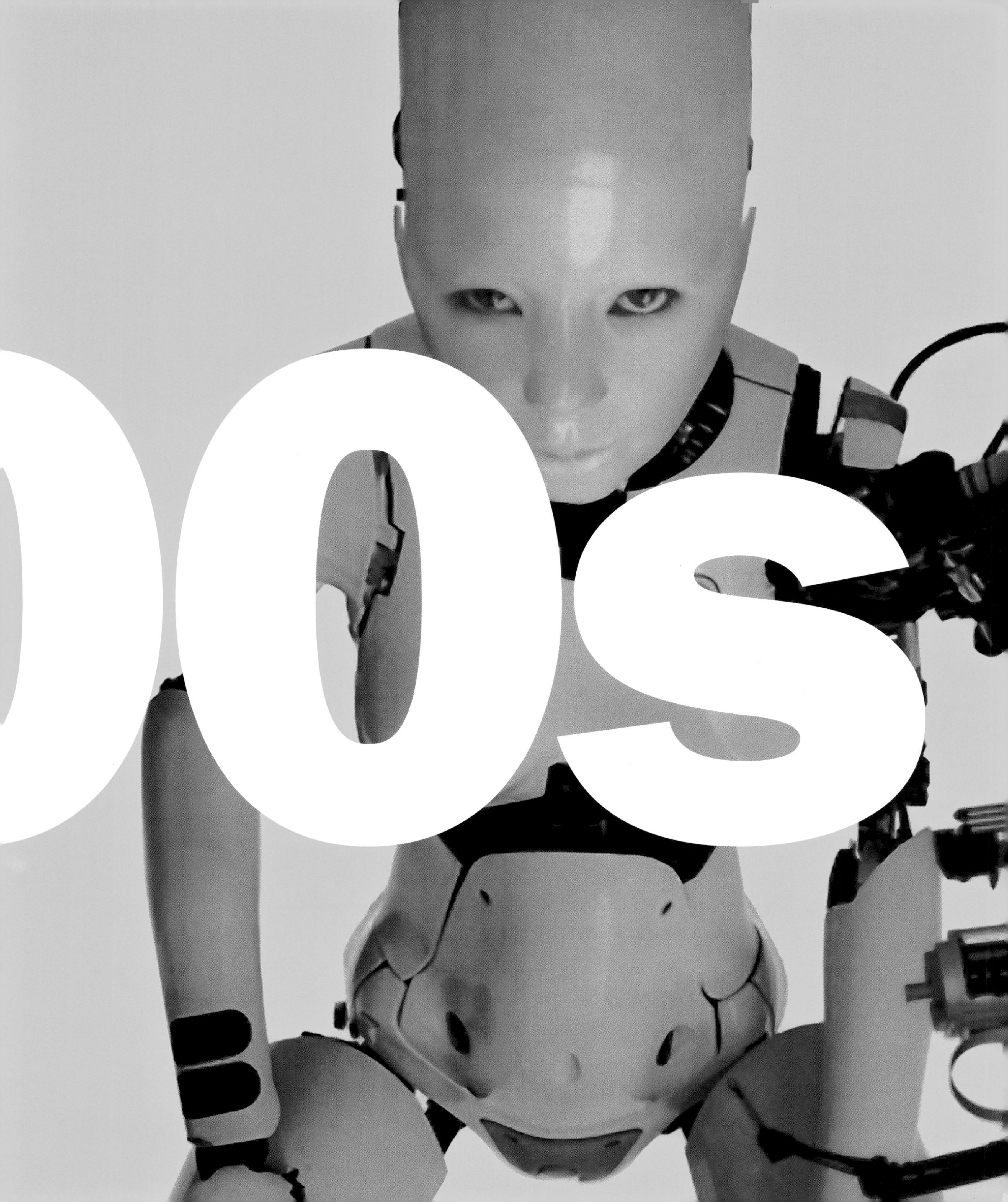
00s

After nearly four decades of social, economic and technological flux, the design and advertising industries entered the new millennium with an array of skills and experiences unprecedented in the history of D&AD. Many of the frailties and flaws identified amid the giant wobble at the end of the eighties had seemingly been fixed. Rapid strides in digital technology had simplified and shortened the production process. Measurement techniques had strengthened the business case for creativity. And new alliances had extended the international reach of the communication sector. (In making the global media village a smaller and more intimate place, designers and art directors brought closer Nicholas Negroponte's prediction about 'the death of distance'.)

The landmark of the millennium itself provided an impetus for creative work, especially in the British design industry which was stimulated by investment from National Lottery funding and by the Labour government's obsessive determination to extract some shiny symbolism from the dawn of a new century. The stand-out projects included a millennium wheel designed by architects David Marks and Julia Barfield, which won a D&AD Gold Award for Environmental Design & Architecture, and a set of 48 Millennium Stamps from the Royal Mail which were commissioned to celebrate 1,000 years of British history and achievement.

2000.01
Designer: **Karl Shanahan**
Publisher: **Phaidon Press**
Century brings together photographic images from world-wide sources to record the astonishing events and advances of the twentieth century.

2000.02
Design group: **CDT Design**
Client: **Royal Mail**
This landmark millennial project was described by D&AD juror Lynn Trickett of Trickett & Webb as 'a last hurrah for illustration'.

2001.01
Architectural design: **Marks Barfield**
Client: **The London Eye Company**
Built without the aid of public money or government subsidy, the aim of the London Eye was to inspire and delight. Great views aside, it is a triumph of engineering. Incredibly light, it is cantilevered out and over the River Thames, and supported on one side only. Aerodynamic wind-shedding passenger capsules give passengers a 360 degree panoramic view when they reach the summit. An example of architecture as advertising – a 3D logo for London.

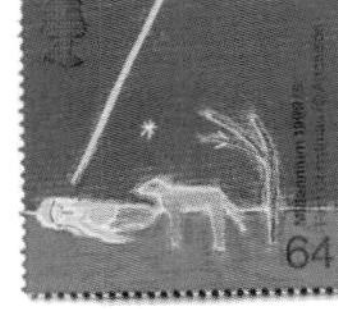

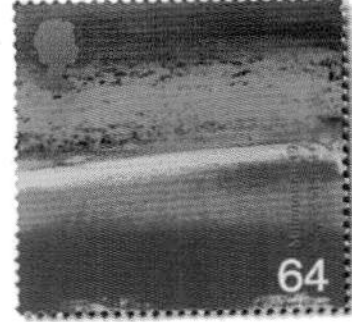

CITY CRUISES 0171 237 5134
A voyage through history to the home of
Westminster to Greenwich

Design group CDT worked with 48 of the most significant British image-makers of the past 40 years, including Peter Blake, Lord Snowdon, Don McCullin, Ralph Steadman, David Gentleman and Bridget Riley, harnessing diverse styles within a generic typographic approach. Meanwhile, the millennium wheel project, called the 'London Eye', overcame a succession of technical hitches which delayed its launch beyond the New Year's Eve deadline. It achieved a level of enduring popularity that revealed the shortcomings and vacuity of the infinitely more expensive Millennium Dome at Greenwich. The London Eye was described in the 2001 D&AD Annual by the organization's chairman Anthony Simonds-Gooding as 'almost a metaphor for creativity at D&AD – an idea which is entrepreneurial and fraught with risk, which is nearly consumed by doubt and cynicism, but which wins through spectacularly in the end.'

But for all the soundbite optimism engendered by the millennium, and for all the undoubted gains of the previous decade, underlying questions remained unanswered about the future of design and advertising. Those questions remain today. Seasoned observers expected to see a new cloud on the horizon and it immediately took shape in the form of a seminal new book, *No Logo: Taking Aim at the Brand Bullies*, by a young Canadian activist called Naomi Klein. In *No Logo*, published in January 2000, Klein linked design and branding with labour abuses and anti-corporate resistance at precisely the moment that popular movements against corporate globalization were emerging around the world, mostly because of the violent anti-World Trade Organization protests in Seattle.

2000.02
Design group: **CDT Design**
Client: **Royal Mail**
The list of image-makers commissioned to contribute to the Millennium Stamps project reads like a *Who's Who* of D&AD, starting with Lord Snowdon who opened the first D&AD exhibition in 1963. Snowdon's startling monochrome portrait of a Dalek, the villainous robot in the popular BBC TV series *Dr Who*, was very nearly something else entirely. Snowdon apparently misheard the brief and thought he'd been asked to photograph a garlic. Meanwhile, Don McCullin, the famous war photographer, spent a week in a field in northern France waiting for the right moment to photograph war graves [see page 426]. After a powerful focus on digital photography throughout the 1990s, illustrators and artists as diverse as Jeff Fisher, George Hardie, Andrzej Klimowski, Peter Blake, Ralph Steadman and Antony Gormley were invited to usher in the new century with drawing of real quality.

opposite

2001.02
Agency: **Saatchi & Saatchi**
Client: **monster.com (Europe)**

2000.03
Agency: **Saatchi & Saatchi**
Client: **COI/The Army**

Two Silver-winning Saatchi projects that owed their cutting edge to the arrival of Antipodean creative director David Droga, one of the youngest in the world. The monster.co.uk press work was part of a campaign for a job recruitment website to 'beware the voices' telling you to do crazy things in the workplace. The scratch cards extended the famous, award-winning Army recruitment campaign into new territory.

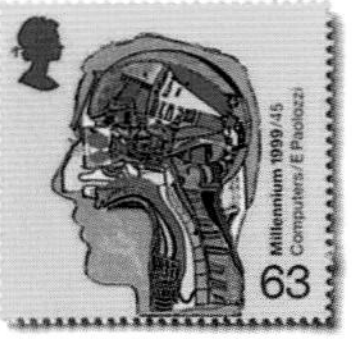

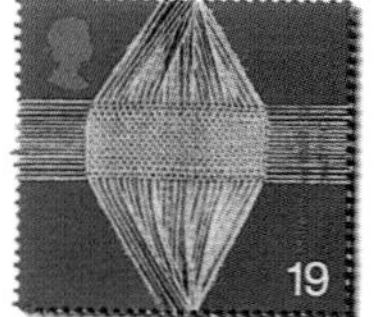

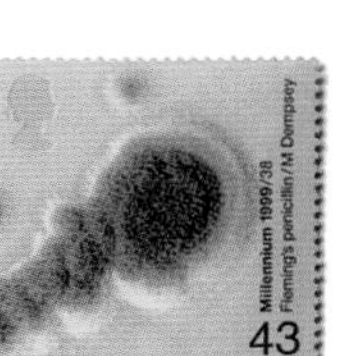

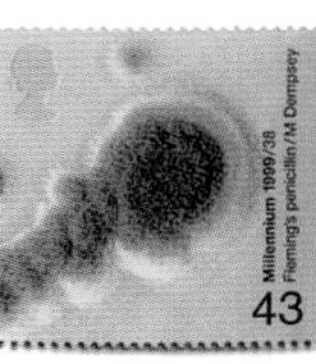

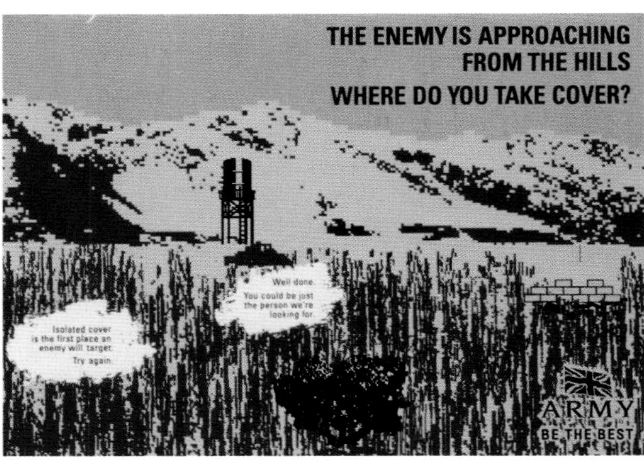

A *Time Europe* review of *No Logo* by Robin Knight in January 2000 explained that 'Klein charges international companies – especially those enjoying high brand recognition – with exploitation, environmental pillage, human rights abuses, hypocrisy, kowtowing to repressive regimes, disowning their homebase workforces, driving down wages and much more besides.' According to *Time*, this fast-selling, anti-capitalist screed was 'one of those totemic, defining works that ultimately transcend fact and acquire a reality of their own.' '*No Logo*,' said the review, 'lacks perspective but it explains why the mobs are angry.' Generation X, a term which came to prominence in the nineties, was now becoming Generation Why.

Naomi Klein, who addressed a D&AD conference on ethics in communication called SuperHumanism in May 2001, immediately became the figurehead of a new movement which implicated design and advertising in the giant conspiracy of corporate globalization. Companies like Nike, that had been garlanded as heroes at D&AD in the nineties, were now right in the firing line. The mood was unsettling, even if the recent trend towards less glossy, more gritty communication had already laid the ground for brands to adopt a less provocative profile in the face of international activism.

Meanwhile, other stormclouds were gathering. A slowdown in the American economy began to alarm the British communication industry which was more dependent than ever before on its state of health. The financial boom in stocks of new media companies, which had followed the revolution in digital media, turned into a disastrous nosedive dubbed 'dot.gone' in Silicon Valley. Escalating media costs and falling audiences for network television forced global clients to cut spending on TV commercials.

When WPP Group chief executive Sir Martin Sorrell, owner of the world's largest design and marketing services group, addressed a D&AD seminar in September 2001, he tried to put a positive spin on the dip in television advertising. Speaking just days before the September 11th atrocities in New York and Washington briefly threatened to reduce the entire communication industry to ground zero, Sorrell argued that client budgets diverted from TV advertising would significantly enhance prospects in below-the-line areas such as direct marketing, interactive media and sales promotion.

As we survey the emerging trends of the noughties less than three years into the new decade, it is impossible to say whether Sorrell's argument will be proven. Such proximity to current events hampers any measured analysis through an inevitable lack of perspective. We can only describe what is currently happening and make an educated guess about the future. But work most recently selected by D&AD juries appears to support the view that these below-the-line disciplines are, indeed, growing in creative stature and potential.

In direct marketing, for example, a witty Granada Media mailer by Tucker Clarke-Williams to promote a Tom Jones TV show among advertisers and journalists catapulted a pair of black cotton knickers out from a vintage sixties record sleeve-style invite, in a homage to the knicker-throwing fans of the Welsh singer. (The creative team tried silk briefs first but they fell parachute-like and lacked the range of the cotton ones.) A direct mail piece for the Alabama Veterans Memorial by Slaughter Hanson took the form of a Western Union telegram – the way Alabama families discovered their loved ones had died serving their country. And an innovative Vodaphone campaign by direct marketing agency Harrison Troughtman sent spoof soccer match tickets, wedding invites and booze bills to households across the UK to persuade people to switch on their voice mail.

 2000.04
Design group:
Tucker Clarke-Williams Creative
Client: **Granada Media**

2000.06
Design group: **The Partners**
Client: **Thrislington Cubicles**

2000.05
Agency: **Slaughter Hanson**
Client: **Alabama Veterans Memorial**

Three Silver-winning projects from 2000 that demonstrated renewed creative vigour and fresh thinking in direct marketing and sales promotion. Tom Jones' famous association with knickers was put to use for Granada Media. A calendar made of soap was part of a long-running campaign masterminded by The Partners for a toilet cubicle manufacturer, while a Western Union telegram was mailed to people in Alabama to inform them of a special memorial service for war veterans.

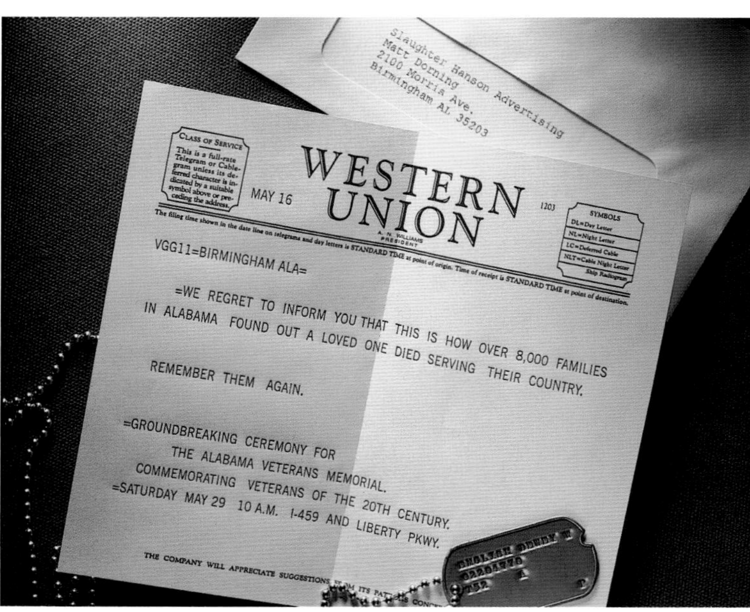

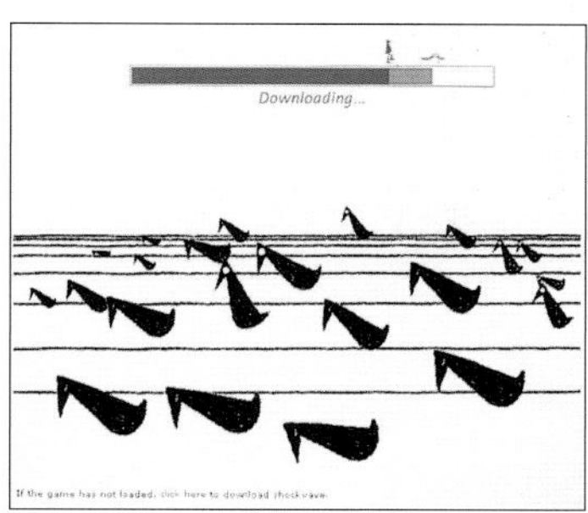

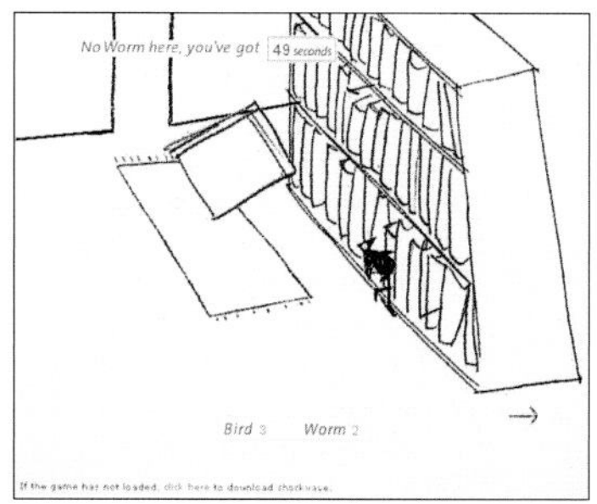

Award-winning sales promotion work included another Thrislington Cubicles calendar designed by The Partners, based on the old 'soap on a rope' idea, with a soap 'tablet' for each day of the year to be broken off and used to 'wash away the 20th century'. As for interactive media, even old-timers like John Webster of BMP DDB entered the fray with an engaging online 'Bird Game' for Compaq, while projects like Studio AKA's Caffeine Society lent web design a new narrative sophistication.

As agencies continued to search for new and different ways to reach more consumers without incurring the rising costs of TV advertising, the area of ambient media – another of D&AD's Cinderella disciplines – also broke into the spotlight. The idea of planting advertising messages directly into the physical environments and onto objects all around us has been around for a while, but apart from one or two outstanding outdoor billboard ideas, the medium had never been exploited to the full. In 2000, a campaign by The Jupiter Drawing Room for South African radio station KFM, a strong supporter of gun control, filled old vending machines with realistic-looking replica firearms and placed them on campuses and in supermarkets. The vending machines bore signs that read: 'This is how easy it is to get hold of a gun in South Africa.' People could readily donate their small change to the gun control lobby by inserting coins in the vending machines.

2000.07
Production companies:
aka PIZAZZ, Edwards Churcher
Clients: **Compaq, BMP DDB**
John Webster showed he could still cut it in the internet age, creating an on-screen Bird Game character for Compaq's website every bit as appealing as the Honey Monster or Cresta Bear.

2001.03
Design group: **Studio AKA**
Client: **IdN Magazine**
While much screen-based design remained mechanistic in structure, this website for IdN magazine introduced a new lyricism in scene setting and storytelling.

2000.08
Agency: **The Jupiter Drawing Room**
Client: **KFM Radio**
Ambient media sprang to the fore as a creative discipline with this powerful campaign for gun control in South Africa.

Clever though this Silver-winning South African ambient media campaign was, even better was to come at D&AD the following year. Mother was asked to create a launch advertising campaign for britart.com, a new venture which aimed to offer an alternative to traditional art galleries and to become the world's largest internet art gallery. Unable to afford TV airtime, the agency opted to use a range of techniques including flyposting art gallery captions onto paving stones, railings and street furniture to create 'instant art'. The idea was that anything the flyposters were affixed to automatically became art, thus conveying the message that britart.com can make original art both accessible and affordable.

The whole premise of britart.com as a dotcom brand was reinforced by a new corporate identity based on the red dot, the small circular sticker used by conventional galleries to show that a piece of artwork has been sold. This irreverent campaign, including mailers of such items as an 'art beard', 'art pencil' and 'preview specs' to further send up the pretentious art world, had an immediate and dramatic effect. In just six weeks, britart.com page views per month rose from 40,000 to 300,000 and monthly sales grew 20-fold.

The britart.com campaign won a Gold Award in the 2001 D&AD Awards, an unprecedented achievement for a low-budget project which gave a huge boost to the unsung discipline of ambient media. But the signs are that other disciplines have begun to benefit from agencies and clients becoming more wary about rushing into make expensive TV commercials.

After years in the creative doldrums when cinematic big-brand imagery ruled, radio advertising looked to be on the up again – although the major players at D&AD were from overseas. There were Silver Awards for Publicis Wellcare Mojo's achingly powerful Australian campaign for the Red Cross Blood Bank and for DDB Chicago's 'Real American Heroes' series for Budweiser Light. 'Heroes' also ran on TV but actually worked better on radio where the under-stated absurdity of the characters was captured more successfully in a series of brilliantly crafted scripts. (Among the 'Real American Heroes' campaign is Mr Horse-drawn Carriage Driver: 'No one knows the guts it takes to ride the subway to work dressed as a foppish dandy from the eighteenth century.')

<u>REAL AMERICAN HEROES</u>

ANNOUNCER: Bud Light Presents...Real Men of Genius.
SINGER: Real Men of Genius.
ANNOUNCER: Today we salute you...Mr. Horse Drawn Carriage Driver.
SINGER: Mr. Horse Drawn Carriage Driver!
ANNOUNCER: You start your day with a tip, tip! and a cheerio!, which is odd because you're from Brooklyn.
SINGER: Jolly Old Brooklyn!
ANNOUNCER: While most people sit behind a desk, you proudly sit two feet behind a four-legged manure factory.
SINGER: Oooh!
ANNOUNCER: No one knows the guts it takes to ride the subway to work dressed as a foppish dandy from the eighteenth century.
SINGER: Hey foppish dandy!
ANNOUNCER: Blaring horns, profanity, vicious insults all met with a courtly tip of your stovepipe hat.
SINGER: Cheerio!
ANNOUNCER: So crack open an ice cold Bud Light, Buggy Boy. (SFX: BOTTLE OPEN) Because the way you say giddy-up makes us say whoa.
SINGER: Whoa! Whoa! Whoa!
ANNOUNCER: Bud Light Beer. Anheuser-Busch. St. Louis Missouri.

<u>Busy Mum</u>

SFX: Telephone conversation.
MOTHER: Hello.
DOCTOR: Mrs Wilson?
MOTHER: Yes?
DOCTOR: It's Doctor Fraser from St George Hospital, Mrs Wilson. I'm afraid your son Matthew's been in an accident, madam.
MOTHER: (shocked) What? What? Matthew?
DOCTOR: (calmly) Now he's going to be all right, but he needs an urgent blood transfusion.
MOTHER: (progressively more hysterical as the doctor explains the situation) Oh my God! Oh my God! Is he all right?
DOCTOR: Yeah he's fine. He's OK.
MOTHER: Oh Matthew! What happened?
DOCTOR: Look, unfortunately, we have no supplies of AB negative blood.
MOTHER: Oh my God! Oh my baby...(suddenly realising what the doctor has just said) I'm AB negative!
DOCTOR: (relieved) That is fantastic. When can you get down to the hospital?
MOTHER: Well it's just that um, I've got this hair appointment, and it's really hard to get into this salon.
DOCTOR: (surprised) Er, Mrs Wilson...
MOTHER: Oh, and then I've got lunch with Jane...
DOCTOR: Mrs Wilson! Your son will die if you do not give blood!
MOTHER: Oh, um all right. Um...pause) what if I come down in the morning after tennis?
SON: Someone desperately needs your blood right now. Call the Red Cross Blood Bank on 13 14 95. Or are you too busy?

2002.01
Agency: **DDB Chicago**
Client: **Anheuser Busch**

2000.09
Agency: **Publicis Wellcare/Mojo**
Client: **Red Cross**

Two Silver Award-winning radio commercials reflecting renewed creative focus on the power of the medium. The influx of work by American and Australian agencies at the start of the noughties showed the growing global status of the D&AD Awards.

this page

2001.04
Agency: **Mother**
Client: **britart.com**
Winning Gold was an unprecedented achievement for this low-budget project that largely avoided paid-for media and used the relatively unsung discipline of ambient media.

'Britart.com is the definitive ambient campaign,' according to D&AD jury foreman Tim Ashton. Britart marketing director Richard Murphy commented, 'Before this advertising we didn't exist as an organization. The idea was to build a strong brand for the art world and art-buying novices alike. Most internet brands just mark a territory. We wanted to communicate real brand values. It had to work on lots of different levels. It was a brave move by us and by Mother too. They pushed us hard into an area where we didn't feel comfortable. But that is exactly where we wanted to be – and it worked. If the agency isn't giving you that stomach-churning feeling, they're not doing their job.'

Pavement 1962

concrete slabs, cement, shoe prints,
dog excrement, chewing gum.
8000 x 15050 x 10cm

Regimented mosaic.
Companion piece to road by the same artist.

art you can buy **britart.com**

Lamp Post 1981

steel pole (hollow), glass,
dog urine.
200 x 10 x 10cm

Totemistic work representing man's beacon
in the existential world.

art you can buy **britart.com**

Wall 1946

mixed media installation: bricks,
tiling, wood, insulation, nails.
2256 x 425cm

Rebuilt 1956.

art you can buy **britart.com**

Cashpoint 1983

glass, steel,
fingerprints, breath.
100 x 150cm

Interactive installation piece. Theme - consumerism.

art you can buy **britart.com**

Car Park 1975

tarmac, oil, urine, cigarette packets,
used condoms.
6000 x 8000 cm

Monumental canvas stained with
the droppings of iron sheep.

art you can buy **britart.com**

Tree 1901

wood, leaves, birds.
500 x 50 x 50cm

Organic sculpture generating oxygen.
A metaphor for life itself.

art you can buy **britart.com**

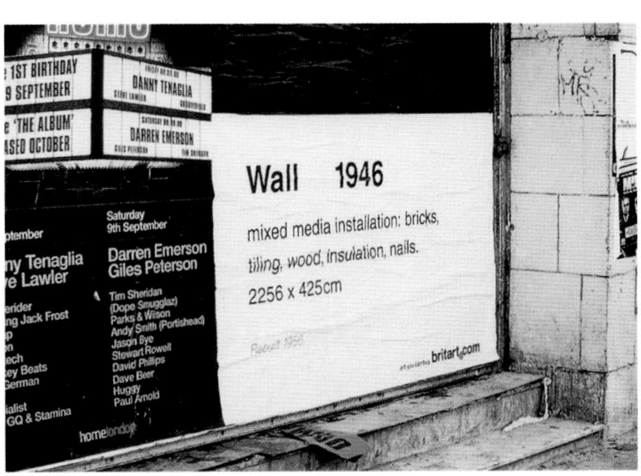

Like the radio medium, packaging design also offered big-selling brands a viable alternative to TV advertising. A campaign by Leo Burnett (Chicago) for Heinz tomato ketchup used the iconic status of the bottle itself to present a series of saucy labels bearing such lines as 'Your Hot Dogs Will Thank You' and 'On A First Name Basis With Onion Rings'. To print cheeky advertising messages on such a famous label (which normally just carries statutory information with the brand name) represented a brave shift of creative strategy.

The Heinz project won a D&AD Silver in 2002 but it wasn't the only packaging work to suggest new directions in the field. Williams Murray Hamm's Wild Brew bottle in the competitive spirit/mixer sector communicated the 'outrageously wild' brand idea with a tiger-skin sleeve. And Lovegrove Studio's plastic mineral water bottle for Ty Nant, bevelled at different angles to represent a piece of ice, expressed the idea of a drink as cool as a mountain stream.

2002.02
Design group: **Leo Burnett (Chicago)**
Client: **H J Heinz Company**
With lines like '14 million French fries can't be wrong', Heinz gambled with the idea that packaging is the advertising that keeps on working, on the supermarket shelf and the kitchen table.

2002.03
Design group: **Coley Porter Bell**
Client: **Chivas & Brothers**
This packaging project developed an original thought by Sedley Place on the spinning Chivas Regal bottle.

opposite

2001.05
Design group:
Williams Murray Hamm
Client: **Interbrew UK**
A classic message – a drink for the party animal. Wild Brew's new look sent sales shooting up.

2002.04
Design group: **Lovegrove Studio**
Client: **Ty Nant**
Ice-cool packaging from Ross Lovegrove for a Welsh mineral water.

Both the Wild Brew and Ty Nant projects were essentially pieces of product design that required no graphic information whatsoever to communicate the core idea. Indeed, it was in product design that the greatest waves were being made at D&AD in the new millennium. All the signs had been there at the end of the nineties, as creative industry commentators began to talk about a new trend – the integration of advertising and product design. This trend reflected the idea that the product itself could intrinsically embody the advertising message in its form and design. For instance, the fabulous range of five different coloured Apple iMacs needed no advertising message other than to be photographed against a simple white background with the copyline 'Yum'. And the Audi TT needed only to be shown driving down a road for the integration of advertising and automotive styling to be complete.

By the start of the new millennium, both Apple and Audi had established powerful visual languages that worked directly on the level of advertising – and D&AD juries were not slow to reward their efforts. Indeed, D&AD's love affair with the work of industrial design chief Jonathan Ive at Apple Computer began to border on the insatiable, with three Golds in the first three years of the noughties for Apple's Cinema Display, Pro Mouse and Apple iPod (a beautifully functional MP3 player). In addition, there were Silvers for the iBook, Pro Speakers, G4 Cube and Titanium PowerBook G4. Little wonder that in 2002, Apple founder and CEO Steve Jobs turned up at the D&AD Awards alongside Jonathan Ive to collect the prizes and share in the applause.

Amid this abundance of awards, D&AD jury members were eager to explain Apple's hot innovation streak. According to Design Council director of design and innovation Clive Grinyer, 'God is in the detail and Apple understands that more than most. They spend extended periods of time with their suppliers and a great amount of effort to achieve what to us appears so simple and beautiful. There's an incredibly innovative approach that goes right through from shape and style to material and manufacturer.' Dick Powell of Seymour Powell added, 'You see gorgeous thick translucent mouldings that take great skill and knowledge to make and this ability puts Apple in the lead. Other companies find it much harder to follow because they just don't know how to do these things.'

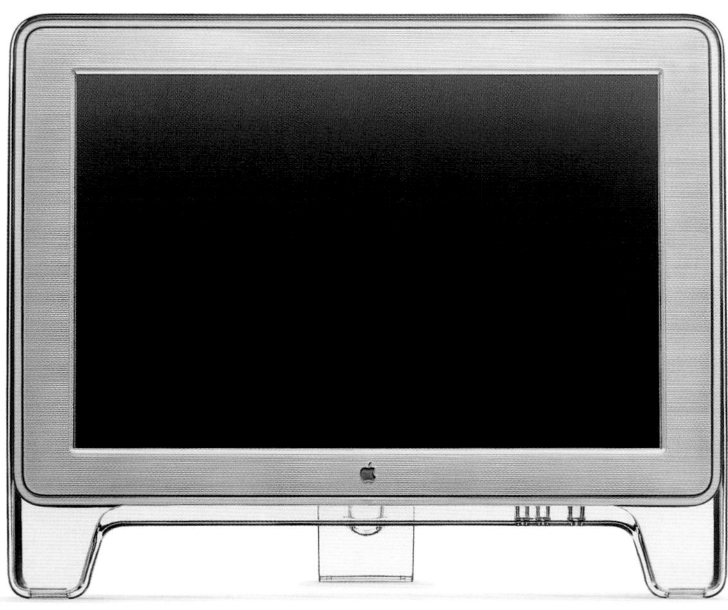

2000.10
Design group: **Apple Industrial Group**
Client: **Apple Computer**

this page

2001.06
Design group: **Apple Industrial Group**
Client: **Apple Computer**

2001.07
Design group: **Apple Industrial Group**
Client: **Apple Computer**

2001.08
Design group: **Apple Industrial Group**
Client: **Apple Computer**

Apple's Cinema Screen won a Gold Award in 2000, and in 2001 they won Silvers for the G4 Cube and Pro Speakers and another Gold for the Pro Mouse. The message from Apple about its products is, whatever the cost, we don't launch anything until every last detail has been perfected. According to Jonathan Ive, Apple's vice-president of industrial design and a master of understatement, 'Apple has a pretty unique culture with a set of beliefs that are really special.'

● 2002.05
Design group: **Apple Industrial Group**
Client: **Apple Computer**
The Gold-winning iPod MP3 player holds 1,200 tracks in a box the size of a deck of cards. According to Apple's industrial design chief Jonathan Ive, 'How the iPod works and how it looks become the same question. This product is a good example of how we design at Apple.'

● 2002.06
Design group: **Apple Industrial Group**
Client: **Apple Computer**

● 2002.07
Design group: **Apple Industrial Group**
Client: **Apple Computer**

In the land of the Apple laptop, small and slender is beautiful. Apple founder Steve Jobs is listed among the design credits on both the iBook and the Titanium PowerBook G4.

2001.09
Design group: **Audi**
Client: **Audi**
Was the market ready for an all-aluminium small people-mover from the Audi stable? The company evidently thought so and invested heavily in the project under design director Peter Schreyer. The car was designed to combine low fuel consumption and low emissions with good looks, prompting *What Car?* magazine to enthuse, 'Audi's all-aluminium baby has already delighted the style-conscious with a conscience.'

2002.08
Design group: **BMW AG**
Client: **BMW AG**
It may belong to BMW but this exuberant and commercially successful reworking of the Mini Cooper heritage under chief designer Bart Hildrebrand is as British as the Union Jack.

Having recaptured Apple's status as a creative pioneer in the early noughties, Steve Jobs signalled his unwillingness to relinquish it again in an interview with *Design Week*. 'No Apple product goes out until every design detail is absolutely right,' he explained, 'whatever the cost of delay. If you are willing to miss the deadline for the launch,' said Jobs, 'that's the moment of truth whether you really care about design as a company.' Jobs was credited on the design team for many Apple D&AD-winning projects, a reflection of the holistic way things work within the company. 'So much of our design process is a design conversation, about a story,' according to Ive.

Audi, too, stayed on a winning course. It followed up its award for the Audi TT Coupe in 1999 with another D&AD Silver for the Audi A2 in 2001. The A2's creative brief was to 'transport four people from Stuttgart to Milan on a single tank of petrol'. The vehicle, which utilizes the company's expertise in aluminium technology, marked Audi's entry into the small MPV (Multi-Purpose Vehicle) market. What excited the D&AD jury was the design language – the A2 is very recognizably an Audi, even though Audi has never built a small MPV before. According to jury foreman Paul Priestman of product design group Priestman Goode, 'Audi has achieved the trick of making the vehicle appear as if it has been hewn out of a solid material.' Less coldly futuristic and more warmly nostalgic was the new Mini Cooper, nominated for a Silver Award in 2002.

Having understudied the main graphic design disciplines at D&AD from the late eighties onwards and having amounted to little more than a diverting side show, three-dimensional design suddenly found itself centre-stage. The pure product brilliance of Apple Computer was part of the reason, but environmental design also found its level at D&AD. 2001 was the big breakthrough year with four landmark schemes getting in among the prizes and two of them – the London Eye and the ...Comment wall at the Science Museum – winning Gold.

The idea of a building as brand statement was writ large in each of the four projects, as architecture itself became a form of communication or advertising. Indeed, the London Eye is as much a logo for London as a three-dimensional piece of engineering, just as Sir Norman Foster's Great Glass House in the National Botanic Garden of Wales, is an integral part of a new image for Wales and Will Alsop's Peckham Library and Media Centre a symbol of inner-city regeneration.

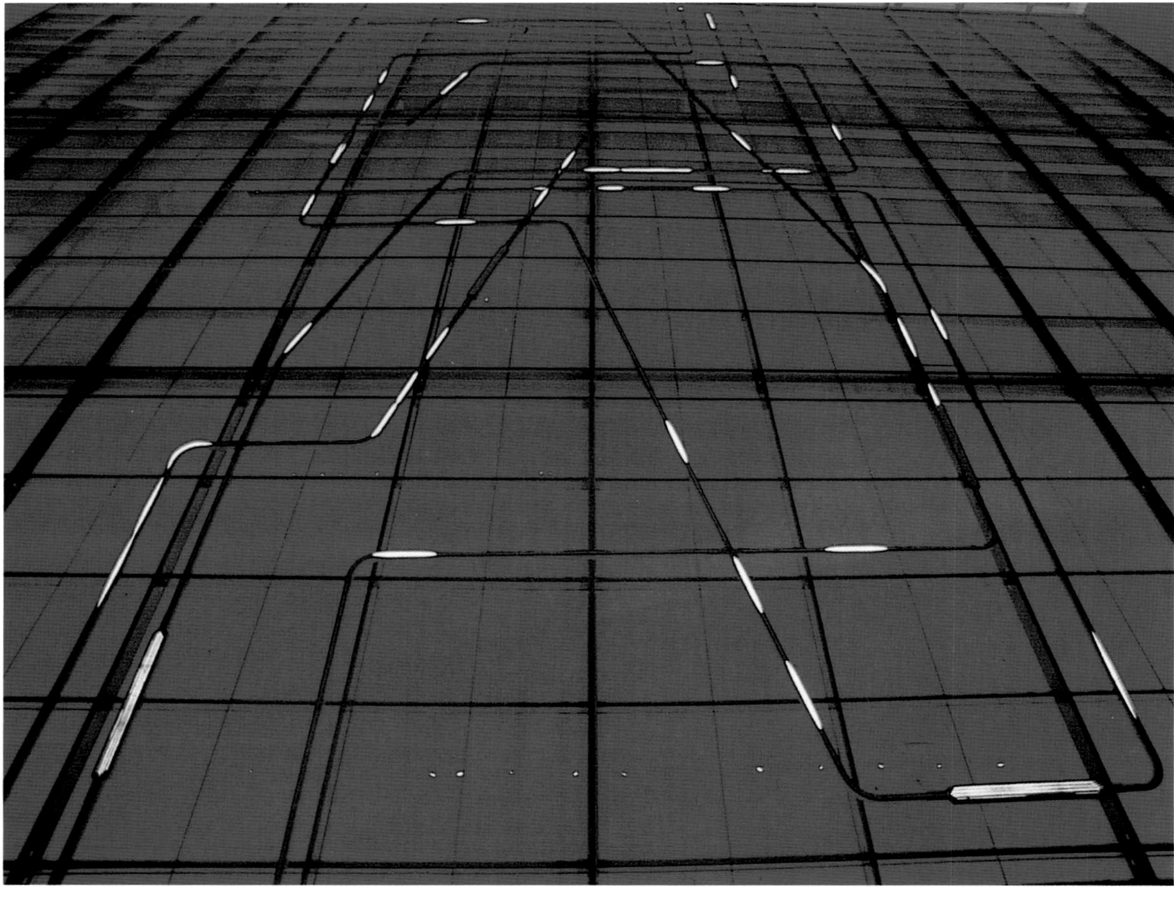

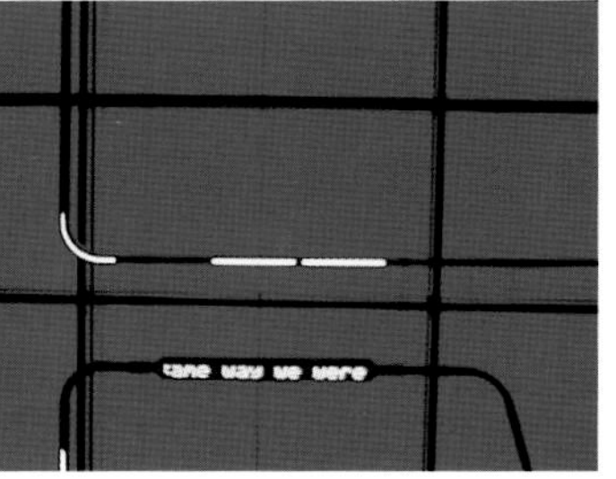

2001.11
Design group: **Alsop Architects**
Client: **Southwark Council**
This library and media centre in Peckham, one of the most socially deprived areas of London, radiates optimism for the future in its bold coloured facade.

2001.12
Design group: **Foster and Partners**
Client: **National Botanic Garden of Wales**
The building as billboard. A skilful interplay of technology and nature for Wales, designed by Britain's most astonishingly prolific high-tech architect Sir Norman Foster.

2001.10
Design groups: **Casson Mann, Itch**
Client: **The Science Museum**
In architect Richard McCormack's Wellcome Wing, a building sealed off from daylight and flooded with blue light, the ...Comment wall takes visitor comments from the Science Museum's feedback system, edits them and displays them as moving 'trains of light' on a giant installation. Still think science is boring? 'A bulletin board for all that is most exciting in the onward rush of science' is how *The Times* described the entire attraction.

According to Science Museum head of design Tim Molloy, 'The wall fits in with and isolates itself from everything else. It works with and against the building – that's what makes it so special.'

this page

2002.09
Architect: **Wilkinson Eyre Architects**
Client: **The Magna Trust**
Working with architects Wilkinson Eyre, lighting designer Jonathan Spiers used coloured effects to make the Magna Centre in Rotherham a memorable experience. In the new crop of environmental schemes at D&AD, lighting would become as ubiquitous to the message as type to a poster.

The giant ...Comment installation, meanwhile, was designed by exhibition designer Casson Mann and interactive media specialist Itch to hang on the back wall of the new £50 million Wellcome Wing of the Science Museum in London, which opened in July 2000. Bathed by a deep blue light, it is 26 metres high and looks like a giant train set featuring small lines of light shooting up and down the tracks. These 'light trains' are digitized information – taking visitor comments inputted into terminals and turning them into a stunning visual display.

...Comment combined graphic communication, exhibition design and interactive media in a single architectural concept, capturing the growing mood of convergence across the design disciplines. Its powerful effects were echoed in the Magna Project, another recipient of National Lottery millennial largesse which won Silver in 2002. This scheme is a conversion of the redundant site that was once Britain's largest steelworks in Rotherham, South Yorkshire; it creates a popular science centre while retaining a sense of the danger, drama and darkness of the original plant.

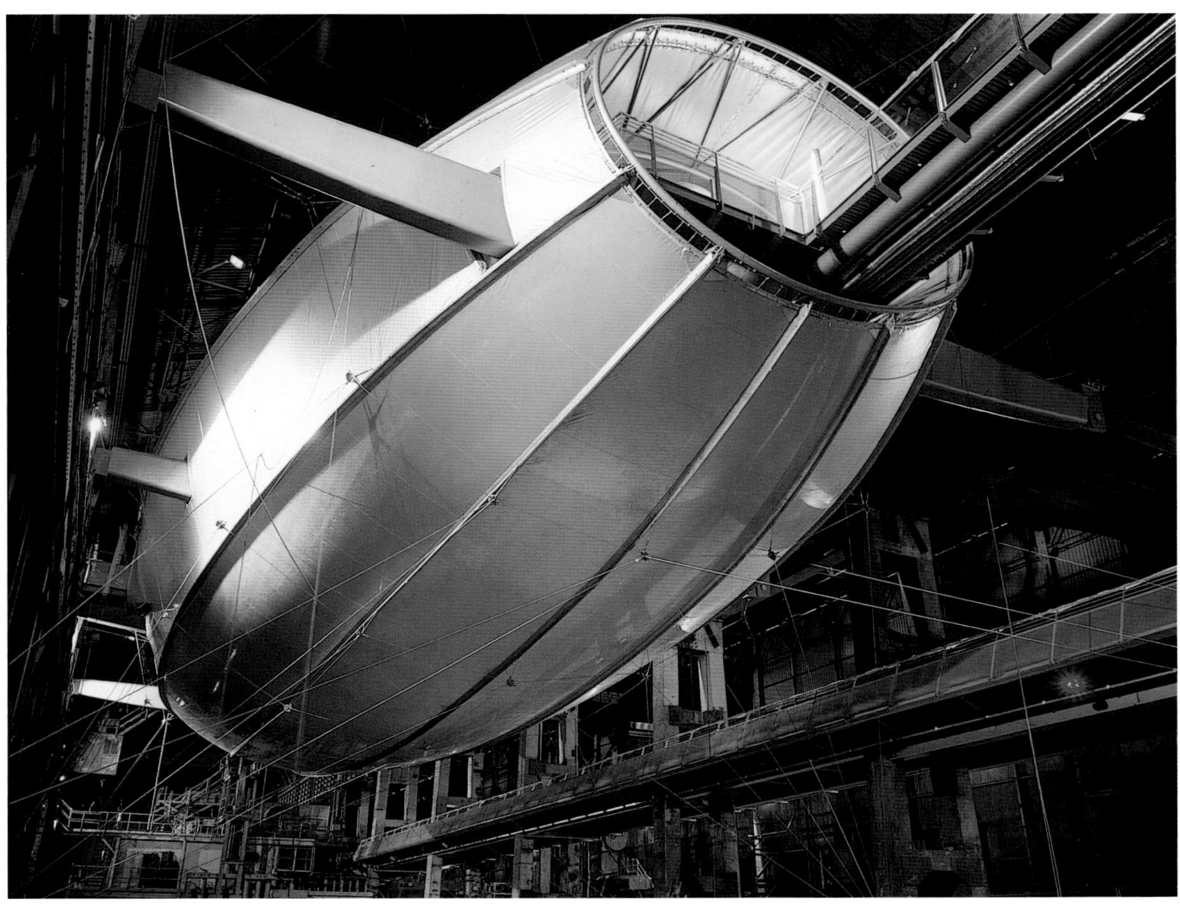

Other environmental schemes recognized by D&AD were more conventionally interior-like than the science projects in the Wellcome Wing or at Magna. There were hotels, bars and shops, some of them – like the oki-ni store in Savile Row by 6a Architects or Yo! Below Bar in Soho by Simon Condor Associates – bearing those minimalist Japanese credentials seemingly essential for success at D&AD. Whatever one's view of the results, it became clear that architects, exhibition designers and interior designers had at last found a place within the communication arts.

2000.11
Design groups:
Agence Starck, Ian Schrager Design
Client: **Ian Schrager Hotels**
The only known sighting of Frenchman Philippe Starck, widely regarded as the world's most important designer of furniture and interiors, at D&AD. Starck's studio collaborated with London architects Harper Mackay to create this project for hotel magnate Ian Schrager, so bringing a style made famous at the Royalton in New York to London.

opposite

2002.10
Design group: **6a Architects**
Client: **oki-ni**
A tailored concept for clothes retailing. You choose the material and the clothes are mailed to you later. How Japanese and minimal can you get? D&AD juries proved that they couldn't get enough of this kind of work.

2000.12
Design group:
Simon Condor Associates
Client: **Yo! Sushi (Soho)**
This project marked a new venture from Yo! Sushi entrepreneur Simon Woodroffe. The concept is gimmick drinking combined with good design: a bar where customers can pour their own beer at low tables, utilizing a computer-controlled beer supply system. Designer Simon Condor overcame the problem of a dark, damp space with low ceilings by sinking the tables into a raised floor.

The graphic design disciplines, however, entered the new century on much less of a high. Across the sector, there seemed an uncertainty and a search for new ideas destined to lead nowhere in particular. Some of D&AD's legacy of craft excellence lived on in special edition book projects such as Aboud.Sodano's volume about fashion designer Paul Smith for Violette Editions (entitled *You Can Find Inspiration in Everything*) and Trickett & Webb's publication to celebrate the Royal Mail Millennium Stamps. The stamp book used 'a thousand words' (by writer Michael Benson) and a stamp perforation timeline to discuss the 48 stamps in the collection. An expensively bound item and a *tour de force* of typographic and printing finesse, the book was conceived as a continuously bound concertina so that type could weave across spreads. It won a D&AD Silver Award in 2000.

The problem-solving tradition also endured at D&AD in the shape of work like Lippa Pearce's 'Children at War' poster for the charity Witness. This was designed for an awareness event highlighting the plight of child soldiers around the world. It is based on the shocking incongruity of scale between a gun and a child, and is reinforced by the typographic twist on the word 'Infantry'. Martin Lambie-Nairn also won a Silver Award for a rational and intelligent identity scheme for BBC Television in response to the multi-channel proliferation of the digital age.

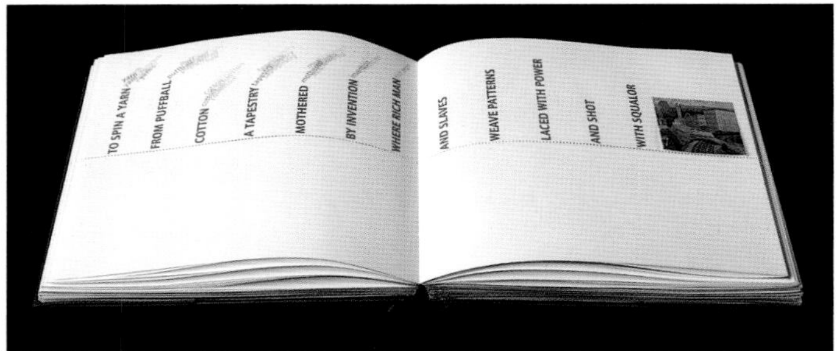

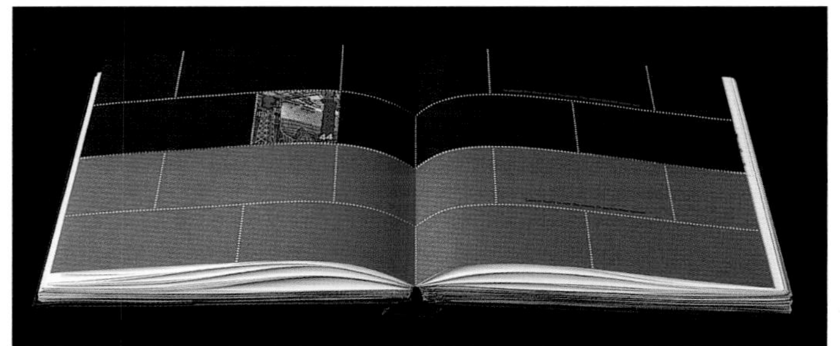

2000.14
Design group: **Trickett & Webb**
Client: **Royal Mail**
A companion piece to the Millennium Stamps project, this expensively bound book is a sensitive and rewarding piece of typographic and printing finesse.

2000.13
Design group: **Lambie-Nairn**
Client: **BBC Television**
Martin Lambie-Nairn took BBC Television into the multi-channel digital age with this identity programme. 'If ever there was a project that looked unsolvable, this was it,' he remarked. The most common comment is always – how on earth did you get it through with all the disparate factions at the BBC?'

2002.11
Design group: **Aboud.Sodano**
Publisher: **Violette Editions**
Book design and beyond. There are 30 different cloth covers as well as a magnifying glass within the polystyrene cover (designed by Apple's Jonathan Ive). Design director Alan Aboud said the project took him years – but only a complete *tour de force* could do justice to Paul Smith's magpie-like eclecticism as a fashion designer.

2001.13
Design group: **Lippa Pearce Design**
Client: **Witness**

2001.14
Design group:
Four IV Design Consultants
Client: **Burberry**

Lippa Pearce's poster for Witness used a brilliantly simple trick to highlight the horrors of children at war. Four IV is a design firm better known for its interiors but that didn't stop a Silver Award in graphic design coming its way.

2001.15
Designer: **Bruce Mau Design Inc.**
Publisher: **Phaidon Press**
Building on the success of his book project with Rem Koolhaus (S,M,L,XL), Bruce Mau neatly camouflaged a book about his studio's work with polemical treaties and quasi-intellectual rigour. How many people actually read the book is highly debatable, but its influence on the designer-as-author debate is unavoidable.

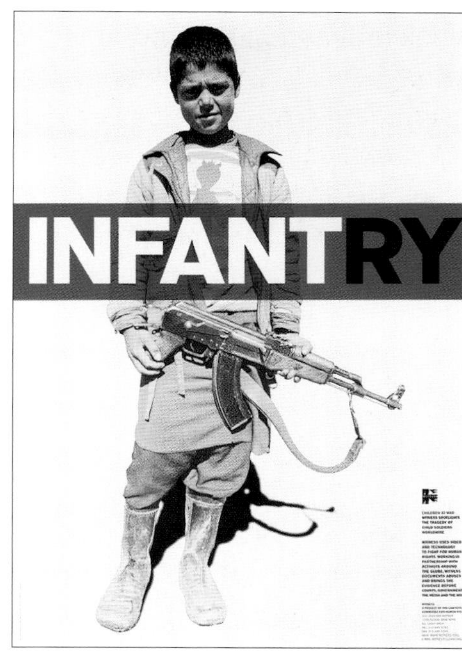

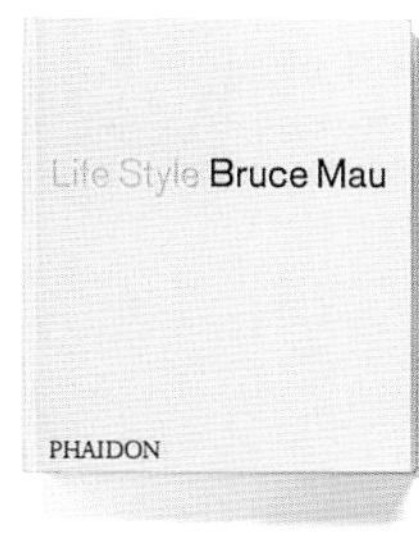

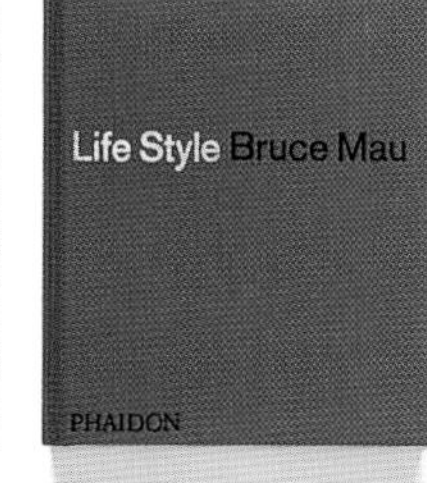

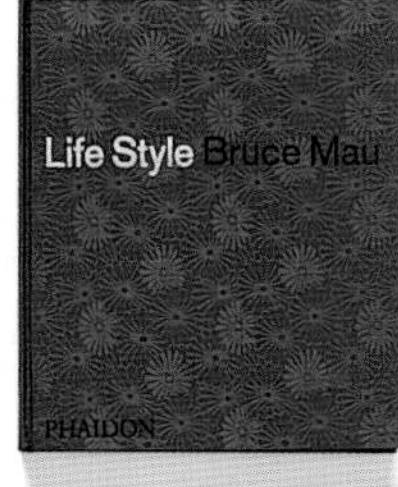

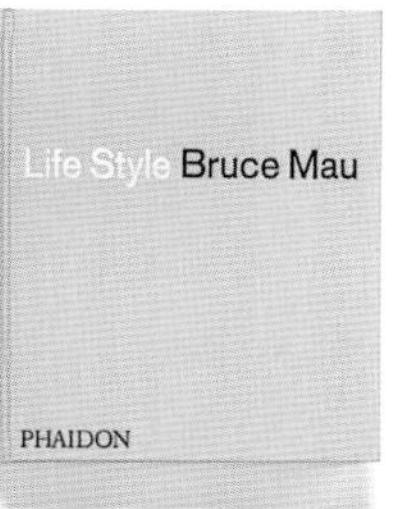

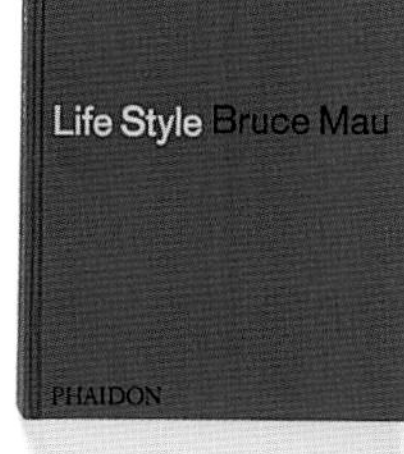

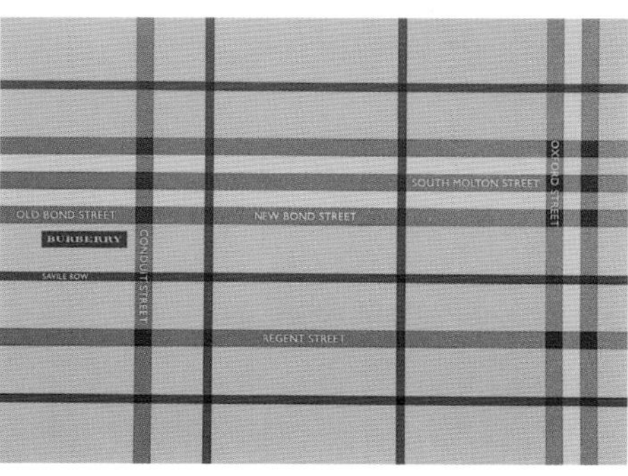

Elsewhere, the dark mood of the late nineties reached its sharpest point – literally – with a poster by Sagmeister Inc. to promote an AIGA Detroit/Cranbrook Academy of Art lecture by Stefan Sagmeister. This showed the naked designer displaying all the details of the event (right down to the sponsor credits) gouged directly into his skin with what looked like a rusty nail. The bloodied Sagmeister is holding a box of sticking plaster. An ironic commentary on how designers suffer for their art? As D&AD jury foreman Michael Beirut of Pentagram observed: 'Perhaps the most telling piece is the one that breaks the mould. Stefan Sagmeister's frozen bit of performance art ignores not just the last half-century of graphic design but a half-millennium of communications technology going back to Gutenberg. And all for a speech in Michigan!'

2000.15
Agency:
Saatchi & Saatchi Wellington
Client: **New Zealand Symphony Orchestra**
When the *Rite of Spring* by Igor Stravinsky was premiered in 1913, it shocked the audience so much that a riot broke out. To demonstrate the power of a live performance by the New Zealand Symphony Orchestra, this ad presented a spirited typographic interpretation of Stravinsky's music, in the form of a dinner party conversation that gets progressively louder and more chaotic as the instruments talk to each other and fragments of conversation literally take flight.

opposite

2000.16
Design group: **Sagmeister Inc.**
Client: **AIGA Detroit**
A gruesome image to promote a lecture by designer Stefan Sagmeister which turned the printing clock back to the Dark Ages while providing an ironic commentary on how designers suffer for their art. Conspiracy theorists claimed that he faked the savagery in Photoshop but they should not be believed. Sagmeister maintains he still bears the scars – especially when he goes out in the sun.

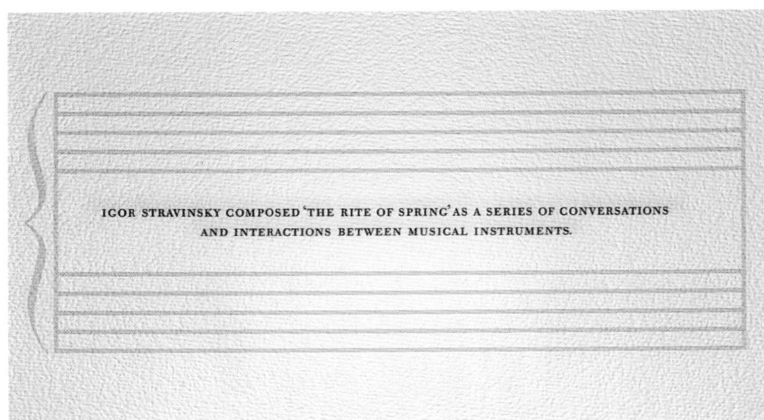

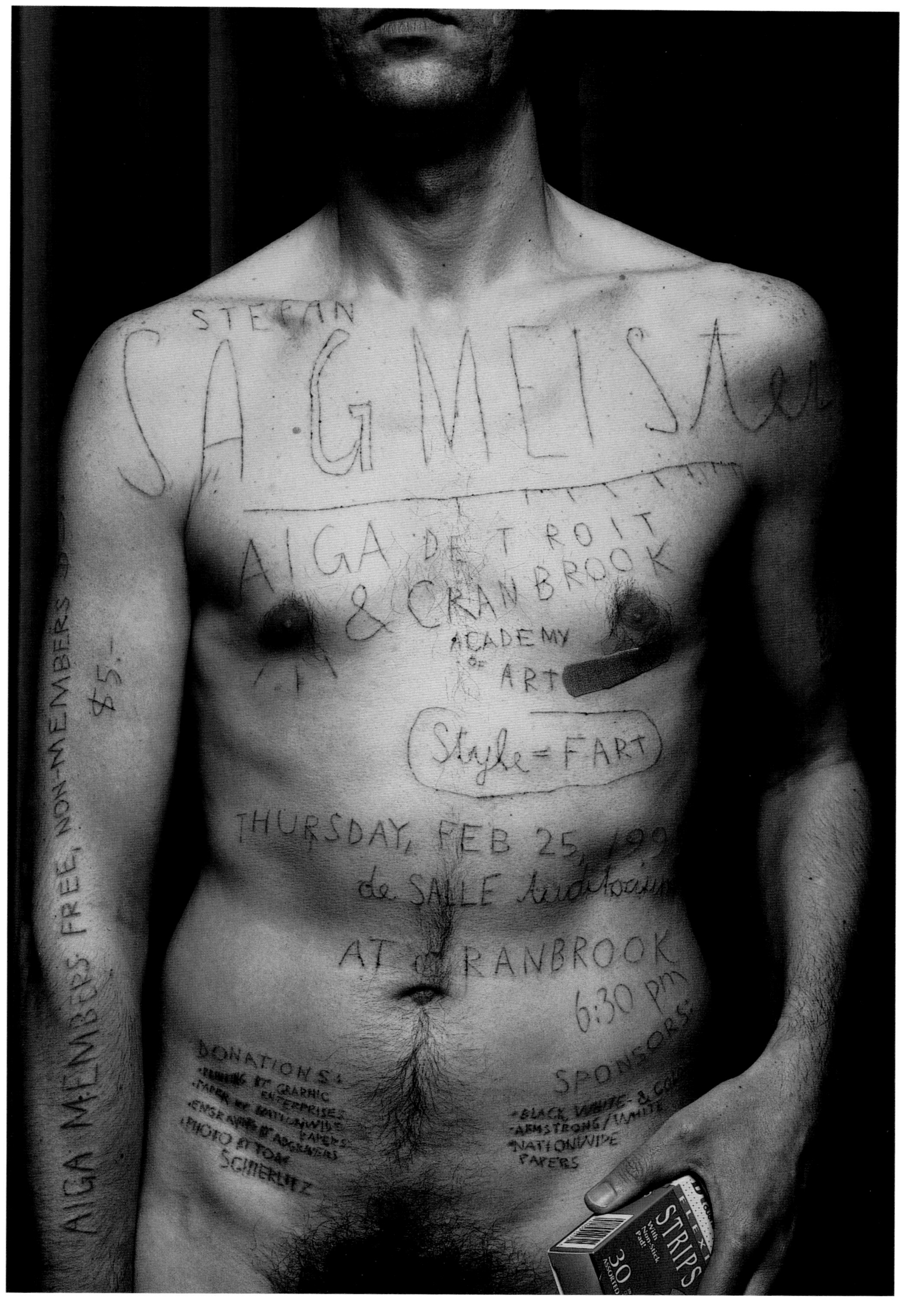
STEFAN
SAGMEIS
AIGA DETROIT
& CRANBROOK
ACADEMY OF ART
Style = FART
THURSDAY, FEB 25, 199
de SALLE
AT CRANBROOK
6:30 pm
SPONSORS:
ARMSTRONG/WHITE
NATIONWIDE PAPERS
DONATIONS:
PAPER BY NATIONWIDE PAPERS
PHOTO BY TOM SCHIERLITZ
AIGA MEMBERS: FREE, NON-MEMBERS $5.-
STRIPS
30

Sagmeister's painful Silver-winning poster shouted 'look at me', in contrast to a more Zen-like mood which subsequently descended on graphic design at D&AD. A Farrow Design CD cover for Spiritualized with a calming embossed face, a johnson banks brochure for a paper company with an expanse of white lab nothingness and 'Vapour Trail', a TV ident for Channel 4, hinted at the drift away from work which seeks attention to work which simply says 'let it be'. The unaffected line drawings in Julian Opie's work for a Blur album cover, designed by Vent, and in Jon Rogers' seemingly old-fashioned illustrations for a Guinness Extra Cold poster campaign by Abbott Mead Vickers (AMV) further caught the mood of stepping right back from straining for effect. It appeared that graphic design had exhausted itself after years and years of trying to be clever and novel. Many practitioners now seemed to be pausing for breath, recognizing that doing less may achieve more, and that this was no bad thing.

Press and poster advertising in the noughties also rode the Zen-like trend, but in a different way. After all those experiments with busy collages and intrusive editorial-style shock tactics in the nineties, much of the new work observed the maxim 'less is more'. Some campaigns began to drop headlines (and even logos) in favour of imagery which relied on the visual double-take.

2002.12
Design group: **Farrow Design**
Clients: **Arista, Spaceman**
Don Brown's sculpture, called Yoko, is the centrepiece of this CD packaging design for Spiritualized.

opposite

2002.13
Design group: **Spin**
Client: **Channel Four**
Channel 4's identity was once synonymous with in-your-face computer graphics. Here, the flowing bars were given a new twist, replaced by vapour trails from passing jets. The result was a serene bit of breathing space between programmes.

2002.14
Designers: **Greg Stogden, Jay Hess**
Client: **Tank Publications**
Andreas Laufer's art direction for Tank Publications doesn't strain for effect.

2002.15
Design group: **johnson banks**
Client: **Smurfit Townsend Hook**
A spoof brochure for a real product. The paper is called Fab and is made in Snodland (near Maidstone in Kent), a place which sounds Scandinavian. The brochure features a geeky hero called Björn who dreams up a new paper. Many people were fooled by the piece.

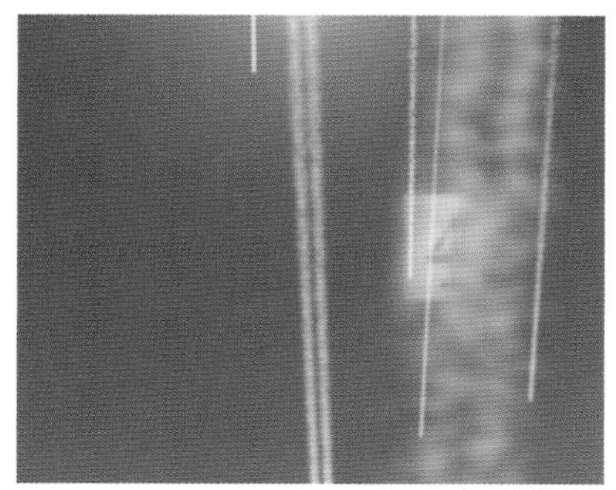

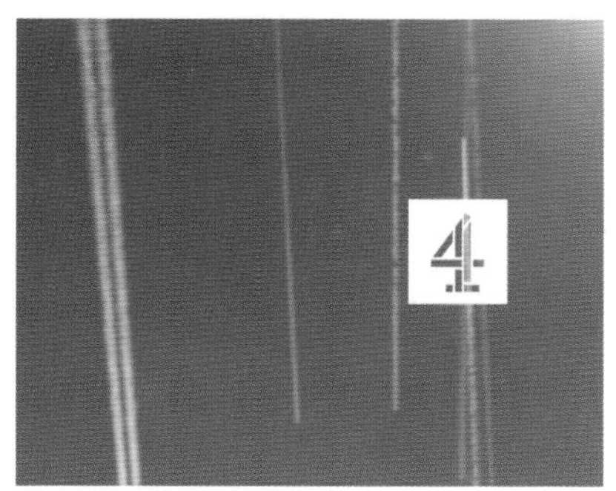

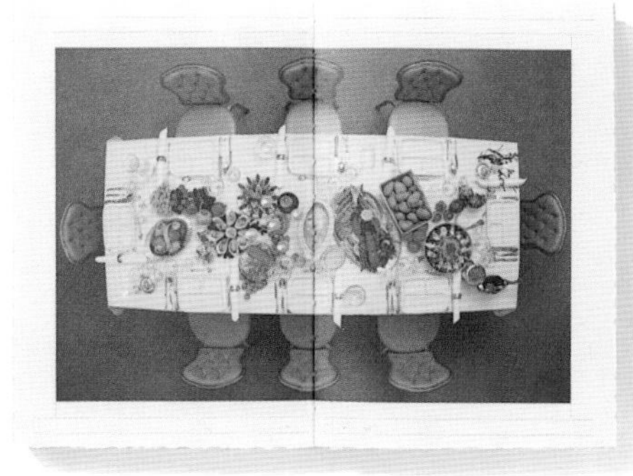

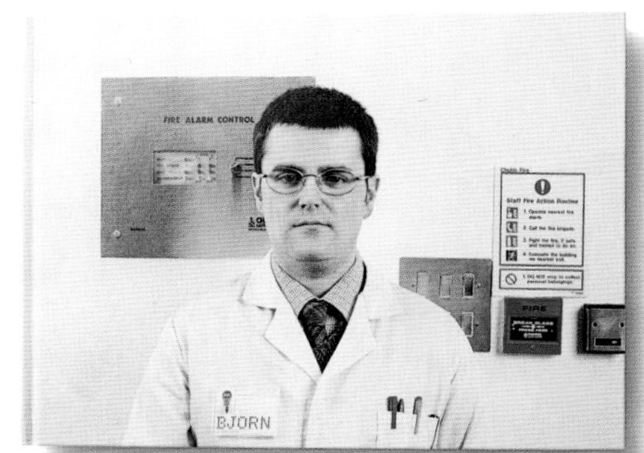
FIRE ALARM CONTROL
BJORN

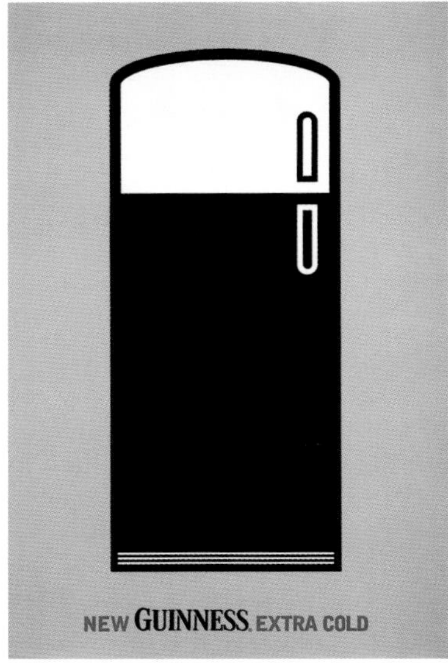
NEW GUINNESS EXTRA COLD

NEW GUINNESS EXTRA COLD

NEW GUINNESS EXTRA COLD

NEW GUINNESS EXTRA COLD

GUINNESS
EXTRA COLD

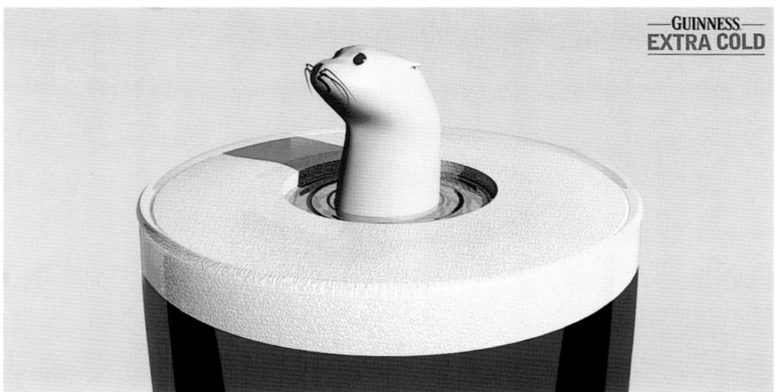
GUINNESS
EXTRA COLD

blur

2000.17
Agency: **Abbott Mead Vickers.BBDO**
Client: **Guinness**
Jeremy Carr's work on this Guinness Extra Cold poster campaign introduced a new simplified language with the interplay of black and blue. The illustrator was Jon Rogers.

2002.16
Agency: **Abbott Mead Vickers.BBDO**
Client: **Guinness**
The award-winning campaign continued, this time with illustration by Faiyaz Jafri in a style which looks computerized.

2001.16
Design group: **Vent**
Client: **Parlophone Records**
Julian Opie's simple portrait of Blur, which captures a prevalent mood, owed much to a revival of interest in the work of artist Patrick Caulfield.

2002.17
Agency: **Abbott Mead Vickers.BBDO**
Client: **The Economist**
The *Economist* campaign doesn't even need to mention the title of the publication, so firmly fixed is the brand language in the viewer's mind.

this page

2001.17
Agency: **TBWA\Paris**
Client: **Sony Computer Entertainment Europe**
Blasphemous or brilliant? Or both? This press ad is from the creative team of Jorge Carreno and Eric Helias.

2001.18
Agency: **TBWA\London**
Client: **Sony Computer Entertainment Europe**
Another provocative project by Paul Belford and Nigel Roberts. Stand right back and this poster reveals a (Freudian) face. Stand forward and it shows only the PlayStation symbols.

In a press ad for Sony by TBWA\Paris, a figurine of Lara Croft replaced Jesus Christ on a boy's bedroom wall as he sleeps beneath the icon. A poster for John West by Leo Burnett had a fishing line cast into the centre of the tin, shot by photographer Andy Roberts to resemble a rippling pool. A press campaign for the Whitbread Beer Company by Lowe Lintas showed priceless design classics like a Charles Eames chair being used casually as a bottle opener for a reassuringly expensive bottle of Stella Artois. A Saatchi & Saatchi campaign for Club 18-30 used photo-manipulation (and the viewer's dirty mind) to suggest that more is going on at the beach and in the bar than at first seems evident.

Meanwhile, the long-running *Economist* poster campaign by AMV became even more minimalist, if that is possible. Already working in the tightest of creative straitjackets, the agency stripped back even more to reveal two Silver-winning gems: 'Smarties', which used the caps of Smarties sweet tubes to spell out 'The Economist', and 'Missing Piece', which removed one jigsaw piece from a giant red poster. This approach worked on the balance sheet as well as the billboard. With this campaign AMV succeeded in breaking one of the cardinal rules of advertising which says that you can't build a brand through posters. The financial results of the poster campaign brooked no argument. Between 1988 and 2000, worldwide circulation of *The Economist* doubled and advertising revenue increased by 250 per cent.

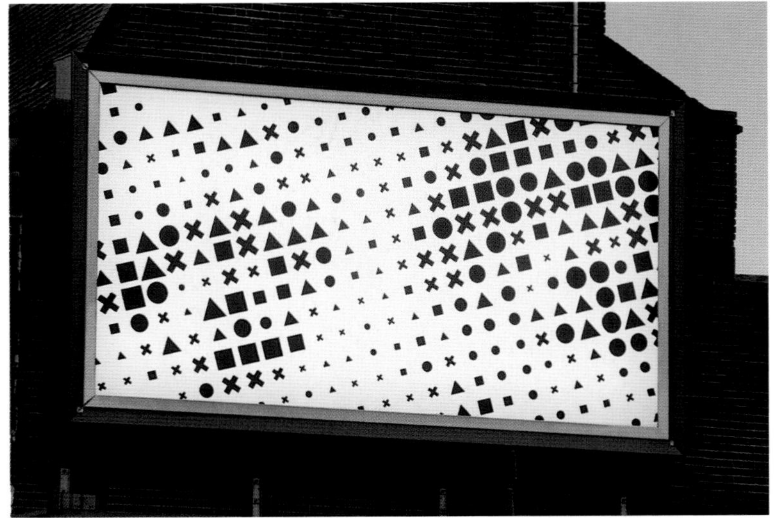

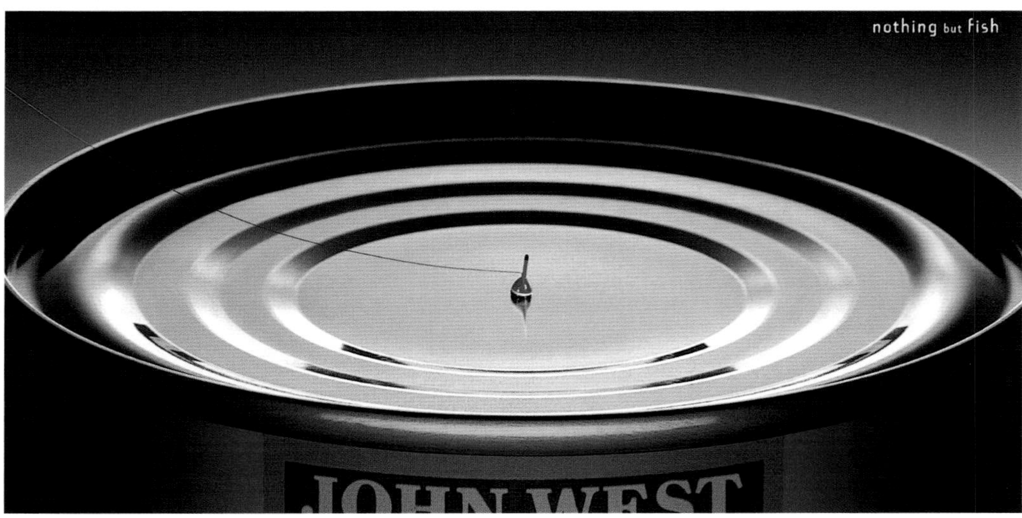

2001.19
Agency: **Leo Burnett**
Client: **John West**
An arresting visual image to complement the John West line 'nothing but fish' in this poster from Leo Burnett.

2000.18
Agency: **Lowe Lintas**
Client: **Whitbread Beer Company**
This press campaign begged the question, what item would you be willing to damage to open your reassuringly expensive bottle of Stella Artois?

opposite

2002.18
Agency: **Saatchi & Saatchi**
Client: **Club 18-30**
If you don't see the fairly crude visual *double entrendres* in this poster campaign then you haven't got a dirty enough mind to go on a racy Club 18-30 holiday. Self-selecting advertising, really. Apparently these ads ran in Ibiza, a classic case of preaching to the converted.

club
18-30
www.club18-30.co.uk

club
18-30
www.club18-30.co.uk
IBIZA

club
18-30
www.club18-30.co.uk

If posters could cut it commercially in the noughties, along with such disciplines as ambient media, packaging design, radio advertising and direct marketing, then what price the blockbuster television commercial in an age of fragmenting TV audiences? As is the way of these things, just as its obituary was being prepared, the TV advertising category at D&AD immediately produced an absolute classic. 'Surfer', a thrilling commercial for Guinness by AMV filmed in Hawaii using local surfers, again featured the talents of copywriter Tom Carty and art director Walter Campbell working with director Jonathan Glazer. The line 'good things come to those who wait' was used in the context of a champion surfer waiting for, and then riding, the ultimate wave of crashing water, foam and wild-eyed white horses. 'Surfer' won two Golds in 2000 for television advertising and direction.

According to Peter Souter, the agency's executive creative director and D&AD's President in 2002, the script was hardly extensive, 'Men stand on beach. Men wait for waves. Men go in and fight waves. Men stop fighting waves. There may be horses. So it's quite a challenge to the imagination to see how that might work.' The client, Guinness marketing director Gary Haigh, was clearly up to the task: 'It sent a shiver down my spine because of the shots that Jonathan captured of waves, of power and surfing, of celebration, communion and bonding. It was better than anything I had expected and that was even without the horses who went on later in a lab. I thought the horses would make it 10 per cent better but they made it 50 per cent better and it was pretty good to start with.'

'Surfer' took Guinness to new heights. 'Beer advertising has always been dominated by four guys in a pub and something funny happening,' explained D&AD jury foreman Dave Waters of Duckworth Finn Grubb Waters. 'This commercial rewrites the rules for the entire sector and does so with such *élan* and style.' Other Guinness work also caught the eye at D&AD. Art director Rob Oliver's stylish work on television sponsorship credits for the Rugby World Cup, playing smoothly on the black and white theme, won a Silver. So did another atmospheric Guinness commercial by Campbell and Carty, 'Bet On Black', set at a Cuban snail race and featuring authentic Cuban music by Beny Moré.

2000.19
Agency: **Abbott Mead Vickers.BBDO**
Client: **Guinness**
Directed by Jonathan Glazer, 'Surfer' was the first ever TV commercial to win two Gold Awards at D&AD in one year. The hero of the film was not cast in London but discovered on location on the beach in Hawaii. He looked right but apparently wasn't a great surfer. Then the waves weren't high enough and the production team had to plead with the client for more time. It all came right in the end. As Guinness discovered, good things come to those who wait.

GOOD THINGS COME TO THOSE WHO WAIT.

GOOD THINGS COME TO THOSE WHO WAIT.

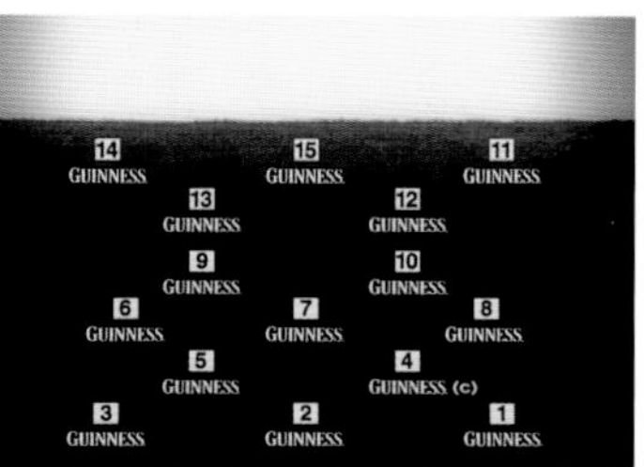

2000.20
Agency: **Abbott Mead Vickers.BBDO**
Client: **Guinness**
A Cuban snail race was the setting for director Frank Budgen's atmospheric commercial for Guinness. It combined cinematic values with the 'ugly' real-life casting that is *de rigeur* for modern advertising.

2002.19
Agency: **Lowe**
Client: **Reebok UK**
Reebok's 'Sofa' ad (directed by Frank Budgen) featured a homicidal piece of furniture preventing our hero getting out for some exercise.

2000.21
Agency: **Abbott Mead Vickers.BBDO**
Client: **Guinness**
Not the All Blacks exactly, but Guinness used its brand cleverly in TV sponsorship credits for the Rugby World Cup.

opposite

2002.20
Agency: **Bartle Bogle Hegarty**
Client: **Levi Strauss**
Another commercial which signalled the confirmation of Frank Budgen as a major directing talent. Levi's 'Twist' showed a car's youthful passengers unwinding (literally) at a roadside diner.

2001.20
Agency: **Bartle Bogle Hegarty**
Client: **Levi Strauss**
Levi's wins a Silver Award at D&AD for Photography and Image Manipulation with this shot by Rankin, suggesting the idea of 'twisted to fit.'

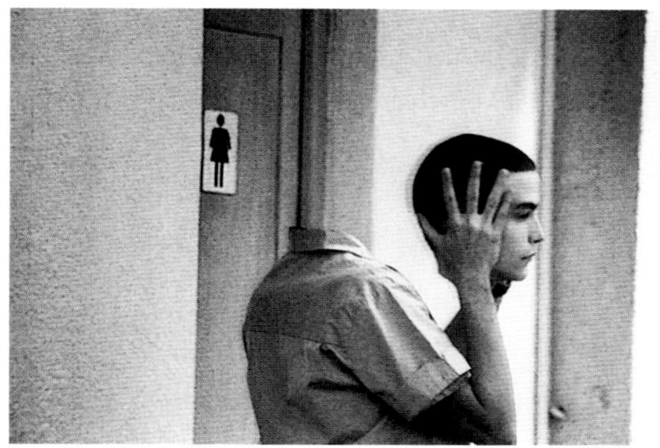

'Bet On Black' was superbly directed, not by Jonathan Glazer but by Frank Budgen, a rising star of the new millennium. It was Budgen's surreal work on Bartle Bogle Hegarty's (BBH) Levi's commercial 'Twist', winner of a D&AD Gold in 2002, that has really brought him to prominence. 'Twist' introduced a new genre in commercials, giving the ugly-edgy look that had been around for a while a new high-style sheen. The film shows a gang of young, thin, beautiful people turning up at an urban diner at night and generally twisting their body parts – even swapping heads – while having fun. The effect is weirdly compelling and highly original. As you'd expect from a Levi's commercial, the whole thing was brilliantly edited with a stunning soundtrack from Pepe Deluxe.

2002 was a big year for Budgen, who also picked up Silver Awards for 'Sofa', a Reebok commercial from the Lowe agency in which a manically animated sofa tries to prevent a young man from going to the gym, in the style of a mini-Hitchcock horror flick, and for 'Tag', a Nike commercial from Wieden + Kennedy USA in which city commuters play a schoolyard game of tag across the metropolis. Not only did these TV ads demonstrate Budgen's cinematic versatility but they also confirmed that the sportswear brand war remained as real as ever – despite the noises off from *No Logo* and its army of disciples.

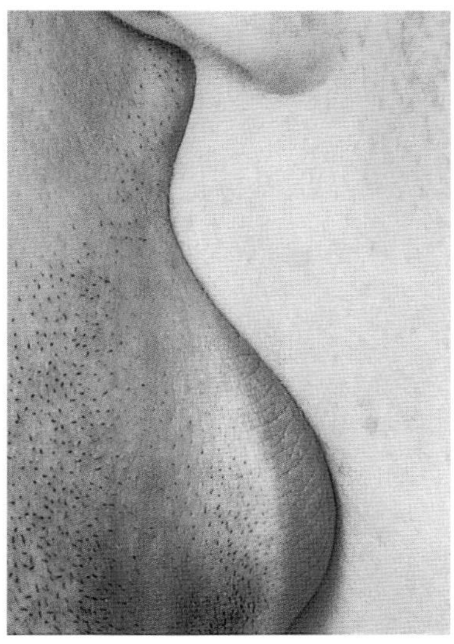

Elsewhere in TV and cinema advertising and graphics, the phenomenon labelled 'oddvertising' by Warren Berger, author of *Advertising Today* (Phaidon Press, 2001), continued to flourish. A succession of offbeat characters up to weird things populated the award-winning work at D&AD in the early noughties – from the hopelessly deluded wannabe musician in a Mother campaign for Q Television, to the Jukka Brothers, three troll-like figures living in the woods, who became cult figures in spots to promote MTV as a global brand. The Jukka Brothers, the antithesis of cool, want to be where it's at so they watch MTV all day in their hut. In one scene, Little Jukka, who constantly contravenes the cool code, is spanked by his big brothers with a ping-pong paddle until the MTV logo appears red-raw on his ass. This was branding in its original sense.

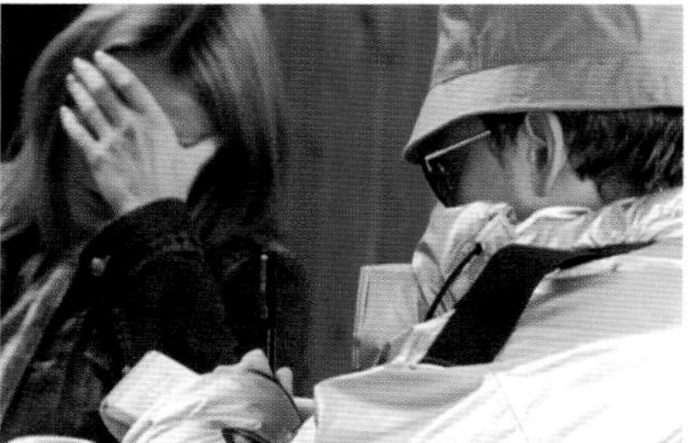

2001.21
Director: **Garth Jennings**
Client: **Parlophone**
This Pop promo for Bentley Rhythm Ace, 'Theme From Gutbuster', was set in Arctic wastelands and starred a breakdancing Eskimo. It was all part of a broader creative trend towards expressing an exhausted white nothingness.

2001.22
Agency: **Mother**
Client: **EMAP On Air**
Brilliantly acted, this series of spots for the rock music cable station QTV, featured a delightfully deluded rock'n'roll wannabe dressed in Liam Gallagher-esque garb and talking complete drivel to cab drivers and guitar shop owners.

2000.22
Agency: **Fallon McElligott NY**
Client: **MTV Networks**
A flagship of the American theatre of cruelty in advertising from Fallon McElligott NY. The elder Jukka brothers torture their younger sibling in their hut in the woods if he doesn't live up to the popular culture expectations beamed in by MTV. Ridiculous stuff, but a cult.

2002.21
Director: **Michel Gondry**
Client: **Virgin Records**
A Gold Award was given to director Michael Gondry for his hypnotic music video for the Chemical Brothers track 'Star Guitar'. This video was edited so that every beat of the music is synched exactly to the view of passing objects, such as chimneys and bridges, seen from a train travelling cross-country.

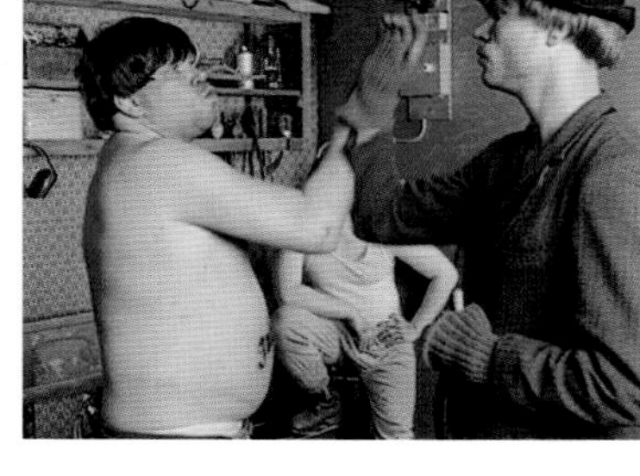

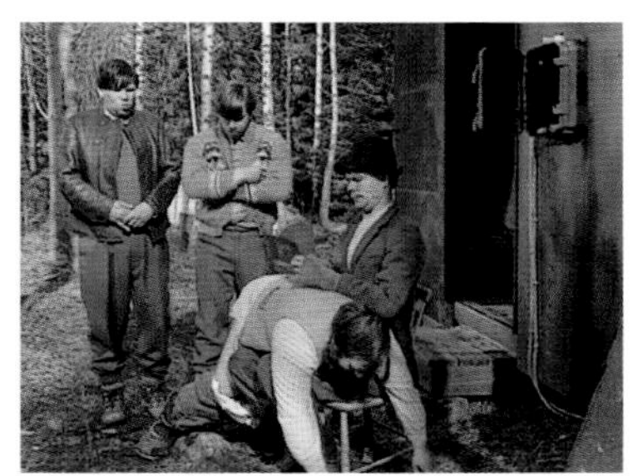

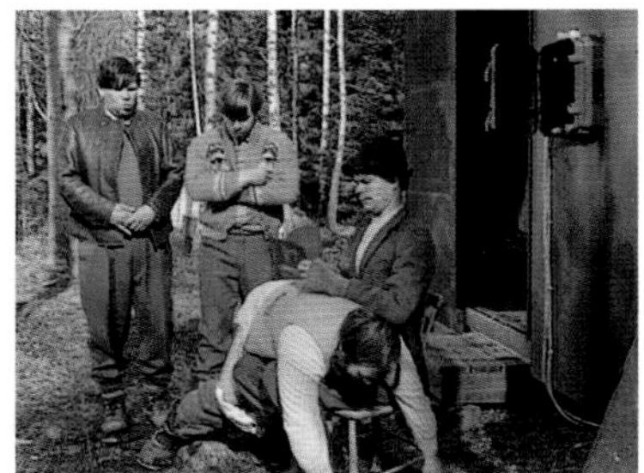

Much of this vicious, counter-cultural work was American. Fox Sports, a well-known master of cruelty, was responsible for a series of hilarious commercials by TWBA\Chiat\Day advising consumers to beware of 'things made in October'. The reason for this warning is that factory workers will have been distracted by Fox's coverage of the baseball play-offs and we see the enjoyably violent results of leaf blowers, pleasure boats and nail guns which malfunction.

In a spot by Butler Shine & Stern for the San Francisco Jazz Festival, a trio of gangbangers in an open-top car are listening to jazz when they draw up at the lights next to a white boy and switch channels to angry rapper music just to scare him. A Leo Burnett commercial for John West features a fight with a grizzly bear over fish. And even when a wholesome sporting hero like Tiger Woods is introduced alongside a line of weekend hackers on the local golf course, in a Nike film by Wieden + Kennedy Amsterdam, the story strikes a discordant note. Tiger's 'magic' immediately influences the amateurs, who all begin to swing in perfect synch with the young star, to the sound of Strauss's *Blue Danube*. But when Tiger leaves, they quickly lose their rhythm. Balls fly everywhere.

At a time when the enormous potential and ethical problems of genetic engineering were being widely discussed in the media, TV commercials also began to explore themes in the field of bio-technology and genetically modified people. 'Twist' and another Levi Strauss commercial, 'Odyssey', hinted at this idea of enhanced human performance, while a BMP DDB commercial for Volkswagen's new Lupo car presented a bionic, turbo-charged infant in 'Demon Baby'.

It all begged the question of where the communication industry would head next in its effort to arouse consumer interest. Of course, the digital technology to create such ideas is now mature, but how long before computer models are replaced by the genetically modified real things?

2000.23
Agency:
Wieden + Kennedy Amsterdam
Client: **Nike**
Even a commercial featuring a wholesome celebrity like Tiger Woods has to have a darker side, as in this spot for Nike, directed by features director Lasse Hallström.

this page

2002.22
Agency: **TBWA\Chiat\Day**
Client: **Fox Sports**
Cliff Freeman & Partners set the style with the Outpost.com campaign [see page 361], TBWA\Chiat\Day carried the torch forward. These cruel but hilarious ads tell viewers to 'beware of things made in October' because their production will have been adversely affected by Fox Sports' coverage of the baseball. Work of this type has become the new comedy default in America.

Beware of things made in October.

Beware of things made in October.

CHEVROLET

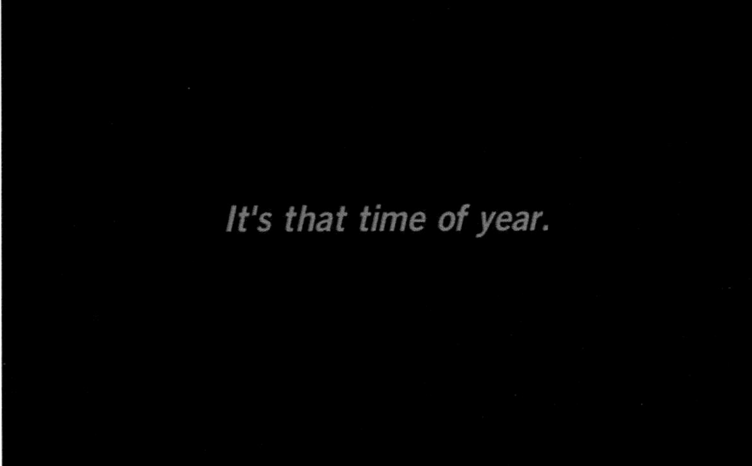
It's that time of year.

SAN FRANCISCO
JAZZ FESTIVAL
PRESENTED BY INFINITI

2001.23
Agency: **Butler Shine & Stern**
Client:
San Francisco Jazz Organization
Directed by Brandon Dickerson, the 'Lowriders' commercial for a jazz festival shows three smiling jazz-lovers cruising in a convertible. When they slow down next to a man on the street, they switch channels, transforming instantly into scowling hip-hop gangsters to scare him. Once out of earshot, they switch the music back. Beautifully done.

this page

2001.24
Agency: **Leo Burnett**
Client: **John West**
Tinned fish isn't the easiest product to sell but this spot cleverly sent the John West fisherman into Kung Fu-style combat with a grizzly bear in order to get the best fish.

2002.23
Agency: **BMP DDB**
Client: **Volkswagen UK**
The idea of VW's new Lupo car being a 'tough little baby' was expressed in this television commercial via a frighteningly bionic infant escaping through what appeared to be a sinister mental hospital. Not exactly heart-warming, but in keeping with a prevailing style towards cold, hard futures in advertising.

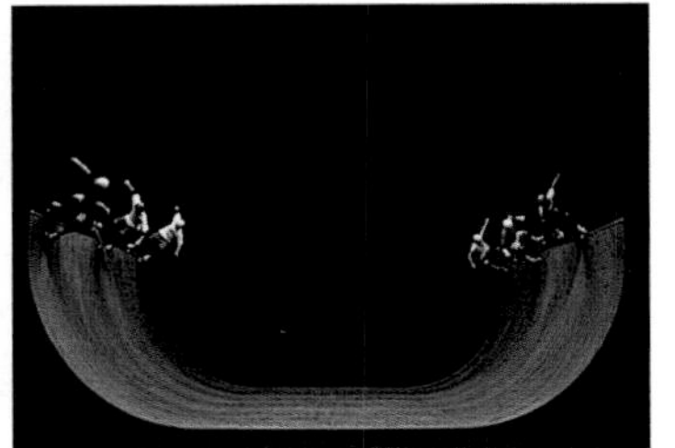

2002.24
Agency:
Wieden + Kennedy USA
Client: **Nike**

2002.25
Agency:
Wieden + Kennedy Amsterdam
Client: **Nike**

2002.26
Agency:
Wieden + Kennedy Amsterdam
Client: **Nike**

Jeff Elmassian won two Silvers (just missing out on a third) for his sound design for these television ads for Nike, 'Freestyle Basketball', 'Freestyle Football' and 'Freestyle Skateboard', which introduced a new balletic style to sports advertising. Sound, skill and choreography were seamlessly integrated to quite mesmerizing effect against a simple black background.

opposite

2000.24
Director: **Chris Cunningham**
Client: **One Little Indian Records**
Directed by self-confessed 'robot nut' Chris Cunningham, this stunning music video for Björk explores the idea of unattainable and doomed love on the production line.

overleaf

2000.25
Agency: **TBWA**
Client: **Sony PlayStation**
Alien and disturbing it may have been but Sony's 'Mental Wealth' ad, directed by Chris Cunningham, was made in seven different languages. Suffice to say, the chosen model didn't look anything like this before the production team digitally enhanced every frame.

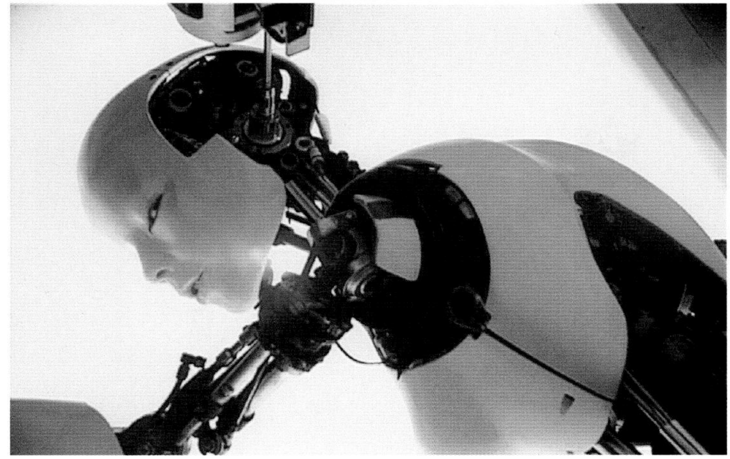

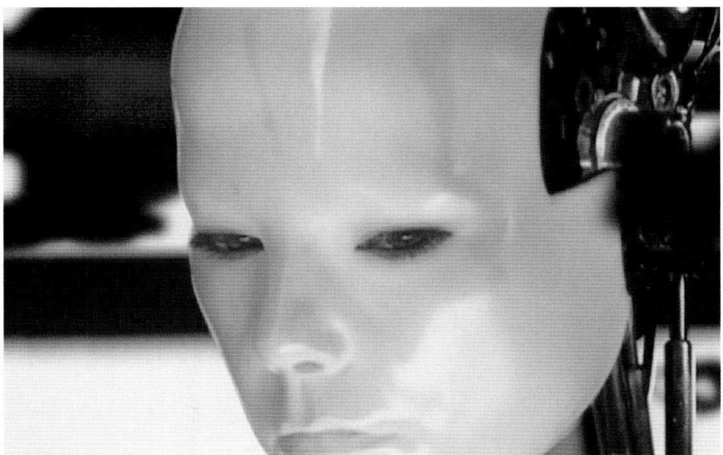

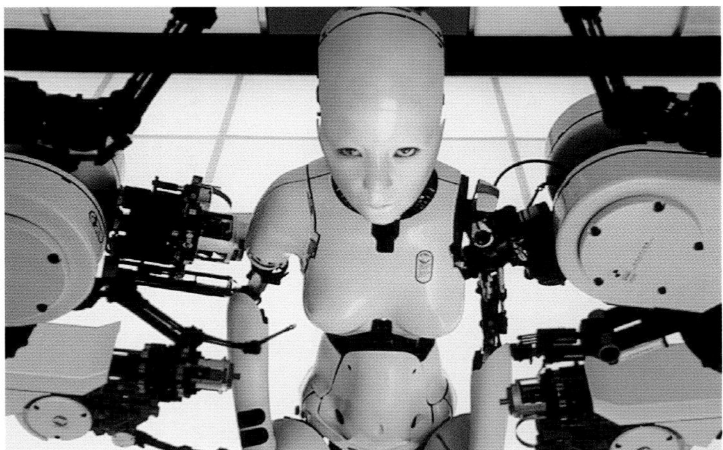

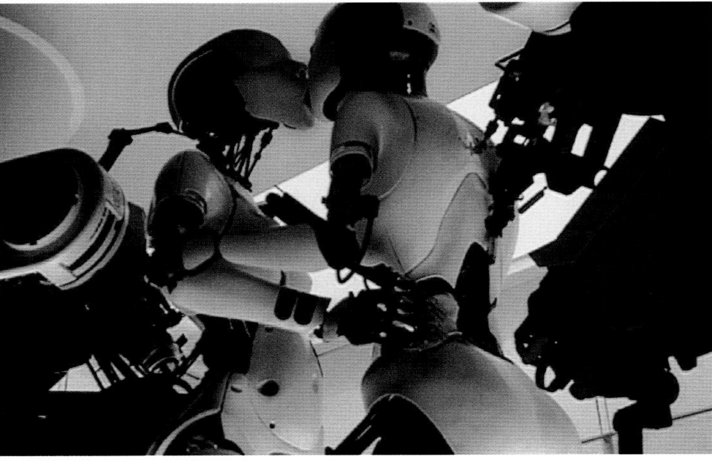

Some of this fascination with bio-technology was clearly derived from the music industry, where pop video directors like Chris Cunningham have been free to develop visually arresting, but morally alarming, theses on the meeting and merging of human and automaton. Cunningham directed a disturbing TBWA commercial called 'Mental Wealth' for Sony PlayStation, featuring a computerized young alien girl called Fifi. This won Silver at D&AD for special effects. But his outstanding work of the new decade was a Gold-winning pop video for Björk's 'All is Full of Love', which not only enhanced the singer's ethereal music but also, more broadly, suggested future directions for image-makers of all kinds.

In 'All is Full of Love', Cunningham drew on his teenage obsession with the sleek bodywork of Japanese motorbikes to fashion a mesmerizing film in which two robots act out a scene of ideal love. When he received his Gold Award in 2000, he remarked of the creative process, 'There's a definite day of pure excitement when you can see all the possibilities ahead and then from that point on to the point at which it is finished, everything else is pure torture.'

As the practitioners responsible for creating D&AD's remarkable archive of design and advertising reflect on the association reaching the memorable milestone of 40 years, that comment could easily have been made by any one of the designers, art directors, copywriters, film-makers, animators, architects, illustrators, photographers, typographers, lighting cameramen and special effects experts who have contributed so richly to the association's awards over the past four decades.

06:59:13:23

Last word on the future
Jeremy Bullmore

A friend of mine, as a young copywriter, was once despatched to New York to learn more about advertising. He was allocated to a huge group of creative people working on a single huge account: so huge that no single person could have the slightest idea of what was going on.

It was my friend's exclusive responsibility to write only the headlines … for one product only … and only for ads to appear in *The Reader's Digest*. That was his job in its entirety. So, despite working for one of America's largest and most famous agencies, he learnt nothing at all about advertising. It was then that I began to appreciate the fearsome dangers not only of size itself but also of its inevitable consequence: specialization.

That young copywriter would have learned a great deal more if he'd spent the same period of time working for the agency that advertises itself on the only platform of my tiny local railway station.

It offers a full range of services and almost certainly delivers them. It employs less than ten people – but I bet they know a great deal more about the real basics of the business than your average second-tier account handler in a mega London agency.

The growth of specialization is probably the most significant change to have taken place in our trade over the last 40 years or so. Forty years ago, in both the US and the UK, there was no such thing as the marketing communications industry – let alone this ugly infant 'MarComms'. Instead, there were advertising agencies – a few of them enormous.

The largest agency in London, at its peak, employed 1,200 people, three times the number employed today. And, yes, it planned and produced advertising – but it also had multiple departments which specialized in packaging, sales promotion, product design, direct mail, direct marketing, conference planning and production, PR, presentation, experimental film production, home economics (I promise), creative research, media planning and buying, business and brand consultancy – and probably another five or six. Long before 'one-stop shopping' was heard of, half-a-dozen London agencies could, and did, provide it. They were, without challenge, their clients' senior business advisers.

The people working in these specialist departments were often extremely talented but many rightly thought their talent unappreciated.

While the commission system held, agencies could afford to provide such services: it was how they competed. But the commission system didn't hold for long.

As margins shrank, those in-house departments thought to be less than central were disbanded; independent companies replaced them; and the specialist talent joined them willingly, at last to enjoy the prominence and rewards they'd been previously denied. That the staff numbers of many agencies are now a third of the size of 30 years ago is not because they're doing less advertising – in fact, they're doing more. They're simply doing very much less of everything else.

And the arrival of D&AD, and its growing influence, helped heighten industry consciousness of the importance of the specialist disciplines and how confidently they could live when freed from the dominant influence of old mother advertising. Once, there were only awards for advertising. Now, there are awards for everything. (Of all major media categories, only fridge magnets, shamefully, still go unrecognized.)

I believe this transformation of our business has been wholly good for practitioners: for their status, for their rewards and for the quality of the work they produce. Even if possible, I wouldn't want to see the tide turned back. But like most change, it leaves some remedial work to be done.

All this has happened at exactly the time that the value of communications consistency and brand coherence has never been more widely recognized. We may not much like the term integrated communication – but we accept its importance. Yet, at precisely the moment that brand owners expect their brands' communications to be seamlessly complementary, the suppliers of those communications have become irrevocably splintered.

There are those who can argue powerfully for the value of television advertising, of a new pack design, of viral marketing, of direct mail or of PR. But who is there left who can stand back from these invaluable finishing skills, track back to the beginning of the planning cycle and ask those most fundamental of questions; Where is this brand? Who is this brand? Where could it be? And how can we get there?

Increasingly, clients question the ability of specialist companies to answer these questions. Specialist companies are believed, often accurately, to favour their own specialist skill as the answer to every problem. It's not that they're villains: that's where their passion resides; that's the skill that gives them confidence.

When client and creative supplier collaborate well, there's a shared sense of excitement about the business of business; about making, distributing and selling good things at a respectable profit. In their pursuit of this aim, the client companies delight in the talents of the specialist companies; and the specialist companies delight to see those talents put to such measurable ends.

But there has to be this overlap. Without it, a great gap will develop between clients and their communication advisers. Clients will begin to despair at the failure of their suppliers to grasp the most basic realities of doing business; and the creative suppliers, disengaged from interest in their clients' markets, will see themselves more and more as makers of attractive artefacts with scant regard for function.

Over the next 40 years, as always, there will be winners and losers. The winners will be those who continue to combine an informed and intuitive sense of business with an alchemist's ability to turn strategy into enviable execution. These are the companies that will make their clients successful, earn themselves authority and thereby fully justify their premium price. The losers will be those who turn their backs on the business of business in the sole pursuit of some unanchored concept called creativity.

Cover story

Covers from left to right

1963
Design Group: Fletcher/Forbes/Gill

1964
Designer: George Daulby
Photographer: Len Fulford

1965
Designer: Peter Wildbur
Photographer: Bob Brooks

1966
Designers: Alan Aldridge & Lou Klein
Photographer: Len Fulford

1967
Designers: Mario Lippa & David Newton
Artist: Peter Blake

If D&AD had the chance to rewind back through its history it might have approached things differently.

The Gold Award, for example, might have been gold. The Silver Award, silver, little things like that. And the yearly task of producing the D&AD Annual cover? Well, that could have been much, much simpler. Maybe it could have featured a blow-up of the year's stand-out project, or a big bit of type on a colour, with just the date changing, year after year.

But no, that's not the way it happened. A little haphazardly at first, but now officially, designing the annual cover has developed a life of its own and has become a kind of award in itself.

It's become one of the President's duties; handing someone the cover baton to run off to a quiet corner somewhere, perspiring quietly, knowing that some of the profession's biggest names have done it before and also knowing that the arrival of the new annual is subjected to the fiercest of critiques in studios the world over.

Each year, the brief is the same: 'We'd like a cover, please, for the world's pre-eminent annual celebration of the finest design and art direction, which has hundreds of projects in it, of which a couple of dozen have won a prize. Oh yes, the prize is yellow and pencil-shaped. And don't forget the logo.'

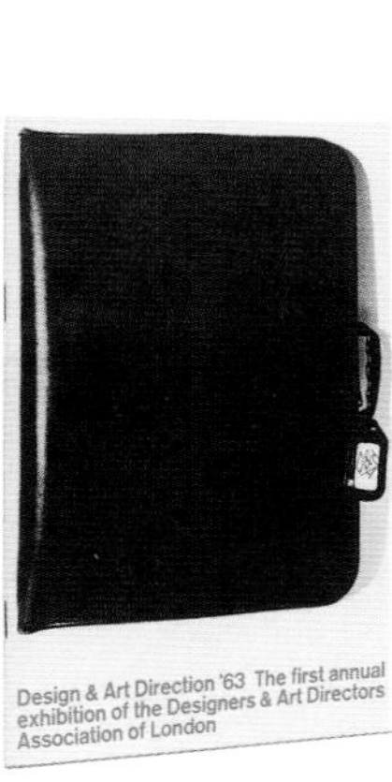

Design & Art Direction '63 The first annual exhibition of the Designers & Art Directors Association of London

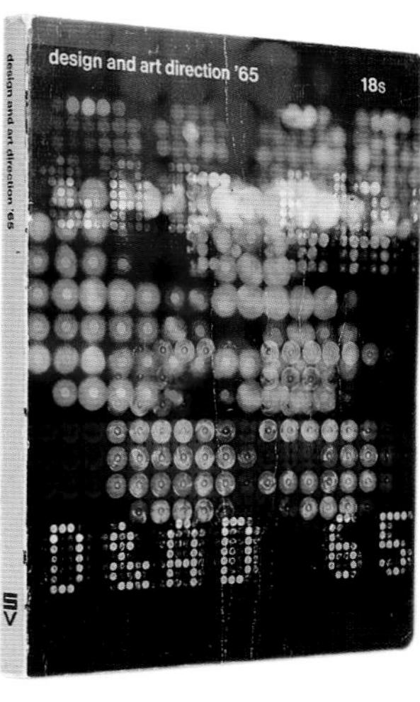

Covers from left to right

1968
Designer: Bob Gill

1969
Designer: Lou Klein
Photographer: Julian Cottrell

1970
Design Group: Shirt-Sleeve Studio
Photographer: Alain Le Garsmeur

1971
Artist: Gray Joliffe

1972
Artist: Allen Jones

The next question is where it gets tricky – 'what should it be about?' – because the answer, at least originally, was 'whatever you want'. Our confused but honoured creative can, at least at this point, take solace in his or her bookshelf, because there are now 39 previous attempts staring them in the face.

Looking back at them all after 40 years, how have they fared? After a perfectly straightforward start of a black portfolio case with the D&AD logo on it (by Fletcher/Forbes/Gill), the first twelve covers concern themselves with whatever seemed to take the designer or art director's fancy.

Some deal metaphorically with the nature of the award scheme ('picking the reddest apple' in 1964, 'biting the dangling carrot' in 1969, or 'achieving the impossible' with 1970's self-abusing hammer). All pretty painful stuff, in every sense, and as for rumours that the 1969 annual (the carrot) sold so poorly that after 500 sales the remainder were duly pulped, well, I couldn't possibly comment. Thankfully, there are at least some early signs of healthy cynicism with the 1968 cover designed to resemble a cheap soap powder packet and Gray Joliffe's navel gazing 1971 offering.

Ten years later, Rod Springett took a subtle pop at the silliness of it all by comparing the creative community to monkeys grasping at wooden bananas, not pencils, employing hairy heroes already made famous by starring in TV ads for a certain best-selling tea brand.

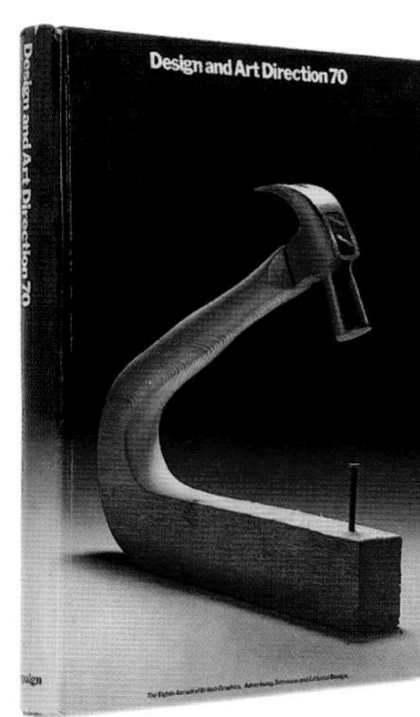

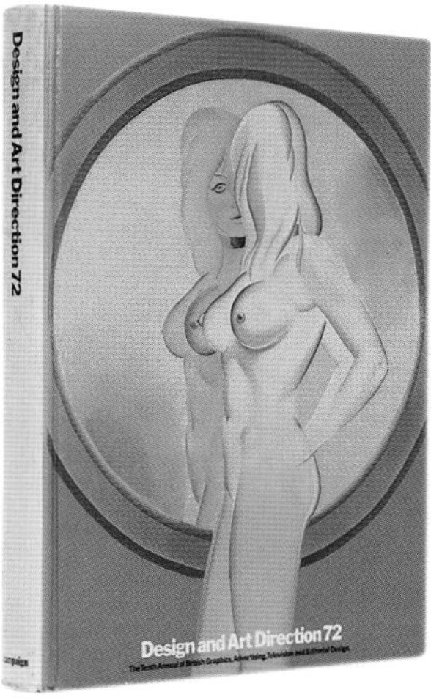

Some seem bizarrely obscure; briefed to ‘do whatever he wanted’ Tony Meeuwissen’s reaction in 1973 was to draw an illustration of, well, whatever he wanted. At the time an avid ephemera collector, he developed a visual *mélange* of a matchbox, a monkey, a ship, a lighthouse, a seagull and mice. The 1974 cover featuring eight zen gardens may have seemed like a good idea once but it hasn’t really stood the test of time.

No-one seems to be quite sure why the 1976 cover features type carved into a black obelisk (I can only guess that it is a hint at carving out the scheme’s highest prize, the black ‘Gold’ Award).

But the finest ‘expression of the time and hang the consequences’ must go to pop artist Allen Jones’ 1972 offering of an archetypically pneumatic blue-bodied girl admiring herself in a yellow glowing mirror. For probably the first time (but definitely not the last), we see the D&AD Annual cover holding a mirror to some of the creative community’s attitudes of the time.

Finally, however, someone cracked. It’s true, 13 years after its inception, an art director put a pencil on the cover (in this case his own, hard-fought-for black one) with 13 vicious little notches carved out of one edge. Neil Godfrey, the cover’s designer, had in one fell swoop written the brief for decades to come, by finally including the organization’s most famous prize.

The fact that the most precious award had been defaced only made it more telling. Godfrey remains one

Covers from left to right

1973
Artist: Tony Meeuwissen

1974
Designer: Tony Evans
Photographer: Tony Evans

1975
Designer: Neil Godfrey
Photographer: Tony May

1976
Designer: Colin Craig
Sculptor: Liam Neary
Photographer: David Thorpe

1977
Designers: *David Driver,* Robert Priest, Derek Ungless, Claudine Meissner, Peter Laws
Photographer: Tony Evans

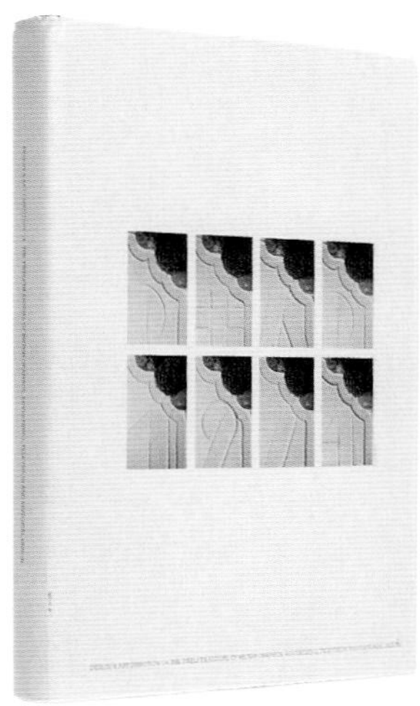

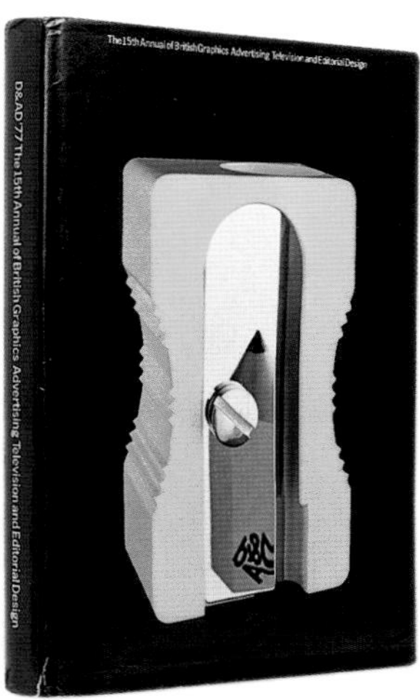

Covers from left to right

1978
Design group: Trickett & Webb: Lynn Trickett, Brian Webb, Colin Sands, Colin Eusden, Liz Arratoon, Andrew Thomas
Photographer: Tony Evans

1979
Designer: Eric Pratt
Photographer: Steve Garforth

1980
Design group: Rod Springett Associates: Rod Springett & Pete Green
Photographer: John Clarke

1981
Design group: Minale Tattersfield & Partners
Art directors: Marcello Minale, Brian Tattersfield, Alex Maranzano
Designers: Alex Maranzano, Dimitri Karavias
Photographer: Ian Stokes

1982
Design group: Larkin, May & Company
Photographer: Peter Hall
Modelmaker: Wrightson Raymond

of a select band who have actually been involved in designing two covers – he returned to the brief with his enigmatic 'can of beans' cover in 1993, a metaphorical reminder that however self-obsessed the profession became, it all still came down to selling more commodity products, tinned or otherwise.

Once the floodgates had opened, for 25 years much of the action focused on the scheme's wooden ambassador. We've had pencil sharpeners (twice), pencils as mountain ranges, pencils as honeycombs (with attendant bees), pencils sawn in half (revealing the scheme's age in rings), pencils as medallion ribbons, pencil boxes, pencils as rockets (OK, I made the last one up but it wouldn't have surprised you, would it?).

Even when given to the then relatively unknown Nick Bell in 1992, in the midst of flocking birds and spinning windmills we still see a gaggle of, you guessed it, pencils, flying across a cloudy sky.

To be fair to Bell, his original concept was based on photographic analogies of energy and movement and contained no pencils at all – the addition of the yellow flock came after a frosty reception to his original designs from the committee, and an all-night session searching for a compromise.

Some designers have chosen to make the winning of the pencil the idea itself – Trickett & Webb's 1978 cover is simply a crowing cockerel – that year's award winners waking to their golden sunrise, perhaps?

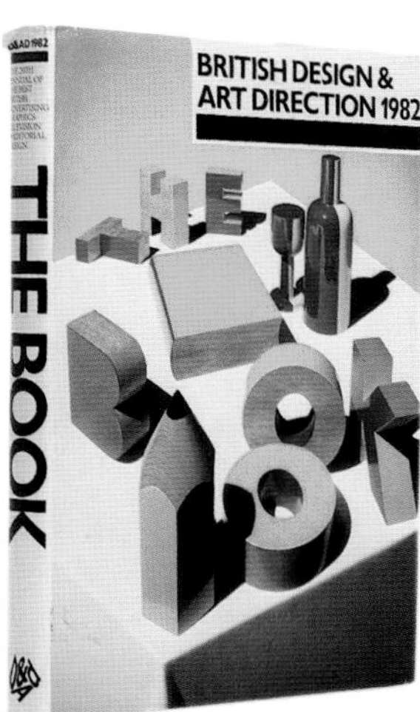

Apparently, to crow correctly *and* raise himself to the right height for the meticulously prepared painted background (this is pre-computer, remember; it had to be done 'in-camera') our feathered lothario had to be surrounded by the fluffiest and horniest hens.

By 1990, John McConnell had simply placed a pencil drawing into the grasp of a piece of clip-art to make a similar point – 'I've got mine, so there' the unwritten caption. When Farrow Design was given the brief, it coincided with a President who wanted a book that felt more like a product – enter, stage left, generous sponsor to help produce a steel slipcase. But it's under the steel that the best idea lies; 17,107 tiny pin pricks cover the surface (representing that year's total entries) of which 36 are silver, and one gold, the brutal statistics of the world's toughest award scheme meticulously brought to life.

Some drew unwittingly from the same inspiration – both the 1984 'blow-up' cover and 1994's 'pencil case' cover took the work of American pop-artist Claes Oldenburg as their starting points but finished at completely different ones.

Malcolm Gaskin's marvellous piece of plastic engineering included a valve that allowed the blind embossed, heat sealed, translucent dust jacket to be inflated, so the purchaser could at least play with their own air-filled friend (perhaps in the absence of the real thing?). Little did unwitting inflators know, the jacket

Covers from left to right

1983
Designer: Malcolm Gaskin
Design Consultant: Barry Lowenhoff

1984
Design group: Lloyd Northover:
Dawn Clarkson, Shawen Hayman, Martyn Hey, John Lloyd, Linda Loe, Jim Northover

1985
Designer: Roger Pearce
Assistant designer: Stephen Kettell

1986
Design group:
Carrol Dempsey Thirkell:
Michael Dempsey & Michael Lindley
Photographer: Peter Lavery

1987
Designer: Dave Horry
Artwork & Illustration: Glen Baxter
Typography: Len Cheeseman

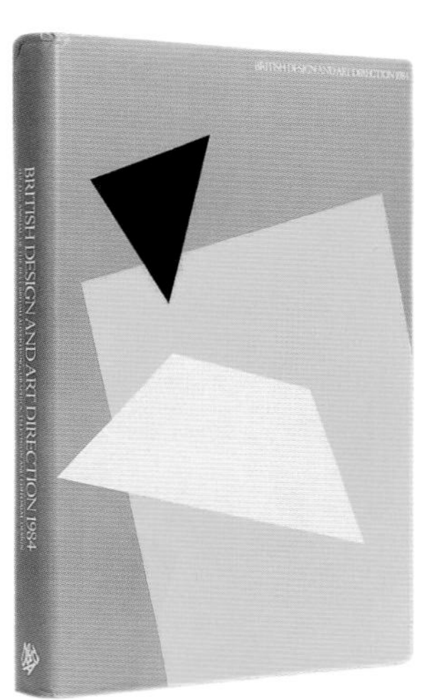

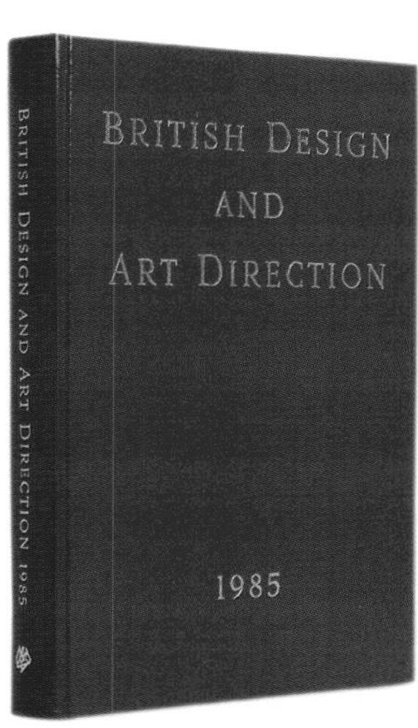

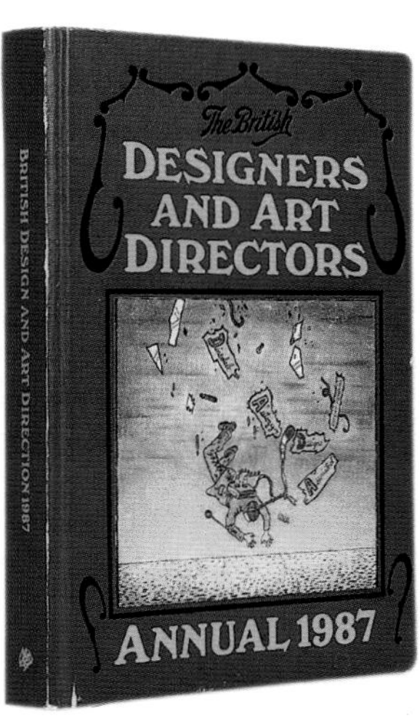

Covers from left to right

1988
Design Group: Lewis Moberly:
Judy Veal, Mary Lewis, Ann Marshall
Illustrator: Geoffrey Appleton
Photographer: Laurie Evans

1989
Designer: Nigel Rose
Modelmaker: Matthew Wurr
Photographer: Kevin Summers

1990
Design director: John McConnell
Designers: John McConnell
& Jason Godfrey

1991
Designer: Graham Watson
Photographer: John Parker

1992
Designer: Nick Bell
Photographer: Andy Rumball
Image manipulation: Peter Crowther

had a non-return valve – once inflated, it stayed that way. This dust jacket also tended to be stolen, so many creatives went through college thinking of this cover as 'the one with the boring yellow printed cover', not realizing what they had been missing.

1994's pencil-case cover turned the entire casing into a yellow, padded rubber extravaganza with brown webbing and a black zip, a metaphorical and physical case for the printed pencils inside. Whilst approved by all at D&AD Towers, this design met with fierce resistance from the legally contracted printer at the time. Only when it became clear that thousands of metres of yellow sou'wester material had, indeed, been purchased by a printer in the far east did it become possible, albeit adding £10 to the price of the book (and arriving six months late in the process).

Sometimes, the core colours of D&AD have been enough – in 1981 Minale Tattersfield simply superimposed two pantone colour chips and that was enough to say 'D&AD' – an early example of how the organization's colours had become ingrained in the collective pysche of the then UK's, and now world's, creative community. Lloyd Northover expressed the graphic *zeitgeist* of 1984 (you remember that cut-out Matisse aesthetic, I'm sure) with flying shards of white, yellow and black on the obligatory grey background.

In 1996 Tony Kaye only had to place the thinnest of yellow slivers behind the forbidding blank white page

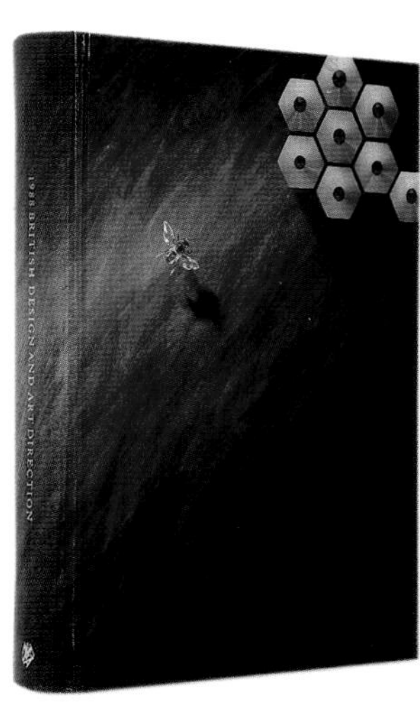

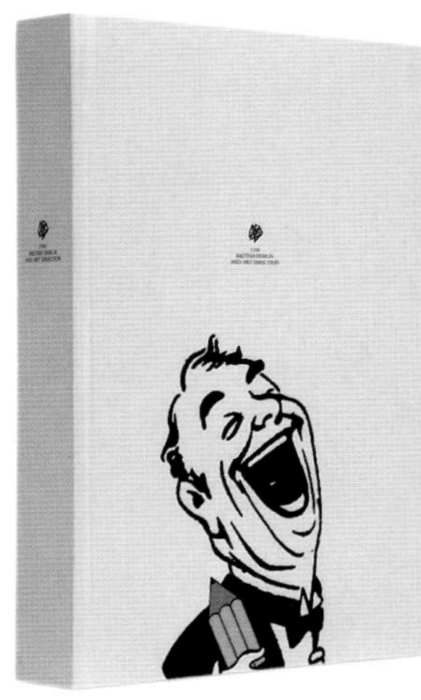

of an unused pad to sum up the feelings of many starting a new project – 'Will this be the one that wins? Am I good enough? Help!'

By 2002, Gregory Bonner Hale (GBH) simply created a dust jacket from yellow duster material (with the help of a Bangladeshi T-shirt manufacturer) and it was still pretty clear whose book this was on the bookshelves of the world. Like Carrol Dempsey Thirkell's 'British Bulldog' cover in 1986 that took dog food jokes into the interior of the annual, GBH extended its 'polishing' idea within the book, merrily mining the references to a famous British metal polish throughout.

Perhaps the onset of pencil fatigue explains the increasingly oblique references to the competition's most famous symbol – throughout the second half of the nineties pencils have been used, but as subtly as possible, either as computer keys, reflected into a creative's pupil, or embedded into the super-enlarged DNA of creative code.

But what few will know is that at least two of the recent covers were produced in haste after the controversial withdrawal of the original proposals. It's not the place to name names, but suffice it to say that two pencils crossed to symbolize the creative 'bible' was deemed a step too far at the time.

As it happens, the Bible analogy had already been explored. In 1985 Roger Pearce placed a few simple lines of gold embossed capitals onto maroon

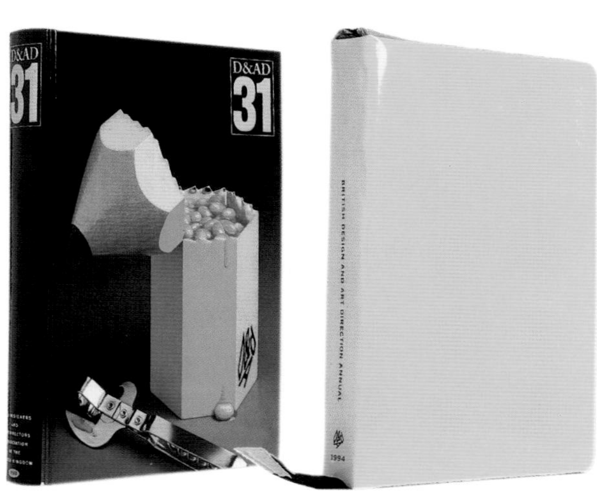

Covers from left to right

1993
Designer: Neil Godfrey
Typographer: Jeff Merrells
Modelmaker: Simon Lunn
Photographer: Neil Barstow

1994
Designer: Michael Johnson
Modelmaker: Wesley West

1995
Designer: John Gorham

1996
Designer: Tony Kaye

1997
Art director: Mike Dempsey
Designer: Fernando Guitérrez

Covers from left to right

1998
Designer: Paul Pickersgill
Photographer: Paul Zak
Retoucher: Anthony Crossfield
Typographer: Andy Dymock

1999
Design group: Farrow Design

2000
Designer: Vince Frost

2001
Design Group: GBH

2002
Designers: Mother

leatherette, a subtle piece of anti-packaging for many people's bible of creative thinking. And actually one of my personal favourites, but I'm forever being asked what the 'real' cover was, because people assume there was once a dust jacket that had either got lost or been discarded (missing the point entirely).

Mother's 2002 entry to the annual cover hall of fame takes Pearce's idea one stage further by creating a journey into the bizarre, not for D&AD but its Victorian cousin, Dulverton & Asquith-Drake. Just to confuse potential purchasers even further, we're told these are 'the unfortunate findings of the collective for the abolition of reason' on the spine.

Mother's side-stepping of the brief reveals one of the new difficulties of this project – designing the cover gets progressively harder and harder. Today's recipient of the cover brief is now expected to produce something that shows what a modern, more grown-up D&AD stands for, and expresses its values, something that booms out of the bookshelves and becomes an instant talking point. I'm not sure that some of the old ones would have stood up to that kind of scrutiny (but then that's probably part of their pre-strategy, pre-marketing charm).

Come to think of it, we'll need someone to design an annual cover soon. Know anyone who might be interested?

Michael Johnson

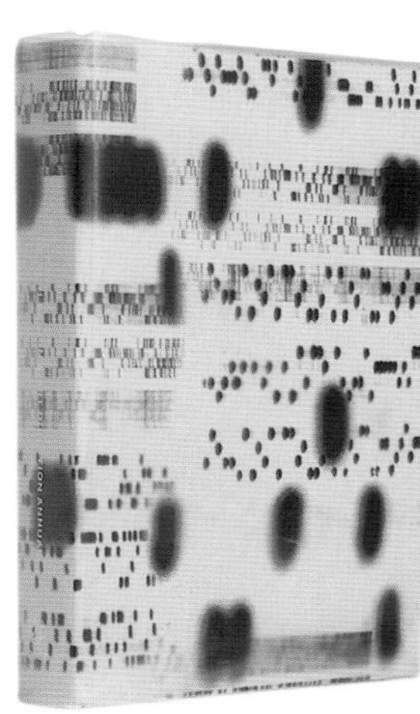

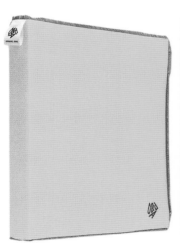

FACT

FILE

& index

The fact file is an alphabetical listing of credits for all work selected by the editors. The award status is shown, followed by the category and/or sub-categories in which the work was recognized. The categories have changed and expanded since D&AD's first award scheme in 1963, alongside the growth and trends in the communications industry, which is reflected in the different category names used here. Each piece of work is listed for the highest award received; in some cases, works received multiple awards of the same status and these listings are numbered.

1963

1963.01
Poster Design
Client
Young Commonwealth Artists
Copywriter
Barrie Bates
Designer
Barrie Bates

1963.02
Advertising Design
Advertising Agency
Colman Prentis & Varley
Art Director
Angela Landels
Client
Yardley
Copywriter
Ian Rankin
Photographer
Len Fulford

1963.03
TV & Cinema Advertising: Show Openings & Station Breaks
Designer
Geoff Brayley
Production Company
BBC TV

1963.04
TV & Cinema Advertising: Show Openings & Station Breaks
Art Director
Arnold Schwartzman
Photographer
Arnold Schwartzman
Production Company
Associated-Rediffusion

1963.05
TV & Cinema Advertising: Show Openings & Station Breaks
Art Director
Arnold Schwartzman
Photographer
Arnold Schwartzman
Production Company
Associated-Rediffusion

1964

1964.01
Advertising Design: Trade & Professional Magazines
Advertising Agency
Benton & Bowles
Art Director
Bob Brooks
Client
IBM
Designer
Bob Brooks
Photographer
John Eriksen

1964.02
Advertising & Graphic Design for TV & Cinema: Television Commercials
Agency Producer
John Heyer
Art Director
Nicholas Spargo
Client
Shell International X-100
Designer
Nicholas Spargo
Production Company
Nicholas Cartoons

1964.03
Advertising & Graphic Design for TV & Cinema: Television Commercials
Art Director
Erik Dibbern
Client
Shell International Gasoline
Designer
Erik Dibbern
Photographer
Erik Willumsen
Producer
John Heyer
Production Company
nordisk reklamefilm

1964.04
Book Jackets & Paperback Covers
Client
Penguin Books
Design Group
Fletcher/Forbes/Gill

1964.05
House Style: Trademarks & Stationery
Client
International Scientific Systems
Design Group
Fletcher/Forbes/Gill

1964.06
Editorial Design: Consumer Magazines
Art Director
Max Maxwell
Client
Queen
Photographer
Bert Steinhauser
Publisher
Stevens Press

1964.07
Editorial Design: Consumer Magazines
Art Director
Tom Wolsey
Client
Town
Designer
Tom Wolsey
Photographer
John Bulmer
Publisher
Cornmarket Press

1964.08
Poster Design
Advertising Agency
Thomson Organisation
Art Director
John Donegan
Client
The Sunday Times
Designer
John Donegan

1964.09
Book Jackets & Paperback Covers
Art Director
Derek Birdsall
Artist
Derek Birdsall
Designer
Derek Birdsall
Publisher
Penguin Books

1964.10
Advertising & Promotional Matter
Advertising Agency
Waddicors & Clark Wilkinson
Art Director
Neville Eldridge
Client
Spicers
Designer
Derek Birdsall
Photographer
Robert Freeman

1964.11
Book Jackets & Paperback Covers
Art Director
Germano Facetti
Artists
George Daulby
Romek Marber
Designers
George Daulby
Romek Marber
Publisher
Penguin Books

1964.12
Applied Graphic Design
Client
Ministry of Transport
Design Group
Kinneir Associates
Designers
Margaret Calvert
Jock Kinneir

1964.13
Poster Design
Agency/Publisher
Robert Brownjohn
Art Director
Robert Brownjohn
Client
Robert Fraser Gallery
Designer
Robert Brownjohn
Photographer
Robert Brownjohn

1964.14
Advertising Design: Consumer Magazines
Advertising Agency
McCann-Erickson
Art Directors
Robert Brownjohn
Ross Cramer
Client
Taylor-Woods
Designer
Robert Brownjohn
Photographer
John S Clarke

1964.15
Feature Film Titles
Art Director
Robert Brownjohn
Client
Apple & Pear Publicity Council
Designers
Trevor Bond
Robert Brownjohn
Photographer
David Watkins
Producer
Hugh Hudson
Production Company
Cammell-Hudson Associates

1964.16
Television Programme Titles
Art Director
Bernard Lodge
Client
BBC TV Graphics
Designer
Bernard Lodge
Photographer
Bernard Lodge
Production Company
BBC TV

1965

1965.01
Advertising Campaigns
Advertising Agency
Doyle Dane Bernbach
Art Director
Neil Godfrey
Client
Remington Electric Shavers
Copywriter
John Withers
Designer
Neil Godfrey
Photographer
Duffy

1965.02
Design for Print: Art & Photography
Client
EMI Records
Designer
Robert Freeman
Photographer
Robert Freeman

1965.03
Design for Print: Direct Mail Announcements
Art Director
Roger Denning
Artist
Bob Gill
Client
The Kynoch Press
Designer
Bob Gill
Publisher
The Kynoch Press

1965.04
Design for Print: Editorial Design – Consumer Magazines
Art Director
Barry Trengove
Designer
Barry Trengove
Publication
Harper's Bazaar
Publisher
National Magazine Company

1965.05
Design for Print: Editorial Design – Consumer Magazines
Art Director
Michael Rand
Designer
Brian Haynes
Photographer
Graham Finlayson
Publication
Sunday Times Colour Magazine
Publisher
Thomson Newspapers

1965.06
Design for Print: Symbols & Logotypes
Art Director
Milner Gray
Client
British Railways Board
Design Group
Design Research Unit
Designer
Gerry Barney

1965.07
Design Programmes
Art Director
Ron Baker
Artist
Juliet Glynn Smith
Client
Habitat
Copywriter
Caroline Conran
Design Group
Conran *Design Group*
Designer
Dudley Bootes Johns

1965.08
Design for Print: Stationery
Client
Zandra Rhodes
Designer
Richard Doust

1965.09
Advertising & Graphics for Cinema & Television: Graphics – Feature Film Titles
Art Director
Robert Brownjohn
Client
Eon Productions
Designer
Robert Brownjohn
Director
Robert Brownjohn
Lighting Cameraman
David Watkins
Production Company
Dart Films
Stills Photographer
John Donaldson

1965.10
Advertising & Graphics for Cinema & Television: Cinema Commercials
Advertising Agency
Collett Dickenson Pearce & Partners
Agency Producer
Raymond Barker
Art Director
Colin Millward
Client
Chemstrand
Copywriter
Ben Duncan
Designer
Colin Millward
Director
Dick Lester
Lighting Cameraman
David Watkins
Production Company
James Garrett & Partners

1965.11
Advertising Campaigns
Agency
Papert Koenig Lois
Art Director
Tony Palladino
Client
J Player & Sons
Copywriter
Ron Holland
Designer
Tony Palladino
Photographer
Adrian Flowers

1965.12
Design for Print: House Journals
Art Director
Churchill/Holmes/Kitley
Designer
Churchill/Holmes/Kitley
Photographer
Ken Phillips
Publication
Shell BP News
Publisher
Shell-Mex & BP

1965.13
Advertising Campaigns
Agency
Young & Rubicam
Art Directors
Rosemary Oxley
David Newton
Client
Cadbury Brothers
Copywriter
Colin Pearson
Photographer
Tom Belshaw

1966

1966.01
Advertising Design: Newspapers
Advertising Agency
Doyle Dane Bernbach
Art Director
Douglas Maxwell
Client
Remington Electric Shavers
Copywriter
Dawson Yeoman
Photographer
Stephen Coe

1966.02
Film Media Advertising & Graphics: Television Commercial
Advertising Agency
Doyle Dane Bernbach
Agency Producer
Vicki Sanders
Animators
Johnny Morrice
Leslie Nutt
Art Director
David Larson
Client
Remington Electric Shavers
Copywriter
John Withers
Director
Leslie Nutt
Lighting Cameraman
Johnny Morrice
Production Company
Dart Syncromation Films

1966.03
Design for Print
Advertising Agency
Charles Hobson & Grey
Art Director
Lou Klein
Artist
Alan Cracknell
Client
Reed Paper & Board Sales
Copywriter
Tom Boyd
Designer
Patrick Tofts

1966.04
Print Media: Direct Mail
Advertising Agency
Charles Hobson & Grey
Art Director
Lou Klein
Client
Spicers
Copywriter
Tom Boyd
Designer
Lou Klein
Photographer
Bob Brooks

1966.05
Editorial: Consumer Magazines
Art Director
Michael Rand
Artist
Alan Aldridge
Designers
Alan Aldridge
Brian Haynes
Photographer
Dennis Rolfe
Publication
Sunday Times Magazine
Publisher
Thomson Newspapers
Writer
Derek Jewell

1966.06
Editorial: Consumer Magazines
Art Director
Harri Peccinotti
Designer
Harri Peccinotti
Photographers
Harri Peccinotti
Clive Arrowsmith
Bill Silano
Michel Certain
Publication
Nova
Publisher
George Newnes
Writer
Dennis Hackett

1966.07
Print Media: Technical Literature
Assistant Designer
Roy Walker
Client
British Railways Board
Consultant Designer
Milner Gray
Design Group
Design Research Unit
Designer
Collis Clements

1966.08
Editorial Art & Photography: Consumer Magazines
Art Director
Terence Whelan
Copywriter
Georgina Boosey
Designer
Terence Whelan
Photographer
Helmut Newton
Publication
Vogue
Publisher
Condé Nast

1966.09
Television Programme Titles
Client
BBC Television
Designer
Alan Jeapes
Director
Alan Jeapes
Production Company
BBC Television
Stills Photographer
Michael Sanders

1966.10
Print Media: Posters
Advertising Agency
Young & Rubicam
Art Director
Rosemary Oxley
Client
Cadbury
Copywriter
Ceri Jones
Designer
Rosemary Oxley
Photographer
Tom Belshaw

1967

1967.01
Advertising Design: Consumer Magazines – Colour
Advertising Agency
Doyle Dane Bernbach
Art Director
Neil Godfrey
Client
Tern Consulate
Copywriter
John Withers
Designer
Neil Godfrey
Photographer
Stephen Coe

1967.02
Advertising Design: Newspapers
Advertising Agency
Doyle Dane Bernbach
Art Director
Neil Godfrey
Client
Remington Electric Shavers
Copywriter
Mike Mangano
Designer
Neil Godfrey
Photographer
Tony Evans

1967.03
Television Commercial
Advertising Agency
Doyle Dane Bernbach
Art Director
Jack Sheridan
Client
Remington Electric Shavers
Copywriter
John Withers
Director
Abel Goodman
Lighting Cameraman
Stephen Coe
Producer
Vicki Sanders
Production Company
James Garrett & Partners

1967.04
Symbols
Art Directors
Marcello Minale
Brian Tattersfield
Client
The Ocean Oil Company
Design Group
Minale Tattersfield Provinciali
Designers
Marcello Minale
Brian Tattersfield

1967.05
Design for Print: Direct Mail
Advertising Agency
Charles Hobson & Grey
Art Director
Lou Klein
Artist
Ilene Astrahan
Client
Reed Paper Group
Copywriter
A E Southcott
Designer
Lou Klein

1967.06
Design for Print: Direct Mail
Art Director
Lou Klein
Client
Time International
Copywriter
Charles Isitt
Design Group
Louis Klein
Designer
Lou Klein

1967.07
Editorial Design: Complete Unit
Art Director
Harri Peccinotti
Assistant Art Director
Bill Fallover
Editor
Dennis Hackett
Publication
Nova
Publisher
George Newnes

1967.08
Editorial Art & Photography: Consumer Magazines – Editorial Colour Photography
Art Director
Harri Peccinotti
Designer
Harri Peccinotti
Photographer
Jean-Loup Sieff
Publication
Nova
Publisher
George Newnes
Writer
Molly Parkin

1967.09
Editorial Design: Consumer Magazines – Editorial Feature
Art Director
Harri Peccinotti
Artist
Roger Law
Designer
Roger Law
Publication
Nova
Publisher
George Newnes
Writer
Norman Price

1967.10
Package Design
Client
Mary Quant Cosmetics
Design Group
Fargo Design Associates
Designer
David McMeekin

1967.11
Package Design
Agency
McLaren Dunkley Friedlander
Client
Fisons Foods
Designers
Robert Brownjohn
Bob Gill
Photographer
Adrian Flowers

1967.12
Advertising Design: Consumer Magazines
Advertising Agency
Collett Dickenson Pearce
Art Director
Edwin Brigdale
Client
Chemstrand
Copywriter
Phoebe Hichens
Designer
Edwin Brigdale
Photographer
Helmut Newton

1967.13
Package Design: Point of Sale or Merchandising
Advertising Agency
Collett Dickenson Pearce
Art Director
Michael Peters
Artist
Alan Cracknell
Client
Chemstrand
Designers
Alan Cracknell
Michael Peters

1967.14
Advertising Design: Newspapers
Advertising Agency
John Collings & Partners
Art Director
John Hegarty
Client
El Al Israel Airlines
Copywriter
Dennis Hackett
Designer
John Hegarty

1967.15
Advertising Campaigns
Advertising Agency
Collett Dickenson Pearce
Art Director
Ross Cramer
Artist
Ross Cramer
Client
Selfridges
Copywriter
Charles Saatchi
Designer
Ross Cramer
Photographer
David Montgomery

1967.16
Advertising Design: Consumer Magazines – Black & White
Advertising Agency
Davidson Pearce Berry & Tuck
Art Director
David Newton
Client
Wates
Copywriter
Paul Hoppe
Designer
David Newton
Photographer
John Knill

1967.17
Poster Design
Advertising Agency
Young & Rubicam
Art Director
Jean Bird
Client
H J Heinz
Copywriter
Mo Drake
Photographer
Tony Copeland

1967.18
Poster Design
Advertising Agency
Young & Rubicam
Art Director
Rosemary Oxley
Client
Cadbury Brothers
Copywriter
Ceri Jones
Designer
Bob Wilson
Photographer
Norman Gold

1967.19
Poster Design
Advertising Agency
Young & Rubicam
Art Director
Terry Badham
Client
Cadbury Brothers
Copywriter
Bob Wilson
Designer
Bob Wilson
Photographer
Tom Belshaw

1968

1968.01
Advertising Art & Photography: Newspapers – Black & White Photography
Advertising Agency
Doyle Dane Bernbach
Art Director
Jerry Caggiano
Client
Uniroyal
Copywriter
Malcolm Gluck
Designer
Jerry Caggiano
Photographer
Donald Silverstein

1968.02
Advertising Design: Consumer Magazines – Colour
Advertising Agency
Doyle Dane Bernbach
Art Directors
Jerry Caggiano
Peter Kettle
Client
Tern Consulate
Copywriter
Malcolm Gluck
Designer
Jerry Caggiano
Photographer
David Montgomery

1968.03
Design for Print: Calendar
Art Directors
Marcello Minale
Brian Tattersfield
Client
Osram-GED
Design Group
Minale Tattersfield Provinciali
Designers
Chris Keeble
Marcello Minale
Brian Tattersfield

1968.04
Design Programmes
Art Director
Michael Wolff
Artist
Maurice Wilson
Client
Hadfields (Merton)
Design Group
Wolff Olins & Partners
Designers
Kit Cooper
Richard Peskett

1968.05
Editorial Design: Consumer Magazines – Editorial Art
Art Director
Michael Rand
Artist
Michael Leonard
Designers
David King
Gilvrie Misstear
Feature Editor
Peter Crookston
Publication
Sunday Times Magazine
Publisher
Times Newspapers

1968.06
Editorial Design: Consumer Magazines – Covers
Art Director
Bill Fallover
Artist
Barry Fantoni
Designer
Bill Fallover
Publication
Nova
Publisher
George Newnes
Writer
Dennis Hackett

1968.07
Editorial Design: Consumer Magazines – Fashion and Editorial Colour Photography
Art Director
Bill Fallover
Designer
Bill Fallover
Photographer
Hans Feurer
Publication
Nova
Publisher
George Newnes
Writer
Caroline Baker

1968.08
Poster Design
Advertising Agency
The KMP Partnership
Art Director
David Holmes
Client
Salvation Army
Copywriter
Bob Connor
Designer
David Holmes
Photographer
Ray Rathborne

1968.09
Cinema Commercials
Advertising Agency
Collett Dickenson Pearce
Agency Art Director
Ross Cramer
Agency Producer
Raymond Barker
Art Director
Leo Austin
Client
Monsanto
Copywriter
Charles Saatchi
Directors
Charles Jenkins
Clive Rees
Lighting Cameraman
Peter Jessop
Production Companies
Trickfilms
Ocelot Productions

1968.10
Advertising Art & Photography: Consumer Magazines – Advertising Colour Photography
Advertising Agency
Collett Dickenson Pearce
Art Director
Chris Burgess
Client
John Harvey & Sons
Copywriter
John Salmon
Designer
Chris Burgess
Photographer
Henry Sandbank

1968.11
Package Design: Point of Sale or Merchandising Scheme
Advertising Agency
Collett Dickenson Pearce
Art Directors
Lou Klein
Michael Peters
Client
Sexton Shoe Company
Design Group
Klein Peters
Designers
Lou Klein
Michael Peters
Photographer
Terence Donovan

1968.12
Television Graphics
Client
BBC Television
Designer
Bernard Lodge
Director
Bernard Lodge
Electronic Engineer
Ben Palmer

1968.13
Advertising Design: Newspapers – Advertising Art
Advertising Agency
John Collings & Partners
Art Director
John Hegarty
Artist
Roy Carruthers
Client
El Al Israel Airlines
Copywriter
Lindsay Dale
Designer
John Hegarty

1968.14
Advertising Design: Newspapers
Advertising Agency
Doyle Dane Bernbach
Art Director
Doug Maxwell
Client
Uniroyal
Copywriter
David Abbott
Designer
Doug Maxwell
Photographer
Tony Evans

1968.15
Advertising Design: Newspapers – Campaign
Advertising Agency
Doyle Dane Bernbach
Art Director
Doug Maxwell
Client
Uniroyal
Copywriter
Dawson Yeoman
Designer
Doug Maxwell
Photographer
Tony Evans

1968.16
Advertising Design: Newspapers
Advertising Agency
Pritchard Wood
Art Director
John Webster
Client
National Provincial Bank
Copywriters
Brian Mindel
John Webster
Designer
John Webster

1968.17
Design Programme: Covers
Art Director
Richard Hollis
Designer
Romek Marber
Photographer
Romek Marber
Publication
New Society
Publisher
New Science Publications

1968.18
Editorial Design: Complete Feature in a Consumer Magazine
Art Director
Michael Rand
Artist (Cover)
David King
Designer
David King
Feature Editor
Peter Crookston
Publication
Sunday Times Magazine
Publisher
Times Newspapers

1968.19
Poster Design
Advertising Agency
Young & Rubicam
Art Director
Bob Isherwood
Client
Cadbury Brothers
Copywriter
Maurice Drake
Designer
Bob Isherwood
Photography
Gilchrist Brothers

1969

1969.01
Design for Print, Art & Photography: Illustration Design for Print
Art Director
Derek Burton
Artist
Harry Willock
Client
Immediate Records
Copywriters
Small Faces
Designers
Derek Burton
Small Faces
Harry Willock

1969.02
Art & Photography: Art Poster
Art Director
Alan Aldridge
Artists
Alan Aldridge
James Marsh
Bob Smithers
Client
Arts Laboratory
Design Group
Ink Studios
Designer
Alan Aldridge
Photographer
Donald Silverstein

1969.03
Design Programmes: Design for Print
Artists
Peter Bentley
Stewart Burnett
Michael Farrell
Client
Bosie's
Design Group
Bentley/Farrell/Burnett
Designers
Peter Bentley
Stewart Burnett
Michael Farrell

1969.04
Art & Photography: Newspapers – Advertising and Black & White Photography
Advertising Agency
Doyle Dane Bernbach
Art Director
Doug Maxwell
Client
London Weekend Television
Copywriter
David Abbott
Photographer
Donald Silverstein

1969.05
Advertising Campaigns: Newspaper Advertisement
Advertising Agency
Doyle Dane Bernbach
Art Director
Martyn Walsh
Client
Christian Aid
Copywriter
Malcolm Gluck
Designer
Martyn Walsh
Photographer
Donald Silverstein

1969.06
Design for Corporate Identity
Art Director
Michael Wolff
Client
Bowyers (Wiltshire)
Design Group
Wolff Olins
Designers
John Larkin
Tony Meeuwissen
Richard Peskett

1969.07
Editorial Design: Consumer Magazines – Editorial Feature
Art Director
Michael Rand
Artist
Richard Weigand
Designers
David King
Gilvrie Misstear
Editors
Peter Crookston
Derek Jewell
David Sylvester
Photographers
Diane Arbus
John Bulmer
Walker Evans
Robert Freson
David Montgomery
Publication
Sunday Times Magazine
Publisher
Times Newspapers

1969.08
Editorial Design: Editorial Feature in a Newspaper
Art Director
Jeanette Collins
Artist
Barry Zaid
Designer
Jeanette Collins
Publication
The Times Women's Page
Publisher
Times Newspapers
Writer
Prudence Glynn

1969.09
Editorial Art & Photography: Consumer Magazines
Art Director
Michael Rand
Author
Don McCullin
Designer
David King
Photographer
Don McCullin
Publication
Sunday Times Magazine
Publisher
Times Newspapers

1969.10
Advertising Design: Newspapers
Advertising Agency
Geer Du Bois
Art Director
Jim Muscatt
Client
Mental Health Trust
Copywriter
Kim Mukerjee
Designers
Kim Mukerjee
Jim Muscatt
Photographer
David Montgomery

1969.11
Design Programmes
Art Director
John McConnell
Client
Biba
Design Group
John McConnell
Designer
John McConnell
Photographer
Donald Silverstein

1969.12
1. Advertising Design: Consumer Magazines – Colour
2. Best Written Consumer Advertisement of the Year
Advertising Agency
Collett Dickenson Pearce
Art Director
Ron Collins
Client
Dunn & Co
Copywriter
John Salmon
Designer
Ron Collins
Photographer
Adrian Flowers

1969.13
TV & Cinema Advertising: Cinema Commercials Colour
Advertising Agency
Pritchard Wood & Partners
Agency Art Director
John Webster
Agency Producer
Maggi Randall
Client
National Provincial Bank
Copywriter
Brian Mindell
Lighting Cameraman
Bob Paynter
Production Company
N Lee Lacy

1969.14
Advertising Campaigns
Advertising Agency
Vernon Stratton
Art Director
Bob Marchant
Client
Debenham & Freebody
Copywriter
Leonard Weinreich
Designer
Bob Marchant
Photographer
Tony Evans

1969.15
Art & Photography: Photography in a Black & White Trade Advertisement
Advertising Agency
Davidson Pearce Berry & Tuck
Art Director
Mario Lippa
Client
Ilford
Copywriter
Jeremy Best
Designer
Mario Lippa
Photographer
Alan Boyd

1969.16
TV & Cinema Advertising: Television Commercials – Black & White
Advertising Agency
Geers Gross
Agency Art Director
John Kean
Agency Producer
Ivan Robinson
Client
Spillers
Copywriter
Tom Bussman
Director
Tony Cattaneo
Production Company
Wyatt Cattaneo Productions

1969.17
TV & Cinema Advertising: Television Commercials – Black & White
Advertising Agency
J Walter Thompson
Agency Producer
Roger Holland
Client
Findus Eskimo Food
Copywriter
Tom Rayfield
Designer
Alan J Withey
Director
Tony Sims
Lighting Cameraman
Manny Wynne
Production Company
Film Contracts

1969.18
1. Cinema Commercial: Colour
2. Copywriting in Print & Films
Advertising Agency
J Walter Thompson
Agency Art Director
Ken Done
Agency Producers
Ken Done
David Norton
Client
Beecham Products (UK)
Copywriters
Bill Oddie
Graeme Garden
Director
John Perkins
Lighting Cameraman
John Perkins
Production Company
Streich Fletcher Perkins

1969.19
Editorial Design: Newspapers
Art Director
Roland Schenk
Designers
Michael Jackson
Roland Schenk
Publication
Campaign
Publisher
Haymarket Publishing Group

1970

1970.01
Design for Print: Direct Mail
Artists
Eric Boman
Steve Thomas
Client
Biba
Copywriter
Leslie Lake
Design Group
John McConnell
Designer
John McConnell
Photographer
Sarah Moon

1970.02
Poster Design
Advertising Agency
Cramer Saatchi
Art Director
Bill Atherton
Client
The Health Education Council
Copywriter
Jeremy Sinclair
Designer
Bill Atherton
Photographer
Alan Brooking

1970.03
Poster Copy
Agency
Cramer Saatchi
Art Director
John Hegarty
Client
The Health Education Council
Copywriters
Michael Coughlan
Charles Saatchi
Designer
John Hegarty

1970.04
Cinema Commercial
Advertising Agency
Collett Dickenson Pearce
Agency Art Director
Bob Byrne
Agency Producer
Alan Marshall
Client
Gallaher
Copywriter
Alan Tilby
Designer
Brian Morris
Director
Bob Brooks
Lighting Cameramen
Mike Seresin
Production Company
Brooks Baker & Fulford

1970.05
Television Commercials: Black & White – Campaigns
Agency
Collett Dickenson Pearce
Agency Art Director
Paul Windsor
Agency Producer
Raymond Barker
Client
General Post Office
Consultant Cameraman
Paul Windsor
Consultant Director
Alan Parker
Copywriter
Alan Parker
Designer
Robert Laing
Director
D Rankin
Lighting Cameraman
R Dinsdale
Production Company
Signal Films

1970.06
TV & Cinema Advertising: Television Commercials – Black & White
Advertising Agency
J Walter Thompson
Agency Producer
Adrian Rowbotham
Client
Guinness
Copywriter
Tom Rayfield
Director
Terence Donovan
Lighting Cameraman
Terry Permane
Production Company
Terence Donovan Productions

1970.07
Packaging Design
Art Directors
Marcello Minale
Brian Tattersfield
Artist
Brian Tattersfield
Client
Harrods
Design Group
Minale Tattersfield Provinciali
Designers
Marcello Minale
Brian Tattersfield

1970.08
Book Jackets & Paperback Covers
Art Director
David Pelham
Artist
Peter Bentley
Author
Evelyn Waugh
Design Group
Bentley/Farrell/Burnett
Designer
Peter Bentley
Publisher
Penguin Books

1970.09
Design for Print: Design Programme
Client
Brooks Baker & Fulford
Design Group
Crosby/Fletcher/Forbes
Designers
Crosby/Fletcher/Forbes
Photographers
Bob Brooks
Len Fulford

1970.10
Stationery Range
Client
Guest & Hughes
Design Group
Crosby/Fletcher/Forbes
Designers
Crosby/Fletcher/Forbes

1970.11
Design for Print: Technical & Industrial Literature
Art Directors
Crosby/Fletcher/Forbes
David Collins
Artists
John Gorham
George Hoy
Client
Mears Caldwell Hacker
Design Group
Crosby/Fletcher/Forbes
Designers
Crosby/Fletcher/Forbes
Photographer
Jean Louis Bloch-Laine

1970.12
Design for Print: Direct Mail
Client
Crosby/Fletcher/Forbes
Copywriters
Crosby/Fletcher/Forbes
Design Group
Crosby/Fletcher/Forbes
Designers
Crosby/Fletcher/Forbes

1970.13
Packaging Design
Art Director
David Juniper
Artist
David Juniper
Client
Atlantic Records
Design Group
Wurlitzer
Designer
David Juniper

1970.14
Editorial Design: Editorial Feature in a Consumer Magazine
Art Director
Michael Rand
Artist
Burt Silverman
Designer
David King
Publication
Sunday Times Magazine
Publisher
Times Newspapers
Writer
Alan Rake

1970.15
Editorial Design: Consumer Magazine
Art Directors
David King
Michael Rand
Designers
Andrew Dark
Gilvrie Misstear
Terence Seago
Editor
Godfrey Smith
Publication
Sunday Times Magazine
Publisher
Times Newspapers

1971

1971.01
Advertising Design: Newspapers
Advertising Agency
Saatchi & Saatchi
Art Director
John Hegarty
Client
The Health Education Council
Copywriter
Chris Martin
Designer
John Hegarty

1971.02
Copy: Consumer Advertisements
Agency
Saatchi & Saatchi
Art Director
Ross Cramer
Client
The Health Education Council
Copywriter
Charles Saatchi
Designer
Ross Cramer

1971.03
Advertising Design: Newspapers – Campaigns
Advertising Agency
Saatchi & Saatchi
Art Directors
Ross Cramer
John Hegarty
Bill Atherton
Client
The Health Education Council
Copywriters
Mike Coughlan
Chris Martin
Charles Saatchi
Jeremy Sinclair
Designers
Bill Atherton
Ross Cramer
John Hegarty
Photographers
Kokon Chung
Ray Rathbone

1971.04
Advertising Design: Newspapers
Advertising Agency
Doyle Dane Bernbach
Art Director
Brian Byfield
Client
Volkswagen Motors
Copywriter
David Abbott
Designer
Brian Byfield

1971.05
Advertising Design: Newspapers
Advertising Agency
Doyle Dane Bernbach
Art Director
Neil Godfrey
Client
Lufthansa Airlines
Copywriter
Dawson Yeoman
Designer
Neil Godfrey
Photographer
Tony Elliott

1971.06
Advertising Design: Consumer Magazines – Colour
Advertising Agency
Collett Dickenson Pearce
Art Director
Bob Byrne
Client
Pretty Polly
Copywriter
Alan Tilby
Designer
Bob Byrne
Photographer
Eve Arnold

1971.07
Poster Design: Outstanding Photograph of 1971
Advertising Agency
Collett Dickenson Pearce
Art Director
Richard Dearing
Client
Hovis
Copywriter
Alan Parker
Designer
Richard Dearing
Photographer
Peter Webb

1971.08
Design for Print: Corporate Identity Programme
Art Directors
Marcello Minale
Brian Tattersfield
Client
Baric Computing Services
Design Group
Minale Tattersfield Provinciali
Designers
Alex Maranzano
Marcello Minale
Richard Sears
Brian Tattersfield

1971.09
Direct Mail
Advertising Artwork Author
Arnold Schwartzman
Art Director
Arnold Schwartzman
Artists
Arnold Schwartzman
Tony Meeuwissen
Mike Reid
Client
Kinney Record Group
Design Group
Arnold Schwartzman Productions
Designer
Arnold Schwartzman

1972

1972.01
Print & Editorial Design: Record Label Design
Art Director
Iain MacMillan
Client
Apple Records
Creative Director
Allan Steckler
Designer
Noah Slutsky
Photographer
Iain MacMillan
Publisher
Apple Records

1972.02
Poster Design
Advertising Agency
Doyle Dane Bernbach
Art Director
Martyn Walsh
Client
Volkswagen (GB)
Copywriter
David Brown
Designer
Martyn Walsh
Photographer
Martin Thompson

1972.03
Packaging Design
Advertising Agency
Collett Dickenson Pearce
Art Director
Vernon Howe
Artists
Jim Coley
Tony Meeuwissen
Client
Birds Eye Foods
Design Group
Michael Peters & Partners
Designers
Ian Butcher
Leyland Gomez
Geoff Hockey
Michael Peters
Colin Robinson
Suzanna Strauss
David Tirrell

1972.04
TV & Cinema: 30 Second Television Commercial in Colour
Advertising Agency
Collett Dickenson Pearce
Agency Art Director
Vernon Howe
Agency Producer
Julia Lisney
Art Director
David Bill
Client
Birds Eye Foods
Copywriter
Tony Kenrick
Director
Alan Parker
Lighting Cameraman
Mike Seresin
Production Company
Alan Parker Film Company

1972.05
TV & Cinema: Television Campaign – Colour
Advertising Agency
Dorland Advertising
Agency Producer
Tony Brown
Art Director
Alan Parker
Client
HJ Heinz
Copywriters
Dorland Group
Alan Parker
Director
Alan Parker
Lighting Cameraman
Mike Seresin
Production Company
Alan Parker Film Company

1972.06
TV & Cinema: Television Commercial – Colour Over 45 Seconds Duration
Advertising Agency
Collett Dickenson Pearce
Agency Producer
Raymond Barker
Art Director
Geoff Kirkland
Client
Gallaher
Copywriter
Lindsay Dale
Director
Ridley Scott
Lighting Cameraman
Peter Suschitzky
Production Company
Ridley Scott Associates

1972.07
Advertising Design: Consumer Magazines
Advertising Agency
Young & Rubicam
Art Director
David Tree
Client
International Distillers & Vintners
Copywriter
John Bacon
Designer
David Tree
Photographer
Hans Feurer

1972.08
TV & Cinema: Television Campaign – Colour
Advertising Agency
J Walter Thompson
Agency Producer
Keith Godman
Client
Arthur Guinness Son & Company
Copywriters
Tom Rayfield
Chris Wilkins
Director
Brian Cummins
Lighting Cameraman
Ousama Rawi
Production Company
Cummins Signal

1972.09
TV & Cinema: 30 Second Television Commercial in Colour
Advertising Agency
J Walter Thompson
Agency Art Director
Julian Sambrook
Agency Producer
Keith Godman
Client
Arthur Guinness Son & Company
Copywriters
Tom Rayfield
Chris Wilkins
Director
Cliff Owen
Lighting Cameraman
Frank Tidy
Production Company
Sierra Productions

1972.10
Art & Photography: Consumer Magazines – Editorial
Art Director
David Hillman
Client
Nova
Copywriter
Caroline Baker
Designer
David Hillman
Photographer
Sarah Moon
Publisher
IPC Magazines

1972.11
Art & Photography: Photography for Print
Art Director
Derek Forsyth
Client
Pirelli
Design Group
The Derek Forsyth Partnership
Designer
Celia Philo
Photographer
Sarah Moon

1972.12
Print & Editorial Design: Menu Card
Art Director
George Hardie
Artist
George Hardie
Client
Mr Freedom
Design Group
Nicholas Thirkell Associates
Designer
George Hardie

1972.13
Print & Editorial Design: Calendar
Art Director
John McConnell
Client
Face
Design Group
John McConnell
Designers
John McConnell
Howard Brown

1972.14
Editorial Design: Book Jackets & Paperback Covers
Art Director
David Pelham
Artist
David Pelham
Designer
David Pelham
Publisher
Penguin Books

1972.15
Design for Print: Calendar
Art Director
Alan Fletcher
Artists
Bentley & Farrell
Derek Birdsall
Mel Calman
Crosby/Fletcher/Forbes
Michael Foreman
Bob Gill
John Gorham
Lou Klein
John McConnell
Enzo Raggazzini
Arnold Schwartzman
Herbert Spencer
Philip Thompson
Client
Robert Norton
Design Group
Pentagram Design Partnership
Designer
Alan Fletcher

1972.16
Print & Editorial Design: Technical or Industrial Literature
Advertising Agency
Aalders Marchant Weinreich
Artist
Tony Meeuwissen
Authors
C J Slunder
W K Boyd
Client
Zinc Development Association
Designer
Mervyn Kurlansky
Publisher
Zinc Development Association

1972.17
Art & Photography: Record Label
Art Director
Paul Leaves
Client
Transatlantic Records
Designer
Tony Meeuwissen

1972.18
Print & Editorial Design: Stationery
Art Director
Tony Meeuwissen
Artist
Tony Meeuwissen
Client
Kinney Records
Design Group
Kinney Records
Designer
Tony Meeuwissen

1972.19
Print & Editorial Design: Record Cover
Art Directors
Nigel Holmes
Douglas Maxwell
Client
Island Records
Design Group
Douglas Maxwell
Designer
Nigel Holmes
Illustrator
Alan Cracknell
Photographer
Ray Rathbone

1972.20
Art & Photography: Consumer Magazines – Editorial
Art Director
Michael Rand
Author
Francis Wyndham
Client
Sunday Times Magazine
Designer
David King
Photographer
Don McCullin
Publisher
Times Newspapers

1972.21
Art & Photography: Consumer Magazines – Editorial
Art Director
Michael Rand
Authors
Don McCullin
Francis Wyndham
Client
Sunday Times Magazine
Designer
Gilvrie Misstear
Photographer
Don McCullin
Publisher
Times Newspapers

1973

1973.01
Art & Photography: Newspaper Advertisement – Photography
Advertising Agency
Collett Dickenson Pearce & Partners
Art Director
Peter Cherry
Client
Gallahers
Copywriter
Mike Doyle
Designer
Peter Cherry
Photographer
Bruce Brown

1973.02
TV & Cinema: Television Advertising Campaign
Advertising Agency
J Walter Thompson
Agency Producers
Howard Eldridge
Terry Taylor
Art Director
Philip Harrison
Client
F S Matta
Copywriter
Adam Rowntree
Director
Karel Reisz
Lighting Cameraman
John Coquillon
Production Company
Film Contracts

1973.03
TV & Cinema: Television Commericals
Advertising Agency
Dorland Advertising
Agency Art Director
Mike Bradshaw
Agency Producer
Paul Mezulianik
Client
Cadbury Schweppes
Copywriter
Roy Taylor
Director
Hugh Hudson
Lighting Cameraman
John Alcott
Production Company
RSA Productions

1973.04
Print & Editorial Design: Calendar Design
Art Director
Derek Forsyth
Artist
Allen Jones
Client
Pirelli
Design Group
The Derek Forsyth Partnership
Designers
Malcolm Storey
Bob Celiz

1973.05
Print & Editorial Design: Design Programme
Art Directors
Ian Butcher
Geoff Hockey
Michael Peters
Artists
Camden Playcentre
Keishu H Careless
Phillip Castle
Barry Craddock
John Gorham
Hargreave Hands
Allan Manham
Tony Meeuwissen
Arthur Robbins
Nicholas Thirkell
Client
Winsor and Newton
Consultant Designer
John Gorham
Design Group
Michael Peters & Partners
Designers
Ian Butcher
Geoff Hockey
Michael Peters

1973.06
TV & Cinema: Television Campaigns – Animation
Advertising Agency
Boase Massimi Pollitt
Agency Art Director
John Webster
Agency Producer
David Bastin
Client
Schweppes
Copywriters
John Webster
Chris Wilkins
Director
Richard Williams
Designer
John Webster
Production Company
Richard Williams Animation

1973.07
TV & Cinema: 45 Second Television Commercial
Advertising Agency
Young & Rubicam Benelux
Agency Art Director
Renee van Rossom
Agency Producer
Gilbert King
Client
Levi-Strauss
Director
Hugh Hudson
Lighting Cameraman
John Alcott
Production Company
RSA Productions

1973.08
Art & Photography: Posters
Art Director
Nancy Fouts
Client
General Post Office
Design Group
Shirt Sleeve Studio
Designers
Nancy Fouts
Malcolm Fowler
Photographers
Nancy Fouts
Malcolm Fowler

1973.09
Print & Editorial Design: Books
Art Directors
Tony Evans
Brian Rice
Authors
Tony Evans
Brian Rice
Clients
Tony Evans
Brian Rice
Designer
David Hillman
Photographer
Tony Evans
Publisher
Mathews Miller Dunbar

1973.10
Print & Editorial Design: Technical or Industrial Literature
Client
Pirelli
Design Group
Pentagram Design Partnership
Designer
Georg Staehelin

1973.11
Print & Editorial Design: Design of a Symbol
Art Director
Mervyn Kurlansky
Artist
Madeleine Bennett
Client
Roche Products
Copywriter
Alan Clews
Design Group
Pentagram Design Partnership
Designer
Mervyn Kurlansky

1973.12
Print & Editorial Design: Paperback Covers
Art Director
David Pelham
Client
Penguin
Designer
John McConnell
Publisher
Penguin Books

1973.13
Advertising Design: Packaging
Art Directors
Gerry Barney
David Bristow
Terence Griffin
Jenny Sebley
Crispin Tweddell
Client
R & G Cuthbert
Copywriters
Terence Griffin
Clay Jones
Francesca Zeissl
Design Group
Wolff Olins
Designers
Gerry Barney
David Bristow
Terence Griffin
Jenny Sebley
Crispin Tweddell
Illustrators
Norman Barber
Henry Barnett
David Baxter
Leonora Box
Patricia Caley
David Cook
Patrick Cox
Pauline Ellison
Peter Goodfellow
Leslie Greenwood
John Hadfield
Vera Ibbett
Ron Kirby
Kristin Rosenberg
Kathleen Smith
George Thompson
Faith Tofts

1973.14
Print & Editorial Design: Corporate Identity Programme
Art Director
FHK Henrion
Client
British European Airways
Design Group
Henrion Design Associates
Designers
FHK Henrion
Chris Holt
Roger Marsden
Alan Parkin

1973.15
Print & Editorial Design: Record Cover Design
Art Director
John Kosh
Client
Family
Design Group
John Kosh
Designers
Peter Howe
John Kosh
Photographer
Peter Howe

1974

1974.01
Posters
Advertising Agency
Saatchi & Saatchi
Art Director
John Hegarty
Client
Health Education Council
Copywriter
Chris Martin
Photographer
Tony Evans

1974.02
Advertising: Consumer Magazines – Colour
Advertising Agency
Collett Dickenson Pearce
Art Directors
Neil Godfrey
Bob Isherwood
Bob Wilson
Client
Birds Eye Foods
Copywriters
Tony Brignull
David Brown
Dave Watkinson

Designers
Neil Godfrey
Bob Isherwood
Bob Wilson
Photographer
David Thorpe

1974.03
1. Newspaper Colour Advertisement
2. Consumer Campaign
Advertising Agency
Collett Dickenson Pearce
Art Director
Neil Godfrey
Client
G A Dunn & Company
Copywriter
Tony Brignull
Designer
Neil Godfrey
Photographer
David Thorpe

1974.04
TV & Cinema Advertising: 60 Second Television Commercial
Advertising Agency
Collett Dickenson Pearce
Agency Producer
Judy Hurst
Art Director
Phil Mason
Client
John Harvey & Son
Copywriter
Geoffrey Seymour
Director
Alan Parker
Lighting Cameraman
Mike Seresin
Production Company
Alan Parker Film Company

1974.05
TV & Cinema Advertising: 45 Second Television Commercial
Advertising Agency
Collett Dickenson Pearce
Agency Producer
Polly Kilminster
Art Directors
Phil Cherrington
Alec Wignall
Client
Gallaher
Copywriters
Phil Cherrington
Alec Wignall
Director
Alan Parker
Lighting Cameraman
Peter Suschitzky
Production Company
Alan Parker Film Company

1974.06
TV & Cinema Advertising: Animation
Advertising Agency
The Boase Massimi Pollitt Partnership
Agency Producer
Wendy Ward
Animator
Dick Purdon
Art Director
John Webster
Client
Ferrero UK
Director
Richard Williams
Editor
Rod Howick
Production Company
Richard Williams Animation

Set Designer
Rowland Wilson
Writer
Graham Collis

1974.07
TV & Cinema: Art Direction
Advertising Agency
The Boase Massimi Pollitt Partnership
Agency Producer
Roger Shipley
Art Director
John Webster
Client
Cadbury Typhoo Foods
Copywriter
Chris Wilkins
Director
Bob Brooks
Lighting Cameraman
Peter Biziou
Production Company
Brooks Fulford Cramer
Set Designer
Peter Richardson

1974.08
TV & Cinema Advertising: Television Commercials
Advertising Agency
The Boase Massimi Pollitt Partnership
Agency Producer
Roger Shipley
Art Director
Judy Cross
Client
Schweppes
Copywriters
Dave Trott
Chris Wilkins
Director
John Alcott
Lighting Cameraman
Ronnie Anscombe
Production Company
Ridley Scott Associates

1974.09
Newspaper: Black & White Advertisement
Advertising Agency
The Boase Massimi Pollitt Partnership
Art Director
David Christensen
Client
The Labour Party
Copywriters
Dave Trott
Chris Wilkins
Designer
David Christensen

1974.10
Graphic Design: Technical Literature
Client
Nederlandse Spoorwegen
Design Group
TEL Design Associated
Designers
Gert Dumbar
Gert-Jan Leuvelink
Frans van Mourik

1974.11
Graphic Design: Gift Pack
Art Director
Alan Fletcher
Client
Reuters
Design Group
Pentagram
Designer
Alan Fletcher

1974.12
TV & Cinema Graphics: Programme Titles
Agency Producer
David Griffiths
Copywriter
Leonard Bernstein
Client
Amberson Video
Director
Pat Gavin
Graphic Designer
Pat Gavin
Production Company
TV Cartoons

1974.13
TV & Cinema Graphics: Cinema
Cameraman
John Williams
Client
The Righteous Apple
Designer
Mick Crane
Director
George Dunning
Production Company
TV Cartoons

1974.14
TV & Cinema Graphics: Programme Titles
Client
Thames Television
Graphic Designers
John Stamp
Ian Kestle
Production Company
Caravel Films
Producer
Jeremy Isaacs

1975

1975.01
Newspaper: Public Service Advertisement
Advertising Agency
Saatchi & Saatchi
Art Director
Ron Mather
Client
The Health Education Council
Copywriter
Andrew Rutherford
Photographer
John Thornton

1975.02
Newspaper: Black & White Advertisement
Advertising Agency
Collett Dickenson Pearce
Art Director
Arthur Parsons
Client
Metropolitan Police
Copywriter
John Salmon
Photographer
Alan Brooking

1975.03
Advertising: Newspaper Campaign
Advertising Agency
Collett Dickenson Pearce
Art Directors
Neil Godfrey
Arthur Parsons
Client
Central Office of Information
Copywriters
Tony Brignull
John Salmon
Photographer
Alan Brooking

1975.04
TV & Cinema Advertising: Film Photography
Advertising Agency
Collett Dickenson Pearce
Agency Producer
Judy Hurst
Art Director
Ronnie Turner
Client
Hovis
Copywriter
David Brown
Director
Ridley Scott
Lighting Cameraman
Terry Bedford
Production Company
RSA Productions
Set Designer
Mike Seymour

1975.05
1. TV & Cinema Advertising: Direction
2. TV & Cinema Advertising: 60 Second Television Commercial
Advertising Agency
Collett Dickenson Pearce
Agency Producer
Judy Bird
Client
Gallaher
Copywriter
Lindsay Dale
Director
Bob Brooks
Lighting Cameraman
Peter Suschitzky
Production Company
Brooks Fulford Cramer
Set Designer
Geoff Kirkland

1975.06
TV & Cinema Advertising: Television Campaign
Advertising Agency
The Boase Massimi Pollitt Partnership
Agency Producers
Roger Shipley
Wendy Ward
Art Directors
Graham Rose
John Webster
Client
Unigate Dairies
Copywriters
Graham Collis
John Webster
Directors
Mike Blum
Brian Mindel
Eric Wylan
Photographers/Lighting and Rostrum Cameramen
Don Cohen
Ted Gerald
Steven Goldblatt
Set Designer
Bruce Grimes
Production Companies
Roger Cherrill
Mindel Stone and Howe
Phos-Cine

1975.07
Packaging Design: Book Jackets
Art Director
David Pelham
Client
Penguin Books
Designer
John Gorham

1975.08
Symbols & Logotypes
Art Directors
John Gorham
John McConnell
Client
Face Photosetting
Designers
John Gorham
John McConnell

1975.09
Print: Corporate Identity
Art Directors
David Bristow
Terence Griffin
Michael Wolff
Client
Bovis
Design Group
Wolff Olins
Designers
Gerry Barney
Bob Celiz
Adrian Harwood
Illustrator
Ken Lilly

1975.10
Packaging Design: Point-of-Sale Material
Art Director
Vincent McEvoy
Client
RSO Records
Copywriter
Vincent McEvoy
Designer
Vincent McEvoy
Illustrators
Wurlitzer Studio

1975.11
Packaging Design: Book Jackets
Art Director
Pearce Marchbank
Client
Music Sales
Designer
Pearce Marchbank
Illustrator
Oliver Williams

1975.12
Editorial Design: Magazines – Weekly
Art Director
Pearce Marchbank
Designer
Pearce Marchbank
Photographer
Roger Perry
Publication
Time Out
Writers
Jerome Burne
Roger Hutchinson

1975.13
Editorial Design: Specialist Feature
Art Director
David Driver
Authors
Barry Davies
Brian Gearing
Peter Gillman
Jimmy Hill
John Motson
Jack Rollin
Designers
David Driver
Derek Ungless
Illustrators
Peter Brookes
Richard Draper

Photographers
Allan Ballard
Michael Brennan
Tony Evans
Roger Jones
Dimitri Kasterine
Robert McFarlane
Keith McMillan
Publication
Radio Times World Cup Special
Publisher
BBC Publications

1976

1976.01
Consumer Poster
Agency
Collett Dickenson Pearce
Art Director
Alan Waldie
Client
Pretty Polly
Copywriter
Paul Weiland
Photographer
John Swannell

1976.02
Posters: 4-48 Sheet Consumer
Advertising Agency
Collett Dickenson Pearce
Art Director
Paul Smith
Client
Whitbread
Copywriters
Tony Brignull
Terry Lovelock
Designers
Tony Brignull
Paul Smith
Illustrator
Phillip Castle

1976.03
TV & Cinema Advertising: Television Campaigns
Advertising Agency
Collett Dickenson Pearce
Agency Producers
Sarah Helm
Kathy O'Carroll
Art Director
Vernon Howe
Client
Whitbread
Copywriter
Terry Lovelock
Director
Vernon Howe
Lighting Cameramen
Mike Seresin
David MacDonald
Producer
Alan Marshall
Set Designers
David Bill
Geoff Kirkland
Production Companies
Alan Parker Film Company
Mindel Stone & Howe

1976.04
TV & Cinema Advertising: 45 Second Television Commercial
Advertising Agency
Collett Dickenson Pearce
Agency Producer
Judy Bird
Art Directors
David Horry
Ronnie Turner
Client
The Parker Pen Company
Copywriters
David Brown
Paul Weiland

Director
Alan Parker
Lighting Cameraman
Frank Tidy
Set Designer
Brian Morris

1976.05
TV & Cinema Advertising: 60 Second Television Commercial
Advertising Agency
Collett Dickenson Pearce
Agency Producer
Judy Hurst
Art Director
Neil Godfrey
Client
Bird's Eye Foods
Copywriter
Tony Brignull
Director
Bob Bierman
Lighting Cameraman
Derek van Lint
Production Company
Bierman & Randall
Set Designer
Evan Hercules

1976.06
Packaging Design: Individual Pack
Client
Harrods
Design Consultancy
Minale Tattersfield Provinciali
Designers
Marcello Minale
Brian Tattersfield

1976.07
1. Trade Magazine Advertising Campaign
2. Written Trade Advertisement
3. Advertising Art
Advertising Agency
Boase Massimi Pollitt
Art Director
David Christensen
Client
Unigate Foods
Copywriter
Graham Collis
Illustrator
Michael Terry
Photographer
Peter Barbieri

1976.08
Direct Mail
Advertising Agency
Davidson Pearce Berry & Spottiswoode
Art Director
Brian Bridge
Client
International Wool Secretariat
Copywriter
David Little

1976.09
Symbols & Logotypes
Client
Milton Keynes Development Corporation
Design Consultancy
Minale Tattersfield Provinciali
Designers
Marcello Minale
Brian Tattersfield
Illustrator
Brian Tattersfield

1976.10
Symbols & Logotypes
Art Directors
Marcello Minale
Brian Tattersfield
Client
Hospital Design Partnership
Design Consultancy
Minale Tattersfield Provinciali
Designers
Alex Maranzano
Marcello Minale
Brian Tattersfield
Illustrator
Ian Grindle

1976.11
1. Poster Photography
2. Record Sleeve Photography
Client
Goldhawke Records
Copywriter
Roger Daltrey
Designer
Graham Hughes
Photographer
Graham Hughes

1976.12
Editorial Design
Art Editor
David Driver
Art Editor (Programmes)
Robert Priest
Designers
David Driver
Robert Priest
Editor
Geoffrey Cannon
Publication
Radio Times
Publisher
BBC Publications

1977

1977.01
Consumer Poster
Advertising Agency
Collett Dickenson Pearce
Art Director
Paul Smith
Client
Wall's Meat Company
Copywriter
Terry Lovelock
Designer
John O'Driscoll
Photographer
Ed White

1977.02
Newspapers: Colour Advertisement
Advertising Agency
Collett Dickenson Pearce
Art Director
Alan Waldie
Client
Whitbread
Copywriters
Mike Cozens
Terry Lovelock
Illustrator
Bob Wilson
Typographer
Jeff Merrells

1977.03
Newspapers: Black & White Advertisement
Advertising Agency
Collett Dickenson Pearce
Art Director
Gordon Smith
Client
Barclaycard
Copywriter
Patrick Woodward
Photographer
John Thornton
Typographer
Maggie Lewis

1977.04
Advertising: Campaigns
Advertising Agency
Collett Dickenson Pearce
Art Directors
Neil Godfrey
Bob Isherwood
Client
The Parker Pen Company
Copywriters
Tony Brignull
Peter Lorimer
Dave Watkinson
Photographers
Bob Cramp
Barney Edwards
David Thorpe
Typographers
Bob Isherwood
Maggie Lewis
Jeff Merrells

1977.05
Advertising: Typography
Agency
Collett Dickenson Pearce
Art Director
Bob Isherwood
Client
The Parker Pen Company
Copywriter
Dave Watkinson
Photographer
David Thorpe
Typographers
Bob Isherwood
Maggie Lewis

1977.06
Advertising: Copy
Advertising Agency
Collett Dickenson Pearce
Art Director
Neil Godfrey
Client
The Parker Pen Company
Copywriter
Tony Brignull
Photographer
Barney Edwards
Typographer
Neil Godfrey

1977.07
TV & Cinema Commercials: Direction
Advertising Agency
Collett Dickenson Pearce
Agency Producer
Judy Hurst
Art Director
John O'Driscoll
Clients
Beaverbrook Newspapers
Daily Express
Copywriter
John Kelly
Director
Alan Parker
Editor
Gerry Hambling
Lighting Cameraman
Mike Seresin
Production Company
Alan Parker Film Company
Set Designer
Brian Morris

1977.08
Packaging Design: Range of Packaging
Art Director
Michael Peters
Client
Penhaligon's
Design Group
Michael Peters & Partners
Designer
Madeleine Bennett
Illustrator
Howard Milton
Typographer
Madeleine Bennett

1977.09
Packaging Design: Range of Packaging
Art Director
Michael Peters
Client
Winsor & Newton
Design Group
Michael Peters & Partners
Designer
Bev Whitehead
Illustrators
Guy Beggs
Ginetto Coppola
Bill Dare
John Davies
Roy Ellsworth
John Gorham
John Rose
Colin Salter
David Sharp
Jan Stringer

1977.10
TV & Cinema Commercials: Television Campaign
Advertising Agency
The Boase Massimi Pollitt Partnership
Agency Producer
Peter Valentine
Art Director
John Webster
Client
Quaker Oats
Copywriters
Graham Collis
John Webster
Director
Berny Stringle
Editor
Geoff Muller
Lighting Cameraman
Peter Jessop
Production Company
N S & H Creative Partnership International
Set Designer
Tony Noble

1977.11
TV & Cinema Advertising: Television Commercial
Advertising Agency
Young & Rubicam
Agency Producer
Mike Gilmour
Art Director
Mike Stephenson
Client
Levi-Strauss (London)
Copywriter
Derek Apps
Director
Ridley Scott
Editor
Nick Lewin
Photographer
Frank Tidy
Production Company
RSA Productions
Set Designer
Peter Hampton

1977.12
1. TV & Cinema Advertising: Film Photography
2. Music
Advertising Agency
Saatchi & Saatchi Garland-Compton
Agency Producer
Michael Russell Hills
Art Director
Adrian Lyne
Client
Brutus
Copywriter
Bob Gabriel
Director
Adrian Lyne
Editor
Alan Blake
Lighting Cameraman
Derek van Lint
Music Composer
David Dundas
Production Company
Jennie & Company
Set Designer
Geoff Kirkland

1977.13
Logotypes
Client
Bugsy Malone Productions
Designer
John Gorham

1977.14
Graphics: Complete Book
Author
David Pelham
Client
Penguin Books
Designer
David Pelham
Illustrator
Andrew Holmes
Photographer
Harri Peccinotti

1977.15
Graphics: Poster
Client
Royal College of Art
Designer
Nick Wurr

1977.16
Direct Mail
Client
Klaus Wuttke & Partners
Designers
John George
Klaus Wuttke

1977.17
Graphics: Design Programme
Client
Clarks Shoes
Design Group
Pentagram
Designers
Howard Brown
John McConnell
David Pearce

1977.18
Packaging: Record Sleeve Photography
Art Director
Storm Thorgerson
Client
Peter Grant, Swansong
Design Group
Hipgnosis/NTA Studios
Designers
Peter Christopherson
George Hardie
Storm Thorgerson
Illustrator
George Hardie
Photographer
Aubrey Powell

1977.19
Packaging: Record Sleeve Illustration
Client
Black Sabbath
Design Group
Hipgnosis
Designers
George Hardie
Storm Thorgerson
Illustrators
George Hardie
Richard Manning
Photographer
Aubrey Powell

1977.20
Editorial Design: Illustration
Art Editors
David Driver
Robert Priest
Author
Gavin Millar
Illustrator
Ralph Steadman
Publication
Radio Times
Publisher
BBC Publications

1977.21
TV & Cinema Graphics: Television Programme Title
Director
Bernard Lodge
Production Company
BBC Television
Stills Photographers
Bernard Lodge
Mike Sanders

1978

1978.01
TV & Cinema Commercials: Television Commercials
Advertising Agency
Collett Dickenson Pearce
Agency Producer
Peter Levelle
Art Director
Paul Smith
Client
Olympus Optical Company (UK)
Copywriter
Mike Everett
Director
Alan Parker
Editor
Roger Cherill
Lighting Cameraman
Ben Knoll
Photographer
Ben Knoll
Production Company
Alan Parker Film Company

1978.02
Illustration & Photography: Poster Campaign Photography
Advertising Agency
Collett Dickenson Pearce
Art Directors
Alan Waldie
Graham Watson
Client
Gallaher
Copywriters
Mike Cozens
John O'Donnell
Photographers
Duffy
Adrian Flowers
Typographer
Maggie Lewis

1978.03
Posters
Advertising Agency
Collett Dickenson Pearce
Art Director
Neil Godfrey
Client
Fiat (UK)
Copywriter
Tony Brignull
Photographer
Alan Brooking
Typographer
Maggie Lewis

1978.04
48-Sheet Poster
Advertising Agency
Collett Dickenson Pearce
Art Director
Neil Godfrey
Client
Fiat Motor Company (UK)
Copywriter
Tony Brignull
Photographer
Alan Brooking
Typographer
Maggie Lewis

1978.05
Newspapers: Black & White Advertisement
Advertising Agency
Boase Massimi Pollitt
Univas Partnership
Art Director
Paul Garrett
Client
Renault
Copywriter
Susan Trott
Typographer
Ed Church

1978.06
TV & Cinema Advertising: Film Photography
Advertising Agency
McCann-Erickson Advertising
Agency Producer
Dorothy Booth
Art Director
Roger Manton
Client
Levi Strauss
Copywriter
Andy Rork
Director
Adrian Lyne
Editor
John Hall
Lighting Cameraman
Howard Atherton
Photographer
Howard Atherton
Production Company
Jennie & Company

1978.07
TV & Cinema Advertising: Direction
Advertising Agency
Zetland Advertising
Agency Producer
Robert King
Art Director
Brian Morris
Client
Berlei (UK)
Copywriter
Nick Evans
Director
Tony Scott
Editor
Pamela Power
Photographer/Lighting Cameraman
Frank Tidy
Production Company
RSA Productions

1978.08
Packaging Design: Individual Pack
Advertising Agency
J Walter Thompson
Art Director
Graeme Norways
Client
Rowntree Mackintosh
Copywriter
Madeleine Andersen
Designer
John Gorham
Illustrator
John Gorham
Typographer
John Gorham

1978.09
Direct Mail & Sales Promotion: Direct Mail
Client
Ruck Ryan Linsell
Design Group
Rod Springett & Associates
Designer
Rod Springett
Illustrator
Rod Springett

1978.10
Graphics: Architectural Graphics – Murals
Client
British Airport Authority
Design Group
Minale Tattersfield & Partners
Designers
Alex Maranzano
Marcello Minale
Brian Tattersfield
Illustrator
Brian Tattersfield

1978.11
Illustration & Photography: Complete Book
Art Director
Storm Thorgerson
Author
Mike Phillips
Client
Thames Television
Designers
Peter Christopherson
George Hardie
Storm Thorgerson
Illustrators
Peter Christopherson
George Hardie
Storm Thorgerson
Typographer
George Hardie

1978.12
Editorial Design: Newspapers – Complete issue
Art Director
David Litchfield
Client
Ritz
Designer
David Litchfield
Editors
David Bailey
David Litchfield

1978.13
Illustration & Photography: Illustration in an Advertisement
Advertising Agency
TBWA
Art Director
John Hegarty
Client
Newsweek International
Copywriter
Neil Patterson
Illustrator
Guy Gladwell
Typographer
Brian Hill

1978.14
Design for Television & Cinema: Arts Programme Titles
Art Director
Pat Gavin
Client
London Weekend Television
Director
Pat Gavin
Music Composer
Andrew Lloyd Webber
Producer
Melvyn Bragg
Production Company
Jerry Albert

1978.15
Design for Television & Cinema: Sports Programme Titles
Art Director
Pauline Talbot
Client
BBC Television Sports Department
Director
Pauline Talbot
Illustrator
Bob Cosford
Producers
Martin Hopkins
Jonathon Martin
Alec Weeks
Production Company
BBC Television
Scenic Artist
Graham Barkley

1978.16
Illustration & Photography: Photographic Editorial Feature
Art Director
Michael Rand
Client
Sunday Times Magazine
Designer
Gilvrie Misstear
Photographer
Lord Snowdon
Publisher
Times Newspapers

1979

1979.01
Illustration & Photography: Posters
Advertising Agency
Collett Dickenson Pearce
Art Director
Neil Godfrey
Client
Gallaher
Copywriter
Tony Brignull
Photographer
Jimmy Wormser

1979.02
TV & Cinema Advertising: Film
Advertising Agency
Collett Dickenson Pearce
Agency Producer
Judy Hurst
Art Director
Alan Waldie
Client
Gallaher
Copywriter
Mike Cozens
Director
Hugh Hudson
Editor
Stuart Taylor
Lighting Cameraman
Mike Molloy
Music Arrangement
Lol Creme
Kevin Godley
Set Designer
Geoff Kirkland
Production Company
Alan Parker Film Company

1979.03
Posters
Advertising Agency
Boase Massimi Pollitt
Univas Partnership
Art Director
Derrick Hass
Client
Barker & Dobson
Copywriter
David Trott
Illustrator
Larry Learmont

1979.04
Poster Campaign
Advertising Agency
French Cruttenden Osborn
Art Director
Graeme Norways
Client
White Horse Distillers
Copywriter
Nick Hazzard
Photographer
Lester Bookbinder
Typographer
Graeme Norways

1979.05
TV & Cinema Advertising: 30 Second Television Commercial
Advertising Agency
The Boase Massimi Pollitt
Univas Partnership
Agency Producer
Fred Robinson
Art Director
David Christensen
Client
Barker & Dobson
Copywriter
Graham Rose
Directors
Denis Russo
Ken Turner
Editor
John Farrow
Lighting Cameraman
Terry Permane
Music Arrangement
Joe Campbell
Production Company
Clearwater Film Company
Set Designer
Denis Russo

1979.06
TV & Cinema Advertising: 45 Second Television Commercial
Advertising Agency
The Boase Massimi Pollitt
Univas Partnership
Agency Producer
Roger Shipley
Art Director
John Webster
Client
L'Oréal
Copywriter
John Webster
Director
Tony Scott
Editor
Roger Wilson
Lighting Cameraman
Derek van Lint
Music Arrangement
Billy Gray
Production Company
RSA Productions

1979.07
TV & Cinema Advertising: Television Campaign
Advertising Agency
The Boase Massimi Pollitt
Univas Partnership
Agency Producer
Roger Shipley
Art Director
John Webster
Client
Courage Brewing
Copywriter
John Webster
Director
Peter Webb
Editor
Peter Beston
Lighting Cameraman
Iain MacMillan
Music Arrangement
Library Music
Production Company
Park Village Productions

1979.08
Advertising: Consumer Magazines – Colour
Advertising Agency
Boase Massimi Pollitt
Univas Partnership
Art Director
Gordon Smith
Client
Renault
Copywriter
Patrick Woodward
Photographers
Graham Ford
Geoff Senior
Typographer
Ed Church

1979.09
Graphics & Editorial Design: Stationery
Design Group
Wurr & Wurr
Designer
Nick Wurr
Client
Nick Wurr

1979.10
Design for Television: Television Programme Identity
Client
London Weekend Television
Designer
Pat Gavin
Director
Pat Gavin
Production Company
London Weekend Television
Set Designer
Michael Turney

1979.11
Design for Television: Documentary Titles
Agency Producer
Tony Edwards
Client
BBC Television
Designer
Roger Kennedy
Director
Roger Kennedy
Laser Company
Holoco
Lighting Cameraman
Peter Chapman
Production Company
BBC Television

1979.12
Design for Television: Documentary Titles
Agency Producer
Patricia Uden
Client
BBC Television
Designer
Charles McGhie
Director
Charles McGhie
Editor
Rod Longhurst
Lighting Cameraman
Les Paul
Production Company
BBC Television
Set Designer
Colin Lowery

1979.13
Posters: Public Service
Advertising Agency
Hall Advertising
Art Director
Jim Downie
Client
Scottish Health Education Unit
Copywriter
Tony Cox
Photographer
Tony May
Typographer
Jim Downie

1979.14
1. Consumer Magazine: Black & White Advertisement
2. Newspapers: Public Service
Advertising Agency
Saatchi & Saatchi
Garland-Compton
Art Director
Ron Mather
Client
Health Education Council
Copywriter
Andrew Rutherford
Illustrator
Ron Mather
Typographer
Olaf Liunberg

1979.15
Posters: up to 48 Sheet
Advertising Agency
Saatchi & Saatchi
Garland-Compton
Art Director
Martyn Walsh
Client
Conservative Central Office
Copywriter
Andrew Rutherford
Photographer
Bob Cramp
Typographer
Roger Kennedy

1980

1980.01
Packaging Design
Art Director
Peter Windett
Client
Crabtree & Evelyn Limited
Design Group
Peter Windett Associates

Designer
Peter Windett
Illustrator
Graham Evernden

1980.02
Posters: up to 20" x 30"
Client
Liberty's of London
Designer
Dan Fern
Illustrator
Dan Fern

1980.03
Television Graphic Design: Drama Titles
Art Director
Douglas Burd
Client
BBC Television Drama Department
Director
Douglas Burd
Editor
Roderick Longhurst
Lighting Cameraman
Victor Cummings
Music Composer
Geoffrey Burgon
Production Company
Caravel Film Services

1980.04
TV & Cinema Advertising: 45 Second Commercial
Advertising Agency
The Boase Massimi Pollitt Univas Partnership
Agency Producer
Tony Sherwood
Art Director
John Webster
Client
Courage Brewing
Copywriter
Dave Trott
Director
Hugh Hudson
Editor
Stuart Taylor
Lighting Cameraman
Bob Krasker
Music Composers
Chas 'n' Dave
Production Company
Hudson Films

1980.05
TV & Cinema Advertising: 45 Second Commercial
Advertising Agency
Collett Dickenson Pearce
Agency Producer
Peter Levelle
Art Director
David Horry
Client
Fiat Motor Company UK
Copywriter
Paul Weiland
Director
Hugh Hudson
Editor
Stuart Taylor
Lighting Cameraman
John Alcott
Music Composer
Rossini
Music Arrangement
Vangelis
Marion Lowe
Production Manager
Hudson Films

1980.06
TV & Cinema Advertising: 30 Second Commercial
Advertising Agency
Collett Dickenson Pearce
Agency Producer
Judy Hurst
Art Director
Rob Morris
Client
Gallaher
Copywriter
Alfredo Marcantonio
Director
Paul Weiland
Editor
Stuart Taylor
Lighting Cameraman
Harvey Harrison
Production Company
Alan Parker Film Company
Set Designer
Evan Hercules

1980.07
Posters
Advertising Agency
Doyle Dane Bernbach
Art Director
Peter Harold
Client
Volkswagen (GB)
Copywriter
Barbara Nokes
Photographer
Geoff Senior
Typographer
Peter Harold

1980.08
Advertising: Newspapers – Campaign
Advertising Agency
Doyle Dane Bernbach
Art Director
Bill Thompson
Client
Commercial Union Assurance
Copywriters
Dave Druiff
Suzie Henry
Photographer
Max Forsythe
Typographer
Simon Pemberton

1980.09
TV & Cinema Advertising: Television Campaign
Advertising Agency
Doyle Dane Bernbach
Agency Producer
Peter Valentine
Art Director
Bill Thompson
Client
Commercial Union Assurance
Copywriter
Suzie Henry
Director
Peter Webb
Editor
Peter Beston
Lighting Cameraman
Ian McMillan
Production Company
Park Village Productions
Set Designer
Tony Noble

1980.10
1. Advertising: Consumer Magazines – Colour
2. Advertising: Consumer Campaigns
Advertising Agency
Cherry Hedger & Seymour
Art Director
Tony Muranka
Client
Standard Brands
Copywriter
Geoffrey Seymour
Illustrator
Warren Madill
Typographer
Keith Mackenzie

1981

1981.01
Graphics: Design Programme
Art Director
Michael Peters
Client
Elsenham Quality Foods
Copywriter
Patricia Kershaw
Design Group
Michael Peters & Partners
Designer
Madeleine Bennett
Illustrators
Steve Adams
Peter Bentley
Graham Berry
Roy Coombes
Peter Goodfellow
Rory Kee
Typographer
Madeleine Bennett

1981.02
Direct Mail: Sales Promotion
Art Director
John Blackburn
Client
Gallaher
Copywriter
Derek Hodgetts
Design Group
John Blackburn & Partners
Designers
John Blackburn
Joe Gillespie
Photographer
Paul Grater
Typographer
Cliff Owen

1981.03
Graphics: Industrial Leaflets
Advertising Agency
Saatchi & Saatchi
Art Director
James Woollett
Client
Manpower Services Commission
Copywriter
Jeff Stark
Design Group
Carroll & Dempsey
Designers
Ken Carroll
Mike Dempsey
Photographer
Mark Edwards

1981.04
Graphics: Stationery Range
Art Director
Heleen Tigler Wybrandi
Client
Studio Dumbar
Design Group
Studio Dumbar
Designer
Ko Sliggers

1981.05
Design for Television
Costume Designer
Reg Samuel
Director
Simon Langton
Graphic Designer
Stefan Pstrowski
Lighting
Howard King
Music Composer/Arrangement
Patrick Gower
Producer
Jonathan Powell
Production Company
BBC Television
Programme Company
BBC Television
Set Designer
David Myerscough-Jones

1981.06
TV & Cinema Graphics: Graphic Inserts
Client
BBC Television
Graphic Designers
Douglas Burd
Rod Lord
Production Company
Pearce Studios
Writer
Douglas Adams

1981.07
Record Sleeves
Art Director
Peter Saville
Client
Dindisc Records
Design Group
Peter Saville
Designers
Ben Kelly
Peter Saville
Typographer
Peter Saville

1981.08
Record Sleeves
Art Director
Peter Saville
Client
Factory Records
Design Group
Peter Saville
Photographer
Charles Meecham
Typographer
Peter Saville

1981.09
Record Sleeves
Art Director
Peter Wagg
Client
Chrysalis Records
Designers
Gordon Ogilvie
John Sims
Illustrator
Geoff Halpin

1981.10
1. TV & Cinema Advertising: Campaigns
2. TV & Cinema Advertising: Use of Music
Advertising Agency
The Boase Massimi Pollitt Univas Partnership
Agency Producer
Tony Sherwood
Art Directors
Tina Morgan
John Webster
Client
Courage Brewing
Copywriter
John Pallant
Director
Len Fulford
Editor
Pamela Power
Lighting Cameraman
Bob Krasker
Music Composers
Chas & Dave
Producer
Richard Burge
Production Company
Brooks Fulford Cramer Seresin
Set Designer
Mike Seymour

1981.11
TV & Cinema Advertising: Film
Advertising Agency
TBWA
Agency Producer
Jane Bearman
Animator
Denis Russo
Art Director
Graham Watson
Client
Lego (UK)
Copywriter
Mike Cozens
Director
Ken Turner
Editor
Patrick Udale
Lighting Cameraman
Tom Harrison
Modelmaker
David Lyall
Producer
David Mitten
Production Company
Clearwater Films

1981.12
TV & Cinema Advertising: 45 Second Commercial
Advertising Agency
Collett Dickenson Pearce
Agency Producer
Judy Hurst
Art Director
John O'Driscoll
Client
Whitbread & Company
Copywriter
John Kelley
Director
Charles Jenkins
Editor
Charles Jenkins
Lighting Cameraman
Bev Roberts
Producer
Charles Jenkins
Production Company
Trickfilm

1981.13
Posters: Super Sites & Specials
Advertising Agency
Collett Dickenson Pearce
Art Director
Neil Godfrey
Client
Gallaher
Photographer
Neil Godfrey

1981.14
Posters
Advertising Agency
Collett Dickenson Pearce
Art Director
John Horton
Client
The Parker Pen Company
Copywriter
Richard Foster
Photographer
Graham Ford
Typographer
Maggie Lewis

1981.15
Press Advertising: Consumer Magazines – Colour
Advertising Agency
Wight Collins Rutherford Scott
Art Director
Ron Collins
Client
Chefaro Proprietaries
Copywriter
Andrew Rutherford
Photographer
Terence Donovan
Typographer
Mike Rix

1981.16
Press: Consumer Advertisement
Advertising Agency
Collett Dickenson Pearce
Art Director
David Horry
Client
Olympus Optical Company (UK)
Copywriter
Alfredo Marcantonio
Photographers
Don McPhee
Graham Wood
Typographer
Nigel Dawson

1981.17
Press: Consumer Campaign
Agency
Advertising and Marketing Services
Art Director
Neil Godfrey
Client
Albany Life Assurance
Copywriter
Tony Brignull
Photographer
Jimmy Wormser
Typographer
Nigel Dawson

1981.18
Newspapers: Black & White Advertisement
Advertising Agency
TBWA
Art Director
Malcolm Gaskin
Client
Land Rover
Copywriter
Neil Patterson
Design Group
Minale Tattersfield & Partners
Illustrator
Ian Grindle
Photographer
Geoff Senior
Typographer
Brian Hill

1981.19
Director Mail: Sales Promotion
Art Director
John McConnell
Client
Fios
Copywriter
Barry Delaney
Design Group
Pentagram
Designers
Mark Biley
Keren House
John McConnell
Illustrator
Dan Fern

1982

1982.01
Packaging: Range of Packaging
Art Director
Madeleine Bennett
Client
Penhaligon's
Design Group
Michael Peters & Partners
Designer
Madeleine Bennett
Typographer
Madeleine Bennett

1982.02
Magazines: Covers
Art Director
Keith Ablitt
Client
Design Magazine
Design Group
Design Magazine
Editor
James Woudhuysen
Illustrator
Donna Muir
Photographer
Tim Quallington
Publisher
The Design Council

1982.03
Graphics: Corporate Identity
Art Directors
Marcello Minale
Brian Tattersfield
Ian Delaney
Philip Carter
Client
Heal & Son
Design Group
Minale Tattersfield & Partners
Designers
Marcello Minale
Brian Tatttersfield
Typographer
Ian Delaney

1982.04
Photography & Illustration: Consumer Magazines
Art Director
Susan Mann
Client
Condé Nast
Photographer
Barry Lategan
Typographer
John Hind

1982.05
Photography & Illustration: Print Photography
Advertising Agency
The Yellowhammer Company
Art Director
Jeremy Pemberton
Client
Olympus Optical Company (UK)
Photographer
Barry Lategan
Typographer
Frances Berger

1982.06
Editorial & Books: Complete Book
Author
David Pelham
Designer
David Pelham
Illustrator
David Pelham
Publisher
Pan Books
Typographer
David Pelham

1982.07
Graphics: Corporate & Brand Identity
Art Director
Gert Dumbar
Client
Westeinde Hospital, The Hague
Design Group
Studio Dumbar
Designers
Michel de Boer
Rik Comello
Gert Dumbar
Heleen Tigler Wybrandi-Raue
Photographer
Lex van Pieterson

1982.08
Graphics: Institutional Poster Campaign
Art Director
Heleen Tigler Wybrandi-Raue
Client
Rijksmuseum
Design Group
Studio Dumbar
Designers
Rik Comello
Ko Sliggers
Typographers
Rik Comello
Ko Sliggers

1982.09
Record Sleeves
Art Director
Neville Brody
Client
Fetish Records
Illustrator
Neville Brody
Typographer
Neville Brody

1982.10
Television Titles
Client
BBC Television
Director
Marc Ortmans
Editor
Simon Morice
Executive Producer
Michael Hurll
Lighting Cameraman
Douglas Adamson
Music Composers/Arrangers
Phillip Lynnot
Midge Ure
Production Company
Stewart-Hardy Films

1982.11
TV & Cinema Advertising: Film
Advertising Agency
The Boase Massimi Pollitt
Univas Partnership
Agency Producer
Roger Shipley
Art Director
John Webster
Client
Courage Brewing
Copywriter
John Webster
Director
Ian McMillan
Editor
Simon Cheek
Lighting Cameraman
Peter Jessop
Music Composer/Arrangement
Clive Hicks
Producer
Abigail Sloggett
Production Company
Park Village Productions
Set Designer
Tony Noble

1982.12
Posters: Campaigns
Advertising Agency
Gold Greenlees Trott
Art Directors
Axel Chaldecott
Andy Lawson
Gordon Smith
Client
London Weekend Television
Copywriters
Paul Grubb
Steve Henry
Dave Trott
Designers
Axel Chaldecott
Andy Lawson
Gordon Smith
Illustrator
Bill Sanderson
Photographer
Ian Giles

1982.13
Press: Trade Colour Advertisement
Advertising Agency
TBWA
Art Director
Malcolm Gaskin
Client
Lego (UK)
Copywriter
Neil Patterson
Illustrator
David Lisle
Photographer
John Lawrence-Jones
Typographer
Brian Hill

1982.14
Press: Consumer Campaign
Advertising Agency
Abbott Mead Vickers/SMS
Art Director
Ron Brown
Client
J Sainsbury
Copywriter
David Abbott
Photographers
Steve Cavalier
Stuart Mcleod
Derek Seagrim
Martin Thompson
Typographer
Joe Hoza

1982.15
Posters: 4-Sheet Consumer Poster
Advertising Agency
Carter Hedger Mitchell & Partners
Art Director
Glen Clarke
Client
Romix Foods
Copywriter
Geoffrey Seymour
Illustrator
Patrick Hughes
Typographer
Robin Brown

1983

1983.01
Packaging: Range of Packaging
Art Directors
Brett Haggerty
Colin Robinson
Clients
Harrison Cowley
Advertising (Bristol)
Readymix Drypack
Design Group
Robinson Lambie-Nairn
Designer
Brett Haggerty
Illustrator
Peter Moore
Typographer
Brett Haggerty

1983.02
Direct Mail
Art Directors
Marcello Minale
Brian Tattersfield
Client
Cubic Metre Furniture
Copywriters
Marcello Minale
Brian Tattersfield
Design Group
Minale Tattersfield & Partners
Illustrator
Brian Tattersfield
Typographer
Alex Maranzano

1983.03
Editorial & Books: Book Jackets & Paperback Covers
Art Director
John McConnell
Client
Faber & Faber
Design Group
Pentagram
Designers
Phoa Kia Boon
John McConnell
Illustrators
Phoa Kia Boon
John McConnell

1983.04
1. Graphics: Symbols & Logotype
2. Graphics: Corporate Identity
Client
International Coffee Organisation
Design Group
Michael Peters & Partners
Designer
Madeleine Bennett
Illustrator
Madeleine Bennett

1983.05
Graphics: Corporate Identity
Client
Channel Four Television
Design Group
Robinson Lambie-Nairn
Designer
Martin Lambie-Nairn
Typographer
Martin Lambie-Nairn

1983.06
TV & Cinema Graphics: Television Drama
Client
BBC Television
Director
Stewart Austin
Editor
David Farlie
Graphic Designer
Stewart Austin
Lighting Cameraman
Douglas Adamson
Music Composer
Patrick Gowers
Producer
Jonathan Powell
Production Company
BBC Television

1983.07
TV & Cinema Graphics: Television Arts Programme
Client
BBC Television
Director
Darrell Pockett
Editor
Simon Morice
Graphic Designer
Darrell Pockett
Lighting Cameraman
Victor Cummings
Modelmaker
Stephen Greenfield
Music Composer
George Fenton
Producer
Christopher Martin
Production Company
BBC Television

1983.08
TV & Cinema Graphics: Television Documentaries
Client
Blackrod
Director
Bernard Lodge
Editor
Colin Cherrill
Graphic Designer
Bernard Lodge
Illustrator
Isabel Willock
Lighting Cameraman
Douglas Adamson
Music Composer
Carl Davis
Producers
Lyn Gambles
Jill Roach
Production Company
Lodge/Cheesman Productions

1983.09
TV & Cinema Graphics: Animated Film
Animators
Stephen Weston
Robin White
Client
Channel Four Television
Editor
John Cary
Director
Dianne Jackson
Graphic Designers
Raymond Briggs
Jill Brooks
Lighting Cameraman
Peter Turner
Music Composer
Howard Blake
Producer
John Coates
Production Company
Snowman Enterprises

1983.10
Record Promotion
Art Director
Kate Hepburn
Client
Francis Dreyfus Music
Copywriter
Jean-Michel Jarre
Illustrator
Kate Hepburn
Photographer
Mark Fisher
Typographer
Kate Hepburn

1983.11
Record Sleeves
Art Director
Jean-Paul Goude
Client
Island Records
Illustrator
Jean-Paul Goude
Photographer
Jean-Paul Goude
Typographer
Rob O'Connor

1983.12
TV & Cinema Advertising: 45 Second Television Commercial
Advertising Agency
Collett Dickenson Pearce
Agency Producer
Mark Andrews
Art Director
Paul Smith
Client
Bluebell Apparel
Copywriter
Mike Everett
Directors
Lol Creme
Kevin Godley
Editor
Ben Rayner
Lighting Cameraman
Howard Atherton
Music Composers
Lol Creme
Kevin Godley
Producer
John Cigarini
Production Company
Brooks Fulford Cramer Seresin
Set Designer
Roger Hall

1983.13
TV & Cinema Advertising: Television Campaign
Advertising Agency
The Boase Massimi Pollitt
Univas Partnership
Agency Producer
Maggie Doyle
Art Director
John Webster
Client
Courage Brewing
Copywriter
John Webster
Director
Roger Woodburn
Editor
Peter Beston
Lighting Cameraman
Roy Smith
Music Composer
Paul Hart
Producer
Mike Stones
Production Company
Park Village Productions

1983.14
Radio
Advertising Agency
The Leagas Delaney
Partnership Limited
Agency Producer
Paul Bagnall
Client
Philips Video Division
Concept Creator
Tim Delaney
Copywriters
Griff Rhys Jones
Mel Smith
Music Composer
Charles Williams

1983.15
TV & Cinema Advertising: 30 Second Television Commercial
Advertising Agency
Gold Greenlees Trott
Agency Producer
Diane Croll
Art Director
Axel Chaldecott
Client
William Levene
Copywriter
Steve Henry
Director
Paul Weiland
Editor
Ian Weil
Lighting Cameraman
Tony Pierce-Roberts
Producer
Glynis Murray
Production Company
Weiland and Lee
Set Designer
Tony Noble

1983.16
TV & Cinema Advertising: 2 Minute Television Commercial
Advertising Agency
Doyle Dane Bernbach
Agency Producer
Howard Spivey
Art Director
Peter Garrett
Client
Corona Soft Drinks
Copywriter
Nick Hazzard
Director
Graham Rose
Editor
Kathy O'Shea
Lighting Cameraman
Stuart Harris
Music Arrangement
Joe Campbell
Paul Hart
Producer
John Hackney
Production Company
Rose Hackney Productions
Set Designer
Norris Spencer

1983.17
TV & Cinema Advertising: Over 45 Seconds
Advertising Agency
Wight Collins Rutherford Scott
Agency Producer
Randi Waagen
Art Director
Ken Hoggins
Client
BMW (GB)
Copywriter
Giles Keeble
Director
Roger Woodburn
Editor
Simon Cheek
Lighting Cameraman
Mike Garfath
Music Composer
Kenneth Freeman
Producer
Mike Stones
Production Company
Park Village Productions

1983.18
TV & Cinema Advertising: Television Campaign
Advertising Agency
Hedger Mitchell Stark & Partners
Agency Producer
Suzie Rodgers
Art Director
Chris Monge
Client
Watney Mann & Truman Brewers
Copywriter
Rowan Dean
Director
David Ashwell
Editor
Greg Willcox
Lighting Cameraman
Howard Atherton
Producer
Jan Roy
Production Company
David Ashwell
Set Designers
Roger Burridge
Mike Hall

1983.19
Posters: Super Sites & Specials
Advertising Agency
FCO Univas
Art Director
Ian Potter
Client
Ciba Geigy
Copywriter
Rob Kitchen
Typographer
Stephen Legate

1983.20
Posters: 4, 16 & 48 Sheet
Advertising Agency
Gold Greenlees Trott
Art Director
Axel Chaldecott
Client
Time Out
Copywriter
Steve Henry
Photographer
Derek Seagrim
Typographer
Ros Walters

1983.21
Press Advertising: Newspapers
Advertising Agency
Lowe & Howard-Spink
Art Director
David Christensen
Client
Albany Life Assurance
Copywriter
Alfredo Marcantonio
Photographer
Jimmy Warner
Typographer
Brian Hill

1983.22
Press Advertising: Newspapers
Advertising Agency
Saatchi & Saatchi
Art Director
Alan Midgley
Client
NSPCC
Copywriter
John Bacon
Photographer
Barney Edwards
Typographer
Roger Pearce

1983.23
Retail Store Design: Exterior Applied Graphic Design
Art Director
David Hillman
Client
Wakefield Fortune (Travel)
Design Group
Pentagram
Designers
Josie Close
David Hillman
Richard Mott
Illustrator
Bob Norrington

1984

1984.01
1. TV & Cinema Advertising: 60 Second Television Commercial
2. TV & Cinema Advertising: Direction
3. TV & Cinema Advertising: Film Photography
Advertising Agency
Chiat/Day
Agency Producer
Richard O'Neil
Art Director
Brent Thomas
Client
Apple Computer
Copywriter
Steve Hayden
Director
Ridley Scott
Editor
Pamela Power
Lighting Cameraman
Adrian Biddle
Producer
Nadia Owen
Production Company
RSA Films
Set Designer
Mike Seymour

1984.02
Packaging
Client
Le Nez Rouge Wine Club
Design Group
Pearce Marchbank Studio
Designer
Pearce Marchbank
Illustrator
Pearce Marchbank
Typographer
Pearce Marchbank

1984.03
Graphics: Poster Campaign
Art Director
Alan Fletcher
Client
IBM Europe
Design Group
Pentagram Design
Designers
Alan Fletcher
Andrew Pengilly
Illustrator
Alan Fletcher

1984.04
Editorial & Books: Book Jackets
Art Director
John McConnell
Client
Faber & Faber
Design Group
Carroll & Dempsey
Designers
Ken Carroll
Mike Dempsey
Typographers
Mike Dempsey
Paul Jenkins

1984.05
Editorial & Books: Single Magazine Feature
Art Director
Wendy Harrop
Client
The World of Interiors
Photographer
James Wedge
Publisher
Pharos Publications Limited

1984.06
Photography
Advertising Agency
Saatchi & Saatchi
Art Director
Paul Arden
Client
Alexon & Company
Copywriter
Tim Mellors
Photographer
Richard Avedon
Typographer
Roger Kennedy

1984.07
Photography: Black & White Advertising
Advertising Agency
Saatchi & Saatchi
Art Director
Paul Arden
Client
Alexon & Company
Copywriter
Tim Mellors
Photographer
Terence Donovan
Typographer
Roger Kennedy

1984.08
Editorial & Books: Complete Magazine
Advertising Agency
Anderson & Lembke
Art Director
David Hillman
Authors
Robert Babatz
Raymond Birri
Graham Bunting
Jan Duffy
Catherine Marenghi
John McQuillan
Brian Murphy
Raymond Panko
Sue Pomfret
Ulla Pyndt
Horst Santo
Ralph Sprague
David Stevens
Hedley Voysey
Terence Westgate
Client
Ericsson Information Systems
Design Group
Pentagram Design
Designers
David Hillman
Bruce Mau
Illustrators
Su Huntley
Peter Knock
Russell Mills
Donna Muir
Jenny Powell
Wolf Spoerl
Ralph Steadman
Publication
Information Resource Management

1984.09
Editorial & Books: Complete Book
Art Directors
Jeremy Cox
David Pelham
Author
Dr Jonathan Miller
Client
Jonathan Cape
Design Group
Pentagram Design
Designer
David Pelham
Illustrator
Harry Willock
Typographer
David Pelham

1984.10
Posters
Art Directors
Howard Brown
John Gorham
Client
Goldcrest Films & Television
Photographer
Tony Evans
Typographers
Howard Brown
John Gorham

1984.11
Television Graphics: Titles
Animator
Reg Lodge
Director
Pat Gavin
Editor
John Cary
Graphic Designer
Pat Gavin
Music Arrangement
The Three Courgettes
Producers
Bob Bee
Kim Evans
Production Company
Jerry Hibbert Animation
Programme Company
London Weekend Television

1984.12
Video Promos: Direction
Choreographer
Arlene Philips
Director
Russell Mulcahy
Editor
Stephen Priest
Lighting Cameraman
John Metcalfe
Music Composer/Arranger
Elton John
Producer
Jacqui Byford
Production Company
MGMM
Writer
Russell Mulcahy

1984.13
TV & Cinema Advertising: Television Campaign
Advertising Agency
Gold Greenlees Trott
Agency Producer
Diane Croll
Art Director
Axel Chaldecott
Client
Holsten Distributors
Copywriter
Steve Henry
Director
Richard Sloggett
Editor
Ben Rayner
Lighting Cameraman
Tony Pierce-Roberts
Music Composers/Arrangement
Joe Campbell
Paul Hart
Producer
John Cigarini
Production Company
Brooks Fulford Cramer Seresin
Set Designer
Roger Burridge

1984.14
TV & Cinema Advertising: Television Commercial up to 60 Seconds
Advertising Agency
Abbott Mead Vickers/SMS
Agency Producer
Mike Griffin
Art Director
Ron Brown
Client
British Telecom/Yellow Pages
Copywriter
David Abbott
Director
Bob Brooks
Editor
Ben Rayner
Lighting Cameraman
Mostyn Rowlands
Music Composer/Arrangement
Richard Walter
Producer
John Cigarini
Production Company
Brooks Fulford Cramer Seresin
Set Designer
Mike Seymour

1984.15
Posters: Super Site
Advertising Agency
FCO
Art Director
Rob Kitchen
Client
Ciba Geigy
Copywriter
Robert Janowski
Typographer
Stephen Legate

1984.16
Posters: Poster Campaign
Advertising Agency
Bartle Bogle Hegarty
Art Director
John Hegarty
Client
James Robertson & Sons
Copywriter
Barbara Nokes
Illustrator
Andrew Hammond
Typographer
John Hegarty

1984.17
Press Advertising: Colour Consumer Magazine
Advertising Agency
Abbott Mead Vickers/SMS
Art Director
Andy Arghyrou
Client
Cow & Gate
Copywriter
Chris O'Shea
Photographer
Steve Cavalier
Typographer
Joe Hoza

1984.18
Press Advertising: Colour Consumer Magazine
Advertising Agency
Abbott Mead Vickers/SMS
Art Director
John Horton
Client
Volvo Concessionaires

Copywriter
Richard Foster
Photographer
Graham Ford
Typographer
Joe Hoza

1984.19
1. Press Advertising: Consumer
2. Typography
Advertising Agency
Saatchi & Saatchi
Art Directors
Noel Farrey
Derek Miller
Client
Cunard Line
Copywriters
James Lowther
Richard Myers
Michael Petherick
Designer
Roger Pearce
Photographer
Rolph Gobits
Typographer
Roger Pearce

1985

1985.01
TV & Cinema Graphics: Television Graphics
Client
Central Independent Television
Director
Peter Harris
Editor
Mike Milne
Graphic Designer
Brian Becker
Music Composer/Arrangement
Phil Pope
Producer
Brian Becker
Production Company
Research Recordings

1985.02
Press Advertising: Public Service Campaigns
Advertising Agency
The Boase Massimi Pollitt
Univas Partnership
Art Director
Peter Gatley
Client
Greater London Council
Copywriter
John Pallant
Typographer
Tony Pashley

1985.03
Packaging: Range of Packaging
Client
J A Sharwood & Company
Design Group
Smith & Milton
Designer
Howard Milton
Illustrator
Brian Grimwood
Typographer
Jay Smith

1985.04
Illustration: Poster Illustration
Advertising Agency
The Boase Massimi Pollitt
Univas Partnership
Art Director
Joanna Wenley
Client
Greater London Council
Copywriter
Tim Riley
Designer
Joanna Wenley
Illustrator
Bush Hollyhead
Typographer
David Wakefield

1985.05
Editorial & Books: Complete Dook Design
Art Directors
Ken Carroll
Mike Dempsey
Client
The Post Office
Copywriter
Mike Barden
Design Group
Carroll & Dempsey
Designers
Mike Dempsey
Pamela Guest
Photographers
Phil Sayer
Andy Seymour
Typographer
Mike Dempsey

1985.06
Editorial & Books: Series of Illustrated Book Jackets
Art Director
Cherriwyn Magill
Client
Penguin Books
Design Group
Cooper Thirkell
Designer
Nicholas Thirkell
Illustrator
Lawrence Mynott
Typographers
Paul Fielding
Bob Rowinski
Nicholas Thirkell

1985.07
Editorial & Books: Book Jacket
Art Director
Pearce Marchbank
Design Group
Pearce Marchbank Studio
Photographer
Nick Knight
Publisher
Omnibus Press

1985.08
TV & Cinema Advertising: Animation
Advertising Agency
Collett Dickenson Pearce
Agency Producer
Alec Ovens
Animator
Graham Ralph
Art Director
Rod Waskett
Client
Gallaher
Computer Animation
CAL Video Graphics
Copywriter
Paul Weinberger
Designer
Anna Hart
Directors
Anna Hart
Martin Lambie-Nairn
Editors
John Cary
Nigel Hadley
Music Arrangement
Jacques Loussier
Music Composers/Arrangement
Joe Campbell
Paul Hart
Producer
Sarah Davies
Production Company
Robinson Lambie-Nairn

1985.09
Design for Television: Design for a Comedy Programme
Client
Central Independent Television
Director
Peter Harris
Editor
John Baldwin
Producer
John Lloyd
Production Company
Spitting Image Productions
Set Designer
Ken Ryan
Writers
Ian Hislop
Nick Newman

1985.10
Pop Promo Videos
Directors
Lol Creme
Kevin Godley
Editors
Rod Aiken
Lol Creme
Kevin Godley
Lighting Cameraman
Peter Sinclair
Music Composers/Arrangement
Frankie Goes to Hollywood
Trevor Horn
Producers
John Gaydon
Lexi Godfrey
Production Company
Medialab
Set Designers
Lol Creme
Kevin Godley
Writers
Lol Creme
Kevin Godley

1985.11
TV & Cinema Advertising: Television Campaign
Advertising Agency
Gold Greenlees Trott
Agency Producer
Gré Dilkes
Animators
Barry Baker
Chris Caunter
Bobby Clennell
John Miller
Paul Vester
Art Director
Gordon Smith
Client
Toshiba (UK)
Copywriter
Dave Trott
Directors
Richard Sloggett
Paul Vester
Editors
Tony Fish
Peter Hearne
Lighting Cameraman
John Taylor
Music Composers/Arrangement
Joe Campbell
Paul Hart
Alexei Sayle
Producer
Suzanne Stewart
Production Company
BFCS
Set Designers
Barry Baker
Mark Shepherd
Paul Vester

1985.12
TV & Cinema Advertising: 30 Second Television Commercial
Advertising Agency
The Boase Massimi Pollitt
Univas Partnership
Agency Producer
Barnaby Spurrier
Client
Sony (UK)
Copywriter
John Webster
Director
Roger Woodburn
Editor
Simon Cheek
Lighting Cameraman
Keith Goddard
Music Composer/Arrangement
Alan Williams
Producer
Abigail Sloggett
Production Company
Park Village Productions

1985.13
TV & Cinema Advertising: Film Editing
Advertising Agency
Bartle Bogle Hegarty
Agency Producer
David Trollope
Art Director
Graham Watson
Client
Levi Strauss (UK)
Copywriter
Mike Cozens
Director
Tony Scott
Editor
Pamela Power
Lighting Cameraman
Caleb Deschenal
Music Composer/Arrangement
Jeremy Healy
Producer
Mike Hayes
Production Company
RSA Productions
Set Designer
John Marguettes

1985.14
1. TV & Cinema Advertising: 60 Second Television Commercial
2. TV & Cinema Advertising: Public Service Television Commercial
Advertising Agency
The Boase Massimi Pollitt
Univas Partnership
Agency Producer
Maggie Campbell
Animator
Gerry Hibbert
Art Director
Peter Garrett
Client
Central Office of Information
Copywriter
Nick Hazzard
Director
Paul Weiland
Editor
Ian Weil
Lighting Cameraman
Ian Cassie
Music Composer/Arrangement
John Altman
Producer
Glynis Murray
Production Company
Paul Weiland Film Company
Set Designer
Tony Noble

1985.15
Posters: 48 Sheet
Advertising Agency
Boase Massimi Pollitt
Univas Partnership
Art Director
Peter Gatley
Client
Greater London Council
Copywriter
John Pallant
Typographer
Gary Whipps

1985.16
Press Advertising: Consumer Campaign
Advertising Agency
The Boase Massimi Pollitt
Univas Partnership
Art Directors
Peter Gatley
Paul Leeves
Client
Greater London Council
Copywriters
John Pallant
Alan Tilby
Photographer
Jimmy Wormser
Typographers
Tony Pashley
Richard Taylor
David Wakefield

1985.17
Mixed Media: Advertising Campaign
Advertising Agency
Lowe Howard-Spink
Campbell-Ewald
Art Director
Ray Brennan
Client
Whitbread & Company
Copywriter
Phil Dearman
Photographer
Max Forsythe
Typographers
Brian Hill
Peter Rowley

1985.18
Poster Campaign
Advertising Agency
Ogilvy & Mather
Art Director
Martyn Walsh
Client
Bovril
Illustrator
Mick Brownfield

1985.19
Mixed Media: Advertising Campaign
Advertising Agency
Saatchi & Saatchi
Art Directors
Adrian Kemsley
Alan Midgley
Client
The National Maritime Museum
Copywriters
John Bacon
Charles Hendley
Illustrators
Robin Jacques
Melvyn Redford
Typographers
Moira Greaves
Roger Kennedy

1985.20
Retail: Retail Design Programme
Art Directors
Rob Davie
Paul Mullins
Michael Peters
Client
Dar Salons
Design Group
Michael Peters & Partners
Designers
Paul Browton
Paul Mullins

1986

1986.01
TV & Cinema Advertising: Film Advertising
Advertising Agency
The Yellowhammer Company
Art Director
Jeremy Pemberton
Client
Greenpeace
Copywriter
Alan Page
Director
David Bailey
Editor
Pamela Power
Lighting Cameraman
Adrian Biddle
Music Composer/Arrangement
Vangelis
Producer
Glynis Murray
Production Company
Paul Weiland Film Company
Set Designer
Gerry Judah

1986.02
1. TV & Cinema Advertising: Campaigns
2. TV & Cinema Advertising: Television Commercial up to 30 Seconds
3. Film – Video Craft: Use of Video
Advertising Agency
Collett Dickenson Pearce
Agency Producer
Mark Andrews
Art Director
Paul Collis
Backgrounds
Steve Lowe
Client
Radio Rentals
Copywriter
John O'Donnell
Directors
Annabel Jankel
Rocky Morton
Editor
Roo Aiken
Lighting Cameraman
Malcolm Copp-Taylor
Producers
Kevin Maloney
Vivien Munt
Production Company
Cucumber Productions

1986.03
Interior Design
Client
Next
Design Group
David Davies Associates
Designers
Stuart Baron
James Buchanan
Ben Burke

David Davies
Richard Greenleaf
Louise Hosker
Brian Johnson
Peter Kent

1986.04
1. Posters: Poster Campaign
2. 48-Sheet Poster
Advertising Agency
Doyle Dane Bernbach
Art Director
Warren Brown
Client
Bryant & May
Copywriter
Bruce Crouch
Photographers
James Cotier
Otto Dyar
Elmar Fryer
George Hurrell
Eugene Richee
Bert Six
Scottie Welbourne
Typographer
Neil Archer

1986.05
Editorial & Books:
Promotional Magazine
Art Director
Nick Wurr
Client
The Royal Shakespeare
Company
Copywriter
Margaret Gaskin
Design Group
The Partners
Designer
Clare Boam

1986.06
Packaging Design
Client
Penhaligon's
Design Group
Michael Peters & Partners
Designer
Madeleine Bennett

1986.07
Graphics: Symbols & Logotypes
Client
Jones
Design Group
Autograph Design Partnership
Designers
Paul Hiscock
Mark Osbourne
Illustrator
Richard Rockwood

1986.08
Editorial & Books: Book Design
Client
Victoria & Albert Museum
Design Group
Cooper Thirkell
Designer
Nicholas Thirkell
Publisher
Nicky Bird
Typographers
Paul Fielding
Nicholas Thirkell

1986.09
Editorial & Books: Illustration
Art Directors
Phyllis Hunt
John McConnell
Shirley Tucker
Author
Ted Hughes
Client
Faber & Faber
Design Group
Faber & Faber
Designers
Louise Millar
Shirley Tucker
Illustrator
Andrew Davidson
Typographer
Louise Millar

1986.10
Editorial & Books:
Complete Magazine
Art Director
Simon Esterson
Client
Blueprint Magazine
Designers
Stephen Coates
Martin Colyer
Simon Esterson
Illustrator
Paul Cox
Photographers
John Barlow
Peter Cook
Ian Dobbie
Ian Lambot
Steve Moors
Sheila Rock
Philip Sayer

1986.11
TV & Cinema Graphics:
Arts Programme Graphics
Computer Animators
Louise Hadley
Bill Keehner
Director
Richard Markell
Editor
Rob Bannochie
Graphic Designer
Richard Markell
Music Composer/Arrangement
Dave Vorhaus
Producer
John Wyver
Production Company
English Markell Pockett
Programme Company
Illumination

1986.12
Pop Promo Videos: Direction
Directors
Lol Creme
Kevin Godley
Editors
Roo Aiken
Lol Creme
Kevin Godley
Lighting Cameraman
Bryan Loftus
Music Composers/Arrangement
Lol Creme
Kevin Godley
Producers
John Gaydon
Lexi Godfrey
Production Company
Media Lab
Record Company
Polydor
Writers
Lol Creme
Kevin Godley

1986.13
1. Press Advertising: Mixed Media Campaigns
2. TV & Cinema Advertising: Television Campaigns
3. TV & Cinema Advertising: Television Commercial up to 60 Seconds
Advertising Agency
Lowe Howard-Spink Marschalk
Agency Producer
Mike Griffin
Art Director
Alan Waldie
Client
Whitbread & Company
Copywriter
Adrian Holmes
Director
Paul Weiland
Editor
Ian Weil
Lighting Cameraman
Phil Meheux
Music
C Tucker
J Saunders
Producer
Nadia Owen
Production Company
Paul Weiland Film Company
Set Designer
Geoff Woodbridge

1986.14
1. TV & Cinema Advertising: 60 Second Television Commercial
2. TV & Cinema Advertising: Direction
3. TV & Cinema Advertising: Use of Music
4. TV & Cinema Advertising: Set Design
Advertising Agency
Bartle Bogle Hegarty
Agency Producer
Jonathon Ker
Art Director
John Hegarty
Client
Levi Strauss UK
Copywriter
Chris Palmer
Director
Roger Woodburn
Editor
Simon Cheek
Lighting Cameraman
Arthur Ibbetson
Music Composers
Karl Jenkins
Mike Ratledge
Producer
Mike Stones
Production Company
Park Village Productions
Set Designer
Roger Burridge

1986.15
1. TV & Cinema Advertising: 60 Second Television Commercial
2. TV & Cinema Advertising: Television Campaigns
Advertising Agency
Bartle Bogle Hegarty
Agency Producer
Jonathan Ker
Art Director
John Hegarty
Client
Levi Strauss Europe
Copywriter
Barbara Nokes
Director
Roger Lyons
Editor
Ian Weil
Lighting Cameraman
Richard Greatrex
Music Arrangement
Karl Jenkins
Mike Ratledge
Producer
Greg Mills
Production Company
Mike Dufficy & Partners
Set Designer
Arthur Max

1986.16
TV & Cinema Advertising: Television Campaign
Advertising Agency
Grey
Agency Producer
Heather Andrews
Art Director
Su Sareen
Client
Beecham Proprietaries
Copywriter
Jan Heron
Editor
Nick Thompson
Facility House
The Moving Picture Company
Music Composers
Art of Noise
Craig Major
Yello
Producer
Roger Randall-Cutler
Video Tape Editor
Alan Young

1986.17
TV & Cinema Advertising: Public Service Cinema Commercial
Advertising Agency
Saatchi & Saatchi
Agency Producer
Sarah Baker
Art Director
Fergus Fleming
Client
The Samaritans
Copywriters
Simon Dicketts
Mark Williams
Designer
Rupert Ashmore
Director
Barney Edwards
Editor
Terry Jones
Lighting Cameraman
Tim Spence
Music Composer/Arrangement
Roger Waters
Producer
Mervyn Lloyd
Production Company
Edwards Baker Swannell

1986.18
1. TV & Cinema Advertising: Public Service Television Commercial
2. TV & Cinema Advertising: Use of Photography
Advertising Agency
FCO
Agency Producer
Lizzie O'Connell
Art Director
Ray Barrett
Client
Central Office of Information
Copywriter
Rob Janowski
Director
Barry Myers
Editor
Terry Jones
Lighting Cameraman
John Stanier
Music Composer/Arrangement
John Altman
Producer
Tim White
Production Company
Spots Films Services
Set Designer
Simon Waters

1986.19
Posters
Advertising Agency
Lowe Howard-Spink Marschalk
Art Director
Mike Stephenson
Client
Whitbread & Company
Copywriter
Derek Apps
Photographer
Geoff Senior
Typographer
Brian Hill

1986.20
Press Advertising:
Colour Trade Advertisement
Advertising Agency
Boase Massimi Pollitt
Partnership
Art Director
Bill Gallacher
Client
Fisher Price
Copywriter
Frank Budgen
Photographer
Ian Giles
Typographer
Tony Pashley

1986.21
Copy: Consumer Campaign
Advertising Agency
Bartle Bogle Hegarty
Art Director
John Hegarty
Client
Smith & Nephew
Consumer Products
Copywriters
Barbara Nokes
Chris Palmer
Photographers
Stak Aivaliotis
Camilla Jessel
Typographer
John Hegarty

1986.22
Press Advertising:
Consumer Campaign
Advertising Agency
Boase Massimi Pollitt
Partnership
Art Director
Paul Leeves
Client
CPC (UK)
Copywriter
Alan Tilby
Illustrator
Carol Jonas
Photographer
Steve Cavalier
Typographer
David Wakefield

1986.23
1. Press Advertising: Newspapers – Colour
2. Illustration: Magazines – Colour
Advertising Agency
Collett Dickenson Pearce
Client
Scottish & Newcastle Breweries
Creative Director
David Hughes
Design Group
The Fine White Line
Designer
Siobhan Noonan
Illustrator
Barry Craddock
Typographer
Siobhan Noonan

1986.24
Press Advertising: Newspapers – public service
Advertising Agency
Saatchi & Saatchi
Art Director
Adrian Kemsley
Client
NSPCC
Copywriter
Rita Dempsey
Photographer
John Moffatt
Typographer
Roger Kennedy

1987

1987.01
Retail & Environmental:
Retail Design Programme
Client
Thresher Wine Merchants
Design Group
Fitch & Company
Design Consultants
Designers
Paul Bennett
Paul Jarvis
Mark Landini
Gabriel Murray

1987.02
Packaging: Individual Pack
Client
Fine Fare
Design Group
Michael Peters & Partners
Designer
Glenn Tutssel
Illustrator
Rory Kee
Typographers
Peter Horridge
Roman Huszak
Glenn Tutssel

1987.03
Packaging: Range of Packaging
Client
Waitrose
Design Group
Michael Thierens Design
Designers
Domenic Lippa
Harry Pearce
Michael Thierens
Illustrator
Lucilla Scrimgeour
Typographer
Michael Thierens

1987.04
1. Graphics
2. Illustration
Art Directors
Brigid McMullen
David Stuart
Client
Wood & Wood International
Signs for Courage
Design Group
The Partners
Illustrators
Geoffrey Appleton
Mick Brownfield
Debbie Cook
Andrew Davidson
John Gorham
Robert Kettell

1987.05
Corporate Identity: Signage Programmes
Art Director
Gert Dumbar
Client
Rijksmuseum, Amsterdam
Design Group
Studio Dumbar
Designers
Michel de Boer
Runi Hamid
Typographer
Runi Hamid

1987.06
Record Sleeve & Promotion: Individual Single Sleeve
Clients
The Pet Shop Boys
Parlophone
Design Group
Three Associates
Designers
Mark Farrow
Chris Lowe
Neil Tennant
Photographer
Eric Watson
Typographer
Mark Farrow

1987.07
Pop Promo Videos
Animators
Richard Goleszowski
Peter Lord
Stephen Johnson
Nick Park
Stephen Quay
Timothy Quay
Director
Stephen Johnson
Editor
Colin Green
Lighting Cameraman
David Sproxton
Music Composer
Peter Gabriel
Producer
Adam Whittaker
Production Company
Limelight Films
Record Company
Virgin Records
Set Designers
Peter Lord
Stephen Johnson
Stephen Quay
Timothy Quay
Writers
Peter Gabriel
Stephen Johnson

1987.08
TV & Cinema Advertising: 60 Second Television Commercial
Advertising Agency
Collett Dickenson Pearce
Agency Producer
Linda Downs
Art Director
Garry Horner
Client
Gallaher
Copywriters
Rowan Dean
Philip Differ
Director
Graham Rose
Editor
David Garland
Lighting Cameraman
David Walsh
Music Composer/Arrangement
Jacques Loussier
Producer
John Hackney
Production Company
Rose Hackney Productions
Set Designer
Tony Noble

1987.09
TV & Cinema Advertising: 30 Second Television Commercial
Advertising Agency
The Boase Massimi Pollitt Partnership
Agency Producer
Barnaby Spurrier
Art Director
John Webster
Client
The Guardian
Copywriter
Frank Budgen
Director
Paul Weiland
Editor
Ian Weil
Lighting Cameraman
Tony Pierce-Roberts
Producer
Glynis Murray
Production Company
Paul Weiland Film Company

1987.10
1. Press Advertising: Consumer Campaign
2. Press Advertising: Consumer Magazines
Advertising Agency
Saatchi & Saatchi
Art Director
Mike Wells
Client
Dickens & Jones
Copywriter
Richard Grisdale
Photographer
Clive Arrowsmith
Typographer
Roger Kennedy

1987.11
Copy: Public Service & Charities – Campaigns
Advertising Agency
The Boase Massimi Pollitt Partnership
Art Directors
Tony Davidson
Bill Gallacher
Client
War on Want
Copywriters
Frank Budgen
Kim Papworth
Illustrators
Tony Davidson
Bill Gallacher
Kim Papworth
Typographer
David Wakefield

1987.12
Consumer Magazine: Public Service Advertisement
Advertising Agency
Saatchi & Saatchi
Art Director
Mike Shafron
Client
Guide Dogs for the Blind
Copywriter
Jeff Stark
Photographer
Peter Lavery
Typographer
Roger Kennedy

1987.13
Retail & Environment: Complete Retail Design Programme
Client
Midland Bank
Design Group
Fitch & Co Design Consultants
Designers
Henry Coelho
Mark Landini

1988

1988.01
Retail & Environmental: Environmental Design
Client
Issey Miyake UK
Design Group
Stanton Williams
Designers
David Gomersall
Tony O'Neill
Alan Stanton
Paul Williams
Photographer
Peter Cook

1988.02
Photography: Editorial Photography
Art Director
Michael Rand
Copywriter
Rob Tyrer
Designer
Ian Denning
Photographer
Sebastião Salgado
Publisher
Sunday Times Magazine

1988.03
Packaging: Packaging Range
Art Director
Mary Lewis
Calligrapher
Kathy Miller
Client
Asda Stores
Design Group
Lewis Moberly
Designers
Mary Lewis
Kathy Miller
Illustration
20th Century Original Print
Illustrators
Dan Fern
Liz Pyle
Photographer
Sue Lanzon
Typographers
Mary Lewis
Kathy Miller

1988.04
Graphics: Annual Reports
Art Director
Kate Stephens
Client
ABSA
Copywriters
Lucy Stout
Colin Tweedy
Designer
Kate Stephens
Illustrator
Brian Grimwood

1988.05
Symbols & Logotypes
Art Director
Michael Denny
Client
BR Railfreight
Design Group
Roundel Design Group
Designers
John Bateson
Michael Denny

1988.06
Direct Mail Campaign: Promotional Magazine
Art Director
Peter Davenport
Client
Rosehaugh Stanhope Developments
Copywriter
Les Hutton
Design Director
Hadn Davies
Design Group
Davenport Designs
Designers
Russell Bell
Peter Davenport
Neil Morgan
Illustrator
Ron Sandford
Photographer
Brian Griffin
Typographer
Peter Davenport

1988.07
Posters: Cross Track Poster
Advertising Agency
The Fine White Line Communications Company
Client
London Underground
Creative Director
David Hughes
Designer
David Booth
Modelmakers
Malcolm Fowler
Nancy Fowler
Photographers
John Hammond
Siobahn Noonan
Typographer
David Booth

1988.08
1. Corporate Identity: Design Programme
2. Graphics: Poster Design
Art Director
Robert Makata
Client
Holland Festival
Design Group
Studio Dumbar
Designer
Ton van Bragt
Photographer
Lex van Pieterson
Typographer
Ton van Bragt

1988.09
1. TV & Cinema Advertising Crafts: Use of Music
TV & Cinema Advertising: Television Commercial up to 60 Seconds
Advertising Agency
DDB Needham Worldwide
Agency Producer
Howard Spivey
Art Director
Graham Featherstone
Client
VAG (UK)
Copywriter
Barry Greensted
Director
David Bailey
Editor
Andrea MacArthur
Lighting Cameraman
Adrian Biddle
Music Composer/Arrangement
Alan Price
Producer
Mary Francis
Production Company
Paul Weiland Film Company
Set Designer
Tim Dann

1988.10
TV & Cinema Advertising: 30 Second Commercial
Advertising Agency
Collett Dickenson Pearce
Agency Producer
Mark Andrews
Art Director
John Foster
Client
Gallaher
Copywriter
Adrian Holmes
Director
Bernard Lodge
Editor
Martin Hicks
Music Arrangement
Jacques Loussier
Paintbox Artist
Rob Hodgson
Producer
Sloan Hickman
Production Company
The Moving Picture Company

1988.11
Press Advertising: Consumer Magazines
Advertising Agency
Saatchi & Saatchi
Art Director
Alexandra Taylor
Client
Gallaher
Copywriter
Michael Petherick
Modelmaker
Nancy Fouts
Photographer
Graham Ford

1988.12
1 Press Advertising: Consumer Magazines
2. Press Advertising: Trade & Professional Magazines
Advertising Agency
Saatchi & Saatchi
Art Director
Alexandra Taylor
Client
Gallaher
Copywriter
Michael Petherick
Modelmaker
Nancy Fouts
Photographer
Graham Ford

1988.13
International: Film Advertising
Advertising Agency
Ogilvy & Mather
Art Director
Mark Shap
Client
Media Advertising Partnership for a Drug Free America
Copywriter
Veronica Nash
Director
Leslie Dektor
Producer
Tina Raver
Production Company
Petermann/Dektor

1988.14
Press Advertising: Consumer Advertising Campaign
Advertising Agency
Leagas Delaney
Art Director
Steve Dunn
Client
Linguaphone Institute
Copywriter
Tim Delaney
Photographer
Graham Cornthwaite
Typographer
Steve Dunn

1988.15
Press Advertising: Mixed Media Campaign
Advertising Agency
Leagas Delaney
Art Director
Steve Dunn
Client
Harrods
Copywriter
Tim Delaney
Photographer
Daniel Jouanneau
Typographer
Steve Dunn

1988.16
Copy: Charity Advertisement
Advertising Agency
Collett Dickenson Pearce
Art Director
Neil Godfrey
Client
Great Ormond Street Hospital
Copywriter
Tony Brignull
Photographer
Neil Barstow
Typographer
Len Cheeseman

1988.17
Press Advertising: Colour Consumer Advertisment
Advertising Agency
Collett Dickenson Pearce
Art Director
Graham Fink
Client
Metropolitan Police
Copywriters
Jeremy Clarke
John Salmon
Photographer
Don McCullin
Typographer
Len Cheeseman

1988.18
1. Press Advertising: Mixed Media Charity Advertising Campaign
2. TV & Cinema Advertising: Charity Cinema Commercial
Advertising Agency
Ogilvy & Mather
Agency Producer
Ros McClellan
Art Director
Derrick Hass
Client
Royal National Institute for the Deaf
Copywriter
Howard Fletcher
Director
Dave Brown
Editor
Paul Jones
Lighting Cameraman
Chris Parker

Producer
Sarah Bell
Production Company
Spots Films Services

1989

1989.01
International: Television Campaign
Advertising Agency
J Walter Thompson (USA)
Agency Producer
Craig Allen
Art Directors
Bert Markland
Shanaz Tajbakhsh
Client
US Sprint
Copywriters
Steve Miller
Jim Sanderson
Joe Sedelmaier
Director
Joe Sedelmaier
Editor
Peggy Delay
Lighting Cameraman
Joe Sedelmaier
Music Composer/Arrangement
Dick Boyell
Producer
Marsie Wallach
Production Company
Sedelmaier Film Productions

1989.02
Packaging Design: Range of Packaging
Client
Tesco Packaging Design Studio
Design Group
CYB Design Consultants
Designers
Steve Davis
Liz Watson
Jonathan Brown
Richard Tilley
Robin Hall
Illustrator
Jim Hansen

1989.03
Packaging Design: Range of Packaging
Art Director
Philip Carter
Client
Katsouris Brothers
Design Group
Carter Wong
Designer
Philip Carter
Typographer
Philip Carter

1989.04
Illustration
Client
Minneapolis College of Art, Minnesota
Designer
Jeff Fisher
Illustrator
Jeff Fisher
Typographer
Jeff Fisher

1989.05
Photography: Photography in a Book
Client
Brian Griffin
Copywriter
Brian Griffin
Designer
Peter Davenport
Photographer
Brian Griffin
Typographer
Peter Davenport

1989.06
Design of a Complete Newspaper
Art Director
David Hillman
Design Editor of The Guardian
Michael McNay
Design Group
Pentagram Design
Designers
Leigh Brownsword
David Hillman
Illustrators
Steve Bell
Berke Breathed
Sue Huntley
Bryan McAllister-Gibbard
Garry Trudeau
Photographers
Martin Argles
Matthew Harris
Douglas Jeffery
Frank Martin
Don McPhee
Michael Putland
Graham Turner
Publisher
The Guardian Newspaper

1989.07
TV & Cinema Graphics: Television Graphics
Animators
Temple Clark
Sheila Dunn
Matt Forrest
Director
Matt Forrest
Graphic Designer
Matt Forrest
Lighting Cameraman
Hugh Gordon
Producer
David Botterell
Production Companies
Snapper Films
Initial Film & Television

1989.08
Compact Disc & Record Sleeve
Clients
Parlophone Records
Pet Shop Boys
Design Group
Three Associates
Designers
Mark Farrow
Chris Lowe
Neil Tennant
Photographers
Peter Andreas
Cindy Palmano
Michael Roberts
Eric Watson
Typographer
Mark Farrow

1989.09
Compact Disc & Record Sleeve
Art Director
Peter Saville
Client
Factory Communications
Design Group
Peter Saville Associates
Designer
Peter Saville
Photographer
Trevor Key
Typographers
Peter Saville
Brett Wickens

1989.10
Compact Disc & Record Sleeve
Art Director
Mike Dempsey
Clients
Virgin Records
The London Chamber Orchestra
Design Group
Carroll Dempsey & Thirkell
Designers
Mike Dempsey
Charlotte Richardson
Photographers
Paul Bradforth
Mike Dempsey
Andy Seymour
David Timmis
Typographer
Charlotte Richardson

1989.11
1. TV & Cinema Advertising: Cinema Commercial
2. TV & Cinema Advertising Crafts: Film Photography
Advertising Agency
Bartle Bogle Hegarty
Agency Producer
Kate O'Mulloy
Art Director
Graham Watson
Client
Speedo Europe
Copywriters
Chris Herring
Graham Watson
Director
Mike Portelly
Editor
Mike Kaufman
Lighting Cameraman
Mike Portelly
Music Composers/Arrangement
Karl Jenkins
Mike Ratledge
Producer
Amos Manasseh
Production Company
Halton Roy Productions
Set Designer
Steve Smithwick

1989.12
TV & Cinema Advertising: 40 Second Television Commercial
Advertising Agency
Saatchi & Saatchi
Agency Producer
Arnold Pearce
Animator
John Challis
Art Director
Paul Arden
Client
British Rail
Director
Tony Kaye
Editor
Peter Hearn
Lighting Cameraman
Hugh Gordon
Music Composer/Arrangement
Leon Redbone
Producer
Merriam Shear
Production Company
Tony Kaye Films
Set Designer
Celia Barnett

1989.13
International: Television & Cinema Crafts – Direction
Advertising Agency
Cliff Freeman & Partners
Agency Producer
Susan Scherl
Art Directors
Doris Cassar
Joe Sedelmaier
Client
Little Caesars Enterprises
Copywriters
Jeff Alpin
Cliff Freeman
Joe Sedelmaier
Director
Joe Sedelmaier
Editor
Peggy Delay
Lighting Cameraman
Joe Sedelmaier
Music Composer/Arrangement
Dick Boyell
Producer
Marsie Wallach
Production Company
Sedelmaier Film Productions
Set Designer
Glen Nielson

1989.14
1. TV & Cinema Advertising: 30 Second Television Commercial
2. TV & Cinema Advertising Crafts: Direction
Advertising Agency
Saatchi & Saatchi
Agency Producer
Suzie Rodgers
Art Director
Adrian Kemsley
Client
Chamber of Coal Traders
Copywriter
Charles Hendley
Director
Tony Kaye
Editor
Jim Bambrick
Lighting Cameraman
Steve Bernstein
Music Composer/Arrangement
Carole King
Producer
Merriam Shear
Production Company
Tony Kaye Films
Scenic Artist
Shane Kenny

1989.15
Posters: Poster Campaign
Advertising Agency
BMP Davidson Pearce
Art Director
Peter Gausis
Client
Courage
Copywriter
Tim Riley
Modelmaker
Matthew Wurr
Photographers
Jack Bankhead
Sanders Nicholson
Typographer
David Wakefield

1989.16
Copy: Posters
Advertising Agency
Abbott Mead Vickers SMS
Art Director
Ron Brown
Client
The Economist
Copywriter
David Abbott
Typographer
Joe Hoza

1989.17
1. Press Advertising: Colour Advertisment in a Consumer Magazine
2. Copy: Consumer Advertisement
3. Photography: Use of Black & White Photography
Advertising Agency
Collett Dickenson Pearce
Art Director
Neil Godfrey
Client
Metropolitan Police
Copywriter
Indra Sinha
Photographer
Don McCullin
Typographer
Len Cheeseman

1989.18
1. Press Advertising: Consumer Magazine Charity Advertisement
2. Posters: Tube Cards
Advertising Agency
Saatchi & Saatchi
Art Directors
Fergus Fleming
Judyth Greenburgh
Client
The Samaritans
Copywriter
Judyth Greenburgh
Photographer
John Turner
Typographer
Olaf Liunberg

1989.19
Retail & Environmental Design: Store Design
Client
Anna Federici
Design Group
Eva Jiricna Architects
Designers
Eva Jiricna
Jon Tollit

1989.20
Product Design
Design Company
Kinsman Associates
Designer
Rodney Kinsman

1989.21
Product Design: Design for Working Environments
Design Company
Wharmby Associates
Designer
Andy Davey

1990

1990.01
TV & Cinema Advertising: Animation
Advertising Agency
D'Arcy Masius Benton & Bowles
Agency Producer
Cydney Barker
Animator
Oliver Harrison
Art Director
Mark Waites
Client
Royal Mail Letters
Copywriters
Neil Pavitt
Mark Williams
Director
Oliver Harrison
Music Composers/Arrangement
Nucci Bongiovanni
Rossie-Testoni
Orchestra of S Andry
Producer
Debbie Mendoza
Production Company
Mendoza Productions

1990.02
1. Press Advertising: Newspapers – Charity
2. Copy
Advertising Agency
Abbott Mead Vickers SMS
Art Director
Ron Brown
Client
RSPCA
Copywriter
David Abbott
Photographer
Derek Seagrim
Typographer
Joe Hoza

1990.03
Press Advertising: Consumer Campaign and Colour Consumer Magazine Advertisement
Advertising Agency
Saatchi & Saatchi
Art Director
Antony Easton
Client
Kitchenware Merchants
Copywriter
Adam Kean
Photographer
Sebastião Salgado
Typographers
Andy Dymock
Jeff Merrells

1990.04
1. Press Advertising: Newspapers – Public Service
2. Newspapers: Black & White
Advertising Agency
BMP DDB Needham Worldwide
Art Director
Peter Gatley
Client
Health Education Authority
Copywriter
Frank Budgen
Photographer
David Bailey
Typographer
David Wakefield

1990.05
Posters
Advertising Agency
Lowe Howard-Spink
Art Directors
Tim Ashton
David Christensen
Client
Reebok UK
Copywriter
Jamie Way
Photographer
Peter Cawthorn Lavery
Typographer
Simon Warden

1990.06
TV & Cinema Advertising: Television Commercial Over 60 Seconds
Advertising Agency
BMP DDB Needham Worldwide
Agency Producer
Howard Spivey
Art Director
Gary Betts
Client
VAG (UK)

Copywriters
Tony Cox
Malcolm Green
Creative Director
Tony Cox
Director
Tony Kaye
Editor
Peter Goddard
Lighting Cameraman
Tony Kaye
Music Composers/Arrangement
Arthur Herzog Jnr
Billie Holliday
Producer
Merriam Shear
Production Company
Tony Kaye Films

1990.07
TV & Cinema Advertising Crafts: Use of Music
Advertising Agency
Howell Henry Chaldecott Lury
Agency Producer
Jane Fuller
Art Director
Tim Ashton
Client
Maxell (UK)
Copywriter
Naresh Ranchandani
Creative Directors
Axel Chaldecott
Steve Henry
Directors
Martin Brierley
Steve Lowe
Editor
Paddy Payne
Lighting Cameraman
Nic Morris
Music Composers/Arrangement
Stuart Adamson
Richard Jobson
Producer
Bruce Williamson
Production Company
Hutchins Film Company

1990.08
TV & Cinema Advertising Crafts
Advertising Agency
WCRS Mathews Marcantonio
Agency Producer
Lesley Wallington
Art Director
Jonathan Greenalgh
Client
Bass
Copywriter
Kes Gray
Creative Director
Alfredo Marcantonio
Director
Roger Woodburn
Editor
Mark Richards
Lighting Cameraman
Mike Garfath
Music Composers/Arrangement
Joe Campbell
Paul Hart
Producer
Mike Stones
Production Company
Park Village Productions
Set Designer
Stuart Rose

1990.09
International: Poster in Graphics
Client
Frascati Theatre
Design Group
Koeweiden-Postma
Designers
Jacques Koeweiden
Paul Postma
Photograph Inserts
Wim Wenders
Photographer
Bruce Weber
Typographers
Jacques Koeweiden
Paul Postma

1990.10
Corporate Identity
Client
PTT Nederland NV
Copywriter
Gerrit Glas
Design Group
Studio Dumbar
Designers
Hélène Bergmans
Michel de Boer
Marc van Bokhoven
Ton van Bragt
Harmine Louwé
Eric Nuyten
Heleen Raue
Henri Ritzen
Ming Tung
Esther Vermeer
Illustrator
Berry van Gerwen
Photographer
Lex van Pieterson
Typographers
Marc van Bokhoven
Ton van Bragt
Eric Nuyten
Henri Ritzen

1990.11
Graphics: Annual Reports
Client
API Corporation
Designers
Siobhan Keaney
Karen Wilks
Photographers
Siobhan Keaney
Robert Shackleton
Karen Wilks
Typographers
Siobhan Keaney
Karen Wilks

1990.12
Editorial & Books: Complete Magazine
Client
i-D Magazine
Design Group
3st (Thirst)
Designer
Stephen Male
Typographer
Stephen Male

1990.13
Illustration: Illustration Concept for Stamps
Design Directors
Mark Pearce
Michael Peters
Design Group
Michael Peters & Partners
Designer/Concept Creator
Mark Pearce
Illustrators
Bill Dare
Colin Elgie
Kevin Hauff
Peter Huggins
The Louvre/Bridgeman Art Library London
Ian Murray
Jim Pearce from reference supplied by Vintage Magazine Company
Harry Willock (after Sir John Tenniel)
Susan Winfield
Photographer
Peter Higgins
Typographer
Mike Pearce

1990.14
Packaging: Range of Packaging
Client
Safeway
Design Director
Mary Lewis
Design Group
Lewis Moberly
Designer
Bruce Duckworth
Typographer
Bruce Duckworth
Photographer
Laurie Evans

1990.15
Packaging: Individual Pack
Client
D'Amico & Partners
Design Directors
Michael Peters
Glenn Tutssel
Design Group
Michael Peters & Partners
Designer
Glenn Tutssel
Illustrator
Harry Willock
Typographer
Glenn Tutssel

1990.16
Environmental Design: Non-Retail Interior Design
Client
Nicole Farhi
Design Director
John Harvey
Design Group
Din Associates
Designer
Kirstie Moon
Project Designer
Lesley Batchelor

1990.17
Product Design: Health & Leisure
Client
UAD Company
Design Group
Rodd Industrial Design
Designer
Tim Rodd

1991

1991.01
International: Consumer Posters
Advertising Agency
The Martin Agency
Art Director
Jelly Helm
Client
Bernie's Tattooing
Copywriter
Raymond McKinney
Photographer
Roy Boy
Typographer
Owen Wachter

1991.02
TV & Cinema Graphics: Television Graphics
Animator
Rob Harvey
Client
BBC Television
Creative Director
Martin Lambie-Nairn
Design Directors
Daniel Barber
Martin Lambie-Nairn
Editor
SVC Television
Lighting Cameraman
Doug Foster
Modelmakers
Mark Curtis
Bob Hinks
Steve Wilshire
Music Composer/Arrangement
Anthony & Gaynor Sadler
Producer
Celia Chapman
Production Company
Lambie-Nairn & Company
Senior Producer
Sarah Davies

1991.03
Photography
Advertising Agency
BMP DDB Needham
Art Director
Mark Reddy
Client
Multiple Sclerosis Society
Copywriter
Richard Grisdale
Photographer
Branka Jukic
Typographer
David Wakefield

1991.04
Posters: Super Sites & Specials
Advertising Agency
McCann Erickson
Art Director
Roger Akerman
Client
Friends of the Earth
Copywriter
John Lewis
Director
David Gee
Illustrator
Phil Say
Photographer
Neil Mills
Typographer
Rob Wallis

1991.05
Posters: Public Service Advertisement
Advertising Agency
Smith-Dennison
Art Directors
Richard Dennison
Markham Smith
Client
North West Ash
Copywriters
Richard Dennison
Markham Smith
Typographers
Markham Smith
Richard Dennison

1991.06
Press Advertising: Consumer Magazine Charity Advertisment
Advertising Agency
Marr Associates
Art Director
Tim Robertson
Client
Action on Smoking & Health (Scotland)
Copywriter
Will Taylor
Photographer
Rod Campbell
Typographer
Carol Rigby

1991.07
TV & Cinema Advertising Crafts: Use of Music
Advertising Agency
Saatchi & Saatchi
Agency Producer
Martha Greene
Art Director
Graham Fink
Client
British Airways
Copywriter
Jeremy Clark
Creative Director
Paul Arden
Director
Hugh Hudson
Editor
Patrick Moore
Lighting Cameraman
Bernard Lutic
Music
Nessum Dorma, Puccini, sung by Pavarotti
Producer
John Garland
Production Company
Hudson Film

1991.08
1. TV & Cinema Advertising: Television Campaign
2. TV & Cinema Advertising: Television Commercial up to 60 Seconds
Advertising Agency
GGT
Agency Producer
Diane Croll
Art Director
Jonathon Prime
Client
Taunton Cider Company
Copywriter
Pete Lewtas
Creative Director
Tim Mellors
Director
John Lloyd
Lighting Cameraman
Clive Tickner
Music Arrangement
Richard Myhill
Producer
Caroline Warner
Production Company
Limelight Productions

1991.09
TV & Cinema Advertising: Animation
Advertising Agency
GGK London
Agency Producer
Joanne Cresser
Animator
Nick Park
Art Directors
Phil Rylance
Newy Brothwell
Client
Electricity Association
Copywriters
Paul Cardwell
Kim Durdant-Hollamby
Creative Director
Nick Fordham
Director
Nick Park
Editor
Rod Howick
Lighting Cameraman
David Sproxton
Producer
Chris Moll
Production Company
Aardman Animations
Set Designer
Michael Wright

1991.10
Graphics: Posters
Client
Wordsearch
Copywriter
Steven Taylor
Design Group
Cartlidge Levene
Designers
Simon Browning
Ian Cartlidge
Adam Levene
Sean Perkins
Editor
Rick Poyner
Photographer
Richard Burbridge
Typographers
Sean Perkins
Simon Browning

1991.11
Editorial & Books: Magazines
Designers
Paul Elliman
Peter Miles
Editors
Paul Elliman
Peter Miles
Photographer
Richard Preston
Publisher
Paul Elliman & Peter Miles
Typographer
Simon Josebury

1991.12
TV & Cinema Advertising: Cinema Commercial – Charity
Advertising Agency
Simons Palmer Denton Clemmow & Johnson
Agency Producer
Jane Fitch
Animator
Andy Staveley
Art Director
Mark Denton
Client
Terrence Higgins Trust
Copywriter
Chris Palmer
Creative Directors
Mark Denton
Chris Palmer
Director
Simon Fellows
Editor
Terry Brown
Graphic Designer
Phil Healey
Lighting Cameraman
Graham Pettit
Music Composer/Arrangement
Roger Jackson
Producer
James Studholme
Production Company
Blink
Set Designers
Phil Hunt
Joan Ashworth

1991.13
Editorial & Books: Book Jackets
Designer
Jeff Fisher
Illustrator
Jeff Fisher

Publisher
Bloomsbury Publishers
Typographer
Jeff Fisher

1991.14
Packaging: Range of Packaging
Client
The Boots Company
Design Director
Mary Lewis
Design Group
Lewis Moberly
Designers
David Booth
Amanda Lawrence
Mary Lewis
Lucilla Scrimgeour
Illustrator
Lucilla Scrimgeour
Typographers
Amanda Lawrence
Nicky Perkins

1991.15
Environmental Design: Store Design
Client
Joseph Ettedgui
Design Team
David Chipperfield
Renato Benedetti
Jorge Carvalho
Dieter von Gemingen
Maha Alusi
Designer
David Chipperfield Architects

1991.16
Product Design: Work
Client
Qubit UK
Design Group
Ideo
Design Team
Oliver Bayley
Jorge Davies
Paul Duff
Roger Penn
Robin Sarre
Paul South
Suzy Stone
Designer
Robin Sarre
Manufacturer's Design Team
Hugh Agnew
Rob Mast
Gwyn Parfitt
Roger Woolley

1991.17
Product Design: Industry & Transport
Client
Technophone
Design Group
Seymour Powell
Design Team
Nick Oakley
Dick Powell
Richard Seymour
Adam White
Technical Designer
Chris Sheldrake

1992

1992.01
Advertising Crafts: Use of Photography – Campaigns
Advertising Agency
Doyle Advertising
& Design Group
Art Director
John Doyle
Client
The Dunham Company
Copywriter
Ernie Schenck
Photographer
Nadav Kander

1992.02
1. Advertising Crafts: Use of Typography
2. Use of Photography: Individual
3. Press Advertising: Consumer Magazines – Colour
4. Newspapers: Colour
Advertising Agency
Bartle Bogle Hegarty
Art Director
Rooney Carruthers
Client
Haagen Dazs UK
Copywriter
Larry Barker
Photographer
Jean Loup Sieff
Typographer
Matthew Kemsley

1992.03
Public Service and Charities: Advertisment
Advertising Agency
Saatchi & Saatchi
Art Director
Jerry Hollens
Client
NSPCC
Copywriter
Mike Boles
Photographer
Graham Cornthwaite
Typographer
Andy Dymock

1992.04
1. Press Advertising: Consumer Magazines – Colour
2. Newspapers: Colour
Advertising Agency
Bartle Bogle Hegarty
Art Director
Mike Wells
Client
The Whitbread Beer Company
Copywriter
Tom Hudson
Photographer
Tif Hunter
Typographer
Nigel Dawson

1992.05
1. Posters: 48 & 96 Sheet
2. Press Advertising: Colour Newspaper Advertisement
Advertising Agency
Abbott Mead Vickers BBDO
Art Director
John Horton
Client
The Economist
Copywriter
Richard Foster
Typographer
Joe Hoza

1992.06
1. Press Advertising: Consumer Campaign
2. Newspapers: Black & White
Advertising Agency
Saatchi & Saatchi
Art Director
Antony Easton
Client
The Habitat Group
Copywriter
Adam Kean
Photographer
Andrew McPherson
Typographer
Roger Kennedy

1992.07
TV & Cinema Advertising: Television Commercial up to 60 Seconds
Advertising Agency
Lowe Howard-Spink
Agency Producer
Amanda Dicks
Art Director
John Merriman
Client
Reebok UK
Copywriter
Chris Herring
Creative Director
Paul Weinberger
Director
David Garfath
Editor
Simon Willcox
Lighting Cameraman
Roger Pratt
Music Composer/Arrangement
Chris Blackwell
Producer
Mary Francis
Production Company
Paul Weiland Film Company
Set Designer
Mike Hall

1992.08
1. Advertising Crafts: Illustration – Campaigns
2. Illustration: Individual
3. Posters: Campaign
Advertising Agency
BSB Dorland
Art Director
Gerard Stamp
Client
H J Heinz Company
Copywriter
Loz Simpson
Illustrator
Robin Heighway-Bury

1992.09
Posters: Campaigns
Advertising Agency
Saatchi & Saatchi
Art Director
Alexandra Taylor
Client
Allied Breweries
Brands Marketing
Copywriters
Alan Thompson
Rachel Heatherfield
Photographer
Peter Lavery
Typographer
Andy Dymock

1992.10
1. TV & Cinema Advertising: Television Commercial up to 60 Seconds
2. TV & Cinema Advertising: Cinema Commercial
Advertising Agency
Bartle Bogle Hegarty
Agency Producer
Philippa Crane
Art Director
Rooney Carruthers
Client
Levi Strauss UK
Copywriter
Larry Barker
Creative Director
John Hegarty
Director
Tarsem
Editor
Andrea McArthur
Lighting Cameraman
Paul Laufer
Music Composer/Arrangement
Noel Coward
Producer
Robert Campbell
Production Company
Spots Films
Set Designer
Alex McDowell

1992.11
TV & Cinema Advertising: Television Commercial up to 40 Seconds
Advertising Agency
Howell Henry Chaldecott Lury
Agency Producer
Jane Fuller
Art Director
Trevor Robinson
Client
Britvic Soft Drinks
Copywriter
Alan Young
Creative Director
Steve Henry
Director
Matt Forrest
Lighting Cameraman
Nic Morris
Producer
Storr Redman
Production Company
Limelight Commercials

1992.12
Public Service and Charities: Film
Advertising Agency
Charity Projects
Client
Charity Projects
Copywriter
Paul Weiland
Director
Paul Weiland
Editor
Ian Weil
Lighting Cameraman
Roger Pratt
Producer
Mary Francis
Production Company
Paul Weiland Film Company
Set Designer
Mike Hall

1992.13
Graphic Design: Self-Promotional Items – Budgets Under £40,000
Cartography
Dirk Fortuin
Client
Ando/Bloem/UNA
Amsterdam
Copywriter
Govert Schilling
Design Directors
Hans Bockting
Will de l'Ecluse
Design Group
UNA Amsterdam
Designers
Hans Bockting
Vero Crickx
Will de l'Ecluse
Typographer
Will de l'Ecluse

1992.14
Identity: Logotypes
Client
English National Opera
Design Director
Mike Dempsey
Design Group
Carroll Dempsey & Thirkell
Designer
Mike Dempsey
Typographer
Mike Dempsey

1992.15
Identity: Corporate Identity Programme
Client
English National Opera
Design Director
Mike Dempsey
Design Group
Carroll Dempsey & Thirkell
Designers
Steven Carter
Ian Chilvers
Mike Dempsey
Fernando Gutiérrez
Barbro Ohlson
Illustrator
Liz Pyle
Photographers
Michael Banks
Richard Burbridge
Mike Laye
Lewis Mulatero
Typographers
Steven Carter
Ian Chilvers
Mike Dempsey
Fernando Gutierrez
Barbro Ohlson

1992.16
Graphic Design: Poster Campaign
Client
C.O.O.B '92
Design Director
Brent Oppenheimer
Design Group
Addison Design Consultants
Designers
Madeleine Bennett
Brent Oppenheimer
Director
Jaume Masferrer
Typographer
Madeleine Bennett
Retoucher
Jones Bloom

1992.17
Graphic Design: Applied Graphic Design
Client
SC Properties
Copywriter
Johnny Bruce
Design Director
Stephen Gibbons
Design Group
The Partners
Designer
Janice Davison
Typographer
Janice Davison

1993

1993.01
Photography: Black & White Photograph Series
Client
James Cotier
Designer
Kevin Thomas
Photographer
James Cotier
Typographer
Jasvir Garcha

1993.02
1. Press Advertising: Consumer Campaign
2. Colour Consumer Magazine Advertisement
Advertising Agency
Bartle Bogle & Hegarty
Art Director
John Gorse
Client
Levi Strauss & Company, Europe
Copywriter
Nick Worthington
Photographers
John Gorse
Nick Worthington
Typographer
Nigel Dawson

1993.03
Press Advertising: Mixed Media Campaign
Advertising Agency
Simons Palmer Denton
Clemmow & Johnson
Art Director
Andy McKay
Client
Nike UK
Copywriters
Tony Barry
Chris Palmer
Tim Riley
Typographer
Barry Brand

1993.04
Posters: Campaign
Advertising Agency
Lowe Howard-Spink
Art Director
Simon Morris
Client
Imperial Tobacco
Copywriter
Geoff Smith
Photographer
Tim O'Sullivan
Typographers
Jasvir Garcha
Simon Warden

1993.05
Posters
Advertising Agency
WCRS
Art Director
Simon Pyrke
Client
Prudential
Copywriter
Terence Bly
Photographer
Richard Mummery
Typographer
Kim Le Liboux

1993.06
Public Service & Charities: Film
Advertising Agency
Street Smart Advertising NY
Art Directors
Peter Cohen
Leslie Sweet
Client
Coalition for the Homeless
Copywriters
Peter Cohen
Leslie Sweet
Director
Laura Belsey

Producers
Peter Cohen
Leslie Sweet
Production Company
First Light

1993.07
Public Service & Charities: Film
Advertising Agency
Saatchi & Saatchi, Singapore
Agency Producer
Anthony Lee
Art Director
Francis Wee
Client
Traffic Police
Copywriter
Dean Turney
Creative Director
Francis Wee
Director
Larry Shiu
Editor
James Ashburn
Harry Editor
Kevin Ryan
Lighting Cameraman
Ben Wu
Producer
Aleck Woo
Production Company
Shooting Gallery

1993.08
TV & Cinema Advertising: Television Commercial Campaign
Advertising Agency
Wieden + Kennedy
Agency Producer
Donna Portaro
Animator
Duck Soup
Art Director
Larry Frey
Client
McKenzie River Corporation
Copywriter
Stacy Wall
Creative Directors
David Kennedy
Dan Wieden
Director
Alex Proyas
Director of Photography
Darek Wolski
Editor
Craig Wood
Executive Producer
Johnathon Ker
Music Composer/Arrangement
Mark Vieha
Producer
Margot Fitzpatrick
Production Company
Limelight

1993.09
1. TV & Cinema Advertising: Television Commercial up to 30 Seconds
2. TV & Cinema Advertising Crafts: Special Effects
Advertising Agency
BSB Dorland
Agency Producer
Barry Stephenson
Art Director
Tom Notman
Client
Woolworths
Copywriter
Alistair Wood
Creative Directors
Chips Hardy
Rodger Williams

Director
Richard Dean
Editor
Andy Kemp
Lighting Cameraman
Keith Goddard
Music Composer/Arrangement
Will Malone
Producer
Charlie Crompton
Production Company
Moving Picture Company

1993.10
Illustration: Illustration in Design
Clients
The Beautiful South
Go Discs
Designer
Simon Ryan
Illustrator
David Cutter

1993.11
Editorial & Books: Complete Magazine
Art Director
Stephen Coates
Client
Wordsearch Publishing
Designer
Stephen Coates
Editor
Rick Poynor
Illustrator
Andrzej Klimowski
Photographer
Julian Broad

1993.12
Graphics: Individual Poster
Advertising Agency
Simons Palmer Denton Clemmow & Johnson
Art Director
Gary Martin
Client
The Terrence Higgins Trust
Copywriter
Mark Goodwin
Photographer
Lewis Mulatero
Typographer
Barry Brand

1993.13
Typography
Client
James McNaughton Paper
Copywriters
Prof William Barrett
Michael Johnson
Nikita Khruschev
Harold MacMillan
Henry Miller
Bertrand Russell
Rabbi Hyman Schachtel
Angus Wilson
Design Group
Smith & Milton
Designer
Michael Johnson
Hand Lettering
Mike Pratley
Photographers
Martin Barraud
Sheena Land
Derek Lomas
Paul Morgan
Typographer
Michael Johnson

1993.14
Illustration: Illustration in Editorial & Books
Client
Nicholas Dawe

Copywriter
Tony Meeuwissen
Design Director
Tony Meeuwissen
Designer
Tony Meeuwissen
Illustrator
Tony Meeuwissen
Illustrator's Agent
Folio
Publishers
Philadelphia Pavilion Books
Running Press
Typographers
Tony Meeuwissen
Tony Spaul

1993.15
Packaging: Range of Packaging
Client
W H Smith Office & Supplies
Design Directors
Frances Newell
John Sorrell
Design Group
Newell & Sorrell
Designers
Mark-Steen Adamson
Illustrator
Charles Barsotti

1993.16
Packaging: Range of Packaging
Client
Harvey Nichols
Design Directors
Anthony Michael
Stephanie Nash
Design Group
Michael Nash Associates
Designers
Anthony Michael
Stephanie Nash
Teresa Roviras
Photographer
Matthew Donaldson

1993.17
Product Design: Health & Leisure
Client
Seiko Corporation Japan
Design Group
TKO
Design Team
TKO Studio Noi
Designer
Andy Davey
Technical Designers
Andy Davey
Yozo Yajima

1993.18
Product Design: Industry & Transport
Client
Muz
Design Group
Seymour Powell
Design Team
Richard Seymour
Adam White
Designers
Richard Seymour
Adam White
Technical Designers
Richard Seymour
Adam White

1993.19
Product Design: Home
Client
Bisque Radiators
Design Group
Priestman Associates
Designer
Paul Priestman
Technical Design
Priestman Associates

1994

1994.01
Advertising Crafts: Photography
Advertising Agency
Wieden + Kennedy Amsterdam
Art Director
Warren Eakins
Client
Nike International
Copywriter
Evelyn Monroe Gude
Photographer
Nadav Kander
Typographer
Warren Eakins

1994.02
TV & Cinema Graphics: Programme Content
Animator
Steve Burrell
Client
BBC Television
Design Group
BBC Bristol Graphic Design Department
Directors
Steve Burrell
Richard Kwietniowski
Editor
Ian Haynes
Graphic Designer
Steve Burrell
Penny Delmon
Lighting Cameraman
Oliver Curtis
Producers
Roland Keating
Peter Symes
Production Company
BBC Television
Set Designer
Steve Burrell

1994.03
TV & Cinema Graphics: Brand Identity – Budgets Over £40,000
Animator
Fred Reed
Client
BBC Presentation
Design Group
BBC Graphic Design Department
Directors
Mark Chaudoir
Iain Greenway
Jason Harrington
Maylin Lee
Tim Platt
Jane Wyatt
Editors
Tim Burke
Rob Harvey
Graphic Designers
Mark Chaudoir
Iain Greenway
Jason Harrington
Maylin Lee
Tim Platt
Jane Wyatt
Lighting Cameramen
George Theophanous
Karl Watkins
Modelmakers
Asylum
Music Composer/Arrangement
The Music Sculptors
Producer
Mike Villiers-Stuart
Production Company
BBC TV Presentation Graphics

1994.04
1. Press Advertising: Newspaper Campaign
2. Advertising Crafts: Illustration Campaign
Advertising Agency
Bartle Bogle Hegarty
Art Director
Graham Watson
Client
The Whitbread Beer Company
Copywriter
Bruce Crouch
Illustrator
Janet Woolley
Typographers
Sid Russell
Graham Watson

1994.05
Press Advertising: Colour Newspaper Advertising
Advertising Agency
Abbott Mead Vickers BBDO
Art Director
Paul Brazier
Client
The Economist
Copywriter
Peter Souter
Typographer
Joe Hoza

1994.06
Press Advertising: Campaigns – Mixed Media
Advertising Agency
Simons Palmer Denton Clemmow & Johnson
Art Directors
Mark Denton
Gary Martin
James McKay
Client
Nike UK
Copywriters
Tony Barry
Mark Goodwin
Photographers
Malcolm Venville
Kerry Wilson
Typographers
Barry Brand
Alan Dempsey

1994.07
Posters: Any Other
Advertising Agency
Abbott Mead Vickers BBDO
Art Director
Paul Briginshaw
Client
The Economist
Copywriters
David Abbott
Malcolm Duffy
Photographer
Neil Evans
Typographer
Joe Hoza

1994.08
TV & Cinema Advertising: Television Commercial up to 40 Seconds
Advertising Agency
Lowe Howard-Spink
Agency Producer
Charles Crisp
Art Director
Charles Inge
Client
Tesco Stores
Copywriter
Phil Dearman
Creative Director
Paul Weinberger

Director
Frank Budgen
Editor
Sam Sneade
Lighting Cameraman
Adrian Wild
Music Composer/Arrangement
David Motion
Producer
Paul Rothwell
Production Company
Paul Weiland Film Company
Set Designer
Sophie Becher

1994.09
TV & Cinema Advertising Crafts: Use of Music
Advertising Agency
Saatchi & Saatchi
Agency Producer
David Eddon
Art Director
Jim Saunders
Client
British Telecom
Copywriter
Patricia Doherty
Creative Director
Simon Dicketts
Director
Gerard De Thame
Editor
Peter Goddard
Lighting Cameraman
Pascal Lebegue
Music Composer/Arrangement
Angelo Badalamenti
Producer
Fabyan Daw
Production Company
Helen Langridge Associates

1994.10
1. TV & Cinema Advertising Crafts: Direction
2. TV & Cinema Advertising: Use of Music
Advertising Agency
Abbott Mead Vickers BBDO
Agency Producer
Francine Linsey
Art Director
Walter Campbell
Client
SP Tyres UK
Copywriter
Tom Carty
Creative Director
David Abbott
Director
Tony Kaye
Editor
Peter Gooard
Lighting Cameraman
Tony Kaye
Music Composer/Arrangement
The Velvet Underground
Producer
Jenny Selby
Production Company
Tony Kaye Films
Set Designer
Stuart Stacking
Sound Designer
Lloyd Billing

1994.11
1. TV & Cinema Advertising: Television Commercial Over 60 Seconds
2. TV & Cinema Advertising: Cinema Commercial
Advertising Agency
Bartle Bogle Hegarty
Agency Producer
Philippa Crane

Art Director
John Gorse
Client
Levi Strauss Europe
Copywriter
Nick Worthington
Creative Director
John Hegarty
Directors
Vaughan Arnell
Anthea Benton
Editor
Duncan Shepherd
Lighting Cameraman
Joe Yacoe
Music Composer/Arrangement
Peter Lawlor
Producer
Adam Saward
Production Company
Lewin & Watson

1994.12
TV & Cinema Advertising: Cinema Commercial
Advertising Agency
Still Price Lintas
Agency Producer
Nick Peers
Animator
Ken Lidster
Art Directors
Stephen McKenzie
Jason Gormley
Client
Van Den Berghs & Jurgens
Copywriters
Jason Gormley
Stephen McKenzie
Creative Director
Rob Kitchen
Director
Ken Lidster
Editor
Tim Fulford
Lighting Cameraman
Peter Murphy
Modelmaker
Andy Baker
Producer
Glenn Holberton
Production Company
Bare Boards Productions

1994.13
TV & Cinema Advertising: Television Commercial up to 30 Seconds
Advertising Agency
BMP DDB Needham
Agency Producer
Lucinda Ker
Art Director
John Webster
Client
Courage
Copywriters
Jack Dee
John Webster
Creative Director
John Webster
Director
Mandie Fletcher
Editor
Alistair Jordan
Lighting Cameraman
Richard Greatrex
Music Composer/Arrangement
Vince Pope
Producers
David Morley
Madeleine Sanderson
Production Companies
Fletcher Sanderson Productions
Open Mike Productions

1994.14
Editorial & Books: Complete Magazine
Art Editor
Vince Frost
Client
Big Location
Design Group
Frost Design
Designer
Vince Frost
Story Editor
Peter Galvin
Photographers
The Douglas Brothers
Don Freeman
Guzman
David Lachapelle
Steven Meisel
Harold Roth
Bert Stern
Publisher
Marcelo Junemann
Typographers
Vince Frost
Alan Kitching

1994.15
Graphic Design: Annual Report
Client
Crafts Council
Design Director
John Rushworth
Design Group
Pentagram Design
Designer
Nick Finney
Photographer
Giles Revell
Typographer
John Rushworth

1994.16
Graphic Design: Poster Campaign
Client
Interior Design International
Design Director
David Hillman
Design Group
Pentagram Design
Designer
Lucy Holmes
Photographer
Peter Wood
Typographer
David Hillman

1994.17
Graphic Design: Calendar
Client
Thrislington Cubicles
Design Director
Aziz Cami
Design Group
The Partners
Designers
Bryan Hook
Greg Quinton
Typographers
Greg Quinton
Bryan Hook

1994.18
Environmental Design: Store Design
Client
Mujirushi Ryohin Europe
Design Group
Harper Mackay
Design Team
Peter Fearon Brown
Fiona McDaniel
Designer
Richard Woolf

1994.19
Environmental Design: Exhibition Design
Client
The South Bank Centre
Design Group
Stanton Williams
Designers
Michael Langley
Alan Stanton
Paul Williams

1994.20
Product Design: Home
Client
Dyson Appliances
Design Group
Dyson Design
Designer
James Dyson

1995

1995.01
TV & Cinema Advertising Crafts: Photography
Advertising Agency
WCRS
Agency Producer
Brenda Dykes
Art Director
Rooney Carruthers
Client
Hutchison Telecom
Copywriter
Larry Barker
Creative Directors
Larry Barker
Rooney Carruthers
Director
Frank Budgen
Editor
Sam Sneade
Lighting Cameraman
Alexander Witt
Music Composer/Arrangement
Philip Glass
Producer
Paul Rothwell
Production Company
Paul Weiland Film Company
Set Designer
Lauren Leclere

1995.02
1. Advertising Crafts: Typography – Campaigns
2. Typography: Individual
Advertising Agency
Faulds Advertising
Animators
Jonathan Barnbrook
Sarah Lewis
Agency Producer
Tim Maguire
Art Director
Lindsey Redding
Client
BBC Radio Scotland
Copywriter
Adrian Jeffery
Creative Directors
Andrew Lindsay
Simon Scott
Director
Jonathan Barnbrook
Editor
Jon Hollis
Music Composer/Arrangement
Logorhythm
Producer
Yvonne Chalk
Production Company
Tony Kaye Films

1995.03
Public Service and Charities: Charity Mixed Media Campaigns
Advertising Agency
Abbott Mead Vickers BBDO
Art Director
Paul Brazier
Client
Queen Elizabeth's Foundation for Disabled People
Copywriters
Paul Brazier
Peter Souter
Photographer
Mike Parsons
Recording Studio
Magmasters
Typographer
Joe Hoza

1995.04
1. Press Advertising: Newspapers: Colour
2. Consumer Magazines: Colour
Advertising Agency
Young & Rubicam
Art Director
Graeme Norways
Client
Pirelli
Copywriter
Ewan Paterson
Photographer
Annie Leibovitz
Typographer
Barry Brand

1995.05
1. Public Service and Charities: Press Advertising
2. Copy
Advertising Agencies
Antennae Communications
Collett Dickenson Pearce
Art Director
Guy Moore
Client
Satinath Sarangi
Copywriter
Indra Sinha
Photographer
Raghu Rai
Typographer
Jeff Merrells

1995.06
Posters: 48 & 96 Sheet
Advertising Agency
Simons Palmer Denton
Clemmow & Johnson
Art Director
Andy McKay
Client
Nike UK
Copywriter
Giles Montgomery
Photographers
Seamus Ryan
Norbet Schaner
Typographer
John Tisdall

1995.07
Posters: Campaigns
Advertising Agency
TBWA
Art Director
Nigel Rose
Client
Playtex UK
Copywriter
Nigel Rose
Creative Director
Nigel Rose
Photographer
Ellen Von Unwerth
Typographer
Tivy Davies

1995.08
1. Advertising Crafts: Photography Campaigns
2. Press Advertising: Newspaper Campaign
Advertising Agency
Abbott Mead Vickers BBDO
Art Director
Walter Campbell
Client
British Telecom
Copywriter
Tom Carty
Photographer
Tony Kaye
Typographer
Ashley Payne

1995.09
TV & Cinema Advertising Crafts: Editing
Advertising Agency
Abbott Mead Vickers BBDO
Agency Producer
Lindsay Hughes
Art Director
Walter Campbell
Client
Volvo Cars UK
Copywriter
Tom Carty
Director
Tony Kaye
Editor
Peter Goddard
Lighting Cameraman
Tony Kaye
Music Composer/Arrangement
Jenkins & Ratledge
Producers
Yvonne Chalk
Miranda Davis
Production Company
Tony Kaye Films
Sound Designers
Malcolm Bristow
Warren Hamilton
Rohan Young

1995.10
1. TV & Cinema Advertising: Commercials up to 60 Seconds
2. TV & Cinema Advertising Crafts: Special Effects
Advertising Agency
Ogilvy & Mather
Agency Producer
John Montgomery
Animators
Grahame Andrew
Ben Hayden
Laurent Huguenoit
Paul Kavanagh
Art Director
Brian Fraser
Client
Guinness Brewing GB
Copywriter
Simon Learman
Creative Directors
Brian Fraser
Simon Learman
Director
Doug Foster
Editor
Tim Burke
Lighting Cameramen
Doug Foster
David Wynn Jones
Music Composer/Arrangement
John Barry
Producer
Michelle Jaffe
Production Company
Blink Productions
Set Designer
Assheton Gorton

1995.11
TV & Cinema Advertising: Cinema Commercials
Advertising Agency
Cowan Kemsley Taylor
Agency Producer
Suzie Rodgers
Art Director
Graham Cappi
Client
Taunton Cider
Copywriter
Alan Moseley
Creative Directors
Graham Cappi
Alan Moseley
Director
Sean Hines
Lighting Cameraman
Sean Hines
Music Composer/Arrangement
Fern Kinney
Producer
David Burgess
Production Company
Harry Films

1995.12
Graphic Design: Compact Disc & Record Sleeve Campaigns
Client
Circa Records
Design Directors
Anthony Michael
Stephanie Nash
Design Group
Michael Nash Associates
Designers
Anthony Michael
Stephanie Nash
Photographer
Matthew Donaldson

1995.13
Graphic Design Crafts: Typography
Client
Big Life Records
Design Group
David James Associates
Design Director
David James
Designer
David James
Photographer
Trevor Key
Typographer
David James

1995.14
Graphic Design: Compact Disc & Record Sleeve
Client
Pet Shop Boys
Design Directors
Mark Farrow
Chris Lowe
Neil Tennant
Design Group
Farrow
Designers
Mark Farrow
Rob Petrie
Phil Sims
Photographer
Richard J Burbridge
Typographers
Mark Farrow
Rob Petrie
Phil Sims

1995.15
Graphic Design: Poster
Client
Pet Shop Boys
Design Directors
Mark Farrow
Chris Lowe
Neil Tennant
Design Group
Farrow
Designers
Mark Farrow
Rob Petrie
Phil Sims
Photographer
Richard J Burbridge
Typographers
Mark Farrow
Rob Petrie
Phil Sims

1995.16
Graphic Design: Annual Report
Client
Chicago Board of Trade
Copywriters
Anita Liskey
Michael Oakes
Design Director
Dana Arnett
Design Group
VSA Partners
Designer
Curt Schreiber
Photographer
François Robert

1995.17
Graphic Design: Direct Mail
Client
Polaroid UK
Copywriter
Peter Lester
Design Director
John Rushworth
Design Group
Pentagram Design
Designers
Vince Frost
John Rushworth
Chiew Yong
Typographers
Vince Frost
John Rushworth
Chiew Yong

1995.18
Graphic Design: Direct Mail
Clients
Advertising Law International
The Simkins Partnership
Copywriter
Neil Mattingley
Design Group
Trickett & Webb
Designers
Steve Edwards
Lynn Trickett
Brian Webb

1995.19
Packaging: Individual Pack
Client
Harveys of Bristol
Copywriter
Derek Hodgetts
Design Director
John Blackburn
Design Group
Blackburn's
Designer
John Blackburn
Illustrator
Douglas Sheldrake
Typographer
Matt Thompson

1995.20
Packaging: Range of Packaging
Advertising Agency
Wieden + Kennedy, USA
Client
The Coca-Cola Company
Copywriter
Peter Wegner
Design Director
Todd Waterbury
Designer
Todd Waterbury
Illustrators
Calef Brown
Charles Burns
Daniel Clowes
David Cowles
Typographer
Todd Waterbury

1995.21
Environmental Design: Exhibition Design
Client
Royal College of Art
Design Director
Daniel Weil
Design Team
First Year Industrial
Design Students
Jean Pierre Généreux
Designer
Daniel Weil

1995.22
Product Design: Health & Leisure
Client
Glaxo Research
and Development
Design Group
Glaxo Research and
Development, Device
Development Unit
Design Team
Peter Brand
Nick Cole
Ian Cude
Phil Farr
Andrew Grant
Richard Walker
Designers
David J Hearne
Paul K Rand

1996

1996.01
TV & Cinema Graphics: Title Sequence
Clients
David Fincher
New Line Cinema
Design Agency
R/Greenberg Associates
Designers
Kyle Cooper
Jennifer Shainin
Director
Kyle Cooper
Director of Photography
Harris Savides
Editor
Angus Wall
Executive Producer
Peter Frankfurt
Special Image Engineer
Findlay Bunting

1996.02
1. Press Advertising: Consumer Magazines – Campaigns
2. Art Direction
Advertising Agency
Lowe Howard-Spink
Art Director
Brian Campbell
Client
Olympus Cameras
Copywriter
Ben Priest
Creative Director
Paul Weinberger
Photographers
Dawid
Raymond Meeks
Mark Power
Typographer
Adam Whittaker

1996.03
Posters: Campaigns
Advertising Agency
Bartle Bogle Hegarty
Art Director
Tiger Savage
Client
Levi Strauss (UK)
Copywriter
Paul Silburn
Photographer
Malcolm Venville
Typographers
Robert Hales
Sid Russell
Tiger Savage

1996.04
TV & Cinema Advertising Crafts: Direction
Advertising Agency
Abbott Mead Vickers BBDO
Agency Producer
Frank Lieberman
Art Director
Walter Campbell
Client
Volvo Cars UK
Copywriter
Tom Carty
Creative Director
David Abbott
Director
Tony Kaye
Editor
Peter Goddard
Lighting Cameraman
Tony Kaye
Music Composer/Arrangement
Ann Dudley
Producer
Amy Appleton
Production Company
Tony Kaye Films
Sound Designers
Lloyd Billing
Warren Hamilton

1996.05
TV & Cinema Advertising: Commercial up to 40 Seconds
Advertising Agency
BMP DDB Needham
Agency Producer
Howard Spivey
Art Director
Tony Davidson
Client
Volkswagen Group
Copywriter
Nick Gill
Creative Director
Tony Cox
Director
Mick Rudman
Editor
John Osborn
Lighting Cameraman
Mick Rudman
Music Composer/Arrangement
Spike Jones
Producer
Basil Stephens
Production Company
The Annex Films

1996.06
TV & Cinema Advertising Crafts: Direction
Advertising Agency
Ogilvy & Mather
Agency Producer
Sue Lee
Art Director
Paul Angus
Client
Golden Wonder
Copywriter
Ted Heath
Creative Directors
Jerry Gallaher
Clive Yaxley
Director
Chris Palmer
Editor
Paul Watts
Lighting Cameramen
Kate Robinson
Peter Thwaites
Music Composers/Arrangement
Joe Campbell
Paul Hart
Producer
Tim Marshall
Production Company
Gorgeous
Set Designer
Amanda McArthur

1996.07
Radio Advertising: Charity
Advertising Agency
Hunt Lascaris TBWA
Agency Producer
Sally Wilson
Client
Childline
Concept Creators
Tony Granger
Samantha Koenderman
Copywriter
Samantha Koenderman
Production Company
Audiolab

1996.08
1. TV & Cinema Advertising: Television Commercial Over 60 Seconds
2. TV & Cinema Advertising: Cinema Commercial
3. TV & Cinema Advertising Crafts: Direction
4. TV & Cinema Advertising Crafts: Editing
Advertising Agency
Paul Marciano Advertising
Art Director
Paul Shearer
Client
Guess?
Copywriter
Rob Jack
Creative Director
Paul Marciano
Director
Andy Morahan
Lighting Cameraman
Joe Yacoe
Music Composer/Arrangement
The Blue Hawaiians
Producer
Laura Gregory
Production Company
Great Guns
Set Designer
Ben Morahan

1996.09
Pop Promo Videos: Direction
Client
Epic
Director
Mark Romanek
Director of Photography
Harris Savides
Editor
Rob Duffy
Music Composers/Arrangement
Janet Jackson
Michael Jackson
Producer
Cean Chaffin
Production Company
Satellite Films
Production Designer
Tom Foden
Special Effects
Richard 'Doc' Baily
Erik Bertellotti
Ashley Clemens
Alexander Frisch
Fusebox
Image Savant
Geoff McAuliffe
Nerv
525 Post Production
Chris Staves
Ann de Vilbiss

1996.10
Graphic Design: Compact Disc, Tape or Record Sleeve
Client
Cream
Designers
Mark Farrow
Rob Petrie
Phil Sims

1996.11
Graphic Design: Individual Poster
Client
Polygram Filmed Entertainment
Copywriter
Mark Blamire
Design Directors
Mark Blamire
Rob O'Connor
Design Group
Stylorouge
Designer
Mark Blamire
Photographer
Lorenzo Agius

1996.12
Environmental Design: Non-Retail Interior Design
Client
The National Museum of
Science & Industry
Design Group
Ben Kelly Design
Design Team
Helen Abadie
Kevin Brennan
Ben Kelly
Angela Kyriacou
Kirk Levoi
Bill Shorten
Jonathon Williams
Graphic Design & Signage
Assorted Images
Mechanical & Electrical Consultants
Andrew Sale Associates

1996.13
Product Design: Health & Leisure
Client
Connolly
Design Group
Studio X
Designer
Ross Lovegrove
Technical Designer
Neil Glen

1996.14
Product Design: Work
Client
NEC Home Industries
Design Group
IDEO Product Development
Design Team
Naoto Fukasawa
Thomas Meyerhoffer
Gary Schultz
Designer
Tim Brown

1997

1997.01
Advertising Crafts: Photography
Advertising Agency
Bartle Bogle Hegarty
Art Director
Steve Hudson
Client
Levi Strauss (UK)
Copywriter
Victoria Fallon
Creative Director
John Hegarty
Photographer
Nick Knight
Typographer
Andy Bird

1997.02
Direct Marketing: Mixed Media Campaign
Advertising Agency
Saatchi & Saatchi
Agency Producers
Mark Hanrahan
Rosemary Poole
Art Directors
Ian Gabaldoni
Dave Lang
Duncan Marshall
John Messum
Stuart Mills
Nik Studzinski
Alexandra Taylor
Richard Worrow
Client
COI/The Army
COI Producers
Simon Blaxland
Barbara Simon
Copywriters
Richard Baynham
Matthew Byrne
Ian Edwards
Jason Fretwell
Martin Gillan
Rupert Jordan
Adam Kean
Tristian Price
Jo Tanner
Howard Willmott
Creative Directors
Adam Kean
Alexandra Taylor
Directors
David Garfath
Mike Stephenson
Alexandra Taylor
Editors
Peter Goddard
Cyril Metzger
Simon Willcox
Lighting Cameramen
Alan Almond
Adrian Biddle
Steve Blackman
Tom Ingle
Music Composers/Arrangement
Paul Hart
Scramble Sound
The Tape Gallery
Photographers
First Base
Liam Kennedy

Fouad El Khoury
Gilles Peress
Dean Steadman
Chris Steele-Perkins
Producers
Johnnie Frankel
Paul Rothwell
Production Companies
Paul Weiland Film Company
UK Radio
Set Designer
Tony Burrough
Sound Designers
Grand Central
Scramble Sound
Typographers
Roger Kennedy
Tim Quest
Website Designer
Corsellis Montford

1997.03
Art Direction
Advertising Agency
Saatchi & Saatchi
Art Directors
Nik Studzinski
Alexandra Taylor
Client
COI/The Army
Copywriters
Jason Fretwell
Adam Kean
Creative Directors
Adam Kean
Alexandra Taylor
Photographers
First Base
Liam Kennedy
Fouad El Khoury
Dean Steadman
Chris Steele-Perkins
Typographer
Roger Kennedy

1997.04
Interactive Media: Interactive Kiosk
Client
Levi Strauss & Co Europe
Copywriters
Andrew Cameron
Sophie Pendrell
Creative Consultants
Jason Kedgeley
Dylan Kendle
Creative/Design Director
Tom Roope
Graphic Designers
Andrew Cameron
Luke Pendrell
Illustrator
Joe Stephenson
Interactive Designers
Sophie Pendrell
Nick Roope
Tom Roope
Programmers
Andrew Allenson
Tom Roope
Photographer
Jeremy Murch
Music Composer
Andrew Allenson
Production Company
Antirom
Video Directors
Andrew Polaine
Nick Roope
Video Producers
Helen Aver
Rob Le Quesne

1997.05
Press Advertising: Campaign in a Consumer Magazine
Advertising Agency
Saatchi & Saatchi
Art Directors
David Hillyard
Adrian Rossi
Keith Terry
Client
Flying Colours
Copywriters
Mark Fretton
Bill Gallacher
Alex Grieve
Robin Murtough
Ed Robinson
Creative Director
Adam Kean
Deputy Creative Director
Alexandra Taylor
Typographer
Mark Cakebread

1997.06
Posters: 48 & 96 Sheet
Advertising Agency
BMP DDB
Art Director
Jerry Hollens
Client
Volkswagen
Copywriter
Mike Boles
Creative Director
Tony Cox
Photographer
Mike Parsons
Typographer
Kevin Clarke

1997.07
TV & Cinema Advertising: Television Commercial up to 60 Seconds
Advertising Agency
Wieden + Kennedy
Agency Producer
Peter Cline
Art Director
David 'Jelly' Helm
Client
Nike EHQ
Copywriter
Glenn Cole
Creative Directors
Bob Moore
Michael Prieve
Director
Tarsem
Editor
Robert Duffy
Producer
Tommy Turtle
Lighting Cameraman
Paul Laufer
Music Composer/Arrangement
Jim Bredouw
Production Company
Spot Films
Set Designer
Ged Clarke

1997.08
TV & Cinema Advertising: Television Commercial over 60 Seconds
Advertising Agency
HHCL & Partners
Agency Producer
Peter Muggleston
Art Director
Jim Bolton
Client
Britvic Soft Drinks
Copywriter
Chas Bayfield
Creative Director
Axel Chaldecott
Director
Colin Gregg
Editor
Steve Gandolfi
Lighting Cameraman
Giles Nuttgens
Music Composers/Arrangement
Jenkins/Thomas/Richardson/Scott/Felix
Producers
Harry Rankin
Anthony Taylor
Production Company
Eclipse Productions
Set Designer
Jim Clay

1997.09
1. TV & Cinema Advertising Crafts: Use of Music
2. TV & Cinema Advertising Crafts: Special Effects
Advertising Agency
Bartle Bogle Hegarty
Agency Producers
Richard Packer
Tim Page
Animator
Pierre Buffin
Art Director
John Gorse
Client
Polaroid Europe
Copywriter
Nick Worthington
Creative Director
John Hegarty
Director
Michel Gondry
Editor
Russell Icke
Lighting Cameraman
Tim Maurice-Jones
Music Composer/Arrangement
Jake Jackson
Producer
Toby Courlander
Production Company
Partizan Midi Minuit
Special Effects
Pierre Buffin

1997.10
TV & Cinema Advertising Crafts: Direction
Advertising Agency
Abbott Mead Vickers BBDO
Agency Producer
Carol Powell
Art Director
Greg Martin
Client
Bayer
Copywriter
Patricia Doherty
Creative Director
David Abbott
Director
Roger Woodburn
Editor
Bobby Holmes
Lighting Cameraman
Keith Goddard
Producer
Irene Douglas
Production Company
Park Village Productions
Sound Designer
Johnnie Burns

1997.11
TV & Cinema Advertising Crafts: Direction
Advertising Agency
Lowe Howard-Spink
Agency Producer
Charles Crisp
Art Director
Vince Squibb
Client
Whitbread Beer Company
Copywriter
Paul Silburn
Creative Director
Paul Weinberger
Directors
Vaughan Arnell
Anthea Benton
Editor
Rick Russell
Lighting Cameraman
Pascal Raubaud
Music Composer/Arrangement
Jean-Claude Petit
Producer
Adam Saywood
Production Company
Federation Productions

1997.12
TV & Cinema Advertising: Television Sponsorship Credits
Advertising Agency
BMP DDB
Agency Producer
Anni Cullen
Art Director
Richard Flintham
Client
Walkers Snack Food
Copywriter
Andy Mcleod
Creative Director
Tony Cox
Directors
Richard Flintham
Andy Mcleod
Editor
Robbie Hartwell
Sound Composers/Arrangement
Tape Gallery

1997.13
1. Pop Promo Videos: Animation
2. Individual Pop Promo Video with Budget Over £40,000
Animators
Sergio Delfino
Olly Reid
Paul Smith
Artist
Tina Turner
Client
Parlophone Records
Creative Director
Dilly Gent
Director
Bill Mather
Editor
Jill Garrett
Lighting Cameraman
Frank Passingham
Producers
Julie Lockhart
Susie Mercer
Production Company
Aardman Animations
Set Designer
Bill Mather

1997.14
Identity: Stationery Range
Client
Cow Lane Garage
Design Group
Hughes & Moulton
Designers
John Hughes
Thomas Andrew Moulton
Photographer
Chris Harrison
Typographer
Thomas Andrew Moulton

1997.15
Identity: Stationery Range
Client
Canna Kendall & Co
Design Director
Michael Johnson
Design Group
johnson banks
Designer
David Jones
Photographer
Mike Parsons

1997.16
Identity: Corporate Identity Programme
Client
The Type Museum
Copywriter
Susan Shaw
Design Director
Phil Cleaver
Design Group
Cleaver et Al
Designers
Eiichi Kono
Aurobind Patel
Susan Shaw
Typographer
Phil Cleaver

1997.17
Graphic Design Crafts: Image Manipulation
Client
The Savoy Group of Hotels & Restaurants
Design Director
John Rushworth
Design Group
Pentagram Design
Designers
Annnabel Chartereris
Giles Revell
John Rushworth
Photographer
Giles Revell

1997.18
Environmental Design: Design for the Workplace
Client
Prospect Pictures
Design Group
Buschow Henley
Design Team
Gavin Hale Brown
Ralph Buschow
Simon Henley
Ken Rorrison

1997.19
Product Design: Health & Leisure
Client
Nike
Design Group
IDEO Product Development
Designer
David Peschel
Technical Designer
Ed Pearce

1997.20
Product Design: Industry & Transport
Client
Eurostar UK
Design Group
Jones Garrard
Designers
Roger Jones
Michael Rodber
Technical Designer
Paul Glover

1997.21
Product Design: Work
Client
Apple Computer
Product Design Engineer
John Tang
Senior Designer
Thomas Meyerhöffer

1998

1998.01
1. TV & Cinema Advertising: Cinema Commercials
2. TV & Cinema Advertising: Television Commercial up to 60 Seconds
3. TV & Cinema Advertising Crafts: Direction
Advertising Agency
TBWA Simons Palmer
Agency Producer
Jo Sayer
Art Director
Guy Moore
Client
Nike
Copywriter
Tony Malcolm
Creative Directors
Tony Malcolm
Guy Moore
Director
Jonathan Glazer
Editors
Emily Dennis
Rick Lawley
Lighting Cameraman
Ivan Bird
Music Composer/Arrangement
Blur
Producer
Nick Morris
Production Company
Academy Commercials

1998.02
1. Press Advertising: Public Service & Charities Campaigns
2. Art Direction
3. Copy
Advertising Agency
Saatchi & Saatchi
Art Directors
Colin Jones
John Messum
Client
Department of Health/COI
Copywriter
Mike McKenna
Creative Directors
Adam Kean
Alexandra Taylor
Photographer
Graham Cornthwaite
Typographer
Roger Kennedy

1998.03
TV & Cinema Advertising Crafts: Use of Music
Advertising Agency
Leagas Delaney
Art Director
Ian Ducker
Client
BBC Television
Copywriter
Will Farquhar
Creative Director
Tim Delaney
Director
Gregory Rood from the Paul Weiland Film Company
Editor
Matthew Wood
Executive Producer
Steve Kelynack
Lighting Cameramen
Steve Blackman
Julian Court
Georgio Scali
Peter Thwaites
Colin Waldeck

Vincent Warin
Music Composer/Arrangement
Lou Reed
Music Directors
The Music Sculptors
Producers
Edel Erickson
Stephanie Vanider Hill
Production Company
BBC
Set Designer
Alistair Kay

1998.04
TV & Cinema Graphics: Title Sequence
Agency/Design Group
Imaginary Forces
Art Director
Michael Riley
Clients
Columbia Pictures
Jersey Films
Design Director
Kyle Cooper
Director of Photography
Slawomir Idziak
Editor
Kurt Mattila
Feature Director
Andrew Niccol
Feature Producers
Michael Shamberg
Stacy Sher
Danny De Vito
Music Composer/Arrangement
Michael Nyman
Producer
Peter Frankfurt
Production Company
Imaginary Forces

1998.05
Press Advertising: Colour Consumer Magazine
Advertising Agency
BDDP GGT
Art Director
Paul Belford
Client
Waterstone's Booksellers
Copywriter
Nigel Roberts
Creative Directors
Trevor Beattie
Tom Hudson
Photographer
Laurie Haskell
Typographers
Paul Belford
Alison Wills

1998.06
Posters: Consumer Posters – Transport
Advertising Agency
BMP DDB
Art Director
Richard Flintham
Client
London Transport
Copywriters
Nick Gill
Andy McLeod
Ewan Paterson
Creative Director
Tony Cox
Photographer
Giles Revell
Typographer
David Wakefield

1998.07
TV & Cinema Advertising: Television Campaigns
Advertising Agency
BMP DDB
Agency Producer
Howard Spivey
Art Director
Andrew Fraser
Client
Volkswagen Group
Copywriter
Andrew Fraser
Creative Director
Jeremy Craigen
Director
Paul Gay
Editor
Adam Spivey
Lighting Cameraman
Barry Ackroyd
Producers
Robert Campbell
Jason Kemp
Production Company
Outsider

1998.08
1. TV & Cinema Advertising: Television Campaigns
2. TV & Cinema Advertising: Television Commercial up to 30 Seconds
Advertising Agency
Cliff Freeman & Partners
Agency Producer
Liz Graves
Art Director
Roger Camp
Client
Fox Network
Copywriters
Jeff Bitsack
Eric Silver
Creative Director
Cliff Freeman
Director
Christopher Guest
Editor
Gavin Cutler
Production Company
Moxie Pictures

1998.09
1. Pop Promo Video Crafts: Direction
2. Pop Promo Video with Budget Under £40,000
Artist
Aphex Twin
Director
Chris Cunningham
Editor
Gary Knight
Lighting Cameramen
Alex Barber
Simon Chaudoir
Producer
Cindy Burnay
Production Company
RSA/Black Dog
Record Company
Warp Records

1998.10
Graphic Design: Any Other
Client
Joe Kerr
Design Group
Studio Myerscough
Designer
Morag Myerscough

1998.11
Corporate & Brand Identity
Client
RAC
Design Group
North
Designers
Paul Austin
Rupert Bassett
Tim Beard
Simon Browning
Ben Parker
Sean Perkins
Mason Wells
Photographer
Fi McGhee

1998.12
Graphic Design Crafts: Typography
Artist
Richard Wentworth
Client
Association for Business Sponsorship of the Arts (ABSA)
Designer
Kate Stephens
Photographer
Mike Parsons
Typographer
Kate Stephens

1998.13
Interactive Media: Distributed Data
Client
Diesel
Copywriter
Bob Shevlin
Creative/Design Director
Tony Brook
Graphic Designers
Jim Birchenough
Tony Brook
Gary Butcher
Viv Cherry
David Rainbird
Programmer
Brad Lowry
Photographers
Peter Hill
Andy Cameron
Music
Wall of Sound
Production Company
Spin
Technical Designer
David Rainbird

1998.14
Graphic Design Crafts: Illustration – Series or Sequence
Client
The Folio Society
Design Director
Joe Whitlock-Blundell
Illustrator
Geoff Grandfield

1998.15
Packaging Design: Brand Label Range of Packaging
Client
Seattle Coffee Company
Copywriter
Janet Brades
Design Directors
David Beard
Mark Wickens
Design Group
Wickens Tutt Southgate
Designers
David Beard
Clem Halpin
Illustrator
Colin Shearing
Photographer
Andy Flack
Typographers
David Beard
Clem Halpin

1998.16
Packaging Design: Brand Label Individual Pack
Client
National Portrait Gallery
Design Director
Andy Bone
Design Group
Four IV Design Consultants
Designers
Kim Hartley
Jane Stanyon

1998.17
Packaging Design: Brand Label Individual Pack
Client
Joseph
Design Director
Teresa Roviras
Design Group
Teresa Roviras
Designer
Teresa Roviras
Photography
Michael Roberts

1998.18
Music Packaging & Print Promotion: Individual Compact Discs, Tapes & Record Sleeves
Client
Dedicated Records
Copywriters
Jonathon Jeffrey
J Spaceman
Design Director
Mark Farrow
Design Group
Farrow Design
Designers
Mark Farrow
Jonathon Jeffrey
J Spaceman
Typographers
Mark Farrow
Jonathon Jeffrey

1998.19
Environmental Design: Retail Design
Client
Harvey Nichols
Design Group
Heatherwick Studio
Designer
Thomas Heatherwick
Lighting
Elektra

1998.20
Product Design: Industry & Transport
Client
JCB Industrial
Designer
Simon Ratcliffe
Technical Designer
Peter Drake

1999

1999.01
TV & Cinema Advertising: Cinema Commercials
Advertising Agency
Lowe Howard-Spink
Agency Producer
Charles Crisp
Art Director
Charles Inge
Client
The Independent
Copywriter
Charles Inge
Creative Director
Paul Weinberger
Director
Rob Sanders
Editor
Tim Fulford
Lighting Cameraman
Robert Pendar-Hughes
Music Composers
Joe Campbell
Paul Hart
Producer
Helen Langridge
Production Company
HLA
Sound Design
Joe & Co

1999.02
TV & Cinema Advertising Crafts: Sound Design
Advertising Agency
Saatchi & Saatchi
Agency Producer
Sally-Ann Dale
Art Director
Alexandra Taylor
Client
COI/The Army
COI Producer
Barbara Simon
Copywriter
Adam Kean
Creative Directors
Adam Kean
Alexandra Taylor
Director
Alexandra Taylor
Editor
John Smith
Lighting Cameraman
Henry Braham
Music Composer/Arrangement
Tot Taylor
Producer
Fran Ratcliffe
Production Company
Paul Weiland Film Company
Set Designer
Andrew Sanders
Sound Designers
Raja Sehgal
Tot Taylor

1999.03
Graphic Design: Self-Promotional Items
Advertising Agency
Mother
Client
Mother
Copywriters
Ben Mooge
Mark Waites
Design Director
Franklin Tipton
Designers
Libby Brockhoff
Paul Bruce
Richard Walker
Illustrator
Hugh Beattie
Modelmaker
Paul Baker
Producer
Paul Adams
Typographer
Ian Hutchings

1999.04
Interactive Media: Internet
Clients
Carat Interactive
Volkswagen
Copywriter
Ralph Pearce
Creative/Design Directors
Fred Flade
David Streek
Graphic Designer
Fred Flade
Interactive Designers
Pete Everett
Fred Flade
Music Composers
Pete Everett
Fred Flade
Photography
Panormania
Production Company
Deepend
Programmers
Gabriel Bucknall
Pete Everett

1999.05
TV & Cinema Graphics: Title Sequences
Clients
Alan Cohn
MTV Films
Copywriters
Adam Bluming
Karin Fong
Creative Director
Peter Frankfurt
Design & Production Company
Imaginary Forces
Designers
Adam Bluming
Karin Fong
Director
Karin Fong
Editors
Doron Dor
Kurt Mattila
Executive Producer
Saffron Kenny
Illustrator
Wayne Coe
Music
David Bowie
Marilyn Manson
Producer
Maureen Timpa

1999.06
1. Art Direction: Campaigns
2. Copy
Advertising Agency
TBWA
Art Director
Paul Belford
Client
Waterstone's Booksellers
Copywriter
Nigel Roberts
Creative Director
Trevor Beattie
Illustrators
Paul Belford
Mick Brownfield
J Otto Seibold
Photographer
Laurie Haskell
Typographers
Paul Belford
Alan Dempsey
J Otto Seibold
Nigel Ward
Alison Wills

1999.07
Art Direction: Campaigns
Advertising Agency
TBWA
Art Director
Paul Belford
Client
Tate Gallery
Copywriter
Nigel Roberts
Creative Director
Trevor Beattie
Photographers
Paul Caponigro
Michael Liam Cumiskey
Andreas Heumann
Peter Knapp
Bruno Munari
Tessa Traeger

Typographer
Paul Belford

1999.08
Art Direction: Campaigns
Advertising Agency
BMP DDB
Art/Creative Director
Dave Dye
Client
Volkswagen
Copywriter/Creative Director
Sean Doyle
Illustrators
Jeff Fisher
Peter Grundy
Tilly Northedge
Christopher Wormell
Typographer
David Wakefield

1999.09
Press Advertising: Newspapers – Colour
Advertising Agency
BMP DDB
Art Director
Neil Dawson
Client
Volkswagen
Copywriter
Clive Pickering
Creative Director
Jeremy Craigen
Photographer
Paul Reas
Typographer
FGDS

1999.10
TV & Cinema Advertising Crafts: Direction
Advertising Agency
Abbott Mead Vickers BBDO
Agency Producer
Yvonne Chalkley
Art Director
Walter Campbell
Client
Guinness
Copywriter
Tom Carty
Creative Director
David Abbott
Director
Jonathan Glazer
Editor
Rick Lawley
Lighting Cameraman
Ivan Bird
Music Composer/Arrangement
Perez Prado
Producer
Nick Morris
Production Company
Academy
Sound Designer
Tony Rapaccioli

1999.11
1. TV & Cinema Advertising Crafts: Direction
2. TV & Cinema Advertising Crafts: Editing
Advertising Agency
TBWA
Agency Producer
Diane Croll
Art Director
Ed Morris
Client
Sony Computer Entertainment
Copywriter
James Sinclair
Creative Director
Trevor Beattie
Director
Frank Budgen
Editor
John Smith
Lighting Cameraman
Frank Budgen
Music Composer
Fauré
Producer
Paul Rothwell
Production Company
Gorgeous
Sound Designer
Hass Hassan

1999.12
TV & Cinema Advertising: Television Campaigns
Advertising Agency
Cliff Freeman & Partners
Agency Producer
Nick Felder
Art Directors
Roger Camp
Gary Feil
Ed Walsh
Client
outpost.com
Copywriter
Eric Silver
Creative Director
Eric Silver
Director
John O'Hagan
Editor
Gavin Cutler
Producer
Lisa Timmons
Production Company
Hungry Man
Set Designers
Gary Feil
Ed Walsh

1999.13
Pop Promo Video Crafts: Direction
Artist
UNKLE
Director
Jonathan Glazer
Editor
Rick Lawley
Lighting Cameraman
John Mathieson
Music Composers/Arrangement
J Davis
Thom York
Producer
Nick Morris
Production Company
Academy
Record Companies
Island Records
Mo'Wax
Set Designer
Dan Betteridge

1999.14
Music Packaging & Print Promotion: Posters
Clients
Circa/Virgin Records
Design Group
Tom Hingston Studio
Design Directors
Tom Hingston
Robert Del Naja
Designers
Tom Hingston
Robert Del Naja
Photographer
Nick Knight

1999.15
Graphic Design Crafts: Illustration – Series or Sequence
Client
Alibaba Verlag
Copywriter
David Hughes
Design Director
Ben Casey
Design Group
The Chase
Designers
Ben Casey
David Hughes
Tommy Shaughnessy
Illustrator
David Hughes
Typographer
Tommy Shaughnessy

1999.16
Editorial & Books: Book Covers
Design Director
Angus Hyland
Design Group
Pentagram Design
Designer
Angus Hyland
Publisher
Canongate Books

1999.17
Corporate Branding: Identity
Client
Go Fly Limited
Copywriters
Robbie Laughton
Joseph Mitchell
Jane Speller
Adam Throup
Design Director
Doug Hamilton
Design Group
Wolff Olins
Designers
Robbie Laughton
Joseph Mitchell
Adam Throup
Illustrators
Robbie Laughton
Adam Throup
Photography
Network Photographers
Typographers
Robbie Laughton
Miles Newlyn
Adam Throup

1999.18
Graphic Design Crafts: Typography – Typeface Design
Client
Yellow Pages
Design Director
Michael Johnson
Design Group
johnson banks
Production Company
The Foundry
Type Designers
David Quay
Freda Sack
Jürgen Weltin
Typographers
Harriet Devoy
Michael Johnson

1999.19
Interactive Media: Distributed Data
Client
Glasgow 1999: UK City of Architecture and Design
Copywriters
Sam Davy
Tim Fendley
Creative/Design Director
Tim Fendley
Design Group
MetaDesign London
Graphic Designers
Sam Davy
David Eveleigh
Frances Jackson
Interactive Designers
Sam Davy
David Eveleigh
Frances Jackson
Music Composer
David Eveleigh
Programmer
David Eveleigh

1999.20
Graphic Design: Brochures & Catalogues
Client
Jill Ritblat
Creative Director
Richard Smith
Design Directors
Richard Smith
Cara Gallardo
Design Group
Area
Designers
John Dowling
Richard Smith
Editor
Robert Violette
Photographer
Toby McFarlan Pond
Publisher
Violette Editions
Typographers
John Dowling
Richard Smith

1999.21
Graphic Design Crafts: Design Writing
Client
WPP Group
Copywriter
Jeremy Bullmore
Design Director
Peter Chodel
Design Group
Addison
Designer/Typographer
Tammy Kustow
Illustrator
Benoît Jacques

1999.22
Product Design: Home
Architect
Isobel Coomber
Client
Ideal Standard
Design Group
Queensberry Hunt Levien
Designers
Robin Levien
David Tilbury
Technical Designer
Nick Swann

1999.23
Product Design: Industry & Transport
Client
Audi
Designer
Peter Schreyer
Technical Designer
Dr Werner Mischke

1999.24
Product Design: Home
Client
Apple Design Group
Designers
Bart Andre
Danny Coster
Richard Howarth
Daniele de Iuliis
Jonathan Ive
Steve Jobs
Doug Satzger
Cal Seid
Christopher Stringer
Photography
Hunter Freeman Studio
Technical Design
Apple Design Group

2000

2000.01
Editorial & Books: Book Covers
Art Director
Alan Fletcher
Designer
Karl Shanahan
Editor
Bruce Bernard
Publisher
Phaidon Press

2000.02
Graphic Design Crafts: Illustration – Series or Sequence
Client
Royal Mail
Design Directors
Mike Dempsey
Barry Robinson
Jane Ryan
Design Group
CDT Design
Designers
Mike Dempsey
Simon Elliot
Jane Ryan
Image Makers
Craigie Aitchison
Barbara Baran
Zafar Baran
Peter Blake
Peter Brookes
John Byrne
Peter Collingwood
Richard Cooke
Christopher Corr
Michael Craig-Martin
Mark Curtis
Andrew Davidson
Mike Dempsey
Allan Drummond
Sara Fanelli
Jeff Fisher
David Gentlemen
Antony Gormley
Colin Gray
George Hardie
Ray Harris Ching
David Hockney
Howard Hodgkin
Peter Howson
Allen Jones
Rod Kelly
Natasha Kerr
Alan Kitching
Andrzej Klimowski
John Lawrence
Susan MacFarlane
Don McCullin
Wilson McLean
Clare Melinsky
Lisa Milroy
Brendan Neiland
Brody Neuenschwander
Eduardo Paolozzi
Gary Powell
Bridget Riley
Bill Sanderson
Lord Snowdon
Ralph Steadman
Tessa Traeger
David Tress
Mike White
Christopher Wormell
Catherine Yass
Typographers
Mike Dempsey
Simon Elliot

2000.03
Mixed Media: Public Service & Charity Campaigns
Advertising Agency
Saatchi & Saatchi
Agency Producer
Sally-Ann Dale
Art Director
Duncan Marshall
COI Producers
Brian Jenkins
Barbara Simon
Clients
COI/The Army
Copywriter
Howard Willmott
Creative Director
David Droga
Director
Paul Gay
Editor
Piers Douglas
Illustrator
Jasper Goodall
Lighting Cameraman
Paul Gay
Producer
Jason Kemp
Production Company
Outsider
Set Designer
Mark Lavis
Typographer
Scott Silvey

2000.04
Graphic Design: Direct Mail
Cardboard Engineer
Debbie Morris
Client
Granada Media
Copywriters
Dave Simpson
Sue Strange
Design Director
Phil Skegg
Design Group
Tucker Clarke-Williams Creative
Designers
Dave Palmer
Dave Simpson
Phil Skegg
Retoucher
Dave Black
Typographers
Dave Simpson
Phil Skegg

2000.05
Graphic Design: Direct Mail
Client
Alabama Veterans Memorial
Copywriter
Dave Smith
Creative Director
Terry Slaughter
Design Director
Marion English
Design Group
Slaughter Hanson
Designer
Marion English
Typographer
Marion English

2000.06
Graphic Design: Calendars
Client
Thrislington Cubicles
Design Director
Greg Quinton
Design Group
The Partners

Designers
Martin Lawless
Steve Owen
Tony de Ste Croix
Illustrator
Tony de Ste Croix
Typographer
Tony de Ste Croix

2000.07
Interactive Media: Online Advertising
Clients
BMP DDB
Compaq
Copywriter
John Webster
Creative/Design Directors
Neil Churcher
Philip Hunt
Graphic Designers
Grant Orchard
James Stone
Illustrator
Grant Orchard
Interactive Designers
Javier Garcia Flynn
James Stone
Music Composer
Aphex Twin
Producer
Sue Goffe
Production Companies
aka PIZAZZ
Edwards Churcher
Programmers
Javier Garcia Flynn
James Stone
Video Directors
Mario Cavalli
Dominic Griffiths
Grant Orchard

2000.08
Ambient Media
Advertising Agency
The Jupiter Drawing Room
Art Director
Graham Lang
Client
KFM Radio
Copywriter
Anton Visser
Creative Director
Ross Chowles
Photographer
Wayne Rochat
Typographer
Graham Lang

2000.09
Radio Advertising: Public Service & Charity Campaigns
Advertising Agency
Publicis Wellcare/Mojo
Agency Producer
Amanda Peters
Client
Red Cross
Copywriters
Pat Richer
Denis Koutoulogenis
Production Company
Stellar Sound

2000.10
Product Design: Work
Client
Apple Computer
Design Group
Apple Industrial Group
Designers
Bart Andre
Danny Coster
Richard Howarth
Daniele de Iuliis
Jonathan Ive
Steve Jobs
Matthew Rohrbach
Doug Satzger
Christopher Stringer

2000.11
Environmental Design: Design for Leisure
Client
Ian Schrager Hotels
Design Groups
Agence Starck
Ian Schrager Design
Designers
Anda Andrei
Philippe Starck
Executive Architect
Harper Mackay

2000.12
Environmental Design: Design for Leisure
Client
Yo! Sushi (Soho)
Design Group
Simon Condor Associates
Designers
Gerry Allbury
Simon Condor

2000.13
Corporate & Brand Identity: Large Identity Schemes
Client
BBC
Creative Director
Martin Lambie-Nairn
Design Group
Lambie-Nairn
Designers
Adrian Burton
Gary Holt
Gareth Mapp
TV Design Directors
Charlotte Castle
Jason Keeley

2000.14
Editorial & Books: Complete Book
Clients
London Institute
Royal Mail
Copywriter
Michael Benson
Design Directors
Lynn Trickett
Brian Webb
Design Group
Trickett & Webb
Designers
Katja Thielen
Lynn Trickett
Brian Webb
Publisher
Camberwell Press

2000.15
Advertising Crafts: Typography
Advertising Agency
Saatchi & Saatchi Wellington
Agency Producer
Tom Ackroyd
Animators
Jason Bowden
David Colquhoun
Tom Eslinger
Brian Merrifield
Tristram Sparks
Art Director
Len Cheeseman
Client
New Zealand Symphony Orchestra
Copywriters
Oliver Maisey
Nigel Richardson
Creative Director
Gavin Bradley
Director
Len Cheeseman
Typographers
Len Cheeseman
Hayden Doughty

2000.16
Graphic Design: Posters
Client
AIGA Detroit
Design Director
Stefan Sagmeister
Design Group
Sagmeister Inc
Designers
Hjalti Karlsson
Martin Woodtli
Photographer
Tom Schierlitz
Typographers
Stefan Sagmeister
Martin Woodtli

2000.17
Posters: Consumer Posters – Campaigns
Advertising Agency
Abbott Mead Vickers BBDO
Art Director
Jeremy Carr
Client
Guinness
Copywriter
Jeremy Carr
Creative Director
Peter Souter
Illustrator
Jon Rogers
Typographer
Brian McHale

2000.18
Advertising Crafts: Photography
Agency
Lowe Lintas
Art Directors
Andy Amadeo
Mick Mahoney
Client
Whitbread Beer Company
Copywriters
Andy Amadeo
Mick Mahoney
Creative Director
Charles Inge
Photographer
Jenny van Sommers
Typographer
Mark Cakebread

2000.19
1. TV & Cinema Advertising: Television Commercial Over 60 Seconds
2. TV & Cinema Advertising Crafts: Direction
Advertising Agency
Abbott Mead Vickers BBDO
Agency Producer
Yvonne Chalkley
Art Director
Walter Campbell
Client
Guinness
Copywriter
Tom Carty
Creative Director
Peter Souter
Director
Jonathan Glazer
Editor
Sam Sneade
Lighting Cameraman
Ivan Bird
Music Composers/Arrangement
Neil Barnes
Paul Daley
Music Consultant
Peter Raeburn
Post Production
The Computer Film Company
Producer
Nick Morris
Production Company
Academy
Sound Designer
Johnny Burns
Special Effects
Richard Clarke
Tom Debenham
Paddy Eason
Dan Glass
Dominic Parker
Alex Payman
Joe Pavlo
Rachael Penfold
Gavin Toomey
Adrian de Wet

2000.20
TV & Cinema Advertising Crafts: Use of Music
Advertising Agency
Abbott Mead Vickers BBDO
Agency Producer
Yvonne Chalkley
Animators
Mike Eames
Jimmy Kiddell
Quentin Mills
Porl Perrott
Dave Throssell
Art Director
Walter Campbell
Client
Guinness
Copywriter
Tom Carty
Creative Director
Peter Souter
Director
Frank Budgen
Editor
Paul Watts
Lighting Cameraman
Peter Biziou
Music Composer/Arrangement
Antar Daly
Post Production
The Mill
Producer
Paul Rothwell
Production Company
Gorgeous
Special Effects
Barnsley
Liz Brown
Phil Crowe
Chris Knight
Adam Scott

2000.21
TV & Cinema Graphics: Television Sponsorship Credits
Advertising Agency
Abbott Mead Vickers BBDO
Art Director
Rob Oliver
Client
Guinness
Copywriter
Rob Oliver
Directors
Ian Cross
Stuart Hilton
Editor
Art Jones
Lighting Cameraman
Tim J M Green
Producer
Richard Price
Production Company
Picasso Pictures

2000.22
TV & Cinema Graphics: Brand Identity
Advertising Agency
Fallon McElligott NY
Agency Producer
Beth Barrett
Art Director
Paul Malmström
Client
MTV Networks
Copywriter
Linus Karlsson
Creative Director
Jamie Barrett
Director
Traktor
Editor
Dick Gordon
Lighting Cameraman
Tim Maurice-Jones
Music Composer/Arrangement
Thad Spencer
Producer
Olé Sanders
Production Company
Partizan
Set Designer
Robbie Freed

2000.23
TV & Cinema Advertising: Television Commercial up to 60 Seconds
Advertising Agency
Wieden + Kennedy
Agency Producers
Vic Palumbo
Shannon Worley
Art Director
Hal Curtis
Client
Nike
Copywriter
Chuck McBride
Creative Directors
Hal Curtis
Chuck McBride
Director
Lasse Hallström
Editor
Peter Wiedensmith
Lighting Cameraman
Lance Accord
Music Arrangement
APM
Producers
Jeff Kohr
Susanne Preissler
Production Company
Propaganda/Satellite
Set Designers
John Dexter
Richard Heinrichs

2000.24
Pop Promos: Direction
Animator
James Mann
Art Director
Chris Oddy
Artist
Björk
Director
Chris Cunningham
Editor
Gary Knight
Lighting Cameraman
John Lynch
Post Production
Glassworks
Producer
Cindy Burnay
Production Company
Black Dog Films
Record Company
One Little Indian Records
Robot Effects
Paul Catling
Set Designer
Julian Caldow
Set Effects
Ben Hall
Special Effects
Paul Catling
Ben Hall
Pasi Johansson
James Mann

2000.25
TV & Cinema Advertising Crafts: Special Effects
Advertising Agency
TBWA
Agency Producer
Diane Croll
Art Director
Bil Bungay
Client
Sony Playstation
Copywriter
Trevor Beattie
Creative Director
Trevor Beattie
Director
Chris Cunningham
Editor
Tony Kearns
Lighting Cameraman
Chris Cunningham
Post Production
The Mill
Producer
Cindy Burnay
Production Company
RSA Films
Set Designer
Chris Oddy
Special Effects
Barnsley
Chris Knight
Dave Phillips

2001

2001.01
Environmental Design & Architecture: Design for Leisure
Architects
John Ahern
Frank Anatole
Joanna Bailey
Nic Bailey
Julia Barfield
Margarita Bodman
Steve Chitton
Malcom Cook
David Marks
Mark Sparrowhawk
Architectural Design
Marks Barfield
Checking Engineer
Babtie Allot & Lomax
Client
The London Eye Company
Engineering Companies
Atelier One
Beckett Ranking Partnership
Dewhurst McFarlane & Partners
Ove Arup & Partners
Tony Gee & Partners
Environmental Design Consultancy
Loren Butt Consultancy
Photographers
Ian Lambot
Nick Wood

2001.02
1. Writing for Advertising: Individual
2. Writing for Advertising: Campaign
Advertising Agency
Saatchi & Saatchi

Art Director
Nik Studzinski
Client
monster.co.uk
Copywriter
Gavin Kellett
Creative Director
David Droga
Illustrator
Graham Carter
Typographer
Roger Kennedy

2001.03
Interactive & Digital Media: Any Other
Client
IdN Magazine
Copywriter
Mario Cavalli
Creative Director
Mario Cavalli
Design Group
Studio AKA
Designers
Jo Billingham
Mario Cavalli
Mic Graves
Grant Orchard
Interactive Designer
Adam Hoyle

2001.04
Ambient Media
Advertising Agency
Mother
Art Directors
Markus Bjurman
Cecilia Dufils
Kim Gehrig
Client
britart.com
Copywriter
Joe De Souza
Creative Directors
Robert Saville
Mark Waites
Typographer
Ian Hutchings

2001.05
Packaging: Brand Label Individual Pack
Client
Interbrew UK
Design Director
Garrick Hamm
Design Group
Williams Murray Hamm
Designers
Garrick Hamm
Simon Porteous
Photographer
Phil Hurst

2001.06
Product Design: Work
Client
Apple Computer
Design Group
Apple Industrial Design
Designers
Bart Andre
Danny Coster
Richard Howarth
Daniele de Iuliis
Jonathan Ive
Steve Jobs
Duncan Kerr
Matthew Rohrbach
Doug Satzger
Cal Seid
Christopher Stringer
Eugene Whang

2001.07
Product Design: Work
Client
Apple Computer
Design Group
Apple Industrial Design
Designers
Bart Andre
Danny Coster
Richard Howarth
Daniele de Iuliis
Jonathan Ive
Duncan Kerr
Matthew Rohrbach
Doug Satzger
Cal Seid
Christopher Stringer
Eugene Whang

2001.08
Product Design: Work
Client
Apple Computer
Design Group
Apple Industrial Design
Designers
Bart Andre
Danny Coster
Richard Howarth
Daniele de Iuliis
Jonathan Ive
Steve Jobs
Duncan Kerr
Matthew Rohrbach
Doug Satzger
Cal Seid
Christopher Stringer
Eugene Whang

2001.09
Product Design: Industry & Transport
Client
Audi
Design Director
Peter Schreyer
Design Group
Audi
Designer
Derek Jenkins
Technical Designer
Luc Doncker-Woake

2001.10
Environmental Design & Architecture: Exhibition Design
Architect
Will Alsop
Client
Southwark Council
Design Group
Alsop Architects

2001.11
Environmental Design & Architecture: Design for Leisure
Client
National Botanic Garden of Wales
Design Group
Foster & Partners
Designers
Foster & Partners
Mechanical and Electrical Engineers
Max Fordham & Partners

2001.12
Environmental Design & Architecture: Design for Leisure
Client
The Science Museum
Design Groups
Casson Mann
Itch
Designers
Durrell Bishop
Roger Mann

2001.13
Graphic Design: Posters
Client
Witness
Copywriter
Andy Mosley
Design Directors
Domenic Lippa
Harry Pearce
Design Group
Lippa Pearce Design
Designers
Andy Mosley
Harry Pearce
Photography
Panos Pictures
Typographers
Andy Mosley
Harry Pearce

2001.14
Graphic Design: Direct Mail
Client
Burberry
Design Director
Andy Bone
Design Group
Four IV Design Consultants
Designers
Julie Austin
Marion Hare

2001.15
Editorial & Book Design: Complete Book
Design Director
Bruce Mau
Design Group
Bruce Mau Design Inc.
Designer
Bruce Mau
Photography
Bruce Mau Design
Armin Linke
See Spot Run
Publisher
Phaidon Press
Typographers
Archetype
Bruce Mau

2001.16
Graphic Design: Music Packaging & Print Promotion – Compact Discs, Tapes & Record Sleeves
Artist
Julian Opie
Client
Parlophone Records
Design Director
Jeremy Plumb
Design Group
Vent
Designers
Jeremy Plumb
Dan Poyner

2001.17
Press Advertising: Trade & Professional Magazines – Colour
Advertising Agency
TBWA\Paris
Art Director
Jorge Carreno
Client
Sony Computer Entertainment Europe
Copywriter
Eric Helias
Creative Directors
Jorge Carreno
Eric Helias
Photographer
Joe Magrean

2001.18
1. Graphic Design: Posters
2. Art Direction
Advertising Agency
TBWA\London
Client
Sony Computer Entertainment Europe
Copywriter
Nigel Roberts
Design Director
Paul Belford
Designer
Paul Belford
Illustrator
Paul Belford
Mac Operator
Dan Beckett

2001.19
Posters: 48 or 96 Sheet
Advertising Agency
Leo Burnett
Art Director
Richard Connor
Client
John West
Copywriter
Julie Adams
Creative Directors
Nick Bell
Mark Tutssel
Photographer
Andy Roberts
Typographer
Alison Greenway

2001.20
Photography and Image Manipulation: Advertising
Advertising Agency
Mother
Agency Producer
Hayley Irow
Client
EMAP On Air
Copywriters
Ben Mooge
Jim Thornton
Graham Linehan
Creative Directors
Robert Saville
Mark Waites
Director
Graham Linehan
Editor
Adam Jenkins
Lighting Cameraman
Barry Ackroyd
Producer
Peter Nice
Production Company
Talkback
Sound Designer
Owen Griffiths

2001.21
TV & Cinema Advertising: Television Campaigns
Advertising Agency
Bartle Bogle Hegarty
Art Directors
Verity Fenner
Claudia Southgate
Client
Levi Strauss Europe, Middle East & Africa
Copywriters
Verity Fenner
Claudia Southgate
Creative Consultant
Alan Aboud
Creative Directors
Bruce Crouch
Russell Ramsey
Photographer
Rankin

Typographers
Andy Bird
Nigel Pullum

2001.22
Music Videos: Direction
Artist
Bentley Rhythm Ace
Director
Garth Jennings
Editor
Ming
Producer
Nick Goldsmith
Production Company
Hammer & Tongs
Record Company
Parlophone
Special Effects
Truss

2001.23
TV & Cinema Advertising: Television Commercial up to 60 Seconds
Advertising Agency
Butler Shine & Stern
Agency Producer
Stephanie Bunting
Art Director
Stephen Goldblatt
Client
San Francisco Jazz Organization
Copywriter
Ryan Ebner
Creative Director
John Butler
Director
Brandon Dickerson
Editor
Angelo Valencia
Lighting Cameraman
Norman Bonney
Producer
Lauren Schwartz
Production Company
Kaboom! Productions

2001.24
TV & Cinema Advertising: Television Commercial up to 30 Seconds
Advertising Agency
Leo Burnett
Agency Producer
Charlie Gatsky
Art Director
Paul Silburn
Client
John West
Copywriter
Paul Silburn
Creative Directors
Nick Bell
Mark Tutssel
Director
Daniel Kleinman
Editor
Steve Gandolfi
Lighting Cameraman
Steve Blackman
Producer
David Botterell
Production Company
Spectre

2002

2002.01
Radio Advertising: Campaigns
Advertising Agency
DDB Chicago
Agency Producer
Chris Bing
Chief Creative Officer
Bob Scarpelli
Client
Anheuser Busch

Copywriters
John Immesoete
Bob Winter
Creative Directors
Bill Cimino
Mark Gross
Group Creative Director
John Immesoete
Music Composer
Sandy Torano

2002.02
Packaging: Brand Label – Range of Packaging
Client
H J Heinz Company
Copywriters
Jim Bosilijevac
Dave Reger
Design Directors
Dave Reger
Mike Straznickas
Design Group
Leo Burnett (Chicago)
Designers
Kevin Butler
Mike Straznickas

2002.03
Packaging: Brand Label – Individual Pack
Client
Chivas & Brothers
Design Director
Martin Grimer
Design Group
Coley Porter Bell
Designer
David Jenkins
Typographer
David Jenkins

2002.04
Packaging: Physical Shape
Client
Ty Nant
Design Group
Lovegrove Studio
Designer
Ross Lovegrove
Photographer
John Ross

2002.05
Product Design: Health & Leisure
Client
Apple Computer
Design Group
Apple Industrial Design
Designers
Bart Andre
Danny Coster
Richard Howarth
Daniele de Iuliis
Jonathan Ive
Steve Jobs
Duncan Kerr
Matthew Rohrbach
Doug Satzger
Cal Seid
Christopher Stringer
Eugene Whang

2002.06
Product Design: Work
Client
Apple Computer
Design Group
Apple Industrial Design
Designers
Bart Andre
Danny Coster
Richard Howarth
Daniele de Iuliis
Jonathan Ive
Steve Jobs
Duncan Kerr

Matthew Rohrbach
Doug Satzger
Cal Seid
Christopher Stringer
Eugene Whang

2002.07
Product Design: Work
Client
Apple Computer
Design Group
Apple Industrial Design
Designers
Bart Andre
Danny Coster
Richard Howarth
Daniele de Iuliis
Jonathan Ive
Steve Jobs
Duncan Kerr
Matthew Rohrbach
Doug Satzger
Cal Seid
Christopher Stringer
Eugene Whang

2002.08
Product Design: Industry & Transport
Chief Designer
Bart Hildebrand
Client
BMW AG
Design Group
Mini Design Team
Design Team
Mini Design Team

2002.09
Environmental Design & Architecture: Design for Leisure
Architect
Wilkinson Eyre Architects
Client
The Magna Trust
Director in Charge
Chris Wilkinson
Exhibition Designer
Event Communications
Lighting Design
Spiers and Major
Architectural Team
Matt Appleton
Marc Barron
John Coop
Graham Gilmour
Bosco Lam
James Parkin
Chris Poulton
Sebastien Ricard
John Smart
Chris Wilkinson

2002.10
Environmental Design & Architecture: Retail Design
Client
oki-ni
Design Group
6a Architects
Designers
Tom Emerson
Steph Macdonald
Lee Marsden
Graphic Design
Fuel

2002.11
Editorial & Book Design: Complete Book
Design Director
Alan Aboud
Design Group
Aboud Sodano
Designers
Alan Aboud
Jonathan Ive
Emma Jones
Maxine Law
Ellie Ridsdale
Zoe Symonds
Mark Thomson
Publisher
Violette Editions

2002.12
Graphic Design: Music Packaging & Print Promotion – Individual Compact Discs, Tapes & Record Sleeves
Clients
Arista
Spaceman
Design Group
Farrow Design
Designers
Mark Farrow
Jonathon Jeffrey
J Spaceman
Gary Stillwell
Nick Tweedie
Sculpture
Yoko by Don Brown

2002.13
TV & Cinema Graphics: Brand Identity
Client
Channel Four
Creative Director
Jon Stevens
Design Group
Spin

2002.14
Editorial & Book Design: Complete Magazine
Design Director
Andreas Laeufer
Designers
Jay Hess
Greg Stogden
Publishers
Masoud Golsorkhi
Andreas Laeufer
Tank Publications
Typographer
Andreas Laeufer

2002.15
Graphic Design: Brochures & Catalogues
Client
Smurfit Townsend Hook
Copywriters
Harriet Devoy
Michael Johnson
Design Director
Michael Johnson
Design Group
johnson banks
Designers
Harriet Devoy
Michael Johnson
Modelling Consultant
Luke Gifford
Photographer
Piers North
Typographer
Harriet Devoy

2002.16
Illustration for Advertising: Campaigns
Advertising Agency
Abbott Mead Vickers BBDO
Art Director
Jeremy Carr
Client
Guinness GB
Copywriter
Jeremy Carr
Creative Director
Peter Souter
Illustrator
Faiyaz Jafri
Typographers
Brian McHale
Robin Warrington

2002.17
Posters: 48 or 96 Sheet
Advertising Agency
Abbott Mead Vickers BBDO
Art Director
Martin Casson
Client
The Economist
Copywriter
Matthew Abbott
Creative Director
Peter Souter

2002.18
Art Direction: Campaigns
Advertising Agency
Saatchi & Saatchi
Art Director
Antony Nelson
Client
Club 18-30
Copywriter
Mike Sutherland
Creative Director
David Droga
Illustrator
Scott Silvey
Photographer
Trevor Ray Hart

2002.19
TV & Cinema Advertising Crafts: Direction
Advertising Agency
Lowe
Agency Producer
Charles Crisp
Art Director
Vince Squibb
Client
Reebok UK
Copywriter
Tony Barry
Creative Director
Paul Weinberger
Director
Frank Budgen
Editor
Russell Icke
Lighting Cameraman
Alwin Kuchler
Modelmaker
Asylum Models & Effects
Music Composer
Toby Anderson
Producer
Paul Rothwell
Production Company
Gorgeous
Set Designer
Gavin Bocquet
Sound Designer
Nigel Crowley

2002.20
TV & Cinema Advertising Crafts: Direction
3D Artist
Russell Tickner
Advertising Agency
Bartle Bogle Hegarty
Agency Producer
Andy Gulliman
Art Director
Tony McTear
Client
Levi Strauss Europe, Middle East & Africa
Copywriter
Mark Hunter
Creative Director
Russell Ramsey
Director
Frank Budgen
Editor
Paul Watts
Flame Artists
Barnsley
Chris Knight
Jason Watts
Flame Assistants
Salima Needham
Gavin Wellsman
Lighting Cameraman
John Lynch
Music Composers
Bartle Bogle Hegarty
Pepe Deluxe
Warren Hamilton
Post Production
The Mill
Producer
Paul Rothwell
Production Company
Gorgeous
Set Designer
Mark Guthrie
Sound Designer
Warren Hamilton
Telecine
Adam Scott

2002.21
Music Videos: Direction
Artist
Chemical Brothers
Director
Michel Gondry
Editor
Twist
Producers
Dan Dickenson
Julie Fong
Production Company
Partizan
Record Company
Virgin UK
Special Effects
Twist

2002.22
TV & Cinema Advertising: Television Campaigns
Advertising Agency
TBWA\Chiat\Day
Agency Producer
Betsy Beale
Art Directors
Eric King
Jeff Labbé
Client
Fox Sports
Copywriters
Eric King
Jeff Labbé
Scott Wild
Creative Director
Chuck McBride
Director
Baker Smith
Editors
Hank Corwin
Paul Martinez
Lighting Cameraman
John Stainer
Producers
Lauren Bayer
Bonnie Goldfarb
Production Company
Harvest Productions
Set Designer
Michael Deal
Sound Design
Jeff Payne

2002.23
TV & Cinema Advertising Crafts: Direction
Advertising Agency
BMP DDB
Agency Producer
Michael Parker
Animator
Henson's Creature Shop
Art Director
Joanna Wenley
Client
Volkswagen UK
Copywriter
Jeremy Craigen
Creative Director
Andrew Fraser
Director
Fredrik Bond
Editor
Rick Russell
Lighting Cameraman
Ben Seresin
Music Composer
Leftfield
Producer
Helen Williams
Production Company
Harry Nash
Set Designer
Dominic Watkins
Sound Designer
Rowan Young

2002.24
TV & Cinema Advertising: Television Commercial up to 60 Seconds
Advertising Agency
Wieden + Kennedy USA
Agency Producer
Vic Palumbo
Art Directors
Hal Curtis
Tim Hanrahan
Client
Nike Europe
Copywriter
Jimmy Smith
Creative Directors
Hal Curtis
Jim Riswold
Director
Paul Hunter
Editor
Adam Pertofsky
Music
Afrika Bambaataa
Hydraulic Funk
Music Composers
Afrika Bambaataa
Steve Brown
Jeff Elmassian
Production Company
HSI

2002.25
TV & Cinema Advertising Crafts: Sound Design
Advertising Agency
Wieden + Kennedy Amsterdam
Agency Producer
Jasmine Kimera
Art Director
Paul Shearer
Client
Nike
Copywriter
Jimmy Smith
Creative Director
Glenn Cole
Director
Charles Randolph-Wright
Editor
Adam Pertofsky
Producer
Kate Sutherland
Production Company
@radical.media
Sound Designer
Jeff Elmassian

2002.26
TV & Cinema Advertising Crafts: Sound Design
Advertising Agency
Wieden + Kennedy Amsterdam
Agency Producer
Jasmine Kimera
Art Director
Paul Shearer
Client
Nike
Copywriter
Jimmy Smith
Creative Director
Glenn Cole
Director
Charles Randolph-Wright
Editor
Adam Pertofsky
Producer
Kate Shearer
Production Company
@radical.media
Sound Designer
Jeff Elmassian

Page numbers in italics refer to picture captions.

A
Aardman Animations
  Parlophone Records 368, *369*
Aardman Animations and the Brothers Quay
  Virgin Records 244, *244*
Abba 154
Abbott, David *72*, 73, 77, 82, 179, 252
  J Sainsbury 276, *278*
  RSPCA 321, *321*
Abbott Mead Vickers (AMV) 72, 179 *358*
  British Telom 344
  Cow & Gate 280, *280*
  The Economist 274–5, *275*, 328,*329*, 337, *337*, 451, *451*
  Guinness 350, 448, *451*, 454, *454*, *456*, 457, 460
  J Sainsbury 276, *278*
  Queen Elizabeth's Foundation for Disabled People *321*, 362, *363*
  RSPCA 321, *321*
  Sony 179
  SP Tyres 344, 346, *347*
  Volvo 179, 280, *280*, 344, *347*, 348, *348*
Abbott Mead Vickers (AMV)/SMS
  Action on Smoking & Health 330, 340, *341*
  Yellow Pages 252, *252*
Adams, Douglas 230
Addison
  WPP Group *399*
Addison Design Consultants
  COOB'92 390, *390*
Adidas 302, 330
Advertising & Marketing Services
  Albany Life Assurance 280, *282*
AIGA Detroit 446, *446*, 448
aka PIZAZZ 431, *431*
Alabama Veterans Memorial 430, *430*
Alan Parker Film Company 104, 105, *105*, *112*, *259*
Albany Life Assurance 280, 282, 290
album sleeves *see* record sleeves
Aldridge, Alan 82, *468*
  Warhol's *Chelsea Girls* poster 18, *19*
Alexon & Company 214, *214*
Ali, Muhammad *128*
Alibaba Verlag 372, *374*
Alka Seltzer 356, *358*
Allen Brady & Marsh 82
Allied Breweries 342, *343*
Allied International Designers 189, 198
Alsop, Will
  Southwark Council 440, *441*
Amberson Video *171*
ambient media 270, 432, 454
Ambre Solaire *128*
Amelio, Gil *421*
American new wave 222
Andre, Carl
  'Equivalent VII' 97
Anglia Television 229
Anheuser Busch 432, *433*
animation 171, 185, 244, *244*
  computer 245
  Cresta bear 125–6, *127*, 179
  The Snowman 230, *230*
  Spitting Image 176, 182, 228, *228*
  Wired title sequence 232, *232*
anti-capitalism 15, 428–9
anti-design and anti-advertising 15
Antirom
  Levi Strauss 308, *309*
Antonioni, Michelangelo 61
Aphex Twin 368, *370*, 372
API Corporation 376, *377*
Apicella, Enzo 83
Apple & Pear Publicity Council *60*
Apple, Billy (aka Barrie Bates) 82
Apple Computer 194, *194*, 303, 311, 421, *421*, 423, 435–6, *437*, *438*, 439–40
Apple Records *86*
Appleton, Geoffrey *473*
Araldite 269, *270*
Arbus, Diane *40*
Archer, Jeffrey 229
architecture 194, 440–1
Arden, Paul
  Alexon & Company 214, *214*
Area
  Jill Ritblat 396, *399*
Arista 448, *448*
Armstrong-Jones, Anthony (Lord Snowdon) 83
The Army 96, *98*, 304, *305*, 306, *306*, *428*
Arnold, Eve 94
Arnold Schwartzman Productions
  Kinney Record Group *154*
Arratoon, Liz *471*
Arrowsmith, Clive 83, *285*
Art Deco *57*
Arts and Crafts movement 11–12
'Aryan Art' 194, 284, *287*
Ashton, Tim 354, *433*
Associated-Rediffusion *69*
Association for Business Sponsorship of the Arts *209*, 392, *392*
Aston, John 314
Atherton, Bill 179
Atlantic Records *156*
Audi 303, 418, *420*, 435–6, 439, *439*
Austin, Stewart
  BBC Television *229*
Autograph Design Partnership
  Jones identity 207, *207*
Auton, Denis 82
Avedon, Richard
  Alexon & Company *214*
Avid 311
Avis 179

B
Bach, Johann Sebastian *259*
Bacon, John
  International Distillers & Vintners (Smirnoff) *115*
Bailey, David 83, *106*, 179
  Greenpeace 186, *186*
  Health Education Authority *331*
  VAG UK *250*
Bailey, Dennis 83
Baker, Andy *361*
Baker, Jim 179
Balding & Mansell 29, 82, 83
Ballard, JG
  Crash 153
Barclaycard 96, *97*
Barfield, Julia
  London Eye 426, *426*, 428, 440
Baric Computing Services *150*, 151
Barker & Dobson
  Hacks *128*
  Victory V 115, *115*
Barker, Larry 352, *352*
Barnbrook, Jonathan *311*
Barney, Gerry *54*
Baron, Stuart *191*
Barsotti, Charles 402, *403*
Bartle Bogle Hegarty (BBH) 71, 268, 269, 333
  Barnardo's *50*
  Häagen-Dazs 318, *318*
  James Robertson & Sons *275*
  Levi Strauss *240*, 255–6, *255*, *257*, 300, *300*, 323, *323*, 333, *333*, 352, *352*, *456*, 457
  Polaroid 356, *357*
  Smith & Nephew 280, *280*
  Speedo 258, *260*
  Whitbread Beer Company 322, *323*, 324, *327*, 328
Bartram, Harold 82
Barstow, Neil *474*
Bass 364, *365*
Bass, Saul 69, 82
Batchelor, Lesley 409
Bates, Barrie (aka Billy Apple)
  Young Commonwealth Artists 31, *31*
Baxter, Glen *472*
Baxter, Stanley *105*
Bayer 356, *358*
BBC 52, 69, *69*, 82, 170
  BBC identity 444, *444*
  BBC1 identity 232
  BBC2 identity 227–8, 232, 312, *313*, 314, *314*
  The Body in Question 175
  Bristol Graphic Design *314*
  Dr Who credits 66, *67*
  Graphic Design 314, *314*
  The Hitchhiker's Guide to the Galaxy 230, *230*
  Horizon titles *172*
  Omnibus 232
  'Perfect Day' 313, *313*
  Playhouse 175
  Radio Times 162, *162*, 164
  Smiley's People 229
  Sports Department *173*
  Teletale titles 66, *67*
  Therese Raquin 229, *229*
  Tinker Tailor Soldier Spy 229, *229*
  Top of the Pops 239, *239*
BDDH
  RAC 376
BDDP GGT
  Waterstone's Booksellers 324
The Beatles 18, 82, 86, 179
  album covers 28, *28*
  Hard Day's Night 66, 86
  Help! 66, 86
  Lennon and McCartney song books 160, *160*
  Yellow Submarine 172
Beattie, Trevor
  French Connection 337
  Playtex 337, *337*
The Beautiful South 372, *372*
Beck's Beer 284, *287*
Beckwith, Carol *214*
Beecham Proprietaries *81*, 258, *260*
Beirut, Michael 446
Belford, Paul 324, *324*, *327*, *451*
Bell, Nick 471, *473*
Bell, Tim 82
Benn, Tony 276, *276*
Bennett, Alan 170
Bennett, Madeleine 204
  COOB'92 390, *390*
  Elsenham Foods 196, *196*
  International Coffee Organisation 220, *221*
  Penhaligon's 124, 196, *196*, 203, *203*
Benson & Hedges 96, 109–10, *110*, *112*, *176*, 177, 179, *197*, 240
Benson, Michael 444
Bensons 116
Bentley & Farrell *144*
Bentley/Farrell/Burnett
  Bosie's *19*
  Penguin Books 134, *134*
Bentley Rhythm Ace *458*
Benton, Anthea *365*
Benton Bowles 82
  IBM computers *21*
Bergasol 270, *271*
Berger, John 82
Berger, Warren 458
Berkeley Hotel 396
Berlei *133*
Bernbach, William 21, 179, 250, *285*
  Traffic Police *363*
  Volkswagen 21
Berners-Lee, Tim 310
Bernie's Tattooing *298*
Bernstein, David 82, 83
Bernstein, Leonard
  Trouble in Tahiti 171
Berry, Norman 82
Biba *57*, 83, 87, *87*
Big Life Records 380, *380*
Big magazine 384, *387*
Binder, Maurice 82
Bird's Eye Foods 96, *102*, 105, *105*, 179
Birdsall Daulby Mayhew Wildbur (BDMW) 82
Birdsall, Derek *26*, 40, 82, 83, *144*, *374*
  Penguin Books 53, *53*
Bisque Radiators 416, *417*
Bisto Kids 13
Björk *464*, 465
Black, Misha 54, 82
Black Sabbath 156, *158*
Black Star 364, *366*
Blackburn, John 196
  Gallaher *197*
  Harveys of Bristol 404, *405*
Blackrod *230*
Blackwell, Lewis *374*
Blair, Lionel 83
Blair, Tony 303
Blake, Peter 82, 428, *468*
Bloomsbury Publishers 396, *396*
Blow Up 82
Bluebell Apparel *240*
Blueprint magazine 218, *219*
Bluming, Adam *317*
Blur *303*
BMP Davidson Pearce
  Courage 274, *274*
BMP DDB 431
  London Transport 342, *342*
  Volkswagen 328, *329*, 342, 343, *349*, 354, *354*, 460, *463*
  Walkers Snack Foods 364, *366*
BMP DDB Needham
  Courage 368, *369*
  Health Education Authority *331*
  Multiple Sclerosis Society *321*
  Volkswagen 354, *354*
BMW 256, *256*, 439, *439*
Boase Massimi Pollitt (BMP) 82, 125–9, 179, 250, 268
  Barker & Dobson (Victory V) 115, *115*
  Cadbury Typhoo Foods 126, *127*, 179
  CPC *285*
  Ferrero *127*
  Fisher Price *280*
  Labour Party *130*
  Quaker Oats *127*, 129, 179
  Schweppes 125–6, *127*, *128*, 129
  Unigate Dairies *128*
  Unigate Foods *30*
  War on Want 288, *288*
Boase Massimi Pollitt Univas
  Barker & Dobson *128*
  Central Office of Information 266, *266*
  Courage Brewing *128*, *244*, 245, 248, 250, *251*
  Greater London Council *184*, 185, *208*, 269, *269*, 270, 271
  The Guardian 266, *266*
  L'Oréal *128*
  Renault *130*
  Sony 252, *252*
Boddingtons Bitter 324, *327*, 328
Boer, Michel de *225*
Boles, Mike *321*
book design 33, 53, 134, *136*, *149*, 211, 216, 220, 444
Bookbinder, Lester 82
  White Horse Distillers *118*, 179
Booth-Clibborn, Edward 30, 83
Boots 200, 400, *400*
Borge, Victor 104
Bosie's *19*
Boty, Pauline 82
Bovis *150*, 151
Bovril *272*, 273
Bowie, David 242
Bowyers *34*, 102
Boxer, Mark 38, 83
Bradbery, Ian 83
Bragg, Melvyn 170
brand building 275
brand management 14, 298, 302
'brand vocabulary' 304
branding 13, 203–7, 440, 451
Braniff 179
Brayley, Geoff
  BBC *52*
Brazier, Paul *321*
Brent Oppenheimer 390
Briggs, Raymond
  The Snowman 230, *230*
Brignull, Tony 96, 103, 109, 348
  Albany Life Assurance *282*
  Bird's Eye Foods *105*
  Gallaher *263*
  Parker Pen Company *100*
  Whitbread (Heineken) *97*, 103–4, *103*, 105
britart.com 432, *433*
British Airport Authority *150*
British Airways 344, *344*, 378
British European Airways 152, *153*
British Rail 54, *54*, 210, *210*, *266*, 267
British Telecom 207, 344, *345*, 378
Britpop 303

Britvic Soft Drinks *249*, 356, *356*
Broccoli, Cubby
Goldfinger 61, *61*
Brody, Neville 238
Fetish Records 238, *238*
Brookes, Peter 164
Brooks Baker & Fulford 83, 142, *143*, 179
Brooks, Bob *36*, 82, 83, 179, *468*
Gallaher *97*, 110
Yellow Pages 252, *252*
Brooks, Jill
The Snowman 230, *230*
Brown, David
Birds Eye 96
Parker Pen Company *105*
Royal National Institute for the Deaf *291*
Brown, Don *448*
Brown Holdings 294, *294*
Brown, Howard
Goldcrest Films & Television 220, *221*
Brown, Ron 321, *321*
Brown, Warren
Bryant & May *192*
Brownfield, Mick 273
Browning, Simon *377*
Brownjohn, Robert *26*, *31*, 82, 83
Apple & Pear Publicity Council *60*
Eon Productions 61, *61*
Fisons Foods *60*
Pickerings 124
Robert Fraser Gallery *60*
Bruce Mau 445
Brutus *133*
Bryant & May 192, *192*
Brylcreem 258, *260*
BSB Dorland
HJ Heinz Company 340, *341*
Woolworths 368, *369*
Budgen, Frank *331*
Guinness *456*, 457
Hutchison Telecom 304, *305*
Levi Strauss *456*, 457
Nike 457
Reebok *456*, 457
Tesco Stores 344
Budweiser 432, *433*
Bullmore, Jeremy 82, 396, *399*, 467
Burberry *445*
Burbridge, Richard *380*
Burd, Douglas
BBC Television 229–30, *229*, 230
Burton, Derek
Small Faces *18*
Bus Stop 87
Buschow Henley
Prospect Pictures 408, *410*
Buschow, Ralph *410*
Butler, Shine & Stern
San Francisco Jazz Organization 460, *463*

C
Cadbury Brothers 78, 78, *80*, 81
Cadbury Schweppes
Dubonnet 116, *117*
Cadbury Typhoo Foods
Smash Martians 126, *127*, 179
Caine, Michael 179
Callaghan, James 179, *276*
Calman, Mel *144*
Calvert, Margaret 54, *55*, 82
Cammell-Hudson Associates 62
Apple & Pear Publicity Council *60*
Campaign magazine 81, *81*
Campbell, Walter 344, 348
Guinness 350, 454
SP Tyres *347*
British Telecom *345*
Canna Kendall & Co *389*
Cannon, Dennis 83
Cannon, Geoffrey 162
Canongate Books 372, *374*
Cantona, Eric 333, *333*, *349*
Caravel Film Services
BBC Television *229*
Carling Black Label 364, *365*
Carr, Jeremy *451*
Carreno, Jorge *451*
Carroll & Dempsey
English National Opera 378, *379*
Faber & Faber 211, *212*
Manpower Services Commission *216*
Post Office 211, *211*
Carroll Dempsey Thirkell (CDT) 211, *472*, 474
Virgin Records & The LCO 236, *236*
Carroll, Ken *212*, *216*
Carruthers, Rooney *352*
Carter Hedger Mitchell & Partners
Romix Foods 284, *286*
Carter Wong
Katsouris Brothers 203, *203*
Cartlidge Levene
Wordsearch *382*, 384
Carty, Tom 344, 348
Guinness 350, 454
SP Tyres *347*
British Telecom *345*
Casey, Ben *374*
Casson Mann
Science Museum 440, 441, *441*
catchphrases 78, 81
Cattaneo, Tony *80*
Caulfield, Patrick *451*
CDT Design
Royal Mail 426, *426*, 428, *428*
celebrities, use of 81
Central Independent Television
Spitting Image 182, *182*, 228–9, *228*
Central Office of Information 262, *262*, 266, *266*
Central Saint Martins College of Art & Design 82, 314
Chaldecott, Axel
Holsten Pils 246
Time Out *272*, 273
William Levene *249*
Chamber of Coal Traders *266*
Channel Four Television
identity 182, 226–8, *227*, 448, *448*
Max Headroom 189–91, *190*
The Snowman 230, *230*
Wired 232, *232*
Chaplin, Charlie 364
charity accounts 288–91, 330, 362
Charles Hobson & Grey 36, *36*, 82
Chas 'n' Dave *244*, 251
The Chase
Alibaba Verlag 372, *374*
Cheeseman, Len *289*, *472*
Chefaro Proprietaries *270*
Chemical Brothers *459*
Chemstrand *63*, *64*
Cherry Hedger & Seymour
Standard Brands 284, *286*
Chiat, Jay 290
Childline 362, *362*
Chipperfield, David
Joseph Ettedgui/Kenzo *408*
Chivas & Brothers *434*
Christensen, David *282*
Christian Aid *25*
Christopherson, Peter 156
Chrysalis Records *238*
Churchill/Holmes/Kitley
Shell BP News *74*
Ciba Gelgy 269, *270*
cinema *see* film
Cinzano *109*
Circa Records 372, *372*, 380, *380*
Clapton, Eric *154*
Claridge, John *291*
Clark, Ossie 83
Clarke, John *471*
Clarks Shoes 148, *149*
Clarkson, Dawn *472*
Cleaver, Phil
The Type Museum 395, *395*
Cliff Freeman & Partners 11
Fox Network 361, *361*, *461*
Little Caesars Enterprises *266*, 267
outpost.com 361, *361*
Club 18-30 318, *318*, 451, *452*
CND 82
Coalition for the Homeless 362, *362*
Coates, Stephen *219*
Wordsearch 384, *384*
Coca-Cola Company 404, *405*
Cold War 255, *255*
Cole, George *106*, *110*
Cole, John 83
Coley Porter Bell
Chivas & Brothers *434*
Collett Dickenson Pearce (CDP) 14, 36, 62, 82, 92, 94–115, 179, 268, 333
Barclaycard 96, *97*
Beck's 284
Benson & Hedges 109–10, *110*, *112*, 177
Bird's Eye Foods 96, *102*, 105, *105*
Central Office of Information *98*
Chemstrand *63*, *64*
Cinzano 109
Daily Express 109
Dunn & Co *64*, *103*
Fiat 109, *112*, 256, *256*
Gallaher 97, 109, 110, 112, 227, 227, 258, *259*, *263*
General Post Office 105, *106*
Great Ormond Street Hospital 288, *288*
Hovis *94*, *109*
John Harvey & Sons *64*
Metropolitan Police 96, *97*, 288, *289*
Monsanto *63*
Olympus Optical Company *106*, 276, *276*
Parker Pen Company *100*, *101*, *105*, *268*, 269
Pretty Polly *94*, *97*
Radio Rentals (Max Headroom) 190, *190*
Satinath Sarangi 330, *330*
Scottish & Newcastle Breweries (Beck's) *287*
Selfridges *71*
Wall's Meat Company *94*
Whitbread *97*, 103–4, *103*, *105*, 177, *259*
Collett, John 94
Collins, Jeanette
The Times Women's Page *40*
Collins, Jesse 82
Collins, Joan 109
Collins, John 83
Collins, Ron *270*
Collis, Graham
Unigate Dairies *128*
Collis, Paul *190*
Colman Prentis & Varley
Yardley 31, *31*
colour printing 40
Commander, John *29*, 83
Commercial Union 245, 276, *277*
Compaq 431, *431*
computer graphics *see* digital technology
Condé Nast *215*, 238
Condor, Simon
Yo! Sushi 442, *442*
Connolly *415*
Conran Design Group
Habitat 56, *57*
Conran, Shirley 83
Conran, Terence 56, 59, 82, 189, 191, 292
Conservative Party *176*, 177, 182
COOB'92 390, *390*
Cooper, Kyle
Gattaca titles 316, *317*
Se7en titles 316, *317*
Cooper Thirkell
The Independent 218
Penguin Books 211, *211*
Victoria & Albert Museum 211, *211*
Cooper-Clark, John *298*
Cornmarket 38, 40, 81
Cornthwaite, Graham *285*, *306*
Corona Soft Drinks *249*
Coronation Street 105
cosmetics 31, *31*, 59, *59*
Cotier, James 300, *300*
Cottrell, Julian *469*
counter culture 31
The Country Diary of an Edwardian Lady 192, *195*
Courage Brewing *128*, *244*, 245, 248, 250, *251*, 274, *274*, 368, *369*
pub signs 213, *213*
Cow & Gate 280, *280*
Cow Lane Garage *389*
Cowan Kemsley Taylor
Ginsters Pies *358*
Taunton Cider 356, *358*
Cozens, Mike 109
Lego 252
Levi Strauss *255*
CPC *285*
Crabtree & Evelyn 195, *195*
Craddock, Barry
Scottish & Newcastle Breweries 284, *287*
Crafts Council 387, *387*
Craig, Colin *470*
Cramer, Ross 71
Cramer Saatchi 71, 83, 88
Cunard Line 284, *285*
Health Education Council 88, *88*
Crawfords 34, 40
Cream 380, *380*
Creative Review magazine 238, 248, 292
Creme, Lol 239–40, 242
'An Englishman in New York' 240
Benson & Hedges 240
Bluebell Apparel *240*
Frankie Goes to Hollywood 240, *240*
Polydor ('Cry') 242, *242*
Cresta bear 125–6, *127*, 179
Crosby/Fletcher/Forbes 142, *143*, *144*, 146
Brooks Baker & Fulford 142, *143*
Guest & Hughes *143*
Mears Caldwell Hacker *143*
Crosby, Theo 33, 82, 142, 146
Cross, Judy 129
Crossfield, Anthony *475*
Crouch, Bruce
Bryant & May *192*
Crowther, Peter *473*
Cubic Metre Furniture 204, *204*
Cucumber Products *190*
Cunard Line 284, *285*
Cunningham, Chris
One Little Indian Records *464*, 465
Sony *464*, 465
Warp Records 368, *370*, 372
Cuthbert, R & G *150*
Cutter, David
Go Discs 372, *372*
CYB Design Consultants
Tesco *198*, 199

D
Daily Express 83, *109*, 164
Daltrey, Roger *158*
D'Amico & Partners 402, *403*
Dandelion Records *154*
Dar Salons 292, *293*
D'Arcy Maslus Benton & Bowles
Royal Mail Letters 314, *314*
Daulby, George 83, *468*
Davenport Designs
Rosehaugh Stanhope Developments 216, *217*
Davenport, Peter 216, *217*
Brian Griffin 216, *217*
Davey, Andy 294, *294*, 414, *415*
David Davies Associates
Next 191, *191*
David, Elizabeth 82
Davidson, Andrew
Faber & Faber *212*
Davidson Pearce Berry & Spottiswoode
International Wool Secretariat *140*
Davidson Pearce Berry & Tuck (DPBT) 82
Ilford *77*
Wates *77*
Davidson, Tony *354*
Davies Baron *191*
Davies, David 191, *191*
Davies, George 190
DDB Chicago
Anheuser Busch 432, *433*
DDB Needham Worldwide
VAG UK 250, *250*
De Majo, Willy 82
De Stijl 238
De Thame, Gerard *345*
Dean, Richard *369*
Debenham & Freebody *74*
Dedicated Records 406, *406*
Dee, Jack 368, *369*

Deepend
Volkswagen *309*, 395
Deighton, Len 82, 83
Del Naja, Robert *372*
Delaney, Tim 179, *246*, *285*
Dempsey, Mike *212*, *216*, *472*, *474*
English National Opera 236, *236*, 378, *379*
Penguin Books 211, *211*
Virgin Records & The LCO 236, *236*
Derek Forsyth Partnership
Pirelli 120, *120*, 122, *122*
Design & Art Directors Association (D&AD) 28–9
Ambient Media 270
annuals 10, 29
awards 10, 15, 26, 29, *29*, 31, 36, 37
formation 83
identity *28*, 29
Interactive Media 308, 395
President's Award 71
Product Design 414–22
purpose 26, 29
Design Council 12
Design magazine *204*
Design Museum 189
Design Research Unit (DRU) 54, 82
British Railways 54, *54*
Design Review magazine 191
Design Week magazine 81
Dickens & Jones 284, *285*
Dickenson, Ronnie 94, 105
Dickerson, Brandon *463*
Diesel 395, *395*
digital technology 14, 15, 190, 194, 226–8, 298, 308–16, 390, 423, 426
computer animation *245*
Din Associates
Nicole Farhi 408, *409*
Dindisc Records *234*
direct marketing 430
Dixon, Peter 198
Domus magazine *219*
Donovan, Janet 83
Donovan, Terence 83
Guinness *117*
Doritos 364, *366*
Dorland Advertising
Cadbury Schweppes 116, *117*
H J Heinz 105, *106*
Doust, Richard
Zandra Rhodes *58*
Doyle Advertising & Design Group
Dunham Company 302, *302*
Doyle Dane Bernbach (DDB) 11, 82, 92, 179
Bryant & May 192, *192*
Christian Aid *25*
Commercial Union 245, 276, *277*
Corona Soft Drinks (Tango) *249*
London Weekend Television *21*
Lufthansa Airlines *92*
Remington Electric Shavers *22*, *25*
Tern Consulate *21*, *25*
Uniroyal *22*, *72*, 73
Volkswagen *92*, 115, 177, 179, 268–9, *268*
Doyle, John *302*
Drake, Mo
HJ Heinz 78, *78*
Driver, David *470*
Radio Times 162, *162*, 164, 165, *165*
The Times Saturday review 165
Droga, David *428*
Dubonnet 116, *117*
Duffy (Brian) 83
Dumb Animals 186, *186*
Dumbar, Gert 139, 222, *223*, 225, 376, 378
Nederlandse Spoorwegen 139, *139*
PTT Nederland NV 376, *377*
Dundas, David
'Jeans On' *133*
Dunham Company 302, *302*
Dunlop Tyres 344, 346, *347*
Dunn & Co *64*, *103*
Dunn, Steve *323*
Dunning, George
The Righteous Apple 172
Yellow Submarine 172
Dylan, Bob *354*
Dymock, Andy *475*
Dyson, James 416–17, *417*

E
Eames, Charles 21
Eames, Ray 21
Eckersley, Tom 82
The Economist magazine 72, 274–5, *275*, 324, 328, *329*, 337, *337*, 451, *451*
Edelman, Heinz 82
Edmonson, Adrian 368, *369*
Edwards, Barney
The Samaritans *262*
Edwards Churcher *431*
eighties 14, 15, 180–294
EL Al Israel Airlines 71, *71*
Electricity Association 368, *369*
Elfer, Arpad 82
Ellman, Paul 384, *384*
Elmassian, Jeff 464
Elsenham Quality Foods 196, *196*
EMAP On Air 458, *458*
Emperor Rosko 129
English, Bob 232
English Markell Pockett 232
English, Michael 82
English National Opera 236, *236*, 378, *379*
environmental design 15, 33, 408–13, 426, 440–2
Epic 368, *370*
Ericsson Information Systems (*The Guardian*) 218, *219*
Esquire magazine *45*
Esterson, Simon *219*
Blueprint 218, *219*
Domus 219
Eurostar 418, *419*
Eusden, Colin *471*
Evans, Harry 83
Evans, Laurie *473*
Evans, Tony *146*, *470*, *471*
Debenham & Freebody *74*
Evans, Walker *40*
Evansky, Rose 83
Eye magazine *219*, *382*, 384, *384*
Eyre, Richard 213

F
Faber & Faber 211, *212*
The Face magazine 182, 238
Face Photosetting 136, *136*, *149*
Facetti, Germano *26*, 82, 83
Penguin Books 53, *53*
Factory Communications *235*
Factory Records 234, *234*
Fallon McElligott
MTV Networks 458, *459*
Fallover, Bill
Nova 45, *48*
Family *158*
Fantoni, Barry *45*
Fargo Design Associates
Mary Quant Cosmetics 59, *59*
Farhi, Nicole 408, *409*
Farrow Design 472, *475*
Arista, Spaceman 448, *448*
Farrow, Mark 234, *234*, *235*, 236, 238
Cream 380, *380*
Dedicated Records 406, *406*
PSPB 380, *380*
Faulds Advertising
BBC Radio Scotland *311*
Faure *358*
Federici, Anna 292, *293*
Fendley, Tim *394*
Fern, Dan 200, *200*, 208
Liberty's of London *208*
Ferrero *127*
Festival of Britain 21
Fetish Records 238, *238*
Feurer, Hans *48*
International Distillers & Vintners *115*
Fiat 109, *112*, 256, *256*
FIFA 306
fifties 14, 21, 26
film 18, 19, 61–2, *61*, 179
Absolute Beginners 242
Bladerunner (Scott) *262*
The Blair Witch Project 310
Blow Up 82
Bugsy Malone (Parker) 104, 105, 134
Chelsea Girls (Warhol) 18, 19
cinema advertising 66
Crocodile Dundee 259
The Dambusters 364, *365*
Dead Men Don't Wear Plaid 246
Dead Man on Campus 316
The French Lieutenant's Woman 117
Gattaca 316, *317*
Goldfinger title sequence (Brownjohn) 61, *61*
Hard Day's Night (Lester) 66, 82, 86
Help! (Lester) 66, 86
Highlander 242
The Italian Job 256
Jaws 255
Jean de Florette 364
The Knack (Lester) 66
Red Monarch 220, *221*
Saturday Night and Sunday Morning 117
Se7en 316, *317*
The Swimmer 352
Trainspotting 380, *382*
Tron 226
Yellow Submarine 82
Fincher, David
Se7en 316, *317*
Findus Eskimo Food 80, *80*
Fine Fare *198*, 199, 210
The Fine White Line Communications Company
London Underground 220, *221*
Scottish & Newcastle Breweries 284, *287*
Fink, Graham 104, 310
Metropolitan Police *289*
Fior, Robin 82
Fischer, Carl 164
Fisher, Gregor *259*
Fisher, Jeff 208, *428*
Bloomsbury Publishers 396, *396*
Minneapolis College of Art 209–10, *209*
Fisher Price *280*
Fisons Foods *60*
Fitch & Company Design Consultants 189
Midland Bank 292, *293*
Thresher Wine Merchants *189*
Fitch, Rodney 82, 189
Fleckhaus, Willy 83
Fleming, Fergus *289*
Fletcher, Alan 29, 33, *61*, 71, 78, 82, 146, 209
Brooks Baker & Fulford 142, *143*
IBM Europe *208*
Reuters identity 142, *143*
Fletcher/Forbes/Gill 33, 82, 83, 142, 146, *468*, 469
D&AD catalogue *29*
D&AD poster *29*
International Scientific Systems *33*
Penguin Books 33, *33*
Fletcher, Howard 290, *291*
Flintham, Richard 342
Doritos 364, *366*
Fluck, Peter 48, 164, 176
Spitting Image 182, *182*, 228–9, 228
Flying Colours 318, *318*
Folio Society 396, *396*
Fong, Karin *317*
Foot, Michael 276
Forbes, Colin 82, 83, 146
D&AD identity *28*, 29, 33
foreign-language award entries 15
Foreman, Michael *144*
Forrest, Matt
Britvic Soft Drinks 356, *357*
Initial Film & Television 232, *232*
Forsyth, Derek 82, 83
Forsythe, Max *277*
Foster, Doug 350, *351*
Foster, Norman 194
National Botanic Garden of Wales 440, *441*
Fosters 258, *259*, 342, *343*
The Foundry 395
Four IV Design Consultants
Burberry *445*
National Portrait Gallery 402, *403*
Fox Network 361, *361*
Fox Sports 460, *461*
fractals 190
Francis Dreyfus Music 236, *236*
Frankie Goes to Hollywood 240, *240*
Frascati Theatre *376*
Freeman, Robert *53*, 82
Beatles 28, *28*
French Connection 337
French Cruttenden Osborne (FCO)
Central Office of Information 262, *262*
Ciba Gelgy 269, *270*
White Horse Distillers 116, *118*
French Gold Abbott *72*, 82
French, John 83
French, Richard 262
Fretwell, Jason *306*
Friedeberger, Klaus 82
Friends of the Earth 337, *337*
Froshaug, Anthony 82
Frost, Vince 384, *387*, *475*
Fuel 310
Fulford, Len 179, *468*
FutureBrand *191*

G
Gabriel, Peter 244, *244*
Galbraith, J K
American Capitalism 33, *33*
Gallaher *97*, *109*, *110*, *112*, *197*, 227, *227*, 240, 258, *259*, *263*
Games, Abram 82
Garfath, David *331*
Garforth, Steve *471*
Garland, Ken 82
Garnett, Alf 80, *80*
Garrett, James 83
Gascoigne, Bamber 83
Gaskin, Malcolm 472, *472*
Land Rover *287*
Gatley, Peter *331*
Greater London Council *184*
Gavin, Pat
Amberson Video (*Trouble in Tahiti*) *171*
London Weekend Television 170, *171*, 230, *230*
Gay, Paul 354
Gaye, Marvin 256
GBH 474, *475*
Geer Du Bois
Mental Health Trust *50*
Geers, Bob 82, 83
Geers Gross 82
Spillers 80, *80*
Gentleman, David 428
George, Adrian 164
George, John *140*
GGK London
Electricity Association 368, *369*
Gill, Bob 33, 82, 83, 142, *144*, 146, *469*
'Bob Gill's New York' *33*
Fisons Foods *60*
Gill, Nick *354*
Gillard, John 82
Ginsters Pies *358*
Girobank 152
Gladwell, Guy *165*
Glasgow 1999: UK City of Architecture and Design *394*, 395
Glaxo *417*
Glazer, Jonathan
Guinness 350, *351*, 454
Island Records 368, *370*, 372
Nike 303, *303*
globalization 14–15, 298, 303–4, 349, 428–9
Gluck, Malcolm *25*
Go Discs 372, *372*
Go fly 378, *379*
Godard, Keith 83
Godfrey, Jason *473*
Godfrey, Neil *21*, 96, 109, 470, *470*, *474*
Albany Life Assurance *282*
Bird's Eye Foods *102*, *105*
Gallaher *263*
Lufthansa Airlines *92*
Metropolitan Police 289
Parker Pen Company *100*
Whitbread *97*, 103–4, *103*, *105*
Godley, Kevin 239–40, 242
'An Englishman in New York' 240

Benson & Hedges 240
Bluebell Apparel *240*
Frankie Goes to Hollywood 240, *240*
Polydor ('Cry') 242, *242*
Gold Greenlees Trott (GGT) 250, 268, 333
Holsten Distributors 192, 246, *246*, 248
London Weekend Television 272, *272*
Taunton Cider Company 364, *365*
Time Out 272, 273
Toshiba 248, *249*
William Levene *249*
Goldcrest Films & Television 220, *221*
Golden Wonder 356, *358*
Goldhawke Records *158*
Gondry, Michael
Virgin Records *459*
Gorbachev, Mikhail 11
Gorham, John 82, 134, 136, *144*, *474*
Bugsy Malone identity 134, *134*
Face Photosetting *149*
Goldcrest Films & Television 220, *221*
'Lion' chocolate bar 134, *134*
Gormley, Antony *428*
Gorse, John *323*
Goude, Jean-Paul
Island Records 236, *236*
Granada Media 430, *430*
Grandfield, Geoff
Folio Society 396, *396*
Grange, Kenneth 82, 146
Graphis magazine 83
Gray, Milner 54, 82
Great Ormond Street Hospital 288, *288*
Greater London Council *184*, 185, *208*, 269, *269*, *270*, 271
Green, Pete *471*
Greenburg, David 316
Greenburgh, Judith *289*
Greenlees, Michael 246
Greenpeace (Dumb Animals) 186, *186*
Greg Stogden, Jay Hess
Tank Publications *448*
Gregory Bonner Hale (GBH) 474
Gregory, Laura *366*
Greiman, April 222
Grey
Beecham Proprietaries 258, *260*
Griffin, Brian 216, *217*
Grimwood, Brian 204, 208, 209, *209*
Grinyer, Clive 436
Gross, Bob 82, 83
The Guardian 218, *219*, 266, *266*
Guess Jeans 364, *366*
Guest & Hughes *143*
Guide Dogs for the Blind 288, *290*
Guinness 116, *117*, 350, *351*, 448, *451*, 454, *454*, *456*, 457
Gutiérrez, Fernando 379, *474*

H
Häagen-Dazs 318, *318*
Habitat 56, *57*, 82, 214
The Habitat Group 330, *330*
Hackett, Denis 45, 83
Hacks *128*
Hadfields 34, *34*
Haggerty, Brett
Readymix Drypack 203, *203*
Hall Advertising
Scottish Health Education Trust *176*, 177
Halpin, Geoff *238*
Hamilton, Paula *250*
Hamilton, Richard 82
Hamlet 96, 227, *227*, 258, *259*
Hamlyn, Paul 82
Hammett, Dashiell *53*
Hardie, George *428*
Black Sabbath 156, *158*
Mr Freedom 134, *134*
Thames Television 158
Harley Davidson 302
Harper Mackay
Ian Schrager Hotels *442*
Mujirushi Ryohin Europe 408, *408*
Harper's Bazaar magazine 39
Harrison, Oliver 314
Harrison Troughtman
Vodaphone 430
Harrods 124, *124*, *200*, 284, *285*
Harrop, Wendy 214, *214*
Hart, Anna 227
Hart, Malcolm *26*, 82, 83
Harvey, Cy 195
Harvey Nichols *380*, 400, 404, *405*, 413, *413*
Harveys of Bristol *64*, 404, *405*
Hass, Derrick 104
Barker & Dobson 115, *115*, 128
Royal National Institute for the Deaf 290, *291*
Hastings, Max *219*
Havindon, Ashley 82
Hawkey, Ray 83
Hawkins, Stephen 344, *345*
Hayman, Shawen *472*
Haymarket Publishing Group
Campaign magazine 82, *82*
Hazzard, Nick
White Horse Distillers *118*
HDA International 152
Heal & Son 210, *210*
Healey, Denis 276, *276*
Health Education Authority 331
Health Education Council 88, *88*, *91*, *176*, 177
Heartfield, John 152
Heath, Edward 152–3, 179
Heatherwick, Thomas
Harvey Nichols 413, *413*
Hedgecoe, John 83
Hedger Mitchell Stark
Watney Mann & Truman Brewers 258, *259*
Hefner, Hugh 82
Hegarty, John 82, 179, *268*, 269
EL Al Israel Airlines 71, *71*, 77
Health Education Council *88*
Levi Strauss 255, *257*
Smith & Nephew 280
Heighway-Bury, Robin 340
Heineken 96, *97*, 103–4, *103*, 105, 177, 250, *251*, 269, *269*, 271
Heinz 78, *78*, 105, *106*, 179, 340, *341*, 434, *434*
Helias, Eric *451*
Hellmann's Mayonnaise 284, *285*
Henley, Simon *410*
Henrion Design Associates 152
British European Airways 152, *153*
Henrion, FHK 82, 152
Henrion, Ludlow & Schmidt *153*
Henry, Steve
Holsten Pils 246
Time Out 272, 273
William Levene *249*
Henry, Suzie *279*
Hepburn, Kate
Francis Dreyfus Music 236, *236*
Heseltine, Michael 40, *82*
Hey, Martyn *472*
Hillman, David 82, 83, *146*, 165, *293*
The Guardian 218, *219*
Interior Design International *388*
Him, George 82
Hingston, Tom *372*
Hipgnosis 156
Black Sabbath 156, *158*
Led Zeppelin 156, *156*
Pink Floyd 156
historical pastiche 191–216, *260*, 292
HMV dog 13
Hobsbawn, Eric 196
Hockney, David 82, 179
Hogan, Paul 258, *259*
Hogarth, Paul 82
Hoggins, Keith 256
Holiday, Billie 348, *349*
Holland Festival 225, *225*
Hollens, Jerry 342
Hollis, Richard 40, 82
Hollyhead, Bush 208, *208*, 209
Holmes, Adrian
Whitbread & Company *251*
Holmes, Nigel
Island Records *155*
Radio Times 162, 164
Holsten Pils 192, 246, *246*, 248
Homepride 80, *80*
Honey Monster 125, *127*, 129, 179
Horn & Hardart 179
Horry, David 104, 109, *472*
Fiat *256*
Horton, John *329*
Hospital Design Partnership *150*
Hovis 94, *109*
Howe, Vernon 104
Howell Henry Chaldecott Lury (HHCL) *272*
Britvic Soft Drinks *249*, 356, *356*
Maxell 354, *354*
Hoza, John 280
Hudson, Hugh 62, 109, 179
Benson & Hedges 109, *112*, 179, 240
British Airways 344, *344*
Cinzano 109
Courage Brewing 250, *251*
Fiat 109, 256, *256*
Levi Strauss *132*
Hughes & Moulton
Cow Lane Garage *389*
Hughes, David 372, *374*
Hughes, Graham
Roger Daltrey *158*
Hughes, Ted
The Iron Man 211, *212*
Hulanicki, Barbara 87
Hunt Lascaris TBWA
Childline 362, *362*
Hurrell, George *192*
Hutchison Telecom 304, *305*
Huygens, Frederique 292
Hyland, Angus 372, *374*

I
IBM computers 21, *21*, 208
ICA 82
i-D magazine 238, 384, *384*
Ideal Standard *419*
Identica Partnership *238*
IDEO 417–18
NEC 416, *417*
Nike 418, *418*
Qubit *415*
IdN Magazine 431, *431*
Ilford *77*
Illumination 232, *232*
illustration 204, 207–13, 273, 284–8, 300
Imaginary Forces
Dead Man on Campus titles 316
Immediate Records *18*
Imperial Tobacco 340, *341*
The Independent 182, 218, *298*
Independent Television (ITV) identity 232
The Industrial Design Partnership 54
Initial Film & Television 232, *232*
Ink Studios
Andy Warhol's *Chelsea Girls* poster 18, *19*
interactive media 15, 308, *309*
Interbrew 434–5, *434*
Interior Design International *388*
International Distillers & Vintners 115, *115*
International Scientific Systems *33*
International Wool Secretariat *140*
internet 11, 310
Isaacs, Jeremy 227
Isherwood, Bob 81, 104
Parker Pen Company *100*
Island Records *155*, 236, *236*, 368, *370*, 372
Italian Institute of Foreign Trade 151
Itch
Science Museum 440, 441, *441*
Ive, Jonathan 421, *421*, 423, 436, *437*, 438
Violette Editions *445*

J
J Player & Sons *64*
J Sainsbury 276, *278*
J Walter Thompson (JWT) 30, 82, 83, 188, 333
Beecham Products *81*
Findus Eskimo Food 81, *81*
Guinness 116, *117*
Smarties 227
US Sprint *188*, 267
Jackson, Michael and Janet 368, *370*
Jaeger *200*
Jafri, Faiyaz *451*
James, Clive 170
James, David
Big Life Records 380, *380*
James McNaughton Paper 392, *392*
James Robertson & Sons *275*
Jankel, Annabel
Max Headroom 189–91, *190*
Jarre, Jean-Michel 236, *236*
Jarvis, Paul *189*
JCB Teletruk 418, *419*
Jeapes, Alan 69
BBC *69*, 312
Jeffries, Desmond 82
Jenkins, Karl *255*
Jennings, Garth
Parlophone *458*
Jiricna, Eva 292, *293*
Jobs, Steve 421, *421*, 436, *438*, 439
John Blackburn & Partners
Gallaher *197*
John Collings & Partners
EL Al Israel Airlines 71, *71*
John, Elton
'I'm Still Standing' 242, *242*
John Harvey & Sons *64*
John Smith's Yorkshire Bitter *244*, 245, 248, 274, *274*, 368, *369*
John West 451, *452*, 460, *463*
johnson banks
Canna Kendall & Co *389*
Smurfit Townsend Hook 448, *448*
Yellow Pages 394, *395*
Johnson, Michael 7, 207, *474*, 475
Johnson, Stephen
Virgin Records 244, *244*
Jolliffe, Gray 104, 469, *469*
Jones, Allen 82, *469*, 470
Pirelli 122, *122*
Jones Garrard
Eurostar 418, *419*
Jones, Geoffrey
Shell 29, 31
Jones, Grace 236, *236*
Jones identity 207, *207*
Jones, Terry 238
Jones, Tom 83, 430
Joseph 406, *406*
Joseph Ettedgui 408, *408*
Joy Division 234, *234*, *235*
Judah, Gerry *186*
Juniper, David
Atlantic Records *156*
The Jupiter Drawing Room
KFM Radio 431–2, *431*

K
Kalman, Tibor 14, 191
Kamen, Nick 256, *257*
Kander, Nadav 302, *302*
Karavias, Dimitri *471*
Katsouris Brothers 203, *203*
Kaye, Tony 7, 267, 344, 473, *474*
British Rail 266, *267*
British Telecom 344
Chamber of Coal Traders *266*, 267
Nike 348
SP Tyres 344, *347*
British Telecom *345*
Volkswagen 348, *349*, 354
Volvo *347*, 348, *348*
Kean, Adam *306*
Keaney, Siobhan
API Corporation 376, *377*
Keeler, Christine 82
Keith, Penelope *105*
Kelly, Ben *234*
National Museum of Science & Industry 411, *412*
Kennedy, Roger *306*
BBC (*Horizon* titles) *172*
Kenny, Sean 82
Kenzo 408, *408*
Kerr, Joe 372, *374*
Kestle, Ian
Thames Television (*The World at War*) *173*
Kettle, Stephen *472*
Key, Trevor 235

KFM Radio 431–2, *431*
King, David 40, 83
  The Sunday Times magazine 77, *77*, 164
King, Sidney 83
King, Stephen 310
Kingsley, David 83
Kingsley Manton & Palmer 83
Kinneir Associates
  road signs 54, *55*
Kinneir, Jock 54, *55*, 82, 83
Kinney Record Group *154*, *155*
Kinsman Associates
  OMK Design 294, *294*
Kirkwood, Ronnie 82
Kitchenware Merchants 322, *323*
Kitching, Alan *387*
Klause Wuttke & Partners *140*
Klein Design 36
Klein, Lou 36, 82, 83, *144*, *468*, *469*
  D&AD awards design 10, 36, 37
  Reed Paper Group 36, *36*, 37
  Sexton Shoe Company 36, *64*
  Spicers 36, *36*
  Time International 37
Klein, Naomi
  No Logo: Taking Aim at the Brand Bullies 15, 428–9
Klein Peters 36, *64*
  Sexton Shoe Company 36, *64*
Klimowski, Andrzej *428*
KLM 152
KMP Partnership 82
  Salvation Army 50, *50*
Knight, Nick
  Circa, Virgin Records 372, *372*
  Levi Strauss 300, *300*
  Skinhead 216, *216*
Knight, Robin 429
Koewelden-Postma
  Frascati Theatre 376, *376*
Koolhaas, Rem *445*
Kosh, John
  Family *158*
Kurlansky, Mervyn 82, 146
  Roche Products *146*
  Zinc Development Association *146*
Kwok, Bert *249*
Kynoch Press *33*

L
Labour Party *130*
Labovitch, Clive 40
Lambie-Nairn, Martin *69*, 230, 232
  BBC identity 444, *444*
  BBC1 identity 232
  BBC2 identity 227–8, 232, 312, *313*, 314
  Channel 4 identity 182, 226–8, 227
  Gallaher 227, *227*
  Smarties 227
  Spitting Image 228–9
Land Rover 284, *287*
Landels, Willy 82
Larkin May & Company *471*
Larsen *343*
Lassie 364
Lategan, Barry
  Condé Nast *215*
  Olympus Optical Company *215*
Laufer, Andreas *448*
Lavery, Peter *472*
Law, Roger *48*, 83, 164, 176
  Spitting Image 182, *182*, 228–9, *228*
Laws, Peter *470*
Layton Awards 83
Le Creuset 322, *323*
Le Garsmeur, Alain *469*
Le Nez Rouge Wine Club 203, *203*
Leagas Delaney
  Adidas 330
  BBC 313, *313*
  Harrods 284, 285
  Linguaphone 284, *285*
The Leagas Delaney Partnership
  Philips Video Division 246, *246*
Learmont, Larry
  Barker & Dobson *128*
Led Zeppelin *156*
Lee, Bruce 364
Lee, Harper
  To Kill a Mockingbird 53, *53*
Leeves, Paul 284
Lego 252, *252*, 276, *276*
Lennon, John 86, 160, *160*
Leo Burnett
  HJ Heinz 434, *434*
  John West 451, *452*, 460, *463*
Leonard, Michael *41*
Lester, Richard 61, *62*, 82
  Chemstrand 62, *63*
  Hard Day's Night 66, 86
  Help! 66, 86
  The Knack 66
Levi Strauss *132*, 182, *240*, 255–6, *255*, *257*, 300, *300*, 302, 308, *309*, 323, *323*, 333, *333*, 352, *352*, *456*, 457, 460
Levitt, Theodore *399*
Lewin, Nick *255*
Lewis, Carl *327*
Lewis, Juliette *366*
Lewis, Maggie *268*
  Parker Pen Company *100*
Lewis, Mary *473*
  Asda 200, *200*
  Boots 400, *400*
Lewis Moberly *199*, 400, 402, *473*
  Asda 200, *200*
  Boots 400, *400*
  Safeway 400, *400*
Liberty's of London *208*
Lidster, Ken *361*
Liebovitz, Annie *327*
Lilly, Ken
  Bovis *150*
Lindley, Michael *472*
Linguaphone 284, *285*
Linklater, Magnus 165
'Lion' chocolate bar 134, *134*
Lippa, Dominic *199*
Lippa, Mario *468*
Lippa Pearce *199*
  Witness 444, *445*
Litchfield, David
  Ritz 165
Little Caesars Enterprises *266*, 267
Live Aid *288*
Livingstone, Ken *184*, 185, 271
Lloyd, John *472*
Lloyd Northover *472*, 473
Lodge, Bernard 69, 82
  BBC *Dr Who* credits 66, *67*
  BBC *Playhouse 175*
  BBC *Teletale* titles 66, *67*
  Blackrod 230, *230*
  Hamlet 258
Loe, Linda *472*
Logan, Nick 238
Lois, George 45, *64*
London Chamber Orchestra *236*
London Eye 426, *426*, 428, 440
London Transport 342, *342*
London Underground *80*, 220, *221*, *285*
London Weekend Television *21*, 170, *171*, *230*, 272, *272*
  The South Bank Show 170, *171*
Lord, Rod
  BBC Television *230*
L'Oréal *128*
Lovegrove, Ross *415*
Lovegrove Studio
  Ty Nant 434–5, *434*
Lovelock, Terry
  Whitbread 96, *97*, 103–4, *103*, *105*
Lowe
  Reebok *456*, 457
Lowe, Chris 234
Lowe, Frank 82, 104, 109
Lowe Howard-Spink
  Albany Life Assurance 280, *282*
  Imperial Tobacco 340, *341*
  The Independent 298
  Olympus Cameras 322, *323*
  Reebok 330, *331*
  Tesco Stores 344, *344*
  Whitbread 250, *251*, 364, *365*
Lowe Howard-Spink Campbell-Ewald
  Whitbread & Company *270*, 271
Lowe Howard-Spink Marschalk
  Whitbread & Company 269, *269*
Lowe Lintas
  Whitbread Beer Company 451, *452*
Lowenhoff, Barry *472*
Luchford, Glen 302
Lufthansa Airlines *92*
Lumsden, Norman 252
Lunn, Simon *474*
Lyne, Adrian 62
  Levi Strauss *132*
Lynott, Phil 239
Lyons, Roger
  Levi Strauss 256, *257*

M
MacLaren, Malcolm 344
McCabe, Ed 179
McCann-Erickson 82
  Friends of the Earth 337, *337*
  Levi Strauss *132*
  Taylor-Woods: Lifelons *60*
McCartney, Paul
  'Frog Chorus' 185
McConnell, John 82, 83 *144*, 146, 148, 160, *212*, 472, *473*
  Biba *57*, 87, *87*
  Face Photosetting *136*, *149*
  Penguin Books *149*
McCormack, Richard *441*
McCullin, Don 50, 83, 164, *169*, 179, 288, *289*, 428, *428*
McEvoy, Vincent
  RSO Records *154*
McEwan, Ian 213
McGhee, Henry 129
McGhie, Charles
  BBC (*The Body in Question*) *175*
McKay, Andy *333*
McKenzie River Corporation 364, *366*
McLaren Dunkley Friedlander
  Fisons Foods *60*
McLeod, Andy
  Doritos 364, *366*
McLuhan, Marshal 82
McMillan, Ian 245
Macmillan, Iain
  Apple Records *86*
Madill, Warren
  Romix Foods 284, *286*
magazines 13, 38–50, *60*, *63*, 160–9, 176, 182, 186, 214, 218, 238, 384–7
Magna Trust 441, *441*
Magritte, René *115*
Main, Jimmy 34
Major, John 298
Male, Stephen 384, *384*
Manpower Services Commission *216*
Maranzano, Alex *471*
Marber, Romek 82, 83
Marcantonio, Alfredo *282*
Marchbank, Pearce
  Music Sales 160, *160*
  Omnibus Books *160*, 216, *216*
  Time Out 160, *160*
Markell, Richard 232
  Illumination 232, *232*
Marks & Spencer *200*
Marks Barfield
  London Eye Company 426, *426*, 428, 440
Marks, David
  London Eye 426, *426*, 428, 440
Marr Associates
  Action on Smoking & Health *341*
Marshall, Ann *473*
The Martin Agency
  Bernie's Tattooing *298*
Mary Quant Cosmetics 59, *59*, 96
Massive Attack 372
Mather & Crowther *72*
Matisse, Henri 194, 204, 207
Mau, Bruce *219*, *445*
Max Headroom 189–91, *190*
Maxell 354, *354*
Maxwell Clark 62
Maxwell Doug *72*
Maxwell, Max
  Queen 39
May, Tony *470*
Mayhew, George 83
Mayle, Peter 82, 83
Mead & Vickers 179
Mears Caldwell Hacker *143*
Media Advertising Partnership for a Drug Free America 26, *266*
Media Laboratory 242, 308
Meeuwissen, Tony *102*, *154*, 470, *470*
  Kinney Records *155*
  Philadelphia Pavilion Books 396, *396*
  Transatlantic Records *155*
Meissner, Claudine *470*
Mellors, Tim *347*
  Alexon & Company *214*
Memphis 192
Mental Health Trust *50*
Merrells, Jeff *474*
MetaDesign London
  Glasgow 1999: UK City of Architecture and Design *394*, 395
Metropolitan Police 96, *97*
Meyerhöffer, Thomas
  Apple Computer 421, *421*, 435
Michael, Anthony 380, 404, *405*
Michael Nash Associates 406
  Circa Records 380, *380*
  Harvey Nichols 404, *405*
Michael Peters & Partners 125, 189, 389–90, 396
  D'Amico & Partners 402, *403*
  Bird's Eye Foods *102*
  Dar Salons 292, *293*
  Elsenham Quality Foods 196, *196*
  Fine Fare *198*, 199, 210
  International Coffee Organisation 220, 221
  Penhaligon's *124*, 196, *196*, 203, *203*
  Royal Mail Stamps *388*, 389
  Winsor & Newton *124*, 125, 136
Michael Thierens Design
  Waitrose 199, *199*
Michelin Man 13
Midland Bank 292, *293*
Miles, Peter 384, *384*
Milla, Gavin 164
Miller, Jonathan *262*
Millward, Colin 82, 83, 94, 105, 179
Milton, Howard *204*
  Penhaligon's *124*
Milton Keynes Development Corporation *150*, 151
Minale, Marcello 32, *32*, 82, *471*
Minale Tattersfield 32, 83, 151, *471*, 473
  British Airport Authority *150*
  Cubic Metre Furniture 204, *204*
  D&AD award design *37*
  Heal & Son 210, *210*
  Italian Institute of Foreign Trade 151
  Land Rover 284, *287*
  Ocean Oil Company 32, *32*
  Osram-GEC *32*
Minale Tattersfield Provinciali
  Baric Computing Services *150*, 151
  Harrods 124, *124*
  Hospital Design Partnership *150*
  Milton Keynes Development Corporation *150*, 151
Mini Cooper 439, *439*
minimalism *184*, 185, 234, 292, *380*, 408
Ministry of Information 152
Ministry of Transport 54, *55*
Minneapolis College of Art 209–10, *209*
Misstear, Gilvrie *169*, 176
Miyake, Issey *184*, 185, 292
Moberly, Robert 200
modernism 12, *236*
Molloy, Tim *441*
Monsanto *63*
monster.com *428*
Montgomery, David *25*, 83
Montgomery, Giles *333*
Moon, Sarah
  Nova 120
  Pirelli 120, *120*
Morahan, Andy *366*
Moré, Beny 454
morphing *86*, 242, *242*
Morris, Ed 342

Morton, Rocky
Max Headroom 189–91, *190*
Mother 306, *306*, 475, *475*
britart.com 432, *433*
EMAP On Air 458, *458*
Mr Freedom 134, *134*
MTV 238, 458, *459*
Muir, Donna 208
Design magazine *204*
Muir, Frank 271
Mujirushi Ryohin Europe 408, *408*
Mulcahy, Russell 242
Elton John 242, *242*
multi-disciplinary consultancies 54, 306
Multiple Sclerosis Society *321*
Muranka, Tony
Romix Foods 284, *286*
Murphy, Richard *433*
Murphy's Bitter 322, *323*
Music Sales 160, *160*
music videos *see* pop promos
MuZ 417, *417*
Myers, Barry
Central Office of Information 262, *262*
Myerscough-Jones, David
BBC Television *229*
Mynott, Lawrence 211

N
Nabokov, Vladimir 134, *134*
Nakata, Robert *225*
The Naked Ape 82
Napster 310
Nash, Stephanie 380, 404, *405*
Nathanson, David *40*
National Botanic Garden of Wales 440, *441*
National Maritime Museum *285*
National Museum of Science & Industry 411, *412*, 440
National Portrait Gallery *402*, 403
National Power 194
National Provincial Bank 73, *74*
National Theatre 152, *411*
Neary, Liam *470*
NEC 416, *417*
Nederlandse Spoorwegen 139, *139*
Negroponte, Nicholas 308, 426
neo-classicism 194
new brutalism 216, *219*
New Order *235*
New Society magazine 73, *74*
New York Art Directors' Club 29
New Zealand Symphony Orchestra *446*
Newell & Sorrell
British Airways 378
WH Smith 402, *403*
newspapers 13, 165, 182, 218–19, *298*
Sunday supplements 40, *40*, 50, 164–5, *169*, *176*, *184*, 185
Newsweek International *165*
Newton, David *468*
Newton, Helmut *63*, 122
Next 182, 190–1, *191*, 292
Nicholas Cartoons
Shell International 31
Nicholas Thirkell Associates
Mr Freedom 134, *134*
Nielsen, Leslie 364, *365*
Nike 302–3, *302*, *303*, 330, *332*, 333, *333*, 348, *349*, 418, *418*, 457, 460, *461*, *464*
nineties 14–15, 294, 295–423
Nokes, Barbara *257*
Smith & Nephew *280*
Volkswagen 268–9, *268*
Nordisk reklamefilm
Shell International *31*
North
RAC 376, *377*
Northover, Jim *472*
Norways, Graeme
Pirelli *327*
White Horse Distillers *118*
noughties 424–67
Nova magazine 40, 45, *45*, *46*, *48*, 83, *120*, 122, 218
NSPCC 288, *288*, *321*, 330

O
Observer 170
Ocean Oil Company 32, *32*
'oddvertising' 458
O'Donnell, John *190*
Ogilvy & Mather 78, 82, 188, 333
Bovril *272*, 273
Golden Wonder 356, *358*
Guinness 350, *351*
Media Advertising Partnership for a drug free America 266, 266
Royal National Institute for the Deaf 290, 291
Ohlson, Barbro *379*
oki-ni 442, *442*
Oldenburg, Clæs 472
Olins, Wally 34, 83, 151
Oliver, Rob 454
Olivetti 82
Olympus Cameras 322, *323*
Olympus Optical Company *106*, *215*, 276, *276*
OMK Design 294, *294*
Omnibus Books *160*, 216, *216*
One Little Indian Records *464*, 465
Opie, Julian
Parlophone Records 448, *451*
Orange 304, *305*
Orchestral Manoeuvres in the Dark 234
Ortman, Marc 239
O'Shea, David 280, *280*
Osram-GEC *32*
outpost.com 361, *361*
Oz magazine 83

P
packaging 124, 148, 195–207, 400–7, 434–5
brand 13, 203–7
own-label 196, 198–200, *198*, *199*, *200*, 203
Page, Alan
Greenpeace 186, *186*
Palladino, Tony 82
Pallant, John
Greater London Council *184*
Palmer, Ben 66
Palmer, Brian 82
Palmer, Chris *358*
Pan Books 220, *221*
Papanek, Victor 82
Papert Koenig Lois
J Player & Sons *64*
Park, Nick 368
Parker, Alan 62, 71, 82, 83, *97*, 104–5, 109, 179, 266
Bird's Eye Foods 105, *105*, 179
Bugsy Malone 104, *105*, 134
Daily Express 109
General Post Office 105, *106*
H J Heinz 105, *106*, 179
Whitbread 104, *105*
Parker, John *473*
Parker Pen Company *100*, *101*, *105*, *268*, 269
Parlophone Records *234*, *235*, 368, *369*, 448, *451*, 458
The Partners 139
Royal Shakespeare Company *196*
SC Properties *406*
Thrislington Cubicles 392, *392*, *430*, 431
Wood & Wood International 213, *213*
Patterson, Neil
Land Rover *287*
Paul Marciano Advertising
Guess Jeans 364, *366*
Pearce, Harry *199*
Pearce, John *26*, 83, 94, 105
Pearce Marchbank Studio
Le Nez Rouge Wine Club 203, *203*
Pearce, Mark 389
Pearce, Roger *472*, 474
Peccinotti, Harri 83
Nova 45, *45*, *46*, *48*
Peckham Library 440, *441*
Peel, John *154*
Pelham, David 82
The Human Body 220, *221*
Kites 136, *136*, 220
Pan Books 220, *221*
Penguin Books *134*, 136, *136*
Pemberton, Jeremy
Greenpeace 186, *186*
Penguin Books 33, *33*, 53, *53*, 82, 134, *134*, 136, *136*, *149*, 153, 211, *211*
Penhaligon's *124*, 196, *196*, 203, *203*
Pentagram Design 33, 142–9, 208, *411*
Canongate Books 372, *374*
Clarks Shoes 148, *149*
Crafts Council 387, *387*
A Dictionary of Graphic Clichés 148
Ericsson Information Systems (*The Guardian*) 218, *219*
Faber & Faber *212*
Interior Design International *388*
The Pessimist Utopia 148
Pirelli *146*
Polaroid 384, *387*
Robert Norton *145*
Roche Products *146*
Savoy Group of Hotels 296, *396*
Wakefield Fortune 292, *293*
Pepe Deluxe 457
Peperami 360, *361*
Pepsi *128*, 129
Perkins, Sean 376, *377*
Pet Shop Boys *234*, *235*, 380
Peter Grant
Swansong *156*
Peter Saville Associates
Factory Communications *235*
Peter Windett Associates 195
Crabtree & Evelyn 195, *195*
Peters, Michael 36, *64*, 82, 83, *102*, 125, 189, *238*
Pethick, Bob *26*, 82
Petrie, Rob *380*
Pevsner, Nikolaus
Pioneers of the Modern Movement 12
Pickersgill, Paul *475*
Phaidon Press *426*, *445*
Philadelphia Pavilion Books 396, *396*
Philips, Arlene *242*
Philips Video Division 246, *246*
photojournalism 40, 50
photomontage *74*, 142, 152
photosetting *136*
Pickerings 124
Pictorial Publicity 94
Pieterson, Lex van 225
Pink Floyd 156, 262
Pinter, Harold 82
Pirelli 82, 120, *120*, 122, *122*, *146*, 324, *327*
pixillation 244
Planters 284, *286*
Playtex 337, *337*
Pockett, Darrell
BBC Television *230*, 232
Pocknell, David 82
Polaroid 356, *357*, 384, *387*
political parties, advertising by *130*, *176*, 177
Polydor 242, *242*
Polygram Filmed Entertainment 380, *382*
pop 15
pop art 82
pop promos 238–45, 310, 342, 368, 372–3, 465
Post Office 105, *106*, *140*, 152, 211, *211*
post-modernism 15, 194
Powell, Aubrey 156
Powell, Dick 416, 417, 436
Power, Pamela *133*
Poynor, Rick *219*, 384
Prada 302
Pratt, Eric *471*
press advertising 321–30
Pretty Polly *94*, *97*
Price, Alan 250
Priest, Robert *470*
Radio Times 162, *162*, *165*
Priestman, Paul 416, *417*, 439
Pringle, Bryan *106*, 250
Pritchard Wood
National Provincial Bank *74*
Private Eye magazine 83
'problem solvers' 378, 380
product design 194, 294, 414–23, 43–40
Prospect Pictures 408, *410*
Proyas, Alex *366*
Prudential 194, 207, 342, *343*
Pryce, Jonathan 213
PTT Nederland NV 376, *377*
pub signs 213, *213*
Publicis Wellcare Mojo
Red Cross 432, *433*
punk 15, 154
Puttnam, David 71, 83, 104

Q
QTV 458, 458
Quaker Oats 127, 129, 179
Quant, Mary 18, 59, *59*, 83, 87, 179
Quantel Paintbox 194
Qubit 415
Queen Elizabeth's Foundation for Disabled People 321, 362, 363
Queen magazine 38, 39, 40, 83
Queensberry Hunt Levien
Ideal Standard 419

R
RAC 376, *377*
radio advertising 246, 432
Radio Rentals (Max Headroom) 190, *190*
Radio Times magazine 162, *162*, *164*, *165*, 176
Ragazzini, Enzo *144*
Rand, Michael 40, 83, 164
The Sunday Times magazine 40, *41*, *50*, *77*, 164–5, *165*, *169*, 176
Rand, Paul 21
Rankin *456*
Ratledge, Mike *255*
Ray, Man *235*
raytracing 190
Readymix Drypack 203, *203*
Reagan, Ronald 280, 290
record sleeves *18*, 28, *86*, 154–60, 234–8, 448, *451*
Red Cross 432, *433*
Red Rock Cider 364, *365*
Reddy, Mark *321*
Reebok 302, 330, *331*, *456*, 457
Reed, Lou 312, *313*
Reed Paper Group 36, *36*, *37*
Regal Cigarettes 340, *341*
Reid, Jamie
Sex Pistols 154
Reisz, Karel *117*
Remington Electric Shavers *22*, *25*
Renault *130*
Reuters identity 142, *143*
Revell, Giles *342*, 396
Rhodes, Zandra 58, 83
Rhys Jones, Griff 192, 246, *246*
Rice, Brian
The English Sunrise 146
Rice Davis, Mandy 82
Ridley Scott Associates (RSA)
Pepsi 129
Rijksmuseum 222, *223*, *225*
Riley, Bridget 82, 428
Ritblat, Jill 396, *399*
Ritz magazine *165*
road signs 54, *55*
Robert Fraser Gallery *60*
Robert Norton *145*
Roberts, Andy 451
Roberts, Nigel 324, *324*, *327*, *451*
Robins, Arthur 82
Robinson, Barry *428*
Robinson Lambie-Nairn
Channel Four Television 182, 226–7, *227*
Readymix Drypack 203, *203*
Roche Products *146*
Rockwood, Richard
Jones identity 207, *207*
Rod Springett & Associates *471*
Ruck Ryan Limited *140*
Rodd Industrial Design
UAD Company 414, *415*
Rogers, Jon 448, *451*

Rogers, Richard 194
The Rolling Stones 18, 82, 179, 242
Rollings, Gordon *128*
Romanek, Mark
  Epic 368, *370*
Romek Barber
  New Society 74
Romix Foods 284, *286*
Ronseal 203
Rood, Gregory
  BBC 312, *313*
Roope, Nick *309*
Roope, Tom *309*
Rorscharch blots 66, *67*
Rose, Graham
  Corona Soft Drinks *249*
  Hamlet 258
Rose, Nigel 337, *473*
Rosehaugh Stanhope Developments 216, *217*
Rossini 256, *256*
Rossiter, Leonard 109
Rot, Dieter 82
Roundel Design Group
  BR Railfreight 210, *210*
Roviras, Teresa
  Joseph 406, *406*
Rowntree Mackintosh
  'Lion' chocolate bar 134, *134*
Royal Automobile Club (RAC) 189
Royal College of Art 139, *139*, *411*
Royal Court 82
Royal Mail 314, *314*, *388*, 389, 426, *426*, 428, 444, *444*
Royal National Institute for the Deaf *290*, 291
Royal Shakespeare Company *196*, 211
RSA 62
RSO Records *154*
RSPCA 321, *321*
Ruck Ryan Limited *140*
Rudman, Mick 354, *354*
Rumball, Andy *473*
Russell, Ken 61, 82
Rutherford, Andrew *270*

S
Saatchi & Saatchi 71, 88, 186, 188, 292
  Alexon & Company 214, *214*
  Allied Breweries 342, *343*
  The Army 304, 305, 306, *306*, 428
  British Airways 344, *344*
  British Rail *266*, 267
  British Telecom 344, *345*
  Chamber of Coal Traders *266*, 267
  Club 18-30 318, *318*, 451, *452*
  Dickens & Jones 284, *285*
  Flying Colours 318, *318*
  Gallaher *263*
  Guide Dogs for the Blind 288, *290*
  The Habitat Group 330, *330*
  Health Education Council 88, *88*, *91*
  monster.com *428*
  National Maritime Museum *285*
  NSPCC 288, *288*, *321*
  The Samaritans 262, *262*, 288
  Traffic Police 362, *363*
  Victoria and Albert Museum 292
Saatchi & Saatchi Garland-Compton *130*, 177
  Brutus *133*
  Conservative Central Office *176*, 177, 182
  Health Education Council *176*, 177
Saatchi & Saatchi Wellington
  New Zealand Symphony Orchestra *446*
Saatchi, Charles *63*, 71, 83, 88, 179
Saatchi, Maurice 88
Safeway 400, *400*
Sagmeister, Stefan
  AIGA Detroit 446, *446*, 448
Sainsbury's 198
St Ivel *30*
Salgado, Sebastião
  Kitchenware Merchants 322, *323*
  The Sunday Times magazine 184, 185
Salmon, John 82
  Metropolitan Police 96, *97*
Salvation Army 50, *50*
The Samaritans 262, *262*, 288
San Francisco Jazz Organization 460, *463*
Sands, Colin *471*
Sassoon, Vidal 82
Satinath Sarangi 330, *330*
Savage, Tiger 333, *333*
Saville, Peter 234, *235*, 236, 238
  Dindisc Records *234*
  Factory Records 234, *234*
Savino, Mike 82
Savoy Group of Hotels 296, *396*
Sayle, Alexei 248, *249*
SC Properties *406*
Schenk, Roland
  Campaign 81, *81*
Schleger, Hans 82
Schrager, Ian *442*
Schreyer, Peter
  Audi 418, *420*, 435
Schwartzman, Arnold 82, 83, 144, *154*
  Associated-Rediffusion *69*
Schweppes 78
  Cresta bear 125–6, *127*, 179
  Pepsi *128*, 129
Science Museum 411, *412*, 440, 441, *441*
Scott, Ridley 62, 82, 83, 179, 266
  Apple Computer 194, *194*
  Bladerunner 262
  Boy & Bicycle 109
  Gallaher *109*
  Hovis *94*, *109*
  Levi Strauss *132*
  Pepsi 129
Scott, Tony 255, *255*
  Berlei *133*
  L'Oréal *128*
Scottish & Newcastle Breweries 284, *287*
Scottish Health Education Trust *176*, 177
Scrimgeour, Lucilla *199*
Seattle Coffee Company 402, *403*
Sedelmaier, Joe 267
  Little Caesars Enterprises *266*, 267
  US Sprint *188*, 267
Segal, Erich
  Love Story 153
Seiko Corporation 414, *415*
seventies 14, 15, 84–179
Sex Pistols 154
Sexton Shoe Company 36, *64*
Seymour, Andy *236*
Seymour Powell 376, 416–17
  MuZ 417, *417*
  Technophone 414, *415*
Seymour, Richard 414, 416, 417, 423
Shafron, Mike *290*
Shainin, Jennifer *317*
Shanahan, Karl *426*
Sharwood & Company 204, *204*, 207
Shell BP News *74*
Shell International 31, *31*
Shirt Sleeve Studio *469*
  General Post Office *140*
shops and shopping 56–7, 59, 87, 190–1, 292, 294, 408, 498
  own-label packaging 196, 198–200, 203
Sieff, Jean-Loup *46*
Silk Cut *263*
Silverstein, Donald *22*, 82, 120
Simkins Partnership *388*
Simonds-Gooding, Anthony 428
Simons Palmer Denton Clemmow & Johnson
  Nike 330, *332*, 333, *333*
  Terence Higgins Trust 390, *390*
Sims, Phil *380*
Sinclair, James 342
Sinclair, Jeremy 179
Sinha, Indra *330*
Siren *154*
Six, Bert 192
6a Architects
  oki-ni 442, *442*
sixties 14, 15, 16–83
The Skids 354, *354*
Sky Television 348
Slaughter Hanson
  Alabama Veterans Memorial 430, *430*
Sliggers, Ko *223*
Sloggett, Richard
  Holsten Pils 246, *246*
  Toshiba 248, *249*
Small Faces *18*
Smarties 227
Smash Martians 126, *127*, 179
Smashing Pumpkins 352
Smirnoff Vodka 115, *115*
Smith & Milton *203*
  JA Sharwood & Company 204, *204*, 207
  James McNaughton Paper 392, *392*
Smith & Nephew 280, *280*
Smith, Clark
  The Case of Torches 53
Smith, Mel 246, *246*
Smith, Paul *103*, 380, 444, *445*
Smith-Dennison
  North West Ash 340, *341*
Smurfit Townsend Hook 448, *448*
Snowdon, Lord 29, 83, 428, *428*
  The Sunday Times magazine 176, *176*
Snowman Enterprises 230, *230*
Sodano, Aboud 380
  Violette Editions 444, *445*
Sony 179, 252, *252*, 272, 356, *358*, 451, *451*, 464, 465
Sorrell, Martin 146, 188, 429–30
Sottsass, Ettore 192
Souter, Peter *321*, 454
South Bank Centre 411, *411*
The South Bank Show 170, *171*
Southern Electric 194
Southwark Council 440, *441*
Spaceman 448, *448*
Speedo 258, *260*
Spencer, Herbert 82, 83, *144*
Spicers 36, *36*
Spiers, Jonathan *441*
Spillers 80, *80*
Spin
  Channel 4 *448*
  Diesel 395, *395*
Spiritualized 406, 448, *448*
Spitting Image 176, 182, 228, *228*
Spoerl, Wolf 83, *219*
Springett, Rod 469, *471*
Staehelin, Georg
  Pirelli *146*
stage photograph 225, *225*
Stamp, John
  Thames Television (*The World at War*) *173*
Standard Brands 284, *286*
Stanton, Harry Dean 364, *366*
Stanton Williams
  Issey Miyake *184*, 185
  National Theatre *411*
  South Bank Centre 411, *411*
Starck, Philippe
  Ian Schrager Hotels *442*
Stark, Jeff *290*, 292
stationery *58*, *139*, 142, *142*, *155*, *207*, 222, *389*
Steadman, Ralph *219*, 428, *428*
  Radio Times 164, 176
Steele, David *182*
Stella Artois 364, *365*, 451, *452*
Stephens, Kate 209, *209*
  ABSA 392, *392*
Stevens, Jocelyn 38, 83, 225
Stevens Press 38
Stevenson, John 83
Stewart-Hardy Films
  BBC Television 239, *239*
Stiff Records 238
Still Price Lintas 330
  Van Den Berghs & Jurgens 360, *361*
stock market listing of Design Groups 189
Stokes, Ian *471*
Storehouse 191
Strauss, Johann 460
Street Smart
  Coalition for the Homeless 362, *362*
Stuart, David 400
Studio AKA
  IdN Magazine 431, *431*
Studio Dumbar 139, 222, *223*, 225, 236
  Holland Festival 225, *225*
  PTT Nederland NV 376, *377*
  Rijksmuseum 222, *223*, *225*
  Westeinde Hospital 222, *223*
Studio Myerscough
  Joe Kerr 372, *374*
Studio X
  Connolly *415*
'style counsellors' 378, 380
Stylorouge
  Polygram Filmed Entertainment 380, *382*
Sudjic, Deyan
  Blueprint 219
  Domus 219
  Glasgow 1999: UK City of Architecture and Design *394*, 395
Sugar Puffs 125, *127*, 129, 179
Summers, Kevin *473*
The Sun newspaper *332*
The Sunday Times magazine 40, *40*, *41*, *50*, *77*, *77*, 164–5, *165*, *169*, *176*, *184*, 185, 218
The Sunday Times weekend review 165
Super Mario Brothers 368
Sylvester, Victor 83

T
Talbot, Pauline
  BBC Sports Department *173*
Tango *249*, 356, *356*
Tank Publications *448*
Tarsem 348, 352, *352*
Tate & Lyle 152
Tate Gallery 324, *327*
Tattersfield, Brian 32, *32*, 82, *471*
Taunton Cider Company 356, *358*, 364, *365*
Taylor, Alexandra
  Allied Breweries 342, *343*
  The Army *305*
  Gallaher *263*
Taylor-Woods: Lifelons *60*
TBWA 71, 342
  Land Rover 284, *287*
  Lego 252, *252*, 276, *276*
  Newsweek International 165
  Playtex 337, *337*
  Sony 356, *358*, 451, *451*, *464*, 465
  Tate Gallery 324, *327*
  Waterstone's Booksellers 324, *324*
TBWA\Chiat\Day 11, 461
  Fox Sports 460, 461
TBWA Simons Palmer
  Nike *303*
techno-modernism 234
Technophone 414, *415*
TEL Design Associated 222
  Nederlandse Spoorwegen 139, *139*
television 14–15, *52*, 62, 66–9, 105, 170–5, 186, 194, 228–34, 239, 248
  BBC identity 444, *444*
  BBC1 identity 232
  BBC2 identity 227–8, 232, 312, *313*, 314, *314*
  Channel 4 identity 182, 226–8, *227*, 448, *448*
  ITV identity 232
  MTV 238
  music videos 238–45
television characters, use of 81, 342
Temple, Julien 242
Tennant, Neil 234
Tern Consulate *21*, *25*
Terrence Higgins Trust 390, *390*
Terry, Quinlan 194
Tesco Stores 198–9, *198*, 344, *344*
Thames Television *158*
  The World at War 173
Thatcher, Margaret 14, 152–3, 177, 179, 182, *182*, 185, 228, 271, 298
'third wave' 333
Thomas, Andrew *471*
Thompson, Bill *277*
Thomson, John 364
Thomson Organisation
  The Sunday Times 40
Thorgerson, Storm 156
  Thames Television *158*
Thornton, Jim 328
Thorpe, David *470*
Three Associates (3a)
  i-D Magazine 384, *384*
  Parlophone Records *234*, *235*
3i 207
Thresher Wine Merchants *189*
Thrislington Cubicles 392, *392*, *430*, 431
Tilby, Alan 284

Time International *37*
Time magazine 82, 146
Time Out magazine 160, *160*, *272*, 273
The Times 83, 165
TKO
Seiko Corporation 414, *415*
Tom Hingston Studio
Circa, Virgin Records 372, *372*
Tomato *309*, 310, *311*
Topolski, Felix 82
Toshiba 248, *249*
Town magazine 38, *39*, 81
Traffic Police 362, *363*
Trainspotting 380, *382*
Transatlantic Records *155*
Trengrove, Barry *26*, 83
Harper's Bazaar *39*
Tricket & Webb 471, *471*
Royal Mail 444, *444*
Simkins Partnership *388*
Trickett, Lynn *426*, *471*
Trident 152, *153*
Trott, Dave 129, 179, *249*, 250, 252, 290
Barker & Dobson 115, *115*, *128*
Courage Brewing *251*
London Weekend Television 272, *272*
Toshiba 249, *249*
William Levene *249*
Tucker Clarke-Williams Creative
Granada Media 430, *430*
Turner, Tina 368, *369*
Turney, Michael *171*
Tutsell, Glenn 199, 210, 402
Twen magazine 83
Twiggy 18, 83
two-thousands 424–67
Ty Nant 434–5, *434*
The Type Museum
Cleaver, Phil 395, *395*
Typographica magazine 83

U
UAD Company 414, *415*
'ugly casting' 300
UNA Amsterdam 376, *376*
Ungless, Derek 162, *470*
Unigate 30, *128*
Uniroyal 22, *72*, 73
UNKLE *155*, 236, *236*, 368, *370*, 372
Ure, Midge 239
US design and advertising 11, 14, 21, 179, 387, 460
US Sprint *188*, 267

V
VAG UK 250, *250*
Van Den Berghs & Jurgens 360, *361*
Vaughan and Anthea 352, *352*
Stella Artois 364, *365*
Veal, Judy *473*
Vent
Parlophone Records 448, *451*
Venturi, Robert 194
Vernon Stratton
Debenham & Freebody *74*
Victoria and Albert Museum 7, 211, *211*, 292, 396, *396*, 399
video art 232
videos, music *see* pop promos
Violette Editions 444, *445*
Virgin Records 236, *236*, 244, *244*, 372, *372*, 459
Vodaphone 430
Vogue magazine *63*, 195
Volkswagen 21, *92*, 115, 177, 179, 250, *250*, 268–9, *268*, *309*, 324, 328, *329*, 342, *343*, 348, *349*, 354, *354*, 395, 460, *463*
Volvo 179, 280, *280*, 344, *347*, 348, *348*
VSA Partners
Chicago Board of Trade 387, *387*

W
Waddlcors & Clark Wilkinson
Spicers *53*
Wagg, Peter
Chrysalis Records *238*
Waitrose 199, *199*
Wakefield, David 285
Wakefield Fortune 292, *293*
Waldie, Alan 109
Benson & Hedges 96
Whitbread & Company *251*
Wales, Charles, Prince of 194
Walkers Snack Foods 364, *366*
Wall's Meat Company *94*
Walsh, Martyn *25*, 273
War on Want 288, *288*
Warhol, Andy 164, *333*
Chelsea Girls 18, *19*
Warp Records 368, *370*, 372
Washington, Dinah 352
Waskett, Rod 227
Waterbury, Todd
Coca-Cola Company 404, *405*
Waters, Dave 454
Waterstone's Booksellers 324, *324*
Wates *77*
Watney Mann & Truman Brewers 258, *259*
Watson, Graham *473*
Lego 252, *252*
Levi Strauss *255*
Waugh, Evelyn 134, *134*
Wayne, John 364
Webb, Brian *471*
Webb, Peter *277*
Webber, Andrew Lloyd *242*
Webster, John 77, 125–6, 178, 248, 250, 348
Cadbury Typhoo Foods 126, *127*
Compaq 431, *431*
Courage Brewing 128, *244*, 245, *251*, 369
Ferrero *127*
National Provincial Bank 73, *74*
Quaker Oats 125, *127*, 129, 179
Schweppes 125–6, *127*, 179
Sony 252, *252*, 272
Unigate Dairies *128*
Weil, Daniel *411*
Weiland, Paul 109, 179
BBC *313*
Central Office of Information 266, *266*
Fiat *256*
The Guardian 266, *266*
Hamlet 96, *259*
Parker Pen Company *105*
Whitbread & Company 250, *251*
William Levene *249*
Weinberger, Paul 227
Welcome, John
Stop at Nothing *53*
Weldon, Fay 78
Welland, Paul 368, *369*
Wells, Mary 179
Welsh, Irving 380
Wesker, Arnold 82
West, Wesley *474*
Westeinde Hospital 222, *223*
Westwood, Vivienne 83
WH Smith 402, *403*
Wharmby Associates
Brown Holdings 294, *294*
Whelan, Terence
Vogue *63*
Whitbread *97*, 103–4, *103*, *105*, 250, *251*, 269, *269*, 270, 322, 323, 324, *327*, 328, 364, *365*, 451, *452*
White, Barry 368
White Horse Distillers 116, *118*, 179
Whitfield, June 96
Wickens, Brett *235*
Wickens Tutt Southgate
Seattle Coffee Company 402, *403*
Wieden + Kennedy 11
Coca-Cola Company 404, *405*
McKenzie River Corporation 364, *366*
Nike 302, *302*, 348, *349*, 457, 460, *461*, *464*
Wight Collins Rutherford Scott (WCRS) 333
Bass 364, *365*
BMW 256, *256*, 268
Chefaro Proprietaries *270*, 271
Hutchison Telecom 304, *305*
Prudential 342, *343*
Wild Brew 434–5, *434*
Wildbur, Peter 82, 83, *468*
Wilkins, Chris 129
Wilkinson Eyre Architects
Magna Trust 441, *441*
Wilks, Karen 377
William Levene *249*
Williams Murray Hamm
Interbrew 434–5, *434*
Williams, Richard 198–9
Ferrero *127*
Schweppes 126, *127*, 179
Willock, Harry
Small Faces *18*
Wilson, Harold *74*, 153, 179
Wilson, Tony 234
Windett, Peter 204
Crabtree & Evelyn 195, *195*
Winsor & Newton *124*, 125, 136
Wise, Robert 160
Withers, John *25*
Witness 444, *445*
Wolfe, Tom 195
Wolff Main 34
Wolff, Michael 34, 83, 125, 151, *390*
Bowyers *34*
Wolff Olins 34, *34*
Wolff Olins 34, *54*, 83, 151, *227*
Bovis *150*, 151
Bowyers *34*, *102*
British Telecom 207, 378
Go fly 378, *379*
Hadfields 34, *34*
Orange 304
Prudential identity 207
R & G Cuthbert *150*
3i 207
Wolsey, Tom 26, 38, 40, 83, 195
The Sunday Times magazine 77
Town *39*
Wonderbra 337, *337*
Wood & Wood International (Courage) 213, *213*
Woodburn, Roger
Bass *365*
Levi Strauss 255
Woodroffe, Simon *442*
Woods, Tiger 460
Woolf, Richard 408
Woolley, Janet 322
Woolworths 368, *369*
Wordsearch *382*, 384, 384
The World of Interiors magazine 182, 214, *214*, 218
Wormser, Jimmy *263*, *282*
Worthington, Nick *323*
WPP Group 146, 188, *399*, 429
Wrangler *240*
Wright, Edward 82
Wright, Ian 333, 348
Wurr & Wurr *139*
Wurr, Matthew *473*
Wurr, Nicholas *139*
Royal College of Art 139, *139*
Royal Shakespeare Company *196*
stationery *139*
Wuttke, Klause *140*
Wynette, Tammy 312

Y
Yardley 31, *31*
Yeoman, Dawson *72*
Yellow Pages 252, *252*, *394*, 395
Yellow Submarine 82
Yellowhammer Company
Greenpeace 186, *186*
Yentob, Alan 312
'yestertech' 194
Yo! Sushi 442, *442*
Young & Rubicam (Y&R) 32, 82
Cadbury Brothers 78, *78*, 80
H J Heinz 78, *78*
International Distillers & Vintners 115, *115*
Levi Strauss *132*
Pirelli 324, *327*
Young Commonwealth Artists 31, *31*

Z
Zak, Paul *475*
Zetland Advertising
Berlei *133*
Zinc Development Association *146*

This project could not have been achieved without the willingness of so many people who have donated their time and copies of their work. The authors of *Rewind*, Jeremy Myerson and Graham Vickers, and D&AD would like to thank all of the companies and individuals involved for their ceaseless generosity. In particular we would like to mention:

Jeremy Bullmore, Alan Fletcher, Richard Seymour, John Webster and Peter York, each of whom rose to the challenge of providing personal insight and recollections of a given decade.

Everyone at johnson banks for their support, but especially Luke Gifford and Michael Johnson.

Campaign & *Creative Review* for opening up their archives.

Tim Mellors at Grey, James Sinclair and Ed Morris at TBWA\London, Richard Williams of Williams Murray Hamm and Tony Muranka for their reflections and insights on key projects and campaigns.

Arnold Schwartzman for so generously donating his personal copies of works relating to the beginnings of D&AD.

Pauline Gorham and Mike Dempsey for their kind help in supplying images of John Gorham's work.

We would also like to thank:
Eliza Brownjohn
Victoria Clarke
Anna Davis
Matthew Donaldson
David Driver
David Kester
Lou Klein
Chris Macleod
Pearce Marchbank
Kathryn Patten
Harri Peccinotti
Phaidon Press
Michael Rand
Amanda Renshaw
Richard Schlagman
Pauline Shakespeare
Paul Tozer
The Victoria and Albert Museum
Sally Waterman
Yolanda Zappaterra

Further mention should go to Sarah Brownrigg of D&AD for her energetic project management of this publication.